to Chuck

best wishes

Simon

Frenk

OXFORD MONOGRAPHS ON LABOUR LAW

General Editors: PAUL DAVIES, KEITH EWING,
MARK FREEDLAND

The Law of the Labour Market

Industrialization, Employment and Legal Evolution

Oxford Monographs on Labour Law

General Editors: Paul Davies, Cassel Professor of Commercial Law at London School of Economics; Keith Ewing, Professor of Public Law at King's College, London; and Mark Freedland, Fellow of St John's College, and Professor of Employment Law in the University of Oxford.

This series is the first new development in the literature dealing with labour law for many years. The series recognizes the arrival not only of a renewed interest in labour law generally, but also the need for a fresh approach to the study of labour law following a decade of momentous change in the UK and Europe. The series is concerned with all aspects of labour law, including traditional subjects of study such as industrial relations law and individual employment law, but it will also include books which examine the law and economics of the labour market and the impact of social security law upon patterns of employment and the employment contract.

Titles already published in this series

The Right to Strike
K. D. EWING

Legislating for Conflict
SIMON AUERBACH

Justice in Dismissal
HUGH COLLINS

Pensions, Employment, and the Law
RICHARD NOBLES

Just Wages for Women
AILEEN MCCOLGAN

Women and the Law
SANDRA FREDMAN

Freedom of Speech and Employment
LUCY VICKERS

International and European Protection of the Right to Strike
TONIA NOVITZ

The Law of the Labour Market

Industrialization, Employment and Legal Evolution

SIMON DEAKIN

and

FRANK WILKINSON

OXFORD

UNIVERSITY PRESS

OXFORD
UNIVERSITY PRESS

Great Clarendon Street, Oxford OX2 6DP

Oxford University Press is a department of the University of Oxford.
It furthers the University's objective of excellence in research, scholarship,
and education by publishing worldwide in

Oxford New York

Auckland Cape Town Dar es Salaam Hong Kong Karachi
Kuala Lumpur Madrid Melbourne Mexico City Nairobi
New Delhi Shanghai Taipei Toronto

With offices in

Argentina Austria Brazil Chile Czech Republic France Greece
Guatemala Hungary Italy Japan South Korea Poland Portugal
Singapore Switzerland Thailand Turkey Ukraine Vietnam

Published in the United States
by Oxford University Press Inc., New York

British Library Cataloguing in Publication Data

Data available

Library of Congress Cataloging in Publication Data
Deakin, S. F. (Simon F.)
The law of the labour market : industrialization, employment, and legal evolution /
Simon Deakin and Frank Wilkinson.
p. cm. — (Oxford monographs on labour law)
Includes bibliographical references and index.
ISBN 0–19–815281–7 (hard cover : alk. paper) 1. Labor laws and legislation—
England—History. 2. Labor laws and legislation—Economic aspects z England. I.
Wilkinson, Frank. II. Title. III. Series.
KD3009. D434 2005
344. 4101—dc22

2004028615

ISBN 0–19–815281–7 (Hbk.)

1 3 5 7 9 10 8 6 4 2

Typeset by Newgen Imaging Systems (P) Ltd., Chennai, India
Printed in Great Britain
on acid-free paper by
Biddles Ltd., King's Lynn

General Editors' Preface

The aim of our series of labour law monographs has been to publish works which are, on the one hand, of the highest quality of scholarship, and which are, on the other hand, innovative or experimental, serving to expand the boundaries of the subject or to throw bright new light upon established areas of discussion. We have been fortunate in having contributors who have enabled that high standard to be maintained. On this occasion we feel very confident that the work we are introducing will be judged to have done so. Some years ago we had the opportunity to arrange for the eventual publication of a projected monograph, still very much in the making, to be co-authored by a labour lawyer, Simon Deakin, and an applied economist specializing in labour economics, Frank Wilkinson. Their interests were already converging upon the economic and legal theory of labour and management studies, and have continued to do so more and more closely. Their project involved the drawing together or interweaving of various strands of history and theory in the fabric of employment and social security law—within the canvas, therefore, of what would be conceived of as 'social law' in continental European legal taxonomies. They could deploy both a deep knowledge of and a novel insight into the interrelations between the law of the contract of employment and other parts of individual and collective labour law, the poor law and its antecedents and successors in social security provision, and the evolution of the theory and the practice of labour economics.

The remarkable phenomenon is that, in various ways, while their project was developing, so that study and theory of labour law was tending in the same general direction, increasingly breaking its banks and flooding over the same broad plains. Despite their apparently eclectic choice of particular topics, Simon Deakin and Frank Wilkinson were in fact at the head of, perhaps even ahead of, the field in the task of generalizing and theorizing this tendency. They arrive at their destination in time to present what is, despite their disclaimers, a very convincing expansion and recasting of (British) labour law as the law of labour market regulation. We are very pleased to present the resulting work, which we are sure will come to be viewed as a very distinguished addition to our series of monographs.

Paul Davies, Keith Ewing, and Mark Freedland
November 2004

Preface

We live in a time in which the predominant currents of thought tend to venerate and mystify the market. The market is seen, in essence, as pre-institutional; that is to say, as somehow natural or primordial. The efforts of public and collective actors to regulate market processes and outcomes are presented as illegitimate 'interferences' or 'distortions'. The result is to call into question all institutions which operate according to a non-market logic. For some, the application of the principle of deregulation must continue until every obstruction to the operation of free competition and exchange has been removed.

In truth, the market itself is an institution, a complex system of interlinked practices, conventions and norms. While some of these norms have a spontaneous and customary quality, many others are codified and expressed in a public–regulatory form. The most basic economic exchanges presuppose a minimal normative order for the protection of expectations; the highly advanced division of labour which supports the productive capacity of modern, industrialized societies requires a correspondingly extensive and articulated institutional framework for its coordination.

Legal *rules* encapsulate information capable of aiding decision making by agents acting under conditions of uncertainty, thereby enhancing efficiency in exchange. A legal *system* has, in this regard, a wider function, namely the preservation and reproduction of categories of knowledge which make economic coordination possible. The emergence, through legislation and adjudication, of a conceptual language or discourse which is distinctively legal or 'juridical' is one aspect of this process. In this respect, as in others, the legal system may complement the institution of the market, without thereby being reduced to it.

Industrialization is the process through which modern societies have been able to mobilize previously untapped human and material resources, making possible a step-change in the level of economic development. The relationship between legal change and industrialization is understood, at best, only incompletely. The dominant tradition was established early on, in the political economy and historiography which accompanied the industrial revolution in the first industrial nation, Britain. Industrialization was identified with the removal of the last vestiges of 'medieval' legal controls over production and exchange, while the progress of society was measured by the extent of its movement from status to contract.

Today, that tradition is alive and well in the neoliberal claim that it is both possible and desirable to return to a market order based on the relations of private law alone. For developed countries, the regulatory state, and, more precisely, the welfare state of the mid-twentieth century, should be stripped away, to reveal once again the institutions of property, contract and tort on which a free economy and a just social order depend. For developing countries, protection for property rights and the shrinking of the public realm are presented as the institutional preconditions of economic growth.

These claims have obscured an alternative narrative which stresses the public–regulatory character of the legal changes accompanying industrialization. The role of publicly-organized forms of legislation and bureaucratic regulation in shaping economic relations is evident, above all, in the pivotal case of the labour market. The transition from an agricultural economy based on the use of the land to provide subsistence income, to one in which the vast majority of the population was dependent on wage labour in the context of an urbanized and industrial economy was not brought about by reliance on contract and property alone. In Britain, two disciplinary mechanisms—the master–servant regime and the poor laws—complemented the emergence of 'free labour' throughout the period of industrialization, and informed the structure and content of the emerging juridical forms through which the law gave expression to wage labour.

However, it was not until the advent of the welfare state, in the first decades of the twentieth century, that the concept clearly recognizable to modern labour lawyers as 'the contract of employment' was definitively established as the foundation of the law governing the labour market. The juridical form of the contract of employment had embedded within it the societal compact of that time: in effect, inequality within the enterprise (the employee's 'subordination' to managerial prerogative) was traded off in return for certain social guarantees of stable employment and protection against risks arising from injury, illness, unemployment and old age. The employment model took shape against the background of the vertical integration of the enterprise and the traditional division of labour within the nuclear family. The power of the nation state to regulate social and economic relations through legislation was more or less taken for granted. In all these respects, the contract of employment was a product of a particular mid-twentieth century consensus which is now being called into question. The disintegration of the enterprise, changing family structures, and the realization of limits to the effectiveness of social legislation together mean that the employment model is increasingly unable to fulfil its essential role of ensuring social protection and cohesion while also providing a framework for the governance of work relations.

There are two possible responses to this situation. One is to hasten the end of the employment model, on the grounds that it has outlived its usefulness. That is the path of labour market deregulation. The neoliberal objective of a completely 'free' or 'flexible' labour market, untainted by regulation, is, of course, unattainable. One of the deepest paradoxes of deregulatory policies, in Britain as in other countries over the past two-and-a-half decades, is the sharp increase in the volume and intensity of regulation which they have produced. This is not an accident, but a structural feature of neoliberal political economy and its forebears. History shows us that the legal regulation of labour has been at its most restrictive (and on occasions repressive) in precisely those periods when free market ideas were regarded as orthodoxy by intellectuals and policy makers.

The alternative path is to consider ways in which the function of the contract of employment, and the values which it expressed, can be renewed in a new form. This implies the reinvention of the welfare state and the inscribing of fundamental social rights at the core of work relations. (This book is intended as a contribution to that task of institutional reconstruction.)

We have incurred many debts in the course of completing this work. We are very grateful for the support which we have received over the long course of the project from the editors of the Oxford Monographs on Labour Law series, Paul Davies, Keith Ewing and Mark Freedland, and above all to Mark for his advice on both the structure and substance of the book, which has been invaluable at every stage. We would also like to thank Catherine Barnard, Jude Browne, Bill Cornish, Jackie Cremer, David Feldman, Richard Hobbs, Sue Konzelmann, Dave Lyddon, Gill Morris, Ulrich Mückenberger, Wanjiru Njoya, Ralf Rogowski, Robert Salais, Paul Smith, Alain Supiot and Noel Whiteside for most helpful discussions on particular aspects of the research. We have benefited greatly from the institutional support provided for inter-disciplinary work by the Centre for Business Research at Cambridge University and we would like to thank its director, Alan Hughes, and our other CBR colleagues for providing a stimulating and collegiate research environment. We are, in addition, deeply indebted to Gwen Booth and John Louth of OUP for allowing us the time and flexibility we needed to finish the work and for their advice on the completion of the manuscript, and to Louise Kavanagh for overseeing the final production stages.

We are grateful to the following copyright holders for permission to reproduce previously published material: Oxford University Press, Joanne Conaghan, Michael Fischl and Karl Klare (material from S. Deakin, 'The many futures of the contract of employment', in J. Conaghan, M. Fischl and K. Klare (eds.) *Labour Law in an Era of Globalisation: Transformative Practices and Possibilities* (Oxford: OUP, 2002), 177–196); Oxford University Press (material from S. Deakin, 'The changing nature of the employer in labour law' *Industrial Law Journal*, 30: 72–84, 2002 and 'Private law, economic rationality and the regulator state', in P. Birks (ed.) *The Classification of Obligations* (Oxford: Oxford University Press, 1997), 283–304); Keele University Centre for Industrial Relations and the editors of *Historical Studies in Industrial Relations* (material from S. Deakin and F. Wilkinson, 'The evolution of collective *laissez-faire*' *Historical Studies in Industrial Relations*, 17: 1–43, 2004, and S. Deakin, 'The contract of employment: a study in legal evolution' *Historical Studies in Industrial Relations*, 11: 1–36, 2001); Gillian Morris (material from S. Deakin and G. Morris, *Labour Law* (3rd ed., London: Butterworths, 2001), ch. 1); Hart Publishing Co. Ltd. and Sarah Worthington (material from S. Deakin, 'Interpreting employment contracts: judges, employers and workers' in S. Worthington (ed.) *Commercial Law and Commercial Practice* (Oxford: Hart, 2003), 433–455); and Hart Publishing Co., Tamara Hervey and Jeff Kenner (material from S. Deakin and J.Browne, 'Social rights and the market order: adapting the capability approach' in T. Hervey and J. Kenner (eds.) *Economic and Social Rights under the European Charter of Fundamental Rights* (Oxford: Hart, 2003), 28–43).

Simon Deakin and Frank Wilkinson
Cambridge
15 November 2004

Contents

Table of Cases

Table of Statutes

1

Labour Markets and Legal Evolution

1. Introduction

The idea of a 'labour market' implies not just competition and mobility of resources, but more specifically the institution of 'wage labour' and its legal expression, the contract of employment. This book studies the evolution of the contract of employment in Britain through an examination of mutations in legal form since the period of industrial revolution. We will argue that, in respect of work relations, the nature of the legal transition which accompanied industrialization and the subsequent rise of the welfare state in Britain was more complex than has hitherto been thought. What emerged from the industrial revolution was not a general model of the contract of employment which could be applied to all wage-dependent workers, but instead a hierarchical model of service, which originated in the Master and Servant Acts and was assimilated into the common law. It was only gradually, as a result of the growing influence of collective bargaining and social legislation and with the spread of large-scale enterprises and of bureaucratic forms of organization, that old distinctions lost their force, and that the term 'employee' began to be applied to all wage or salary earners. The concept of the contract of employment which is familiar to modern labour lawyers is thus a much more recent phenomenon than is widely supposed. This has important implications for the way in which we conceptualize the modern labour market and for the way in which proposals to move 'beyond' the employment model are addressed.

The scope of our study is wider than that conventionally ascribed to the term 'labour law' that is used to describe the forms of legal regulation of work relations which are found in market economies. The discipline of labour law derives from the early twentieth century and its structure reflects its origins in a particular political project of social reform.[1] It has more recently been acknowledged that the accepted parameters of labour law do not necessarily capture a wide range of phenomena which are associated with the construction and governance of labour markets. For some, this gives rise to a need to 'redefine' the scope of the discipline;[2]

---

[1] See B. Hepple (ed.) *The Making of Labour Law in Europe* (London: Mansell, 1986); A. Supiot, *Critique du droit du travail* (Paris: Presses Universitaires de France, 1994), ch. 1.

[2] R. Mitchell (ed.) *Redefining Labour Law* (Melbourne: Centre for Employment and Labour Relations Law, 1995).

for others, labour law's 'productive disintegration' implies an engagement with other disciplines and areas of study.[3] While these perspectives are not universally accepted, there has undoubtedly been, since the early 1980s, a reorientation of research and scholarship towards the labour market as a focus of study for labour lawyers.[4] This reorientation can be understood as a response to the relative decline in the importance of collective bargaining as a mode of regulation over this period, and to the corresponding rise of individual employment law, the growing influence of the European Union, the role played by active employment policy, and, more generally, the efforts of successive governments to align legal rules with the policy goals of 'deregulation' or, in some contexts, 're-regulation' of the labour market.

There is not, as yet, general agreement on the contours of a 'law of the labour market' which might offer a new juridical frame of reference for labour market regulation. We can, however, see that if we wish to understand the legal forces which influence labour market structure, we have to look beyond the core labour law institutions of collective bargaining and the individual employment relationship. In particular, it is necessary to incorporate into the analysis some aspects of social security law and active labour market policy, in so far as they seek to regulate, or have the effect of regulating, the conditions under which individuals enter the labour market. Certain features of commercial, competition and company law may be relevant since they serve to define the legal form of the business enterprise. Fiscal law and family law may also have an impact on labour market structure. It is not our aim to chart, in detail, all the areas of law which may have a bearing on the labour market, although reference to certain aspects of those just cited will be made at various points in the text. Nor do we aim to cover every aspect of 'core' labour law. We will concentrate instead on those aspects of legal doctrine which have had a particularly prominent role in determining the juridical nature and structure of the employment relationship, as the core institution of the labour market. In this respect, the link between labour law and social security law will be of particular importance to our study. This is in keeping with the historical perspective which we seek to adopt: the poor law, dating from the late Middle Ages, reformed and revised at regular intervals and completely abolished only in 1948, played a pivotal role in regulating the labour supply throughout our period of study. The incomplete separation of wages and poor relief for much of this period was reflected in the tendency for the poor law to be simultaneously a law governing the work relationship and a body of regulation

---

[3] H. Collins, 'The productive disintegration of labour law' (1997) 26 *Industrial Law Journal* 295–309.

[4] See in particular P. Davies and M. Freedland, *Labour Law: Text and Materials* (London: Weidenfeld and Nicolson, 1st ed., 1980, 2nd ed., 1984); B. Hepple, 'A right to work?' (1981) 10 *Industrial Law Journal* 65–83; M. Freedland, 'Labour law and leaflet law: the Youth Training Scheme of 1983' (1983) 12 *Industrial Law Journal* 220–235; Lord Wedderburn, 'Labour law now—a hold and a nudge' (1984) 13 *Industrial Law Journal* 73–85, and *The Worker and the Law* (Harmondsworth: Penguin, 3rd ed., 1986), ch. 1.

determining access to non-waged income. Thus it is above all to the poor law that we have to look in order to understand the way in which the law described labour market relationships in the period when, in Britain, the transition to the first industrial society and economy was taking place.

Legal concepts consist of the abstract categories and formulations which make up the building blocks of legal discourse; as such they provide an epistemological frame of reference, a 'cognitive map' of social and economic relationships.[5] The historical record of decided cases and statutory texts, together with the wider body of public discourse on legislative policy in the form of reports of select committees, boards of inquiry, governmental commissions, and so on, provides us with an opportunity to study how this juridical map of the labour market has changed over time. These legal and institutional texts will provide the principal raw material of our study. This does not mean that we will neglect the role played by factors outside the law, ranging from political movements and ideologies to the influence of technology on the form of production, and the role played by economic theory. Nor are we suggesting that an analysis of legal concepts necessarily provides us with a *direct* understanding of the conditions under which the law 'in action' was operating at a particular time or in a particular place. Our starting point is the observation that an examination of changes in legal form over time—*legal evolution*—may provide an important source of knowledge of the historical processes which accompanied the emergence of modern labour markets. Notwithstanding the enormous body of historical research which exists on industrialization and the growth of the welfare state, and in particular the important contributions which a number of economic and legal historians have made to our understanding of the role of legal change within these processes, the evolutionary analysis of law, in the sense that we intend to use it here, remains an under-utilized resource. In particular, the observation that there have been different conceptual maps of the work relationship at different periods is, we believe, one with the potential to throw new light on the nature of the transition to an industrial society, a process which, in fundamental respects, is still going on today.

At the centre of our analysis will be an examination of the concept of the contract of employment, its antecedents, and its current evolutionary path. Against the background of claims that the employment model does not adequately describe a wide range of work relationships, and that its inability to do so threatens to undermine not only its own effectiveness but that of the various forms of labour law regulation which depend upon it,[6] this choice of perspective might seem hard to defend. In fact, it is justified by the very same concerns which inform the contemporary critique of the employment model. It is precisely because the contract of employment no longer seems fitted to its purpose that it is relevant to examine the historical conditions under which it emerged and by

[5] G. Samuel, *Epistemology and Method in Law* (Aldershot: Ashgate, 2003).
[6] See P. Gahan, 'Work, status and contract: another challenge for labour law' (2003) 16 *Australian Journal of Labour Law* 249–258.

virtue of which it came to occupy a focal point in the conceptual structure of labour law (and also of related aspects of social security and tax law). From this perspective, the problems which the employment model is currently encountering are the result, not simply of a changing labour market environment, but of the contingent and specific historical circumstances which accompanied its emergence. It also remains the case that forms of work which fall on the edges of, or completely outside, the scope of the employment contract—forms such as self-employment, outwork or homework, agency work, temporary work and (to some degree) part-time work—derive their seemingly marginal or excluded status by reference to the particular features of that model. Thus to understand the causes of the fragmentation and conceptual confusion currently afflicting labour law, it is necessary, paradoxically, to look more closely at the paradigm form whose disintegration is now being so widely anticipated.

This chapter sets out the framework of our analysis. The following section considers the nature of the employment model, and to this end combines functional and historical perspectives. We then look more closely at the meaning of the term 'industrialization' in economic and legal history and consider the relevance to our theme of the timing and nature of industrial change in Britain and the subsequent rise of the welfare state. Finally we set out in more detail what we mean by the expression 'legal evolution' and discuss a number of methodological issues arising from our approach.

2. The Institutional Nature of the Contract of Employment

It is no exaggeration to think of the classification of work relationships as the central, defining operation of any labour law system. This is not just an abstract process, it is also a practical one. Without classification, the law cannot be mobilized. It is an operation which any agent acting in a legal context—a category which may include not just judges and practising lawyers, but also labour inspectors, trade union officers, shop stewards, personnel managers, and so on—must inevitably undertake when considering the application of a labour law norm to a given set of facts. The outcome may, in the vast majority of cases, be obvious, or the process may require only a minimal investment of resources for the result to become clear, but in either case the process cannot be avoided *if* the rule is to be applied in a consistent way. Classification is therefore both condition and consequence of the maintenance of 'system order'. The requirement of legal consistency provides a built-in mechanism by which the law's internal 'cognitive map'—the juridical taxonomy through which social and economic relations are described and understood—is continuously being reproduced and renewed.

That 'cognitive map' need not, and in practice almost certainly will not, correspond precisely to the meanings which are ascribed to a given set of social practices by actors outside the context of the application or implementation of the law. The principal reference point here is not the external 'reality' of, for present purposes, work relationships, but what autopoietic theories of law refer to as the legal system's self-constructed rule of internal order. As Gunther Teubner puts it,

law refers to social meanings in a variety of ways, as well as to constructs of reality and social values. In a self-referentially closed legal system, however, these forays into current social values assume the guise of normativisation in its legal form. Their normative content is produced from within the law itself, by constitutive norms which refer back to those values. It is a condition of all forays into current social values that they be subject to legal reformulation. As soon as they are in dispute, a decision has to be made about them according to criteria established by the law itself.[7]

Thus the conceptual framework of the law is not simply, or even principally, a reflection of a wider social or economic reality; it is, above all, the result of a search for the internal consistency which is an aspect of the fundamental value of 'legality', a notion, as Philip Selznick has suggested, can be thought of as a 'synonym for the rule of law':[8]

The effort to see in law a set of standards, an internal basis for criticism and reconstruction, leads us to a true *Grundnorm*—the idea that a legal order faithful to itself seeks progressively to reduce the degree of arbitrariness in positive law and its administration. By 'positive law' we mean those public obligations that have been defined by duly constituted mechanisms, such as a legislature, court, administrative agency, or referendum. This is not the whole of law, for by the latter we mean the entire body of authoritative materials—'precepts, techniques and ideals'—that guide official decision-making.[9]

The existence of an internal legal discourse based on distinctive 'precepts, techniques and ideals'[10] is at the core of a certain type of law, one based on the value of rationality and calculability. Concepts are linguistic devices which inform legal decision making; they are a means by which consistency, and hence legitimacy in the exercise of authority, are sought. If this ideal of the rule of law is one which serves to underpin what Max Weber called 'the modern form of capitalism, based on the rational enterprise',[11] it is also, as Selznick stresses, part of a wider legal-political project, founded on 'aspirations that distinguish a developed legal order

---

[7] G. Teubner, *Law as an Autopoietic System* (Oxford: Blackwell, 1993), at p. 81. A very important contribution in demonstrating the applicability of autopoiesis to labour law is that of Ralf Rogowski and Ton Wilthagen, 'Reflexive labour law: an introduction', in R. Rogowski and T. Wilthagen (eds.) *Reflexive Labour Law* (Deventer: Kluwer, 1994).

[8] P. Selznick, *Law, Society and Industrial Justice* (New Brunswick, NJ: Transaction Books, 1980), at p. 11.   [9] Ibid., at p. 12.

[10] This reference, quoted by Selznick, ibid., is to R. Pound, *Jurisprudence* (St. Paul, MN: West Publishing Co., 1959), at p. 107. See Teubner, *Law as an Autopoietic System*, op. cit., at p. 44: 'abstract legal thought, dogmatics, and construction as self-descriptions of the legal system have to become central to legal-sociological analyses in such a way that would have appeared impossible in the wake of sociological disillusionment over law'.

[11] M. Weber, 'The origins of industrial capitalism in Europe', in W.G. Runciman (ed.) and E. Matthews (transl.), *Max Weber. Selections in Translation* (Cambridge: Cambridge University Press, 1978), at p. 339 (originally published as *Gesammelte Aufsätze zur Religionssoziologie* (Tübingen: Mohr, 2nd ed., 1922)).

from a system of subordination to naked power'.[12] In this context it is relevant to note that:

even a cursory look at the legal order will remind us that a great deal more is included than rules. Legal ideas, variously and unclearly labeled 'concepts', 'principles' and 'doctrines', have a vital place in authoritative decision.[13]

It is undoubtedly the case that 'the development and application of these materials requires a continuing assessment of human situations' and that 'the transition from general principle to specific rule requires a confrontation of social reality'.[14] The doctrinal content of legal thought cannot afford to become too far detached from the features of the social relationships which the law seeks to regulate. However, this is very far from saying that the law can or should map *directly* on to those particular features. On the contrary, the value of legal consistency requires that doctrinal descriptions of the 'external' world must be mediated through those linguistic forms which represent the principles or precepts which guide legal judgment.

It follows that a legal concept can be regarded as describing a certain social relationship without being reducible to, or becoming synonymous with, that relationship. Thus the juridical notion of 'employment' can be understood as linked to, but at the same time separate from, notions of employment which operate outside the legal frame of reference, in the context of economic exchange or of enterprise-level relations.

The terms used by labour lawyers to describe and define the employment relationship—expressions such as 'mutuality of obligation', 'integration', 'control'—arise in the context of attempts to classify work relations for regulatory purposes. They have a juridical meaning which arises in a particular normative context. The definitions of employment which are used in the social sciences do not have this particular purpose or rationale. In various ways, they try to capture the meaning attributed to employment by social actors for whom the concept serves as a reference point for practice. One particularly influential approach is that of new institutional economics. This offers an account of how the practice of employment could emerge as the result of the interactions of individual agents engaged in the repeated exchange of work for wages. More specifically, this body of work offers a functional account of the employment relationship as a transaction-cost minimizing device which facilitates large-scale production within the vertically integrated firm. It is this functionality which, in turn, is said to account for the prevalence of employment as a social practice. As David Marsden puts it:

Two great innovations lie behind the rise of the modern business enterprise: limited liability and the employment relationship. The first revolutionized company finance, opening up a vast new supply of capital. The second has revolutionized the organisation of labour services, providing firms and workers with a very flexible method of coordination and a platform for investing in skills. Today, nine tenths of workers with jobs in industrialized

[12] Selznick, *Law, Society and Industrial Justice*, at p. 8.　　[13] Ibid., at p. 27.　　[14] Ibid.

countries are engaged as employees. Despite the sometimes rapid growth in contingent employment, there is no evidence that the open-ended employment relationship is about to lose its preeminence.[15]

This analysis combines two ideas, both of which are familiar to labour lawyers, even if the terminology used is different. The first is the suggestion that the employment form offers the employer inherent flexibility which derives from the power to alter the mode of work organization after the employment has begun. Viewed from a contractual perspective, employment minimizes the costs which would otherwise arise from the need to renegotiate the contract in the light of changing circumstances. This is the idea which labour lawyers refer to as 'managerial prerogative' and which some economists, following R.H. Coase,[16] call the 'organising authority' which is present in employment but absent from the independent provision of labour services. Employment gives management the implicit power to direct labour, as Coase puts it, 'within certain limits',[17] the limits being determined, informally, by the parties' mutual expectations of the nature of the 'job' being undertaken and, more formally, by the express terms of the contract they enter into.

The second idea builds on this observation: this is the claim, advanced by Herbert Simon,[18] that the employment form offers something to the employee, namely a certain degree of continuity and security of employment. In legal terms, this is characterized by the open-ended and indeterminate duration of the contract of employment. The expectation of continuity makes it possible for the employee to invest in firm-specific skills which have limited value in other economic contexts, and more generally to offset some of the social and economic risks, in terms of exposure to loss of income and employment, which arise from dependence on one particular employer.

More generally, the employment contract can be understood as embodying a set of social norms or tacit conventions which together represent solutions to the problems of strategic interaction which arise when economic agents engage in a pattern of repeated economic exchange. These conventions make it possible for the parties to engage in a form of complex cooperation which generates a surplus by comparison to other modes of work organization. The nature of the relevant conventions can, it is claimed, be deduced from first principles, that is to say, by starting from certain assumptions about the ability of the parties to contract and about the context or environment in which they find themselves, assumptions which are realistic enough to command general assent while also being straightforward enough to generate predictive models of behaviour.[19] One crucial assumption is

[15] D. Marsden, *A Theory of Employment Systems: Micro-Foundations of Societal Diversity* (Oxford: Oxford University Press, 1999), at p. 4. Our argument here builds on S. Deakin, 'The many futures of the contract of employment', in J. Conaghan, R.M. Fischl and K. Klare (eds.) *Labour Law in an Era of Globalization* (Oxford: Oxford University Press, 2001) 177–196.

[16] R.H. Coase, 'The nature of the firm' (1937) 4 *Economica* (NS) 386–405.

[17] Ibid., at p. 391.

[18] H. Simon, 'A formal theory of the employment relation' (1951) 19 *Econometrica* 293–305.

[19] Marsden, A *Theory of Employment Systems*, op. cit.

that the parties are 'boundedly rational', that is, that they act in a calculative manner to further their self-interest, while at the same time being aware of the limits to calculation: they know that they cannot necessarily foresee the future and, above all, that they cannot accurately compute the costs and benefits of all relevant future courses of action. In addition, they operate in an environment which is characterized by a high degree of uncertainty. Under these circumstances, the parties know that they can profit from cooperation based on reciprocity, but each one also knows that the cooperation of the other cannot be guaranteed; it may be in the self-interest of each to act uncooperatively at some future point. The employment form serves to counter this threat of 'opportunism' or non-reciprocation.[20]

The precise source of the norms or conventions upon which cooperation within employment depends can be understood in a number of different, if possibly complementary, ways. One approach is to assume that the parties to the employment relationship simply strike a deal each time labour is hired, the terms of which reflect the basic trade-off between coordination and continuity. But a more realistic suggestion is that the social norms which are associated with employment arise, to a large degree, independently of the will of the parties in any particular case. This reflects the sense, which conforms to empirical observation, that there is a generally accepted understanding, in industrial societies, of what employment entails: a certain irreducible element of continuity and security on the one side and the right to manage on the other. Although the parties are free to negotiate, either individually or through their representatives, *within* the framework of this understanding, in the absence of one or, arguably, both of these elements, the relationship would not be one of employment, but would instead fall into the category of the independent provision of labour services.

One of the most important claims made by proponents of the new institutional economics or 'comparative institutional analysis' in the course of the past two decades is that social norms of this kind can form in the absence of any centralized legal or other rule-making authority. Norms or conventions, understood as regular patterns of behaviour, may arise 'spontaneously' on the basis of repeated interactions between boundedly rational agents.[21] In the absence of a major change in the external context or environment, inter-related behavioural strategies may take on the character of stable equilibria, because no individual agent has a good reason to believe that any of the others is going to change their strategy in the future. Once established, norms can spread thanks to the presence of 'network externalities': a norm may be worth following for any given agent, simply because large

[20] O. Williamson, M. Wachter and J. Harris, 'Understanding the employment relation: understanding the economics of idiosyncratic exchange' (1975) 6 *Bell Journal of Economics and Management Science* 250–278; O. Williamson, *The Economic Institutions of Capitalism* (New York: Free Press, 1985), ch. 9.

[21] See, in particular, A. Schotter, *The Economic Theory of Social Institutions* (Cambridge: Cambridge University Press, 1981); R. Sugden, *The Economics of Rights, Cooperation and Welfare* (Oxford: Blackwell, 1986); and H.P. Young, *Individual Strategy and Social Structure: An Evolutionary Theory of Institutions* (Princeton, NJ: Princeton University Press, 1998).

numbers of others are doing the same. The transaction costs of searching from scratch for a new solution may be too great, even if, in theory, the search might result in a superior pay-off.[22]

From this point of view, an economic institution arises from a combination of behavioural strategies and rational expectations. In this very basic sense, it is simply 'the equilibrium outcome of a game',[23] that is, of a process of strategic interaction. As such, an institution contains in a 'compressed' form the information which agents need to coordinate on a successful plan of action: 'information compression embodied in an institution will make it possible for boundedly rational agents to efficiently collect and utilize the information necessary to their actions to be consistent with changing internal and external environments'.[24] In the context of the labour market, this type of analysis has been used to explain, among other things, the emergence of norms relating to job definitions and patterns of skill formation,[25] and conventions governing the supply of labour, such as the 'reservation wage' below which unemployed workers will refuse offers of employment.[26]

What are the implications, for our understanding of the law, of a theory which claims to account for the emergence and stabilization of social norms without reference to intervention by a public, authoritative law-making body? It does not necessarily follow, from this approach, that the law can only ever be a peripheral force in shaping employment relations. It may well be the case that the law is indeed quite often peripheral to the conduct of workplace relations, but there is nothing in the theory to rule out an instrumental role for law in certain instances, even if, to be effective, the law has to go with the grain of social norms. However, there is another, more fundamental point being made here by the proponents of comparative institutional analysis. This is that the law itself should properly be regarded as a kind of 'meta-convention' which arises on the basis of multiple layers of iteration between agents. From a sociological or economic perspective, law is not an external or exogenous 'given' whose existence can simply be assumed; it is endogenous to the same processes of norm formation which give rise to non-binding conventions. The law is just as much a product of a given society as an instrument for shaping it. It follows that there is a limit to what formal law can achieve in determining outcomes:

the effectiveness of formal third-party mechanisms may lie primarily in their complementary support of private-order mechanisms but less so in entirely replacing them. Thus the role of the government in market governance may be viewed as endogenously determined by its overall arrangements rather than an autonomous determinant of it.[27]

---

[22] For a more detailed explanation of the relevant game-theoretical concepts of 'Nash equilibrium', 'subgame-perfect equilibrium' and 'evolutionarily stable strategy', see M. Aoki, *Toward a Comparative Institutional Analysis* (Cambridge, MA: MIT Press, 2001), ch. 1.

[23] Ibid., at p. 2.   [24] Ibid., at p. 14.

[25] Marsden, *A Theory of Employment Systems*, op. cit.

[26] R. Solow, *The Labour Market as a Social Institution* (Oxford: Blackwell, 1990).

[27] Aoki, *Towards a Comparative Institutional Analysis*, op. cit., at p. 89.

But is law then simply a reflection or consequence of the underlying strategies of the actors? In claiming, as Masahiko Aoki does, that 'statutory laws or institutions may induce an institution to evolve, but they themselves are not institutions',[28] is new institutional economics in danger of reproducing, in a fresh context, the Marxian distinction between an economic 'base' which represents the 'real foundation' of society, and a legal 'superstructure' which is one of a number of 'ideological forms'?[29] That distinction is problematic because it implies that legal change is only ever a symptom or expression of an underlying economic logic: 'laws and legal systems are regarded as mere surface phenomena'.[30] To take a sceptical view of this claim is not necessarily to deny the role of spontaneous forces in the formation of institutions, or the limits of legal regulation, or, indeed the potential significance of certain long-run historical forces shaping capitalist economic relations; it is simply to question whether such reductive approaches adequately capture the significance of law as an independent site of social and economic change.

If 'institutions' can, in general, be understood as bundles of norms and conventions of varying degrees of formality and rigidity, which function to guide the behaviour of agents, then juridical institutions such as the contract of employment are institutions of a particular type.[31] The 'compressed information' which they contain is 'encoded' on the basis of specifically legal processes, in particular litigation, adjudication and legislation. A social convention, however widespread, can only be 'instituted' in legal form once it has been mediated through these processes, just as the influence of a legal idea on society depends upon the presence of mechanisms, at the level of the enterprise or industry, for the reception and 'translation' of juridical notions. Thus the appearance of a convention or social norm of 'employment' at the level of social or economic relations offers only a partial explanation for the emergence of 'employment' as a juridical category. We cannot directly infer the nature of one from that of the other. Just as we should resist the temptation to imagine that social relations are instrumentally shaped by

[28] Aoki, *Towards a Comparative Institutional Analysis*, op. cit., at p. 20.

[29] K. Marx, *A Contribution to the Critique of Political Economy* ed. M. Dobb, transl. S. Ryazanskaya (London: Lawrence and Wishart, 1971) (originally published 1859), at pp. 20–21.

[30] G. Hodgson, 'The enforcement of contract and property rights: constitutive versus epiphenomenal conceptions of law', paper presented to the CRIC Polanyi conference, Manchester, October 2002, at p. 2.

[31] It would be consistent with Aoki's approach to regard legal institutions, in common with others, as norms in the sense of a set of shared beliefs concerning strategies and interactions, while acknowledging, as he does (in *Toward a Comparative Institutional Analysis*, op. cit.), that the public–legal sphere constitutes a distinctive 'domain' in which the state appears as a unique, focal agent, endowed with a set of action choices which are asymmetric to other, 'private' agents. The relationship between the 'domain' of the state and those of 'organization' (including the firm) and 'trade' (including the market) is defined by Aoki in terms of co-evolving 'complementarities' across institutions. This view is perhaps capable of reconciliation with the one we advance in the text; however, we would not go as far as Aoki appears to go in positing an all-embracing logic of individual interaction which ultimately defines *both* the economic *and* the legal domain. See further our discussion of the methodology of social systems theory, Section 4, below.

legal concepts drawn from abstract categories of juridical thought, so we should also avoid reducing legal categories to the level of 'surface' phenomena which simply 'express' the 'underlying reality' of the economic relationships to which they superficially correspond.

From this perspective, a major problem with the new institutional economics is that it affords too little weight to the role of formal, public institutions in shaping market relations. An alternative view would start from the proposition that labour markets and capital markets are, in part at least, legally and institutionally constituted.[32] This pattern of 'constitution' or institutional formation is too complex, and too specific to particular constraints of time and space for its nature to be deduced axiomatically from first principles. Thus law and the economy stand on the same ontological plane:

'the economy' is no more real than 'legal ideas'. It's an assemblage of conventions of which 'legal ideas' such as property, contract, promissory and fiduciary obligation, not to mention money itself, are indispensable elements and propagators.[33]

This point of view, in turn, has epistemological implications, in the sense of informing our understanding of what we can know about society through an examination of the law. If law is one of a number of 'constitutive' elements in the formation of market relations, the forms of legal–conceptual thought are, in and of themselves, evidence for the basic structure of a society or economy:

it is just about impossible to describe any set of 'basic' social practices without describing the legal relations among the people involved—legal relations that don't simply condition how the people related to each other, but to an important extent define the constitutive terms of the relationship, terms such as lord and peasant, master and slave, employer and employee, ratepayer and utility, and taxpayer and municipality . . . in actual historical societies, the law governing social relations—whenever invoked, alluded to, or even consciously much thought about—has been such a key element in the constitution of productive relations that it is difficult to see the value (aside from vindicating a wholly abstract commitment to 'materialist' world views) of trying to describe these relations apart from the law.[34]

If, in addition, there is no set of economic forces to which the law must conform, since the law is one of the constitutive forces which create 'the economy' and the institutions within it, it further follows that close attention should be paid to the historical conditions shaping the development of the law. There is no single, or pre-ordained, evolutionary path for the law, either as a result of the deterministic effects of historical forces, or by virtue of a supposedly inherent tendency for it to

---

[32] See F. Wilkinson, 'Productive systems' (1984) 7 *Cambridge Journal of Economics* 413–29, and 'Productive systems and the structuring role of economic and social theories', in B. Burchell, S. Deakin, J. Michie and J. Rubery (eds.) *Systems of Production: Markets, Organisations and Performance* (London: Routledge, 2003) 10–39. The account of the law–economy relation which we outline in the text builds on the 'productive systems' analysis; see further ch. 5, below.

[33] R. Gordon, 'Critical legal histories' (1984) 36 *Stanford Law Review* 57–125, at p. 117.

[34] Ibid., at pp. 102–4.

reproduce or express 'efficient' solutions to coordination problems. Instead, legal institutions are shaped by the historical circumstances of their formation; a *teleological* analysis, stressing evolution to efficiency, is replaced by a *genealogical* one, stressing the importance of origins and initial conditions.[35]

In this respect, Marsden's comparison between limited liability and the employment relationship is a highly revealing one. Each of these 'institutions' can be seen, in broad terms, as having a functional relationship to the emergence of the large-scale, vertically integrated enterprise. An argument can therefore be made for regarding each of them as an efficient response to the needs of economic agents for mechanisms which could overcome opportunism. In each case, however, the historical record suggests not just that public–legal interventions played a highly significant role in 'instituting' the social and economic practices on which these outcomes depended but, in addition, that the process was very far from being one of smooth adaptation of the law to economic needs. In each case, economic forms were 'instituted' by legal processes which were conditioned by historical circumstances and which subsequently evolved alongside the economic relations which they were regulating.[36]

Limited liability is one of a number of features of the modern business corporation to which functional analysis ascribes the role of reducing the costs of contracting, in particular the 'agency costs' which arise from asymmetries of information in long-term economic relations:

Consider, in this regard, the basic legal characteristics of the business corporation . . . there are five characteristics, most of which will be easily recognizable to anyone familiar with business affairs. They are: legal personality, limited liability, transferable shares, delegated management under a board structure, and investor ownership. These characteristics are . . . induced by the economic exigencies of the large modern business corporation. Thus corporate law everywhere must, of necessity, provide for them.[37]

Limited liability for shareholders makes it possible for equity investors to subscribe their capital to the enterprise without facing the possibility of personal claims for the firm's trading debts (beyond the amount of any share capital not yet

[35] W.N. Njoya, 'Employee ownership and efficiency: an evolutionary perspective' (2004) 30 *Industrial Law Journal* 211–241.

[36] This is an illustration of what Mark Harvey, building on Karl Polanyi's work, calls 'instituted economic process': see M. Harvey, 'Productive systems, market and competition as "instituted economic process"', in B. Burchell, S. Deakin, J. Michie and J. Rubery (eds.) *Systems of Production: Markets, Organisations and Performance* (London: Routledge, 2003) 40–59; K. Polanyi, 'The economy as instituted process', in K. Polanyi, C. Arensberg and H. Pearson (eds.) *Trade and Market in the Early Empires* (New York: Free Press) 243–270. Harvey points out that an 'instituted' view of economic relations is fundamentally different from one which stresses their 'embeddedness' in interpersonal relations, a view which he suggests has the effect of 'sociologising the economy out of existence' ('Instituted economic process', at p. 43). The principal reference for the 'embeddedness' approach is M. Granovetter, 'Economic action and social structure: the case of embeddedness' (1985) 91 *American Journal of Sociology* 481–510.

[37] H. Hansmann and R. Kraakman, 'What is corporate law?', in R. Kraakman, P. Davies, H. Hansmann, G. Hertig, H. Kanda, K. Hopt and E. Rock (eds.) *The Anatomy of Corporate Law: A Comparative and Functional Approach* (Oxford: Oxford University Press, 2003), at p. 1.

paid up). Because shareholders now no longer have to monitor each other's wealth or behaviour, the potential pool of risk capital available to companies is greatly expanded.[38] Yet, for reasons we shall explore in more detail in Chapter 2 below, for most of the period of early British industrialization, limited liability was simply not available to the vast majority of firms. It was not possible for parties to contract for it, because of the existence of significant legal obstacles, and although there were substitutes which came close to replicating its effects, they were deficient in a number of ways, and recognized as such at the time.[39] The constituent elements of what later became recognized as the standard corporate form originated independently of each other, and only converged in stages. The institution of joint stock, the forerunner of freely transferable shares, had origins in the structure of the chartered corporations, some of which dated from the late sixteenth and early seventeenth centuries; however, for much of the period prior to the mid-nineteenth century, share ownership did not confer limited liability. In a period when incorporation via royal charter was highly restricted, most early industrial enterprises were run as 'unincorporated companies', in effect partnerships under which owner-managers and investors retained personal liability for debts of the business. It was only in 1844 that a low-cost registration procedure made incorporation generally available, and as late as 1856 that it was followed by the provision of limited liability, without significant strings attached, for this new corporate form.[40] Thus public–legal intervention, in this case in the form of legislation, was the precondition for the emergence of this pivotally important mechanism for the mobilization of risk capital. Even then, its use remained limited in most manufacturing industries; it was only in the last decades of the nineteenth century that a significant movement towards consolidation began. Thus it is difficult to see the enactment of corporate laws underpinning the business enterprise as an efficient response to economic needs. Whatever its efficiency properties may have been, during this period the limited liability form evolved in a way which was distinctly out of synch with the evolution of the business enterprise. Moreover, as we explore in more detail later, this 'asynchronic' evolution had real effects, both for the law and for the development of industrial enterprise in Britain.[41]

The same prominence for public–legal intervention and the same kind of asynchronic relationship with economic and social change can also be seen in the development of the contract of employment. The innovation of the

---

[38] See F. Easterbrook and D. Fischel, *The Economic Structure of Corporate Law* (Cambridge, MA: Harvard University Press, 1991), ch. 2.

[39] See R. Harris, *Industrializing English Law: Entrepreneurship and Business Organization 1720–1844* (Cambridge: Cambridge University Press, 2000), ch. 1.

[40] By virtue, respectively, of 7 & 8 Victoria c. 110, and 19 & 20 Victoria c. 47. See W.R. Cornish and G. de N. Clark, *Law and Society in England 1750–1950* (London: Sweet & Maxwell, 1989), at pp. 254–257; Harris, *Industrializing English Law*, op. cit., ch. 10, and our discussion in Ch. 2, below.

[41] The idea of asynchronic evolution is extensively developed in the context of English company law by A.S.Y. Lee, 'Law, economic theory, and corporate governance: the origins of UK legislation on company directors' conflicts of interests, 1862–1948' Ph.D. thesis, University of Cambridge, 2002.

contract of employment was not simply a matter of matching the law to economic needs. Rather, it depended upon a public articulation of a societal compromise or compact which went beyond the level of the enterprise, described by Alain Supiot, writing in the context of western European labour law as a whole, as follows:

Under the model of the welfare state, the work relationship became the site on which a fundamental trade-off between economic dependence and social protection took place. While it was of course the case that the employee was subjected to the power of another, it was understood that, in return, there was a guarantee of the basic conditions for participation in society.[42]

In the same way that the different elements of the legal concept of the corporation converged in a series of steps, the employment contract was the result of several, distinct steps in legal evolution. The concepts used by nineteenth century British judges and legislators to describe employment relationships in the common law world—independent contractor, casual worker, servant, labourer, workman—do not map neatly on to 'binary divide'[43] between employees and the self-employed which labour lawyers are familiar with today. In both the common law and the civil law, the apparently fundamental classification between employment and self-employment only assumed its modern form at the end of the nineteenth century.

Employment relations in the early phases of industrialization were only partially 'contractual'. In common law systems the juridical form of this idea can be found in the 'master–servant' model which reached its height in the mid-nineteenth century while in civilian systems, during the same period, the employer's unilateral powers of control were with some difficulty grafted on to the traditional Roman law concept of the contract of hire (the *locatio conductio*).[44] Both in Britain and on the continent, criminal law provisions and sanctions defined the extent of managerial prerogative, rather than contract alone. In time, the employer's right to give orders became rationalized, in the English common law and in systems closely influenced by it, as an implied contract term, so cloaking managerial prerogative in contractual form. However, this was a twentieth century development which occurred only some time after the point, starting in the 1870s, at which criminal sanctions for breach of the contract of service were repealed in most of the common law world. As we shall see in more detail in Chapter 2, it is highly doubtful that nineteenth-century judges regarded the source of the employer's unilateral power as contractual.

---

[42] A. Supiot, 'Introduction', in A. Supiot (ed.) *Au delà de l'emploi. Transformations du travail et devenir du droit du travail en Europe* (Paris: Flammarion, 1999) 7–24, at p. 10.

[43] This expression is explained and developed by M. Freedland, 'The role of the contract of employment in modern labour law', in L. Betten (ed.) *The Employment Contract in Transforming Labour Relations* (Deventer: Kluwer, 1995) 17–27, at p. 19.

[44] B. Veneziani, 'The evolution of the contract of employment', in B. Hepple (ed.) *The Making of Labour Law in Europe* (London: Mansell, 1986) 31–72.

The 'contractualization' of the employment relationship was associated above all with the gradual spread of social legislation in the fields of workmen's compensation, social insurance and employment protection. The terms 'contract of employment' and 'employee' came into general use as a description of wage-dependent labour only as a result of this process. Contractualization, in this sense, had two aspects: the placing of limits on the employer's legal powers of command, limits which, as we have just noted, were given a contractual form as either express or implied terms; and the use of the employment relationship as a vehicle for channelling and redistributing social and economic risks, through the imposition on employers of obligations of revenue collection, and compensation for interruptions to earnings. This process made it more plausible for the courts to visualize employment as a 'relational' contract, based on mutual commitments to maintain the relationship over a period of time.[45]

The role of the vertical integration of the enterprise in this process was a complex one. The emergence of large-scale business provided the occasion for the extension of social protection within the model of the employment relationship, at least as much as the functional necessity for it. As vertical integration replaced sub-contracting as the predominant form of economic organization, a process which began in the final quarter of the nineteenth century and was still going on at the mid point of the twentieth century, workplace rules emerged to deal with the problem of how to specify the limits to managerial prerogative within the context of the open-ended employment relationship.[46] These rules were a response to the increase in employer power which arose with the end of the subcontracting system and the associated removal of many traditional forms of workers' control over the pace and organization of work. Under these circumstances, 'for workers who distrusted the intentions of particular employers, an open-ended contract would have seemed a recipe for exploitation: and so it only became acceptable as various protections were incorporated into it'.[47] The solutions found—such as the categorization of grades according to work tasks, craft skills, professional qualifications and, more recently, to flexible job functions—were context-specific in the sense that they differed according to the degree to which work in different countries and industries was organized along the lines of 'occupational' or craft labour markets, or according to bureaucratic or enterprise-based systems of control. The process was also both contingent and cumulative, in

[45] On the notion of the 'relational' contract, see I. Macneil, 'The many futures of contracts' (1974) *Southern California Law Review* 691–816.

[46] See S. Jacoby, *Employing Bureaucracy: Managers, Unions, and the Transformation of Work in American Industry 1900–1945* (New York: Columbia University Press, 1985); P. Cappelli, 'Market-mediated employment: the historical context', in M. Blair and T. Kochan (eds.) *The New Relationship. Human Capital in the American Corporation* (Washington DC: Brookings Institution, 2000) 66–90; Marsden, *A Theory of Employment Systems*, op. cit.; J. Saglio, 'Changing wages orders: France 1900–1950' in L. Clarke, P. de Gijsel and J. Jansenn (eds.) *The Dynamics of Wage Relations in Europe* (Dordrecht: Kluwer, 2000) 44–59.

[47] D. Marsden, 'Breaking the link: Has the employment contract had its day?' *Centrepiece* (1999) winter, 20–25, at p. 21.

the sense that existing rules and practices were put to new purposes. Hence, in the cumulative manner of 'path-dependent' evolution, rules which had initially been deployed for the purposes of management, such as job classification rules, were then used by unions to defend established working patterns, since 'defining people's jobs also makes clear the limits on their obligations'.[48]

Labour law gradually came to support many of the norms arrived at by labour and management by codifying them in the form of terms incorporated from collective agreements, common law implied terms and statutory employment protection rights, but the single most significant form of legislative intervention in the labour market was in the area of social security law, and, more specifically, the law of social insurance. The growth of large-scale enterprise provided the opportunity for redistributive policies which operated through the mechanisms of taxation and social security system, of which national insurance became the most prominent. As individuals and households became increasingly dependent on continuous, waged employment for access to income, they were vulnerable to the effects of any prolonged interruptions to earnings. State intervention, by imposing responsibility for these wider social risks on employers, then provided further incentives for the growth, in its turn, of the vertically integrated firm, which was best placed to deal with the costs of regulatory compliance.

This is not to deny that the contract of employment has been 'a remarkable social and economic institution';[49] but it is to suggest that, in seeking to understand the nature of its current trajectory, an analysis of its public–regulatory character is at least as important as one which is focused on enterprises and industries, and that an historical perspective should be incorporated into functional analyses. When the public–regulatory dimension is taken into account, it becomes clear that the state became the implicit third party to the contract, channelling the risks of economic insecurity throughout the workforce as a whole through the social insurance system, and using social security contributions and income taxation to support the public provision of welfare services. The complex interaction of these different governance mechanisms was then reflected in the juridical form of the contract of employment. Given the multiple tasks of classification, regulation and redistribution which it was called on to perform, it is perhaps the durability of the contract of employment, rather than the dysfunctionality which some contemporary critiques identify,[50] which above all requires explanation.

---

[48] D. Marsden, 'Breaking the link: Has the employment contract had its day?' *Centrepiece* (1999) winter, 20–25, at p. 22.   [49] Ibid., at p. 20.

[50] See H. Collins, 'Independent contractors and the challenge of vertical disintegration to employment protection law' (1990) 10 *Oxford Journal of Legal Studies* 353–380, at p. 369 ('dysfunctional'), and 'Market power, bureaucratic power and the contract of employment' (1986) 15 *Industrial Law Journal* 1–15, at p. 2 ('artificial and unpersuasive doctrinal explanations'); J. Clark and Lord Wedderburn, 'Modern labour law: problems, functions and policies', in Lord Wedderburn, R. Lewis and J. Clark (eds.) *Labour Law and Industrial Relations: Building on Kahn-Freund* (Oxford: Clarendon Press, 1983) 147–242 ('anarchy' and 'crisis of concepts').

What we have called a 'genealogical' analysis makes it possible to see why it is that the contract of employment could be, at one and the same time, the 'cornerstone'[51] of the modern labour law system, joining the enterprise to the welfare state just as it connected the common law of contract and property to social legislation, *and* the source of anachronisms, confusions and crises in the application of the law. On the one hand, it spoke to the inclusive agenda of the welfare state, aiming for an ideal of social citizenship which could mirror the notion of political and civil rights, completing the democratic project by extending the conditions of social existence in the same way that the conditions of civil and political participation were extended through the franchise. On the other, it was constructed on a set of contingent social and economic circumstances which soon began to unravel, thereby endangering the project of democratic emancipation which it embodied.

This was because, in the first place, the contract of employment looks back to the model of economic subordination which was contained in the master–servant relation. This has meant, among other things, that many of the objectives of economic democracy and worker participation in decision-making within the enterprise which inspired labour law reform at the turn of the twentieth century have remained unfulfilled; they have been addressed neither by the reforms to employment law which aimed to regulate the employer's powers of discipline and dismissal, nor by the predominant emphasis on wage determination and related distributional issues within collective bargaining.

Secondly, the contract of employment, at least in its classic form, incorporated an anachronistic notion of the division of household labour. This was done by formalizing the notion of the male breadwinner wage through collective bargaining, and by ensuring the primacy of the single (male) earner within social insurance. In the traditional model of social insurance, women were rarely in a position to claim unemployment or retirement benefits in their own right, either because their occupations were excluded from the coverage of the contributory schemes, or because their contributions records were inadequate on account of low earnings and interruptions to employment. Conversely, their most substantial rights were those derived from dependence on a male earner through marriage or other family connection.

Finally, the contract of employment has been premised on a model of regulation which makes a series of assumptions about the power of legal centralism which no longer hold. Part of this represents the undermining of the idea of the nation state as a more or less self-contained political entity, insulated from the pressures of transnational economic migration and integration. 'Full employment in a free society', Beveridge's programme for economic inclusion and social citizenship,[52] was a strategy principally addressed to national government. The focus, for

---

[51] O. Kahn-Freund, 'Servants and independent contractors' (1951) 14 *Modern Law Review* 504–509.

[52] W. Beveridge, *Full Employment in a Free Society* (London: Liberal Publications Department, 1944, and Allen and Unwin, 2nd ed., 1967).

example, on *national* insurance set clear jurisdictional limits to the notion of social inclusion which the contract of employment was capable of representing. When, in the 1970s, governments began to liberalize rules on the movement of capital, the bases upon which they had previously assumed powers of regulation and taxation were undercut. In practice, the extent to which the increasing inter-dependence of national economies from the point of view of trade makes it more difficult for them to regulate labour and product markets is an open question. It is possible that governments are no longer able to coordinate their national macroeconomic policy interventions as they did in the past; however, many of the institutional changes which have led to a weakening of national regulatory regimes were initiated by these same national governments. More generally, legal centralism as a form of regulation is challenged by the perception that there is a set of rival and competing modes of regulation or governance, ranging from transnational codes of practice to forms of professional and occupational self-regulation which no longer take the state as their point of reference. The result is a 'de-centred' labour law system, within which not just mandatory social legislation but also established modes of collective bargaining have come under challenge.[53]

Thus an historical, and even more precisely, an *evolutionary* perspective, is essential for understanding the current 'crisis of concepts' in labour law. The emergence of the contract of employment has been a complex process involving many actors and influences. It was not 'invented' by a single draftsman or judge, nor even as the result, solely, of the collective efforts of lawyers and advocates. Pressures and opportunities for legal change were derived from outside the legal system in the form of political mobilization, and changes in the predominant form of economic organization, and shifts in the structure of the family and the composition of the labour force. These made up the background against which strategies for legal change were formulated and implemented. Instead of the adjustment of legal rules to economic needs, there has been at best a confusing, at times disjointed, and fundamentally asynchronic *co-evolution* of legal and economic forms.[54] The functional and dysfunctional features of the contract of employment alike are the consequence of this very particular trajectory.

3. Industrialization and Freedom of Contract

The implication of the analysis which we have just presented is that the juridical form of the contract of employment is the result of two linked, but historically distinct, developments. The first was the process of industrialization which led to

---

[53] U. Mückenberger, 'Alternative mechanisms of voice representation' presentation to joint Columbia University/Institute of Advanced Legal Studies seminar, London, July 2004 (using the term 'decentration').

[54] See Lee, 'Law, economic theory and corporate governance' op. cit. for a similar argument in the context of company law.

the institution of formally free labour, as workers were separated from the land and other traditional sources of subsistence, and labour became the subject of exchange relations but also of a specific, hierarchical form of legal control. The second was the advent of the welfare state, which provided a basis for organizing and spreading the risks inherent in the shift to an industrial society, in which wage labour had become the principal source of subsistence for the large majority of the population. The contract of employment reflects within its structure the tension between these two ideas, between, that is, the two functions of economic coordination on the one hand and risk redistribution on the other. This structural tension is, moreover, the result of a particular historical process of institutional formation, in which the new model of employment was superimposed on the older notion of service.

What does this analysis imply for our understanding of the legal transition which accompanied industrialization? This is a pivotal issue for British legal and economic history. The British industrial revolution, suggests E.A. Wrigley, 'is the centrepiece of world history over recent centuries, and *a fortiori* of the country in which it began'.[55] In the historiography of the industrial revolution, moreover, the role of legal and institutional factors has played a major part from the very inception of the field. Arnold Toynbee, the first historian to use the term 'industrial revolution' in lectures he gave in the 1880s, defined it by reference to several, linked features: the marked increase in the overall size of the population in the course of the eighteenth and early nineteenth centuries; the decline of the agricultural population during the same period and the growth of towns; the replacement of the domestic system of manufactures by the factory; the expansion of trade which was made possible by improvements in communication; and those 'altered conditions in the production of wealth' which 'necessarily involved an equal revolution in its distribution'.[56] But in Toynbee's view, the most fundamental change of all was *institutional*: 'the essence of the Industrial Revolution is the substitution of competition for the medieval regulations which had previously controlled the production and distribution of wealth'.[57]

Toynbee's analysis has particular resonance in the context of the removal of legislative support for guild controls and the abolition of statutory wage fixing, which occurred in 1814 and 1813 respectively. Together with the laws governing poor law settlements, these were measures which Adam Smith, writing in the mid-eighteenth century, had described as 'obstructions' to the 'free circulation' of labour and stock.[58] In addition, the poor law Amendment Act of 1834,[59] which

[55] E.A. Wrigley, *Continuity, Chance and Change: The Character of the Industrial Revolution in England* (Cambridge: Cambridge University Press, 1988), at p. 8.
[56] A. Toynbee, *Lectures on the Industrial Revolution in England*, ed. with an introduction by T.S. Ashton (Newton Abbott: A.M. Kelley, 1969) (originally published 1884), at p. 92.
[57] Ibid., at p. 85.
[58] A. Smith, *An Inquiry into the Nature and Causes of the Wealth of Nations*, ed. with an introduction by J.S. Nicholson (London: T. Nelson and Sons, 1886) (originally published 1776), volume 1, ch. 10, at p. 57.   [59] 4 & 5 William IV, c. 76. See further Ch. 3, below.

put an end to the allowance system of the old poor law and instituted the principle of 'less eligibility', was for Toynbee 'perhaps the most beneficent Act of Parliament which has been passed since the Reform Bill [of 1832]'.[60] The idea that the industrial revolution was characterized by a shift from protection to competition, from regulation to contract, and from collective to individual forms of property, has remained a point of reference in the debate ever since.

One reason for this association is that the period between 1760 and 1830 which is often regarded as the critical period of economic transition was, undeniably, a period of intense institutional change during which the liberalizing influence of the theory of political economy was particularly strong. In the 1960s, W.W. Rostow's theory of the 'take-off' into industrial growth identified industrialization with the same period,[61] thereby adding further force to the link between economic growth and the removal of regulatory 'constraints' on production. More recent scholarship has revised the 'take-off' theory. It is now generally agreed that the half century after 1750 was one of relatively slow rates of growth, in terms of both output and incomes per head, in comparison to the period from the mid-seventeenth to the mid-eighteenth century, which had seen rapid improvements in agricultural productivity, allowing the movement of population into towns and cities.[62] The economy as a whole did not grow at more than three per cent per annum until the 1830s, and the pace of industrial change and the adoption of machine technologies, outside a few industrial sectors, were limited up to this point.[63] By 1850, relatively few workers were employed in factories; only a small proportion worked in technologically advanced industries such as cotton, iron and steel, and metalworking; and the full impact of steam power in transport and production was yet to be felt.

By the mid-nineteenth century, a decisive shift had nevertheless occurred in the direction of an industrialized economy in which sustained increases in output per head were able to support a growing population, which, in a virtuous circle, provided a source of rising demand. As Wrigley explains, the process by which this was arrived at was a complex and protracted one, involving a transition from an 'advanced organic economy' which, notwithstanding the rise in agricultural productivity, remained dependent upon limited resources to sustain a growing population, to a 'mineral-based energy economy' in which the use of coal and steam-based technologies released new productive powers:

The essential nature of the contrast . . . was that between negative and positive feedback systems. An organic economy, however advanced, was subject to negative feedback in the

---

[60] *Lectures on the Industrial Revolution*, op. cit., at p. 111.

[61] W.W. Rostow, *The Stages of Economic Growth, A Non-Communist Manifesto* (Cambridge: Cambridge University Press, 1961).

[62] Wrigley, *Continuity, Chance and Change*, op. cit., ch. 1; M. Daunton, *Progress and Poverty: An Economic and Social History of Britain 1700–1850* (Oxford: Oxford University Press, 1995), ch. 2.

[63] N.F.R. Crafts, *British Economic Growth during the Industrial Revolution* (Oxford: Clarendon Press, 1985).

sense that the very process of growth set in train changes that made further growth additionally difficult because of the operation of declining marginal returns in production from the land…Each step taken made the next a little more painful to take. In parts of an organic economy, because of the effect of the specialisation of function, increasing returns were available, and positive feedback existed, but, since each round of expansion necessarily increased pressure on the land by raising demand for industrial raw materials, as well as food, in the system as a whole negative feedback tended to prevail. In a mineral-based energy economy, in contrast, freed from dependence on the land for raw materials, positive feedback could exist over a large and growing sector of economic activity. Each step taken made the next easier to take. The system as whole could gain an increasing momentum of growth. Real wages were not permanently constrained to remain close to the minimum set by the prevailing norms of society.[64]

This more complex view of the timing of industrial development implies a reconsideration of the nature of the legal transition to industrialization, in which the role of the old poor law is pivotal. As we examine in greater detail in Chapter 3, up to 1750 the system of poor law settlements functioned to provide poor relief in the event of an interruption to earnings through sickness, old age, or other loss of employment. Income replacement rates were high by modern standards, expenditure was on a greater scale than in any other western European country at the time, and although administration was carried out at parish level, national legislation provided a public–institutional framework for the collection of the local taxes on which the system depended. Labour mobility was encouraged by the legal guarantee that a young, unmarried worker could acquire a settlement by hiring under a yearly contract of service, and by a system of certificates under which 'home' parishes undertook to meet the costs of poor relief administered by 'host' parishes. Although the settlement system began to decline after 1750, its demise was the result of increasing casualization of employment and the effects of rural overpopulation, rather than any readjustment of the economy towards a more market-orientated legal framework. On the contrary, the old poor law can be seen as underpinning the emergence of wage labour at a time when reduced access to the land and related legal and social changes were increasing the degree of wage dependence experienced by the still largely rural population:

It might be nearer the truth to say that the development of capitalism in England was conditional upon the existence of an efficient and ubiquitous welfare system than to say that it could only flourish by undermining the old system of welfare provision. The system of support created by the old poor law covered much the same range of life-cycle hazards as are covered by the state today, sometimes on a scale uncannily similar to that current nowadays . . . Viewed in this light the creation and elaboration of the poor law system from the reign of Elizabeth onwards was an important reason for the development of a capitalist system in England, affording the kind of provision for those in need which gave individuals a degree of protection against the hazards of life that in typical peasant cultures was provided by kin.[65]

[64] *Continuity, Chance and Change*, op. cit., at pp. 29–30.　　[65] Ibid., at p. 120.

Thus the state had, in effect, already replaced the extended family as the basis for welfare support, *prior to* the period traditionally identified with industrialization.

When the framework of relief through poor law settlements began to break up, it was replaced by various versions of the allowance or 'Speenhamland' system, under which outdoor relief, paid by reference to a sliding scale based on the price of bread, was used to subsidize low-paid and casualized forms of employment. How far the allowance system was the cause, and how far the consequence, of the break-up of stable employment in agriculture, continues to be a matter of dispute between historians.[66] What is not in doubt is that the widespread adoption of the allowance system filled a void left by the demise of annual service and the *de facto* ending of wage regulation in agricultural areas in the 1790s. The subsequent substantial rise in poor relief was a principal factor in the pressure which eventually led to the legislative abrogation of the old poor law and the adoption of the principle of 'less eligibility' in the administration of poor relief, following the passage of the poor law Amendment Act 1834. Statutory and administrative enforcement of 'less eligibility', while slow to take effect in the years following 1834, had achieved considerable momentum by the 1870s, and was to form the centrepiece of poor law policy up to, and in some ways even beyond, the first national insurance legislation of the early twentieth century.

How is this process of institutional change to be assessed by reference to the concept of industrialization? Was the old poor law a vestige of pre-industrial regulation? In *The Great Transformation* Karl Polanyi presented Speenhamland as holding back the emergence of a modern labour market: 'during the most active period of the Industrial Revolution, from 1795 to 1834, the creating of a labour market in England was prevented through the Speenhamland law'.[67] The outcome was a social catastrophe: 'the attempt to create a capitalistic order without a labour market had failed disastrously'.[68] The new poor law was designed on the assumption that once outdoor relief was denied to those able to work (the 'able-bodied' poor), wages would once again rise to a level which reflected subsistence needs. In that sense, the Act of 1834 was indeed the harbinger of a labour market based purely on exchange relations, in which there were no impediments to the free operation of supply and demand. But there is also a sense in which Speenhamland was a mechanism for the destruction of a system of poor relief, based on the twin institutions of settlement and the yearly hiring, which had been complementary to the emergence of a modern labour market. As Polanyi himself put it, 'if human society is a self-acting machine for maintaining the standards on which it was built, Speenhamland was an automaton for demolishing the standards on which any kind of society could be built'.[69] The reaction to the negative consequences of the allowance system (which were real enough to contemporaries, however imaginary

[66] See our discussion of this point in Chapter 3, below.
[67] K. Polanyi, *The Great Transformation. The Political and Economic Origins of our Time* (Boston: Beacon Press, 1957) (originally published 1944), at p. 77.   [68] Ibid., at p. 80.
[69] Ibid., at p. 99.

some now claim them to have been) was so severe that the idea of wage regulation and the use of the poor relief system to underpin basic labour market standards was ruled out for the rest of the nineteenth century, in favour of dogmatic adherence to the precepts of classical political economy; and while 'less eligibility' was intended to be an expression of the doctrine of laissez-faire, in practice it required the creation of an extensive bureaucratic apparatus of poor law administration for the ideal of a self-regulating market to be made effective.[70]

What of the law regulating the content of the employment relationship and the organization of work during this period? The political economists of the period saw the removal of guild controls and the suppression of centuries-old constraints on the use of machinery as part of the process of freeing up productive forces. Later commentators, including those critical of or sceptical towards laissez-faire such as Polanyi, have tended to regard mechanization and contractualization as the linked processes which brought about an irrevocable shift from household and guild forms of labour to factory employment.[71] E.P. Thompson's account of the cultural shift from a 'moral economy' of customary rights to a system of 'political economy',[72] in which the formality of contractual relations was coupled with the new time-based work-discipline of factory labour, is in a similar vein.[73]

Weber, likewise, described the transition from pre-modern forms of service to 'formally free labour' as lying at the foundations of the emergence of industrial capitalism. The 'modern West', he argued, displayed 'a completely different form of capitalism, which has developed nowhere else in the world: the rational capitalist organization of (formally) free labour'. The rational organization of the capitalist enterprise would not have been possible without 'the separation of the household from the place of work'.[74] Echoing this point, Selznick has influentially drawn a contrast between the master–servant law of the pre-industrial age, and the contractual model of the employment relationship, which he dated to the early nineteenth century. On the one hand:

The old law of master and servant looked to the household as a model and saw in its just governance the foundation of an orderly society. The household model made sense in an overwhelmingly agricultural economy where hired labour, largely permanent, supplemented the work of family members and all were subject to the tutelage of the father-manager. The model also fit the early pattern of work and training among skilled artisans. In this setting, the relation of master and servant was highly diffuse and paternalistic. Work was carried out in the house of the master or in a small shop nearby. The workman lived as a member of the household and often remained for life with the same master. It was against this background that the law of master and servant developed.[75]

[70] See generally Ch. 3, below.   [71] Polanyi, *The Great Transformation*, op. cit., at p. 75.
[72] E.P. Thompson, 'The moral economy of the English crowd in the eighteenth century' (1971) 50 *Past and Present* 76–136.
[73] E.P. Thompson, 'Time, work-discipline, and industrial capitalism' (1967) 38 *Past and Present* 36–97.   [74] 'The origins of industrial capitalism in Europe', op. cit. at p. 336.
[75] *Law, Society and Industrial Justice*, op. cit., at p. 123.

The arrival of industrialization marked the removal of legal obstacles to freedom of contract:

A truly contractual theory of employment did not emerge until the concept of a free market gained ascendance in economic life. In the late eighteenth and early nineteenth centuries, the idea of contract heralded a new age in politics as well as in trade. Contract was the solvent and the surrogate for a new political community rooted in traditional and unquestioned authority. It was the key to growth and freedom for an economy bound and fettered by privileged guilds, chartered corporations, and the heavy hand of state control. With contract as master image and touchstone of legitimacy, the old constraints on political freedom, freedom of movement, and freedom of trade could be removed.[76]

This description is not necessarily inaccurate as the representation of the movement from one ideal type of production to another. However, it truncates a process of historical development which, in practice, was both more complex and considerably more elongated than the passages just quoted appear to suggest. In the England of the seventeenth or eighteenth century, just prior to industrialization, the extended family had ceased to be common: 'the small conjugal family had been the normal co-residential unit in England for many centuries'.[77] Service in the course of a yearly hiring was normally undertaken prior to marriage and so was not intended to give rise to a permanent or lifelong employment, but was just one part of the customary life cycle of employment. Employment in the form of day labouring or on the basis of a weekly hiring was already common by this point.

Nor is the description an accurate account of what happened as industrialization began to gather pace, at the turn of the nineteenth century. As we explain in more detail in Chapter 2 below, the role of the master–servant law did not *diminish* as industrialization gathered pace; significant legislative innovation in the course of the eighteenth and nineteenth centuries meant that the scope, force and severity of this body of law *intensified* at this point. It was not until the 1870s that criminal sanctions were removed from the law of the individual service relationship, and even then a form of specific performance at the employer's behest remained in place. Conceptually, too, contract played a limited role in governing the work relationship for most industrial and agricultural workers; the source of the master's right to give orders was conceptualized as an adjunct of the particular status created by the legislation.

Three points stand out from the critique that we develop in more detail in later chapters. The first is that there was a labour market in England *before* the transition to an industrial society and economy took place. Land enclosure and the movement of the population into towns and cities ensured that a substantial proportion of the population was already dependent on wages, directly or indirectly, for subsistence. Secondly, the institutions of wage labour were supported by legal provisions of various kinds, many of which gave expression to customary

---

[76] *Law, Society and Industrial Justice*, op. cit., at p. 130.
[77] Wrigley, *Continuity, Chance and Change*, op. cit., at p. 118.

expectations, but which at the same time supported market mechanisms. The poor law provided a framework for the encouragement and regulation of labour mobility and the provision of welfare support; guild rules and apprenticeship regulations sought to regulate competition in production and maintain standards of quality. These were not simply remnants of a medieval pattern of economic regulation; they had evolved to meet the conditions of an emerging industrial economy. Thirdly, although the period between 1750 and 1830 did indeed see the removal both of the poor law (in its traditional form), the repeal of guild-based forms of apprenticeship and labour regulation and the suppression of attempts, such as those of the Luddites, to maintain traditional controls over production, this was not a process which can be straightforwardly characterized in terms of 'contractualization' or, in modern terminology, 'deregulation'. What was involved here was the *redefinition* of property rights and the *reconstitution* of public–regulatory law, rather than a simple shift from paternalist control to market-based contractualism. As Martin Daunton has recently put it:[78]

The response of workers should not be interpreted in terms of disorder and ineffectuality, but as part of a well-developed and articulate 'corporate discourse' which stressed stability, regulation, and the need to observe strict limits to innovation which threatened independence and accountability. Workers threatened by the rise of 'dishonourable trades' appealed for the state to protect their property in skill in the same way as other property, and to recognize their social value. The rejection of legislative support for this set of assumptions was political, and workers continued to press for its restoration. Luddites who continued to urge the implementation of laws which no longer existed were, according to some historians, not adjusting to new realities. This fails to comprehend their attitudes and assumptions, and gives priority to the ideology of their opponents.

To sum up: the relationship between industrialization and the emergence of the contract of employment was a complex and multi-layered one. To argue that, at the time of the industrial revolution, there was a fundamental shift from status to contract, which was then reversed with the advent of the welfare state, is far too simplistic. Whatever the validity of such a claim in other contexts,[79] it does not apply to the labour market; and given the importance attached to the labour market and in particular to the institution of 'free labour' in the historical analysis of the emergence of capitalism, this is a matter of wider significance. The conceptual history which we will present in greater detail in later chapters indicates that throughout the evolution of the law governing work relationships, it is at each point the *conjunction* of contract and status which stands out. In the nineteenth century it was the status of *service* which was grafted on to the contractual form of

---

[78] *Progress and Poverty*, op. cit., at p. 499.

[79] See generally P.S. Atiyah, *The Rise and Fall of Freedom of Contract* (Oxford: Clarendon Press, 1979). Recognizing the exceptional nature of employment within his larger thesis, Atiyah writes, at p. 523: 'I must begin with the process by which freedom of contract came to apply to contracts of employment in the first place, and we shall then observe the curious fact that this process was never wholly completed at all'. See further our analysis in Ch. 2, below.

the relationship; in the twentieth, the rights-based status of social insurance and employment protection law, a category which approximated to a notion of *social citizenship*. As Supiot has suggested, in the wider context of a comparative analysis of the systems of western Europe, 'the coupling of contract and status should not be understood in the sense of an historical passage from one to the other, but instead in terms of a fundamental structural ambiguity which characterizes labour law'.[80] This 'structural ambiguity' is also a deep-seated functional feature of capitalist labour relations, in which, as Polanyi recognized, public regulation is the inevitable precondition of the operation of the market:

in respect to business, a very similar situation existed as in respect to the natural and human substance of society. The self-regulating market was a threat to them all, and for essentially similar reasons. And if factory legislation and social laws were required to protect industrial man from the implications of the commodity fiction in regard to labour power, and if laws and agrarian tariffs were called into being by the necessity of protecting natural resources and the culture of the countryside against the implications of the commodity fiction with respect to them, it was equally true that the central banking system and the management of the monetary system were needed to keep manufactures and other productive enterprises safe from the harm involved in the commodity fiction as applied to money. Paradoxically enough, not human beings and natural resources only but also the organization of capitalistic production itself had to be sheltered from the devastating effects of a self-regulating market.[81]

4. Legal Evolution

The long-run movement towards industrialization was accompanied not just by substantive changes in the content of the law, but by a gradual shift in the nature of law itself, a movement towards the kind of 'rational structure of law and administration' which made it possible to have 'a rational private enterprise economy with fixed capital and sure calculation'.[82] This in turn implied 'a "rational" legal procedure, based on formalized legal concepts'.[83] The aim of internal conceptual unity was an aspect of the separation, or autonomy, of the legal system, and both arose from, among other things, the growing use of law as an instrument of labour market regulation. This began in England in the later Middle Ages. The administrative and judicial reforms which led to the emergence of a unified system of common law in the twelfth century also stimulated the growth of a formalized type of legislation and the recognition of the distinction between statutory and

---

[80] *Critique du droit du travail*, op. cit., at p. 33.
[81] *The Great Transformation*, op. cit., at p. 132.
[82] Weber, 'The origins of industrial capitalism in Europe', op. cit., at p. 329.
[83] Weber, 'The development of bureaucracy and its relation to law', in Runciman (ed.) and Matthews (transl.) *Max Weber: Selections in Translation*, op. cit., 341–354 (excerpted from Weber, *Wirtschaft und Gesellschaft*, 4th ed., Tübingen: Mohr, 1956 (first published in 1922)), at p. 352.

judge-made law.[84] The Black Death of 1346, and the ensuing labour shortage, was the catalyst for the first national labour legislation, the Ordinance of Labourers of 1349 and the Statute of Labourers of 1351. Prior to this point, wage regulation had been local and largely customary in character. Labour legislation encouraged the growth of the common law writ of *assumpsit* which came to form the basis for the enforcement of promissory undertakings; already, by the second half of the fourteenth century, '*assumpsit*, thus allied with the Statute of Labourers, was part of a considered and controlled governmental policy of coercing working people to work well'.[85] The policy of using legislation and the courts to regulate the labour market continued into the early modern period. Even if there is a sense in which even the great statutes of the Elizabethan period, the Statute of Artificers of 1562[86] and the Poor Relief Act of 1601,[87] were merely formalizing practices which had begun at a lower level,[88] once enacted they were regarded as sources of law in their own right, and active efforts were made to ensure consistency of interpretation and application. The first treatises written by and for the justices of the peace who were principally responsible for the local enforcement of this body of law appeared in the late sixteenth century.[89] By the eighteenth century the image of the justice as the 'gentleman volunteer' was being displaced, a shift symbolized by Richard Burn's legal manual, *The Justice of the Peace and Parish Officer*, which in its very structure 'implicitly reminded the justice that he was preeminently part of the English legal system'.[90] With the development of the prerogative writs, the Court of King's Bench acquired the power to supervise the administration of the law by the justices and in particular, through the writ of *certiorari*, to quash decisions made in excess of jurisdiction.[91] One of the by-products of this process was the extensive (and extensively reported) litigation under the Settlement Acts through which the service relationship acquired its early juridical character.[92]

The autonomy of the legal system creates the material for our study: the emergence of distinctive legal practices and an autonomous body of legal doctrine based on legal continuity makes it possible to trace the evolution of legal concepts over long periods. What exactly is the nature and significance of this evidence?

[84] See P. Brand, *The Making of the Common Law* (London: Hambledon, 1992).

[85] R. Palmer, *English Law in the Age of the Black Death, 1348–1381: A Transformation of Governance and Law* (Chapel Hill, NC: University of North Carolina Press, 1993), at p. 213.

[86] 5 Elizabeth I, c. 4. [87] 43 Elizabeth I, c. 2.

[88] See, for discussion of how far this was the case, R.H. Tawney, 'Assessment of wages in England by the Justices of the Peace' in W. Minchinton (ed.) *Wage Regulation in Pre-Industrial England* (Newton Abbot: David & Charles, 1972) (originally published in 1913).

[89] William Lambard's *Eireanarcha: or the Office of the Justice of the Peace* was first published in 1581 and Michael Dalton's *The Country Justice* in 1618.

[90] N. Landau, *The Justices of the Peace, 1679–1760* (Berkeley: University of California Press, 1984), at p. 340. For a full account of the judicial system of England during the period of industrialization, see W.R. Cornish and G. de N. Clark, *Law and Society in England 1750–1950*, op. cit., at pp. 17–53. [91] See Landau, *The Justices of the Peace*, op. cit.

[92] See below, Ch. 3.

Douglas Hay rightly reminds us that while legal doctrine is 'important for an understanding of both judicial thinking and political conflict', judicial decisions including 'the cases that appear in the Law Reports are highly unrepresentative, in many ways, and especially as guides to enforcement'.[93] Legal concepts are linguistic devices, cultural artefacts which are used for the purposes of determining and applying legal rules. They are not intended to be models for action and they are not synonymous with the social and economic relations which they purport to describe. But nor are they timeless creations of some judicial imagination.

The juridical record which, in the case of English law, has come down to us as the result of several centuries of continuous legal development, is the result of institutional pressures which have brought about the persistence or survival of certain ideas or precepts at the expense of others. The reported decisions are only a fraction of those decided by courts, and these in turn represent a tiny segment of the instances in which disputes were resolved and agreements struck in the shadow of legal rules. If what survives is, almost by definition, unrepresentative of the range and type of relations operating in a society at any given time, it is the very fact of their survival which has the potential to inform us about the society which created them and which ensured their continuation within the body of the public discourse of the law.

To that end, an evolutionary study of the law requires us to take a dual approach: on the one hand, an internal understanding of internal juridical modes of thought and conceptualization; and, on the other, an external perspective on the law as a social institution or mechanism, one which is at times capable of being an active instrument of change, but which is also shaped by the society in which it is located. In this sense, our study, while it takes the body of legal doctrine as its focus, is an interdisciplinary one, which seeks to locate the law with reference to the wider framework of social relations, and which to that end draws on a range of material from beyond the law, concerning changes over time in the organization of work, the structure of worker representation, and the development of the state as an actor in labour market regulation.

The question of whether, and how far, legal institutions matter to economic development in the sense of having substantial and lasting effects on patterns of growth, is an open one, currently much discussed and debated by historians and economists. The argument which we have presented up to this point, and which we expound at greater length in the rest of the book, does not try to claim that legal change is always and everywhere capable of determining, in an instrumental way, a certain set of social and economic outcomes. Nor, conversely, are we attempting to show that the path of legal evolution is rigidly predetermined by the wider social and economic context within which the legal process is located. Both of these possibilities are equally plausible, at first sight. Thus it is entirely possible

---

[93] D. Hay, 'Master and servant in England: using the law in the eighteenth and nineteenth centuries', in W. Steinmetz (ed.) *Private Law and Social Inequality in the Industrial Age: Comparing Legal Cultures in Britain, France, Germany and the United States* (Oxford: Oxford University Press, 2000) 227–264, at p. 232.

to argue, of any particular legislative measure or common law rule, that it may have had certain effects upon the growth path of the economy, and to test such a proposition using quantitative or case study techniques. It is equally possible to argue that a change in the law was itself the product of economic changes which led to the formation of interest groups in a position to lobby for legislation or litigate for a change in case law. Did the passage of the Conspiracy and Protection of Property Act in 1875, for example, cause the subsequent growth in trade union membership by lifting the most significant legal constraints on strike action?; or was the Act itself the result of a combination of economic and political factors, such as the extension of the democratic franchise and the growth of early forms of joint regulation of industry, which together brought about the accommodation, within legislation, of trade union interests, and which led in turn to the further expansion of collective bargaining over the following decades?

Each hypothesis is just as plausible as the other, and there is no straightforward *a priori* way to choose between them. Nor are we greatly helped by the various accounts of evolutionary adaptation which are in common use by historians and economists. If we say that the 'legal system had to adapt to its environment in order to survive', why not reverse the sequence by arguing that 'the environment could also be adapted to the system'? We arrive very quickly at a tautology: 'systems could adapt to the environment if the environment were adapted to the system, and vice versa'.[94] It is not possible to escape from this tautology by simply assuming that it is the system which adapts to its environment, since this introduces an implicit causal sequence, once again reducing the 'legal' to a sub-category of the 'economic'. This technique is what unites instrumentalist Marxist accounts which view law as an element of a 'superstructure' constructed on a base of economic relations, and neo-functionalist law and economic accounts which view legal evolution as the outcome of a selection process dictated by economic requirements, and which in each case severely limits their power to explain legal change.

There is a need, in contrast to these approaches, for a methodological position which can account for the distinctiveness and specificity of legal processes, while recognizing that they are lodged within a wider set of social and economic relations; which can pinpoint the role of contingency in bringing about institutional change, without falling back on ad hoc causal explanations; and which can explain comparative institutional divergences between systems which nevertheless share the common experience of industrialization and the transition to a market-based economic order. This methodology is one in which *legal and economic history* is understood in terms of the *evolution of social systems*.[95]

[94] N. Luhmann, *Social Systems*, translated by J. Bednarz Jr. with D. Baecker (Stanford, CA: Stanford University Press, 1995) (originally published in 1984 as *Soziale System. Grundriss einer allgemeinen Theorie* (Frankfurt am Main: Suhrkamp)), at p. 31.

[95] See M.T. Fögen, 'Legal history—history of the evolution of a social system. A proposal' *Rechtsgeschichte* (2002) September, available on line at: http://www.mpier.uni-frankfurt.de/Forschung/Mitarbeiter_Forschung/foegen-legal-history.htm.

When the process of legal evolution is considered over an extended period of time, as it is in this book, it becomes clear that its relationship to social and economic change is complex and multi-linear. It is not generally possible to posit simple relations of cause and effect, in either direction. Nor do we observe the precise synchronization of legal and economic change. Thus while it is possible to argue, for example, that the advent of the welfare state was a factor in the emergence within labour law of the binary divide between employment and self-employment, this did not happen overnight with the adoption of the first legislative measures of workmen's compensation and social insurance. On the contrary, it took several decades for the modern test to emerge, and it did so in stages, as distinctions between manual and non-manual workers gradually disappeared from the law, and as the language of 'employment' replaced that of 'service'.[96] Nor was this an outcome which the framers of the welfare state necessarily intended to occur, or even gave much thought to. The closest we come to an instrumental relationship between political direction and legal change at the level of conceptual categories is the anticipation, in Beveridge's 1942 report on social insurance, of the separation between employees (Class 1 contributors) and the self-employed (Class 2 contributors) which was later reproduced in the National Insurance Act 1946.[97] Yet even in this case, it is not possible to see Beveridge's report in isolation. Once the report was completed and the decision taken to legislate on the basis of its recommendations, it still remained for the draftsman to make use of particular statutory formulae, and for the courts to give these an interpretation which reflected the classification which the Act had aimed to put in place.[98] It was, at one and the same time, a process which aligned British practice with that of other systems, in both the common law and civil law world, which were also in the process of adopting a binary classification of labour relationships during this period, but also one which reflected institutional and legal practices which were specific to the British courts and Parliament.

The example of the role of the Beveridge report in helping to instantiate the binary classification of employment and self-employment illustrates the *genetic* aspect of legal-conceptual evolution. By this we mean that conceptual mutation occurs as a result of a particular kind of interaction between system, 'code', and environment. This approach has links to biological analogies of the kind which have been developed within systems theory and memetics,[99] and with evolutionary economics, in particular the theory of path dependence.[100] At its core is the

[96] See Chapter 2, below.   [97] See Chapter 3, below.   [98] See Chapter 2, below.

[99] On autopoiesis, see Teubner, *Law as an Autopoietic System*, op. cit., and Fögen, 'Legal history—history of the evolution of a social system', op. cit.; on memetics, see S. Deakin, 'Evolution for our time: a theory of legal memetics' (2002) 55 *Current Legal Problems* 1–42; W. Njoya, 'Employee ownership and efficiency', op. cit. Memetics offers a theory of *cultural* evolution, and must therefore be distinguished from reductionist approaches to legal evolution which see the evolution of cultural forms, such as law, as the *direct* result of *genetic* processes. This latter claim forms no part of our argument; see Deakin, op. cit., at pp. 34–35.

[100] On path dependence, see, in particular, P. David, 'Clio and the economics of QWERTY' (1985) 75 *American Economic Review* 332–337 and 'Why are institutions the "carriers of history"? Path dependence and the evolution of conventions, organizations and institutions' (1994) 5 *Structural*

idea that legal concepts act as mechanisms of cultural inheritance, which work by 'coding' information into conceptual form.

'Abstraction' is the process by which complex social information concerning the social world assumes a conceptual form; by these means, information concerning the implicit codes of the workplace, or the conventions of labour market exchanges, is translated into legal–conceptual terms such as 'contract', 'employment', 'dismissal', 'wage', and so on.[101] The important point here is that information from the social world can only be retained and transmitted within the legal system once it has been conceptually coded. It must be mediated through legal processes for this to occur. The conceptual framework therefore operates as a repository of information, an interpretive resource, but one of a particular kind. If, in general, the information contained in rules—such as information about what constitutes 'reasonable' or acceptable behaviour, or a breach of the rules governing the employment contract—is principally aimed at the addressees of the law, the social and economic actors, then the information contained in concepts is different in nature—it is information addressed above all to the legal actors whose task is to interpret and apply the rules. Concepts such as these thereby become indispensable linguistic aids in preserving the internal order of the legal system. They are deployed with the goal of ensuring that the body of legal doctrine is held together by a series of interlinked principles, and does not simply consist of a mass of individuated rules. On that basis, they provide the basis for continuity in the legal system, that is, for its reproduction across time and space.

At the same time, the unity of the legal order is able to accommodate innovation; but new information from the external environment has to be assimilated using *existing* conceptual devices. In this way, continuity and change are combined. The substance of the law can change while the form often stays the same—'it is because law has to present the appearance of continuity that change comes about behind such screens as unchanging words';[102] while it is normal for *ex post*, functional explanations to be attached to legal forms whose original justification has ceased to apply—'the rule adapts itself to the new reasons which have been found for it, and enters upon a new career'.[103]

Change and Economic Dynamics 205–220; M. Roe, 'Chaos and evolution in law and economics' (1995) 109 *Harvard Law Review* 641–668.

[101] On the evolutionary significance of abstraction with regard to cultural forms in general, see L. Gabora, 'The origin and evolution of culture and creativity' (1997) 1 *Journal of Memetics* 1–27 and Deakin, 'Evolution for our time', op. cit., which we draw on for our discussion in the text. 'Abstraction' can itself be thought of as a technique which has evolved over time with the development of legal method, mirroring the idea of the 'evolvability' of biological evolution: D. Dennett, *Darwin's Dangerous Idea: Evolution and the Meanings of Life* (Harmondsworth: Penguin, 1995), at pp. 221–3.

[102] S.F.C. Milsom, *A Natural History of the Common Law* (New York: Columbia University Press, 2003), at p. 107.

[103] O.W. Holmes Jr., *The Common Law*, ed. M. DeWolfe Howe (London: Macmillan, 1968) (originally published 1881), at p. 8.

Thus to take the case of the Beveridge report: conceptual innovation was triggered by an external event, that is, by a political process set within a wider pattern of far-reaching economic and social changes; on the other, the change occurred through an act of legal interpretation, using procedures specific to the juridical and legal-administrative process. These two sets of explanations are not mutually incompatible. The new rule resulted from the interaction of the legal system with the wider political and economic environment. This interaction can be understood in terms of a particular evolutionary dynamic. Pressures for *selection* came from the external economic and political environment, while the particular stock of precedents available to the draftsman and the courts of the time provided the source of *variation* in the options from which they could choose. The procedures of 'internal' validation within the legal system, in particular the relevant conventions of statutory drafting and rules of precedent for judicial decision-making, constituted the mechanisms of *inheritance* by which the continuity of the new rule (its consistency with existing practice and its binding force for the future) was ensured. The result was a 'new career' for the juridical form of the contract of service, which was in the process of being renamed the contract of employment.

There are a number of implications of this evolutionary approach to understanding legal change. The first is that the logic of linear causation gives way to one of mutual influence between systems. Law and the economy exercise reciprocal influences on each other, in the sense, as we have already suggested, of *co-evolution*. Even then, the impact of change in one system upon the other is unpredictable; a major upheaval in one does not necessarily imply anything for the other.[104] This means that causal claims have to be advanced cautiously, as Marie Theres Fögen explains:

it is insufficient, or even directly misleading, to say: 'trial by formula developed from the *legis actio* procedure', or 'the origins of the criminal law are to be found in ecclesiastic penalties', or, finally, 'the industrial revolution led to the invention of social security'. All these assertions and countless more besides ought to be reformulated as the question: was the *legis actio* procedure one of the conditions of the possibility of establishing the trial by formula? Or, to put it more precisely: did legal structures take shape in the *legis actio* procedure that were capable of further development such that structurally determined selection—in favour of the trial by formula—became possible?[105]

---

[104] An autopoietic presentation of this idea would insist on the impossibility of *direct* communication between self-referentially closed systems (Teubner, *Law as an Autopoietic System*, op. cit.). However, the notion of 'closure' in this sense does not mean that the system is not open to its environment in the sense of receiving certain communications from it (hence the idea of the system's 'cognitive openness'), nor is it suggested that the environment is anything but open-ended and complex. The function of the boundary between system and environment is to enable the system to organize and reduce this external complexity to terms which it can then internally process. In this sense, the issue, paradoxically, is 'how self-referential closure can create openness' (Luhmann, *Social Systems*, op. cit., at p. 9).

[105] Fögen, 'Legal history—history of the evolution of a social system', op. cit., at pp. 3–4.

Secondly, as we have already suggested, the process of evolution is *genealogical* as opposed to *teleological*: it is one which 'links the present state of arrangements with some originating context or set of circumstances and interpolates some sequence of connecting events that allow the hand of the past to exert a continuing influence upon the shape of the present', as opposed to one which supposes 'that the present shape of things can best be explained by considering their function and particularly their function in some future state of the world'.[106] Thus the process is 'not a necessity, but a product of itself', it 'is not linear and is by no means target-orientated … it "serves" nothing and no-one'.[107]

Thirdly, the process can result—indeed, normally will result—in the survival of sub-optimal rules.[108] Through selection, the influence of the external environment is brought to bear on the internal structure of the system. But the 'code' through which the system maintains its continuity must, of necessity, refer back to existing precedents and known forms. Legal concepts are coded for *past* environments: hence, for example, the negative influence of the 'exaggerated continuity of the common law'[109] in the context of modern British labour law.

Fourthly, the process of legal change implied by this account is indeterminate and open-ended. The evolutionary concept of 'punctuated equilibrium'[110] is more appropriate to describe legal evolution than the idea of a smooth progression or adjustment towards optimality: 'if we examine the social system of law over shorter or longer historical periods, we can observe, as we can in organic systems, that there are periods of "calm" (stasis) and periods of relative "unrest"'.[111] Change is likely to be triggered by chance or contingent events; although it may be possible to reconstruct the relevant process afterwards, 'there is no way of *predicting* when or why such factors may produce changes (or, evolutionarily speaking, "variations") in the law'.[112]

It does not follow from the above that an historical analysis of the conditions which led to the emergence of labour market relations rules out the *qualified* use of a functional logic. Functional reasoning may be useful in explaining why certain patterns of behaviour, and particular institutional forms, persist over time. Thus the explanation offered within company law for the emergence and persistence of the modern corporate form—namely that it corresponds to the economic requirements

---

[106] David, 'Why are institutions the "carriers of history"?', op. cit., at p. 206.

[107] Fögen, 'Legal history—history of the evolution of a social system', op. cit., at p. 4.

[108] The law and economics idea that a Darwinian theory of 'natural selection' is one which necessarily results in the emergence of optimal forms rests upon a fundamental misreading (or perhaps non-reading) of Darwin's works, as well as those of modern evolutionary theorists. See G. Hodgson, 'Darwinism in economics: from analogy to ontology' (2002) 12 *Journal of Evolutionary Economics* 250–282, and 'Darwinism and institutional economics' (2003) 37 *Journal of Economic Issues* 85–97.

[109] Lord Wedderburn, 'Companies and employees: common law or social dimension?' (1993) 109 *Law Quarterly Review* 220–262, at p. 253.

[110] See S.J. Gould, *The Structure of Evolutionary Theory* (Cambridge, MA: Belknap Press, 2003), ch. 9; Aoki, *Toward a Comparative Institutional Analysis*, op. cit., at pp. 223–4.

[111] Fögen, 'Legal history—history of the evolution of a social system', op. cit., at p. 2.

[112] Ibid.

of the business enterprise—may well be significant for labour lawyers seeking to explain the (in many ways surprising) longevity of the contract of employment. However, there is a difference between an approach which, on the one hand, simply assumes functionality from the persistence of form, and one, on the other, which examines the historical record of institutional evolution to see how particular patterns emerged, at which point they became established, and how they have changed over time. The danger with the first approach is that it 'projects backward from the end of the story'; it becomes exclusively a 'history of winners'.[113] The second approach, by contrast, stresses the variety of alternatives, the uneven and unpredictable quality of institutional change, and the uncertainty of outcomes. In this perspective, there is an important distinction between functionality and optimality: forms which are efficient enough to survive are not necessarily, for that reason, ideally suited to present environments, nor are they inevitably superior to alternatives which, in the passage of time, have not fared as well.

An historical analysis of concepts can therefore be an aid to the understanding of contemporary legal doctrine. A type of *legal* teleology occurs when a judge or drafter adapts an existing conceptual form or precedent to a new use, while making it appear that there is nothing more at stake than the application of an existing rule. The former meaning of the rule or form, and the context within which it first emerged, is then put to one side. This technique is probably a universal feature of judge-made law; in those legal systems, such as the English common law, which have never been systematically codified, it touches virtually all aspects of legal doctrine. In such a system, as David Ibbetson has shown, 'the inventing of the new is rarely combined with the discarding of the old'. Rather,

legal change occurs through filling in gaps between rules in the way that seems most convenient or most just at the time; through twisting existing rules, or rediscovering old ones, to give the impression that a change in the law is no more than an application of the law that was already in place; through inventing new rules that get tacked on to the existing ones; through borrowing rules from outside the Common Law; through injecting shifting ideas of fairness and justice; and, very occasionally, through adopting wholesale procrustean theoretical frameworks into which the existing law can be squeezed.[114]

This effect is unavoidable in a system which relies upon precedent to ensure consistency and predictability in the application of the law. From the point of view of the practising lawyer or judge, indeed, the capacity to mould existing

---

[113] Harris, *Industrializing English Law*, op. cit. at p. 14. Harris's suggestion that English company law was more or less 'functional' at different times in its development is compatible with the idea of 'asynchronic' evolution which we have discussed in the text (above). However, rather than suggest, as Harris does, that the law was alternately 'autonomous' and 'functional', it is an implication of our approach that the law was always 'autonomous' and that its separation was in a basic sense a precondition of any functionality which it might have possessed.

[114] D.J. Ibbetson, *An Historical Introduction to the Law of Obligations* (Oxford: Clarendon Press, 1999), at p. 294.

concepts to new needs in this way is essential. But it can also lend to the law an appearance, not simply of continuity, but also of a smooth progression towards an efficient outcome, which may be very far from true to the historical record.[115]

Thus legal concepts assist in the transmission of values which, through their association with the juridical process, assume the status of accepted truths. The term 'legal dogmatics' is frequently used in the civil law world to refer to the internal language of juridical concepts. Assuming the pejorative meaning of the term 'dogma', this carries overtones of a closed system of reasoning, dependent on the mechanical application of formal axioms. However, Alain Supiot has pointed to a prior sense of the term 'dogma', which refers to 'what seems self-evident, and therefore has no need to be demonstrated'.[116] In this sense, legal concepts institute and guarantee those dogmatic beliefs which, notwithstanding their often arbitrary character, aid coordination between social actors. The 'closure' of legal concepts, their partial separation from the social and economic realm, is part of the means by which the values which they embody come to acquire legitimacy.

The historical study of legal concepts is therefore an exercise in reconstructing part of the process by which particular ideas acquire legitimacy in a given society, and by which those ideas are contested in their turn. In the course of an historical analysis, the role of contingency in producing a particular outcome, which otherwise has the appearance of permanence and stability, is clarified. In this context, 'traditional modes of inquiry tend to structure our focus by implicitly accepting the underlying assumptions and values of the doctrines analysed'; thus 'assumptions and values about the economic system and the prerogatives of capital, and about the rights and obligations of employees, underlie many labor law decisions'.[117] An historical approach is an essential antidote to approaches which confer a false impression of inevitability and efficiency in the evolution of legal rules.

But at the same time, an evolutionary analysis of law can help us to see not just the limitations of contemporary labour law, but also its potentialities and capabilities. Encoded in labour law are not simply the managerialist and disciplinary values of the service model and the poor law, but also values which reflect the political project of democratic emancipation on which labour law was first constructed. Part of our task is to understand how those values may be renewed today within the framework of an emergent 'law of the labour market'.

---

[115] On the difficulties, but also the opportunities, this creates for legal historians, see S.F.C. Milsom, *A Natural History of the Common Law*, op. cit., at p. xvi: 'the largest difficulty in legal history is precisely that we look at past evidence in the light of later assumptions, including our own assumptions about the nature and working of law itself'.

[116] A. Supiot, 'The labyrinth of human rights: credo or common resource?' (2003) 21 *New Left Review* 118–136, at p. 119.

[117] See J. Atleson, *Values and Assumptions in American Labor Law* (Amherst, MA: University of Massachusetts Press, 1984), at p. 4.

5. The Structure and Argument of the Book

In the remaining chapters of the book we develop our method and our argument as follows. Chapter 2 discusses the historical development of the body of law that is concerned with defining and constituting the employment relationship. We develop in detail our argument that the term 'contract of employment' did not begin to enter widespread use as a general description of wage-dependent labour until the twentieth century. We show that the growing adoption of this term by judges and drafters represented a substantive rather than a purely symbolic change. It was, firstly, the juridical equivalent of changes in the form of private and public sector enterprise, which at this point was becoming increasingly integrated. With vertical integration, it made sense to have a unified model of the employment contract, one which subsumed the independent role previously occupied by labour intermediaries and effaced old status-based distinction between manual and managerial workers. Secondly, the rise of the contract of employment took place alongside the introduction of social legislation in the fields of workmen's compensation, national insurance and employment protection. This legislation took as its premise the need to provide mechanisms to offset the social and economic risks of wage dependence. In this way, the modern system of classification based on the 'binary divide'[118] between employment and self-employment came into being.

The transitions from 'servant' to 'employee' and from 'independent contractor' to 'self-employed' were not straightforward. This is because the purposes for which labour relationships were classified shifted over time. The term 'servant' was not the forerunner of the modern 'employee'; in the nineteenth century, it was an *alternative* to the employee, in the sense that both expressions denoted a particular form of wage-dependent labour, differentiated by status. To stress this point is not to suggest that there is anything *necessarily* illegitimate in the process whereby the courts of today borrow and adapt the old case law of 'master and servant' when deciding employment cases. However, there may be occasions on which it is useful for a court to know that when it reads a nineteenth century decision on the definition of labour relationships, it is doing so against a context which is entirely different from that in which the precedent is now being applied. There is, moreover, a deeper, structural sense in which the legacy of the law's past affects decision-making today. One of the most controversial and difficult tasks facing today's judges, namely the application to work relationships of the tests for identifying a contract of employment, is not made any more straightforward by the confusing multiplicity of tests apparently available to the court. From the analysis which is presented in more detail in Chapter 2, it can be seen that these tests originated at different points in the development of the law governing the employment contract, and that each of them responded to a distinct set of

---

[118] See Freedland, 'The role of the contract of employment in modern labour law', op. cit.

requirements for classification. These in turn are associated with particular phases in the evolution of the enterprise and of the welfare state.

This analysis may help to explain why the current law on employment classifications, consisting as it does of a series of overlapping and potentially contradictory criteria, is quite as confusing as it is, but does it help to clarify it? Perhaps the historical origin of the present-day tests is of no more than antiquarian interest after all. One possible answer to this is that just as 'the medieval ground plan of the Common Law of obligations remains visible'[119] in modern private law, so today's labour law cannot be understood unless the structural influence of successive waves of mutation and adaptation is taken into account. The fact that some of these adjustments are very recent makes it all the more important to appreciate how they came about; such is the pace of legislative change that the memory of certain statutes, such as the Workmen's Compensation Acts of the early twentieth century, has apparently been almost entirely erased from legal consciousness, only decades after their passage.

There is a wider significance in the claims put forward in Chapter 2 which relate to the way in which the role of contract within labour law is understood, and, more specifically, how it relates to conceptions of status. The 'invention' of the concept of the contract of employment can be understood as reflecting, within the sphere of juridical discourse, the institutional tensions which accompanied the rise of a modern labour market. These are to be found within the very conceptual core of labour law. Is the contract of employment based on agreement, or command; is it an exchange, or a relationship; is it a private law transaction or a type of status regulated by public law? Different systems have responded to the challenge of resolving these tensions in particular ways, but they all have in common the 'insertion' of status, in some form, into the framework of the contract.[120]

Thus at every point in the development of the employment relationship in British labour law, contract and status have been intertwined. It has never been possible to give an exhaustive account of the employment relationship using the logic of contract alone. Thus there was no general movement from status to contract at the time of industrialization, nor does the welfare state mark a reversion to pre-modern status forms. In the period of industrialization, contract was complemented by the disciplinary code of master and servant regime and poor law conceptions of the legal duty to work. The effect of the advent of the welfare state and collective bargaining was to add a second, protective element of status, resulting from the application to the individual employment contract of norms deriving from collective agreements, via the concept of incorporation of terms, and social legislation, traditionally through the 'imposition' of extra-contractual obligations but more recently using a wider range of techniques.[121]

---

[119] Ibbetson, *An Historical Introduction to the Law of Obligations*, op. cit., at p. 295.

[120] Supiot, *Critique du droit du travail*, op. cit., at p. 27 *et seq.*

[121] See Chapter 2, below. It should be noted that while these are the principal mechanisms of adjustment used in British labour law, in French labour law, the notion of *ordre public social* operates in a way which is quite distinct from common law techniques for the application of social legislation,

This theme is developed further in Chapter 3, which considers the evolution of the duty to work from the time of the poor law to the present day. The 'old' or pre-1834 poor law gave expression to a set of reciprocal obligations which linked the legal duty to serve to the expectation of relief from the public authorities to mitigate the effects of joblessness, sickness and old age. While poor relief was coupled with various forms of social control and, on occasion, with physical compulsion to work, the old poor law nevertheless operated to encourage the growth of wage labour in an economy increasingly governed by the market principle. When, however, the framework of customary wage regulation was dismantled at the end of the eighteenth century, the resulting burden on the poor law, exemplified above all by the Speenhamland practice of wage subsidization, threatened to undermine wage labour and to create an unsustainable level of claims for relief. This led to the break-up of the system and its replacement by the restrictive code of the 1834 poor law Amendment Act. The 1834 Act was intended to make poor relief conditional upon a labour-market test, administered where possible through the workhouse, or combined in any event with compulsory labour. Through the principle of 'less eligibility', regulation aimed to set relief at a standard below the lowest level of wages available in the labour market; the result, however, was to instigate a cycle of casualization which threatened, once again, to destabilize the employment relationship. This was only brought to an end by the introduction of labour exchanges and the first forms of social insurance at the beginning of the twentieth century; however, the poor law, and the workhouse, did not completely disappear until 1948.

The poor law looms large in any attempt to provide an evolutionary explanation for trends in the British labour market, and it has given rise to a correspondingly extensive historiography which is particularly rich in studies of local poor law administration. We do not try to replicate that methodology here; our focus is on the juridical forms associated with poor relief and with their relationship to poor law policy. The principal regulatory mechanisms through which the poor law Amendment Act 1834 was implemented—the outdoor relief orders made by successive poor law Boards and Commissions—have been little studied. They merit close study, however, because they illustrate how notions of the employment relationship and the family as an economic unit were being constructed through the poor law at a time when the modern labour market was in the process of formation. Thus the concept of a breadwinner wage, although formulated by way of reaction against the poor law's destabilizing effects on family relations, also drew on poor law notions of subsistence and dependence.

Social insurance legislation likewise provides an important source of information on the evolution of the employment relationship during the twentieth century. Social insurance provided a highly juridified and complex set of mechanisms which underpinned the emerging model of indeterminate or open-ended employment.

---

and that in German labour law the same function is served to a certain degree by a 'communitarian' conception of the enterprise. See Supiot, *Critique du droit du travail*, op. cit.

The concepts of 'unemployment' and 'retirement', as they developed within social security law, were the mirror image of the conception of employment as a stable or 'permanent' relationship. The decline of social insurance since the early 1980s has been translated into further changes to these core concepts, just as the practice of stable employment has been in decline. The abolition of unemployment benefit, its replacement by the jobseeker's allowance, and the blurring of the line between employment and retirement, are all part of a fundamental policy shift: the post-war goal of full employment, which implied the stabilization and control of the labour supply, has given way to an 'activation policy' aimed at increasing the employment rate, notwithstanding the negative consequences of this move for stability of employment. In the set of beliefs and institutional mechanisms responsible for this shift, it is not difficult to discern the continuing legacy of the poor law.

Chapter 4 is concerned with the core labour market institution of collective bargaining between trade unions and employers, and with its relationship to social legislation governing conditions of employment. It addresses the paradox of British factory legislation: the earliest type of industrial legislation, in the first society to undergo an industrial revolution, did not bequeath a viable legacy to labour law. Within a few decades of the passage of the first Factory Acts, the standards which they set had been significantly improved upon by voluntary collective bargaining. The preference for voluntarism over statutory control was rooted in a legal and industrial relations culture which came to prioritize the values of contract; 'collective laissez-faire' was a logical extension of this wider philosophy to the sphere of industrial relations. By the mid-twentieth century, the triumph of voluntarism, although contested, implied the marginalization of arguments in favour of comprehensive statutory regulation of the employment relationship. That argument had turned not simply on the issue of fair treatment of workers, but also on the expectation that statutory control would suppress the 'parasitic' trades, sectors in which employers profited from low pay and casual employment, the costs of which were felt by the community at large. The failure of economic arguments for a labour code meant that terms and conditions continued to be set through sector-level bargaining by reference to the needs of the least profitable firms in each sector. That outcome has been little changed by the enactment, at the end of the 1990s, of new statutory standards governing the minimum wage and maximum working time; one of the principal criteria by which these new laws have been judged by government is how little they interfere with the business prospects of low-paying employers.

Collective laissez-faire was recognized to be a distinctively British solution to the problem of how to reconcile independent trade unionism with the dictates of a market economy. As such it reflected the conditions under which both industry and trade unionism developed in Britain during the course of the nineteenth and twentieth centuries, in particular the persistence of small-scale and fragmented forms of production past the point where, in other countries, they had largely been displaced through industrial rationalization and vertical integration. In the absence of legal guarantees for employee representation, collective bargaining was dependent not just upon the varying ability of workers in different trades to control the labour process, but also upon the capacity of employers to control product markets. Much of the stability which collective bargaining achieved by the high point of the middle decades of the twentieth century was the result of fortuitous economic conditions, in particular, full employment and favourable external terms of trade, together with government encouragement for the monopolization and concentration of industry, not least through the post-war programme of nationalization and the expansion of public sector employment. When this particular conjunction of circumstances ceased to hold in the 1980s and 1990s, collective bargaining declined rapidly, exposing employment in large areas of the economy to the unmediated forces of competition.

For British trade unions today, the legacy of collective laissez-faire takes the form of the increasing isolation of the remaining pockets of labour organization. It is also to be found in the relative absence of complementary mechanisms for worker representation of the kind found in other western European systems, which include statutory support for the extension of sectoral collective bargaining and provision for the exercise of employee voice at enterprise level. The experience of implementing the EU Working Time Directive demonstrates that without mechanisms of this kind, there are significant obstacles in the UK to the use of regulatory strategies which have been deployed elsewhere to combine basic labour protections with flexibility of work organization.

The initial conditions attaching to British industrialization were therefore highly influential in shaping the subsequent development of labour market institutions, including those which grew up alongside collective bargaining and the welfare state. This process was reflected in and reinforced by the development of British labour law: it can be seen today in the lingering influence of the master–servant and poor law regimes, the partial and incomplete floor of rights to terms and conditions of employment, and the weakness of mechanisms of collective voice, both for employers and workers. At the same time, the British case can be seen as an illustration of a wider process of adjustment between the legal system and the labour market, which relates to the common experience of all industrializing countries. We have pointed to the 'contingent and circumstantial'[122] nature of the conditions which shaped the emergence of the contract of employment and the binary divide between employees and the self-employed. But this fundamental dichotomy is of course not unique to British labour law; it can be seen as 'a more universal and deeply embedded one which permeates the jurisprudence, as well as the legislation, of many legal systems over very long periods of time'.[123] What are the wider lessons of our analysis for the debate over the future of the contract of employment? In the concluding chapter we consider possible contours of institutional solutions to the current disjunction affecting the employment relationship, solutions suggested by the possible emergence of a 'law of the labour market'.

---

[122] M. Freedland, *The Personal Employment Contract* (Oxford: Clarendon Press, 2003), at p. 19.
[123] Ibid., at p. 20.

2

The Origins of the Contract of Employment

1. Introduction

The essence of the British industrial revolution, according to the historian Arnold Toynbee, was 'the substitution of competition for the medieval regulations which had previously controlled the production and distribution of wealth'.[1] This process culminated in the repeal of the wage-fixing and apprenticeship provisions of the Statute of Artificers, between 1813 and 1814, and in the abolition of the poor law system of settlement by hiring in 1834. As these laws fell into decline, a process which was largely complete by the time the formal statutory repeals took place, their place was taken by the principle of freedom of contract, and the modern labour market was born.

This, at any rate, is the long-standing and conventional view. The transition from a predominantly agricultural society to a modern industrial and commercial one is assumed to have been coterminous with the liberalization of the economy and with the growing pre-eminence of contract in social and economic relations. Conversely, the rise of the welfare state from the late nineteenth century onwards is seen as qualifying the role of contract and introducing new forms of status. A.V. Dicey was among the first, in his *Lectures on the Relation between Law and Public Opinion in England in the Nineteenth Century*,[2] to identify this process and to question its legitimacy. The imagery of contract's 'rise and fall' is still deeply embedded in the legal imagination.[3] Richard Epstein, for example, in arguing that labour legislation 'should be scrapped in favour of the adoption of a sensible common law regime relying heavily upon tort and contract law', appeals to a nineteenth century when 'the area of labor relations was governed by a set of rules that spanned the law of property, contract, tort and procedure'.[4] From the opposite point of view of those

---

[1] A. Toynbee, *Lectures on the Industrial Revolution in England*, ed. with an introduction by T.S. Ashton (Newton Abbot: A.M. Kelley, 1969) (originally published 1884), at p. 92. See Ch. 1, Section 3, above. [2] London: Macmillan, 1905.

[3] See, for example, from differing perspectives, P.S. Atiyah, *The Rise and Fall of Freedom of Contract* (Oxford: Clarendon Press, 1979); F.H. Buckley (ed.) *The Fall and Rise of Freedom of Contract* (Durham, NC: Duke University Press, 1999).

[4] R.A. Epstein, 'A common law for labor relations: a critique of the New Deal labor legislation' (1983) 92 *Yale Law Journal* 1357–1408, at p. 1357.

critical of the role of contract in modern labour law, Hugh Collins has argued that it is still 'the dead weight of tradition in the common law [which] accounts in part for the survival of the simple contractual account of the employment relation'.[5] In each case, the implication is that, for better or worse, a common law system of employment law, based around freedom of contract and respect for private property, can be traced back to the period prior to the advent of the modern welfare state.

A more complex picture begins to emerge from studies which have looked at the historical record more closely. Otto Kahn-Freund's discussion of 'Blackstone's neglected child'[6] dated the appearance of the contract of employment to the period normally attributed to the industrial revolution, between 1750 and 1850, but he also noted the curious 'atrophy' or under-development of the employment contract for much of the nineteenth century. Kahn-Freund's argument has been attacked on the grounds that the development of large-scale industry took place later than he assumed, and that, for the time (the 1760s) in which Blackstone was writing the *Commentaries*,[7] it was fully appropriate for him to use the traditional categories which appear there.[8] This line of attack shifts industrialization to a later period but simply repeats, without questioning, the conventional association between industrialization and the emergence of contractual relations.

A more radical critique has argued that the application of contractual principles to the employment relationship 'is still in formation, rather than a tradition succumbing to gradual erosion'.[9] The basis for this view is the claim that the predominant legal form of work relations in the nineteenth century was not the employment contract, but, instead, the disciplinary and hierarchical model of the master–servant relationship[10]—hence the 'atrophy' of contract to which Kahn-Freund referred. During the nineteenth century, the master–servant code was extended and its effects intensified in most common law jurisdictions in Britain, Australia, New Zealand and North America.[11] Although statutory repeals

---

[5] H. Collins, 'Market power, bureaucratic power, and the contract of employment' (1986) 15 *Industrial Law Journal* 1–15, at p. 14.

[6] O. Kahn-Freund, 'Blackstone's neglected child: the contract of employment' (1978) 93 *Law Quarterly Review* 508–528.

[7] W. Blackstone, *Commentaries on the Laws of England. A Facsimile of the First Edition of 1765–69* (with an introduction by S.N. Katz) (Chicago, IL: University of Chicago Press, 1979).

[8] J. Cairns, 'Blackstone, Kahn-Freund and the contract of employment' (1989) 105 *Law Quarterly Review* 300–314.

[9] A. Merritt, 'The historical role of the law in the regulation of employment—abstentionist or interventionist?' (1982) 1 *Australian Journal of Law and Society* 56–86, at p. 57.

[10] A. Merritt, ' "Control" v "economic reality": defining the contract of employment' [1982] *Australian Business Law Review* 105–124, and 'The historical role of the law in the regulation of employment', op. cit.; K. Foster, 'The legal form of work in the nineteenth century: the myth of contract?', paper presented to the conference on *The History of Law, Labour and Crime*, University of Warwick (1983).

[11] See D. Hay and P. Craven, 'Master and servant in England and the Empire: a comparative study' (1995) 31 *Labour/Le Travail* 175–84, and 'The criminalisation of "free labour": master and servant in comparative perspective' (1994) 15 *Slavery and Abolition* 71–101; D. Hay, 'Master and servant in England: using the law in the eighteenth and nineteenth centuries' in W. Steinmetz (ed.) *Private Law and Social Inequality in the Industrial Age. Comparing Legal Cultures in Britain, France, Germany and the United States* (Oxford: Oxford University Press, 2000) 227–264.

had removed the role of the criminal courts in resolving labour disputes in most systems by, at the latest, the end of the nineteenth century, the master–servant model continued to influence the development of employment law in various ways, and this influence has only recently begun to wane.

The persistence of the master–servant model provides a clue in reconstructing the evolutionary path of the contract of employment, but as we shall see in this chapter, it is only part of the story. A further part of the reconstruction is to be found in the impact upon the employment relationship of two related developments: the rise of vertically-integrated forms of industrial organization, and the influence of the welfare state. These together had the effect of encouraging the growth of the open-ended or indeterminate employment relationship as the paradigm form in which labour was contracted. From the point of view of employers, the higher coordination costs of contracting through labour intermediaries were seen to outweigh the benefits of avoiding a more permanent and stable relationship. From the perspective of the state, the open-ended employment contract provided a more effective basis for the regulation and taxation of the enterprise. The resulting assimilation of a large variety of employment forms into the 'unitary' model of the contract of employment, embracing all forms of wage-dependent labour, took place gradually in the first half of the twentieth century. The juridical focus for this process was the debate about the meaning of the 'control' test for determining the legal status of workers. This process ended comparatively recently—in the case of Britain, it was only with Beveridge's report on social insurance of 1942, and the subsequent National Insurance Act of 1946, that the modern 'binary divide'[12] between employees and the self-employed was definitively established.

The result of the analysis which we will present is, in many ways, to invert the accepted understanding of the origins of the contract of employment. At one level, the transition to an industrial economy was indeed accompanied by a move to freedom of contract, as elements of the 'corporative' system of labour market regulation were removed. Within the law of obligations as a whole, there was a move to a conception of contract based upon the autonomous will of the parties,[13] and employment was not unaffected by this. However, alongside this process, a restrictive master and servant code, whose roots lay in the same pre-modern system of labour regulation, was also being extended and reinforced. As a result, employment could only be partially assimilated to the emerging contractual model, with the result that many aspects of the parties' relations could not be described, even formally, using contractual concepts. Conversely, the effect of the welfare state has not been to de-contractualize employment. Just

---

[12] M. Freedland, 'The role of the contract of employment in modern labour law', in L. Betten (ed.) *The Employment Contract in Transforming Labour Relations* (Deventer: Kluwer, 1995) 17–27, at p. 19.

[13] On the rise of 'will theory' and the influence upon the common law of the natural law theories of, among others, Pufendorf and Pothier, see D.J. Ibbetson, *A Historical Introduction to the Law of Obligations* (Oxford: Clarendon Press, 1999), ch. 12.

the opposite: the modern, open-ended employment contract, with its emphasis on reciprocal, contractual obligations of the parties, could only have emerged against the backdrop of, among other things, the growth of regulatory employment legislation.

Our analysis will also seek to show that the model of the contract of employment which we are familiar with today is the result of a process of accumulation and adaptation of earlier juridical models. At each stage in its development, the law has built on existing conceptual devices and mechanisms. An evolutionary perspective helps to explain much of the ambiguity of the idea of the contract of employment, and the controversy which it engenders in contemporary labour law doctrine. At the same time, it helps us to discern more clearly the multiple functions which the institution of the contract of employment performs in the modern labour market.

The argument is developed in the following way in the rest of this chapter. Section 2 below outlines the forms of employment which were recognized by the pre-industrial labour code of the Statute of Artificers and Settlement Acts, and explains their significance. Section 3 discusses the decline of the system of corporative regulation, and the role played by the courts in precipitating it. Section 4 then shifts the focus to the master–servant model and its links to the common law of employment in the periods both before and after 1875. Section 5 then traces the beginnings of juridical recognition of the open-ended employment contract, and Section 6 describes how collective bargaining combined with the rise of modern social legislation and the vertical integration of production to put in place the conditions for the emergence of the employment relationship. Section 7 considers the place occupied within labour law, as a result of these developments, by the concept of the contract of employment. Section 8 concludes.

2. Pre-capitalist Forms of the Contract of Service

In Britain, the emergence of a wage-dependent class preceded the growth of large-scale industry. John Rule writes that if by a proletariat we understand 'those of the labouring people who depend on selling their labour power, then in England proletarianisation had already proceeded a long way by 1750'.[14] Two-thirds of both the rural and urban labour force can be categorized as wholly or partially wage-dependent as early as the late sixteenth and early seventeenth centuries.[15] From the late Middle Ages the bulk of the rural labour force consisted of labourers or servants with only a limited access to the land or to industrial by-employments, employed by tenant farmers who rented their farms from the landowning gentry. Nor was

---

[14] J. Rule, *The Labouring Classes in Early Industrial England 1750–1850* (London: Longmans, 1988), at p. 18.

[15] L. Clarkson, 'Wage labour 1500–1800', in K. Brown (ed.) *The English Labour Movement 1700–1951* (Dublin: Gill and Macmillan, 1982) 1–27.

agriculture the only significant source of employment; by the early 1700s manufacturing and mining already accounted for between a quarter and a third of the labour force.[16] The movement of labour away from agriculture accelerated after 1750, with agricultural employment declining from over 50 per cent to less than 25 per cent of the labour force a century later.[17] Manufacturing and mining represented over 30 per cent of the workforce in 1811 and over 40 per cent by 1851.

Service in the form of an annual hiring was socially and legally the most significant form of wage labour for most of the eighteenth century, but it was not the exclusive form even for agricultural workers. In the *Commentaries*, which first appeared in 1765, Blackstone divided the class of servants into four: domestic or menial servants, apprentices, labourers hired by the day or the week, and higher servants such as stewards or bailiffs. Blackstone based his classification upon the distinctions between groups of workers made by the Elizabethan Statute of Artificers; the same approach can be found in the successive editions of the legal treatises written for the justices of the peace.[18]

Within the rural labour force the term 'servant' denoted a worker who was normally unmarried, hired for the year, and paid mainly in kind through food, clothes and lodging, while the term 'labourer' denoted one who was hired by the week or the day and paid cash wages. Service under an annual hiring marked a particular period in the life cycle of the agricultural worker: unmarried servants would normally complete a series of annual hirings before leaving the master's home and family to marry and set up their own household, after which they would seek employment as labourers.[19] This pattern of employment was closely linked to the settlement laws which governed the right to poor relief; until changes in local practice and in judicial interpretations in the period from the 1760s onwards, it was widely understood that a yearly hiring carried with it the right to poor relief in the parish where the employment was carried out.[20]

Although the bulk of the rural labour force received wages of some kind, cash wages were inter-mingled with other forms of income. Payment in kind could constitute up to 80 per cent of the live-in servant's remuneration.[21] Equally, the wages of married labourers living out of the farmer's household would be

---

[16] See J. Rule, *The Experience of Labour in Eighteenth Century Industry* (London: Croom Helm, 1981), ch. 1.

[17] N.F.R. Crafts, *British Economic Growth during the Industrial Revolution* (Oxford: Clarendon Press, 1985).

[18] Blackstone, *Commentaries*, op. cit., vol. 1, at pp. 410–420. Michael Dalton's *The Country Justice: Containing the Practice of the Justices of the Peace out of Their Sessions* was first published in 1618 and Richard Burn's *Justice of the Peace and Parish Officer* in 1743. See generally N. Landau, *The Justices of the Peace, 1679–1760* (Berkeley: University of California Press, 1984); on the evolution of the categories used by Dalton, Blackstone and Burn, see C. Tomlins, *Law, Labor and Ideology in the Early American Republic* (Cambridge: Cambridge University Press, 1993), at pp. 232–239.

[19] A. Kussmaul, *Servants in Husbandry in Early Modern England* (Cambridge: Cambridge University Press, 1981).   [20] See our discussion of the settlement laws in Chapter 3, below.

[21] On the conditions of service of farm servants, see generally K.D.M. Snell, *Annals of the Labouring Poor* (Cambridge: Cambridge University Press, 1985), chs. 1 and 2.

supplemented from a variety of sources, including the use of a smallholding, access to common or waste land and industrial by-employments. Family subsistence depended to a large extent on the labour of wives and children, engaged either in agricultural work or domestic manufacturing, to support the cash wage income of the agricultural labourer.[22]

Thus although wage labour was widespread and increasingly normal in the agricultural sector prior to the mid-eighteenth century, dependence upon cash wages as such was only partial. Wage labour was, moreover, supported by the complementary social and legal institutions of the service relationship and the poor law, which operated as substitutes or additions to cash wages at stages in the life cycle.

In the case of urban workers within the artisanal trades, a seven-year apprenticeship was still the traditional requirement for entry into the trade. Apprenticeship, like annual service in farming, involved payment in kind and living in as part of the master's household. Journeymen would in most cases be former apprentices who had served their time, and were paid by the day although usually hired for a longer period. Admission to the group of masters depended upon a journeyman having the resources to set up on his own, but also on the rules of the guild limiting the numbers of masters. The terms 'master' and 'employer' were not necessarily synonymous.[23] What distinguished a 'master', and gave him the right to direct the apprentices and journeymen he employed, was his knowledge of the trade and in many cases his position as a freeman of the relevant guild or city corporation. Masters themselves might be employed as independent contractors or on a regular basis by third parties, such as merchants or wealthy clients.

The distinctive feature of the artisanal system, in contrast to the capitalist forms of employment which developed later, was the preservation of control over the form and pace of work by the 'trade', the collectivity of producers who were subject to the rules of guild membership. A master's relationship with his suppliers and customers was normally that of an independent contractor, while a journeyman, although paid by the day, could only be hired to work within his apprenticed trade and was protected from low wage competition by the restrictions on apprenticeship numbers and by the general controls on entry into the trade. Hence the nature of the 'artisan wage relationship' was that the journeyman 'worked with, nor for, his master, and during slack times he was likely to be kept on for as long as the master could manage'. Equally, the guild rules gave the master a 'protective independence . . . [which] existed within a body of custom and law which prevented competition and encouraged solidarity between producers of the same trade'.[24]

---

[22] I. Pinchbeck, *Women Workers and the Industrial Revolution 1750–1850*, edited with a new introduction by K. Hamilton (London: Virago, 1981) (originally published 1930); M. Berg, *The Age of Manufactures: Industry, Innovation and Work in Britain 1700–1820* (London: Fontana, 1985), p. 175.

[23] R. Leeson, *Travelling Brothers: The Six Centuries' Road from Craft Fellowship to Trade Unionism* (London: Allen & Unwin, 1979), at p. 30.

[24] J. Smail, 'New languages for labour and capital: the transformation of discourse in the early years of the industrial revolution' (1987) 12 *Social History* 54–61, at p. 55.

The legal centrepiece of this 'corporative' system of regulation was the Statute of Artificers of 1562.[25] This Act had consolidated and extended a number of regulations deriving from earlier legislation, most notably the Ordinance of Labourers of 1349 and Statute of Labourers of 1351,[26] and the apprenticeship law of the early fifteenth century.[27] The other major Elizabethan labour statute, the Poor Relief Act of 1601,[28] was equally comprehensive in its scope and aims. Although they were substantially added to, these statutes continued in force with their basic structure more or less intact right up to the early nineteenth century. In many respects they constituted a single body of laws covering labour and employment. The division which later emerged between labour laws, on the one hand, and poor relief or social security on the other, did not exist clearly before the nineteenth century. The principal aim of the 'poor' laws was the regulation of employment, the term 'poor' referring specifically to the wage-dependent status of those who were subject to legislative controls.[29]

The formal origins of the justices' powers to fix wages and to regulate the service relationship can be traced back to the medieval labour statutes passed in the aftermath of the Black Death and the labour scarcity which it engendered. The justices had the power to set maximum wages and to punish servants leaving their service prematurely or without a testimonial from their employer. The prelude to the Elizabethan statute of 1562 was growing labour unrest, again caused by inflation and labour scarcity, which produced various attempts by the central state authorities to control wages. Urban guilds were also under pressure to ease the property qualifications for apprenticeships, a policy opposed by the central government in the interests of preserving the agricultural labour force. In the event, the Statute 'was not a slavish imitator of previous enactments; unworkable parts of obsolete measures were not revived and it was more flexible than many earlier Statutes'.[30] The wage

[25] 5 Elizabeth I c. 4.

[26] The statute of 1351 (25 Edward III Stat. 1 c. 1) formalized and extended the Ordinance of 1349 (23 Edward III c. 1–8). Later statutes of the fourteenth century strengthened the controls over labour mobility, by, among other things, requiring servants to have a testimonial from their master as a condition of leaving employment, and confirmed the justices' jurisdiction to set maximum wage rates (12 Richard II c. 4, 13 Richard II Stat. 1 c. 8). On the background to and enforcement of these early labour statutes, see B. Putnam, *The Enforcement of the Statutes of Labourers in the First Decade after the Black Death 1349–1359* (New York: Columbia University Press, 1908); R. Palmer, *English Law in the Age of the Black Death, 1348–1381: A Transformation of Governance and Law* (Chapel Hill, NC: University of North Carolina Press, 1993).   [27] 7 Henry IV c. 17 (1405–6).

[28] 43 Elizabeth I, c. 2 (see Chapter 3 below).

[29] As Tawney put it, 'villeinage ceases, but the poor laws begin' (R.H. Tawney, *The Agrarian Problem in the Sixteenth Century*, edited with an introduction by L. Stone (New York: Harper & Row, 1967), at pp. 47). The relationship between the ending of villeinage, agrarian change and the poor law in the late medieval period is examined by C. Lis and H. Soly, *Poverty and Capitalism in Pre-Industrial Europe* (Hassocks: Harvester, 1979), chapters 2 and 3. On the relationship between the Statute of Artificers and the poor laws, see K. Polanyi, *The Great Transformation: The Political and Economic Origins of our Time* (Boston: Beacon Press, 1957), at pp. 86–87: the 'neat distinction between employed, unemployed and unemployable is, of course, anachronistic as it implies the existence of a modern wage system, which was absent for another 250 years or so'.

[30] D. Woodward, 'The background to the Statute of Artificers: the genesis of labour policy, 1558–63' (1980) 33 *Economic History Review* 32–44.

regulation provisions were principally designed, as before, to set maximum and not minimum wages, but they gave the justices power to set higher rates than those previously fixed by statute, reflecting the impact of inflation, and to make yearly assessments at quarter sessions, in place of the unsuccessful attempts in previous Acts to lay down national maximum wage rates.[31]

The apprenticeship sections of the Act made the property qualifications applying to parents of apprentices less onerous and introduced a number of exemptions as concessions to the larger corporate guilds.[32] Other aspects of apprenticeship regulation were confirmed, however.[33] Only those who had served a seven-year apprenticeship in one of the regulated trades could exercise that trade or be employed in it, on pain of a fine, and masters in those trades were required to limit numbers of apprentices to three for every one journeyman.[34]

The Act's provisions on labour discipline sought to stabilize employment in agriculture, and, in particular, to provide mechanisms for controlling the movement of labour into and out of the agricultural sector to the urban trades. They required annual hirings in specified trades,[35] and made provision for compulsory service of the young and unpropertied, either in the trades or, for the unapprenticed, in agriculture.[36] Artificers and labourers could be required to work in the fields at harvest.[37] Quarterly notice on either side was required to terminate the contracts of *servants* hired by the year (although this provision did not affect *labourers* hired by the week or the day).[38] The local justices (either at assizes or quarter sessions) were given power to fine or imprison servants departing without notice or refusing to perform their duties, and to fine masters dismissing their servants other than on a quarter's notice without good cause; similarly, labourers or artificers abandoning their work before it was finished were subject to fine or imprisonment.[39]

---

[31] The earlier Acts setting national maximum wage rates were 6 Henry VIII c. 3 (1514) and 7 Henry VIII c. 5 (1515). See also 23 Henry VI c. 13 (1445). The new provisions were enacted in 5 Elizabeth I c. 4, ss. 15–19. Section 15 required the justices at general sessions to set a yearly wage assessment 'respecting the plenty or scarcity of the time', covering 'so many of the said artificers, handicraftsmen, husbandmen or any other labourer, servant or workman, whose wages in time past hath been by any law or statute rated and appointed, as also the wages of all other labourers, artificers, workmen or apprentices of husbandry, which have not been rated as they [the justices] . . . shall think meet by their directions to be rated . . . '. Employers and workers agreeing wages above the rates set by the justices were made liable to imprisonment (ss. 18, 19).

[32] Woodward, 'The background to the Statute of Artificers', op. cit.

[33] 5 Elizabeth I c. 4, ss. 25–41.

[34] The 1562 Statute stood above a host of by-laws concerning apprenticeship, in many cases the expression of long-standing local, customary laws, which were made and enforced by the incorporated urban guilds. Guilds applied their rules through fines and operated the 'right of search' to destroy 'deceitful' goods and unauthorized machinery: see Leeson, *Travelling Brothers*, op. cit., at p. 67. In the City of London, the Acts of Common Council gave the trade companies powers to set prices, enforce entry controls by excluding outsiders, and place upper limits on the numbers of apprentices. These by-laws were the subject of litigation and disputes between the companies and the journeymen's clubs throughout the eighteenth century: see C. Dobson, *Masters and Journeymen: A Pre-History of Industrial Relations* (London, Croom Helm: 1980), ch. 4.

[35] 5 Elizabeth I c. 4, s. 3.   [36] Ibid., ss. 4, 7.   [37] Ibid., ss. 22, 23.   [38] Ibid., s. 8.
[39] Ibid., ss. 8–9, 12, 13–14.

The high point of efforts to enforce the regulatory regime put in place by the Statute of Artificers came during the late Elizabethan monarchy and again during the period of Charles I's extra-parliamentary rule (1629–1640). Dissatisfaction with the efforts of the justices in making wage assessments led to Acts of 1597 and 1603[40] which authorized wage setting at quarter sessions as well as general sessions, clarified the power of justices and magistrates to regulate the wages of urban industrial workers and made it an offence for employers in the clothing trade to pay wages *below* the rates assessed, the first attempt to enforce a statutory minimum.[41] The Book of Orders and Directions of 1631, issued under the royal prerogative, supplemented the statutes with a detailed series of instructions to magistrates and justices on the application of both the poor law and wage and trade regulations.[42] The enforcement of assessed wages as *minimum* rates was most significant during this period of direct executive rule, although it has been suggested that, from the viewpoint of the central government authorities, this 'did not involve any popular sympathies, but simply a desire to prevent agitation by removing the material causes of discontent, and incidentally to put pressure on the middle and upper classes, who were the stronghold of religious and constitutional opposition'.[43] The same need to maintain order in the countryside led to the use at this time of Crown officials, the provost marshalls, to enforce disciplinary martial law powers against the 'wandering poor'.[44]

The weakening of central executive authority in the 1640s, following the Parliamentary victory in the Civil War, had the effect that labour market regulation became more clearly local, and diverse, in character. In the urban trades efforts to enforce minimum rates were reduced and legal wage assessments became less important in practice as a source of rates. The rural magistrates, on the other hand, continued to make wage assessments both during and after the Civil War, in the interests of preserving the stability of the agricultural labour market. In addition to using their powers to set maximum wage levels, the justices were also able to modify wages on an annual basis in order to meet changes in the cost of living. The regulation of wages in line with prices was made necessary by the increasing mobility of the class of landless labourers, to discourage them from leaving their work and living off unenclosed land.[45]

---

[40] 39 Elizabeth I c. 12, 1 James I c. 6, respectively.

[41] 1 James I c. 6, s. 7. The preamble to this Act (s. 1) noted that the Act of 1563 'hath not according to the true meaning thereof, duly been put in execution, whereby the rates of wages for poor artificers, labourers and other persons, whose wages was meant to be rated by the said Act, have not been rated and proportioned according to the plenty, scarcity, necessity and respect of the time . . . '.

[42] B. Quintrell, 'The making of Charles I's Book of Orders' (1980) 95 *English Historical Review* 553–572; P. Slack, 'Books of Orders: the making of English social policy 1577–1631' (1980) 30 *Transactions of the Royal Historical Society* 5th Ser. 1–22.

[43] R.H. Tawney, 'Assessment of wages in England by the Justices of the Peace', in W. Minchinton (ed.) *Wage Regulation in Pre-Industrial England* (Newton Abbott: David & Charles, 1972) (originally published in 1913), at p. 75.

[44] A. Beier, *Masterless Men. The Vagrancy Problem in England 1560–1640* (London: Methuen), ch. 9.

[45] R.K. Kelsall, 'Wage regulations under the Statutes of Artificers', in W. Minchinton (ed.) *Wage Regulation in Pre-Industrial England* 93–197 (Newton Abbot: David & Charles, 1972) (originally published in 1938 (London: Methuen, Associated Book Publishers)), at pp. 167–8.

Thus decentralization was part of the process through which the Elizabethan statutes began to fall into disuse well before their repeal in the first half of the nineteenth century. However, there was no simple fading away of the corporative controls, but rather a complex process in which the laws adapted to the growing wage dependence of the working population. Wage dependence became the norm, not simply in the sense of the continuing growth in the numbers of wage labourers, but also by virtue of the increasing precariousness of work, the removal of supplements to wages in the form of access to land and to poor relief, increased discipline within work, and separation between employers and employed.

Blackstone's *Commentaries* were written at the point when this process was gathering pace. The *Commentaries* are normally read as portraying a quasi-medieval, household or familial system of employment. It was on this basis that Kahn-Freund[46] argued that they were anachronistic for the time in which they were written. In commenting on Kahn-Freund's analysis, John Cairns has argued that, on the contrary, 'to represent the relations of master and servant as essentially familial was for Blackstone totally realistic, and encompassed virtually the entire economic landscape; Kahn-Freund has projected an industrial England too far into the past'.[47] But this critique of Kahn-Freund itself rests on what is arguably a misperception of the nature of household employment in the period prior to industrialization. It is an over-simplification, in particular, to claim that 'well beyond 1765, it was common to conceive of servants as members of the family of their masters . . . [t]he practical realities of social life, legal tradition, and contemporary social theory all stressed the familial nature of the relationship between master and servant'.[48] In fact, household labour in the traditional sense was limited, by the eighteenth century, to specific groups such as apprentices and agricultural servants. Even then, the yearly hiring was a position generally held by young, unmarried farm labourers at a particular stage in the life cycle. Married farm labourers normally worked for cash wages and were hired by the day or the week.[49]

Nor was the household self-sufficient as an economic unit. Access to the land in the eighteenth century was not usually enough to provide a basis for subsistence on its own. There was no large-scale class of independent agricultural producers in pre-industrial England. Rural households were already dependent upon a mixture of incomes: waged income from regular employment by adult males would be supplemented by seasonal work by women and children, access to the common land and to small plots for the production of food for immediate consumption, and in some cases earnings from industrial by-employments based on family

---

[46] 'Blackstone's neglected child', op. cit.

[47] Cairns, 'Blackstone, Kahn-Freund and the contract of employment' op. cit., at p. 307.

[48] Ibid, at p. 313.

[49] See J. Humphries, 'Enclosures, common rights, and women: the proletarianization of families in the late eighteenth and early nineteenth centuries' (1990) 50 *Journal of Economic History* 17–42; Pinchbeck, *Women Workers in the Industrial Revolution*, op. cit.; Kussmaul, *Servants in Husbandry*, op. cit.; Snell, *Annals of the Labouring Poor*, op. cit., chs. 2 and 3.

labour. During this period, 'a model based on family and subsistence, the traditional model of the family economy, is clearly not adequate to the task of analysing the domestic system. For the reality of that system involved the individual and the household, wage labour and family labour, market and custom'.[50]

A better view of Blackstone's text is that it was modelled not on the traditional (and, even then, largely mythical) household system of labour, but more straightforwardly on the *juridical* forms of employment set out, principally, in the Statute of Artificers. That legislation recognized the prevalence, in the early-modern English economy, of wage-dependent labour. It acknowledged the existence of contract: hiring was possible in one of a number of forms, which the Statute identified and sought to regulate. However, it is not possible to point to juridical recognition of a contract of service or employment, for a number of reasons.

Firstly, as we have seen, the service relationship in agriculture was intensively regulated, to the extent that mobility was constrained by law. The hiring process was tightly controlled in the interests of maintaining and stabilizing the agricultural labour supply. Secondly, in many of the urban trades, artisanal employment relationships were still the norm, which implied that producers owned the means of production and that the guild controlled the formation and reproduction of skills. Hence *capitalist* modes of employment—in which the employer was also the owner of the physical assets of production—were not yet widespread within industry.

If the *Commentaries* were not based on the traditional, self-sufficient household, then nor would Blackstone have recognized the integrated capitalist enterprise. The labour market of Blackstone's time was one in which there was considerable reliance on wages for subsistance, partial contractualization of work relations, and intensive localized regulation of wages and labour mobility, but in which the specific configuration of property rights which came to characterize capitalist work relations was largely absent. The redefinition of these property rights was beginning just as the *Commentaries* were completed. The *Commentaries* describe a world which was about to be transformed.

3. The Dismantling of the Corporative System

The demise of the corporative system has already been referred to. However, this was not a straightforward case of the legislation simply lapsing into disuse as it became decreasingly relevant to economic circumstances. The repeals of 1813–14 which removed the wage-fixing and apprenticeship provisions of the Statute of Artificers were not just symbolic. On the contrary, they had been preceded by a concerted and vigorous campaign by the laws' defenders for the provisions' enforcement, a campaign which had employed strike action, parliamentary petitions and recourse

[50] Berg, *The Age of Manufactures*, op. cit., at p. 133.

to the courts.[51] The undermining of the legislation, to which this campaign was a response, had begun in the mid-eighteenth century through a series of Acts which had withdrawn controls from selected trades and imposed constraints on journeymen's combinations. In addition, the courts used the doctrine of restraint of trade and a series of limiting interpretations to narrow down the scope of guild controls and assert the primacy of individual contract. The process of disengagement from market regulation was actively pursued at both statutory and judicial levels.

3.1 Wage fixing

The power to rate wages under section 15 of the Statute of Artificers was the most direct form of state management of the labour market under the corporative system, as it enabled the justices to modify wage rates according to varying degrees of labour scarcity. To a lesser extent it also functioned as a means of linking wages to changes in living standards; this was a way of dealing with the social consequences of food shortages and dearth, rather than an attempt to set a guaranteed minimum wage as such. The annual wage assessments could 'limit, rate or appoint' the wages of workmen or labourers within their scope; the only penalties, however, were for paying and receiving wages over the assessed rate, so that the Act effectively only provided for the enforcement of *maximum* wages. However, at the end of the sixteenth century the courts held that an agricultural worker who could, under the Act, be compelled to serve by the year in husbandry,[52] had the right to bring an action on the Statute for the recovery of the assessed wage and might also seek an order for payment from the justices.[53] His or her right to the standard wage was a function of the legal duty to serve which the Statute imposed at that time. Moreover, as we have seen, the Act of 1603 attempted to enforce a minimum wage for industrial workers by providing for the prosecution of masters paying below the agreed rate.[54]

The enforcement of minima in the urban trades fell away after the ending of centralized state direction in the mid-seventeenth century, while guild controls over wages were undermined by the Rebuilding Act of 1667[55] which gave the King's Bench the power to set 'reasonable' wages for reconstruction work in the capital and outlawed combinations of building workers there.[56] A series of

[51] See E.P. Thompson, *The Making of the English Working Class* (Harmondsworth: Penguin, 1968), in particular Chs. 8 and 14; I. Prothero, *Artisans and Politics in Early Nineteenth Century London: John Gast and His Times* (Folkestone: Dawson, 1979); Dobson, *Masters and Journeymen*, op. cit.; Rule, *The Condition of Labour in Eighteenth Century Industry*, op. cit.

[52] 5 Elizabeth I c. 4, s. 7.

[53] *Watkins* v. *Gomersall* (1598) Moo. KB 698; *R.* v. *London* (1702) 3 Salk. 261; see W.R. Holdsworth, *A History of English Law* (London: Methuen, 1938), at p. 468. *Watkins* v. *Gomersall* concerned a maid servant who was bound to serve by s. 24 of the Act, but in *R.* v. *London* the rule was restricted to servants in husbandry bound to serve by s. 7.   [54] 1 James I c. 6, s. 7.

[55] 18 & 19 Charles II c. 8.

[56] L. Clarke, *Building Capitalism: Historical Change and the Labour Process in the Production of the Built Environment* (London: Routledge, 1992) at pp. 47–48.

judicial decisions then formally cut back the scope of the legislation. First of all, the courts restricted the scope of wage assessment power in the 1562 Act to servants in husbandry;[57] this interpretation was eventually overruled only two years before the Act's repeal.[58] It was also decided that the Statute only applied to workers hired by the year.[59] Thus by the middle of the eighteenth century it was generally understood that for one reason or another, the law had little or no application to industrial workers. As a result, several Acts were passed to regulate specific trades, coupling both minimum and maximum wage regulation with a ban on combinations.[60] However, the success of the Gloucestershire weaving industry in obtaining a minimum wage law in 1756 was immediately reversed in the following session, as a result of pressure from clothing employers.[61]

The legal difficulties in setting and applying rates multiplied at the same time as the law began to be disapplied in practice. In the agricultural sector the number of assessments declined quickly after 1700, although it may be that in some cases this simply represented the continuation in force of customary wage rates.[62] Nevertheless, the completion of enclosure in the second half of the century and the growing over-supply of labour in the south and east limited the need to set maximum rates as a labour discipline device. By the time of the harvest failures of 1795, the uncertainty about the function and legal limits of the justices' powers is illustrated by the decision of the Speenhamland magistrates not to set a new wage rate reflecting the increased price of bread, but instead to authorize the payment of allowances through the poor law. Samuel Whitbread's failed Minimum Wage Bill of the same year sought to make explicit the link between wages and subsistence which under the 1562 Act had been ambiguous at best.[63]

Further attempts to introduce a minimum wage were made by the cotton weavers in the early 1800s; these took the form of petitions to Parliament as well as attempts to revive the Statute of Artificers.[64] The petitions were rejected and the campaign in the courts was stymied by Lord Ellenborough's decision in *R.* v. *Kent Justices* (1811),[65] to the effect that the writ of mandamus would not be issued to require local magistrates to set a rate: their power was only discretionary. Efforts to get magistrates to set rates led to pressure from employers for the complete repeal of the relevant sections of the 1562 and 1603 Acts, which duly followed in 1813.[66] The Spitalfields Acts, providing for the regulation of wages in the London silk weaving trades, survived until 1824 when they too were repealed.

[57] Holdsworth, *History of English Law*, op. cit. at p. 438.
[58] In *R.* v. *Kent Justices* (1811) 14 East 395.
[59] *Snape* v. *Dowse* (1685) Comb. 3; *R.* v. *Champion* (1691) Carth. 156.
[60] These included Acts regulating the journeymen tailors (7 George I Stat. 1 c. 13, 1720 and 8 George III c. 17, 1768), woollen manufacturers and weavers (29 George II c. 33, 1756), and the Spitalfields silk weavers (13 George III c. 68, 1773 and 32 George III c. 44, 1792).
[61] 30 George II c. 12, s. 1, 1757.
[62] Kelsall, 'Wage regulations under the Statutes of Artificers', op. cit.
[63] See further our discussion in Chapter 3, below.
[64] See Rule, *The Labouring Classes in Early Modern England*, op. cit., at p. 272.
[65] (1811) 14 East 395.   [66] 53 George III c. 40.

3.2 Apprenticeship and guild controls

If capitalist economic relations are broadly defined as those in which ownership
of the enterprise is separated from producers or workers, and vested in those
whose principal stake takes the form of financial capital or ownership of the
physical assets of production,[67] the decline of the apprenticeship system paved
the way for the transition to capitalist work relations in Britain, in the sense that
it removed legal supports for producer-owned forms of enterprise. The Statute of
Artificers had made it an offence punishable by repeated fines of forty shillings
for each month for any person to 'set up, occupy, use or exercise any craft,
mystery or occupation now used or occupied within the realm of England and
Wales, except he shall have been brought up therein seven years at the least as an
apprentice'.[68] It was also an offence to employ persons who had not been properly apprenticed in these occupations and to employ more than three apprentices
for each journeyman.[69] More generally, corporations and guilds established by
royal charter could exercise legal controls over local trade and employment,
subject to a requirement to submit their ordinances to examination by the
justices or city governors.[70] Corporate by-laws could be enforced by an action of
debt or by an action on the case for breach of custom, and through the power to
levy distress against the goods of the defendant, but their breach did not give rise
to criminal liability.[71]

The Act of 1562 was narrowly interpreted almost from its inception. However,
it was only from the middle of the eighteenth century that significant erosion
of the apprenticeship clauses took place. This was retrospectively validated as the
culmination of a long process of restrictive interpretation, as in Lord Kenyon's
comments in 1792:

When [the Act] was made, those who framed it might find it beneficial, but the ink with
which it was written was scarce dry, ere the inconvenience of it was perceived; and Judges
falling in with the sentiments of policy entertained by others have lent their assistance to
repeal this law as much as it was in their power.[72]

Under the doctrine of restraint of trade, 'at common law, no man could be
prohibited from working in any lawful trade . . . and therefore the common law
abhors all monopolies'.[73] Only an Act of Parliament or 'ancient custom' could
legitimize such restraints; otherwise, 'ordinances for the good order and government of men of trades and mysteries are good, but not to restrain anyone in his

---

[67] See H. Hansmann, *The Ownership of Enterprise* (Cambridge, MA: Belknap Press, 1996), ch. 1.
[68] 5 Elizabeth I c. 4 s. 21.   [69] Ibid., ss. 31, 33.   [70] Under 19 Henry VII c. 7 (1491).
[71] J. Chitty, *A Practical Treatise on the Law Relating to Apprentices and Journeymen, and to
Exercising Trades* (London: W. Clarke & Sons, 1812), at p. 138.
[72] *Smith v. Company of Armourers and Braziers of the City of London* (1792) Peake 199, 201.
[73] *Case of the Tailors of Ipswich* (1615) 11 Co Rep 53a.

lawful mystery'.[74] Accordingly courts struck down rules imposing additional entry requirements on apprentices and seeking to limit company numbers.[75] It was also decided that the Act did not apply to trades which were not in existence when it was passed.[76] This doctrine was used in the eighteenth century to exclude a number of emerging industrial crafts including cotton spinning, coach building and framework knitting from the scope of regulation. The hosiery trade, which was established after the 1563 Act, was regulated by the by-laws of the Framework Knitters' Company, but in this respect was an exception. It was also decided that the Act only applied to those established trades where in the opinion of the court it could be contended that 'much learning or skill was required'.[77]

For as long as the Act was in force, it effectively made capitalist forms of employment unlawful in the regulated trades; ownership and control of work organization rested with those within the guild, so that an employer setting up in a particular trade had to have completed an apprenticeship in that trade. Nor was it possible, under the Act, for one employer to hire as workmen a number of artisans from different trades, since he would then be exercising trades in addition to his own. After initial hesitation[78] the courts confirmed that qualification in one trade did *not* by itself entitle a person to exercise any of the other trades regulated by the Act.[79]

As a result, the artisanal form of production on which the Act was premised was at odds with emerging forms of factory labour. This can be seen from the relatively early case of *Hobbs* v. *Young* (1689).[80] Here, a merchant employed journeymen clothworkers in his house for a month to make materials for export. He was successfully prosecuted for a breach of the Act. Counsel argued that:

he who cannot use a mystery himself, is prohibited to employ any other men in that trade; for if this should be allowed, then the care which has been taken to keep up mysteries, by erecting guilds or fraternities, would signify little.

The court, by a majority, agreed:

the exercise of [the trade] by journeymen and master workmen, or an overseer for hire, is not an exercise of it by them, but by him that employs them; he provided them materials and tools, and paid them wages: by law, he is esteemed the trader who is to run the loss and

[74] Ibid.: 'without an Act of Parliament, none can be in any manner restrained from working in any lawful trade'; see also *Case of Monopolies* (1602) 11 Co Rep 84b at 87b: only Parliament, under 5 Elizabeth I c. 4, could restrain a person from exercising any trade.
[75] *Case of the Tailors of Ipswich*, above (rule that no person should exercise any of the specified trades until he had appeared before the master and wardens of the society to prove that he had duly served the seven years); *R.* v. *Coopers' Company, Newcastle* (1768) 7 Term Rep 544 (by-law restricting numbers of indentured apprentices: 'a prohibition not to take more than a certain number of apprentices is a bye-law in restraint of trade', per Kenyon CJ); Chitty, *Law of Apprenticeship*, op. cit., at pp. 6–7.
[76] See *Tolley's Case* (1615) Calthrop 9; *R.* v. Housden (1665) 1 Keble 848; *R.* v. *Paris Slaughter* (1700) 2 Salk. 611; *R.* v. *Harper* (1706) 2 Salk. 611; *Pride* v. *Stubbs* (1810) 6 Esp. 131.
[77] *R.* v. *Fredland* (1637) Cro Car 499.   [78] *Re. Statute of 5 Eliz., Apprentices* (1591) 4 Leon 9.
[79] Per Lord Mansfield CJ in *Raynard* v. *Chase* (1756) 1 Burr. 6—'which construction I take not to be law now'.   [80] 1 Show KB 266; 3 Mod.313.

hazard; the whole managery was to be for his profit, and the workmen are to have no advantage but their wages.

This view was steadily undermined by later decisions, so that by the end of the eighteenth century the prohibition on wage labour in the regulated trades was little more than nominal. In *Hobbs* v. *Young* itself the dissenting judge commented that 'no encouragement was ever given to prosecutions upon this Statute . . . it would be for the common good if it were repealed, for no greater punishment can be to the seller than to expose goods for sale ill wrought, for by such means he will never sell more'. The turning point was Lord Mansfield's judgment in *Raynard* v. *Chase* in 1756,[81] which decided that a merchant or supplier of capital could be the owner and employer of a business as the partner of one who was qualified in the relevant trade. This was seen as casting doubt on *Hobbs* v. *Young*, to the extent that it was held that an owner could employ men from more than one trade, as long as those employed were qualified in their respective crafts.[82] In *Smith* v. *Company of Armourers* (1792)[83] the Court of King's Bench ordered the admission to the company of an unqualified manager of an iron foundry, on the grounds that although 'he did not know how to manufacture the commodity by his own personal labour', he had been employed there for seven years 'during the greatest part of which time he conducted the whole of their extensive works, received all the orders, gave directions to the workmen etc. . . . he knew how to conduct the business as well as any master in London'.[84] Finally, just prior to the repeal of the Act, in *Kent* v. *Dormay* (1811)[85] Ellenborough refused to convict an unqualified textile mill owner, alluding to

the valuable mills at Wakefield, Leeds etc., the property of several persons of the first families in this kingdom; but who would be liable to informations, or would be required to serve regular apprenticeships as millers, if the defendant could be considered as within the meaning of the Statute.

The increased unwillingness of the judges to enforce the Act even in the areas where it apparently applied suggests the growing legitimacy and 'normality' of wage labour at this time. Wage labour was developing and increasing in spite of the apprenticeship law. Even accepting that the Act formally restricted wage

[81] 1 Burr. 6.
[82] *Coward* v. *Maberly* (1809) 2 Camp. 127, 128, where it was held that a coachmaker could directly employ a blacksmith to manufacture coach wheels; per Lord Ellenborough CJ: 'blacksmith's work may be required in building a bridge; but the builder who employs a journeyman properly qualified to do that work, is not himself to be considered as carrying on the trade of a blacksmith'.
[83] Peake 199, 200.
[84] It followed that 'serving an apprenticeship' was reduced to time serving, as anyone who worked for seven years without interruption as master, servant or apprentice could now qualify under the Act: Chitty, *Law Relating to Apprentices*, op. cit., at p. 127–9. Earlier cases taking a similar view under the Statute of Apprentices include *R.* v. *Moor and Dibloe* (1674) 3 Keble 400 and *French* v. *Adams* (1763) 2 Wils 168.
[85] Kingston Assizes, August 14, 1811; reported in Chitty, *Law Relating to Apprentices*, op. cit., at p. 122.

labour, its enforcement was another matter. The effectiveness of the legislation was limited by the expense of private prosecutions and by the diminishing force of the fines stipulated in the Act.[86] Courts frequently levied only the 40 shillings fine for one month's breach of the Act, even in cases where illegal employment had continued for longer. Even so, Adam Smith urged the Act's repeal, arguing that it hindered innovation, allowing only the new trades, beyond statutory control for historical reasons, to prosper: 'the manufactures of Manchester, Birmingham and Wolverhampton, are many of them, upon this account, not within the statute, not having been exercised in England before the 5th of Elizabeth'.[87]

The weakening of guild controls in London was concerned more specifically with the enforcement of the City by-laws, the Acts of Common Council. A major breach in the system was brought about by the Rebuilding Act 1667, which, as we have seen, removed the power of the bricklayers' and carpenters' companies to set wage rates and regulate the building trade. The power to assess wages was transferred to the Court of King's Bench, combinations of workmen were forbidden, and the right to work in London was extended to building workers from all over the country, overriding the City customs excluding outsiders. Throughout the eighteenth century a series of rulings by City courts and by the King's Bench limited the impact of the Acts of Common Council, principally by permitting employers to take on more apprentices and others who had not yet acquired the status of freemen of the guilds.[88] Guilds and city corporations continued to exercise the 'right of search' up to the third quarter of the eighteenth century, but instances of its use appear to have declined after that.[89]

Legislative repeals followed. Apprenticeship controls were first repealed in cloth manufacturing in 1733[90] and hat making in 1777[91] and in 1809 Parliament repealed the Weavers Act of 1555 which had incorporated apprenticeship controls for the weaving trade and limited the number of looms which could be operated under one roof.[92] A campaign for the more effective enforcement of apprenticeship controls through prosecutions of employers and through proposals to amend the Act of 1562 was organized by London artisans in 1812–13.[93] This led to the establishment of a House of Commons Select Committee on Apprenticeship which took evidence in 1813, but no Bill to strengthen the apprenticeship clauses was introduced, and in the following session a Bill for their abolition was passed

---

[86] Chitty, ibid., at pp. 130–1, wrote, 'It has been well observed, that it is fortunate that there is not much inducement, from pecuniary considerations, to bring an action on this Statute, as the plaintiff cannot recover for his own use more than twelve pounds, and he must pay his own costs'.

[87] A. Smith, *An Inquiry into the Nature and Causes of the Wealth of Nations*, ed. with an introduction by J.S. Nicholson (London: T. Nelson and Sons, 1886) (originally published 1776), volume I, ch. 10, at p. 50.   [88] Dobson, *Masters and Journeymen*, op. cit., ch. 4.

[89] Holdsworth, *History of English Law*, op. cit., at p. 422.   [90] 6 George II c. 37, s. 3.

[91] 17 George III c. 55, ss. 1, 5, repealing 5 Elizabeth I c. 4, s. 31, 8 Elizabeth I c. 11, and 1 James I c. 17.

[92] 49 George III c. 190, s. 5, which repealed not just the earlier Act (2 & 3 Philip and Mary c. 8) but corporation by-laws regulating the trade.

[93] See generally Prothero, *Artisans and Politics*, op. cit.

instead, following pressure from a group of engineering employers. The remaining powers of city guilds to restrict and regulate trade were formally repealed by the Municipal Corporations Act of 1835.[94]

Underlying the repeal were laissez-faire ideas promoting the effectiveness of 'free' markets in preference to direct legal control. Joseph Chitty's treatise on *The Law Relating to Apprentices* which had appeared in 1812 in response to the demand caused by 'numerous recent prosecutions' cited Smith, Malthus, and Paley in support of the Statute's repeal. The attempts to enforce the law 'have been uniformly instituted, not with a view to any advantage that might result to the public, but purely on behalf of *journeymen*, in order to keep up the *high price of wages*', and repeal would create that 'competition incident to the freedom of employment' which Smith had advocated, and the benefits which would flow from the removal of legislative interference:

> Where there is free competition, the labour and capital of every individual will always be directed by him into the channel most conducive to his own ultimate interest; of that interest *each is himself*, from a thousand circumstances, the best possible judge; and the interests of the whole community must in general be most effectually insured, when that of each individual is most judiciously consulted.[95]

In the same vein, Lord Kenyon asserted that the 'natural reason' of the market, rather than guild controls, was the true constraint upon the manufacture of poor quality goods: '[t]he reason for making [the Act] was that bad commodities might not be spread abroad; but natural reason tells us, that if the manufacture is not good, there is no danger of its having a favourable reception in the world, or answering the tradesman's purpose'.[96] This was an echo of the *Wealth of Nations* in which Adam Smith had written that 'the pretence that corporations are necessary for the better government of the trade, is without any foundation. The real and effectual discipline which is exercised over a workman, is not that of his corporation, but that of his customers'.[97]

3.3 Restrictions on combination

While these protective regulations were being removed, the development of restrictive legislation regulating workers' combinations and enforcing individual discipline in the service relationship gathered pace. The first restraints on combinations were an integral part of Acts which also provided for minimum wage regulation and the control of payment in kind (truck); later, however, these protective provisions fell away and the combination laws were used to undermine extra-legal regulation of apprenticeship and craft controls.

---

[94] 5 & 6 William IV, c. 76.   [95] Chitty, *Law Relating to Apprenticeship*, op. cit., at p. 2.
[96] *Smith* v. *Company of Armourers* (1799) Peake 199, 201.
[97] Smith, *The Wealth of Nations*, op. cit., at p. 55.

Statutory restraints on trade combinations and 'conspiracies' can be traced back to the legislation of the Middle Ages. An Act of 1424 outlawed combinations of masons[98] and an Act of Edward VI made it an offence for workmen to combine to raise wages and for masters to combine to set prices.[99] The Statute of Artificers, on the other hand, made no attempt to regulate combinations as such. The bulk of the restrictive legislation dates from the eighteenth century and can be related to the increasing division, within the urban guilds, between the separate associations of masters and journeymen, which became more pronounced at this time.[100] The first of these measures was the Act of 1720 'for regulating the journeymen tailors' in London, which followed the formation of the London Journeymen Tailors' Union and the strike of the preceding year. According to the Act,

great numbers of journeymen tailors in and about the cities of London and Westminster, and others, who have served apprenticeships, or have been brought up in the art or mystery of a tailor, have lately departed from the services without just cause, and have entered into combinations to advance their wages to unreasonable prices, and lessen their usual hours of work, which is of evil example and manifestly tends to the prejudice of the trade, to the encouragement of idleness, and to the great increase of the poor.[101]

The Act rendered agreements for the purpose of advancing wages or reducing hours null and void, and made it an offence subject to two months' imprisonment to enter into such contracts. It was also made an offence for a journeyman tailor to leave work unfinished or to quit before the end of his agreed term of employment.

Similar legislation, dealing with combinations or work discipline or both, followed in the case of shoemakers (1722), weavers and framework knitters (1725), and glove and shoemakers (1740).[102] These measures were followed by a more general anti-combination law of 1749[103] covering several expanding manufacturing trades including cotton, iron, leather, hat-making and dying and pressing. These laws assumed that combinations to raise wages were unlawful at common law—it was 'contrary to law' for the journeymen weavers 'to enter into combinations, and to make by-laws or orders, by which they pretend to regulate the trade and prices of their goods, and to advance their wages unreasonably'[104]—but the Acts had the advantage over the common law of providing for a summary procedure for conviction. Common law actions for criminal conspiracy were less straightforward to argue and more expensive to bring.[105] The Acts of 1799 and 1800,[106] which imposed a general ban on combinations, went further still by empowering justices to grant a licence to employers to take on labour contrary to the apprenticeship rules of the Statute of Artificers and related legislation, in any

---

[98] 3 Henry VI c. 1, 1424.   [99] 2 & 3 Edward VI c. 15, 1548–9.
[100] See Leeson, *Travelling Brothers*, op. cit.   [101] 7 George I Stat. 1, c. 13, preamble.
[102] 9 George I, c. 27, 12 George I c. 34 and 13 George II c. 8, respectively.
[103] 22 George II c. 27.   [104] 12 George I c. 34, preamble.
[105] Rule, *The Labouring Classes in Early Industrial England*, at pp. 259–60.
[106] 39 George III c. 81 and 39 & 40 Geo. III c. 106.

case where combinations of workmen struck for higher wages or interfered with business; in any case, that is, where

the qualified journeymen and workmen usually employed in any manufacture, trade or business, shall refuse to work therein for reasonable wages, or to work for any particular person or persons, or to work with any particular persons, or shall, by refusing to work for any cause whatsoever, or by misconducting themselves when employed to work, in any manner impede or obstruct the ordinary course of any manufacture, trade or business, or endeavour to injure the person or persons carrying on the same.[107]

In practice, too, the combination laws were substantially directed against collective action of artisans to maintain entry controls and price regulation of the traditional kind. In this respect they were used in conjunction with the common law of conspiracy and the duty-to-work clauses of the Statute of Artificers, in particular section 13 which made it an offence for any artificer or labourer to leave his work before it was finished.[108]

As long as some form of wage and trade regulation remained nominally in force, the law could be presented as enforcing the traditional duty to work at the assessed or customary wage, and associations to raise wages above the customary rate could be regarded as undermining the structure of trade regulation. The polarization of masters and journeymen into separate groups made this argument unrealistic well before the repeals of 1813–14; with those repeals, the traditional justifications for limiting collective worker action were formally replaced by new ones based on laissez-faire and individual contract. The laws were used strategically to undermine union organization within the trades which had seen traditional statutory controls removed. The principal issues in disputes concerned the introduction of machinery, the payment of wages below customary rates and in the form of truck, and the circumvention of limits on entry into trades. The combination and conspiracy laws were used to break the resistance to machinery of West Country shearmen in 1801–2 and to end strikes of the Lancashire handloom weavers in 1808 and 1818.[109] The Luddite protests in Nottinghamshire in 1811–12 began when local magistrates refused to convict hosiery employers acknowledged to be paying below the customary wage; in response, sixty machines belonging to those employers paying 'illegal' wages were destroyed. The combination laws and duty-to-work laws were used again to suppress the

[107] 39 & 40 George III c. 106, s. 15.
[108] Rule, *The Labouring Classes in Early Industrial England*, op. cit., at p. 269.
[109] Thompson, *The Making of the English Working Class*, op. cit., at pp. 553 et seq.; Rule, *The Labouring Classes in Early Industrial England*, ch. 11. Thompson and Rule also discuss the role played by associated criminal laws, such as those making machine-breaking a capital offence and governing the administration of oaths, in the suppression of worker resistance and the breaking of trade customs. The development of the common law of conspiracy during this period is discussed by J. Orth, *Combination and Conspiracy: A Legal History of Trade Unionism 1721–1906* (Oxford: Oxford University Press, 1991), and 'The English Combination Laws reconsidered', in F. Synder and D. Hay (eds.) *Law, Labour and Crime: An Historical Perspective* (London: Tavistock, 1987), examining Dorothy George's sceptical account of the effects of the Combination Acts ('The Combination Laws reconsidered' (1937) *Economic Journal (Supplement) Economic History Series*, no. 2, 214–28).

resistance of the framework knitters in 1813–14. Their leader Gravenor Henson described these laws as a 'tremendous millstone around the neck of the local artisan . . . every act which he has attempted, every measure which he has devised to keep up or raise his wages, he has been told was illegal'.[110]

The resistance of the early craft unions to the attempts of the state and employers together to dismantle the system of producer control of manufacturing looked both forward and back. On the one hand, 'Luddism must be seen as arising at the crisis-point in the abrogation of paternalist legislation . . . a violent eruption of feeling against unrestrained industrial capitalism, harking back to an obsolescent paternalist code'.[111] From the point of view of the artisans, the destruction by the state of trade controls was itself an 'unconstitutional' expropriation of the 'mystery' or property of the trade. Machine breaking had been among the traditional remedies for countering goods produced in breach of trade rules. However, it is not possible to draw a clear line between the craft unions' defence, at the turn of the century, of the decaying framework of guild control, and the later development of collective bargaining. The tradition of control over entry was carried over into workplace union organization in the new manufacturing industries, while the attempts of the framework knitters to reassert control over wage rates and end the payment of truck were to culminate in the establishment of the first organized conciliation boards in the 1860s.[112] But the modern trade unions were to emerge under conditions in which property rights over the process of production and the nature of the business enterprise had been fundamentally reconstituted.

4. The Master–Servant Regime and its Legacy

In addition to the decline of the apprenticeship system, two other fundamental institutional transformations occurred around the turn of the nineteenth century. The first was the mobilization of the labour supply which occurred with the ending of the system of poor law settlements, which is discussed in Chapter 3 (below). The second, which we will now examine, was the generalization of a model of employment based on the *personal subordination* of the worker to the employer, that is to say, a model incorporating an open-ended duty of obedience.

The open-ended duty of obedience is, today, characterized as an implied contract term, and courts increasingly recognize the role of the express contract terms in placing limits on the employer's managerial prerogative.[113] However, the

---

[110] Cited in Thompson, *The Making of the English Working Class*, op. cit., at p. 555.

[111] Ibid., at p. 594. On Luddism, its antecedents and consequences, see A. Randall, *Before the Luddites: Custom, Community and Machinery in the English Woollen Industry, 1776–1809* (Cambridge, Cambridge University Press, 1991); J. Dinwiddy, *From Luddism to the First Reform Bill: Reform in England, 1810–1832* (Oxford: Blackwell, 1987).

[112] See our discussion of this development in Ch. 4, Section 2.1, below.

[113] See this chapter, below, Section 7.

juridical origin of the duty of obedience does not lie in contract. It is to be found instead in the master–servant model which reached its height in the nineteenth century. The master–servant model was recognized, to a certain degree, by the common law, but it was above all a statutory innovation, the product of legislation which was specific to certain types of wage relationship. This legislation had its roots in the corporative code of the Statute of Artificers, but was then subject to a series of legislative innovations which took place during the same period in which other parts of the corporate system were being dismantled. In that sense, the master–servant model was a product of industrialization.

4.1 The juridical form and scope of the Master and Servant Acts

It is possible to identify the antecedents of the master and servant model in aspects of the medieval notion of villeinage or serfdom, which was carried over into the first labour statutes of the fourteenth century,[114] and later in the service provisions of the Elizabethan labour code.[115] However, the element of continuity must not be exaggerated. The passage of the first labour statutes, which were aimed at regulating wages, was an acknowledgement that the old concept of villeinage was beginning to give way to a relationship based on agreement, and that as a result, the parties' basic obligations, including the servant's duty of obedience, now had to be spelled out. In a similar way, the master and servant legislation of the eighteenth and nineteenth centuries, while it emerged out of the framework of the Elizabethan Statute of Artificers, also marked a departure from it. The master and servant legislation was not an attempt to maintain in place a pre-industrial model of household employment. Instead, it aimed to impose a more rigorous system of work discipline upon the growing numbers of labourers, artisans and outworkers employed in manufacturing, as well as maintaining control of the agricultural labour market at a time of considerable upheaval. Thus while Alan Fox, in his seminal analysis of the employment contract,[116] was right to suggest that during the industrial revolution 'in the very heyday of contract the evolving modern law of employment was drawing heavily on the old master–servant law by incorporating the traditional subordination of the workman', the element of subordination introduced by the master and servant laws was more innovative and less traditional than this passage perhaps implies.[117]

---

[114] 23 Edward III c. 1–8 and 25 Edward III Stat. 1 c. 1.

[115] 5 Elizabeth I c. 4, ss. 5–14; see above.

[116] A. Fox, *Beyond Contract: Work, Power and Trust Relations* (London: Allen & Unwin, 1974), at p. 188.

[117] The argument to the effect that the Master and Servants Acts of the eighteenth and nineteenth centuries marked an innovation in the context of the traditional corporative system of the Statute of Artificers is also made by Christopher Tomlins (*Law, Labor and Ideology in the Early American Republic*, op. cit, at pp. 236–8, arguing that the novel sense of 'servant' is reflected in Blackstone's classifications) and by Robert Steinfeld (*Coercion, Contract and Free Labour in the Nineteenth Century* (Cambridge: Cambridge University Press, 2002), ch. 2).

The first of the Master and Servant Acts was enacted in 1747 on the basis that the existing laws for the regulation of servants and the payment of their wages 'are insufficient and defective'.[118] This was a reference to the confusion surrounding the wage and service provisions of the Statute of Artificers, and in particular the question of whether they had any application to industrial workers; it was widely understood at this time that they only applied to servants in husbandry hired for the year and workers whose wages were formally rated by the justices.[119] Thus the justices were given a jurisdiction to examine and rule on disputes between masters and servants in husbandry and between masters and 'artificers, handicraftmen, miners, colliers, keelmen, pitmen, glassmen, potters and other labourers employed for any certain time, or in any other manner' whether or not any rate or assessment of wages had been made for them in that year. They had the power to order payment of wages due and to punish the servant or labourer for any 'misdemeanour, miscarriage or ill behaviour' by abating wages or committing him to the house of correction for up to a month; they could also discharge the servant from the contract. The Act of 1758 extended their jurisdiction to cover servants in husbandry hired for less than one year,[120] and that of 1766 made it an offence for the servant to quit before the end of the agreed term.[121] This last provision was an attempt to bring up to date the similar prohibition in section 15 of the Act of 1562. The Act of 1823 established new crimes of absconding from work and refusing to enter into work under a contract of hiring, and provided for imprisonment of workers for up to three months.[122] Thus far from abandoning this particular part of the Elizabethan labour code, Parliaments of the eighteenth and nineteenth centuries significantly strengthened and extended it.

Complementing the Master and Servant Acts were numerous measures passed specifically to deal with theft and embezzlement by servants, labourers and outworkers. At this point, merchants and middle-men who put out goods for finishing up remained the legal owners of the material or produce throughout the process; these laws gave them powerful procedures for enforcing discipline against the rural manufacturers whom they normally employed on a nominally independent basis.[123] Precedents for these measures exist from the seventeenth century;[124] again, the pace

---

[118] 20 George II c. 19, preamble.   [119] See our discussion above, Section 3.1.

[120] 31 George II c. 11, s. 3.

[121] 6 George III c. 25, s. 4. This was an attempt to impose a general restraint of the kind previously enacted around this time for particular trades, including the journeyman shoemakers (9 George I c. 27, s. 4, 1722), woollen manufacturers and framework knitters (12 George I c. 34 s. 2, 1725), glove and shoe manufacturers (13 George II c. 8, 1740, s. 8). The 1766 Act was stated to apply to any 'artificer, calico printer, handicraftsman, miner, collier, keelman, pitman, glassman, potter, labourer or other person contracting for any time or times whatsoever'.

[122] 4 George IV c. 34, ss. 3, 4 and 5.

[123] On the so-called 'proto-industrialization' model based on the putting-out to production to household forms of labour, see Berg, *The Age of Manufactures*, op. cit.; the evidence for and against 'proto-industrialization' as a distinct mode of production is assessed by M. Daunton, *Progress and Poverty: An Economic and Social History of Britain 1700–1850* (Oxford: Oxford University Press, 1995), ch. 6.

[124] See 13 & 14 Charles II c. 15, 1672–3; 20 Charles II c. 6, 1677; 8 & 9 William III c. 36, 1696–7.

of legislative change increases after the mid-eighteenth century. Under Acts of 1740, 1749, 1777, and 1792[125] it became an offence punishable by imprisonment for persons employed in manufacturing various goods to divert or sell materials sent to them for finishing up, or to detain them for more than twenty-one days after completing the work agreed. Justices could issue a search warrant for the inspection of premises of those convicted or charged of these crimes. Those buying or receiving stolen goods from servants also committed crimes. An Act of 1800, noting that 'it often happens' that colliers and miners breach their contracts 'to the great and lasting prejudice of their employers', made it an offence for persons contracted to raise coal or minerals to do so 'in a different manner to [the owner's] stipulations thereto, and contrary to the directions and against the will of the owner'.[126]

The use of the criminal law to enforce the contractual obligations of labourers and artisans found ready justification. 'Imprisonment may be viewed as a mode of compelling the performance of contracts', wrote J.E. Davis in his account of the Master and Servant Act of 1867.[127] 'In some cases, damages might recompense a master for the breach of a contract by his servant, but the latter is seldom in a position to pay damages, and therefore, in the absence of any other remedy, he might set his employer at defiance'.[128] It was expected that the jurisdiction over employment disputes would be very widely used, and that the regular courts would not be able to cope:

No substitute . . . can be found for the jurisdiction of the magistrates, stipendiary or otherwise, in the case of master and servant. The County Court does not sit sufficiently often for this purpose. In populous districts it is held once a month, so that, to say nothing of frequent adjournments of cases from one court to another, persons would be almost without the means of having their cases heard for many weeks together, instead of having the magistrates' court to resort to every week-day in the most populous districts, and in rural districts seldom less than once in every week.[129]

Court procedure was streamlined and, generally, beneficial to the employer who would normally be the one to bring the complaint. In complaints of neglect of work, which took the form of proceedings for a conviction as opposed to an order, the servant could not be a witness in his or her own defence.[130] The Act of 1867 remedied this and replaced imprisonment with fines as the principal remedy for breach of the Act, although imprisonment remained a possibility for, among other things, 'aggravated' misconduct.[131] Fines also offered an advantage over

---

[125] 13 George II c. 8; 22 George II c. 27; 17 George III c. 56; 32 George III c. 44.
[126] 39 & 40 George III c. 77.
[127] J.E. Davis, *The Master and Servant Act 1867* (London: Butterworths, 1868), at p. 6.
[128] Ibid, at p. 7.   [129] Ibid., at p. 8.   [130] Ibid., at p. 10.
[131] 30 & 31 Victoria c. 141. The principal remedy envisaged by the Act was compensation for non-performance of the contract of service (s. 9), but there was the possibility of imprisonment for up to three months for non-payment of compensation (s. 11) and for aggravated misconduct (s. 14). No wages were to be payable during a period of imprisonment (s. 17). Servants and their spouses were deemed to be competent witnesses by s. 16. On the extensive use, in practice, of powers of imprisonment under this Act, see Steinfeld, *Coercion, Contract and Free Labor*, op. cit., at p. 81.

discharge, which 'although at first sight a desirable course to adopt, was impracticable as a punishment (and therefore impracticable as a remedy) owing to the demand for labour in many branches of manufacturers and the ability of men to get work elsewhere'.[132]

Following the decision in *Lowther* v. *Earl of Radnor* in 1806,[133] the Master and Servant Acts were applied to all servants and labourers, but not to higher status employees such as managers, agents and clerks. The latter were excluded by implication from the wording of the Statute and also by being associated with the separate concept of 'office'.[134] The selective effect of the disciplinary provisions of the Acts was clarified further by the Act of 1867, which expressly stated it was only to apply to the classes of servants and labourers.[135] The test adopted for distinguishing between servants and independent contractors was based on the criterion of 'exclusive service'. Thus it was held that 'the statute . . . applies only to cases of contracts to serve. There may indeed be a service, not for any specific time or wages, but to be within the contract there must be a contract of service to the party exclusively'.[136] This apparently excluded the task contract and the casual hiring from the scope of the legislation.[137] After the abolition of settlement by hiring in 1834, the test of exclusive service was applied rather more flexibly, with the courts no longer persisting with the artificial requirement that the servant should be at the employer's disposal at all hours of the day and night.[138] Instead, it was held to be enough to show that the parties had undertaken mutual obligations to serve and to provide work respectively, for a defined period. In particular, the presence in the contract of long notice periods was used as evidence of the necessary mutuality of obligation.[139] This interpretation had the effect of bringing within the scope of the legislation groups of skilled artisans with a tradition of independence and a large degree of market power.[140] In this way, long periods of hire were frequently used in the early nineteenth century to bind artisans and skilled workers to the firm.

The courts implied into the contract of service employers' obligations to provide work and to maintain the relationship in being through depressions in trade, as the necessary complements to provisions for extended notice or duration. Without such terms, a worker's agreement to serve the employer exclusively for a period of years would be void on the grounds that it was in restraint of trade. The

---

[132] Davies, *The Master and Servant Act 1867*, op. cit., at p. 10.   [133] 8 East 113.

[134] B.W. Napier, 'The contract of service: the concept and its application', Ph.D. Thesis, University of Cambridge, 1975.   [135] S. 3.

[136] *Lancaster* v. *Greaves* (1829) 9 B & C 628, 631–2.

[137] *Hardy* v. *Ryle* (1829) 9 B & C 603 (outworkers); *ex parte Johnson* (1840) 7 Dowl PC 825 (calico printer).   [138] As in *R.* v. *St. John Devizes* (1829) 9 B & C 896.

[139] See *R.* v. *Welch* (1853) 2 E & B 356; *ex parte Gordon* (1856) 1 Jur (NS) 683; *Lawrence* v. *Todd* (1863) 14 CB (NS) 554; *Whittle* v. *Frankland* (1862) 2 B & S 549.

[140] See, for example, *Hartley* v. *Cummings* (1846) 2 Car & K 453 (skilled glass workers); *Pilkington* v. *Scott* (1846) 16 M & W 657 (glass blower); *Lawrence* v. *Todd* (1863) 14 CB (NS) 554 (iron workers employing their own assistants); *re Baily* (1854) 3 E & B 607 (butty workers). For discussion of the background to these cases, see Steinfeld, *Coercion, Contract and Free Labour*, op. cit., at pp. 125–153.

contract might provide for payment on the basis of piece rates or time rates. In an agreement for exclusive service for twelve months with payment on piece rates and provision for three months' notice on either side, the court found a

necessary implication that the employer shall find reasonable work and pay for the articles manufactured . . . The necessity of giving notice clearly shows that there is some obligation on the part of the employer. What is that? To find reasonable employment according to the state of the trade. That is not a unilateral agreement, but a mutual agreement with something to be done on each side.[141]

However, as contract terms for the employee's protection, these obligations were more or less notional. In the principal, reported cases of this period, the higher courts consistently rejected employee's claims for wages based on the employers' duty to find work.[142] They found that the employer had an implied right to lay off without wages, even in the case of an annual pit bond binding the workers to a year's exclusive service.[143] In this sense, long-service agreements effectively benefited only the employer; the worker was bound without having the protection of security of income or employment. The principal purpose of finding mutuality was to trigger the disciplinary provisions of the Act against the worker, or to form the basis for an action by the employer against another employer for enticing away the servant. Moreover, the courts' construction of the contract of employment differed according to the statutory context which they were considering. 'Butty' workers—subcontractors in coal mining—were excluded from the coverage of the protective Truck Acts on the grounds that they were independent workers, while being simultaneously subject to the Master and Servant Acts as servants.[144] Nor did the concept of mutuality extend to the continuation of the master's traditional obligations of care under the service relationship. In this sense, the nineteenth century model of master and servant had little or nothing in common, beyond the use of certain terminology, with persistence of reciprocal obligations which can still be seen in parts of the eighteenth century case-law on the annual hiring.[145] Thus at the turn of the century, the courts passed over the old authorities to find that a master had no obligation to maintain a servant or to provide him or her with medical care and expenses in the event of sickness or injury.[146] These cases suggest that the courts at this time had no consistent

---

[141] *R.* v. *Welch* (1853) 2 E & B 357, per Lord Campbell CJ, above; see also *Pilkington* v. *Scott* (1846) 16 M & W 657.

[142] This is in contrast to case law of the late medieval and early modern period in which claims by servants for wages due in return for being willing to serve frequently succeeded, via an action on the Statute of Labourers of 1351: see D.J. Ibbetson, *An Historical Introduction to the Law of Obligations* (Oxford: Oxford University Press, 1999), at p. 75.

[143] *Williamson* v. *Taylor* (1843) 5 QB 175; see Steinfeld, *Coercion, Contract and Free Labour*, op. cit., at pp. 102–124, for discussion of this case and other decisions in the same vein.

[144] *Sleeman* v. *Barrett* (1863) 2 H & C 934, where the court explicitly rejected an earlier suggestion (made in *Bowers* v. *Lovekin* (1856) 6 E & B 584) that the Truck Acts and the Master and Servant Acts should be interpreted in tandem.   [145] See below, Chapter 3.

[146] *Newby* v. *Wiltshire* (1784) 2 Esp 739; *Wennall* v. *Adney* (1802) 3 B & P 247.

conception of the contract of employment as a legal institution governing the reciprocal obligations of industrial workers and their employers; the classification of work relationships was determined not so much by contractual practices, as by the forms of regulatory legislation which operated on the service relationship.

4.2 Labour discipline and the legal framework of the enterprise

This juridical transformation of the service relationship needs to be set in the context of the organizational and technological transformation of production which was taking place during the late eighteenth and early nineteenth centuries. Although guild-based and independent forms of production were in decline at this time, a process which, as we have seen, was hastened by legislative change and judicial interpretations, they did not give way straight away to directly employed labour. Direct labour relations were by no means the inevitable outcome of technological change; at this time, many of the new technologies, such as those associated with steam power, were used in small workshops and in artisans' cooperatives as well as in factories.[147] Moreover, certain of the pressures favouring the adoption of subordinated labour were not technological in nature. Factory owners took steps to undermine forms of profit-sharing between independent producers: 'some capitalist entrepreneurs had had to fight for a system in which they could keep all the decision-making, all the control, and all the subsistence of the workers in their own hands, and had had to destroy earlier and more equable systems, such as the laws and organisations of the free miners in the Stannaries, the Mendips, Derbyshire, the Forest of Dean, Alston Moor and similar areas of Scotland'.[148] Close supervision and control of the work process were features, by contrast, of conditions in the growing number of pauper factories and workhouses in which those dependent on poor relief were set to work. Pauper apprentices were employed on a similar basis in private industry, often as a condition of their parents continuing to receive relief from the poor law authorities.[149] Thus it was not surprising that independent artisans and outworkers associated factory labour with the workhouse and, as far as they could, resisted it, drawing on a long cultural tradition of hostility to the loss of autonomous status.[150] In sectors where employers did establish direct employment relations, they sometimes took a form not far removed from the 'unfree' labour of the workhouse. This was exemplified by the institution of the pit bond in the north-eastern coal fields, by which colliers were bound by long-term contracts incorporating complex disciplinary codes. Pit bonds were regularly enforced in the courts as a means of breaking strikes and

[147] See generally Berg, *The Age of Manufactures*, op. cit.
[148] S. Pollard, *The Genesis of Modern Management: A Study of the Industrial Revolution in Great Britain* (Cambridge, MA: Harvard University Press), at p. 39.   [149] Ibid., at p. 161.
[150] C. Hill, 'Pottage for freeborn Englishmen: attitudes to wage labour in the sixteenth and seventeenth centuries', in C.H. Feinstein (ed.) *Socialism, Capitalism and Economic Growth: Essays Presented to Maurice Dobb* (Cambridge: Cambridge University Press, 1967) 338–350.

instilling work discipline. This was a nineteenth century practice but it had roots going back to the early modern and late medieval period, when long-term employment contracts akin to a form of industrial serfdom had been widespread in the mining industry of Scotland and parts of the north east of England.

The traditional pit bond was, however, exceptional, and was in any case in decline by the 1830s.[151] In most industries, when the adoption of integrated factory production took place, it did not lead immediately to the establishment of direct employment relations between owners and workers. Factory sites often began as mills to which outworkers and artisans brought goods for finishing up; in practice, there was often an unclear boundary between merchants putting materials out for production, and employers of direct labour. When the transition from independent production occurred it was mediated in most industries by the institution of *internal contracting*, through which artisans or supervisors contracted with the works owner or entrepreneur for the performance of a job in return for piece rates, and were themselves responsible for the employment of the labourers and underhands on time rates.[152] Three forms of the internal contract system emerged: *family control*, in which the sub-contractor would hire members of his own family as assistants, as in the early cotton spinning factories; *craft control*, in which the contractor would be an artisan in the position of a master craftsman who would recruit from apprenticed workers so as to uphold craft rule and entry restrictions, as in early nineteenth century iron working; and *gang work*, exemplified by docks work and the butty-system in coal mining.[153] In each case characteristic elements of pre-factory employment—family labour, on the one hand, and the maintenance of craft control, on the other—were carried over into the workplace, together with related differentiations of workers by family or craft status.

A number of explanations can be given for the persistence of the internal contracting system. From the employer's perspective, it was a control device which could often be more effective as a source of discipline than direct employment relations. This is because internal contracting involved the delegation to the intermediary of a range of managerial functions and a high degree of economic risk. In many cases sub-contracting was unavoidable for employers who lacked the skills and knowledge either to organize the labour force or to manage the production process.

More generally, the persistence of internal contracting represented the absence, at this point, of unified managerial and organizational structures in most firms.

<hr/>

[151] See Steinfeld, *Coercion, Contract and Free Labour*, op. cit., pp. 167–182, on the evolution of contracts in coal mining away from annual bonds and monthly hirings to short-term 'minute contracts' between the 1830s and 1860s.

[152] See Daunton, *Progress and Poverty*, op. cit. ch. 7, for an account of the 'coming of the factory'.

[153] See generally C. Littler, *The Development of the Labour Process in Capitalist Societies: A Comparative Study of the Transformation of Work Organisation in Britain, Japan and the United States* (London: Heinemann Educational Books, 1982), and on the impact of the family-based systems of contract labour on the nature of women's and children's work, see J. Mark-Lawson and A. Witz, 'From "family labour" to "family wage"? The case of women's labour in nineteenth century coal mining' (1988) 13 *Social History* 151–174.

The vast majority of early industrial enterprises employed only a few dozen or at most a few hundred workers. Economies of scale from increased size were difficult to achieve, in part, because there was no generally available mechanism for business incorporation, and because of the absence of limited liability for investors. The typical eighteenth century enterprise was either family-owned or took the form of an unincorporated business association in which a number of merchant-capitalists and managers formed the partners.[154] This 'unincorporated company' form provided a way of linking a number of individual units of production to one another and to their financiers, customers and suppliers; it offered a mechanism for sharing and spreading risk in a period before incorporation and limited liability became widely available to commercial enterprises in the 1850s.[155] Providing managers with a stake in the enterprise as partners also reflected the widespread contemporary view that '[i]t is impossible for a mill at any distance to be managed unless it is under the direction of a partner or superintendent who has an interest in the success of the business'.[156] However, it was, even then, an unwieldy form which, notwithstanding the use of transferable shares, was unable to shield investors effectively from liability for the debts of the business, and which gave rise to problems of continuity of ownership when new partners joined or existing ones left.[157] Large-scale enterprise of the kind which required limited liability for the suppliers of external finance and a unified managerial structure was a feature of companies which were chartered by an Act of Parliament in the canal and railway sectors, but these were specialized cases in which benefits to shareholders 'were sanctioned by Parliament in some sort of a statutory bargain, in which the rights of third parties were protected and the public interest was not overlooked'.[158] This mode was only extended to the manufacturing sector once reforms to company law made incorporation widely available, and even then the process of concentration of ownership did not occur straight away.[159] Thus the slow development of modern, bureaucratic forms of management, in part the result of the state of company law, was a further factor favouring the retention by firms for

---

[154] Pollard, *Genesis of Modern Management*, op. cit., at p. 140.

[155] Incorporation through registration was made available through the Joint Stock Companies Act 1844 (7 & 8 Victoria c. 110) and limited liability for shareholders by the Limited Liability Act 1855 (18 & 19 Victoria c. 133), later further amended by the Joint Stock Companies Act 1856 (19 & 20 Victoria c. 47). Prior to that point, the institution of joint stock, although in widespread use in certain industries (and with roots in the practices of the chartered trading companies and insurance partnerships, going back in some cases to the late sixteenth century), did not normally confer limited liability on shareholders. See R. Harris, *Industrialising English Law: Entrepreneurship and Business Organisation 1720–1844* (Cambridge: Cambridge University Press, 2000), ch. 1; W.R. Cornish and G. de N. Clark, *Law and Society in England 1750–1950* (London: Sweet & Maxwell, 1989), at pp. 246–266.

[156] Sir Robert Peel the elder (the father of the prime minister of the 1830s and 1840s), cited by L. Hannah, *The Rise of the Corporate Economy* (London: Methuen, 2nd ed., 1983), at p. 19. In the late eighteenth century, the Peel family business already owned over twenty mills in Lancashire and the West Midlands of England.   [157] See R. Harris, *Industrialising English Law*, op. cit., ch. 6.

[158] Atiyah, *Rise and Fall of Freedom of Contract*, op. cit., at p. 562.

[159] See this chapter, Section 6, below.

much of the nineteenth century of the internal contracting system, since by these means a direct contractual nexus between the worker and the ultimate employer could be avoided; labour-only subcontractors were simply one of a larger number of suppliers of inputs within the complex nexus of contractual relations making up the firm.

From the workers' perspective, on the other hand, internal contracting was a means by which job differentials and control over the labour process could be maintained by the groups of skilled artisans and supervisors.[160] In cotton spinning, for example, the adoption of the self-acting mule led to the division between the spinners, paid by the piece, and piecers, who were employed by the spinners as their assistants and paid on time rates. The spinners were predominantly male workers who operated rigid entry controls through a closed shop and successfully suppressed the claims of the piecers' unions. In ironworking and metalworking, craft controls were maintained in a similar way despite the abolition of the apprenticeship laws and the move to integrated factory production. Thus internal contracting was not incompatible with the increasing use of wage and work discipline which accompanied mechanization and integration of production; at the same time it marked the preservation within factories and workshops of methods of job control and labour organization which were adaptations of earlier forms of craft-based regulation.

Against this background, the significance of the master and servant legislation lay in providing employers with a mechanism for imposing discipline on workers who otherwise had only a loose organizational connection to the firm, and who would often be in a position to take advantage of labour shortages to push up wages. As we have seen,[161] most of the most contentious mid-nineteenth century decisions on the coverage of the Master and Servant Acts were precisely concerned with the position of skilled artisans and intermediaries such as butty workers; the central issue concerning the scope of the Acts was how far they could be used by employers to discipline skilled workers who otherwise retained a semi-independent status. This was reflected in the practice of enforcement of the Acts. Prosecutions played an important role in relation to the business cycle, by providing employers with a disciplinary weapon to counter the effects of a tight labour market; prosecutions for absconding or refusing to work rose at times of high levels of activity, as workers sought better paid or less dangerous work. In terms of numbers of prosecutions alone, the material impact of the Acts was considerable, in particular in the mining and engineering trades and in certain regions, such as the Potteries.[162] In England and Wales, numbers of prosecutions

---

[160] See Littler, *The Development of the Labour Process*, op. cit.

[161] See this chapter, Section 4.1, above.

[162] D. Simon, 'Master and servant', in J. Saville (ed.) *Democracy and the Labour Movement: Essays in Honour of Dona Tor* (London: Lawrence and Wishart, 1954) 160–200; D.C. Woods, 'The operation of the Master and Servant Acts in the Black Country, 1858–1875' (1982) 7 *Midland History* 109–123; Hay, 'Master and servant in England', op. cit.; Steinfeld, *Coercion, Contract and Free Labour*, op. cit., ch. 2 (discussing the role of the business cycle and the extent to which enforcement was directed against quasi-independent workers).

never fell below 7,000 per year between 1858 and the repeal of the Acts in 1875; a peak of over 17,000 prosecutions was reached in 1872. The historical evidence suggests that the disciplinary mechanism of the Acts were widely used as instruments of economic regulation during a period when modern managerial techniques had yet to develop, and when shifts in the business cycle could lead to considerable fluctuations in the bargaining power of employers and workers.

4.3 The influence of the service model on the common law: insecurity of wages and employment

The wider juridical influence of the master–servant model is visible in the lack of contractual reciprocity in the service relationship during the nineteenth century. Long intervals between wage payments, extended notice periods and long fixed-term hirings were all used by employers as disciplinary devices to retain and control labour. Servants who quit without notice or in the middle of a pay period normally forfeited all wages due under the contract, even for work actually completed. This was the result of a common law rule that an employee who quit voluntarily or who was discharged for good cause in mid-contract had no pro rata claim for wages for work done.[163]

The tightening of the rule against the recovery of wages in long-term contracts at the start of the nineteenth century has been attributed to the growing influence of the 'will theory' of contract in place of traditional notions underpinning the right to compensation for work done and benefits transferred to the employer.[164] However, as we have seen, the courts did not consistently see the contents of the service relationship in contractual terms; this casts doubt on the relevance to the service relationship of a general theory of contractual obligation such as will theory. A better explanation (at least in the English context[165]) is to be found in the more specific influence of the master-and-servant model in reinforcing the employer's control over the payment of wages, and the decline of the model of reciprocal rights and obligations which was associated with the institution of the yearly hiring.

The settlement cases of the eighteenth century indicate that in a fixed-term hiring the employer only had the right to terminate the contract prematurely in

---

[163] *Spain* v. *Arnott* (1817) 2 Stark 256; *Turner* v. *Robinson* (1833) 5 B & A 789; *Ridgway* v. *Hungerford Market Co.* (1835) 3 A & E 171; *Saunders* v. *Whittle* (1876) 33 LT 816.

[164] M. Horwitz, *The Transformation of American Law 1780–1860* (Cambridge, MA: Harvard University Press, 1977), at pp. 186–88.

[165] There were significant differences between the English and American experiences in the transition to formally free labour. Although the master–servant model influenced US case law, the American states did not enact (or re-enact) master and servant legislation along British lines: see C. Tomlins, *Law, Labor and Ideology in the Early American Republic*, op. cit.; R. Steinfeld, *The Invention of Free Labor: The Employment Relation in English and American Law and Culture*, 1350–1870 (Chapel Hill, NC: University of North Carolina Press, 1991), and *Coercion, Contract and Free Labor*, op. cit.

exceptional circumstances,[166] and that in the absence of gross misconduct by the employee the contract was regarded as continuing for the agreed term. It followed that in the event of a *wrongful* dismissal, the employee could sue for the contractual wages under the fiction of 'constructive service'.[167] There are also some indications that even in the event of a *justified* dismissal, the servant might have had a restitutionary action in the form of a *quantum meruit* for work actually performed.[168]

After the repeal of settlement by hiring in 1834, the fiction of constructive service was abandoned.[169] A servant who was wrongfully dismissed was now theoretically entitled to bring a claim for damages for breach of contract, based on the employer's failure to employ him for the period agreed.[170] However, this claim was unlikely to succeed in practice as the courts began to give a wider scope to the employer's contractual power of summary dismissal. In a contract with long notice periods or a long fixed term, the courts applied the principle of 'entire obligations' to require the servant to complete the agreed service in full before being entitled to any payment. Nor could the servant sue in *quantum meruit* for work done as an alternative to a contract action.[171] These common law developments paralleled the magistrates' statutory power to discharge the servant from the contract and abate his or her wages for breaches of discipline. The statutory powers overrode any contractual right to wages, to the extent that a servant convicted under the Act would forfeit wages due as earned and his employer would be released from any obligation to pay for work actually done.[172] It would appear, then, that the statutory context—the repeal of settlement by hiring, on the one hand, and the enactment of the magistrates' wide-ranging powers to abate wages for breaches of discipline, on the other—propelled the common law in the direction of a strict rule against recovery in either contract or *quantum meruit*.

The abolition of settlement by hiring also brought to an end the long-standing presumption that service was for a fixed term of a year. Although there was

[166] See below, Chapter 3.

[167] M. Nolan, *A Treatise of the Laws for the Relief and Settlement of the Poor* (London: Butterworth, 1825), at p. 485 et seq.; *Gandell* v. *Pontigny* (1816) 4 Camp 375.

[168] See the judgment of Lord Mansfield in *R.* v. *Westmeon* (1781) Cald. 129: in a yearly hiring terminated for good cause by the employer shortly before the service was due to end, 'supposing no wages paid, and no agreement, here are four days wanting in the service, and it is by means of his own act that the servant becomes incapable of completing it . . . If an action had been brought for his wages, he could not recover upon a *quantum meruit* for those four days'. This dictum appears to assume that the servant (who had been arrested and imprisoned for fathering a child out of wedlock) could recover on a *quantum meruit* for the period actually served, although he would not have achieved a yearly hiring and service for the purposes of settlement law. J.L. Barton, 'Contract and *quantum meruit*: the antecedents of *Cutter* v. *Powell*' [1988] *Journal of Legal History* 48–63, and P. Karsten, *Heart and Head: Judge-Made Law in Nineteenth Century America* (Chapel Hill, NC: University of North Carolina Press, 1997), at pp. 161–2, both argue that the rule against recovery in long-term contracts pre-dated the decision in *Cutter* v. *Powell* (1795) 6 Term Rep 320, but their analyses do not consider the role of the settlement laws in underpinning the institution of annual service during this period.   [169] *Smith* v. *Hayward* (1837) 7 A & E 544.

[170] Ibid.

[171] See *Turner* v. *Robinson* (1833) 5 B & A 789; *Ridgway* v. *Hungerford Market Co.* (1835) 3 A & E 171.

[172] *Lilley* v. *Elwin* (1848) 11 QB 742; *R.* v. *Biggins* (1862) 5 LT 605.

nominally still a presumption that servants in husbandry were hired for the year, this was easily rebutted by evidence of a common intention or practice to the contrary. In industrial employment and domestic service, contracts were normally regarded as terminable by notice on either side, by reference to the payment period agreed by the parties; the employer did not then need to give a reason for dismissal.[173] At the same time the courts implied a number of wide-ranging duties into contracts of service, with the sanction of summary dismissal in the event of breach. Servants were required to obey all lawful orders on pain of summary dismissal; for industrial and agricultural workers a single act of disobedience or of negligence would be enough to entitle the employer to dismiss.[174]

The Truck Acts, which attempted to secure regular payment of agreed wages without arbitrary deductions or payment in kind, were generally ineffective in providing protection for outworkers and servants alike. Deductions from wages for the 'rent' of tools and machinery and for alleged defects in workmanship were widely used as control devices both against outworkers and against factory labour. Personal and household debt was another mechanism for labour discipline and retention; it could be the result of fines and deductions from wages and high rents on company housing as in coal mining,[175] or of advances to workers for materials and equipment as in the outwork trades.[176] In the hosiery trade it was a widespread practice to make deductions for frame rents and for the use of needles, oil, coal and candles by manufacturing outworkers. The practice of charging rents provided an income for the merchant clothiers and middlemen which was independent of output, and a means of passing on the business risks and capital costs of production to the knitters, in particular at times of business depression. Clothiers refused to deal with knitters who owned their own frames; this, and the high cost of buying and maintaining a frame, made renting necessary for most knitters. The trade was highly competitive and typically overstocked with labour, owing to the difficulties of organizing outworkers who were geographically dispersed and to the demise of trade regulation in the late eighteenth century.

Attempts to regulate the practice of deductions by Act of Parliament were made in the 1770s and again in 1812, when the Framework Knitters' Union sponsored a Bill 'for preventing frauds and abuses in the framework knitting manufacture

---

[173] C.M. Smith, *A Treatise on the Law of Master and Servant* (London: Sweet, 2nd ed., 1860), at p. 47.

[174] *Read* v. *Dinsmore* (1840) 9 C & P 588; *Turner* v. *Mason* (1845) 14 M & W 112; Smith, *A Treatise on the Law of Master and Servant*, op. cit., ch. 2, noted that 'the servant is bound to obey all lawful orders of his master, and to be honest, and diligent, in his master's business', and gives the following four bases for dismissal: wilful disobedience of a lawful order; gross moral misconduct, pecuniary or otherwise; habitual negligence; or conduct calculated to damage the employer's business; and incompetence or disability. See Cornish and Clark, *Law and Society in England*, op. cit., at p. 294.

[175] See R. Church, *The History of the British Coal Industry. Vol. 3, 1830–1913: Victorian Pre-eminence* (Oxford: Clarendon Press, 1986), ch. 3 at pp. 263–274; 277–281.

[176] Rule, *The Experience of Labour in Early British Industry*, op. cit., ch. 5.

and in the payment of persons employed therein'. This was opposed on the grounds of freedom of contract by the M.P. Joseph Hume:

> If it should be more convenient or profitable for a workman to receive payment for his labour partly or wholly in goods, why should he be prevented from doing so? For if such a practice is inconvenient or injurious to any man he will not work a second time for the master who pays him in that manner.[177]

The Bill passed the House of Commons, only to fail in the Lords. The later Truck Act of 1831[178] was chiefly directed at the practice of payment in kind, and failed to regulate deductions. The two leading cases under the Act again involved the framework knitting industry. In *Chawner* v. *Cummings*[179] the Court of Queen's Bench held that deductions agreed in the contract were outside the protective regulations of the Act; they were 'the mode of calculating the amount of wages, nothing more', so that the 'wages payable' to the worker under the Act were formed by the net amount and not the gross rate per piece. This view was upheld in *Archer* v. *James*[180] when the Court of Exchequer Chamber divided equally on the question. The problem of deductions in framework knitting was not satisfactorily dealt with until a tighter statutory formula was introduced by the Hosiery Manufacture Wages Act of 1874.[181]

5. The Employment Relationship after the Repeal of the Master and Servant Acts

At what point did the courts begin to acknowledge the existence of reciprocal obligations within the employment relationship, as part of a wider recognition of its contractual basis? During the nineteenth century, the most important fault-line within employment law was not between employees and the self-employed, but between industrial and manual workers, who were subject to the master–servant regime in its various forms, and higher-level managerial, clerical and professional workers, who were outside the disciplinary reach of that legislation. It was in relation to the latter group that the modern contract of employment, based on true reciprocity of obligation and the placing of limits on the employer's powers of direction, first developed. The extension of this model to other groups of workers only took place as the influence of the master–servant model waned, slowly, in the half century after 1875. In common with other jurisdictions, Britain repealed its master and servant legislation in the second half of the nineteenth century. However, the legacy of the master and servant code was the assimilation by the common law of a hierarchical, disciplinary model of service. The persistence

---

[177] (1812) XXIII *Parliamentary Debates* 1162 at 1175–1176.   [178] 1 & 2 William IV c. 32.
[179] (1842) 8 QB 311.   [180] (1859) 2 B & S 67.
[181] 37 & 38 Victoria c. 48. See further our discussion of the evolution of the hosiery trade in Chapter 4, below, Section 2.2.

of this model owed much to the Employers and Workmen Act 1875, which provided statutory backing for a wide view of managerial prerogative and also for the application of quasi-criminal sanctions against certain categories of workers well into the twentieth century.

5.1 The disciplinary model after 1875: the role of the Employers and Workmen Act

The legislative settlement of the 1870s did not, in itself, give rise to formal contractual equality between employer and employee, or to the assimilation of the service relationship to the general law of contract. Benjamin Disraeli, the then Prime Minister, described the effect of the Employers and Workmen Act in the following terms:

> For the first time in the history of this country the employer and the employed sit under equal laws. No one can now be imprisoned for a breach of contract, while adequate civil remedies have been furnished for that occasion.[182]

However, this apparent parity of remedies did not exclude the use of the magistrates' courts by employers seeking a quick remedy for breach of contract. Under the Employers and Workmen Act these courts retained a special civil jurisdiction to impose damages in the nature of fines upon workers who committed acts of indiscipline or who absented themselves from work. Wage insecurity continued to be a feature of many industrial employments. Throughout the period of the growth of collective bargaining, the Employers and Workmen Act remained in force; it was changes in industrial organization, including the growth of joint procedures, which were responsible for the gradual fading away of this Act as a disciplinary measure and the establishment of a formal contractual equality between employer and employee.

Under the 1875 Act, the powers of magistrates and of the County Courts were not confined to the simple enforcement of civil law obligations arising out of the contract of employment. The Act conferred additional powers in effect to supervise the terms of the contract and the manner of its performance by the worker.[183] section 3(1) of the Act gave these courts the powers to adjust and set off against

---

[182] Speech delivered at the Mansion House on 4 August 1875, reproduced in C. Petersdorff, *A Practical Compendium of the Law of Master and Servant in General and Especially of Employers and Workmen under the Act of 1875* (London: Simpkin, Marshall & Co., 1876), at p. 8.

[183] Section 3 confirmed and extended the jurisdiction of the County Courts, and section 4 applied to Magistrates' Courts all the powers of the County Courts over employment disputes, except that the Magistrates' Courts could not deal with any claim greater than £10, nor could they order damages, or security, in excess of this amount. For an empirical study of the operation of this jurisdiction, which contains evidence on the degree to which it was used by workmen against employers as well as vice versa, see W. Steinmetz, 'Was there a de-juridification of employment relations in Britain?' in W. Steinmetz (ed.) *Private Law and Social Inequality in the Industrial Age. Comparing Legal Cultures in Britain, Germany, France and the United States* (Oxford: Oxford University Press, 2000) 265–312.

each other the separate claims of the parties, enabling the workman's claim in debt for wages due as earned to be reduced or possibly cancelled out altogether by an employer's counter-claim for damages for breach of contract, which the courts would readily award against an absconding or negligent employee. Under section 3(2) the courts had extensive powers to dissolve contracts of service at their discretion and apportion wages or damages between the parties. In *Keates* v. *Lewis Merthyr Consolidated Collieries Ltd.*[184] Lord Robson said of section 3(2),

This is a very unusual power, and shows that the county court judge or magistrate is being entrusted with a jurisdiction and discretion outside the limits of ordinary litigation. It opens a wide field of inquiry beyond the particular claim which one of the parties has brought before him.[185]

Similarly, Lord Atkinson considered that:

the statute of 1875 was passed, as set forth on the face of it,[186] to enlarge the powers of the county courts, not to leave them as they were. And it has enlarged them in a most remarkable way. The court may now, under [section 3] give relief which not only was never claimed by either of the parties litigant, but which is directly in conflict with the relief claimed, and setting at naught the rights they respectively insist upon.[187]

Hence in *Keates* the House of Lords applied the 'remarkable' power of section 3 to enable the court to order (and thereby effectively to ratify) abatement of the workman's wages upon a finding that he was liable to the employer for breach of contract, an abatement which would otherwise have been contrary to the Truck Acts.[188]

   Under section 3(3) of the Act the court had the power to order specific performance against an employee who was in breach of contract, a right not available under the general law of contract either at the time or since. The workman could be made to give security for the unperformed portion of his contract, whereupon the court could then 'order performance of the contract accordingly', in place either of the whole of the damages which would otherwise have been awarded, or some part of such damages'. In principle the consent of the workman was needed but the latter might have little choice in accepting this as a means of meeting the debt to the employer. In the last resort the court could commit the employee to prison for forty days for failure to pay a sum due, using powers under the Debtors Act 1869. This was a measure designed to facilitate the enforcement of small debts, below £50; in the case of *larger* sums only, the debtor could present a petition in bankruptcy in

---

[184] [1911] AC 641.   [185] [1911] AC 641, 646.

[186] This was a reference to the phrase in section 3 of the Act which referred to the County Court being granted powers 'in relation to any dispute between an employer and a workman arising out of or incidental to their relation as such . . . *in addition to any jurisdiction it might have exercised if this Act had not been passed*' (emphasis added).   [187] [1911] AC 641, 643.

[188] The Truck Acts would have outlawed this practice thanks to the earlier House of Lords' decision in *Williams* v. *North's Navigation Collieries* [1906] AC 136, which is discussed below. Remarkably, *Williams* was not cited in *Keates*.

order to obtain his release. According to the treatise writer Charles Petersdorff, referring to the alleged even-handedness of the 1875 Act:

It will be, and is already, unfortunately, being contended by the representatives of the handworkers, that this equality is more apparent than real . . . The wage class contend they may be committed for the non-payment of a demand, however small it may be, for a period not exceeding 40 days, and the claim not only remains undischarged but the penalty of costs, often double and treble the debt, is added . . . The advocates for abolition contend, that though theoretically the law of imprisonment is unaffected by class distinctions, practically its operation is characterised and accompanied by differences that are unjust and irreconcilable.[189]

Under section 3(3), the court had the power, on finding that the workman had committed a breach of contract, to order him or her to give security for the unperformed portion of the contract, and then, as we have seen, 'order performance of the contract, in place, either in whole or in part, of the damages which the court could otherwise have awarded'. In principle, both parties to the contract had to agree to the order being granted. However, the workman's agreement was likely to be forthcoming if this was the only practical means of meeting the debt to the employer. The employer had the option, then, of seeking specific performance of the contract in place of a claim in debt or damages, as an exception to the normal common law rule against the direct enforcement of personal employment contracts. Nor was this option open to the worker in the event of wrongful dismissal.

The power which the employer had had under section 9 of the Master and Servant Act 1867, of making a deduction from wages for breach of contract even if no civil claim for damages would have arisen—in effect, then, a power to issue a disciplinary fine—did not survive into the Employers and Workmen Act. Despite this, damages awards made by the courts under the 1875 Act tended to be in the nature of fines, for the reason that no attempt was usually made to quantify any precise loss flowing to the employer from breach. Again, this was a clear exception to the approach normally followed in the law of contract. Courts routinely awarded damages up to the £10 limit imposed by statute, or awarded some other sum not obviously related to any loss.[190] Defendants also had to pay costs. These powers of the courts, as with the earlier Master and Servant Acts, only applied to contracts of 'workmen'—labourers, artisans or servants; higher status employees were not within the magistrates' jurisdiction.

After 1875 an employee's failure to give notice would still, in most cases, result in a significant loss of wages. Long terms of service, and extended notice periods, were not as common as they had been under the Master and Servant Acts, partly

---

[189] *A Practical Compendium of the Law of Master and Servant*, op. cit., at pp. 55, 59.

[190] In *Bowes & Partners* v. *Press* [1894] 1 QB 602 the court rejected an argument for awarding only nominal damages to the employer in a case where the workman's breach of contract did not clearly lead to any loss; see also *Ayling* v. *London & India Docks Committee* (1893) 9 TLR 409; and see M.R. Freedland, *The Contract of Employment* (Oxford: Clarendon Press, 1976), at pp. 138–139.

because it was no longer necessary to find that the element of 'exclusive service', in the special sense which that concept had developed in the 1840s, was part of the terms of hiring. However, notice periods of a week or a fortnight were common in industrial employment, and were frequently coupled with the practice of late payment and the withholding of wages from any employee who left without giving notice (even though these wages had, in principle, been earned and were therefore a debt owed to the employee). The courts upheld these arrangements, despite employers frequently being unable to point to any loss flowing from the employee's breach.[191]

Section 11 of the Employers and Workmen Act attempted to prohibit such forfeiture in a case where the employer could not show actual damage. In common with much of the protective legislation of the time, this provision only applied to women and young workers falling under the Factory Acts, and was defeated in the same way as the courts undermined the Truck Acts—that is, by the argument that there could not be any forfeiture from wages which, under the terms of the contract, had never been properly earned.[192] The result was reversed only when the courts construed these contracts not as periodic contracts to which the principle of 'entire obligations' applied, but as indeterminate hirings.[193]

The only exception to the generally unfavourable trend in the judicial interpretation of this protective legislation was the 1906 decision of the House of Lords in *Williams* v. *North's Navigation Collieries*,[194] in which it was held that the Truck Act 1831 prohibited the employer making a set-off against wages in respect of damages for breach of contract, with Lord Davey asserting that 'set-off outside the Court means nothing more than a claim of deduction and retention'. However, as we have just seen, this decision was totally outflanked by the decision five years later in the *Keates* case, which allowed the same deduction to be made by order of the magistrates' court. The lingering influence of the master and servant model, given a practical expression in the continuing role of the magistrates as enforcers of discipline, thereby retarded the application of general contractual principles to the service relationship.

5.2 The contract of employment of 'higher status' employees

For the bulk of industrial and agricultural workers in the nineteenth century, the imposition of a restrictive disciplinary code supported by legislation and by the criminal jurisdiction of the magistrates' courts makes it impossible to speak of

---

[191] *Walsh* v. *Walley* (1874) LR 9 QB 367.   [192] *Gregson* v. *Watson* (1876) 34 LT 143.

[193] Most importantly in *Warburton* v. *Heyworth* (1880) 6 QBD 1 and *Parkin* v. *South Hetton Coal Co.* (1907) 98 LT 162. Under the rather complex contractual logic applied by the courts, this meant that the employee had a pro rata claim in debt for service rendered or work performed in respect of particular periods of the employment in question (such as an hour, day or month) and hence would not be penalized for early quitting in breach of contract unless this caused loss to the employer. See this chapter, below, Section 5.3.   [194] [1906] AC 136.

a developed contractual theory of the employment relationship. A contractual model of employment only began to emerge in the case of middle-class, salaried workers, whose position placed them outside the scope of the Master and Servant Acts and, later, the Employers and Workmen Act. Thus although a modern-style contract of employment can be seen developing in the nineteenth century, the scope of its application was limited by notions of social and economic status. One indication of this is the terminology used by the courts; the terms 'employee' and 'servant' denoted different forms of work relationship.[195]

One form of differentiation was concerned with notice periods. In some early cases, high status employees such as managers and clerks successfully argued that they had the benefit of a yearly hiring, so enabling them to claim wages for the whole year in the event of wrongful dismissal.[196] By the 1840s, the presumption of annual hiring was on the way out. In *Baxter* v. *Nurse* (1844)[197] a journalist who had been paid a weekly wage was dismissed shortly after being hired by a magazine which went out of business. He sued for lost wages for the unexpired portion of the year, claiming that he had been hired for twelve months. The Court of Common Pleas rejected the claim and cast doubt on annual hiring by describing it as a presumption which was 'by no means an inflexible rule', and which (according to one judge) would not apply if wages were paid weekly. By the rule that contracts were, in most cases, terminable by notice, the length of notice to which an employee was entitled became an important function of job security. Whereas long notice periods for servants and others could be used to bind the worker to the employer, if necessary by means of the criminal sanctions of the Master and Servant Acts, this was irrelevant in the case of middle-class employees who were beyond the magistrates' jurisdiction.

From this point on, the presumption generally applied by the courts was one of an indeterminate hiring, terminable by notice according to the custom for the trade in question: 'general usages are tacitly annexed to all contracts relating to the business with reference to which they are made, unless the terms of such contracts expressly or impliedly exclude them'.[198] For domestic servants who were formally outside the Master and Servant Acts, a month's notice was normal.[199] For professional and managerial employees, notice of three months or a year was common.[200]

Thus in *Todd* v. *Kerrich* (1852) the Court of Exchequer Chamber found that a governess employed on a yearly salary could not be dismissed on a month's notice, as a domestic servant could: 'the position which she holds, the station she occupies

---

[195] Foster, 'The myth of contract?' op. cit.

[196] *Beeston* v. *Collyer* (1827) 4 Bing 307; *Fawcett* v. *Cash* (1854) 5 B & A 904; *Davis* v. *Marshall* (1861) 4 LT 216; *Foxall* v. *International Land Credit Co.* (1852) 16 LT 637; *Buckingham* v. *Surrey & Hants. Canal Co.* (1882) 46 LT 885.   [197] 6 Man. & G. 936.

[198] *Metzner* v. *Bolton* (1854) 9 Ex. 517, 521 (Parke B.).

[199] *Robinson* v. *Hindman* (1800) 2 Esp. 235.

[200] See *Fairman* v. *Oakford* (1860) 5 H. & N. 635; *Metzner* v. *Bolton* (1854) 9 Ex. 517; *Levy* v. *Electric Wonder Co.* (1893) 9 TLR 495.

in a family, and the manner in which such a person is usually treated in society, certainly places her in a very different situation from that which mere menial or domestic servants hold'.[201] In this way 'the courts made employment security, in the form of reasonable notice, a function of the employee's status and income . . . some salaried employees of relatively high status still had as much security as an annual contract would have provided, although this was not true for those in lower positions'.[202]

The development of a contractual model based on reciprocity and mutuality of obligation can also be observed in cases concerning the employee's rights to be given work and not to be wrongfully dismissed. Contractual notions were used to limit the employer's right to give orders. The modern contract action for wrongful dismissal was synthesized in *Emmens* v. *Elderton* (1853),[203] a case concerning a company solicitor. The basis of the action was the employer's duty to find the employee work for the duration of the contract, in default of which he would be obliged to pay damages for breach of contract. Even in the case of commission agents and others paid on a piece-rate basis, the employer's act of wrongfully preventing the employee from earning his commission amounted to an unjustified repudiation of the contract.[204] The status and skills of the professional set a limit to the work he could be required to do; if he was 'hired as a buyer, he was not bound to perform services not properly appertaining to that character';[205] nor would a single act of disobedience or neglect justify the summary dismissal of a manager or a journalist.[206]

5.3 The partial extension of the contractual model to industrial workers

It is only in decisions of the early twentieth century that the courts can first be seen applying the contractual model, which they had developed for the middle classes, to industrial workers, agricultural labourers and domestic servants. A first step was to protect the right to payment for completed labour by holding that in the case of piece workers, wages were apportionable to work actually done, with the result that an employee leaving before a particular week was completed could nevertheless claim payment for the part of that week actually worked.

The next step was to separate the notice period from the period by reference to which wages were calculated. In *Parkin* v. *South Hetton Coal Co.* (1907) the Court of Appeal held that a contract with a term for fortnightly *notice* was not for that

---

[201] 8 Exch 215.

[202] S. Jacoby, 'The duration of indefinite employment contracts in the United States and England: an historical analysis' [1985] *Comparative Labor Law* 85–128, at p. 1.

[203] 13 CB 495; see Freedland, *The Contract of Employment*, op. cit., at p. 22.

[204] See *Turner* v. *Goldsmith* [1891] 1 QB 544; *re. Rubel, Bronze and Metal Co.* [1918] 1 KB 315; *Healy* v. *S.A. Rubastic* [1917] 1 KB 946.

[205] *Price* v. *Mouat* (1862) 11 CB (NS) 508; Foster, 'The myth of contract', op. cit., at p. 15.

[206] *Cussons* v. *Skinner* (1843) 11 M. & W. 161; *Edwards* v. *Levy* (1860) 2 F. & F. 94.

reason a fortnightly *hiring*; the employee was hired indefinitely, but earned his wages on a day by day basis (that is, he was 'daily paid' as opposed to being paid by reference to the hour or month or some other period). His failure to give notice was a breach of contract, but this did not affect his right to wages for days actually worked; and if the employer made a deduction from wages, he would have to show that the employee's early departure caused him damage.[207] The Divisional Court reached the same conclusion in *George* v. *Davis* (1911),[208] a case concerning a domestic servant. An employee who left without the requisite notice did not thereby automatically forfeit her right to wages:

the wages were payable monthly. At the expiration of the first month one month's wages had accrued to her, and she had then a vested right to be paid those wages, and could have sued for them. If she subsequently committed a breach of contract by leaving without giving proper notice she would not forfeit the wages which had already accrued due to her, though her master might have a cross-claim against her for damages for breach of contract.[209]

Similarly, it was held in *Hanley* v. *Pease & Partners* (1915)[210] that an employer had no implied right to suspend the contract of a workman without pay for incompetence or disobedience. In the absence of an express term providing for suspension, the workman had the right to bring a claim for damages for breach of contract.

The high-water mark of this process of 'contractualizing' the service relationship was the decision of the Court of Appeal in *Devonald* v. *Rosser* (1906).[211] In this case, employees recovered damages equivalent to wages for the employer's failure to provide work before and during a period of notice. The case arose out of the closure of the Cilfrew tinplate works in South Wales, and was brought by a number of rollermen at the works. Rollermen were skilled workers who were in the position of intermediate contractors, employing their own underhands; they were paid a tonnage rate and so were technically piece workers who could not claim wages due as earned if no work was actually done. Their claim was therefore framed as a claim in damages, on the basis that the employer had a duty to provide them with work for the duration of the notice period, which was one month, and for a period of two weeks when the works were closed prior to the employer giving notice. In upholding the claim, the Court of Appeal applied the principle of the parties' mutual obligations under the contract, which it had previously used to support claims for breach of contract by commission agents and other higher status employees. It also relied on the nineteenth century cases on mutuality, which, shorn of their significance as means of invoking the Master and Servant Acts, could now be used for the benefit of the employee. The employer could not avoid the duty to find work simply by claiming that a shortage of orders

---

[207] See 98 LT 162, 164 (Lord Alverstone CJ and Buckley LJ).

[208] [1911] 2 KB 445 this decision may be contrasted to the earlier case of *Moult* v. *Halliday* [1898] 1 QB 125 which, on essentially similar facts, was decided the other way.

[209] [1911] 2 KB 445, 448.   [210] [1915] 1 KB 698.   [211] [1906] 2 KB 728.

left the plant with no work to do, nor would the court imply a custom of lay-off without pay:

That is not a matter which is not in any sense within the knowledge of the employer, who can anticipate in respect of such matters, and who ought to know what is the probable future of the trade and act in time by giving the notice for which the contract provides. It seems to me that it is not reasonable to imply that the risk of that was in the contemplation of both sides as being taken by the workman.[212]

5.4 Employment at will and collective laissez-faire

Decisions such as *Devonald* and *Hanley* did not, however, lead straight to a fully relational model of the contract of employment. As collective bargaining grew in the early years of the twentieth century, there was a time during which it *displaced* the individual relationship to the extent that for most industrial workers the contract of employment became a 'contract at will', that is to say, one which could be terminated on short notice and which gave rise to practically no long-term, reciprocal obligations. In one sense, this lack of contractual protection reflected the insecurity of the employee and the inadequacy of the common law in controlling employer prerogatives. However, unlike in America where the contract at will was used as a device for limiting legal intervention in the employment relationship,[213] in Britain the absence of a stable contractual structure for the individual relationship reflected the increasing success of collective bargaining in removing disputes from the individual level to that of the union–employer relationship. This was to become part of the logic of 'collective laissez-faire', according to which, in Kahn-Freund's rationalization of the 1950s, protection for employees was sought through an equilibrium of social forces, which developed 'beyond' the law and which eclipsed the individual contract as a source of norms.[214]

The phrase 'contract at will' barely appears in the English legal discussion, but so-called 'minute contracts' allowing for practically immediate notice of termination were common in some industries as early as the 1850s. Most of these contracts in fact provided not for immediate notice but for notice of a day. This form of employment was common in Scotland in the mining and construction trades. One result of adopting the minute contract was to neutralize the Master and Servant Acts: as the 1865 Select Committee on Master and Servant was informed, 'the minute's warnings now are generally introduced, and that, of course, to some extent, annuls the law altogether'.[215] Similarly, 'in the minds of some workmen, it

---

[212] [1906] 2 KB 728, 742.

[213] P. Selznick, *Law, Society and Industrial Justice* (New Brunswick, NJ: Transaction Books, 1980), at pp. 134–35.

[214] O. Kahn-Freund, 'Labour law', in M. Ginsberg (ed.) *Law and Opinion in England in the 20th Century* (London: Stevens, 1959), 215–63; see generally Chapter 4, below.

[215] Select Committee on Master and Servant (Elcho) *Report*, Parliamentary Papers (1866) XIII.1, at Q. 701 (Colin Steele, Secretary of Scottish Iron Moulders' Association).

creates a feeling of independence'.[216] The weight of the evidence before the Select Committee tends to suggest that the initiative for the introduction of short notice periods came in most cases from employers, and was initially opposed by workmen on the grounds of reduced job security; the possible advantages, in terms of avoiding restrictive disciplinary laws, was appreciated only later. Even then, minute contracts were not common in England at this stage; fortnightly notice was the more normal rule in the Lancashire coalfield, for example. After 1875, as we have seen, notice periods of between a week or a month were common in most English industrial establishments, and were frequently used by employers in conjunction with the practice of late payment as devices for retaining employees.[217]

Up to the 1870s, both the British and the American courts determined the period of notice in contracts of employment by reference to the payment period, that is to say, the period by reference to which payment was calculated (the hour, day, week or month as the case might be). In a case where there was no express term governing notice, this was thought to be the correct doctrinal approach among US lawyers such as Williston, the author of the leading contract treatise of the time. This had the effect that salaried employees, who were paid at weekly or monthly intervals rather than by the hour, would enjoy for that reason a longer notice period, and thus an enhanced form of job security.[218] Casual employees or workers in trades where short notice was the custom were, on the other hand, construed as having contracts at will.

Where the British and American systems diverged at around this time was over the question of whether *all* employment relationships should be presumed to be at will unless the contrary were stated. The American courts, following *Payne* v. *Western & Atlantic Railroad*[219] and in particular *Martin* v. *New York Life Insurance Co.*[220] which concerned a middle-class employee, began to apply just such a general presumption. The extension of the at-will model to all classes of employment was primarily a product of a constitutional debate over the legitimacy of legislation protecting trade union members from dismissal. The ability of the employer to dismiss workers at will was crucial in practice to halting organization drives. The courts, however, struck down legislation outlawing non-union membership clauses in contracts of employment (the so-called 'yellow dog' contract) and the use of the anti-union blacklist. In this way, the question of the construction of the terms of employment contracts took on a general significance, far beyond the immediate question of rights under the wage–work bargain between employer and employee.[221]

---

[216] Ibid., Q. 2045 (John Ormiston, Manager of Shotts Iron Co.).

[217] See above, Section 4.4.

[218] S. Jacoby, 'The duration of indefinite employment contracts in the United States and England', op. cit.   [219] 81 Tenn. 507 (1884).

[220] 148 NY 117 (1895).

[221] See W.N. Njoya, 'Ownership and property rights in the company: a law and economics analysis of shareholder and employee interests', Ph.D. thesis, University of Cambridge, 2002, at pp. 128–133.

No such presumption developed in Britain, principally because there was no equivalent to the constitutional dimension to the issue which arose in the United States. After the passage of the Trade Disputes Act had confirmed state support for collective bargaining, a gradual process of judicial acceptance of the legislation took place. By the inter-war period the accommodation of the courts to the values of the legislation is clear, in particular in the decisions in *Reynolds* v. *Shipping Federation*[222] and later in the *Crofter* case[223] which limited the common law of tortious interference and upheld the legality of measures taken to enforce the closed shop.

The rise in influence of collective bargaining in Britain saw a shortening of the notice period for most industrial workers. From the vantage point of today's debates concerning job security and the contractual stability of the employment relationship, this development seems counter-intuitive, in so far as it reduced the formal legal rights of individual employees to a measure of job and income security under the contract. However, it achieved two important gains for the trade unions: the neutralization of the disciplinary jurisdiction of the magistrates under the Employers and Workmen Act, and the exclusion of common law restrictions on the right to strike. In relation to the Employers and Workmen Act 1875, Tillyard noted in 1928 that the restrictive provisions of the Act were 'practically a dead letter', principally because 'contracts of service are determinable more and more by short notice, so that powers to rescind and powers to enforce performance for unexpired periods of service are in practice rarely if ever wanted'.[224] The Act continued to be used as a weapon of discipline in the mining industry, and cases arising from its use reached the higher courts as late as the 1940s;[225] however, in most industries it appears to have played a gradually decreasing role with the expansion of collective bargaining.[226]

Individual sanctions against the employee, enforced by law and resting on formal subordination, gave way to collective procedures resting more on a formal 'equality' between the parties:

the inferior status of the worker has disappeared. This is absolutely true as regards the administration of the law, but it is also largely true of other means of settling disputes. On Boards of Conciliation, on Trade Boards, on Courts of Referees, and on other bodies dealing with trade interests, working men and employers meet on an equality.[227]

---

[222] [1924] Ch. 28.　　[223] *Crofter Hand Woven Harris Tweed Co. Ltd.* v. *Veitch* [1942] AC 435.

[224] F. Tillyard, *Industrial Law* (London: A. & C. Black, 1928), at pp. 328–329.

[225] See *Nokes* v. *Doncaster Amalgamated Collieries* [1940] AC 1014. *Nokes* later came to have pivotal importance in the law relating to transfers of undertakings. The decision of the House of Lords, ruling against automatic novation of the contract of employment in the event of a business transfer on grounds related to the adverse implications of this for the personal liberty of the worker (see in particular the speech of Lord Atkin), is much more readily understandable when the statutory background to the case is borne in mind. See also *Dorman, Long & Co. Ltd.* v. *Carroll* (1945) 173 LT 141.

[226] The Act had a curious end. The powers to order specific performance and to order security in return for performance were repealed by the Industrial Relations Act 1971, Sch. 9. The remaining parts of the Act were repealed by the Statute Law (Repeals) Act 1973, Sch. 1.

[227] Tillyard, *Industrial Law*, op. cit, at pp. 17–18.

Underlying this 'equality' was, in the final analysis, the economic power of the union as expressed through strike action. The shortening of notice periods was useful to unions as it meant that strikes would rarely, if ever, involve a breach of contract; short strike notice could be given within the terms of the individual contract, so relieving the strike organizers from tortious liability. The 1891–4 Royal Commission found that while short notice periods originated in many cases from employers' need to deal with 'fluctuations of trade', they were nonetheless supported by the unions for their own reasons: '[a]t the present day the trade unions would seem themselves to be opposed to any system of long notice to terminate engagements because it would interfere with their power to strike all hands simultaneously in a trade at short notice, at the time most convenient for that purpose.'[228]

One effect of collective laissez-faire, then, was that individual litigation over contractual rights declined in significance. The focusing of legal rights (or 'immunities') on trade unions made individual litigation over the terms of the employment contract from one point of view unnecessary, or at least of little purpose. As a result, the progress made in the *Devonald* case towards contractualizing the employment relationship was not continued very far during this period. Formally, the concept of contract now described all forms of the employment relationship.[229] In practice, because the contract at will was hardly a contract at all, the application of contractual analysis to the employment of most industrial workers was severely limited. In *Marshall* v. *English Electric*[230] the Court of Appeal found that the employment relationship of an industrial worker consisted of nothing more than a bare exchange of work for wages. When this stopped, as in the case of a suspension of the employee, there was nothing left of the contract; suspension was in fact a dismissal and re-employment:

What is left . . . of the contract during [the period of suspension]? Everything, say the respondents, except the obligation to work on the one side and to pay on the other. But in the case of the hourly servant are there any rights or obligations left except possibly the obligation to pay for one hour?[231]

The decisions in *Marshall* and in *Hulme* v. *Ferranti Ltd.*[232] which most clearly express the concept of employment at will in the British context arose against the background of the wartime legislation which conferred certain protective rights on munitions employees, in return for constraints on the right to quit and to take industrial action. It is significant that in each case resort to litigation to assert the contractual rights of individual employees took place in exceptional circumstances where the normal economic sanction of the strike was unavailable. Even then the British courts, unlike the American ones, had no consistent approach to

---

[228] Royal Commission on Labour Laws (Devonshire), *Fifth and Final Report*, Parliamentary Papers (1894) XXXV.9, at para. 25.
[229] F.R. Batt, *The Law of Master and Servant* (London: Pitman, 1929), at pp. 14–15.
[230] [1945] 1 All ER 642.   [231] [1945] 1 All ER 642, 645.   [232] [1918] 2 KB 426.

construction. It was possible to find, in *Payzu* v. *Hannaford*,[233] that a departing employee had to give notice in a case where he was being sued by the employer for breach of contract under the Employers and Workmen Act; whereas in *Hulme* and *Marshall* at-will analysis was used to defeat employees' claims for wages.

The different ways in which the courts construed the contract of employment reflected, as did social legislation and the 'control' test, the various ways in which labour was contracted within firms. For industrial workers employed in mass production processes, contractual terms conferred few rights beyond the right to wages for completed labour. Manual workers rarely succeeded in claims for sick pay or lay-off pay,[234] where the courts asserted a principle of 'no work, no pay' notwithstanding *Devonald* v. *Rosser*. By contrast, clerical and managerial staff were more likely to have not only longer notice periods and greater *de facto* security of tenure, but also occupational benefits including pension rights. In their case the source of security was not collective bargaining, but their position of trust and responsibility within the hierarchy of the firm, a position the common law recognized by attaching significant rights of income protection to salaried status. Hence Lord Atkin in *Nokes* v. *Doncaster Amalgamated Collieries* (1940) could compare the position of manual workers 'confined to weekly or fortnightly contracts' with 'the longer term contracts of accountants, managers, salesmen, doctors, and . . . managing directors employed for a term of years'.[235]

6. The Impact of the Welfare State, Collective Bargaining and the Vertical Integration of the Enterprise

The removal of criminal sanctions from the individual employment relationship in the 1870s was soon followed by the first legislative interventions of the welfare state. This wave of 'social legislation' began with the Employers' Liability Act 1880, which mitigated the effects of the doctrine of common employment. This rule held that an employer could not be held vicariously liable in tort where negligence by one employee, acting in the course of employment, caused personal injury to another. The basis for the rule was the fiction that the contract of service contained an implied term under which the employee consented to the risk of being injured by a fellow worker. The 1880 Act made a limited exception, by excluding the common employment rule in a case where the plaintiff was injured as a result of the negligence of a fellow employee exercising managerial or supervisory responsibilities. From this small beginning, the principle that the employer should assume responsibility for social and economic risks arising from the employment

---

[233] [1918] 2 KB 348.
[234] Compare the line of case containing *Marrison* v. *Bell* [1939] 2 KB 187, *Petrie* v. *Macfisheries* [1940] 1 KB 258 and *O'Grady* v. *Saper* [1940] 2 KB 469, with *Orman* v. *Saville Sportswear Ltd.* [1960] 1 WLR 1055.   [235] [1940] AC 1014, 1028.

relationship began to take shape. The first Workmen's Compensation Act was introduced in 1897 and the first National Insurance Act in 1911. The workmen's compensation scheme imposed liability on employers for workplace-related injuries and disease, and prompted the widespread use of employers' liability insurance to spread the risks in question. Social insurance spread the more general risks of interruption to earnings through illness, unemployment and old age throughout the working population through the device of state-run insurance funds. National insurance contributions, levied on employers and employees, introduced a kind of fiscal regulation of the employment relationship which was later extended through the income taxation scheme.[236]

These interventions, by their purpose and nature, presupposed a certain degree of stability and regularity in the employment relationship, so reinforcing tendencies towards the growth in the size of firms. Once the enterprise became a mechanism for the redistribution of social and economic risks, the resulting imposition of regulatory and fiscal costs on to employers created economies of scale which favoured larger firms at the expense of smaller productive units. The welfare state extended its influence alongside increasing vertical integration of production and the emergence of the public sector as a significant employer.

This process can be observed at the juridical level in terms of the decisions of courts called on to determine the scope of social legislation. Early social legislation did not adopt the 'unitary' model of the contract of employment, which emerged only after 1945; instead, it persisted in stratifying the labour force by reference to distinctions drawn from restrictive legislation and from the common law. Hence salaried, non-manual workers were distinguished from hourly or daily-paid wage earners, who were distinguished in turn from casual workers and others with irregular wage relationships. At the core of this process of stratification was the 'control' test, the predominant judicial test of the time for identifying the service relationship.

6.1 Status distinctions in early social legislation

The Employers' Liability Act of 1880 and the Workmen's Compensation Act of 1897 both adopted the term 'workman' rather than 'employee' to describe the workers within their scope. As we have seen, the term 'workman' had a specific meaning, related to manual labour, under the Employers and Workmen Act of 1875; to this extent it was a legacy (if in somewhat attenuated form) of the status distinctions drawn under the master and servant regime. The 1880 Act explicitly adopted the meaning of the term under the Act of 1875, and the two Acts—the one protective, the other restrictive—were subsequently interpreted in tandem. In a further reinforcement of status distinctions, supervisory employees were also expressly excluded from the protection of the 1880 Act. The term 'workman' was also applied to truck legislation following the Truck Amendment Act of 1887.

---

[236] On social insurance, see generally Chapter 3, below.

Following the passage of these Acts, the term 'workman', previously given a wide reading, began to receive a more restrictive interpretation in the courts. In *Morgan* v. *London General Omnibus Company* the courts, in a claim for personal injuries compensation under the 1880 Act, held that a bus conductor 'who earns the wages becoming due to him through the confidence reposed in his honesty', was not a workman:

'labourer' cannot in its ordinary acceptation include an omnibus conductor . . . The mere fact that a man works with his hands is not enough to constitute a workman within [the Act].[237]

Similarly, a locomotive guard was not within the Truck Acts,[238] a sales assistant[239] and a hairdresser[240] were outside the Employers and Workmen Act, and a tramcar driver was outside the Employers' Liability Act.[241] As a result of these decisions, a large class of employees, who were neither supervisory employees within the meaning of the Employers' Liability Act nor managerial employees under the Truck Acts, were excluded from the protective scope of those statutes.

The first Workman's Compensation Act of 1897 adopted a wider definition, referring to a workman as '[including] any person who is engaged in an employment to which this Act applies, whether by way of manual labour or otherwise'. The employments covered by this Act were restricted to the railways, mining and quarrying, and factory and laundry work.[242] However, the attempt to give the Act an extended scope failed to survive the Court of Appeal judgment in *Simpson* v. *Ebbw Vale Steel, Iron & Coal Co.*[243] Here, a widow of a colliery manager sued his former employers for compensation in respect of his death in an underground accident. Her claim was rejected, the court concluding that while it was theoretically possible for a non-manual worker to be within the Act, he 'must still be a workman'. The *Simpson* decision was based on the assumption that protective legislation of this kind was inappropriate for a high status (salaried) worker:

It presupposes a position of dependence; it treats the class of workmen as being in a sense 'inopes consilii', and the Legislature does for them what they cannot do for themselves: it gives them a sort of State insurance, it being assumed that they are either not sufficiently intelligent or not sufficiently in funds to insure themselves. In no sense can such a principle extend to those who are earning good salaries.[244]

Despite the hostile language used here, it should not be thought that it was the courts alone which perpetuated these status distinctions. Such distinctions were

---

[237] The quotations in the text are from judgments of the Court of Appeal ((1884) LR 13 QBD 832, 834 (Brett MR)) and the Divisional Court ((1883) LR 12 QBD 201, 207 (A.L. Smith LJ)), respectively.   [238] *Hunt* v. *Great Northern Railway Co.* [1891] QB 601.
[239] *Bound* v. *Lawrence* [1892] 1 QB 226.   [240] *R.* v. *Louth Justices* [1900] 2 Ir. R. 714.
[241] *Cook* v. *North Metropolitan Tramways Ltd.* (1887) 18 QBD 683, not followed in Scotland: *Wilson* v. *Glasgow Tramways & Omnibus Co.* (1878) 5 SC (4th Ser.) 981; while in *Smith* v. *Associated Omnibus Co.* [1907] 1 KB 916 the court distinguished *Cook* by deciding that a bus driver who had to start his engine with a hand pump and used spanners and wrenches to fix it if it broke down was, for these reasons, a 'workman'.   [242] Workmen's Compensation Act 1897, s. 7.
[243] [1905] 1 KB 453.   [244] [1905] 1 KB 453, 458 (Collins MR).

deeply embedded in the law as a result of the influence of the Employers and Workmen Act, and the levels of compensation established by the Workmen's Compensation Act were low enough to justify a belief that the Act was principally intended for the manual industrial workforce. Lawyers could be explicit about the class distinctions underlying the Acts; in *Simpson* counsel argued that 'the Legislature were contemplating a class of workers who may be described as belonging to the working class in the popular sense of the term—a wage earning class'.[245]

The Workmen's Compensation Act of 1906 established yet another scheme of definition, which in due course formed the basis for the classifications drawn by the legislation of the pre-war and inter-war periods. A 'workman' was now defined as 'any person who enters into or works under a contract of service or apprenticeship with an employer, whether by way of manual labour, clerical work or otherwise, and whether the contract is expressed or implied, is oral or in writing'; but there were significant exceptions, including non-manual workers employed on annual remuneration greater than £250, casual workers employed 'otherwise than for the purposes of their employer's trade or business', outworkers and family workers. This scheme, then, excluded high status workers at the top and casual workers at the bottom.

In similar vein the National Insurance Act of 1911 applied its health insurance provisions to 'employed' persons, who were defined principally as those employed under a contract of service or apprenticeship, but excluding non-manual workers on an annual salary of more than £160, casual workers not dependent on their employer's business, commission agents, and a large class of public sector workers including civil servants, military personnel and teachers, on the grounds that they were better served by state schemes already in existence.[246] Male outworkers were included in the Act,[247] but most female outworkers were initially excluded by the provision excepting outwork employment 'where the person so employed is the wife of an insured person and is not wholly or mainly dependent for her livelihood on her earnings in such employment'.[248] The Insurance Commissioners later exercised delegated powers[249] to bring female outworkers within the Act,[250] but both male and female outworkers remained outside the unemployment insurance part of the scheme. Male industrial workers were also the principal beneficiaries of the unemployment insurance scheme. The 1911 Act applied only to a specified number of industrial trades;[251] women workers were only covered in practice after the extension of insurance in the Unemployment Insurance Act of 1921, and even

---

[245] [1905] 1 KB 453, 456.   [246] See National Insurance Act 1911, s. 1 and Schedule 1.

[247] National Insurance Act 1911, Sch. 1, Part I, para. (d). The courts held that master tailors were within the Act even if they themselves hired others: *re Master Tailors as Outworkers* (1913) 29 TLR 725; and outworkers were held to come under the Trade Boards Act 1909 (*Street* v. *Williams* [1914] 3 KB 537). Statutory definitions of the term 'homeworker' subsequently acknowledged that out-workers employing others could come under protective legislation. See Wages Act 1986, s. 26(1); National Minimum Wage Act 1998, s. 35.

[248] National Insurance Act 1911, Sch. 1, Part II, para. (j).

[249] Contained in s. 1(2) of the 1911 Act.   [250] SR&O 1912/921; SR&O 1914/880.

[251] See National Insurance Act 1911, Sch. 6. The regulated industries were named as: building, con-struction, shipbuilding, mechanical engineering, ironfounding, vehicle construction, and sawmilling.

then the legislation set differential contribution and benefit rates which had the effect of providing women workers with less extensive protection than men.

6.2 The 'control' test

The hierarchical distinction between clerical/managerial workers, industrial workers and casual workers which is to be found in this legislation filtered through into the common law in the form of the 'control' test for identifying the contract of service. 'Control' is traditionally seen in labour law as a test inherited from pre-industrial traditions of employment, and in particular the forms of domestic and artisanal production. This was the sense referred to by Kahn-Freund when he described the control test as:

> based upon the social conditions of an earlier age . . . It reflects a state of society in which the ownership of the means of production coincided with the possession of technical knowledge and skill and in which that knowledge and skill were largely acquired by being handed down from generation to the next by oral tradition and not by being systematically imparted in institutions of learning from universities down to technical schools. The control test postulates a combination of managerial and technical functions in the person of the employer.[252]

Certainly, the control test was close to the test of 'exclusive service' which was the principal test of subordinated employment under the Master and Servant Acts; however, there is little to suggest that it was a remnant of pre-capitalist forms of employment. 'Control' was not an important test until the later nineteenth and early twentieth centuries, and when it began to be used it was in the context of the social legislation of that period and in particular the status distinctions which were being drawn at that time.

An early case referring to 'control' in the context of the master's vicarious liability for the torts of the servant is *Sadler* v. *Henlock* (1855),[253] in which Crompton J. defined the relevant test as 'whether the defendant retained the power of controlling the work. No distinction can be drawn from the circumstance of the man being paid at so much a day or by the job'. In contrast to a servant, an independent contractor 'chooses the mode in which the work is done, and the persons who do it'. This was a case concerning a labourer employed by the defendant to clear a drain on his land. It is unlikely that the control test, as such, was clearly established as a general test of status at this time; up to the repeal of the Master and Servant Acts the judicial focus was on 'exclusive service' and after that on the definition of the term 'workman'. Although 'control' may have been more important in the area of tortious liability for personal injury, the main issues there concerned the scope of the defences—common employment, consent (*volenti non fit injuria*) and contributory negligence—rather than the question of workers' status.

---

[252] 'Servants and independent contractors' (1951) 15 *Modern Law Review* 504–509, at p. 505.
[253] 4 E. & B. 570.

The control test was only clearly asserted later, in cases concerning not the common law of vicarious liability but the scope of social legislation. The leading cases in which the test was established were decided in the twentieth, not the nineteenth century—*Simmons* v. *Heath Laundry*[254] and *Underwood* v. *Perry*[255] in the field of workmen's compensation, and *Scottish Insurance Commissioners* v. *Edinburgh Royal Infirmary*[256] and *Hill* v. *Beckett*[257] in national insurance. The nineteenth century cases which were most frequently cited in support of the test had nothing to do either with vicarious liability or with contractual disputes between employer and employee. The 1873 case of *R.* v. *Negus*,[258] in which Blackburn J. referred to control as the principal test, was concerned with the definition of 'servant' under the Larceny Act 1868. The subsequently much-cited case of *Yewens* v. *Noakes*[259] involved a claim for exemption from inhabited house duty under the Customs and Inland Revenue Act 1869, under which premises used for trade only would be exempt from the tax if they were occupied merely by a caretaker, defined by the Act as 'a servant or other person . . . for the protection thereof'. The Court of Appeal held that a clerk, earning £150 per annum, did not fall into this category.

In both these cases, the judges were clear that the status of 'servant' was distinct from that of high status 'employee', and that the main basis of differentiation was not the knowledge of the trade or craft but the presence of a wide-ranging power of the master to give orders to the servant, something the courts had previously associated with the idea of exclusive service. Blackburn J.'s judgment in *Negus* reflected this, when he said that 'the test is very much this, whether the person is charged and bound to obey the orders of his master. He may be so without being bound to devote the whole of this time to this service; but if bound to devote his whole time to it, that may be very strong evidence of his being under control'.[260] Lord Justice Bramwell evidently had the same distinction in mind when he said in *Yewens* v. *Noakes* that 'a servant is a person subject to the command of his master as to the manner in which he shall do his work'.[261] Lord Justice Thesiger thought it obvious that a salaried clerk was not a servant, any more than would be 'the manager of a bank, a foreman with high wages, persons in the position almost of gentlemen'.[262]

Why did courts, several decades later, alight upon these cases as authoritative guidance to the classification of employment relationships? The answer would not be problematic if the control test had become well established in tort law or in the interpretation of labour statutes, but as we have seen, this does not appear to have been the case. A more convincing explanation is that rediscovery and adaptation of the control test were a doctrinal innovation which was introduced at the same

[254] [1910] 1 KB 543.   [255] [1923] WC & I Rep. 63.   [256] 1913 SC 751.
[257] [1915] 1 KB 578.   [258] (1873) LR 2 CCR 34.
[259] (1880) 6 QBD 530; see Merritt, ' "Control" v "economic reality": defining the contract of employment', op. cit., at p. 113: 'the "control" test has been misapplied almost from the moment of its emergence'.   [260] (1873) LR 2 CCR 34, 37.
[261] (1880) LR 6 QBD 530, 532–533.   [262] (1880) LR 6 QBD 530, 538.

time as the courts were being called on to define the boundaries of regulatory legislation of a novel type. The element of compulsion in the legislation went strongly against the grain of prevailing common law values, as the judgments of the Court of Appeal in *Simpson* v. *Ebbw Vale* make clear. It was in the context of employers' efforts to limit the scope of the legislation and a sympathetic judiciary that the control test was taken up.

The particular effect of the control test was that it reinforced status distinctions between the 'labouring' and 'professional' classes, on the one hand, while excluding casual and seasonal workers, to whom the employer made a limited commitment, on the other. *Simmons* v. *Heath Laundry*[263] concerned the employment status of a young laundry woman who gave piano lessons in her spare time. It was held that in respect of the music lessons she was not a 'workman' [sic], so that when she injured her hand at the laundry she could not claim for diminution of earning capacity as a pianist. Rather than saying that she was an independent contractor for the purposes of the lessons, the Court of Appeal used the control test in order to place her in the category of professional workers: 'the question to be asked is what was the man [sic] employed to do; was he employed upon the terms that he should within the scope of his employment obey his master's orders, or was he employed to exercise his skill and achieve an indicated result in such manner as in his judgment was most likely to achieve success?'[264] In other cases in this line, a lecturer, chemist, nurse, doctor and poor law officers were held to be outside the Act.[265] This exclusion reflected the view that compulsory insurance was inappropriate for salaried or professional employees; it was also a means of reducing the potential liability of poor law guardians and hospitals, at a time when funding was more precarious than it subsequently became.[266]

The position of casual workers was complicated by the prevalence of subcontracting in many industries. The contract system of hiring labour through an intermediary was still the predominant form of industrial organization in road building, construction, shipbuilding, mining and quarrying, and iron and steel. As we have seen, this meant that there was unlikely to be a contractual nexus between workmen hired by the butty worker or foreman, and the ultimate owners of the site, plant or materials on which they worked. It was for this reason that the Factory and Workshop Acts of the period imposed obligations not upon employers in respect of their employees, but upon *occupiers* or owners of factories in

---

[263] [1910] 1 KB 543.   [264] [1910] 1 KB 543, 553 (Buckley LJ).

[265] See, respectively, *Waites* v. *Franco-British Exhibition* (1909) 25 TLR 441; *Bagnall* v. *Levinstein* [1907] 1 KB 531; *Dow* v. *McNeil* [1925] WC & I Rep. 32 (although not followed in *Wardell* v. *Kent County Council* [1938] 2 KB 769); *re South Dublin Union Officers* [1913] WC&I Rep. 245.

[266] In similar vein, the control test could even be used to hold that a nurse was an employee or 'servant' of a hospital for one purpose (administrative duties) but not another (work on the ward): *Hillyer* v. *St. Bartholomew's Hospital* [1902] 2 KB 820, a tort case, not followed in the workmen's compensation case of *Wardell* v. *Kent County Council* [1938] 2 KB 769, and overruled for tort law purposes (but with Greer LJ dissenting) in *Gold* v. *Essex County Council* [1942] 2 KB 293.

respect of workers *on their premises*, regardless of whether there was a contractual relationship between them.[267]

The control test, as applied by twentieth century courts, often had the effect of classifying foremen as independent contractors, given their responsibility for hiring their own gangs;[268] while the gang workers or labourers themselves had no claim against the ultimate users of their labour since the latter did not 'control' the performance of their work.[269] Piecework payments were also treated by the courts as strong evidence of independent contractor status, notwithstanding clear statutory signals that this was not the case.[270] Share fishermen—inshore trawlermen who were paid on a proportion of the profits from individual voyages—were found to be outside the social insurance legislation.[271]

Seasonal and casual workers who were directly employed by the ultimate employer were the subject of particular statutory provisions, specifying that they were to be included in the legislation where they were economically dependent on their employer's business. This did not prevent considerable litigation arising. The courts held that a single, one-off hiring was not necessarily outside the scope of the Acts,[272] and were also prepared to include seasonal workers who returned to their employer on a regular basis[273] and part-time workers with long service.[274] However, in other cases they excluded workers under task contracts,[275] temporary workers[276] and casual workers with short-term service.[277] Trainees and unemployed workers receiving instruction and work experience at government training centres were also beyond the scope of the legislation.[278]

The adoption of the control test enabled employers to avoid responsibility for the social risks of illness, injury and unemployment which it had been the aim of social legislation to impose, at least in part, upon them. The drawing of fine distinctions to defeat the legislation in this way was not universally accepted. The Scottish courts, influenced, perhaps, by the civilian tradition of giving a purposive interpretation to social legislation, were on occasion reluctant to allow employers

---

[267] See Factories Act 1844, ss. 41, 73; Factories and Workshops Act 1878, ss. 93, 94.

[268] The courts reached opposing outcomes in different cases. Butty workers and foremen were found to be within the protection of the Workmen's Compensation Acts in *Evans* v. *Penwelt Dinas Silica Brick Co.* (1901) 18 TLR 58 and *Paterson* v. *Lockhart* (1905) 42 SLR 755, but outside them in *Simmons* v. *Faulds* (1901) 17 TLR 352, *Hayden* v. *Dick* (1902) 40 SLR 95 and *Vanplew* v. *Parkgate Iron & Steel Co.* [1903] 1 KB 851.

[269] *Crowley* v. *Limerick County Council* [1923] 2 Ir. R. 178; *Littlejohn* v. *Brown & Co. Ltd.* 1909 SC 87; although cf. *Dunlop* v. *M'Cready* (1900) 37 SLR 779; *Doharty* v. *Boyd* 1909 SC 87.

[270] Workmen's Compensation Act 1906, s. 13; National Insurance Act 1911, Sch. 1, Part I, para. (a).

[271] *Scottish Insurance Commissioners* v. *M'Naughton* 1914 SC 826.

[272] *Boothby* v. *Patrick & Son* [1918] W.C. & I. Rep. 340.

[273] *Smith* v. *Buxton* [1915] W.C. & I. Rep. 126.   [274] *Dewhurst* v. *Mather* [1908] 2 KB 754.

[275] *Alderman* v. *Warren* [1916] W.C. & I. Rep. 266.   [276] *Stoker* v. *Wartham* [1919] 1 KB 499.

[277] *Knight* v. *Bucknill* [1913] W.C. & I. Rep. 175; *Withams* v. *Larsen Ltd.* [1928] W.C. & I. Rep. 323.

[278] *Broome* v. *Ministry of Labour* [1927] W.C. & I. Rep. 232; *Watson* v. *Government Instructional Centre* [1929] W.C. & I. Rep. 265; re *Leeds Corp. and Chadwick* (1928) 44 TLR 797 (cf. Unemployment Insurance Act 1927, s. 15); *McGeachy* v. *Dept. of Health for Scotland* 1938 SC 282.

to contract out of the Acts by these means (just as, in the nineteenth century, they had been reluctant to accept the doctrine of common employment which held that the worker impliedly accepted the risk of a fellow servant's negligence[279]). In *Paterson* v. *Lockhart*,[280] a case concerning the status of a foreman, Lord McLaren considered that

it would be a serious restriction of the scope of the Act if it were possible by introducing some condition into an agreement to take it out of the category of a pure contract of service and so to avoid liability under the Act . . . It is quite in accordance with custom for a superior workman to choose his own assistants. An engineer may choose his own fireman or a mason his hodman. But that does not prevent their being servants, paid by a common employer.

In *Dunlop* v. *M'Cready*,[281] Lord Adam said of a group of gang workers that 'to call them independent contractors is a mere playing with words'. These were, however, isolated examples of a more tolerant judicial attitude. More typical of the case-law was the finding of the Court of Session in *Littlejohn* v. *Brown*[282] to the effect that a rivet boy, hired by the head riveters in a shipyard, had no contract of service with the main employer: 'if the test is direct and immediate selection, payment and control and power of dismissal, the evidence is all one way, namely, that [the plaintiff] was in the service of Gammell and Lacey, John Brown & Company being only indirectly connected with the boy's employment'.

The 'unitary' model of the contract of employment which, in modern labour law, extends to all categories of wage-earners, only came into being when further reforms were enacted to social legislation, in particular the extension of social insurance which took place in the National Insurance Act 1946. A major aspect of the Beveridge Report was the abolition of distinctions between different categories of employees: henceforth, all wage or salary earners, regardless of their annual income or of their professional status, would come under the same contributory classification.[283] Accordingly, the 1946 Act established two principal classes of contributors: Class I covered 'employed earners', defined as 'any persons gainfully occupied in employment . . . being employment under a contract of service', and Class II covered those employed on their own account.[284] The latter paid a lower rate of contribution and were excluded from the unemployment insurance part of the scheme. In this way the fundamental division between *employees* and the *self-employed* was established. The same distinction was adopted for the purposes of income taxation[285] and, in due course, under the employment

---

[279] It was not until the House of Lords decided *Bartonshill Coal Co.* v. *Reid* (1856) 4 Macq. 266, that the Scottish courts accepted the doctrine, which had its origins in decisions of the English courts.
[280] 42 SLR 755, 757.   [281] (1900) 37 SLR 797, 782.   [282] 1909 SC 169, 174.
[283] *Social Insurance and Allied Services* Cmd. 6404, November 1942, at para. 314.
[284] National Insurance Act 1946, s. 1(2).
[285] The modern division between self-employment and employment in tax law emerged gradually during the inter-war period. The principal division in the Income Tax Act 1918 was between earnings from public-sector employment, which fell under Schedule E, and earnings and profits from all other

protection legislation which was introduced first in the early 1960s.[286] The ending of the old divide between manual and non-manual workers was epitomized by the merging of the concepts of the contract of *service* and of *employment*: for statutory purposes, these were now synonymous with each other.[287]

Faced with this new situation, the courts abandoned the old distinction between low status and high status employees when seeking to identify the contract of service.[288] The control test itself came to be regarded as excessively artificial, and gave way to the tests of 'integration' and 'business reality'. These stressed economic as opposed to personal subordination as the basis of the contract of employment. The test of the worker's 'integration' into an organization was used to explain how professionals such as doctors and journalists could be classified as employees notwithstanding the high degree of autonomy they enjoyed in their work.[289] 'Economic reality' had the effect of extending protection to casual workers and outworkers who were dependent on the business of another, as opposed to being entrepreneurs with a business and employees of their own.[290] By these means, a more inclusive notion of the employment relationship came to be established for the purposes of determining the scope of employers' liabilities in respect of personal injuries, employment protection and social insurance.[291]

6.3 Vertical integration of the enterprise, collective bargaining, and the stabilization of the employment relationship

At the same time as changes to social legislation were cementing the 'unitary' contract of employment in place, the growth of collective bargaining, supported indirectly by the state, was contributing to the same process. Its impact was felt first in the marginalization of the internal contracting system which occurred as a result of the spread of collective representation to the lower occupational grades and ranks. At the same time, changes to company law, coupled with technological

employment, which fell under Schedule D. Schedule D therefore covered both the self-employed and certain groups of private-sector employees. The Finance Act 1922, s. 18, then transferred earnings from private-sector employment into Schedule E, leaving only the self-employed in Schedule D. The Pay-As-You-Earn system of automatic deductions of tax from the earnings of employees was applied to most Schedule E employments by the Income Tax (Employments) Act 1943.

[286] The first such statute was the Contracts of Employment Act 1963; the relevant provision is now contained in the Employment Rights Act 1996, s. 230(1).

[287] See, in the context of social insurance, *Vandyk* v. *Minister of Pensions and National Insurance* [1955] 1 QB 29.

[288] See, in particular, *Stevenson, Jordan & Harrison* v. *McDonald & Evans* [1952] 1 TLR 101.

[289] *Cassidy* v. *Minister of Health* [1951] 2 KB 343; *Roe* v. *Minister of Health* [1954] 2 QB 66; *Beloff* v. *Pressdram Ltd.* [1973] 2 All ER 241.

[290] *Market Investigations Ltd.* v. *Minister for Social Security* [1969] 2 QB 173; *Lee Ting Sang* v. *Chung Chi-Keung* [1990] ICR 409.

[291] See R. Mitchell and J. Howe, 'The evolution of the contract of employment in Australia: a discussion' (1999) 12 *Australian Journal of Labour Law* 113–130, for discussion of how far a similar process of conceptual evolution to that described in the text occurred in Australian labour law during the same period.

change, altered economies of scale and scope so as to encourage the growth of larger firms and the integration of production. As these various changes took effect, the modern, integrated form of corporate organization emerged, and along with it came the open-ended or indeterminate contract of employment.

At the start of the 1870s most industrial enterprises were still independent, family-run firms, employing fewer than a hundred workers. The largest firms in engineering employed only a few thousand men. The averagely sized coal mine in 1869 employed only just over a hundred workers; by 1897 it employed just over two hundred, although the larger firms which made up the Mining Association of Great Britain employed around a thousand men each. In textiles, the average size of a mill was 120 employees in 1870 and 139 in 1890. In engineering, the Royal Commission of 1891–4 reported an average size of around 450 employees per establishment. Ownership also tended to be limited to single or dual establishments; in the 1890s on average each mining firm owned two mines, a pattern which persisted into the inter-war period.[292]

One reason for the relatively small size of industrial enterprises was the restricted and informal nature of capital markets at this point. The establishment of limited liability in the 1850s had provided a degree of security for investors which had previously been lacking, and paved the way for the growth of large-scale corporate enterprises in sectors such as the railways which required large infusions of capital. However, considerable suspicion of limited liability remained, on the grounds that unlimited liability was necessary in order to discourage speculative ventures.[293] Over 30 per cent of the public companies formed between 1856 and 1883 became insolvent, many of them in their first five years.[294] Periodic corporate crises led to a large number of calls on partly paid up shares and a resulting loss of investor confidence.

However, from the mid-1880s public interest in company flotations increased again. Following the high-profile flotations of the Guinness brewing company and the textiles company J. & P. Coats in 1885, the number of UK manufacturing and distribution firms with a London stock exchange quotation went up from 60 in 1885 to over 600 by 1907.[295] Investor interest was encouraged by a reduction in the average size of share denominations. In the years immediately following the introduction of the 1855 Act, when the legitimacy of limited liability was still widely questioned, it had been the practice of many industrial companies to set

---

[292] M. Holbrook-Jones, *Supremacy and Subordination of Labour: The Hierarchy of Work in the Early Labour Movement* (London: Heinemann Educational Books, 1982), ch. 2.

[293] J. Saville, 'Sleeping partnership and limited liability, 1850–1856' (1956) *Economic History Review* 418–433, at p. 425.

[294] See H. Shannon, 'The limited companies of 1866–1933' (1933) *Economic History Review* 290–316. The legal distinction between 'private' and 'public' companies did not arrive until 1908 (by virtue of the Companies Consolidation Act of that year (8 Edward VII c 59)); Shannon used his own definition of 'private' and 'public' companies according to whether the company in question offered its shares to the public (the most salient aspect of the definitions adopted in 1908).

[295] P. Hart and S. Prais, 'The analysis of business concentration: a statistical approach' (1956) 119 *Journal of the Royal Statistical Society Series A (General)* 150–191.

a high share denomination and restrict shareholdings to those with a close family or trading connection to the business. Only 16 per cent of the 3,720 companies formed in the decade after 1856 offered shares for less than £5. This began to change in the 1860s, as a number of mining companies began offering shares for £1 each, and cotton companies followed suit in the 1870s. This practice was, nevertheless, far from universal. Many of the iron and steel, coal, engineering and shipbuilding companies which converted from private ownership to an incorporated business form maintained high share denominations during this period, and offered shares only to a small number of local wealthy families and investors with trade connections;[296] thus incorporation was largely a matter of family-owned firms adapting the corporate form to their own ends.[297]

Nevertheless, around the turn of the century, large combines of firms began to emerge in textiles, coal and engineering. Mergers were encouraged by the possibility of a stock market flotation. The textiles finishing industry was typical of the process: in 1898, 21 firms came together to form the Bradford Dyers' Association; in 1899, 45 firms formed the Calico Printers' Association; in 1900, 52 firms formed the Bleachers' Association, and in 1900, 46 firms made up the British Cotton and Wool Dyers' Association. These combines were the forerunners of large-scale, integrated corporations; in many cases concentration took place gradually as firms at first associated together for the purpose of pooling decisions over distribution and production levels, and only later lost their separate identity as a result of formal merger and incorporation. In the inter-war period a small number of large-scale enterprises established themselves in monopoly or semi-monopoly positions in a number of sectors, largely as a result of a further wave of corporate takeovers and mergers.[298] In 1909 the net share of manufacturing output of the 100 largest firms was 15 per cent; by 1935 it had increased to 24 per cent, and was to go on to reach 50 per cent by 1970.[299] The size of larger firms also increased during this period. In 1907, the largest manufacturing employer was the textiles firm Fine Cotton Spinners & Doublers, which employed 30,000 workers; by the 1930s, there were ten manufacturing firms employing this number, with ICI and Unilever each employing over 50,000.[300]

The increased rate of growth in the size of firms after around 1880 was paralleled by changes in the nature of intra-firm organization. One aspect of this was the development of managerial functions: 'what is perhaps as important as the actual size of concerns is the extent to which, in engineering, growth meant the accretion of fresh layers of clerical, supervisory and managerial staff as a consequence of the "upward drift" of knowledge and power from the shop floor'.[301]

[296] J. Jefferys, 'The denomination and character of shares' (1946) 16 *Economic History Review* 45–55.   [297] Hannah, *The Rise of the Corporate Economy*, op. cit., at p. 125.

[298] E. Hobsbawm, *Industry and Empire* (Harmondsworth: Penguin, 1969), at p. 217.

[299] L. Hannah, 'Managerial innovation and the rise of the large-scale company in interwar Britain' (1974) 27 *Economic History Review* 252–270.

[300] Hannah, *Rise of the Corporate Economy*, op. cit., at p. 101.

[301] Holbrook-Jones, *Supremacy and Subordination of Labour*, op. cit., at p. 23.

With the growth of the management function, firms were able to take over directly the supervisory role previously performed by intermediaries. Technical change played a part in undermining the contract system; internal contracting was often bound up with traditional methods of craft control which came under pressure from increased mechanization in the last quarter of the nineteenth century.[302] The emergence of large-scale 'employment bureaucracies' was also driven by a perception by employers that internal contracting gave too much bargaining power to groups of skilled workers at key points in the production process; the establishment of internal systems of managerial control made forward planning more straightforward.[303]

At the same time, vertical integration was encouraged by the growth of collective bargaining. The increase in the scope of collective bargaining, and in particular its extension to previously unorganized groups of 'underhands', put pressure on employers to agree to direct employment. The underhands opposed the contract system because of its association with forms of 'sweating' and with the control of the skilled workers over the pace of work and over the division of labour; in addition, under the wage system then prevailing the benefits of higher productivity were confined to the contractors, who were paid a piece rate but who employed their own underhands on fixed time rates. In iron and steel the Smelters' Union, established in 1886, and the Millmen's Union, established in 1888, opposed the contract system and sought to negotiate direct employment as an aspect of their recognition by employers. Where this policy was successful it led to the extension of tonnage rates to cover all process workers, and the transformation of the contractors into 'leading hands'.[304] Even then, this process did not take place all at once; the last major dispute took place in 1909–10 at Hawarden Bridge, with the Ironworkers' Union, representing the contractors, resisting the introduction of general piece rates.[305] Although many industries underwent similar changes in the 1890s and 1900s, forms of internal contracting persisted into the 1920s and 1930s; in cotton they were ended only by a collective agreement of 1932. In other industries, such as mining, internal contracting only disappeared with the additional impetus given to industrial concentration by the rise of public enterprise and the post-1945 nationalization wave.

[302] B. Elbaum and F. Wilkinson, 'Industrial relations and uneven development: a comparative study of the American and British steel industries' (1979) *Cambridge Journal of Economics* 275–303; Littler, *The Development of the Labour Process in Capitalist Society*, op. cit., at p. 78.

[303] See S. Jacoby, *Employing Bureaucracy: Managers, Unions, and the Transformation of Work in American Industry 1900–1945* (New York: Columbia University Press, 1985); P. Cappelli, 'Market-mediated employment: the historical context', in M. Blair and T. Kochan (eds.) *The New Relationship. Human Capital in the American Corporation* (Washington DC: Brookings Institution, 2000) 66–90; R. Biernacki, *The Fabrication of Labour: Britain and Germany, 1640–1914* (Berkeley, CA: University of California Press, 1995); D. Marsden, *A Theory of Employment Systems: Micro-foundations of Societal Diversity* (Oxford: Oxford University Press, 1995).

[304] F. Wilkinson, 'Collective bargaining in the steel industry in the 1930s', in A. Briggs and J. Saville (eds.) *Essays in Labour History 1918–1939* (London: Croom Helm, 1977) 102–132.

[305] H. Clegg, A. Fox and A. Thompson, *A History of British Trade Unions since 1889* Volume I (Oxford: Clarendon Press, 1964), at pp. 446–48.

A significant effect of collective bargaining, supported by employment legislation, was to stabilize the employment of industrial workers by discouraging lay-offs and other suspensions of work initiated by the employer and by attacking the practice of workers being hired by the day. Although the common law made some progress towards recognizing the individual worker's right to wages during lay-off caused by lack of work,[306] short-time working and lay-off without pay remained widespread during the inter-war years. In part this was because workers could claim unemployment benefit for short periods without work, so that the risk of short-time working could effectively be displaced on to the unemployment insurance system.[307] However, the wartime Essential Work Order[308] helped limit this abuse in the case of 'scheduled' or essential work, by requiring the employer to find work for the employee and restricting the power of both sides to terminate the contract of employment at will. At the same time the Ministry of Labour actively encouraged the growth of collective bargaining over Guaranteed Week Agreements, and these spread to a number of industries after 1945.[309] Collective bargaining at sector level received significant statutory support through Order 1305, which provided for compulsory arbitration over the application of sector-level terms and conditions to non-union firms, and which remained in place for several years after the end of the war.[310] Casual labour practices in the docks were dealt with through legislation which, somewhat unusually, placed the hiring process on a statutory footing.[311]

These legal controls over hiring and the more general move away from short-term notice periods were central to the post-war conception of full employment. The memorandum of evidence submitted by Political and Economic Planning during the preparation of *Social Insurance and Allied Services* argued for 'greater job security and better organisation of man-power . . . by a compulsory notice period (at least two weeks) in every contract of employment, and compulsory notification of every vacancy and registration of every worker during the period of notice'.[312] In similar vein, Beveridge argued in *Full Employment in a Free Society* in 1944 that:

in one special field, return to the old ways of engaging labour should be definitely made impossible. Industries like docks and harbour services which by practising casual

---

[306] Most notably in *Devonald* v. *Rosser & Son Ltd.* [1906] 2 KB 728, discussed in Section 5, above.

[307] On the 'OXO' system of working, see Szyszczak, *Partial Unemployment: The Regulation of Short-Time Working in Britain* (London: Mansell, 1990), at p. 76.

[308] The Essential Work (General Provisions) (No. 2) Order, SR & O 1942/1594.

[309] Szyszczak, *Partial Unemployment*, op. cit., at pp. 82–83. At the same time, the scope for using the unemployment insurance system to subsidize short-time working was gradually restricted, but it was only with the introduction of statutory guaranteed pay in the Employment Protection Act 1975 that the practice was effectively ended (ibid.).

[310] On Order 1305 see Lord Wedderburn, 'Change, struggle and ideology in British labour law', in Wedderburn, *Labour Law and Freedom* (London: Lawrence and Wishart, 1995), at pp. 8–15.

[311] Dock Workers (Regulation of Employment) Act 1946. The Wages Councils Act 1945 also aimed to combat casualization by a series of extensions to the powers of the Wages Councils, most notably the power to set minimum conditions relating to annual paid leave. (The principle of annual paid leave had been introduced by the Holidays with Pay Act 1938, but its implementation had lapsed with the outbreak of war.) [312] Cmd. 6405, 1042, at p. 36.

employment have been the main generators of chronic under-employment in the past, have been transformed in the war. It may be assumed that the main principle of the transformation will remain in peace, that the men following such occupations will have guaranteed weekly wages, and that this will lead in due course to the organisation of regular work as well as of regular wages, with men working for a single employing agency or for groups of employers, in place of taking their chance with single employers at a number of separate taking-on places. It may be hoped that in many other industries, the former position in regard to the employment of men will be transformed by the substitution of weekly for daily or hourly engagements.[313]

As it was, the proposal for compulsory notice periods had to wait until the Contracts of Employment Act 1963, and notification by employers of vacancies has never been made mandatory. However, the advent of employment protection legislation was to confirm still further the central role of the concept of the contract of employment.

7. The Significance of the Contract of Employment in Contemporary Labour Law

The contract of employment has been called, with justification, 'the fundamental legal institution of Labour Law'.[314] It owes this position, above all, to modern employment protection legislation. That legislation, while appearing at first sight to displace the rules of the common law, has had the paradoxical effect of elevating the contract of employment to a level of importance it had not previously occupied within labour law. This is only in part because employment protection legislation makes widespread use of contractual and language concepts to define key statutory terms. It is also because the legislation, by virtue of its substantive content, focuses attention on the rights of the individual worker or 'employee', to the detriment of perspectives which define workers' rights and interests by reference to collective procedures and mechanisms of dispute resolution.[315] The advent of employment protection legislation is therefore part of a wider process of 'individualization' within labour law which is responsible for the increased doctrinal importance of the individual employment relationship and hence of its juridical form, the contract of employment.

However, this is a process which began only very recently, and is still not complete. Notwithstanding the reference in the Beveridge report on full employment of 1944 to the issue of casualization, the process of applying labour standards to the employment relationship remained in many respects incomplete after 1945.

---

[313] *Full Employment in a Free Society* (London: Liberal Publications Department, 1944), at para. 231.

[314] Lord Wedderburn, *Cases and Materials on Labour Law* (Cambridge: Cambridge University Press, 1967), at p. 1.

[315] See W. Brown, S. Deakin, D. Nash and S. Oxenbridge, 'The employment contract: from collective procedures to individual rights' (2000) 38 *British Journal of Industrial Relations* 611–629.

The regulatory role of labour legislation was confined, with collective bargaining at sector level remaining the principal source of regulation of terms and conditions.[316] Sector-level collective agreements, while providing an effective floor of rights for hourly-paid workers in a majority of industries from the 1940s onwards, did not significantly widen the subject-matter of bargaining, so that there remained a significant gap between manual and non-manual groups in the quality of occupational benefits, notwithstanding their single status as employees for legal purposes.[317] The employment protection legislation of the 1960s and 1970s, on the other hand, marked a significant step towards standardization, in that it introduced important protections in the areas of income security and termination of employment for both manual and non-manual employees.

The choice of the contract of employment as the conceptual point of reference for the protective legislation of the 1960s and 1970s was a logical extension of a process of assimilation between the common law and collective bargaining which was already well established at that point. From the 1930s onwards, judicial decisions had reconciled the common law with the regulatory function of collective agreements by adapting the contractual device of the incorporation of terms.[318] The effect was conceptually striking: the 'normative' terms of the collective agreement, those affecting wages, working time and other terms and conditions, could in an appropriate case take effect as terms of the individual contract and be enforced by either party, without compromising the extra-legal (and non-contractually binding) character of the 'procedural' terms which regulated collective relations between employers and trade unions.

The same conceptual flexibility has characterized the relationship between contract and statutory employment protection. As we have seen, the Contracts of Employment Act 1963 adopted a test of personal scope based on the binary divide between employees and the self-employed, and subsequent employment protection statutes, most notably the Redundancy Payments Act 1965, the unfair dismissal part of the Industrial Relations Act 1971, and the Employment Protection Act 1975, followed suit. The concept of the contract of employment was also used, albeit in adapted form, in the definition of the core statutory notions of 'dismissal', 'redundancy' and 'continuity of employment'.[319] The results were not always greeted enthusiastically by labour lawyers, some of whom argued that the retention of contractual concepts in the structure of this legislation frustrated its protective purpose.[320]

However, the interaction of contract and legislation had effects on the common law, changing the character of the substantive rules governing the employment

---

[316] See our discussion in Chapter 4, below.   [317] See generally Chapter 4, below.

[318] *Young* v. *Canadian Northern Railway* [1931] AC 83; *MacLea* v. *Essex Line Ltd.* (1933) 45 Ll. L. Rep. 254.

[319] For a fuller description of this case law, see Deakin and Morris, *Labour Law* 3rd ed. (London: Butterworths, 2001), at pp. 435–458 (dismissal), 502–8 (redundancy) and 203–5 (continuity of employment).

[320] T. Kerr, 'Contract doesn't live here any more?' (1984) 47 *Modern Law Review* 30–47.

relationship. In strong contrast to the 'at-will' model which some courts had applied to manual employment as late as the 1940s,[321] the idea that the employment relationship had a 'relational' or reciprocal character, which was implicit in modern employment protection legislation, came to influence the common law. One of the catalysts for this development was the large body of case law which grew up around the statutory definition of 'constructive dismissal'; because the appellate courts had decided at an early stage in the exercise of the unfair dismissal jurisdiction that this test was in essence a contractual one—had the employer committed a repudiatory breach of contract?—it was necessary for courts and tribunals, when applying the legislation, to consider the framework of the express and implied terms of the contract.[322]

This process began with the landmark decision in the early years of the unfair dismissal jurisdiction in *Western Excavating (ECC) Ltd.* v. *Sharp*,[323] in which the Court of Appeal decided that for the purposes of this body of legislation, the test for identifying a 'constructive dismissal' was whether the employer had committed what would have amounted, at common law, to a repudiatory breach of contract. Under the Act, such a dismissal occurred where 'the employee terminates [the contract of employment], with or without notice, in circumstances such that he is entitled to terminate it without notice by reason of the employer's conduct'.[324] The Court of Appeal's decision was criticized at the time as an unjustified gloss on the statute which, moreover, had introduced into the law of unfair dismissal an unnecessarily complex and rigid body of case law, the effect of which had been to cloud the employee's rights and thereby undermine the legislation's social purpose.[325]

However, the decision in *Western Excavating* has had unexpected consequences for labour law. By incorporating a common law test into the core of the statutory right to protection against unfair dismissal, it established a new jurisdictional context within which issues of the construction of the contract of employment could be litigated. Gradually, the courts and tribunals used this opportunity to modify the basic structure of the contract of employment itself, by requiring that the employer should observe affirmative duties of 'cooperation' and 'good faith'. It was in a case arising under the Act, for example, that it was said that the employer must not 'without reasonable and proper cause, conduct [itself] in a manner likely calculated to or likely to destroy or seriously damage the relationship of confidence and trust between employer and employee'.[326] These duties are increasingly conceptualized as reciprocal, where previously at common law duties of trust and cooperation only bound, for most practical purposes, the employee. While

---

[321] See this chapter, above, Section 5.

[322] B.A. Hepple and P. O'Higgins, *Individual Employment Law* (London: Sweet & Maxwell, 4th ed., 1981), ch. 9.   [323] [1978] QB 761.

[324] See now Employment Rights Act 1996, s. 95(1)(c).

[325] Kerr, 'Contract doesn't live here any more?', op. cit.

[326] *Woods* v. *W.M. Car Services (Peterborough) Ltd.* [1981] IRLR 347, 350 (Browne-Wilkinson, J.).

this development of the employer's duty could be regarded as inherent in the basic common law structure of the employment relationship, it seems that the intervention of the legislature was, at the very least, the catalyst for this evolution. Approaches to construction which were initially expounded in the statutory context of constructive dismissal have found their way back into decisions which arise out of a purely common law jurisdiction. Although the immediate context for this development was provided by statute, the concepts and values of the good faith term spilled over into common law cases with no statutory element. The result has been the emergence of an extensive jurisprudence exploring the nature of the implied contract term of good faith or mutual trust and confidence.[327] In a comparatively short space of time it has become possible to speak of 'an amalgamation of the common law of the contract of employment and statutory employment law',[328] a fusion which operates at both a substantive and, to some degree, at a jurisdictional level: '[w]e should understand that we are now talking about not so much the common law of employment contracts, as a *common law based* law of employment contracts'.[329]

This is not to suggest that the reciprocal model of the employment contract is without certain, highly significant limits. The survival of the service model and its assimilation into the modern contract of employment account for many of the doctrinal tensions of contemporary labour law. It is unclear, for example, how the open-ended duty of obedience fits together with the notion of 'mutual trust and confidence' which represents the latest stage in the application to the contract of employment of a 'relational' contractual logic. The courts have insisted that the employment relationship, notwithstanding its consensual character, continues to confer upon the employer an essentially extra-contractual power to give orders within certain limits, a power which cannot be easily be reconciled with a contractual logic.[330] Nor can the limitations placed on the common law action for wrongful dismissal by *Addis* v. *Gramophone Co. Ltd.*[331] in the early years of the twentieth century be easily reconciled with the recognition, a century later, of the multiple interests, financial, reputational and psychological, which the employee has in the employment relationship. The judgments in the House of Lords' decision in *Johnson* v. *Unisys Ltd.*[332] indicate that today's judges are prepared, in principle, to extend the common law of wrongful termination of employment

[327] See D. Brodie, 'The heart of the matter: mutual trust and confidence' (1996) 25 *Industrial Law Journal* 121–136; 'Beyond exchange: the new contract of employment' (1998) 27 *Industrial Law Journal* 79–102; 'Mutual trust and the values of the employment contract' (2001) 30 *Industrial Law Journal* 84–100; and 'Legal coherence and the employment revolution' (2003) 117 *Law Quarterly Review* 604–625 and M.R. Freedland, *The Personal Employment Contract* (Oxford: Oxford University Press, 2003), sections 3 and 4.

[328] M.R. Freedland, *The Personal Contract of Employment*, at p. 3.   [329] Ibid., at p. 4.

[330] See, in particular, *Secretary of State for Employment* v. *Aslef (No. 2)* [1972] 2 QB 455, discussed by S. Deakin and G. Morris, *Labour Law*, op. cit, at p. 239 et seq., and by Freedland, *The Personal Employment Contract*, op. cit., at pp. 147–154.   [331] [1909] AC 488.

[332] [2001] IRLR 279, affirmed, notwithstanding a powerful dissent, in *Eastwood* v. *Magnox Electric plc* [2004] UKHL 35.

in a way which would encompass some of these wider interests; but that, for the time being at least, they are unwilling to do so in a way which would extend common law protection beyond that provided by unfair dismissal legislation. In particular, they are not prepared to countenance the application of the notion of mutual trust and confidence to the employer's power to dismiss, where that would have the effect of putting in place a common law jurisdiction governing termination of employment which would largely parallel that created by statute. Since the statutory action is restricted in its turn by the courts' refusal to question decisions of the employer which fall within the 'band of reasonable responses', a test which pegs the legal standard of fairness to a particularly low benchmark, the limits of the relational model in this area of law are clear.[333] It is possible to see in the majority judgments in *Johnson* v. *Unisys Ltd.* the vestiges of a hierarchical conception of employment which entered the common law via the disciplinary labour legislation of an earlier period, and which is now barely able to resist the application of modern contractual logic.

Nor has the development of a relational model of the employment contract under the influence of collective bargaining and protective legislation been without other difficulties. The greater emphasis placed by the courts upon reciprocity between employer and employee, the more problematic it becomes to apply the employment model to casual or irregular forms of work. This may help to explain the rise of popularity of the 'mutuality of obligation' test for determining employee status: according to this test, in order for the court to find a contract of employment, it is necessary not just to show that there has been an exchange of work for wages, but that, in addition, there has been an exchange of mutual undertakings to be available or to work over a period of time, on the employee's part, and to make work available, on the employer's.[334] Although this test could be said to have antecedents in nineteenth century decisions on mutuality and the definition,[335] for master and servant purposes, of 'exclusive service', its modern use appears to date from the period in the 1970s[336] when the courts had the task of interpreting and applying a large body of newly-created statutory rights. In so far as these provided employees with legal expectations of continuing income and employment in the event of interruptions to work on the grounds of lay-off, illness and maternity, as well as compensation for redundancy for unfair dismissal, they assumed a normal pattern of continuous and regular employment. The rise of the mutuality test reflected the difficulty the courts had in applying these rights to relationships which were, by their nature, discontinuous and irregular, such as those involving outworking, task contracts, and frequent re-hirings. At the same time, just as in the context of the early twentieth century

---

[333] See the Court of Appeal decision in *Post Office* v. *Foley*; *HSBC* v. *Madden* [2000] IRLR 827.

[334] See generally Freedland, *The Personal Employment Contract*, op. cit., ch. 1, Section 2; Deakin and Morris, *Labour Law*, op. cit., pp. 161–165.   [335] See above, Section 4.1.

[336] See, in particular, the discussion in *Airfix Footwear Ltd.* v. *Cope* [1978] ICR 1210.

analysis of 'control' and 'integration',[337] the recent case law on mutuality has produced examples of unnecessarily rigid conceptual reasoning,[338] as well as thinly veiled ideological justifications for decisions excluding workers from employment protection.[339]

As the argument over the meaning and legitimacy of the 'mutuality' test has intensified, the numbers employed in casualized forms of work have increased, thereby giving rise to concerns that the concept of the contract of employment is no longer able to deal effectively with the task of defining the scope of protective legislation. Whether the concept is capable of adaptation is an issue we consider in greater detail in a later chapter.[340] For present purposes, it is enough to point to the importance of viewing the modern-day debate in an historical perspective. That perspective informs us that the employment contract, as we know it today, is a relatively recent development, and that it is, moreover, a *contingent* one, in the sense of being linked, in terms of its evolution, to wider institutional changes in the welfare state, collective bargaining, and the structure of the enterprise. It is possible, as Mark Freedland suggests, that the unitary model of the employment relationship 'represented a false unity, perhaps even from the outset' and that labour lawyers have been 'papering over the cracks' ever since its inception.[341] The employment model can therefore be seen as a construction which was imposed upon a number of different types of work relationship at the cost of varying degrees of artificiality, and which was bound, eventually, to unravel. But there is also a sense in which the current uncertainty is simply the latest stage in a cycle of periodic crisis and renewal which can be traced back to the origins of labour law itself.

8. Conclusion: the Legal Genealogy of Employment

This chapter has argued that the nature of the legal transition which accompanied the emergence of the modern labour market in Britain involved a complex and multilinear process of adjustment between the law and the economy. The impact of this process on the legal form of the employment relationship is summed up in Table 2.1.

[337] See above, Section 6.1.

[338] See H. Collins, 'Employment rights of casual workers' (2000) 29 *Industrial Law Journal* 73–78, for a discussion of the courts' reluctance to interpret the 'mutuality' requirement as flexibly as they might have, in the context of the House of Lords' decision in *Carmichael* v. *National Power plc* [2000] IRLR 43.

[339] As in the statement of Fox LJ, in *O'Kelly* v. *Trusthouse Forte plc* [1984] QB 90, 121, to the effect that it was open to a tribunal to find that casual work fell outside the scope of employment protection legislation where it 'was simply the consequence of market forces (in effect, the dominant economic position of the company)'. *O'Kelly* was not a case in which stability of employment presented a functional difficulty, of the kind referred to in the text, in applying the concept of employee, since it was concerned with dismissal on the grounds of trade union membership, a right for which no statutory continuity of employment was required.   [340] See Chapter 5, below.

[341] The *Personal Contract of Employment*, op. cit., at p. 17.

Table 2.1. Legal classifications of work relationships from the eighteenth century to the mid-twentieth century

Period to 1800	
Servant	Worker (typically unmarried) engaged in service under a yearly hiring, entitled to payment in cash or in kind whether or not there was work during the period of the hiring, and with a right to a poor law settlement after the hiring ended
Labourer	Daily or casual manual worker in agriculture or the unregulated trades
Master, journeyman, apprentice	Worker in trades protected by guild regulation
Period from 1800 to 1875	
Servant	Manual worker in industry or agriculture under the disciplinary regime of the master and servant legislation, with little security or wages or employment
Employee	Clerical, managerial or professional worker outside the master–servant regime, with a degree of contractual income and employment security
Independent contractor	Independent artisan outside the scope of master and servant legislation
Period from 1875 to 1950	
Workman	Manual worker subject to the semi-disciplinary provisions of the Employers and Workmen Act 1875, increasingly protected as the period went on by collective bargaining, workmen's compensation and social insurance legislation
Employee	At the beginning of the period, a non-manual worker with managerial or professional status; by the end of the period, a wage or salary-dependent worker, either manual or non-manual
Self-employed	Independent worker not employed under a contract of employment

Prior to the industrial revolution, many aspects of employment were already contractual, and large parts of the population were dependent on wages for subsistence; conversely, wage regulation had been established as one of the principal functions of labour legislation from the late medieval period. As industrialization gathered pace, some of the regulations which characterized the 'corporative' economy of the late medieval and early modern economy were removed. But although legal controls over trade regulations which were protective of producer-owned forms of enterprise were abolished in the late eighteenth and early nineteenth centuries, paving the way for capitalist forms of production, other aspects of the system of labour regulation were reinforced at this time. The Master and Servant Acts, which gave expression to the subordinate status of the worker within the employment relationship, far from repudiating the framework of regulation contained in the Elizabethan Statute of Artificers, grew out of that body of legislation, and were designed to remedy what were seen as some of its central deficiencies in disciplining the labour force. The modern labour market emerged at a time of intense legislative activity, with the law repeatedly being used as an instrument of economic policy.

From a juridical point of view, the result of this process of change was not a general model of the contract of employment which was capable of being applied to all wage-dependent workers, but instead a hierarchical model of service, which originated in the Master and Servant Acts and was gradually assimilated into the common law. In the nineteenth century the courts drew sharp distinctions between categories of workers according to their place within the hierarchy of organization. The idea of the contract of employment as a mechanism for express-ing reciprocal obligations of employer and employee only developed for certain higher status employees, such as professional and managerial workers. Many of these status-based distinctions survived the repeal of the Master and Servant Acts in the 1870s, and were carried over into the first legislative interventions of the welfare state in the period between 1880 and 1914. These distinctions ceased to be meaningful only when collective bargaining and social legislation extended their influence over the employment relationship, and when, as a result of the spread of modern management techniques, the vertically integrated enterprise displaced the internal contracting system. It was against the background of the conjunction of these forces that the term 'employee' came to be applied to all wage or salary earners. Thus the juridical form of the contract of employment, as we know it today, was a product not of the industrial revolution, but of the welfare state of the early and middle decades of the twentieth century.

The redistributive and protective goals of the welfare state gave rise to forms of regulation and taxation which were focused to a large extent on the institution of wage-dependent labour. This legislation sought to establish on a general basis the responsibilities of employers for sharing and spreading social and economic risks arising out of employment (injury, ill-health, unemployment, lack of income in retirement). At first, the courts were reluctant to apply this form of regulation to relationships which in their eyes were more akin to the relationship of employer and independent contractor. This category included, on the one hand, intermedi-ary suppliers of labour services, such as butty men and gang leaders, and, on the other, high-status workers such as managers, professionals and skilled clerical staff. The juridical form given to these status-based distinctions was the 'control' test. Gradually, however, these distinctions faded as the legislation took hold, and the previously separate models of 'service' and 'employment' began to merge into one another. The control test was eclipsed by the 'organization' and 'economic reality' tests. The modern, 'unitary' contract of employment was the result: legally, at least, all employees now had a single status, which was differentiated from that of independent contractors who genuinely worked 'on their own account'.[342]

---

[342] Freedland, 'The role of the contract of employment in modern labour law', op. cit., at p. 21.

The impact of the welfare state, then, was to add a layer of protective 'status obligations' to the employment relationship,[343] in addition to those supplied by the older, hierarchical tradition of master and servant.[344] Far from being inimical to a contractual conception of employment, collective bargaining and social legislation, by stabilizing the employment relationship, made it possible for a contractual model to develop which was based on the recognition of reciprocal rights and obligations and the sharing of economic risk. Even the core of common law rules, the judge-made implied terms, were affected by this process, as the courts gradually came round to the view that the employer, as well as the employee, was bound by the implied duty of cooperation and by the requirement to act in good faith. Common law doctrines, such as the concept of incorporation of terms, were used to give effect to the normative terms of collective agreements (albeit with variable success).

This is not to say that the master and servant model lost all influence. On the contrary, many elements of the earlier tradition of 'service' remain within the modern law. Thus hierarchical notions of the employee's duties of 'obedience' and 'loyalty' remain highly relevant to judicial interpretations, notwithstanding the repeal over a hundred years ago of the restrictive legislation in which they originated. It is the absorption of these statutory concepts into the common law which has ensured their survival. At each successive stage in the legal evolution of the employment relationship, the common law has built upon and incorporated what came before, often using the same concepts and language. The result is the curious overlapping of contract and status which is characteristic of the modern contract of employment, and which helps to explain its elusive and ambiguous nature.

Whatever its shortcomings, the contract of employment remains at the core of the conceptual framework of modern labour law. It is often, mistakenly, seen as having survived into the modern period *in spite of* the growth of collective bargaining and regulatory legislation. This chapter has shown that the opposite is the case, that the contract of employment as we know it today is in many ways the *product* of the welfare state and of changes in the framework of collective bargaining and the enterprise. As such, it inevitably reflects weaknesses in the design of the welfare state, and appears anachronistic at a time when employment relations and the form of the enterprise are in a state of flux. However, it is necessary to draw a distinction here between those features of the employment contract which are essentially contingent, in the sense of being the product of a particular conjunction of policies and institutional forms which came together in the 'mid-century social compromise' of the post-war welfare state,[345] and those of a more enduring nature.

What is remarkable about the employment contract is that it performs two quite distinct, and possibly contradictory, functions at once: through what may be

[343] W. Streeck, *Social Institutions and Economic Performance* (Cambridge: Polity, 1993), ch. 2.
[344] Fox, *Beyond Contract*, op. cit.
[345] Freedland, *The Personal Employment Contract*, op. cit., at p. 17.

called its 'coordination function' it expresses the worker's subordination to the managerial power of the employer within the enterprise, while through its 'risk function' it channels the risks of economic insecurity in such a way as to protect the individual worker against the consequences of that very same dependence on, and subordination to, the employer's superior resources. It is precisely this *linking* of capitalist work relations to the wider risk-sharing role of the welfare or social state which was embodied in the 'compromise' of mid-twentieth century social and economic policy, and coded, juridically, in the contract of employment. This is the idea which was vividly captured in Kahn-Freund's description of the contract as the 'cornerstone' of modern labour law, simultaneously supporting the enterprise and social citizenship.[346] Thus the argument for the contract of employment is, in the final analysis, an argument in favour of an integrative mechanism, or set of mechanisms, which makes it possible for a market economy and a social state to co-exist. Today's conceptual arguments over the protective scope of labour law and the applicability of contractual reasoning within the context of social legislation express, at a juridical level, the tensions which are inherent in this goal.

---

[346] O. Kahn-Freund, 'A note on contract and status in labour law' (1967) 30 *Modern Law Review* 635–644.

3

The Duty to Work

1. Introduction

The economic concept of 'labour supply' has an institutional dimension, consisting of the norms which define when, and under what conditions, individuals are expected to offer their services for hire in the labour market. In neoclassical economic theory, labour supply is a function of the choices individuals make to trade off leisure against work, with wages offered as compensation for the resulting disutility. Whatever the degree of abstraction which may be accorded to this 'choice' as a matter of theory, in practice it is closely framed by the extent to which alternative, non-waged sources of income are available. This in turn depends upon notions of what constitutes a normal life-cycle of labour market participation. In developed market economies, the law of social security defines the circumstances under which it is legitimate for individuals to remain outside waged work in such categories as 'unemployment' or 'retirement'. In the developing industrial society of England in the eighteenth and nineteenth centuries, it was the 'poor law' which established, in a more general fashion, the legal status and condition of those who were dependent on wages for subsistence. As this chapter will show, the history of the English poor law closely tracks the emergence of an industrial economy in which waged employment gradually became the principal means of support, directly or indirectly, for the vast majority of the population.

In purely juridical terms, the English poor law was an institution of remarkable longevity. The instruction to local officers to take on the task of organizing 'poor relief', which was contained in the principal Elizabethan statute of 1601[1] (itself a consolidating measure), was repeated practically word for word in the last major piece of poor law legislation, as late as 1930.[2] The context of those statutory provisions had completely changed in the meantime. However, there were many continuities in the transition from the poor law to social security.

The old poor law gave expression to a dense network of reciprocal obligations which linked together wage labour, the family, and the wider social order. Service was a formal duty for those without independent means of subsistence, but it was also a route to a poor law settlement which conferred the right to relief in the event

---

[1] 43 Elizabeth I c. 2, s. 1.   [2] Poor Law Act 1930, s. 15.

of unemployment or sickness. Through the concept of the 'derivative settlement', the rights of women and children were dependent on those of the principal male earner. Family subsistence also depended, in practice, on access to the land. In the late medieval period, wages were periodic and irregular additions to income from the land; by the eighteenth century, this relationship had been reversed, with wages the more important source of income for most households. However, grazing and gleaning rights served to protect the still largely rural workforce from the extremes of market fluctuations.

The new poor law, formally instituted from 1834 and applied with increasing rigour as the nineteenth century progressed, aimed to sever all connection between wages and relief: wages would henceforth reflect the pure laws of supply and demand. The 'deserving' poor would thereby be freed from reliance on outdoor relief, although not necessarily from private charity. For the 'undeserving' able-bodied poor, as well as the ill and the old, relief was to be organized through the workhouse. Poor law legislation and bureaucratic practice aimed to depress conditions in the workhouse below those of the poorest 'independent' household (the principle of 'less eligibility'), so as to deter claims and avoid 'artificial' interference with the market rate for wages.

This vision failed at the turn of the twentieth century when it became generally accepted that the practices of the new poor law were reinforcing, and not averting, destitution. The way was now clear for the construction of the welfare state. Social security neutralized some of the disciplinary aspects of the new poor law but it did not abolish the duty to work. It inherited from the new poor law a reluctance to allow wages and welfare payments to be combined. Thus the new principle was one of institutional support for the 'breadwinner wage' which, when coupled with social insurance, would guarantee household subsistence. Because the wage earner was assumed to be male, the social security system, while it represented a new phase in the institutional construction of the labour market, also took from the poor law an asymmetric conception of household relations, in which the economic security of women and children was seen as deriving from their relationship to a male breadwinner.

Since 1980, reforms to the social security system, coupled with the move away from the goals of full employment policy as conceived in the 1940s, have led to an erosion of the model of the breadwinner wage, a situation which parallels the wider erosion of the open-ended, indeterminate-duration contract of employment. Increased female participation in employment has severely qualified notions of male priority of access to well-paid work, while legislation has removed most forms of direct and indirect discrimination between men and women in the calculation of contribution and benefit rates. But while formal equality in social security was being achieved, the social insurance principle itself was being undermined. One aspect of this has been the revival of disciplinary aspects of the duty to work, part of the wider package of measures which eventually saw the jobseeker's allowance replace unemployment benefit. At the same time, the security of retirement incomes has been weakened by the break in the link between contributions and earnings for the basic state pension and by the reduction in the value of the second state pension. The notion of social citizenship based on employment which inspired the welfare state reforms of the early and mid-twentieth century is slowly being whittled away.

As a further consequence of recent policy shifts, 'unemployment' and 'retirement' are no longer categories which are clearly demarcated from waged employment. Beginning in the late 1980s, changes to social security law made it possible for both retirement pensions and low-income social security benefits to be combined with income from wages. Since then the range and scale of in-work benefits of all kinds have increased significantly. Thus the most recent changes to the system, although in some senses reminiscent of the pure market philosophy of the new poor law, bear a still more striking resemblance to the final years of the *old* poor law. Then, the failure of wage subsidization policies led to general disenchantment with the tradition of poor relief and a determination to use new mechanisms of labour discipline, above all the workhouse, to restore the 'natural' functioning of the labour market. The fate of more recent experiments remains to be seen. But from an institutional perspective, it is not going too far to talk of many recent changes as anticipating the 'abolition' of unemployment and retirement.

The complex evolution of the duty to work through the poor law and social security will be mapped out in this chapter as follows. Section 2 below looks at the structure of the poor law at the dawn of the industrial revolution and examines the stresses which led to the decline of the twin institutions of annual service and the poor law settlement. Section 3 is concerned with the legal and policy debates surrounding the adoption of the Speenhamland system of in-work benefits and its replacement by the principle of less eligibility in the poor law Amendment Act of 1834. Section 4 focuses on the juridical forms associated with the new poor law, in particular the nineteenth-century poor law orders which governed the administration of relief. Section 5 looks at the transition from the poor law to social security during the twentieth century and examines the more recent erosion of social insurance and the revival of wage supplementation. Section 6 concludes.

2. Institutions of the Old Poor Law: Settlement and Annual Service

2.1 Forms of relief under the old poor law

Under the old poor law, relief by the parish of settlement came to be seen as the 'peculiar privilege', that is to say the particular *right*, 'of the poor'.[3] During this

---

[3] K.D.M. Snell, *Annals of the Labouring Poor: Social Change and Agrarian England 1660–1900* (Cambridge: Cambridge University Press, 1985), at p. 73.

period, the 'poor' were not simply those in immediate need of support but, more precisely, those who depended on wage labour for subsistence. This definition reflected a view that the receipt of relief was not necessarily intended to be stigmatizing. According to Dalton's *Country Justice*, the poor 'are here to be understood not vagabond beggars and rogues, but those who labour to live, and such as are old and decrepit, unable to work, poor widows, and fatherless children, and tenants driven to poverty; not by riot, expense and carelessness, but by mischance'.[4] The expectation of relief did not take the form of a claim-right which individuals could assert against the state in the modern sense of a legal entitlement. Nevertheless, from the sixteenth century onwards, statutes imposed an obligation on parish officers to raise a local rate for the support of poor relief and to suppress indiscriminate giving.[5] Under the Poor Relief Act of 1601 (in this respect consolidating earlier legislation), the local justices were empowered to fine parish officers who neglected their duty and to levy distress against the property of local rate payers who refused to make their contribution.[6] In the first half of the seventeenth century, central government authority in the form of the Privy Council took the initiative of attempting to impose a uniform approach upon counties and parishes; the Book of Orders of 1631 recorded and codified what was regarded as good practice by the county justices in this regard.[7] Although central control receded with the defeat of the monarchy in the civil war, by the end of the seventeenth century virtually every parish in England had set a compulsory rate, and the practice of relief was such that 'it was assumed by managers, magistrates, and the poor themselves, that the poor were entitled to relief if they required it'.[8]

The Act of 1601, largely repeating an earlier, equally comprehensive statute of 1597, imposed a three-fold duty on the parish overseers: to set to work 'all such persons, married or unmarried, having no means to maintain them, and use no ordinary and daily trade of life to get their living by'; to raise 'competent sums of money for and towards the necessary relief of the lame, impotent, old, blind, and such other among them, being poor and not able to work'; and to arrange for the putting to work or putting out to apprenticeships of children whose parents were unable to maintain them.[9] The instruction to set the able-bodied poor to work was not effectively implemented in most parishes for most of the seventeenth and eighteenth centuries, because of the excessive cost of making the necessary arrangements. As a result, relief for the able-bodied and the 'impotent' alike took the form, in practice, of 'outdoor relief', that is, payments in kind or cash payments made to individuals or households.

---

[4] M. Dalton, *The Country Justice: Containing the Practice, Duty and Power of the Justices of the Peace, as Well In as Out of their Sessions* (London: Lintot, 1746), at p. 164.

[5] 27 Henry VIII c. 25 (1536); see P. Slack, *The English Poor Law 1531–1782* (London: Macmillan, 1990), at p. 17.   [6] 43 Elizabeth I c. 2 (1601), ss. 2, 4.

[7] B. Quintrell, 'The making of Charles I's Book of Orders' (1980) 95 *English Historical Review* 553–572.   [8] Slack, *The English Poor Law 1531–1782*, op. cit., at p. 29.

[9] 43 Elizabeth I c. 2, s. 1; this is the formula repeated in the Poor Law Act 1930, s. 15, on which see this chapter, Section 5.1, below.

While some urban and rural parishes had workhouses or equivalent institutions for housing the poor at this time, this was exceptional. The Workhouse Test Act of 1722 empowered (but did not require) parishes to establish a 'house or houses . . . for the lodging, keeping, maintaining and employing any or all such poor in their respective parishes, townships or places, as shall desire to receive relief or collection', and to deny relief to who those who 'shall refuse to be lodged, kept or maintained in such house or houses'.[10] By contrast, the Poor Relief Act of 1782, known as Gilbert's Act after its parliamentary sponsor, the MP Thomas Gilbert, established a regime, for those parishes which chose to opt into it, under which entry into the workhouse was confined to the non-able-bodied, 'such as are become indigent from old age, sickness or infirmities, and are unable to acquire a maintenance by their labour'.[11] Gilbert's Act divided the able-bodied poor into those 'idle or disorderly persons, who are able, but unwilling to work', and those who were 'able and willing to work, but who cannot get employment'; those in the former category were subject to the various punishments set aside for 'vagrants',[12] while individuals in the latter were to be put to work on tasks 'suited to his or her strength or capacity' until such time as regular employment could be obtained.[13] The idea of the workhouse as a mechanism of discipline to be applied to all able-bodied poor who could not find employment came later, after 1834.

In the seventeenth and eighteenth centuries the English poor law system was distinctive in Europe for the extent to which it embodied a nationally-organized, comprehensive and publicly-regulated approach to relief. Expenditure on poor relief grew steadily throughout the eighteenth century, more than keeping up with the growth in population.[14] By 1800, the amount devoted to poor relief had doubled as a proportion of GDP. Although this translates into an increase from only 1 to 2 per cent of national income, it represents seven times the amount spent on poor relief per head of population in France, for example, in the same period.[15] In absolute terms, poor relief did not imply an end to hardship, nor did it do much to redress inequalities. It has been estimated that at the end of the seventeenth century, over a third of households in England were exempt from hearth tax on the grounds of low income and slightly less than a third did not pay local rates; a quarter were in receipt of some form of private charity and a tenth regularly received poor relief. On this basis, judged by the standards of the time, 'about one-quarter of the population lived in some form of poverty and about one-seventh perhaps in or near destitution'.[16] However, replacement rates were more generous than those on the continent at that time.[17] In addition, the

---

[10] 9 George I c. 7 (1722), s. 4.   [11] 22 George III c. 83 (1782), s. 29.   [12] Ibid. s. 32.
[13] Ibid. (1782), s. 33.   [14] Slack, *The English Poor Law 1531–1782*, op. cit., at p. 31.
[15] P. Solar, 'Poor relief and English economic development before the Industrial Revolution' (1995) 42 *Economic History Review* 1–22.
[16] T. Arkell, 'The incidence of poverty in England in the later seventeenth century' (1987) 12 *Social History* 23–47, at p. 47.
[17] Indeed, it is highly likely that average replacement rates for the elderly and single parents were higher not just than they became during the period of the new poor law after 1834, but (in relative

legally-organized character of the relief made it more predictable, lending certainty to the administration of the system.[18] Relief levels varied, but it is thought that at the turn of the eighteenth century, between 5 and 10 per cent of households received relief on a regular basis, and that it was not abnormal for up to 25 per cent of households, around 15 per cent of the population, to receive relief of some kind in the course of a year.[19] Not only was there an expectation of relief, but 'recipients were not a separate, marginal group in society'; rather, 'the fundamental point about relief to the impotent poor was that most families would at some time turn to the parish for assistance'.[20]

It is likely that these factors combined to accelerate the growth in wage labour in England by comparison with other western European economies. At the end of the sixteenth century, wage labour was still seen as a supplementary source of income for most rural households, which continued to have access to the land; by 1800 it had become a much more regular feature of both the rural and urban economies. The existence of poor relief helped to mitigate the risks arising from reliance on wages, which included fluctuations in wage levels arising from variation in food prices and the irregular, seasonal character of much waged work.[21]

2.2 The concept of the poor law settlement

The settlement laws evolved alongside the growth of wage labour. The legal concept of a poor law settlement appears clearly for the first time in legislation of the seventeenth century but the practice of settlement and removal predates these statutes. Eighteenth-century judges speculated that as far back as Saxon and early Norman times, just a few days' residence in a parish had conferred a settlement,[22] while according to Michael Nolan's treatise on the law of settlements, 'where a person could not be removed as a wanderer, it is said to have been the common law from the time of the Mirror, [sic] that the parish was to maintain him when actually chargeable'.[23] 'Vagrancy' described a condition in which an able-bodied

---

terms) were higher than those which applied in the modern, post-war social security system: see D. Thomson, 'The decline of social security: falling state support for the elderly since Victorian times' (1984) 4 *Ageing and Society* 451–82, and K.D.M. Snell and J. Millar, 'Lone parent families and the welfare state: past and present' (1987) 2 *Continuity and Change* 387–422 (see, in particular, their discussion at pp. 409–414, suggesting possible reasons for the relative generosity of outdoor relief under the old poor law, including the restriction of parochial relief to those who were locally settled members of the parish).

[18] Solar, 'Poor relief and English economic development', op. cit.

[19] Arkell, 'The incidence of poverty in England', op. cit.

[20] Daunton, *Progress and Poverty*, at p. 452.   [21] Solar, op. cit., at pp. 8–9.

[22] *R. v. St. Peter's in Oxford* (1795) Fol. 193, Fortescue J.

[23] M. Nolan, *A Treatise of the Laws for the Relief and Settlement of the Poor*, 4th ed. Vol. I (London: Butterworth, 1825), at p. 272, citing Foster J. in *R. v. Aythrop Rooding* (1756) Burr SC 412 (but also noting Lord Mansfield's disagreement on this point); for discussion of the antecedents of the seventeenth-century law, see J.S. Taylor, 'The impact of pauper settlement' (1976) 73 *Past and Present* 42–73, at pp. 47–48.

person without work or other means of subsistence was liable (in addition to corporal punishments of various kinds) to be returned to his or her parish of origin. Fourteenth-century legislation stipulated that itinerant beggars should return to their home parish or hundred[24] and from the mid-sixteenth century, statutes were making provision for their forcible removal.[25] But a resolution of the judges of assize in the time of Elizabeth I confirmed that only 'vagrant rogues' were to be sent back to their place of birth or last habitation,[26] while in the seventeenth century a similar resolution asserted (if somewhat tautologously) that 'the law unsettleth none who are lawfully settled'.[27]

The flurry of legislative activity on the subject of poor law settlement at the end of the seventeenth century coincided with an increase in wage dependence, growing labour migration, and rising costs of poor relief. At parish level, local ratepayers responded by attempting to control migrant labour and displace the costs of relief on to neighbouring areas; in Parliament, their reaction took the form of legislation which sought to redefine the grounds of settlement. The Settlement Act of 1662[28] gave justices of the peace the power to order the removal to the parish of settlement 'any person or persons likely to be chargeable to the parish [they] shall come to inhabit'. Two justices were empowered to act on a complaint by the parish officers, made within 40 days of the person's arrival in the parish 'so to settle as aforesaid in any tenement under the yearly value of ten pounds'. In 1685 an amendment[29] stipulated that the 40 days should only begin to run from the point when the newcomer gave parish officers notice of his or her intention to reside there. In practice, such notice was hardly ever given since it amounted to an invitation to the parish overseers to seek a removal order.[30] At this point, then, a settlement could in effect be obtained, subject to the need to give notice, either by renting property worth £10 per annum (a high threshold which migrant labourers would in practice almost invariably be unable to meet[31]) or by 40 days' uninterrupted residence.[32]

---

[24] 12 Richard II c. 7.

[25] 1 Edward VI c. 3 (1547) (prefigured to some degree by 22 Henry VIII c. 12 (1531) and 27 Henry VIII c. 25 (1536)); 3 & 4 Edward VI c. 16 (1550); 14 Elizabeth I c. 5 (1572); 39 Elizabeth I c. 40 (1597). 7 James I c. 4 (1610) made provision for the construction of 'houses of correction' for 'rogues' and 'idle and disorderly persons'.

[26] Nolan, *Treatise of the Laws for the Relief and Settlement of the Poor*, op. cit., at p. 271.

[27] Nolan, op. cit. at p. 273, referring to the judgment of Holt CJ in *Weston Rivers* v. *St. Peter's Marlborough* (1696) 2 Salk 492. This appears to have been reflected in the practice of the early seventeenth century: see P. Styles, 'The evolution of the law of settlement' (1963–4) 9 *University of Birmingham Historical Journal* 32–63, at p. 43.   [28] 13 & 14 Charles II c. 12 (1662).

[29] 1 James II c. 17 (1685).

[30] See P. Styles, 'The evolution of the law of settlement', op. cit., at p. 48.

[31] 'This high limit was probably fixed with the cities of London and Westminster in mind and cannot have been intended to ease the lot of the majority of rural migrants', Styles, ibid.

[32] Under the Act of 1662, which in this respect (as in a number of others) appears largely to have formalized earlier practice, landlords, employers, the families of migrants, and migrants themselves, could also avoid removal of the migrant by giving a bond or security for the potential cost of relief over a certain period (14 Charles II c. 12, s. 1); see Styles, 'The evolution of the law of settlement', op. cit., at pp. 39–42.

Since most English parishes consisted of areas of only a few square miles (there were over 15,000 of them in the eighteenth century), the possibility of removal to the parish of origin under the settlement laws was in principle a substantial bar to labour mobility. The parish had acquired its position as the unit of settlement more or less by default, once central government authority of the kind exercised by the Privy Council in the first half of the seventeenth century had given way to greater local autonomy after the civil war of the 1640s. There were some advantages to parish level administration: it was more straightforward to levy rates locally; and it has also been suggested that, in relation to the nature of claims, 'moral hazard was unlikely to have been a severe problem in small communities where potential recipients were well known to relief authorities'.[33] The possibility of local discretion in the application of the law was one of the conditions for its legitimacy: the system 'was bound, therefore, to be locally parochial if it was to be nationally uniform—paradoxical as that might seem'.[34] From this perspective, the Settlement Acts are best understood not as restricting migration so much as regulating it in the interests of both promoting and controlling labour mobility.[35]

Thus the Act of 1692[36] added four new methods of acquiring a settlement for which notice was unnecessary: service in a parish office, payment of local rates, yearly hiring (for those who were unmarried), and apprenticeship. A further Act of 1697[37] provided that, under the yearly hiring, it was necessary for the servant to serve out the year in question. This Act took advantage of the practice, already established, of one parish giving a certificate to another accepting liability for the relief of a migrant worker, to promote mobility: if a worker held a certificate of settlement from his or her home parish, they were to be removable only if they actually became a charge on the parish of residence, as opposed to being potentially chargeable. The right not to be removed until the point of being chargeable

---

[33] Solar, 'Poor relief and English economic development', op. cit., at p. 8.

[34] Slack, *The English Poor Law 1531–1782*, op. cit., at p. 20.

[35] For an extended argument that the Settlement Acts regulated the migration of the rural poor in general and not just the situation of those who became destitute, see N. Landau, 'The laws of settlement and the surveillance of immigration in eighteenth-century Kent' (1988) 3 *Continuity and Change* 391–420, 'The regulation of immigration, economic structures and definitions of the poor in eighteenth-century England' (1990) 33 *Historical Journal* 541–572, and 'Who was subjected to the laws of settlement? Procedure under the settlement laws in the eighteenth-century England' (1995) 43 *Agricultural History Review* 139–59. The crux of Landau's argument is that the power of removal under the 1662 Act applied, until 1795, to any individuals *likely to become chargeable*, and not just to those who actually became a charge. After 1795, Landau suggests, parishes used other methods to control and monitor the rural poor, including the roundsman system and other forms of relief in the form of employment ('The regulation of immigration', op. cit., at pp. 570–71; on the roundsman system after 1795, see this chapter, Section 3.2, below). For an historical study of how the poor law regulated migration, which brings the story up-to-date to the 1990s and 2000s with an account of laws governing the benefit entitlements of asylum seekers, see D. Feldman, 'Migrants, immigrants and welfare from the old poor law to the welfare state' *Transactions of the Royal Historical Society*, forthcoming.   [36] 3 William and Mary c. 11.

[37] 8 & 9 William III c. 30.

was extended to all categories of recipient in 1795.[38] The preamble to the 1697 Act addressed the need for greater flexibility in the application of the laws, referring to persons unable to move from their parish 'to any other place where sufficient employment is to be had . . . though their labour is wanted in many other places where the increase of manufactures would employ more hands'.

A considerable volume of historical research has been generated over the past thirty years on the operation of the poor law in general and the Settlement Acts in particular; one reason for this is the understanding that 'the old poor law provides the key to a social understanding of the eighteenth century', since it 'permeated social relationships with its wide-ranging influence over aspects of parish life such as employment and the regulation of wages, price fixing, the grain market, apprenticeship, marriage, settlement, allocation of relief, or the treatment of the elderly'.[39] For our purposes, a further dimension of the Settlement Acts is key, namely that they illustrate the beginnings of a legal discourse concerning the relationship between wage labour, gender relations and the market. The Settlement Acts generated a huge amount of litigation between parishes and hundreds of decisions were reported, leaving us with an important (if under-researched) historical record. A study of this record shows how in testing the limits of the different grounds of settlement, the courts defined the contours of the service and apprenticeship relationships and the link between poor relief and family status.

2.3 Judicial interpretation of the Settlement Acts

A first step was the development of the 'derivative settlement', the idea that the settlement rights of women and children depended on their link to a male wage earner and/or property holder. This began as a judicial gloss on the statutes and became firmly entrenched in the law in the early eighteenth century.[40] Single women were capable of acquiring a settlement in their own right through service or apprenticeship, but upon marriage they acquired the settlement of the husband. Similarly, a child born legitimately took the settlement of the father (thereby displacing the normal rule that a settlement could be acquired by birth).[41] The child and mother would follow the father's new settlement as he moved around,[42] and widows and fatherless children could be removed to the father's last place of settlement prior to his death, even after an interval of many

---

[38] 35 George III c. 101. See generally, Styles, 'The evolution of the law of settlement', op. cit., at pp. 49–53 and 62–63, for an account of the origins of the certificate system and the significance of the 1662, 1697 and 1795 Acts. The certificate did not entitle the holder to a settlement in the host parish, but merely granted protection against removal.

[39] Snell, *Annals of the Labouring Poor*, op. cit., at 104–5.

[40] The certificate system may have played a role in its growth, since the granting of a certificate protected both the individual to whom it related and his immediate family (the case of a principal male earner was generally assumed): see Styles, 'Evolution of the law of settlement', op. cit., at p. 56.

[41] *Cripplegate* v. *St. Saviour's* (1709) Foley 265.

[42] *St. Giles Reading* v. *Everfly Blackwater* (1723) Str. 580.

years. In some cases an individual was removed to the settlement of his last known relative, such as a grandparent.[43] In practice, as the Webbs observed and more recent research has confirmed,[44] removals disproportionately affected poor families, widows, and the elderly, with relatively little impact upon those most likely to be economically active, that is, the single and able-bodied.

Single men and women had considerable opportunities for mobility thanks to the way in which the rules governing the yearly hiring worked. In the early eighteenth century, the yearly hiring became the normal stage in the life cycle of agricultural workers in the southern and eastern counties.[45] A live-in servant could expect to acquire a series of settlements as he or she moved around with their employer. Thanks to the generosity (in relative terms) of parish doles to the elderly, 'young people could move, save, marry late and not rush to have offspring of their own who would care for them in sickness and old age'.[46] The stability of the yearly hiring, in turn, reduced the extent to which the young and able-bodied would become chargeable to poor relief; since the master was, in Blackstone's memorable phrase, responsible for maintaining the servant 'throughout the revolution of the respective seasons: as well as when there is work to be done as when there is not',[47] he would be obliged to keep the servant in board and lodging and to meet the costs of medical assistance. The courts also noted that the young and unmarried were the least likely to claim relief at least in the short-term: 'for such a term as a year, it is not supposed a master would hire one, unless able of body, and so a person not likely to become chargeable'.[48]

For the first half of the eighteenth century, judicial interpretations mostly strove to maintain the stability of the yearly hiring. From a conceptual point of view, the security provided by service and apprenticeship as exceptions to the normal rules on removal was rationalized in terms of the contractual link between the parties to the relationship. According to Burn's legal treatise, the normal rule, enabling the justices to make an order of removal at any time within forty days of the servant's arrival, 'would not avail; for that the justices, upon complaint of the overseers, who are no parties to the contract, cannot make void the contract between the master and servant, by which the servant is bound to continue with his master if he requires it'.[49] In the event of a breach of contract by the servant the master could apply to have the contract discharged, under the Statute of Artificers; only then could the servant be removed from the parish. If, on the other hand, the master was removed, the justices had the power to order the servant to

---

[43] *R.* v. *Bethnal Green* (1759) 2 Bur. 870.

[44] S. Webb and B. Webb, *English Poor Law History: Part I. The Old Poor Law* (London: Longmans, Green & Co., 1927), at pp. 341–2; N. Landau, 'The laws of settlement and the surveillance of immigration in eighteenth-century Kent', op. cit.

[45] Snell, *Annals of the Labouring Poor*, op. cit., at p. 54.

[46] Slack, *English Poor Law 1531–1782*, op. cit., at p. 55.

[47] Blackstone, *Commentaries*, op. cit., at p. 413.   [48] *Dunsford* v. *Ridgwick* (1711) 2 Salk. 535.

[49] R. Burn, *The Justice of the Peace and Parish Officer* (London: Millar, 1764), at p. 51; and on apprenticeship, see p. 37.

go with him *not* under the laws of settlement and removal, but as part of their more general jurisdiction to supervise the performance of the service contract.[50]

The courts also supported the yearly hiring by taking a highly flexible approach to the requirement of annual service. In early cases under the Acts of the late seventeenth century, the courts had taken a flexible view on the twin statutory requirements of a hiring for a year and actual service for a year. In principle there had to be 'an entire contract for at least a complete year's prospective service, consisting of 365 consecutive days'.[51] In practice the courts held that a contract to work for a year could be implied from the fact of a continuous year's service,[52] and disregarded breaks brought about by illness[53] or temporary absence with the employer's permission. Although successive hirings of less than a year were regarded from the inception of the Acts as insufficient,[54] a contract for a year's service with provision on either side to determine the hiring on a month's notice at the end of any quarter was held to confer a settlement, the court commenting that 'if this should be determined not to gain a settlement, it would overturn great numbers of settlements that subsist on such things'.[55]

The courts also disregarded an apparent requirement of the 1697 Act that the twelve months' service should be precisely coterminous with the contract for the yearly hiring: Lord Parker was reported as saying, 'if there was a service for a year, on a hiring from week to week, and then a hiring for a year, and serving for forty days, that he should adjudge that a settlement'.[56] Nor did the hiring have to be coterminous with a year's residence in the parish of employment. As a result, servants and apprentices who moved with their employers from place to place gained successive settlements in each new parish simply on forty days' residence there as long as the service continued without interruption.[57]

2.4 The decline of settlement by hiring

The decline of the institution of annual service can be traced to the 1780s. Historical studies have charted the decline and identified the role played by a combination of institutional and market factors: the rising cost of poor relief, on the one hand, which discouraged employers from agreeing to yearly hirings, and on the other the intensification of cereal farming in the south-eastern counties, which reduced the need for regular, year-round employment.[58] K.D.M. Snell's

[50] Burn, *The Justice of the Peace and Parish Officer*, op. cit., at pp. 51–52.
[51] Nolan, *Treatise of the Laws for the Relief and Settlement of the Poor*, op. cit., at p. 343.
[52] *R. v. Cowhoneybourn* (1808) 10 East 88.   [53] *R. v. Islip* (1720) 1 Str. 423.
[54] *Dunsford* v. *Ridgwick* (1711) 2 Salk. 535.   [55] *Atherton* v. *Barton* (1743) 2 Str. 1142.
[56] *Brightwell* v. *Westhallam* (1714) Foley 143.
[57] Burn, *Justice of the Peace and Parish Officer*, op. cit., at p. 38; *Silverton* v. *Ashton* (1714) Foley 188; *R.* v. *Whitechapel* (1725) Foley 146; *St. Peter's in Oxford* v. *Chipping Wycombe* (1722) Foley 200; *Bishop's Hatfield* v. *St. Peters in St. Albans* (1715) Foley 197; *St. Peters in Oxford* v. *Fawley* (1722) Foley 194.
[58] See, in particular, E. Hobsbawm and G. Rudé, *Captain Swing* (Harmondsworth: Penguin, 1973), ch. 2; Snell, *Annals of the Labouring Poor*, op. cit., ch. 2.

study of settlement records indicates that in the early eighteenth century, half of the yearly hirings in the south-east continued for two or more years; by the 1830s the proportion was less than a sixth. While in 1831 a substantial proportion of the agricultural labour force was still employed as farm 'servants', the clear distinction of an earlier generation between servants and labourers no longer existed, and there had been an increase in the number of daily and weekly hirings.[59]

The decline of annual service as a social institution was mirrored by a gradual move within the law towards a more restrictive reading of the exceptions to the power of removal, which culminated in the statutory abolition of settlement by hiring in the poor law Amendment Act 1834. In the Court of King's Bench this shift occurred both through a more narrow interpretation of the Acts but also through a modification of the prevailing conception of the service relationship. Rather than infer an intention to contract for a yearly hiring, in ambiguous cases the courts regarded the payment of weekly or monthly wages as evidence of a periodic hiring lasting only between payments.[60] Similarly, task contracts were held to be insufficient to give a settlement.[61] The judges also cast doubt on the earlier decisions which had held that the hiring (or contract) and the service (or performance) did not need to be precisely coterminous. The earlier construction, wrote Nolan in 1825,

was given to the Statutes soon after the 8 & 9 Wm. III was passed. It was founded on a strict interpretation of their provisions, which the court would not carry beyond the letter, from an opinion that they were restrictive of the subject's liberty, and in derogation of a common law birth right . . . But judges, who have held themselves bound by the authority of this decision, have questioned its propriety. Indeed, the design of the statute seems to point to a contrary construction; and it has been stated, that the place of settlement can be of no consequence to the pauper, since he is equally entitled to support wherever it may be.[62]

The most serious limitation on settlement was the notion of the 'exceptive hiring'. The rationale for this was put in terms of the master's unqualified right of 'control' over the servant throughout the term of the contract: anything less came

---

[59] Ibid., at pp. 74–84.

[60] *R.* v. *Newton Toney* (1788) 2 Term. Rep. 453; *R.* v. *Mitcham* (1810) 12 East 351; *R.* v. *Droitwich* (1814) 3 M. & S. 243, although cases went both ways, since in other decisions the courts construed indefinite hirings as hirings for a year: *R.* v. *Birdbrooke* (1791) 4 Term. Rep. 245; *R.* v. *Hampreston* (1793) 5 Term. Rep. 205; *R.* v. *St. Andrew in Pershore* (1828) 8 B. & C. 679. Burn, *Justice of the Peace and Parish Officer*, op. cit., at p. 54, argued that a lawful hiring of a servant was by definition a hiring for a year under s. 3 of the Statute of Artificers: 'in general, the law never looks upon any person as a servant, who is hired for less term than one whole year; otherwise they come under the denomination of labourers. Now being lawfully hired, can mean nothing else but being hired according to law. And being hired according to law, is being hired for one whole year, and not otherwise'. But by the end of the eighteenth century the Act of 1562 was less significant in practice than it had been as a means of regulating hiring.   [61] *R.* v. *Woodhurst* (1818) 1 B. & Ald. 325.

[62] Nolan, *Treatise of the Laws for the Relief and Settlement of the Poor*, op. cit., at p. 446, referring to *R.* v. *Aynhoe* (1727) 2 Ld. Raym. 1521. The eighteenth-century case law allowing minor hirings to be connected to a yearly hiring as long as service was continuous throughout was regarded as suspect by the time of *R.* v. *Denham* (1813) 1 M. & S. 221.

to be seen as incompatible with the relationship of service. In this way, the settlement laws helped to initiate the open-ended duty of obedience which later came to characterize the contract of service. Although a servant could not be made to work 'unreasonable hours of the night, and he is punished if he profanes the sabbath day', nevertheless 'an express stipulation in the hiring, even of these seasons, will defeat a settlement'. This was because 'a right of control and authority, at least so far as it relates to the general discipline and government of the servant, must reside in the master at all times during the continuance of the service'.[63]

The distinction in practice between an 'exception' in the contract, which deprived the servant of a settlement, and a 'dispensation' in the actual service, whereby the master gave the servant a temporary leave of absence without affecting his settlement rights, seems in retrospect so slight as to be meaningless; nor was this point lost on judges at the time.[64] The contradiction is easier to understand if it is borne in mind that these two concepts developed at different times and so represent separate stages in the courts' analysis of the service relationship, with the later notion of the master's right of 'exception' being used to discredit the earlier concept of the 'dispensation'. It appears that underlying the growing use of the concept of the exceptive hiring was the increasing number of cases coming before the courts involving industrial and commercial workers whose employment patterns, based on regular hours and work schedules, lacked the open-endedness of the traditional service model.[65] Mill workers and coal miners, who worked long and regular hours and who at other times were seen to be 'at their own liberty', were hence held to gain no settlement by way of yearly hiring.[66]

Thus the rise of the exceptive hiring reflected a shift towards a more hierarchical model of employment, which emphasized both the employer's powers of discipline within the employment relationship and the economic power to use the market to discharge the worker without regard to customary understandings of hiring practice. The earlier cases had relied on a model of service as a relationship based upon reciprocal obligations, going beyond the immediate execution of work, which the courts came to consider anachronistic for all groups of workers, and not simply those engaged in industry or commerce. Under the traditional model, the master had the power to dispense with the servant's labour, being under no duty to find work—'he may compel his servant to work at all lawful seasons, or suffer him to remain unemployed'[67]—but this did not in any way put an end to the wider relationship between them, nor to his duty to maintain the

---

[63] *R.* v. *Wrington* (1748) Burr. S.C. 280, per Foster J.; Nolan, ibid; *R.* v. *Thistleton* (1795) 6 Term. Rep. 185.   [64] See the judgment of Ashhurst J. in *R.* v. *Sulgrave* (1788) 2 Term. Rep. 376.
[65] Napier, 'The contract of service', op. cit., at pp. 65–70, 120–121; R. Cranston, *Legal Foundations of the Welfare State* (London: Weidenfeld and Nicolson, 1985), at p. 45.
[66] *R.* v. *Macclesfield* (1758) Burr SC 458; *R.* v. *Buckland Derham* (1772) Burr SC 694; *R.* v. *Kingswinford* (1791) 4 Term. Rep. 219; *R.* v. *North Tibley* (1792) 5 Term. Rep. 21.
[67] Nolan, *Treatise of the Laws for the Relief and Settlement of the Poor*, op. cit., at p. 386.

servant through cash payments or in kind. It followed that a settlement could be gained not just by actual service but also by fictional or 'constructive' service during the periods when the relationship continued without work.[68] For this purpose the consent of both parties was deemed necessary to discharge the contract, unless in an exceptional case the master could point to 'immorality' or some similar serious breach of contract by the servant as grounds for dismissal without the prior sanction of the magistrates.[69] Not even the master's bankruptcy could dissolve the contract of hiring against the servant's consent.[70]

By contrast, the concept of the exceptive hiring was based on a clear legal recognition of the employer's power to treat the contract as dissolved prior to the completion of the customary year's service. Its application marked the increasing irrelevance in the late eighteenth century of the requirement of yearly hiring for servants which still formally remained in place in the Statute of Artificers. Conversely, the traditional concept of service gave way to one in which only the closest and most complete control of the worker by the employer was sufficient for the Acts to be satisfied: 'if the master has once parted with his control over the servant, so that neither he nor the servant retain power of compelling subsequent performance of the contract, it is dissolved and no settlement gained'.[71] The nineteenth-century judges clearly understood that the result of such an approach would be to undermine settlement by hiring and confine the right to poor relief ever more narrowly. While some judges limited the notion of the exceptive hiring for this very reason,[72] others were more explicitly favourable to such an interpretation:

I should not wish to carry the idea of dispensation further than it has been already carried; which in many of the cases seems to me to have been stretched as far as ingenuity could go, upon the false idea that the servant had a right to acquire in gaining a settlement . . . I am not inclined to carry the decisions further.[73]

In due course Parliament followed the courts in making the law increasingly rigid, and a series of Bills proposed outright abolition of settlement by hiring before this was finally brought about by section 64 of the poor law Amendment Act 1834.[74] The ostensible aim of abolition was to reduce the burden of poor relief upon parishes and to make the yearly hiring once again attractive to

---

[68] Ibid., at p. 385.
[69] Ibid., at p. 437.   [70] *R. v. St. Andrews in Holborn* (1788) 2 Term. Rep. 267.
[71] *R. v. Thistleton* (1795) 6 Term. Rep. 185.
[72] *R. v. Byker* (1823) 2 B. & C. 120; *R. v. St. John Devizes* (1829) 2 B. & C. 896.
[73] *R. v. King's Pyon* (1803) 4 East 351, 354 per Lord Ellenborough CJ.
[74] Although the concept of the 'servant' was being interpreted more restrictively in the context of the right to a settlement, it was being given an expansive interpretation at the same time in tax law, as 'many kinds of domestic and horticultural and agricultural worker [were] being labelled "servant" by the high court judges, in order to render their masters and mistresses liable to the new tax' on domestic servants created in the late eighteenth century: see C. Steedman, 'The servant's labour: the business of life, England, 1760–1820' (2004) 29 *Social History* 1–29, and more generally on the numbers of domestic servants, L. Schwarz, 'English servants and their employers during the

employers by cutting the link with settlement. This was meant to address the complaint, articulated by Adam Smith in *The Wealth of Nations*, that it was 'more difficult for a poor man to pass the artificial boundary of a parish, than an arm of the sea, or a ridge of high mountains, natural boundaries which sometimes separate very distinctly different rates of wages in other countries'.[75] It seems possible that immobility was caused not by any inherent quality of the laws, but in part at least by the construction placed upon by them by the courts from the mid-eighteenth century onwards, which resulted in the ineffectiveness of the yearly hiring as a route to a settlement in the parish of employment. As it was, it was this judicial revision of the Settlement Acts which seeded developments within the concept of the service relationship which included the open-ended duty of obedience and the employer's right to lay off or terminate the relationship at will without retaining the obligation to pay or otherwise 'maintain' the servant.

3. Poor Relief and Wages: From Speenhamland to Less Eligibility

3.1 The crisis of the old poor law

The decline of settlement by hiring reflects a wider crisis which occurred in the administration of the poor law at the turn of the nineteenth century. At the end of the eighteenth century the process of land enclosure which had started at the end of the sixteenth century accelerated towards its completion.[76] 'Enclosure', write Eric Hobsbawm and George Rudé, 'dissipated the haze which surrounded rural poverty and left it nakedly visible as propertyless labour'.[77] Enclosure led to loss of access to the land in a number of ways; squatters on the waste were evicted without compensation and cottagers, small farmers with legal title to the land they farmed were often forced to leave by legal costs, the high costs of fencing their land, and the limited viability of small plots once they were fenced. Common grazing rights and rights to cut turf and glean wood and other materials from the open fields were also cut back at this time, partly by enclosures themselves and partly by restrictive decisions in the courts.

eighteenth and nineteenth centuries' (1999) 52 *Economic History Review* 236–256; see also, on cultural and legal conceptions of domestic service during this period, C. Steedman, 'Servants and their relationship to the unconscious' (2003) 42 *Journal of British Studies* 316–350. Variable interpretation of the term 'servant' according to the statutory context in which the terms arose was also a feature of judicial construction of the Master and Servants Acts and Truck Acts in the mid-nineteenth century: see Chapter 2, Section 4.1, above.

[75] A. Smith, *An Inquiry into the Nature and Causes of the Wealth of Nations*, ed. with an introduction by J.S. Nicholson (London: T. Nelson and Sons, 1886) (originally published 1776), volume I, ch. 10, at p. 59.

[76] J.R. Wordie, 'The chronology of English enclosure, 1500–1914' (1983) 36 *Economic History Review* 483–505.   [77] *Captain Swing*, op. cit., at p. 16.

These losses had an adverse effect on the ability of rural households to survive independently of wage labour. Under the open field system, the wives of cottagers and squatters had been able to supplement the wages of husbands employed as day labourers through the cultivation of small plots of land and the rearing of livestock. While enclosures produced a growth in wage-earning opportunities for women, principally as day labourers in the enclosed fields, increased female participation also led to the intensification of competition and greater precariousness of work and income for men and women alike.[78] Thus for the rural labour force, 'proletarianisation was a gradual process whereby access to resources other than wages was slowly eliminated'.[79] Enclosure also accelerated the move towards large-scale arable farming, which further intensified the decline of the yearly hiring and increased seasonal unemployment for both male and female farm labourers. This in turn led to an increase in poor relief payments which were now needed to supplement wages on a seasonal basis.[80] There was an historically unprecedented rise in expenditure on poor relief in the decades after 1780: by the early 1800s it had increased three-fold in nominal terms. Although the rate of growth was less substantial after taking the rise in population and in prices into account, it was still considerable, and fell particularly heavily on rural ratepayers at a time of agricultural depression.[81]

The immediate effect of the growing insecurity of income and employment in agriculture in the 1790s was to prompt a national debate on the most effective means of avoiding widespread destitution within the rural population. Two solutions were suggested: an expansion of outdoor relief, using the existing mechanisms of the poor law, and the strengthening of the institution of annual service, thereby reversing the effects of the decline which had set in during the second half of the eighteenth century. In particular, defenders of annual service argued for the use of wage-fixing powers to set a minimum wage rate which would reflect the increases in food prices which accompanied a series of bad harvests.

The argument for the minimum wage involved an appeal to elements within the traditional framework of regulation of the service relationship, derived from the Statute of Artificers of 1562. The 1562 Act was used to set rates which were meant to operate as maxima, protecting employers during times of inflation, but in practice could take on the quality of minima too. In the early part of the

---

[78] I. Pinchbeck, *Women Workers and the Industrial Revolution 1750–1850*, edited with a new introduction by K. Hamilton (London: Virago, 1981) (originally published 1930), ch. 2. For an assessment of Pinchbeck's work, concluding that it stands up well in the light of new evidence on the impact of industrialization on female labour and the shift to a male breadwinner conception of the family, see S. Horrell and J. Humphries, 'Women's labour force participation and the transition to the male breadwinner family, 1790–1865' (1995) 43 *Economic History Review* 89–117.

[79] J. Humphries, 'Enclosures, common rights, and women: the proletarianisation of families in the late eighteenth and early nineteenth centuries' (1990) 50 *Journal of Economic History* 17–42, at p. 42.   [80] Snell, *Annals of the Labouring Poor*, ch. 2.

[81] See Slack, *The English Poor Law 1531–1782*, op. cit., at pp. 29–34, and J. Marshall, *The Old Poor Law 1795–1834*, 2nd ed. (London: Macmillan, 1985), at pp. 23–4.

seventeenth century, the central authorities encouraged the idea that the Act should be used to set minima, out of concern for the maintenance of social order against a background of rising prices. An Act of 1603 'made for the explanation of the Statute made in the fifth year of the late Queen Elizabeth's reign, concerning labourers' complained in its recital that 'the said Act hath not according to the true meaning thereof, duly been put into execution, whereby the rates of wages for artificers, labourers and other persons, whose wages were meant to be rated by the said Act, have not been rated and proportioned according to the plenty, scarcity, necessity and respect of the time, which was politicly intended by the said Act'.[82] Accordingly, the 1603 Act sought to clarify the scope of the wage-fixing power, extending it formally to all classes of 'labourers, weavers, spinsters and workwomen whatsoever' so that it would not be confined to servants in husbandry, and making it a criminal offence for masters not to pay the stipulated rates in the clothing trade, effectively setting a minimum. The 1635 edition of Dalton's *Country Justice* noted that 'the Justices of the Peace . . . shall do well to assess the wages in such manner, as that servants etc. may reasonably maintain themselves therewith', and encouraged its readers to 'see the preamble of the Statute 5 Eliz. 4 [the Statute of Artificers], that considering the advancement of prices of all things belonging to servants and labourers, if more reasonable wages and allowances be not given them than is limited by former Statutes, it would be a grief and burden to the poor hired servant and labourer'.[83] However, the influence of central government faded from the mid-seventeenth century, and by the time of debate over poor relief at the end of the eighteenth century, the wage-fixing power, while not formally repealed, had fallen into disuse in many parts of the country.[84]

3.2 The Speenhamland system

The Speenhamland system of wage supplementation emerged from the debate over alternative ways of relieving poverty. The meeting at the Pelican Inn, Speenhamland on 6 May 1795 was originally convened to fix a minimum wage after concern had been expressed at the General Quarter Sessions about the 'miserable state of the labourers and the necessity of increasing their wages to subsistence level, instead of leaving them to resort to the parish officer for support for their families'.[85] However, the resolution proposing a minimum wage was not

[82] 1 James I c. 6 (1603).
[83] M. Dalton, *The Country Justice* (London, 5th ed. 1635), at p. 80.
[84] R.K. Kelsall, 'Wage regulations under the Statutes of Artificers', in W. Minchinton (ed.) *Wage Regulation in Pre-Industrial England* (Newton Abbot: David & Charles, 1972) 93–197 (originally published in 1938, London: Methuen, Associated Book Publishers) (see Chapter 2, Sections 2 and 3.1, above).
[85] J.L. and B. Hammond, *The Village Labourer 1760–1832: A Study of the Government of England before the Reform Act*, 2nd ed. (London: Longmans, Green & Co., 1913), at p. 161.

carried, and what emerged from the meeting was, in modern terms, a minimum income guarantee linked to the price of bread by a sliding scale. Thus:

when the gallon loaf of second flour, weighing 8lbs. 11oz. shall cost 1 shilling, then every poor and industrious man shall have for his own support 3s weekly, either produced by his own or his family's labour or an allowance from the poor rates, and for the support of his wife and every other of his family 1s 6d. When the gallon loaf shall cost 1s 4d, then every poor and industrious man shall have 4s weekly for his own, and 1s 10d for the support of every other of his family.[86]

Essentially, then, the minimum weekly income was to rise or fall by 3d. for the man and 1d. for every other member of his family with every 1d. increase or reduction in the price of a gallon loaf of bread, and any difference between this level and the weekly wage was to be met from parish funds.

The reasons for the failure of the magistrates to fix a minimum wage rate were not recorded. Some members of the Berkshire county bench were disciples of Adam Smith and were opponents of wage regulation on ideological grounds.[87] The failure to proceed under the Statute of Artificers is also explicable by the rarity of wage assessments in the late eighteenth century; if the jurisdiction had not actually died out altogether, it was at least widely regarded as having fallen into abeyance by this time. Some other counties attempted to set wage rates and others, doubtful of their power to set a minimum as opposed to a maximum rate under the Elizabethan statute, petitioned Parliament to introduce an amendment clarifying the law. A Minimum Wage Bill introduced in the House of Commons by the Whig MP Samuel Whitbread would have restored (or restated) the power to rate the wages of workers generally and would have made it an offence for employers to pay wages below those rated. Whitbread argued that the alternative, of expanding the poor relief system, would deprive the agricultural labourer of his autonomy or 'independence'. The Prime Minister, William Pitt the younger, responded in these terms:

By the regulation proposed, either the man with a small family would have too much wages or the man with a large family who had done most service to his country would have too little. So that were the minimum fixed upon the standard of the large family, it might operate as an encouragement to idleness on one part of the community; and if it were fixed on the standard of a small family, those would not enjoy the benefit of it for whom it was intended. What measure then could be found to supply the deficit? Let us . . . make relief, in cases where there are a number of children, a matter of right, and an honour instead of a ground for opprobrium and contempt. This will make a large family a blessing, and not a curse; and thus will draw a proper line of distinction between those who are able to provide for themselves by their labour, and those who after having enriched their country with a number of children, have a claim upon its assistance for support.[88]

[86] The Speenhamland scale, as reproduced in ibid., at p. 163.

[87] See M. Neuman, *The Speenhamland County: Poverty and the Poor Laws in Berkshire, 1782–1834* (New York: Garland, 1982).

[88] Pitt's speech as quoted in K. de Schweinitz, *England's Road to Social Security. From the Statute of Labourers in 1349 to the Beveridge Report of 1942* (New York: A.S. Barnes & Co., 1961) (first published 1943), at p. 88.

Here were the beginnings of a debate which was to come to have a familiar modern ring: the priorities for the governing majority were the market determination of wages, the ineffectiveness of the minimum wage for relieving poverty, and the importance of targeting social welfare so as to avoid possible disincentive effects. The Bill was rejected, in return for an undertaking by Pitt to introduce a Bill amending the poor law (which itself was to fail in due course). In the next session, however, an Act was passed confirming the justices' power to grant outdoor relief notwithstanding the existence in any parish of the power (under the Workhouse Test Act of 1722) to commit claimants to a workhouse as an alternative to outdoor relief.[89] This was an attempt to generalize the provision in Gilbert's Act of 1782 which, as we have seen, had expressly authorized the payment of outdoor relief to the able-bodied unemployed while prohibiting their committal to the workhouse.

The 1795 Act, however, did not give the justices any greater power than before to control the parochial administration of relief, and it was parish officers who retained control over the actual form of payments and the conditions attached to them. Applicants for relief could appeal to the justices against decisions to deny them relief but it was not possible for the justices to exercise more than general supervisory control even then. In Berkshire itself the allowance tables were used as no more than a general guide and many parishes failed to implement them. The allowance table nevertheless achieved widespread attention thanks to the description it received in Eden's treatise *The State of the Poor* (1797).[90]

Moreover, the boom created by the Napoleonic War lasted until 1815 and as long as prices kept up, the full implications of Speenhamland remained hidden. The incomes of the poor were insulated from rising prices by the Speenhamland allowance, but this also served to keep wages down by checking demands for their increase. Therefore, although the working poor were to a degree protected against rising prices by the Speenhamland system, they failed to share in general prosperity which enriched those in receipt of profits, rent and tithes. The ending of the war brought deep recession, with rapidly rising unemployment and falling prices and profits, although poor harvests kept food prices high. It was then that the full implications of Speenhamland became apparent.[91]

In the Speenhamland era there were four ways by which able-bodied workers were aided outside the workhouse: the *allowance in relief of wages* (supplementation of wages by parish relief), the *roundsman* system, the *labour rate* and *public works*. Allowance in relief of wages was the application of the Speenhamland principle to those already in employment, and the other three were applied to the unemployed who looked to the parish for relief. The *roundsman* system included various ways whereby the parish provided workers to local employers and made

[89] 9 George III c. 7.
[90] F. Eden, *The State of the Poor* (London: B. & J. White, 1797). See Neuman, *The Speenhamland County*, op. cit.   [91] Hobsbawm and Rudé, *Captain Swing*, op. cit., ch. 4.

up the difference between what the employer paid and a minimum subsistence income. The system was described in the poor law Report of 1834:

According to this plan, the parish in general makes some agreement with a farmer to sell to him the labour of one or more paupers at a certain price, and pays to the pauper, out of the parish funds, the difference between that price and the allowance which the scale, according to the price of bread and the number of his family, awards to him. It has received the name of the billet or ticket system, from the ticket signed by the overseer, which the pauper, in general, carries to the farmer as a warrant for his being employed, and takes back to the overseer, signed by the farmer as a proof that he has fulfilled the conditions of relief. In other cases the parish contracts with some individual to have some work performed for him by the paupers at a given price, the parish paying the paupers.[92]

The *labour rate* located the responsibility for creating work directly with the employers. This was:

an agreement among the rate-payers, that each of them shall employ and pay out of his own money, a certain number of the labourers who have settlements in the parish, in proportion, not to his real demand for labour, but according to his rental or to his contribution to the rates, or to the number of horses that he keeps for tillage, or to the number of acres that he occupies, or according to some other scale.[93]

Public works were a relatively rare means of creating employment. In 1832 barely 5 per cent of relief expenditures was accounted for by make-work schemes, including road working and compulsory labour in workhouses.[94]

Under the pressure of the widening coverage of in-work benefits, the related fall in wages and the resulting growing burden on the rates, the conditions for receipt of relief were continuously made more restrictive, and allowances were reduced.[95] Thus by 1831 the value of the minimum weekly income guarantee for a family of four had fallen to five gallon loaves from the seven and a half guaranteed by Speenhamland.[96] For the rural workforce in the predominantly arable farming areas of the south, pauperism and destitution fed a rise in crime and social unrest. From 1810 economic crimes, in particular poaching, rose continuously except in years of better harvests when the plight of the poor was temporarily eased. Machine breaking and arson were more sporadic and coincided with times of distress, reaching a peak in 1831 and 1832 with the Swing riots.[97]

Radical opponents of the political establishment were among those who drew a link between Speenhamland and social unrest. William Cobbett opposed the 'comforting system' of 'giving wages in the shape of relief', which he maintained 'implies interference on the one side and dependence on the other'.[98] Cobbett was

---

[92] Commission for Inquiring into the Administration and Practical Operation of the poor laws, *Report*, Parliamentary Papers (1834) (44) XXVII.1, at p. 19.   [93] Ibid., at p. 24.

[94] De Schweinitz, *England's Road to Social Security*, op. cit., at p. 75.

[95] See generally, Hobsbawm and Rudé, *Captain Swing*, ch. 4.

[96] Hammond and Hammond, *The Village Labourer*, op. cit., at p. 185.

[97] See generally, Hobsbawm and Rudé, *Captain Swing*, op. cit.

[98] See G. Himmelfarb, *The Idea of Poverty. England in the Early Industrial Age* (New York: Knopf, 1983), at p. 418.

among those who argued for a return to the stability of the yearly hiring and the implementation of minimum wages. Concern over the consequences of the 'confusion' of wages and poor relief was also expressed in a series of parliamentary select committee reports from the late 1810s onwards, but with implications for policy which were diametrically opposed to those of the political radicals.

3.3 The economic and legal critique of wage subsidization

In 1824 a Select Committee of the House of Commons concluded that the practice of paying wage supplements was responsible for the fall in wages in the southern counties in comparison with the higher wages paid in the north, where the practice was less widely followed.[99] In 1828 a further Select Committee, having found that a surplus or 'redundancy' of agricultural labour 'is the principal source of the low wages and misery of the peasantry', felt it necessary to ask

whether that redundancy is kept up by anything in the [Speenhamland] practices alluded to? because if that *is* the case, it will follow that *low wages give rise to the practice of allowance, and the system of allowance reacts to keep the wages low; so that without some change in that which is alternately cause and effect, the evil may be continued in a vicious cycle almost without limit.*[100] [italics in original]

It was widely believed that Speenhamland had become an unnatural distortion in the workings of the market. For the Select Committee on the poor laws of 1819 it was axiomatic that

the demand and supply of labour have in the natural course of things, such a tendency to regulate and balance each other, unless counteracted by artificial institutions, that any excess of either arising from temporary causes, would, if met by temporary expedients alone, in no long time correct itself.[101]

The discourse of the Parliamentary select committees was inspired by the political economy of the time. There were two sides to classical political economy's labour

---

[99] Select Committee on Labourer's Wages, *Report*, Parliamentary Papers 1824 (392) VI.401. A modern 'revisionist' tradition in economic history maintains that the policy of wage supplementation was not the cause of low wages but was, rather, their effect: see in particular M. Blaug, 'The myth of the old poor law and the making of the new' (1963) 23 *Journal of Economic History* 151–184, and 'The poor law Report re-examined' (1964) 24 *Journal of Economic History* 228–245; A. Digby, *The Poor Law in Nineteenth Century England and Wales* (London: Historical Association, 1982); G. Boyer, *An Economic History of the English Poor Law 1750–1850* (Cambridge: Cambridge University Press, 1990). Consideration of the correctness or otherwise of this claim is beyond the scope of the present work, which is concerned with the impact on the direction of social and economic policy of the very widespread contemporary *perception* of those involved in the poor law reform process, on all sides, that the Speenhamland system was responsible for the effects described in the text. For a valuable methodological discussion of the revisionist position, see K. Williams, *From Pauperism to Poverty* (London: Routledge and Kegan Paul, 1981), ch. 1.

[100] Select Committee on the poor laws (Slaney), *Report*, Parliamentary Papers 1828 (494) IV.137, at pp. 6–7.

[101] Select Committee on the poor laws (Bourne), *Report*, Parliamentary Papers 1819 (529) II.249, at p. 7.

supply side theory and its explanation of poverty. From the late seventeenth century, poverty was regarded by many European writers as a necessary mechanism for obtaining from the growing population of wage-dependent labourers the work necessary to make wealth productive.[102] However, the mass pauperization which occurred in many countries in the later eighteenth century (including England) spawned an alternative theory, popularized by Townsend[103] and systematized by Malthus.[104] This maintained that poverty resulted from population growth, driven by a lack of moral restraint or 'character' on the part of the poor, pressing on the food supply. Food supply grew less rapidly than population because of the diminishing marginal productivity of land, so that starvation kept the labour supply in check. It was further supposed that the demand for labour was constrained by the wage fund—a fixed part of aggregate capital set aside for the payment of wages—which meant that if employment were to rise, wages would need to fall.

Therefore, according to classical political economy, the well-being of the mass of the population was determined by a combination of the natural fertility of the soil, the willingness of the poor to work, their propensity to reproduce, the rate of accumulation of capital, and the fixed wage fund. These forces were expressed in the way supply and demand for labour interacted to determine the level of wages and employment. The legal setting of a minimum wage above that determined by supply and demand would reduce employment because the wage fund was assumed to be *fixed*. But equally, any attempt to interfere with these 'natural' laws by, as in the case of Speenhamland, attempting to alleviate poverty through poor relief, would be countered by an increasing population which would absorb any surplus and generalize the resulting poverty. Hence Malthus's stark conclusion: 'the poor laws of England tend to depress the general condition of the poor'.[105]

The case against wage supplementation became a standard reference point for nineteenth-century political economy. J.S. Mill's *Principles of Political Economy*, first published in 1848, contained a detailed restatement of the arguments.[106] If persisted in, 'taxation for the support of the poor would engross the whole income

---

[102] B. Geremek, *Poverty: A History*, translated by A. Kolakowska (Oxford: Blackwell, 1994).

[103] J. Townsend, *A Dissertation on the Poor Laws: By a Well-Wisher to Mankind* (London: Dilly, 1786).

[104] T.R. Malthus, *An Essay on the Principle of Population, as it Affects the Future Improvement of Society. With Remarks on the Speculations of Mr. Godwin, M. Condorcet, and other Writers* (London: Johnson, 1798).

[105] Ibid., at p. 33. On Malthus's conception of the self-equilibrating nature of a market economy, see E.A. Wrigley and D. Souden, 'Introduction' in E.A. Wrigley and D. Souden (eds.) *The Works of Thomas Robert Malthus* Volume I (London: Pickering, 1986), at p. 28: 'In Malthus's view . . . capitalist organization, with its emphasis on private property, the prevalence of wage-paid labour, a characteristic legal system, and so on, functioned in a way which closely paralleled the west European marriage system . . . [it] promoted a comparatively favourable balance between population and resources by establishing an institutional framework in which the minimum real wage was adequate to the needs of a family. It possessed a tendency for population to be arrested relatively close to the economic optimum.'

[106] On the influence of classical political economy on the workings of the 1834 poor law Commission (the political economist Nassau Senior was a member of the Commission), see A. Picchio del Mercado, *Social Reproduction, the Political Economy of the Labour Market* (Cambridge: Cambridge University Press, 1992).

of the country; the payers and the receivers would be melted down into one mass'.[107] Wage subsidization had the effect of reducing wages below the level they would 'naturally' achieve in the market:

When the labourer depends solely on wages, there is a virtual minimum. If wages fall below the lowest rate which will enable the population to be kept up, depopulation at least restores them to the lowest rate. But if the deficiency is to be made up by a forced contribution from all who have anything to give, wages may fall below starvation point; they may fall almost to zero.[108]

Mill concluded:

All subsidies in aid of wages enable the labourer to do with less remuneration, and ultimately bring down the price of labour by the full amount, unless a change can be wrought in the ideas and requirements of the labouring class; an alteration in the relative values which they set upon the gratification of their instincts, and upon the increase of their comforts and the comforts of those connected with them.[109]

The solution, then, lay in measures to alter the 'character' of the labouring poor. For Bentham, writing in the late eighteenth century (and thereby anticipating the reform of the poor laws by nearly forty years[110]), 'poverty' was the natural state of those who were wage dependent; everyone, that is 'who in order to obtain subsistence, is forced to have recourse to *labour*'. The poor were therefore to be contrasted with the indigent, that is to say, those unable to work or, if working, unable to earn a subsistence wage. The fault of the old poor law was that it had ceased to discriminate between the 'natural' poverty of the wage-earning population and the 'evil' of indigence:

If the conditions of individuals, maintained without property of their own, by the labour of others, were rendered more eligible than that of persons maintained by their own labour, then, in proportion as this state of things were ascertained, individuals destitute of property would be continually withdrawing themselves from the class of persons maintained by their own labour, to the class of persons maintained by the labour of others: and the sort of idleness, which at present is more or less confined to persons of independent fortunes, would thus extend itself sooner or later to every individual of the number of those on whose labour the perpetual reproduction of the perpetually consuming stock of subsistence depends: till at last there would be nobody left to labour at all, for anybody.[111]

[107] J.S. Mill, *Principles of Political Economy, with some of their Applications to Social Philosophy*, edited by with an introduction by W.J. Ashley (London: Longmans, Green & Co., 1909), at p. 364.
[108] Ibid., at p. 368.   [109] Ibid., at p. 369.
[110] On the nature of Bentham's influence in the debate over the poor laws, see J.R. Poynter, *Society and Pauperism: English Ideas on Poor Relief, 1795–1834* (London: Routledge and Kegan Paul, 1969); for an account stressing the role of landed interests in pressing for reform, and the significance of the return of the Whigs to office and the Reform Act of 1832 in paving the way for the poor law Amendment Act of 1834, see P. Mandler, 'The making of the new poor law *redivivus*' (1987) 117 *Past and Present* 131–157.
[111] J. Bentham, 'Essay II. Fundamental Positions in Regard to the Making Provision for the Indigent Poor', in *Essays on the Subject of the Poor Laws* (1796), reproduced in M. Quinn (ed.) *The

The need to distinguish between the 'deserving' and 'undeserving' poor was taken up in the legal and parliamentary discourse of the time. The Select Vestries Act of 1819, in the course of allowing parishes to create local boards (vestries) with the power to control the administration of relief by overseers, empowered the new boards to 'examine into the state and condition of the poor of the parish, and to inquire into and determine upon the proper objects of relief, and the nature and amount of the relief to be given, and to be at liberty to distinguish, in the relief to be granted, between the deserving, and the idle, extravagant and profligate poor'.[112] The role of Speenhamland in 'corrupting' the poor by depriving them of their independence was a consistent theme. For the 1824 Select Committee, 'by far the worst consequence of the system is the degradation of the character of the labouring class'.[113] This was because 'the evil of this practice augments itself; and the steady, hard working labourer, employed by agreement with his master, is converted into the degraded and inefficient pensioner of the parish'.[114] The practice of increasing allowances to provide for the families of the poor 'has a strong tendency to lead to improvident marriages, thus to keep up a redundancy of labourers, and depress artificially the natural rate of wages'.[115]

To address the problem, it was not sufficient simply to restrain the payment of poor relief. The logic of the new system was two-fold. Firstly, it should discriminate more precisely between different categories of the poor. Echoing Bentham, the 1834 poor law Report condemned the old law for its inability to distinguish between poverty and indigence:

in no part of Europe except England has it been thought fit that the provision [of relief], whether compulsory or voluntary, should be applied to more than the relief of *indigence*, the state of a person unable to labour, or unable to obtain, in return for his labour, the means of subsistence. It has never been deemed expedient that the provision should extend to the relief of *poverty*; that is, the state of one who, in order to obtain a mere subsistence, is forced to have recourse to labour.[116]

Collected Works of Jeremy Bentham. Writings on the Poor Laws Volume I (Oxford: Clarendon Press, 2001), at p. 39; on the background to the essays, which Bentham wrote by way of a critique of draft legislation aimed at extending the allowance system, see Quinn, 'Introduction' in ibid., at p. 3. The essays were not published by Bentham but their themes were taken up by Colquhoun in his treatise on indigence (P. Colquhoun, *The State of Indigence, and the Situation of the Casual Poor in the Metropolis, Explained* (London: Baldwin, 1799)). De Mandeville had earlier written: 'All men are more prone to ease and plenty than they are to labour, when they are not prompted to it by pride and avarice, and those that get their living by their daily labour, are seldom powerfully influenced by either: so that they have nothing to stir them up to be serviceable but their wants, which it is prudent to relieve, but folly to cure. The only thing then that can render the labouring man industrious, is a moderate quantity of money, for as too little will, according as his temper is, either dispirit or make him desperate, so too much will make him insolent and lazy'. B. De Mandeville, *The Fable of the Bees*, edited with an introduction by P. Heath (Harmondsworth: Penguin, 1970) (originally published 1714).

[112] 59 George III c. 12, s. 1.

[113] Select Committee on Labourers' Wages (Russell), *Report*, Parliamentary Papers (1824) (392) VI.401, at p. 4.   [114] Ibid., at p. 3.

[115] *Slaney Report* (1828) op. cit., at p. 8.

[116] *Report of the Poor Law Commission* (1834), op. cit., at p. 127.

The second and related condition was that relief of the indigent able-bodied should be such as to make claiming that relief unattractive. As long as poor relief guaranteed a certain level of income to the labourer regardless of whether or not he worked, the necessary motivation for employment would be lacking: 'he, whose subsistence is secure without work, and who cannot obtain more than a mere sufficiency by the hardest work, will naturally be an idle and careless labourer'.[117] Accordingly, in the words of the 1824 Select Committee,

the great object to be aimed at, is, if possible, to separate the maintenance of the unemployed from the wages of the employed labourer; to divide the two classes, which have been confounded; to leave the employed labourer in possession of wages sufficient to maintain his family, and to oblige the rest to work for the parish in the way most likely to prevent idleness.[118]

This last point meant that parish labour had to be 'labour less acceptable in its nature than ordinary labour, and at lower wages than the average rate of the neighbourhood'.[119] But by the time of 1834 Report, the full logic of less eligibility had been spelled out: 'the first and most essential of all conditions' was that the recipient of relief 'on the whole shall not be made really or apparently so eligible as the situation of the independent labourer of the lowest class'—the *lowest* wage being that set by the market according to the laws of supply and demand, not the *average* or *customary* rate of the locality.

For its supporters, then, it was an essential part of less eligibility that external 'interference' in the contract between employer and employed should be removed: 'let the rural magistracy be persuaded or compelled to retire from all interference in the business of agriculture, let master and servant make their bargain without the intervention, direct or indirect, of a law or scale of maintenance'.[120] But in practice it meant the use of statutory compulsion to formalize a national labour market policy and a uniform system of administration based upon legal principles of relief. Only through detailed legal and administrative controls could the principles of discrimination and less eligibility be put into effect: 'in the absence of fixed rules and tests that can be depended upon, the officers in large towns have often no alternative between indiscriminately granting or indiscriminately refusing relief'.[121] Thus the new poor law was accorded the task of bringing into being what the political economists had simply assumed to exist: a functioning labour market.

4. Less Eligibility and the Legal Structure of the New Poor Law

Three principal mechanisms were used after 1834 to implement the principle of less eligibility. Firstly, the law restricted and regulated the conditions under which

---

[117] *Bourne Report* (1824) op. cit., at p. 4.   [118] Ibid., at p. 6.   [119] Ibid., at p. 7.
[120] The poor law reformer C.D. Brereton, cited in P. Mandler, *Aristocratic Government in the Age of Reform: Whigs and Liberals 1830–1852* (Oxford: Clarendon Press,1990), at p. 199.
[121] *Report of the Poor Law Commission* (1834), op. cit., at p. 152.

relief outside the workhouse could be administered. In rural areas, outdoor relief to the able-bodied was prohibited, subject only to a few narrow exceptions, a measure which was enforced with increasing rigour as the nineteenth century progressed. In most urban areas, outdoor relief continued, but subject to the guiding principles that it should not be combined with wages and that, if it were, exceptionally, to be paid to the able-bodied, it should be made conditional upon a 'labour test' aimed at deterring claims. An able-bodied adult's 'wilful' refusal to work, already a crime under the Vagrancy Act 1824, took on a new significance now that low wages could no longer be supplemented by relief: the duty to work applied no matter how low the 'natural' or market rate of wages might fall. Secondly, efforts were made to distinguish conditions in the workhouse from the lowest standard of living available to wage earners. Out of concern that the workhouse might provide a superior level of 'comfort', poor relief orders spelled out in some detail a disciplinary regime intended to depress the quality of life below even that of the poorest 'independent' household. Thirdly, the principle was gradually established that private charity and the family should, wherever possible, bear the costs of supporting those unable to work, with the state providing support which was both residual and repressive. Private charity fulfilled a dual function: on the one hand, it released the public arm of the poor law for the functions of discipline and control, while on the other it made it clear that outdoor relief was no longer the 'privilege' or right of the poor. Private giving could never confer a legal right to relief. At the same time, the law sought to shift the burden of social risks more clearly on to the family and away from public relief by extending to women, children and the elderly some of the punishments initially designed for the encouragement of the male able-bodied. Thus it was not simply the prospect of their *own* confinement in the workhouse which was meant to incentivize wage-earners, but that of their dependants too. Related changes to the law of settlement and removal further redefined the relationship between poor relief, gender and the inter-dependence of family members.

4.1 The legal restriction and regulation of poor relief

The poor law Amendment Act of 1834[122] did not abolish outdoor relief to the able-bodied, but sought, instead, to restrict and regulate it. Section 52 of the Act inveighed against the 'practice . . . of giving relief to persons or their families who, at the time of applying for or receiving such relief, were wholly or partially in the employment of individuals'. Such provision 'is in many places administered in modes productive of evil'. Thus the newly established poor law Commissioners were empowered to make regulations declaring 'to what extent and for what period the relief to be given to able-bodied persons or to their families in any

---

[122] 4 & 5 George IV c. 76. On the 1834 Act and the legal structure underpinning the administration of the new poor law, see generally W.R. Cornish and G. de N. Clark, *Law and Society in England 1750–1950* (London: Sweet & Maxwell, 1989), at pp. 425–435.

particular parish or union may be administered out of the workhouse of such parish or union, by payments in money, or with food or clothing in kind, or partly in kind and partly in money, and in what proportions, to what persons or class of persons, at what times and places, on what conditions, and in what manner such out-door relief may be afforded'. Relief paid contrary to an order of the Commissioners was unlawful and hence 'disallowed'. Local poor relief officers were given a limited power to make emergency payments and to suspend the effect of a poor relief order for thirty days, but could be overridden by the power retained by the Commissioners to respond with a 'peremptory order' disallowing even emergency relief. In its early years the Commission issued a large number of individual orders, directed to particular parishes or poor law unions (groupings of parishes). General orders, which were subject to the scrutiny of Parliament, were not issued until the 1840s.[123]

The most important of the general orders was the Outdoor Relief Prohibitory Order of 21 December 1844.[124] This made outdoor relief presumptively unlawful in those parishes and unions in which a workhouse had been established. Under Article 1 of the Order,

Every able-bodied person, male or female, requiring relief . . . shall be relieved wholly in the workhouse of the union, together with such of the family of every such able-bodied person as may be resident with him or her, and may not be in employment, and together with the wife of every such able-bodied male person, if he be a married man, and if she be resident with him . . .

Exceptions were made on a number of grounds including 'sudden and urgent necessity'[125] and 'any sickness, accident or bodily or mental infirmity affecting [the recipient], or any of his or her family'.[126] The former, according to the Circular Letter issued by the poor law Commissioners along with the Order, applied only to cases of 'destitution requiring instant relief' and did 'not authorize

---

[123] The principal general orders were published and, in some cases, later consolidated by the poor law Commission and its successors, the poor law Board and the Local Government Board. The orders were reproduced, along with related publications of the Commission and Boards, and analysed in a number of contemporary legal texts and treatises: these include W.G. Lumley, *The New General Orders of the Poor Law Commissioners* (London: Shaw & Sons, 1845); J.F. Archbold, *The New Poor Law Amendment Act etc.* (London: Shaw, 1842), and subsequent editions; W.C. Glen, *The General Consolidated Order Issued by the Poor Law Commissioners, 24th July, 1847: with a Commentary* (London: Knight, 1847); R.C. Glen, *The General Orders of the poor law Commissioners, the poor law Board, and the Local Government Board relating to the poor law: with Explanatory Notes elucidating the Orders, Tables of Statutes, Cases and Index* (London: Knight, 1898); H.R. Jenner-Fust, *poor law Orders* (London: P.S. King, 1907; Supplement, 1912). These are the sources used in the account of the Orders which follows in the text. The orders were extensively discussed and analysed by S. and B. Webb, *English Poor Law Policy* (London: Longmans, Green & Co., 1910), pp. 22–87. One of the very few more recent discussions of the Orders, which demonstrates their links to poor law administration in the period during which they were in force, is by Karel Williams, *From Pauperism to Poverty*, op. cit., chs. 2 and 3.   [124] This Order rescinded and largely restated an earlier one of 2 August 1841.

[125] Outdoor Relief Prohibitory Order, 21 December 1844, Art. 1(1).

[126] Outdoor Relief Prohibitory Order, Art. 1(2). Other exceptions related to burial (Art. 1(3)) and imprisonment (Art. 1(6)).

permanent outdoor relief in any case'.[127] The latter principally covered cases of temporary sickness.[128] Moreover, in making these exceptions the Order did not make the payment of out-relief compulsory in their case. Guardians still had a discretion to refuse payment, subject to control by the local magistracy. What the Order did was to *prohibit* out-relief altogether in the non-excepted categories.

Initially, the Prohibitory Order, or variations on it, was mainly applied in rural and agricultural unions in the south and east of the country. Even there, local studies suggest that at least up until the 1870s outdoor relief continued to be paid to the unemployed on a seasonal basis, mainly in the guise of sickness payments.[129] However, restrictions on the practice of paying outdoor relief grew tighter in the final decades of the nineteenth century. In 1871 the Local Government Board issued a circular informing poor law inspectors that 'outdoor relief is in many cases granted by the guardians too readily and without sufficient inquiry, and that they give it also in numerous instances in which it would be more judicious to apply the workhouse test, and to adhere more strictly to the provisions of the orders and regulations in force in regard to out-door relief'. The circular reasserted the principle that 'out-door relief should not be granted to single able-bodied men or to single able-bodied women, either with or without illegitimate children', and insisted that 'in unions where the prohibitory order is in force the workhouse test should be strictly applied'. Where outdoor relief was paid, it was to be limited, in any individual case, to a maximum of three months.[130] In 1878 the Board issued a memorandum recommending the adoption by unions of the regulations drawn up by the Manchester Board of Guardians; these forbade the payment of outdoor relief to the able-bodied except on the ground of sickness, set a six-week limit even then on the payment of outdoor relief to any able-bodied person, and an eight-week limit in all other cases.[131] Thus the 'Great Depression' which lasted from the 1870s to the mid-1890s was accompanied by significant tightening of the poor law regime.

In the case of urban and manufacturing districts, it was considered impractical to impose a general ban on outdoor relief. As a result, two further orders, the Outdoor Labour Test Order of 13 April 1842 and the Outdoor Relief Regulation Order of 14 December 1852 allowed outdoor relief, but made it conditional upon a strict work test. By the late 1840s, the Prohibitory Order was in force in the vast majority of rural unions, a small number of which were also governed by various versions of the

---

[127] *Circular Letter* of 21 December 1844, contained in the *Eleventh Report of the Poor Law Commissioners*, at p. 58 (reproduced in Jenner-Fust, *Poor Law Orders*, op. cit., at p. 151).

[128] *Circular Letter* of 21 December 1844, op. cit.

[129] See A. Digby, *The Poor Law in Nineteenth Century England and Wales*, op. cit., and 'The rural poor law' in D. Fraser (ed.) *The New Poor Law in the Nineteenth Century* (London: Macmillan) 149–170.

[130] Circular to Inspectors on Out-door Relief of 2 December 1871, in *1st Report of the Local Government Board*, 1871–2, at p. 63 (see Jenner-Fust, *Poor Law Orders*, op. cit., at p. 145).

[131] *Memorandum Relating to the Administration of Out-relief*, February 1878, contained in *Seventh Report of the Local Government Board, 1877–78*, Appendix, p. 217 (reproduced in Jenner-Fust, *Poor Law Orders*, op. cit., at pp. 146–7).

Labour Test Order; the Relief Regulation Order applied in urban unions. Over the next seventy years the proportion operating some form of labour test slowly increased until it amounted to half the number of unions, representing three-quarters of the national population.[132] At the same time, as more workhouses were constructed in cities and industrial areas, the coverage of the Prohibitory Order was gradually extended, so that by the early twentieth century it was in force in five-sixths of all unions.[133] In this way, most areas came to operate under a hybrid of the two systems, applying an outdoor labour test during periods of recession and unemployment, and a workhouse test at other times. In some unions, especially restrictive 'test workhouses' were set up specifically for the adult able-bodied.

The underlying principles of the Labour Test Order and Relief Regulation Order were, firstly, that 'no relief shall be given to any able-bodied male person while he is employed for wages or other hire or remuneration by any person';[134] secondly, that where such relief was granted it should be subject to a strict work test, whereby the recipient 'shall be set to work by the guardians, and be kept employed under their direction and superintendence as long as he continues to receive relief';[135] and, thirdly, that at least half the relief granted should be given in kind, that is, 'in articles of food or fuel, or in other articles of absolute necessity'.[136] The logic of the labour test was 'to supply a test of the reality of destitution on the part of the applicant, and thereby to afford him an inducement to seek for independent employment'.[137] As a result, it was 'of primary importance that the paupers should labour under vigilant superintendence'.[138] Just as wages were to be kept separate from relief, so work under the labour test was sharply differentiated from normal employment: labourers 'should be required to execute a task fixed according to their physical ability' and paid in kind according to 'the wants of the applicant, and not by the quantity of labour done'.[139]

In principle, the new poor law was flexible enough to respond to short-run fluctuations in the demand for employment in urban areas. The ban on mixing wages and poor relief meant that 'what it is intended actually to prohibit is the giving of relief at the same identical time as that at which the person receiving it is in actual employment, and in the receipt of wages'.[140] This did not necessarily mean that relief could not be given in the event of short-time working or temporary lay-offs: 'relief given in any other case, as, for instance, in that of a man working or

---

[132] Webb and Webb, *English Poor Law History Part II: The Last Hundred Years*, Vol. I (London: Longmans, Green & Co.: 1929), at p. 151.

[133] See Jenner-Fust, *Poor Law Orders Supplement*, op. cit., at p. 4.

[134] Outdoor Relief Regulation Order of 14 December 1852, Art. 5; cf. Labour Test Order, Art. 1.

[135] Outdoor Relief Regulation Order, Art. 6; cf. Labour Test Order, Art. 2.

[136] Outdoor Relief Regulation Order, Art. 1; cf. Labour Test Order, Art. 1.

[137] *Minute of the Poor Law Commissioners respecting the means of enforcing an out-door labour test*, 31 October 1842, in *Ninth Annual Report of the Poor Law Commissioners*, 1843, at p. 381; see Jenner-Fust, *Poor Law Orders*, op. cit., at p. 167.

[138] *Circular Letter of the Poor Law Board*, 25 August 1852, in *Fifth Report of the Poor Law Board*, 1853, at p. 23; see Jenner-Fust, *Poor Law Orders*, op. cit., at p. 172.   [139] Ibid.

[140] Ibid.

in wages on one day and being without work the next, or working half the week and being unemployed during the remainder, and being then in need in receipt of relief, is not prohibited by the article'.[141] Thus there is evidence of a practice of paying relief even without a labour test to those laid off by short-term fluctuations in trade in the manufacturing towns in the North and Midlands. One reason for this was the expense involved in workhouse relief.[142] However, there is no doubting the major impact of the post-1834 changes on the practice of paying relief to the able-bodied unemployed. In the final decades of the old poor law, there was a 'massive involvement of the institution in assisting the male labourer and his dependants', with in some years the able-bodied and their dependants representing four-fifths of all those in receipt of relief.[143] After 1834, those receiving outdoor relief on account of 'want of work' could only be measured in their tens of thousands, nationally, in any given year: 'the reformed poor law had moved out of large-scale assistance to the unemployed and underemployed which had been the norm before 1834.'[144]

Outside the context of short-term lay-offs, the labour test operated as a device to discipline the workless. Becoming eligible for relief could open up the possibility of conviction under the Vagrancy Act 1824. It was an offence punishable by one month's hard labour to become chargeable to the parish or union in the case of 'every person being able wholly or in part to maintain himself, or his or her family, by work or other means, and wilfully refusing or neglecting to do so'.[145] In earlier vagrancy legislation, dating from 1744, a crime was committed only where there was 'a refusal to work for the usual and common wages given to other labourers in the like work'.[146] In the 1824 Act, the reference to 'usual and common wages' was removed. Thus from this point on, refusal to work on the grounds that the wages

---

[141] Ibid.

[142] 'In Lancashire, during the quarter ended 25 March 1839, as many as 78% of the able-bodied men on outdoor relief were being relieved on account of insufficient wages. Guardians could see no sense in forcing underpaid handworkers and underemployed operatives to give up their inadequate incomes altogether, merely in order to be maintained entirely at the ratepayers' expense': D. Ashworth, 'The urban poor law', in D. Fraser (ed.) *The New Poor Law in the Nineteenth Century* (London: Macmillan, 1976) 128–148, at p. 137; and on the mixture of public relief and charitable giving used to counter the effects of unemployment during the Lancashire 'cotton famine' of the 1860s, see L. Kiesling, 'The long road to recovery' (1997) 21 *Social Science History* 219–243; G. Boyer, 'The evolution of unemployment relief in Great Britain' (2004) 34 *Journal of Interdisciplinary History* 393–433.

[143] Williams, *From Pauperism to Poverty*, op. cit., at p. 147. Williams's estimate of the impact of poor relief on the able-bodied is based on the few systematic attempts to gather national statistics on relief prior to 1834, the poor law returns of 1802–3.

[144] Williams, ibid., at p. 179. Boyer, 'The evolution of unemployment relief', op. cit., gives a different emphasis, suggesting that for the three decades after 1834, the outdoor relief orders were effectively evaded by urban poor law unions, which, nevertheless, had to turn to relief through private charity during cyclical downturns. After the beginnings of the 'crusade against outdoor relief' in 1870, outdoor relief to the unemployed was more tightly controlled, and reliance was again placed on private charity and, increasingly, on trade-union organized unemployment benefits (ibid., at pp. 411–429).

[145] 5 George IV c. 83.

[146] 17 George II c. 5 (1744).

being offered were inadequate or below the commonly accepted rate was effectively a criminal offence; this continued to be the case until the early twentieth century, when the courts, for the first time in cases under the Vagrancy Act, began to place constraints upon the conditions which employers could attach to offers of work.[147] The Vagrancy Acts also reinforced the family responsibilities of parents: a male able-bodied worker deserting his wife or children, with the result that they became a charge to the parish or union, was liable to imprisonment with hard labour for up to three months,[148] and it was also an offence for a mother to abandon her children so as to make them chargeable to relief.[149]

Historical studies have shown how the Vagrancy Acts were used in conjunction with the threat of the workhouse to instil labour discipline. In rural unions, the example of the agricultural districts of East Anglia from the 1820s onwards is indicative of the use of the law. Employers operated a version of the 'ticket system' which carried over some aspects of the 'roundsman system' under the old poor law; applicants for relief were required to offer themselves for work with local employers and could only get assistance from the parish if each employer signed a note to the effect that he had been unable to offer him work. An applicant who refused to work for the wages on offer would be denied relief and prosecuted under the Vagrancy Act. The workhouse was used to house unmarried labourers in the winter months when work was scarce; married workers were normally kept on in jobs in order to avoid the greater cost to the parish in terms of providing indoor relief to an entire family. These forms of labour control continued into the 1870s and were discontinued only with the formation and strengthening of the agricultural trade unions.[150]

In urban unions which operated under the Relief Regulation Order, the increased construction of workhouses led to the use of 'labour yards' for the administration of the outdoor labour test. Section 15 of the poor law Amendment Act 1866 made it a criminal offence under the Vagrancy Act to refuse or wilfully

---

[147] See *Poplar Union* v. *Martin* [1905] 1 KB 728 and *Lewisham Union* v. *Nice* [1924] 1 KB 618, and the discussion of these cases in I. Jennings, *The Poor Law Code: Being the Poor Law Act 1930 and the Poor Law Orders Now in Force* (London: Knight, 2nd ed., 1936), at pp. 238–9.

[148] Vagrancy Act 1824, s. 4.

[149] By virtue of the poor law Amendment Act 1844, amending the Vagrancy Act 1824; see further Section 4.2, below.

[150] A. Digby, 'The labour market and the continuity of social policy after 1834: the case of the eastern counties' (1975) 28 *Economic History Review* 69–83; see also the discussion in Williams, *From Pauperism to Poverty*, op. cit., ch. 2, of the extent to which the continuance of outdoor relief after 1834 was compatible with the disciplinary strategy of the 1834 poor law Report. On the different disciplinary effects of the Speenhamland system and the post-1834 poor law on the regulation of agricultural labour, see I. Pinchbeck, *Women Workers and the Industrial Revolution*, op. cit., ch. 4. Pinchbeck points to the role of the Gangs Act 1867 (30 & 31 Victoria c. 130) and the Education Act 1876 (39 & 40 Victoria c. 79) in putting to an end the employment of young children which was an aspect of 'gang labour' in agriculture. On the relationship between the poor law and migration between 'closed' and 'open' parishes before and after the 1834 reforms, see B.K. Song, 'Landed interest, local government, and the labour market in England, 1750–1850' (1998) 51 *Economic History Review* 465–88.

neglect to perform a task set by the guardians, and as late at 1910 the Local Government Board was encouraging guardians to 'bear in mind that the men should be kept employed for at least 8 hours a day during the whole time they are receiving relief, not so much for the purpose of testing whether they are in need of relief as for the purpose of preventing them from loafing idly about the streets or competing for odd jobs with independent workmen'.[151]

The principle of less eligibility found further legal expression in a series of orders regulating the conditions for indoor (workhouse) relief, the most important of which was the General Consolidated Order of 24 July 1847. As the 1839 *Report on the Continuance of the Poor Law Commission* put it, 'the fundamental principle . . . with respect to the legal relief of the poor is, that the condition of the pauper ought to be, on the whole, less eligible than that of the independent labourer'. Outdoor relief was in general unacceptable because 'money or goods given to paupers to be spent or consumed by themselves, as they may think proper, is in general more acceptable [to them] than an equal value earned as wages; inasmuch as it is unaccompanied by the painful condition of labour'. But indoor relief was also problematic: 'a public establishment, if properly managed, necessarily secures to its inmates a larger amount of bodily comfort than is enjoyed by an ordinary independent labourer in his own dwelling'. A well-run union workhouse would have more spacious rooms, be better ventilated and warmed, and provide better and more regular meals, better healthcare and better clothing than the worst-off 'independent' household could expect to attain. To offset these benefits, the workhouse regime had to be one of repressive discipline:

Thus far, relief in a public establishment violates the principle above adverted to, and places the pauper in a more eligible condition than the independent labourer. And yet humanity demands that all the bodily wants of the inmates of a public establishment should be amply provided for. The only expedient, therefore, for accomplishing the end in view, which humanity permits, is to subject the pauper inmate of a public establishment to such a system of labour discipline and restraint as shall be sufficient to outweigh, in his estimation, the advantages which he derives from the bodily comforts he enjoys. This is the only mode, consistent with humanity, of rendering the condition of the pauper less eligible than that of the independent labourer; and upon this principle the English union workhouse has been organized.[152]

Accordingly the 1847 Order provided for the employment of pauper inmates 'according to their capacity and ability; and no pauper shall receive any compensation for his labour',[153] since this would be to 'confuse' relief and wages. For the

[151] *Local Government Board Circular on the Administration of Outdoor Relief*, 18 March 1910, reproduced in Jenner-Fust, *Poor Law Orders Supplement*, op. cit.

[152] *Report on the Continuance of the Poor Law Commission*, 1839, reproduced in Jenner-Fust, *Poor Law Orders*, op. cit., at p. 4. See Williams, *From Pauperism to Poverty*, op. cit., chs. 2 and 3, for a full account of the way in which the philosophy of the General Consolidated Order was reflected in poor law practice, and in particular in workhouse construction, in the period after 1834.

[153] General Consolidated Order, Art. 112.

same reasons 'boards of guardians should carefully avoid the employment of pauper inmates in such a manner as to cause so much competition with any particular branch of trade as to render it difficult, if not impossible, for the independent labourer to earn a living'.[154] Stone breaking and oakum picking were commonly prescribed, at least until 1898 when the latter was discontinued for regular inmates,[155] although not for casual or migrant paupers. Refusal of inmates to work as ordered was made an offence under the Vagrancy Act, as were failure to work properly, failure to observe the workhouse regulations and the destruction of clothes or other property of the workhouse.[156]

Regulations also sought to ensure that inmates could not come and go as they pleased. Under the Order of 1847 a pauper could quit the workhouse on giving regular notice; later Acts specified that those who frequently discharged themselves could be detained for up to a further week after giving notice.[157] The 'casual' or migrant pauper—the 'destitute wayfarer or wanderer applying for relief'[158]—was the subject of the Pauper Inmates Discharge and Regulation Act of 1871 and a General Order of 1882.[159] Tasks of work for migrants were intended to be especially onerous, in the case of men, the breaking of several hundredweight of stone, and for women, picking oakum. Again, the Vagrancy Act was used to criminalize casual paupers who disregarded or refused to obey the regulations prescribed for them.[160]

4.2 Private charity, the family, and gender relations under the new poor law

The 1870s, which saw the growing regulation and criminalization of the migrant poor in particular in urban areas, was significant in a further respect, namely the stress placed on the subordination of public methods of relief to private and charitable ones. The Local Government Board embarked on what the Webbs later called a 'crusade against out-relief'.[161] This amounted to a reassertion of less eligibility in the sphere of public relief, and the encouragement by government of

---

[154] *Circular Letter of the Local Government Board to Unions and Parishes of the Metropolis*, 31 October 1888; reproduced in Jenner-Fust, *Poor Law Orders*, op. cit., at p. 52.

[155] *Memorandum of the Local Government Board*, 12 January 1898; reproduced in Jenner-Fust, *Poor Law Orders*, op. cit., at p. 52.

[156] Refusal or failure to work was made an offence under the Vagrancy Act 1824, s. 3, and destruction of property an offence under s. 7: poor law Amendment Act 1842, s. 5; Pauper Inmates Discharge and Regulation Act 1871, s. 7.

[157] General Consolidated Order, Art. 115; Pauper Inmates Discharge and Regulation Act 1871, s. 4; poor law Act 1899, s. 4.

[158] General Order—Regulations with Respect to Casual Paupers, 18 December 1882, Art. 16.

[159] Ibid.   [160] 34 & 35 Victoria c. 108, s. 7.

[161] Webb and Webb, *Poor Law History: The Last Hundred Years*, op. cit., at p. 440 et seq. (giving details of the local by-laws adopted by poor law unions to implement the restrictive policy of the period); and on the crusade against poor relief, and its effects, see Williams, *From Pauperism to Poverty*, op. cit., at pp. 86–107.

charitable giving as a means of relieving the pressure of the urban poor on the workhouse. The policy was instituted by the minute circulated to poor law unions in 1869 by the President of the Local Government Board in Gladstone's government. According to the Goschen Minute,

> one of most recognized principles of our poor law is that relief should be given only to the actually destitute, and not in aid of wages . . . no system could be more dangerous, both to the working classes and to the ratepayers, than to supplement insufficiency of wages by the expenditure of public money.[162]

But rather than simply reasserting the logic of the 1834 poor law Report, the Goschen Minute marked a departure from the previously public nature of poor relief by instituting a policy of 'cooperation between Charity and the poor law'. In a tradition going back to the Tudor poor law legislation,[163] a priority of poor law administration had been to suppress the indiscriminate giving of alms in favour of an organized system of relief based on a compulsory local rate. Now, private charity was revived because of its *discriminating* effects. The new policy was expressed through the work of the Charity Organisation Society ('COS'), which the Webbs ironically described as making public opinion 'aware of the social obligation of regarding primarily the effect of philanthropy upon the recipient, and particularly upon his character, and that of his neighbours and acquaintances'.[164] This implied the partial privatization, through delegation to the COS, of the task of discriminating between the deserving and undeserving poor.

The result of the joint 'crusade' of the COS and the inspectorate of the Local Government Board was a large increase in the numbers confined in the workhouse: whereas in the mid-1860s between 12 and 15 per cent of paupers in England and Wales were in receipt of indoor relief, by the 1880s the proportion was 20 per cent. It continued to grow until it reached nearly 30 per cent by the early 1900s.[165] The philosophy of the Goschen Minute was reaffirmed as late as the *Local Government Board Circular on the Administration of Outdoor Relief* of 18 March 1910, which referred to it in terms of 'cooperation between the compulsory and voluntary forces' and stressed its importance for dispelling the idea that the able-bodied poor had any *entitlement* to relief:

> The [Goschen] Minute laid down the principle that the poor law authorities should confine their operations to those persons who were actually destitute and for whom they were legally bound to provide, while the charitable organizations, whose alms could in no case be claimed as a right, would most appropriately assist those who though not actually destitute might for the want of timely assistance become so.[166]

[162] The Goschen Minute is reproduced in Jenner-Fust, *Poor Law Orders Supplement*, op. cit.

[163] See Section 2.1 of this chapter, above.

[164] Webb and Webb, *The Last Hundred Years*, op. cit., at p. 456.

[165] M. McKinnon, 'English poor law policy and the crusade against outdoor relief' (1987) 47 *Journal of Economic History* 603–625.

[166] Reproduced in Jenner-Fust, *Poor Law Orders Supplement*, op. cit.

In addition to using private charity to limit the costs of the public system of poor relief and reinforce its disciplinary function, the new poor law shifted certain costs of insecurity on to households and families. The old poor law had formalized the customary obligation of family members to look after their relatives; section 7 of the Poor Relief Act of 1601 imposed a duty upon the parents, grandparents and children of 'every poor, old, blind, lame and impotent person, or other poor person not able to work', if they had the means to do so, to relieve and maintain them at a rate to be assessed at quarter sessions. In practice, however, under the traditional system of poor law settlements which reached its height in the early eighteenth century, the regular payment of cash doles to the elderly and non-working poor meant that younger family members were free to move in search of work. But by the nineteenth century the law was shifting to a position under which the obligation of family members came before that of the state. Under the Poor Relief Act of 1819 and subsequent legislation, poor law guardians were empowered to seek maintenance orders against parents in respect of their children and their own parents who had become a charge on the parish. Orders for the repayment of up to twelve months' relief could also be made if recipients came into a family inheritance or otherwise received valuable property or security. Nineteenth-century courts also denied claims for relief in cases where family members had the means to provide support.[167]

Under the new poor law, there were complex and multi-layered notions of inter-dependence between family members and in particular between husbands and wives. The law assumed, for most purposes, that women, children and the elderly were dependent on a male wage earner. As we have seen,[168] under the Vagrancy Act 1824 it was an offence for an able-bodied male adult to fail to support his dependent wife and children, and following the passage of the poor law Amendment Act of 1844, it became an offence for either parent to abandon their dependent children. However, the idea that a wife might abandon a dependent husband found no place in the statutory scheme. In general, then, married women were regarded as dependants rather than workers, and if they obtained poor relief, it was in the former capacity. If an adult male claimant was found to be able-bodied, Article 1 of the Prohibitory Order of 1844 forbade the payment of outdoor relief not just to him but to his dependent wife and children too, and it was assumed that they would enter the workhouse with him. A Circular Letter issued by the poor law Commissioners on 5 February 1842, while noting that 'it seems doubtful if the guardians have the power to prevent the wife from leaving the workhouse without her husband', nevertheless considered that 'the husband can, if he thinks fit, detain her in the house by his marital authority; and the guardians would be justified in refusing her permission to quit the house under such circumstances'.[169] Conversely, the General Consolidated Order of 1847

---

[167] During this period, the courts regarded the parents' obligation to maintain their child as 'derived from the poor law': see the judgment of Lord Atkin in *Coventry Corp.* v. *Surrey CC* [1935] AC 199, 205, referring to a dictum of Cockburn CJ in *Bazeley* v. *Forder* (1868) LR 3 QB 559, 565.

[168] In Section 4.2, above.

[169] *8th Report of the Poor Law Commissioners*, 1842, op. cit, at pp. 114–115.

provided that if an able-bodied male pauper did leave the workhouse, his entire family had to go with him.[170]

Female dependence was the consequence of marriage. Single adult women, if able-bodied, were subject to the duty to work just as men were: 'every able-bodied person, male or female'[171] was to be denied outdoor relief unless they fell into one of the exceptions in the Prohibitory Order. Moreover, mothers of children born illegitimately were solely responsible for their own and their children's upkeep: the poor law Amendment Act 1834 provided that, exceptionally, the father of an *illegitimate* child had no legal obligations towards it,[172] and illegitimacy was a grounds for the withdrawal of relief under the Prohibitory Order.[173]

These provisions fulfilled a number of functions: they were meant to deter claims, penalize those who tried to raise families which they could not support and, in particular, punish mothers who gave birth illegitimately. Thus the common link they have is their origin in the Malthusian view that 'intemperate' marriages and births outside wedlock were responsible for overpopulation and the pauperization of the labouring classes. Female dependency had no counterpart in the male *expectation* of a breadwinner wage, as it was to do under the legislation of the welfare state; rather, the prevailing notion was one of male *responsibility* which served the wider disciplinary purposes of the new poor law.[174]

Thus dependence on a male earner did not shield married women from the duty to work to the same, significant degree as it was to do later. Within a short time following widowhood or separation, they were expected to find paid employment. Under the Prohibitory Order, widows and deserted wives without children were prevented from receiving outdoor relief beyond a period of six months following the relevant event, on the grounds that this was 'an adequate interval for the purpose of making such arrangements for their support as their altered condition may require'.[175] Widows with dependent (and legitimate) children could receive outdoor relief without this restriction, but it was expected that they too would seek work. The guardians could order outdoor relief to supplement wages in such a case but were urged to exercise 'great circumspection' in applying this power to cases of widows in employment 'inasmuch as their wages ... are commonly reduced in consideration of the allowance', leading to the danger that 'their labour (thus depreciated at the expense of the ratepayers) may be substituted for the more highly-paid labour of independent labourers'. The Commissioners asserted that widows' earnings were unlikely to be 'so low as not to enable them to support one child at least' and warned poor law guardians that, in any event, they

[170] General Consolidated Order, Art. 115.   [171] Outdoor Relief Prohibitory Order, Art. 1.

[172] This was the effect of the poor law Amendment Act 1834, s. 69 (removing any responsibility of the father) and s. 71 (providing for the responsibility of the mother).

[173] This was the case where a widow who would otherwise qualify for outdoor relief gave birth to an illegitimate child after widowhood: see Outdoor Relief Prohibitory Order, Art. 1(4).

[174] See A. Clark, 'The new poor law and the breadwinner wage: contrasting assumptions' (2000) 34 *Journal of Social History* 262–281.   [175] Circular Letter of 21 December 1844, op. cit.

should not adopt fixed rules for relief based on the number of children in a household, but should consider cases individually.[176]

Similarly, the wives of soldiers and sailors on active service could receive outdoor relief,[177] but 'as a rule, an able-bodied woman with the Government allowance and such assistance as her husband ought to have been able to provide from his deferred pay, or to be able to afford from time to time afterwards with his pay and allowances, should have no difficulty in finding, if not immediately, at least within a reasonable period after her husband's departure, sufficient employment to enable her to maintain adequately herself and her children, if any'.[178] Situations of military service aside, wives whose husbands were 'beyond the seas, or in the custody of the law, or in confinement in a licensed house or asylum as a lunatic or idiot' were to be granted relief on the same basis as widows.[179] In other cases of marital separation the guardians had a discretion to grant either outdoor relief or relief in the workhouse, except where the recipient had a child below the age of seven, in which case outdoor relief was the norm.[180]

The dependent status of married women could also work actively to undermine claims for poor relief, by virtue of the continuing influence of the settlement laws. Although settlement by hiring was abolished by the poor law Amendment Act 1834, other forms of settlement remained relevant as a basis for the determination of liability between administrative units of the poor law, in particular the concept of the 'derivative settlement' under which a woman, on marriage, adopted the settlement of her husband. The lack of a settlement in the parish or union of residence could lead to the forcible removal of the claimant. This meant that a widow or deserted wife could be removed to her husband's parish of settlement. Even if removal did not take place, the poor law orders strictly confined the circumstances under which outdoor relief could be paid to non-resident claimants (that is to say, claimants with a *settlement* in the parish making the payment, but *resident* elsewhere); payments to non-resident widows were permitted, but only up to six months after the death of the husband if the widow were childless and, in other cases, if the presence of a dependent child or children meant that she was unable to earn her livelihood.[181]

The Poor Removal Act of 1846[182] created a new status of 'irremovability' which could be acquired by five years' residence in a parish (later reduced to one year) and also provided that widows could not be removed within the first twelve

---

[176] Circular Letter of 21 December 1844, op. cit.

[177] Outdoor Relief Prohibitory Order, Art. 1(7).

[178] *Letter of the Local Government Board to the Guardians of the Bromsgrove Union*, 24 May 1878; see Jenner-Fust, *Poor Law Orders*, op. cit., at p. 153.   [179] Outdoor Relief Prohibitory Order, Art. 4.

[180] Ibid., Art. 1(8).

[181] See the Outdoor Relief Prohibitory Order, Art. 3(4)–(5) and the Outdoor Relief Regulation Order, Art. 4(2)–(3).

[182] 9 & 10 Victoria c. 66, as amended (or clarified) by the Poor Removal Act 1848 (11 & 12 Victoria c. 111). For a discussion of the effects of this and related Acts in terms of the reduction in the number of removals, see Feldman, 'Migrants, immigrants and welfare', op. cit.

months of widowhood.[183] The Union Chargeability Acts of 1848[184] and 1865[185] further reduced the impact of the settlement law by charging the costs of relieving those with a settlement or with the status of irremovability to the relevant poor law union. The 1865 Act made the union and not the parish the unit of local taxation and effectively of residence for the purposes of relief; later, the county or county borough replaced the union.[186] Prior to this legislation the threat of removal was often seen as even more of a deterrent against applications for relief than the workhouse test. Even after these reforms, however, a married woman continued to derive her status for both settlement and removal purposes from her husband, and a child, unless illegitimate, took his or hers from their father. As a result, widowhood or desertion could make still a woman subject to removal; although widows were irremovable within the twelve months following the death of their husband,[187] they might not easily acquire the necessary period of residence to become irremovable in their own right, particularly since any period in which relief was being received did not count towards the period of residence required under the law. Removals, mainly affecting women, children and the elderly, continued right up to the abolition of the poor law in 1948.[188]

There were other respects in which the wider disciplinary objectives of the new poor law affected family relations. It was intended that, within the workhouse, family members should be separated from one another. The General Consolidated Order of 1847 provided for the classification of paupers into a series of groups: infirm men; able-bodied men and youths over the age of fifteen; boys between seven and fifteen; infirm women; able-bodied women and girls above fifteen, girls between seven and fifteen; and children under seven. Each class was to be housed separately, 'without communication with those of any other class'.[189] A mother or father of any child confined in the same workhouse could be allowed a daily interview with the child, and the guardians were also allowed to grant occasional interviews for family members confined in different locations 'at such time and in such manner as may best suit the discipline of the several workhouses'.[190] Only if a married couple were 'infirm through age or other cause' did the guardians have the discretion to provide them with shared accommodation; while an Act of 1847 provided that if both husband and wife were over 60 years of age, they were not to be separated. Thus 'life in the workhouse was the antithesis of the domestic ideal: families were fragmented, women worked, and men did not provide for their families'.[191]

---

[183] This meant that the obligation to provide relief fell on the parish of residence, not the parish of settlement, so that, notwithstanding the exceptions made for payment of relief to non-resident claimants under the poor law orders, payments by the parish of settlement were not regarded as lawful: *Circular Letter of the Poor Law Board*, 25 August 1852, in *5th Report of the Poor Law Board*, 1853, at p. 22.

[184] 11 & 12 Victoria c. 110.   [185] 28 & 29 Victoria c. 79.

[186] By virtue of the poor law Act 1930.

[187] This was the effect of s. 2 of the Poor Removal Act 1846.

[188] See Jennings, *The Poor Law Code*, op. cit., for an account of the law during this period.

[189] General Consolidated Order, Art. 98.   [190] Ibid., Art. 99(8).

[191] M. Levine-Clark, 'Engendering relief: women, ablebodiedness and the new poor law in early Victorian England' (2000) 11 *Journal of Women's History* 107–130, at p. 122.

The harsh treatment of families and the elderly was not an incidental feature of the new poor law; it was central to the objectives set out at the time of the shift in policy in the 1830s. According to the 1839 *Report on the Continuance of the Poor Law Commission*,[192] it was essential that the workhouse should remain a place of discipline, and not an 'almshouse' for the aged and infirm:

If the condition of the inmates of a workhouse were to be so regulated as to invite the aged and infirm of the labouring classes to take refuge in it, it would immediately be useless as a test between indigence and fraud—it would no longer operate as an inducement to the young and healthy to provide for their later years, or as a stimulus to them, while they have the means, to support their aged parents and relatives . . . If the views of those who desire the conversion of the workhouse into an almshouse were to be carried into effect, not only would all the aged of the labouring class be maintained at the public expense, and the burdens of the community be thus enormously increased, but the habits of forethought and industry in the young, who, exerting themselves for their future benefit, find an immediate reward in the increase of their present welfare—habits which we rejoice to say are daily developing themselves throughout the labouring portion of the community—would be discouraged and finally extinguished.

In the years immediately following the 1834 Act, many parishes, particularly in the North and Midlands, continued to pay poor relief to supplement low wages in times of recession, as well as supplementing the earnings of widows and deserted wives. But over time, greater uniformity and standardization of practice was achieved. The 'crusade' against poor relief was launched in the early 1870s against a backdrop of economic depression and a cholera epidemic, which together led to an upsurge in claims. The COS took on the task of organizing outdoor relief for women and children who were allowed to stay outside the workhouse if they were deemed 'deserving'. By contrast, a family deemed 'undeserving' by reference to the qualities of temperance, cleanliness and thrift would be split up, with the husband entering the workhouse with the older children, and the wife left to seek such 'independent' employment as could support her and the youngest child.[193] In some poor law unions, widows were allowed to receive outdoor relief only if their children were confined in the workhouse, while others were unwilling to separate family members. Where poor law officers permitted the payment of outdoor relief to able-bodied men following a labour test, it was on the basis that these were 'deserving poor' who could be relied on to find work at adequate wages: 'poor law policy was thus used to draw a line between the respectable, who could potentially be breadwinners, and the rough, who lacked responsibility'.[194] Thus even as the new poor law edged towards the notion of the breadwinner wage, it accepted the premise of the disciplinary principle of less eligibility.

[192] Jenner-Fust, *Poor Law Orders*, op. cit., at pp. 4–5.
[193] Clark, 'The new poor law and the breadwinner wage', op. cit., at p. 270, referring to the practice in Whitechapel in the 1880s.   [194] Ibid., at p. 271.

5. Wage Labour and Social Security

The displacement of the poor law by social security in the first half of the twentieth century did not simply involve a growing role for the state in the administration of welfare; it represented a fundamental shift in labour market policy. The institutions of the post-1834 poor law were modelled on the belief that, once freed from the distortions introduced under the Speenhamland model, the labour market would be self-correcting. Destitution and poverty were, therefore, the consequence of a lack of responsibility on the part of the poor themselves.

The premise underlying social security, by contrast, was that the causes of what Beveridge termed 'want' and 'idleness' lay within the economic system; as he put it, unemployment was 'a problem of industry'. The Webbs extended this critique to the poor law itself, which they identified as a principal cause of casualization, under-employment and low pay. Thus the case they mounted against the poor law was not simply or even principally that it was degrading and oppressive but, above all, that it was *inefficient*; as an alternative, they looked to 'the substitution of a deliberately ordered Commonwealth for the present industrial anarchy'.[195]

The 'public organisation of the labour market' envisaged by the Fabian reformers took a specific form, namely the strengthening through regulation of the model of 'permanent' or indefinite employment which was then emerging. This implied a number of measures including an extended role for factories and workshop legislation and collective bargaining, which we examine in a later chapter.[196] There is a sense in which the policy was most clearly articulated in the context which we are currently considering, that of social security, and in the related development of the policy of full employment. The process can be seen, conceptually, in the way in which the categories of 'unemployment', 'retirement' and 'widowhood' developed in the social insurance legislation of the early twentieth century. Each of these categories was constructed so as to be mutually exclusive with a notion of 'employment' which they thereby, implicitly, defined; the model of employment which they took as their reference point was one based on continuous, regular work delivering a male breadwinner wage. This was also the model implicit in the notion of 'full employment' in the *Employment Policy* White Paper of 1944[197] and Beveridge's report, *Full Employment in a Free Society*[198] of the same year.

In essence, social security inverted the poor law: in place of the duty to work at whatever wages the market provided, social insurance and full employment policy together sought to guarantee access to a wage capable, at a minimum, of supporting subsistence. But because this was conceived of as a wage capable of supporting

[195] S. and B. Webb, *The Public Organisation of the Labour Market: Being Part Two of the Minority Report of the Poor Law Commission* (London: Longmans, Green & Co., 1909), at p. xi.
[196] See Chapter 4, below.   [197] Cm. 6527, 1944.
[198] W. Beveridge, *Full Employment in a Free Society* (London: Liberal Party Publications, 1944).

a *male* earner and *his* dependants, it implied the marginalization of married women, children and the elderly from regular waged employment. As a result, although social insurance legislation contained the germ of the idea of social citizenship, the rights which it conferred were far from universal in their coverage. The trajectory of social insurance after 1945 reflected this basic limitation, as well as certain structural weaknesses which arose both from Beveridge's design in *Social Insurance and Allied Services*[199] and from the way in which that design was implemented. The contributory principle began to be eroded in the 1980s and 1990s and this process went hand in hand with the undermining of the full employment model of the immediate post-war years: the aim of *regulating* the supply of labour was replaced by the goal of *activating* it, the previously clear demarcation between employment and the categories of 'unemployment' and 'retirement' was blurred, and social security benefits came to be used, in an echo of Speenhamland, to subsidize low-paid employment.

5.1 The attempt to separate unemployment from the poor law: the 1909 Minority Report and its aftermath

The classical political economy of the first part of the nineteenth century had united Malthus's population theory, notions of the 'natural' indolence of the poor, Ricardo's theory of the diminishing marginal productivity of land, and the 'wage fund' theory to produce what were conceived of as immutable laws of labour supply and demand. During a period when large parts of the population endured economic insecurity and destitution, this theory conveniently cast the responsibility for poverty on to the poor themselves. However, as the nineteenth century progressed, economic advances progressively weakened the empirical foundations of these 'iron laws'. The threat of famine was lifted by technical progress in food production and transport which opened up new fertile land for cultivation. With this increased supply, food prices fell and real incomes rose, but the predicted population explosion did not occur as family sizes also fell.

A decisive blow to classical political economy came with the refutation of the wage fund theory in the 1860s, which turned upon the implausibility of the idea of an invariable fund for the payment of wages.[200] Its refutation lifted the political economy objection to institutional wage determination and this played a part in the campaign to ease legal constraints on trade union activities in the 1870s.[201] At the same time, the notion that the poor were responsible for their own plight was challenged by the research of Charles Booth and, in particular Seebohm Rowntree, who demonstrated that even with 'exemplary' behaviour, a large part of the working population could not reach even the lowest possible subsistence level.

---

[199] Cmd. 6404, 1942.
[200] E. Biagini, 'British trade unions and popular political economy 1860–1880' (1987) 30 *Historical Journal* 811–840.   [201] See Chapter 4, below.

This refutation of Malthusianism opened the way to the development of economic theories supportive of Rowntree's recommended solution to poverty: high wages, full employment and social security.[202]

At the end of the nineteenth century, the recorded numbers in receipt of poor relief amounted to only around 3 per cent of the population.[203] It was against this background that the social surveys of Booth (in 1887) and Rowntree (in 1897) revealed evidence on the much greater extent of poverty and destitution which existed beyond the operation of the poor law.[204] Rowntree's survey of poverty in York was an advance on Booth's London study because it involved a detailed study of a larger number of households. Moreover, it provided an answer to those critics of Booth who believed that he had uncovered a special 'metropolitan problem' of a quite exceptional nature.[205] In preparing his survey Rowntree based his definition of poverty on the nutritional requirements for maintaining individuals, or more precisely families, in a state of *physical efficiency*. This bare subsistence measure allowed him to draw a distinction between *primary poverty*—that of families whose incomes were insufficient to provide the base necessities of physical efficiency, no matter how wisely and carefully their incomes were spent—and *secondary poverty*—that of families who were obviously poverty-stricken although they received incomes large enough to live above 'the poverty-line' if their income had been spent differently. Rowntree used evidence related to workhouse diets and selected as his standard efficiency diet one less generous than that recommended for an able-bodied pauper. This was then re-valued at the prices the poor would have to pay for basic-level goods and services, and to this was added the cost for clothing, rent, light and heat, in turn parsimoniously estimated. Rowntree kept to the very barest of subsistence and wrote of his estimates:

A family living on the scale allowed for in this estimate must never spend a penny on railway fare or omnibus. They must never go into the country unless they walk. They must never purchase a half-penny newspaper or spend a penny to buy a ticket for a popular concert. They must write no letters to absent children, for they cannot afford the postage. They must never contribute anything to their church or chapel, or give any help to a neighbour which costs them money. They cannot save, nor can they join a sick club or Trade

---

[202] A. Briggs, *Social Thought and Social Action: A Study of the Work of Seebohm Rowntree 1981–1954* (London: Longmans, 1961).

[203] A.I. Ogus, 'Great Britain', in P. Köhler and H. Zacher (eds.) *The Evolution of Social Insurance 1881–1981. Studies of Germany, France, Great Britain, Austria, and Switzerland* (London: Pinter, 1982) 150–264, at p. 167.

[204] See Williams, *From Pauperism to Poverty*, op. cit., ch. 3, on the effect which the disciplinary policy of the new poor law had in terms of reducing numbers in receipt of relief at the end of the nineteenth century. The 3 per cent figure did not take into account pauperism among the non-able bodied poor, in particular the elderly; this increased the figure to nearer to 30 per cent in parts of London. Booth's work of classification of the elderly poor demonstrated the ineffectiveness of the policy of restricting, on disciplinary grounds, outdoor relief to the old, and thereby helped pave the way for the introduction of an old age pension based on legal entitlement. Thus 'Booth should be remembered not as the man who discovered poverty, but as the man who diminished pauperism': Williams, *From Pauperism to Poverty*, at p. 344.   [205] Briggs, *Work of Seebohm Rowntree*, at p. 27.

Union, because they cannot pay the necessary subscriptions. The children must have no pocket money for dolls, marbles or sweets. The father must smoke no tobacco and must drink no beer. The mother must never buy any pretty clothes for herself or for her children, the character of the family wardrobe as for the family diet being governed by the regulation: 'nothing must be bought but that which is absolutely necessary for the maintenance of physical health, and that what must be bought must be of the plainest description'. Should a child fall ill, it must be attended by the parish doctor; should it die it must be buried by the parish. Finally, the wage earner must never be absent from his work for a single day. If any of these conditions are broken, the extra expenditure is met, and can only be met, by limiting the diet; or in other words by sacrificing physical efficiency.[206]

Rowntree's research found that 15 per cent of the working-class population, 10 per cent of the total population of York, could not reach even this lowest possible subsistence level and were classified as being in *primary poverty*. A further 18 per cent of York's population was in what he called *secondary poverty*. On this basis he concluded that the average earnings of labourers in York were below the physical efficiency level if they were married with three children.

Rowntree's work directed attention to what was soon understood to be a social problem of enormous dimensions.[207] Public policy came round to the view that a combination of thrift and self-help for the 'deserving' poor and discipline for the rest was an inadequate substitute for a programme based on full employment and social security. But the poor law was slow to fade, and for the first half of the twentieth century it overlapped with the emerging social security system. The first steps in the construction of that system consisted of the introduction of measures intended to provide the unemployed with alternatives to the workhouse and the outdoor labour test. Local 'distress committees' were set up to provide temporary employment and assistance for those displaced from employment by cyclical depressions, a practice first initiated at local government level and then endorsed and extended by the Unemployed Workmen Act 1905. Labour exchanges at which the unemployed could register for work were established on a nationwide basis by legislation of 1909. From 1911, with the passage of the first National Insurance Act, unemployment compensation became available on the basis of contributions paid by individual wage earners. At first, contributory unemployment benefits were restricted to workers in specified industries,[208] but over the course of the inter-war period the scheme was extended to most sectors of industry and agriculture,[209] and the practice of paying unemployment assistance

[206] Quoted in Briggs, ibid., at pp. 38–9.
[207] But for a much more sceptical account of Rowntree's work, suggesting that his 'technicist' approach to the definition of poverty prefigured later difficulties in the operation of the welfare state, see Williams, *From Pauperism to Poverty*, op. cit., ch. 8.   [208] National Insurance Act 1911, Part II.
[209] Following a wartime extension of the scheme to cover munitions workers (which was, nevertheless, ineffective in practice: see N. Whiteside and J. Gillespie, 'Deconstructing unemployment: developments in Britain in the inter-war years' (1991) 44 *Economic History Review* 665–81, at p. 675–6); the Unemployment Insurance Act 1920 extended it again to cover the large majority of manual industrial workers; agriculture was brought within the scheme by the Unemployment Insurance (Agriculture) Act 1936.

to those with an inadequate contribution record received increasing statutory recognition.[210] The contributory model was also used to provide wage earners with access to health insurance, initially through Part I of the National Insurance Act 1911, and to provide pensions in respect of retirement and widowhood, beginning with legislation of 1925.[211] These changes meant that, while the poor law remained in place, it dealt only with those residual cases which fell outside the range of the statutory social insurance schemes.

Even so, the process whereby social insurance displaced the poor law was slow and, for most of the inter-war period, seriously incomplete. In terms of the numbers receiving outdoor relief, the inter-war period, paradoxically, saw an enormous increase in the role of the poor law, as the rules on the payment of relief to the able-bodied unemployed were loosened at the same time as the insurance principle was brought in.[212] Even when this form of outdoor relief metamorphosed into unemployment assistance, after 1934, it was by no means free of the disciplinary tendencies of the poor law; the logic of less eligibility lingered on in the form of the 'wage stop' and the household means test.[213] The complex and extensive body of poor law legislation was reconsolidated as late as 1930,[214] and it was not until 1948 that this legislation was replaced by general provision for social assistance.[215]

Nevertheless, by the time of the 1948 reforms, the intellectual case for the poor law had long since withered. Both the majority and minority reports of the Royal Commission of 1909 recommended the dismantling of the post-1834 system. The Minority Report was drafted by Beatrice and Sidney Webb (Beatrice had been a member of the Commission). Part II of that Report, republished as *The Public Organisation of the Labour Market*, made a case for wide-ranging reform which came to underpin many of the subsequent legislative developments; it is the pivotal text in the early twentieth century reconstruction of labour market regulation.[216] The essence of the Webbs' critique was that the new poor law had failed in

[210] The distinction between unemployment insurance, paid principally to cover short-term interruptions to earnings, and unemployment assistance, a means-tested benefit paid in respect of long-term unemployment, was first clearly established by the Unemployment Act 1934.
[211] The first legislation to introduce contributory retirement and widowhood pensions was the Widows', Orphans' and Old Age Contributory Pensions Act 1925. Prior to that, the Old Age Pensions Act 1908 had made limited provision for a means-tested old age pension payable to those over 70 years old, with an exclusion for those who had been in receipt of poor relief within two years of making their claim.
[212] See Williams, *From Pauperism to Poverty*, op. cit., at p. 180 et seq.; see Section 5.2, below.
[213] See N. Whiteside, *Bad Times: Unemployment in British Social and Political History* (London: Faber, 1991), ch. 4.   [214] Poor law Act 1930; see generally Jennings, *Poor Law Code*, op. cit.
[215] National Assistance Act 1948. National assistance was the forerunner of later means-tested benefits, supplementary benefit (under the Supplementary Benefits Act 1966 and, later, the Social Security Act 1975) and income support (under the Social Security Act 1986 and, now, the much-amended Social Security Contributions and Benefits Act 1992).
[216] For an extended discussion and analysis of the Minority Report and the associated reforms to the poor law and unemployment compensation, see Picchio del Mercado, *Social Reproduction of the Labour Market*, op. cit., ch. 3; for the background to the Royal Commission on the poor laws and its

its own terms: it was unable to discipline the truly 'work shy' or to offer adequate support to 'the respectable able-bodied man or woman'.[217] It was founded on a false premise, namely that destitution was always and everywhere the result of personal irresponsibility, and this was the result in turn of the attention placed in 1834 on 'one plague spot—the demoralization of character and waste of wealth produced in the agricultural districts by an hypertrophied poor law'.[218] For the Webbs, the issue was how to understand more effectively the multiple causes of poverty and destitution and to deal with them appropriately. Their proposal amounted to a conceptual revolution in which the language of 'pauperism' gave way to the 'modern terminology' of *unemployment*.[219]

'Unemployment' connoted a condition of worklessness brought about by the operation of industrial and commercial forces. The Webbs did not believe that the 'personal character' of those in poverty was completely irrelevant; it was 'of vital importance to the method of treatment to be adopted with regard to the individuals in distress'. However, it was not 'of significance with regard to the existence of or the amount of Unemployment'.[220] In this vein, they proposed a four-fold classification of the unemployed, based not on individual characteristics of workers but on the nature of their employment prior to becoming jobless:

(a) Those who have lately been in definite situations of presumed permanency; for instance, an engine driver, a cotton spinner, an agricultural labourer, a carman or a domestic servant.

(b) Those who normally, in their own trades, shift from job to job, and from one employer to another, with more or less interval between jobs, but each one lasting for weeks, and perhaps for months; for example, the contractor's navvy, the bricklayer, the plumber, and plasterer and, indeed, all varieties of artisans and labourers of the building trades, etc.

reports, see B.B. Gilbert, *The Evolution of National Insurance in Great Britain: The Origins of the Welfare State* (London: Michael Joseph, 1966), ch. 5; J. Harris, *Unemployment and Politics: A Study in English Social Policy 1886–1914* (Oxford: Clarendon Press, 1972); K. Woodroofe, 'The Royal Commission on the poor laws 1905–09' (1977) 22 *International Review of Social History* 137–164; A. McBriar, *An Edwardian Mixed Doubles: The Bosanquets versus the Webbs. A Study in British Social Policy 1890–1929* (Oxford: Clarendon Press, 1987); J. Burnett, *Idle Hands. The Experience of Unemployment 1790–1990* (London: Routledge, 1994), ch. 5. On the development of the Webbs' strategy and philosophy of labour market regulation in the period prior to their involvement in the Minority Report, see generally R. Harrison, *The Life and Times of Sidney and Beatrice Webb: The Formative Years 1858–1905* (London: Macmillan, 2000).

[217] *The Public Organisation of the Labour Market*, at p. 96.   [218] Ibid., at p. 4.
[219] Ibid., at p. 3. The term 'unemployment', although certainly known in the early nineteenth century and relied on in parliamentary reports, began to be generally used to describe the condition of joblessness in the 1880s (see Burnett, *Idle Hands*, op. cit., at p. 149); it was legally defined in the 1900s and 1910s, above all in the context of national insurance legislation and the reform of the outdoor relief orders (see below, Sections 5.2 and 5.3); and it was adopted for statistical purposes in the 1920s, replacing the term 'in want of work' (Williams, *From Pauperism to Poverty*, op. cit., at p. 180). The emergence of a political and institutional discourse centred on the notion of 'unemployment' during this period is analysed by M. Mansfield, 'Naissance d'une définition institutionelle du chômage en Grande-Bretagne (1860–1914)' in M. Mansfield, R. Salais and N. Whiteside (eds.) *Aux sources du chômage 1880–1914* (Paris: Belin) 295–323 and by Whiteside and Gillespie, 'Deconstructing Unemployment', op. cit.   [220] Ibid.

(c) Those who normally earn a bare subsistence by casual jobs, lasting only a few hours each, or a day or two; for instance, the dock and wharf labourers, the market porters, and the 'casual hands' forming a fringe round many industries.

(d) Those who have been ousted, or have wilfully withdrawn themselves from the ranks of the workers; for instance, the man broken down by some infirmity or advancing age, the habitual inmate of philanthropic 'shelters' and Casual Wards of the great cities, and the professional Vagrant.

These were, respectively, 'the men from Permanent Situations, the Men of Discontinuous Employment, the Under-Employed and the Unemployable'.[221]

The purpose of the distinction was to diagnose the conditions under which unemployment arose. Those in 'permanent work', although 'enjoying no permanence of tenure and . . . liable to be dismissed at short notice', in practice 'find themselves working, practically without intermission throughout the year, and often for many years, for one and the same employer'. As a result, they were not likely to lose employment unless there was a particular reason such as the bankruptcy of their employer, the trade cycle, new industrial techniques, 'the arbitrariness of a foreman, [or] the hundred and one frictions of industrial life'.[222] By contrast, the discontinuously employed and the under-employed were subjected to joblessness on a regular basis. Although the boundary between these two classes was 'obscure',[223] under-employment, in particular, was seen as parasitic upon society, a 'grave social evil' which caused a 'demoralising irregularity of life' for workers and families.[224] As such, it was 'above all other causes responsible for the perpetual manufacture of paupers'.[225] Beveridge's research on casualization[226] was called in aid to show that 'chronic over supply of casual labour in relation to the local demand was produced and continued, irrespective of any excess of population or depression of trade, *by the method by which employers engaged their casual workers*' (emphasis in original). This 'inevitably creates and perpetuates what have been called "stagnant pools" of labour in which there is nearly always some reserve of labour left, however great may be the employer's demand'.[227] It was continued exposure to the effects of under-employment which precipitated decline into the final and fourth group, a body which, leaving aside 'the rare figure of the ruined baronet or clergyman', consisted of 'those Unemployables who represent the wastage from the manual, wage earning class'.[228]

---

[221] Ibid., at p. 165.   [222] Ibid.   [223] Ibid., at p. 185.
[224] Ibid., at pp. 191, 193.   [225] Ibid., at p. 243.
[226] Published as *Unemployment: A Problem of Industry* (London: Longmans, Green & Co., 1909). On the evolution of Beveridge's approach to social reform, see generally J. Harris, *William Beveridge: A Biography* (Oxford: Clarendon Press, 2nd ed., 1997). For discussion of the relationship of Beveridge's early work to Booth's and S. and B. Webb, see Whiteside, *Bad Times*, op. cit., at p. 62 et seq.; Mansfield, 'Naissance d'une définition du chômage', op. cit.
[227] Webb and Webb, *The Public Organisation of the Labour Market*, op. cit., at p. 200.
[228] Ibid.

The next step in the argument presented by the Minority Report was to link casualization not just to employers' practices in particular industries (the docks were identified as the main culprits), but to the operation of the poor law itself. The workings of the principal institutions of the poor law—the outdoor labour test, the workhouse and the casual ward—were examined with this claim in mind. Thus the outdoor labour test, it was argued, encouraged casualization by virtue of the intermittent work which it provided to the jobless. It thereby 'facilitates and encourages the worst kind of Under-employment, namely, the unorganized, inter-mittent jobs of the casual labourer': the periodic closing of the labour yard 'defeats the object of the Outdoor Labour Test of keeping the paupers in any real sense off the labour market, and positively helps to make it possible for employers to avoid maintaining a regular staff'.[229] The workhouse test for the able-bodied, by 'estab-lishing a worse state of things for its inmates than is provided by the least eligible employment outside', not only engendered 'deliberate cruelty and degradation, thereby manufacturing and hardening the very class it seeks to exterminate'; it also 'protects and, so to speak, standardizes the worst conditions of commercial employment'.[230] The 'fatal ambiguity'[231] of 'less eligibility', therefore, was that standards inside and outside the workhouse, since they were mutually reinforcing, would drive each other down, until 'the premises, the sleeping accommodation, the food and the amount of work exacted, taken together, constitute a treatment more penal and more brutalizing than that of any gaol in England'.[232]

While the poor law exacerbated casual labour, casualization, in turn, made the operation of the poor law problematic. Thus the administrators of the Casual Ward faced a dilemma in setting the standard of discipline: the Ward filled up quickly if less eligibility was taken to refer to 'the lodging and supper of the lowest grade of independent labourers *who are in employment*', because it would then attract 'the limitless mass of Unemployed or Under-employed, including the semi Able-bodied, and the Unemployables of all kind'. But if it adopted a more punit-ive stance, 'the professional Vagrant stays away, and leaves the penal discipline to harden and brutalise the respectable man in search of work'.[233]

The final link in the argument concerned the combined impact of the poor law and casualization on the family, and the further consequences for labour supply. The casualization of male labour led to increased female participation in waged work: '[t]he household of the Casual Labourer, subject to chronic Under-employment, cannot possibly be maintained at all without making use of the wife's earning power'.[234] Equally, the payment of intermittent outdoor relief to a widowed or deserted mother, it was argued, encouraged her to take up casual work and led her to neglect 'her legal obligation to rear her children properly'.[235] Single women of working age should be treated on an equal basis to men: '[w]e see no reason why

[229] Webb and Webb, *The Public Organisation of the Labour Market*, at p. 34.
[230] Ibid., at p. 67.   [231] Ibid., at p. 72.   [232] Ibid., at p. 79.
[233] Ibid., at pp. 87–88.   [234] Ibid., at p. 218.   [235] Ibid., at p. 19.

such able-bodied women, potentially competent to engage in industrial occupations, should not have made for them exactly the same provision that is desirable for men of like capacity'.[236] But in other cases, female employment was seen as inefficient and 'parasitic' because it led to the neglect of domestic responsibilities. Most dangerous of all, in the eyes of the authors of the Minority Report, was the case of married female *breadwinners*: 'the laundry industry offers inducements to the women to become breadwinners of the family; the consequent loss to the home life if seen in the neglect from which the children suffer, and in the wild independence of the older girls'.[237]

The solutions advanced by the Minority Report reflected its diagnosis of the problem. The first aim was to remove the 'able-bodied' from the reach of the poor law. The key mechanisms for achieving this end were labour exchanges. The function of the labour exchange was to provide a register of unemployed which could then be matched with the demands of employers seeking workers. It would thereby reduce the costs of search for the unemployed and under-employed. More than this, supporters of the labour exchange model saw it as breaking the power which employers had to maintain 'pools of labour' in reserve, waiting for work:

What a National Labour Exchange could remedy would be the habit of each employer of keeping around him his own reserve of labour. By substituting one common reservoir, at any rate for the unspecialised labourers, we could drain the Stagnant Pools of Labour which this habit produces and perpetuates.[238]

The Minority Report also addressed the issue of unemployment compensation as an alternative to poor law relief. It argued in favour of a hybrid public–private system, under which government would have the power to subsidize the private insurance schemes already run, at that point, by certain trade unions, and covering around 2.5 million workers.[239] In the event, Part II of the National Insurance Act 1911 went further by instituting a fully state-administered system. However, the form of unemployment compensation which initially emerged was similar to that discussed (but rejected as unfeasible—prematurely, as it turned out) by the Minority Report, namely a system of compulsory insurance 'applied only to particular sections of workers or to certain specified industries, under carefully considered conditions'.[240]

The second and related objective was to put in place a series of measures aimed at 'absorbing the surplus' of employment which caused under-employment and unemployment. Some of these measures were based on the improvement and extension of labour standards; these included proposals to set a maximum working week for railway and transport workers (for whom long hours had been identified as a particular problem), and a general minimum employment age of

---

[236] Ibid., at pp. 18–19.   [237] Ibid., at p. 219.
[238] Webb and Webb, *The Public Organisation of the Labour Market*, at p. 261.
[239] Ogus, 'Great Britain', op. cit., at p. 186.
[240] Webb and Webb, *The Public Organisation of the Labour Market*, op. cit., at p. 291.

15 years. Others were more straightforwardly aimed at limiting labour supply. Thus the 'withdrawal from industrial wage-earning of the mothers of young children' was to be achieved by the combined effect of increasing payments of relief to reflect the full cost of childcare, while banning intermittent and partial relief to those engaged in employment. The logic of this position was that women with domestic responsibilities were not to be regarded as 'able-bodied', in the old terminology, or 'unemployed' in the new.

Under the poor law, the able-bodied were defined as those to whom a work-house or outdoor labour test could be applied; in that sense, they were subject to the wide-ranging duty to work at the available wages which the poor law implic-itly imposed. The Minority Report argued that, as a *matter of administrative practice*, female applicants were more likely to receive partial outdoor relief in order to enable them to work than to be subjected to a labour test; however, it was preferable that '[w]omen having the care of children should, so long as such care is required from them, be wholly excluded from the category of the Able-bodied . . . In no case ought women burdened with the care of young children to be either regarded as Able-bodied, and refused adequate assistance for the children's upbringing, or relieved merely in respect of their own needs'.[241]

The new category of 'unemployment' differed from the concept of 'able-bodiedness' in the way it carefully defined the status of the applicant for relief by reference to the employment which had been lost and to which the applicant was expected to return: as the Minority Report recognized in referring to the inten-tions of the Unemployed Workmen Act 1905, the 'bona fide Unemployed' were 'the men and women who, having been in *full work at full wages*, find themselves without employment through no fault of their own' (emphasis added).[242] This category, in the view of the authors of the Report, necessarily excluded women whose domestic responsibilities prevented them from becoming 'regular and efficient recruits of the industrial army'.[243] Thus in response to the questions 'Are Women Able-Bodied?', posed at the beginning of the Report, and 'Are Women Unemployed?', posed at the end, the same answer was supplied: only if they were 'unencumbered independent wage earners, both supporting themselves entirely from their own earnings and having no one but themselves to support'.[244]

This led logically on to the third main component of the Minority Report's pro-posals, which was, in effect, the institutionalization of the breadwinner wage. In assuming that a consensus in favour of the breadwinner model already existed, the Report presented its conclusions as the inevitable recognition of a social practice. The idea that married women and their children were dependent on a male wage earner was nothing new; as we have seen,[245] it had been recognized, in different

---

[241] Webb and Webb, *The Public Organisation of the Labour Market*, op. cit., at p. 22.
[242] Ibid., at p. 1.   [243] Ibid., at p. 209.
[244] Ibid., at p. 208. For further discussion of the Webbs' analysis of the issue of female 'able-bodiedness', see Picchio del Mercado, *The Social Reproduction of the Labour Market*, op. cit., at pp. 86–94.
[245] Sections 2.3 and 4.2 of this chapter, above.

forms, under both the old and new forms of the poor law, and above all in the law of settlement and removal. Yet the post-1834 poor law system which the Minority Report was seeking to displace, as its authors were well aware, had at its centrepiece the rejection of the idea that institutional means should be used to fix wages at a level which could support family subsistence. Nor (and this was precisely the point made by the Minority Report itself) had the new poor law discouraged female entry into the labour market even in the event of widowhood and desertion; if anything, the opposite had been the case (subject to local variations in the practice paying outdoor relief). Now, however, the Minority Report could assert that

we have chosen so to organise our industry that it is to the man that is paid the income necessary for the support of the family, on the assumption that the work of the woman is to care for the home and the children. The result is that mothers of young children, if they seek industrial employment, do so under the double disadvantage that the woman's wage is fixed to maintain herself alone, and that even this can be earned only by giving up to work the time that is needed by the care of the children. When the bread-winner is withdrawn by death or desertion, or is, from illness or Unemployment, unable to earn the family maintenance, the bargain which the community made with the woman on her marriage— that the maintenance of the home should come through the man—is broken. It seems to us clear that, if only for the sake of the interest which the community has in the children, there should be adequate provision made from public funds for the maintenance of the home, conditional on the mother's abstaining from industrial work, and devoting herself to the care of the children.[246]

The removal of unemployment from the reach of the poor law therefore occurred under precisely defined conditions; traditional notions of family structure remained firmly in place and, indeed, were strengthened by the shift from the new poor law to social security.

What did change, decisively, was the prevailing attitude towards regulation of the employment relationship. The nineteenth century faith in the self-correcting properties of supply and demand could no longer be maintained in the face of evidence of their daily failure. The case advanced by the Minority Report was that even when the administration of the poor law was at its harshest, and outdoor relief most severely restricted, wages did not automatically rise to the point where they coincided with subsistence, and continuous employment remained the exception, not the norm, for those in or near poverty. It was not simply that 'distress from want of employment, though periodically aggravated by depression of trade, is a constant feature of industry and commerce'; it was also the case that 'this misery has no redeeming feature'.[247] Thus while the experience of 'degradation' and humiliation under the unreformed poor law was a disaster for those who came into direct contact with it, all sections of the community, and not just the recipients of relief, were affected: 'a hundred different threads of communication

[246] Webb and Webb, *The Public Organisation of the Labour Market*, op. cit., at p. 211.
[247] Ibid., at pp. 241–2.

connect the slum and the square'.[248] In this way, the case for social security was constructed on an appeal, not only to the general good, but also, specifically, to the interests of the propertied classes.

5.2 Social insurance and full employment

The 1909 Royal Commission, divided as it was between Majority and Minority Reports which diverged on the role to be played by the state in the reconstruction of poor relief, did not produce an immediate blueprint for legislative reform. Part II of the National Insurance Act 1911 went further than the Minority Report had proposed in establishing a publicly-run unemployment insurance scheme based on contributions from workers, employers and national government.[249] However, the Webbs' analysis of the labour market was to have a major influence on the subsequent development of the social insurance model; as unemployment compensation evolved, the separation of unemployment benefit from the poor law was gradually, if haltingly, achieved.

The displacement of the poor law was the result, in the first place, of the widening of the industries and occupations covered by the unemployment insurance scheme which, however, only took place in stages. To begin with, the scope of the insurance scheme was limited and for those outside it the poor law, if anything, became more restrictively administered. Under the Act of 1911, the statutory unemployment insurance system had a coverage of 2.25 million workers, in trades which were identified as, on the one hand, suffering from the effects of cyclical employment but which, on the other hand, were not so badly affected as the casualized and 'sweated' trades in which low pay and intermittent unemployment were understood to be the norm.[250] In a parallel reform to the poor law, the

---

[248] Webb and Webb, *The Public Organisation of the Labour Market*, op. cit, at p. xi.

[249] See E.P. Hennock, *British Social Reform and German Precedents: the Case of Social Insurance 1880–1914* (Oxford: Clarendon Press, 1987).

[250] The designated trades were: building, construction of works, shipbuilding, mechanical engineering, iron and steel, vehicle construction, and sawmilling: National Insurance Act 1911, Sched. 6. Skilled workers in certain trades were already well protected by union-run schemes. In 1908 about 1.5 million workers, 66 per cent of all union members and 12 per cent of the adult workforce, were in union-run schemes; in 1911, it was estimated that the coverage of union schemes was more or less comprehensive in metalworking, engineering, shipbuilding, and printing, and stood at around 67 per cent in construction, 59 per cent in cotton and 38 per cent in mining, but only 5 per cent in general labouring trades; see Boyer, 'The evolution of unemployment relief', op. cit., at p. 414. Unions were given the option, under the 1911 Act, of administering the statutory scheme, and could thereby benefit, in effect, from a state subsidy for their own forms of provision. However this gave rise to a number of tensions since the uniform statutory definition of 'unemployment' did not match the heterogeneous experience of the unions; nor, by excluding those on strike, did it accord with the diverse union practice prior to 1911. See N. Whiteside, 'Définir le chômage: traditions syndicales et politique nationale en Grande-Bretagne avant la Première Guerre mondiale', in M. Mansfield, R. Salais and N. Whiteside (eds.) *Aux sources du chômage 1880–1914* (Paris: Belin) 381–411, and *Bad Times*, op. cit., in particular at p. 127: the imposition of a single definition of unemployment on top of diverse industrial practices 'may have made for administrative simplicity and convenience, but it did not lead to social justice. In its early years the system bred resistance'.

general orders on outdoor relief were revised and reconsolidated in the form of a new version of the Outdoor Relief Regulation Order, issued on 29 December 1911.[251] The Prohibitory Order was formally rescinded, and the new order exempted the non able-bodied poor from any general restriction on payment of outdoor relief. That, however, was a largely symbolic change, since the exclusions and controls contained in the old orders had for the most part been aimed at the able-bodied. In other respects, the 1911 Order was intended to formalize legislative controls over the issuing of poor relief to the unemployed (as they were now termed) and their dependants. Poor law unions were for the first time obliged to keep case papers on recipients of relief, to review all cases of outdoor relief at regular intervals, and to make provision for poor law medical officers to carry out examinations of all applicants claiming relief on the ground of infirmity. In effect, the establishment of national insurance was counter-balanced by greater selectivity in the administration of outdoor relief for those not covered by the insurance scheme, and more systematic monitoring of their condition.[252]

However, the coverage of the system was raised to 4 million by the wartime extension to cover munitions workers, and to 12 million by the Unemployment Insurance Act 1920, which brought virtually all categories of manual workers and non-manual workers earning up to £250 per year within its scope. The remaining exclusions—agriculture, domestic service, public-sector employments, and higher non-manual earners—were, for the most part, brought into the scheme by the late 1930s, at which point 14 million individuals were in insurable employment. Dependants' allowances for unemployment and sickness benefits were introduced from 1921, reflecting the idea that the social insurance scheme should underpin the 'breadwinner' wage. Even so, the extension of the scheme did not immediately result in the phasing out of the poor law. In a practical sense, after 1920 the poor law was more, not less important, as a source of relief for the unemployed, as, in a major shift from pre-war practice, regular payments of outdoor relief were made for those out of work. In 1922 and 1923 nearly 200,000 unemployed men, in trades outside the insurance scheme, were in receipt of this form of poor relief, and the poor law ceased to be a major source of support for the unemployed only after the implementation of the unemployment assistance scheme in the late 1930s.[253]

But the statutory scheme was extended, and it brought with it a shift in philosophical approach which combined collectivist values with the language of individual legal entitlement. On the one hand, social insurance was understood to

[251] The 1911 Order is reproduced in Jenner-Fust, *Poor Law Orders Supplement*, op. cit.

[252] See Williams, *From Pauperism to Poverty*, op. cit., at pp. 130–135; Whiteside, *Bad Times*, at p. 63.

[253] See Williams, *From Pauperism to Poverty*, op. cit., pp. 178–195. Even then, certain significant employments were not insurable, most importantly, domestic service, an exception which had the effect of excluding large numbers of women claimants, while certain long-term claimants (those unemployed for beyond two years) continued to have to resort to poor relief. See Whiteside and Gillespie, 'Deconstructing unemployment', op. cit.

have redistributive and collectivizing effects: '[w]orkers of every grade in every town and village in the country are now banded together in mutual State-aided insurance . . . They are harnessed together to carry the industrial population through every vicissitude'.[254] On the other, the contributory nature of unemployment benefits was stressed: individuals received entitlements in return for their contributions to the Unemployment Fund. The initial scheme was based on a principle of strict reciprocity between contributions and benefits: '[i]nsurance for the purpose of Unemployment Benefit is on a modified deposit system, that is to say, the benefits which the workman can draw are proportionate to the deposits standing to his credit'.[255] Subject to an upper limit on claims, one week's benefit could be drawn for each five weeks of contributions.[256] In other respects, the 1911 Act treated claims as akin to individualized property rights; thus a worker who reached the age of 60 without making a claim for benefit could 'withdraw his own part of the contributions that have been made in respect of him', with interest at 2.5 per cent, if he had previously made the equivalent of ten years' contributions.[257] The right to a return of contributions did not long survive the post-1918 rise in unemployment; however, the legislation of the inter-war years continued to express the idea that social insurance benefits were claimable as a matter of legal entitlement rather than by way of charitable gift.

Thus a sustained effort was made to put the Unemployment Fund on an actuarial basis, with contribution levels linked to expected unemployment rates. This attitude persisted in the face of unprecedentedly high levels of unemployment in the depression which followed the First World War. Applicants who had exhausted their right to the contributory payment received 'uncovenanted' (later called 'extended') benefits on the basis that they would repay the necessary contributions in the future.[258] This was, in essence, a fiction, but it was a convenient one since it avoided a situation in which applicants would have had to fall back on poor relief. The Blanesburgh Committee, which reported in 1927,[259] affirmed the principle that the Unemployment Fund should maintain its solvency over the course of the business cycle, and argued for the restriction of discretionary ministerial powers to alter benefit rates, on the grounds that such powers undermined the rights-based nature of insurance benefits. The Unemployment Insurance Act 1927 went most of the way to meeting these recommendations, and also introduced a system of 'transitional' payments administered by poor law officers to make further provision for the non-insured and long-term unemployed. In the first half of the 1930s, when unemployment rose to even higher levels, the 'extended' and 'transitional' options were seen as excessively artificial, and

---

[254] P. Cohen, *Unemployment Insurance and Assistance in Britain* (London: Harrap, 1938), at p. 10.
[255] A.S. Comyns Carr, G.H.S. Garnett and J.H. Taylor, *National Insurance* (London: Macmillan, 3rd ed., 1912), at p. 31.   [256] This was the effect of National Insurance Act 1911, Sched. 7.
[257] National Insurance Act 1911, s. 95.
[258] This was achieved by the two Unemployment Insurance Acts of 1921.
[259] Committee on Unemployment Relief (Blanesburgh), *Report* (London: HMSO, 1927).

unemployment assistance was introduced, in Part II of the Unemployment Act 1934. The assistance benefit was subject to a household means test and a 'wage stop' which cut off benefit at the point when household income reached the level it had enjoyed when the claimant was in employment (the paradoxical effect of the earlier introduction of dependants' allowances). The effect was to create work disincentives for any household with even a single unemployed member (since additional earnings were cancelled out by reduced benefits) and was, moreover, unevenly administered; it reflected continuing 'assumptions about scrounging and fears that the unemployed would "settle" on the dole'.[260] However, the defenders of unemployment assistance argued that it did not mark a return to the poor law:

A clear line of demarcation has been drawn between insurance and relief, so that the one does not trespass on the other. The bane of the old system by the mixing up of insurance and relief destroyed the insurance principle and put those who had exhausted insurance rights on sufferance. By the new plan applicants for assistance, both the successors of the Transitional Payments system and the new able-bodied entrants formerly under public assistance, are grouped under a Department in a way which preserves their industrial status as potential units of the labour market. There is a complete divorce from the poor law.[261]

It was with the National Insurance Act of 1946 that social insurance acquired its distinctive modern form as a 'comprehensive' system. The contributory scheme of the 1946 Act extended to all persons of working age, although with different types of contribution, and varying degrees of access to benefits, in the cases of the employed, the self-employed, and non-earners. At the same time, the National Health Service Act 1946 swept away the hybrid public–private system of health insurance administered by the Approved Societies, in favour of the fully state-run NHS. The NHS provided health care free at the point of supply and without a contribution requirement; it was funded almost entirely from general taxation, with national insurance contributions playing only a minor role in its financing.

The mature social insurance model, as conceived by Beveridge in his 1942 report for government, *Social Insurance and Allied Services*, was constructed on certain premises concerning the relationship between social security and wage labour. The first was the idea that the risks which social insurance guarded against were those which inevitably attached to the condition of employment in an industrial society. The near-universal dependence of individuals on wage labour for subsistence meant that 'interruption or loss of earning power' was the main cause of 'want'.[262]

The second premise was the converse of the first: the employment relationship was the *principal* mechanism through which the provision of social security would be organized. Thus the principle of joint contribution from employers,

---

[260] Whiteside, *Bad Times*, op. cit., at p. 83; and see Whiteside and Gillespie, 'Deconstructing unemployment', op. cit., for an argument that, notwithstanding the inter-war reforms, wage subsidization remained a widespread practice during this period.
[261] Cohen, *Unemployment Insurance and Unemployment Assistance*, at p. 15.
[262] Cmd. 6404, 1942, at p. 5.

employees and the state, which the 1911 Act had introduced for unemployment compensation, was retained as part of the wider scheme. Rights to benefit were to be based upon the number of contributions made by individual claimants, and for most relevant purposes, this meant their records as wage earners. For this purpose, Beveridge divided the national population into six classes:[263] Class I consisted of 'employees' ('persons whose normal occupation is employment under contract of service'), Class II, 'others gainfully employed' ('including employers, traders and independent workers of all kinds'), Class III, 'housewives' ('married women of working age'), Class IV, others of working age 'not gainfully employed', Class V, those below working age, and Class VI, the retired above working age. Beveridge's intention was that individuals in Classes I, II and IV would pay a weekly social security contribution, with employers in Class I also contributing. Individuals in Class I would be eligible, in return for a certain level of contributions, to receive unemployment and disablement benefits, retirement pensions, and medical and funeral benefits. Those in Classes II and IV would receive all benefits with the exception of unemployment and disablement. With the exception of the separate Class for married women, this classification was carried into the national insurance legislation of the immediate post-war period and continues in use today in the law governing the categories of national insurance contributions, although the structure of contributions and benefits and the conditions of entitlement are now far removed from those originally envisaged.

The contribution structure introduced in the 1946 Act reflected the logic of social citizenship. All citizens of working age came under a duty to contribute, subject to only very narrow exceptions, regardless of the degree to which they were exposed to social and economic risks:

The Act accepts the principle of universality. It brings everyone inside it, including those formerly above the income limit [for contributions], those exempt because they were substantially free from insurable risks and those exposed to risk but who were outside insurance. In addition it abolishes special arrangements such as those for unemployment insurance in agriculture, banking and insurance . . . There is no 'contracting out' except under section 5 in the case of people earning less than £104 a year, and under section 59 in the case of certain married women.[264]

These exceptions, in particular that relating to married women, were to prove significant. But in other respects, the Act came close to realizing a model of employment-based social citizenship.

The link between social insurance and employment was further spelled out in Beveridge's report on employment, *Full Employment in a Free Society*, which appeared in 1944. This was not an official publication but, like the *Social Insurance* report, it was produced with the aid of civil servants and government

[263] Cmd. 6404, 1942, at p. 10.
[264] D. Potter and D. Stansfield, *National Insurance* (London: Butterworth, 2nd ed., 1949), at p. 18.

advisers; it fed into the government White Paper on *Employment Policy*[265] of the same year and subsequently into the conduct of post-war economic policy. In Beveridge's conception, it was a central assumption of social security that 'employment is maintained, and mass unemployment prevented'.[266] It was the responsibility of the state to provide the conditions for full employment: '[i]t must be the function of the State to defend the citizens against mass unemployment, as definitely as it is now the function of the State to defend the citizens against attack from abroad and against robbery and violence at home'.[267] Full employment, in turn, had a specific sense; it meant

having always more vacant jobs than unemployed men, not slightly fewer jobs. It means that the jobs are at fair wages, of such a kind, and so located that the unemployed men can reasonably be expected to take them; it means, by consequence, that the normal lag between losing one job and finding another will be very short.[268]

Thus full employment, implying not just work for all but the provision of regular employment at decent levels of wages, was the condition which made social insurance feasible: the norm of stable employment would enable regular contributions by employers and employees to flow into the National Insurance Fund, while rendering exceptional the circumstances under which benefit would have to be paid out from it.

Beveridge's combined scheme for social security and full employment therefore sought to complete the work of the Minority Report of 1909 in reversing the effect of the poor law. As he put it, 'the labour market should always be a seller's market rather than a buyer's market'. For this, two sets of justifications were given. The first, a 'decisive reason of principle', was that

difficulty in selling labour has consequences of a different order of harmfulness from those associated with difficulty in buying labour. A person who has difficulty in buying the labour that he wants suffers inconvenience or reduction of profits. A person who cannot sell his labour is told that he is of no use. The first difficulty causes annoyance or loss. The other is a personal catastrophe.[269]

The additional justifications were more pragmatic. Thus 'only if there is work for all is it fair to expect workpeople, individually and collectively in trade unions, to co-operate in making the most of all productive resources, including labour, and to forgo restrictionist practices'. Ensuring that labour was in short supply would provide employers with a 'stimulus to technical advance' while, in turn, encouraging workers not to resist technical progress.[270] In this way the possibility of social citizenship was conditioned by an expectation of economic cooperation, in broad terms, between labour and capital.

---

[265] Cmnd. 6527.
[266] W. Beveridge, *Full Employment in a Free Society* (London: Allen & Unwin, 2nd ed., 1967) (originally published 1944), at p. 17. [267] Ibid., at p. 29.
[268] Ibid., at p. 18.   [269] Ibid.   [270] Ibid., at p. 19.

5.3 The conceptual structure of social insurance

The conceptual structure of the principal contributory benefits under the 1946 Act, in particular those relating to unemployment and retirement, reflected the aims of full employment policy. The impermissibility of combining relief with wages had, of course, been the lynchpin of the new poor law; the inability of the poor law administrators to avoid paying intermittent outdoor relief to the under-employed and low paid was one of the charges levelled against it by the Webbs and others. Beveridge's plan continued the principle of strict separation between employment and social security, but in a new context: now the aim was to stabilize the employment contract. As a result, the categories of 'unemployment', and 'retirement' were defined in terms not simply of the absence of work but, more specifically, of stable, regular employment.

'Unemployment' was defined in section 86(3) of the National Insurance Act 1911 which required a claimant to show that 'he is capable of work but unable to find suitable employment'. This succinct formula in effect coupled the traditional poor law test of able-bodiedness or capability for work, with the new principle that the claimant was entitled to benefit if he could not find employment which was *suitable for him*. The application of this test in any given case was a matter for the relevant national insurance officer who under section 100 of the Act was required to take into account the skills of the applicant; more generally, it was understood that section 86(3) 'must be read as a whole and that employment offered must be suitable, having regard to the applicant's capability for work'.[271] Under proviso (b) to section 86, an applicant was deemed not to have failed to fulfil the statutory conditions by reason only that he had declined an offer of employment 'in the district where he was last ordinarily employed at a rate of wage lower, or on conditions less favourable, than those which he habitually obtained in his usual employment in that district, or would have obtained if he had continued to be so employed'. The effect was 'to maintain union rates so far as Trade Union members are concerned, and to empower other workmen to demand their customary rate'.[272] In the case of an offer of employment in another district, proviso (c) stated that he was entitled to refuse to work 'at a rate of wage lower or on conditions less favourable than those generally observed in such district by

---

[271] Comyns Carr et al., *National Insurance*, op. cit., at p. 428.

[272] Ibid., at p. 429; although the legislation, by excluding participation in industrial action from the definition of unemployment, did not go so far as to underwrite unions' own efforts to defend customary conditions of employment. It is also relevant, in this context, that no claim could be made for more than fifteen weeks in a given year. See Whiteside, 'Définir le chômage', op. cit., and Whiteside and Gillespie, 'Deconstructing unemployment', op. cit. Similar assumptions relating to the regularization of employment can be found in the sickness insurance schemes which were initiated by Part I of the National Insurance Act 1911 and carried on during the inter-war periods, prior to their absorption in the National Health Service in 1946. See G. Phillips and N. Whiteside, *Casual Labour: The Unemployment Question in the Port Transport Industry 1880–1970* (Oxford: Oxford University Press, 1986), ch. 1.

agreement between associations of employers and or workmen, or, failing any such agreement, than those generally recognised in such district by good employers'. Even then, the national insurance officer was not *obliged* to find that employment at the standard rate of another district was suitable.[273]

Inter-war legislation changed the statutory formula by stipulating that in order to qualify for unemployment benefit the applicant should be both 'available for work' and 'genuinely seeking whole time employment but unable to find such employment'.[274] Refusal to take up an offer of suitable employment was already, under the scheme initially put in place by the 1911 Act, one of a number of grounds for disqualification from benefit for a limited period (others included voluntarily quitting work and misconduct in employment leading to dismissal). The 'genuinely seeking work' test proved controversial because it was interpreted as placing a duty on applicants to take active steps to look for employment even when, in conditions of economic recession, such a search would be fruitless, and in 1930 it was repealed.[275] In 1946 the basic structure of the inter-war test, without the 'genuinely seeking work requirement' was retained, and this remained in place until the 1980s. Under the slightly revised formula for determining suitability,[276] the claimant was entitled to refuse work outside his usual occupation for such period 'as in the circumstances of the case is reasonable', after which the national insurance adjudicator could require him to take up an alternative line of work; but in no circumstances could he be required to accept an offer on terms and conditions below those set in the relevant district, either by collective agreement or by 'good employers'.[277]

In this way, the administration of unemployment benefit was made to serve the wider goal of labour market regulation and the preservation of fair labour standards. 'Unemployment' signified a status for workers who had lost regular employment through no fault of their own, and who were expected to return, after a short interval, to a similar type of regular employment.

The structure of the long-term benefits for retirement and widowhood also reflected the labour-market aims of employment policy. According to *Social Insurance and Allied Services*, pensions were not to be age-related as such but payable 'only on retirement from work'.[278] By virtue of the statutory *retirement condition*, claimants had to withdraw more or less completely from employment

---

[273] Ibid.

[274] The 'genuinely seeking work' requirement was added by the Unemployment Insurance Act 1921, s. 3(3)(b).

[275] Unemployment Insurance Act 1930, s. 6. See A. Deacon, 'Concession and coercion: the politics of unemployment insurance in the twenties', in A. Briggs and J. Saville (eds.) *Essays in Labour History 1918–1939* (London: Croom Helm, 1937: 9–35). At its height, the test had led to the rejection of around a third of all claims for unemployment benefit: Committee on the Procedure and Evidence for the Determination of Claims for Unemployment Insurance Benefit (Morris), *Report*, Cmd. 3415, 1929; see N. Wikeley, *Ogus, Barendt and Wikeley's Law of Social Security* (London: Butterworths, 4th ed. (2002), at p. 340.

[276] The new definition was contained in ss. 11–13 of the National Insurance Act 1946.

[277] National Insurance Act 1946, s. 13(5).   [278] Cmd. 6404, at p. 11.

upon reaching pensionable age (60 for women, 65 for men) in order to receive the benefit; more precisely, an applicant had to show that he had 'retired from *regular* employment' (emphasis added).[279] Under the principle of *deferral*, an applicant who carried on in regular employment after reaching pensionable age forfeited the right to receive the pension for the period in question, in return for receiving a small increase in entitlements above the basic level.[280] In addition, a strict *earnings rule* operated so as to claw back any earnings from non-regular employment above a certain weekly threshold.[281] All these conditions ceased to operate when the claimant reached the age of 65, in the case of women, or 70 in the case of men; only then could the pension could be combined with regular work. The aim of this complex body of rules was to encourage individuals to carry on working into their late 60s, but the gains from deferral were too small to provide an adequate incentive. In addition, most employers set compulsory retirement ages for male and female workers of 65 and 60 respectively. While this practice was not required by either social security or employment legislation, nor was it prohibited, and it achieved a degree of statutory recognition when, after 1959, the adoption of the state retirement ages became a condition for the contracting-out of occupational pension schemes. With the advent of employment protection law in the 1960s and 1970s, steps were taken to ensure that dismissal on the grounds that the employee had reached the normal retirement age for the relevant employment or, in certain alternative cases, state pensionable age, did not give rise to a claim for either unfair dismissal or redundancy compensation.[282] As a result, it became abnormal for individuals to carry on in regular employment after reaching state pensionable age.

5.4 Social security contributions and the financing of national insurance

Beveridge's conception of social insurance, then, placed regular and stable employment at the core of the system of social security. This was also reflected in the arrangements made for the financing of the national insurance scheme. By virtue of what he called the 'contributory principle',[283] benefits were linked to the contributions paid by an individual over the course of a working lifetime or part of it. This was intended to produce a number of effects. First, building on the

[279] National Insurance Act 1946, s. 20(1)(a).   [280] Ibid., s. 20(4).
[281] Ibid., s. 20(2)(a)(ii), (5).
[282] These provisions are now contained in the Employment Rights Act 1996, s. 109 (unfair dismissal) and s. 156 (redundancy compensation). For unfair dismissal, the age exclusion applies once the employee reaches normal retirement age for that employment, or, if there is no such norm, the age of 65. In the case of redundancy compensation, the age of 65 applies unless there is a lower normal retirement age. Sixty-five is used as the benchmark age for both men and women because of the need to comply with EC law requirements of equal treatment in employment; prior to the Sex Discrimination Act 1986, separate benchmark ages of 60 for women and 65 for men were used, in line with state pensionable age.   [283] Cmd. 6404, at p. 17.

philosophy which informed the development of unemployment compensation in the inter-war years, social insurance would operate as a legal entitlement rather than a form of charity: 'benefits in return for contributions, rather than free allowances from the state, is what the people of Britain want'. Secondly, going beyond the achievements of the inter-war period, the disincentive and demoralizing effects of the household means test would be avoided: '[t]he scheme of social insurance is designed of itself when in full operation to guarantee the income needed for subsistence in all normal cases'.[284]

At the same time, the system was meant to be redistributive. According to Beveridge, state compulsion made it possible to include all earners in a single scheme, pooling the risks of unemployment across different industries and occupational groups. In his 1942 report he argued that the practice of adjusting premiums by reference to risk, a necessary feature of voluntary schemes which had to provide individuals with adequate incentives to participate, could be avoided in the case of an 'insurance made compulsory by the power of the state'.[285] Nor was it necessary for the state scheme to accumulate reserves against future claims. Beveridge recognized that a social insurance scheme of the kind he was proposing would not be 'pre-funded' as private pensions and savings plans were; in the terminology which was used later, it would be a 'pay-as-you-go' scheme under which, in any given tax year, payments were matched not from previous but from *current* contributions. However, it was a potential strength of the scheme, in Beveridge's view, that the state could take on tasks which private insurance was incapable of performing: '[t]he State with its power of compelling successive generations of citizens to become insured and its power of taxation is not under the necessity of accumulating reserves for actuarial risk'.[286] Thus it was precisely the active involvement of the state which made it possible to construct a *comprehensive* social insurance scheme which was able to spread social and economic risks as widely as possible across the whole of the working population.

This vision was articulated against the background of rapidly rising incomes for the lowest paid groups. This transformation can be demonstrated by comparing the results of the 1936 and 1950 Rowntree surveys of poverty in York. Whereas in 1936 17.7 per cent of the total population of York (31.1 per cent of the working-class population) were in the poorest classes A and B, and hence in 'primary poverty', in 1950 only 1.66 per cent of the total population (2.77 per cent of the working-class population) were in such conditions. In no single family was 'poverty', in this sense, due to the unemployment of an able-bodied wage-earner. Old age had become the primary cause of primary poverty, accounting for 68 per cent of the total, and sickness came second with over 21 per cent. Moreover there was a general improvement in living standards at the lower end of the scale and not simply a movement from those previously below the poverty line to a position just above it. If the working-class population was divided into five income classes, the

---

[284] Ibid., at p. 12.   [285] Ibid., at p. 11.   [286] Ibid., at pp. 12–13.

three lowest classes were not only predominantly above the poverty line; they had decreased from 28 per cent of the working-class population to only 13 per cent.

However, there were significant respects in which Beveridge's design failed to put in place the conditions which were needed for the effective redistribution of risk. Although contribution levels were not risk-sensitive for particular groups or industries, because they were maintained at a flat rate, their incidence fell more heavily on the lower paid. In his 1942 report Beveridge had rejected graduated or earnings-related contributions and benefits on the grounds that 'contribution means that in their capacity as possible recipients the poorer man and the richer man are treated alike'.[287] He also wished to retain a place for private initiative:

Social security must be achieved by cooperation between the State and the individual. The State should offer security in return for service and contribution. The State in organising security should not stifle incentive, opportunity and responsibility in establishing a national minimum; it should leave room and encouragement for voluntary action by each individual to provide more than that minimum for himself and his family.[288]

But because flat-rate contributions resembled a regressive tax, there was a limit to how far they could subsequently be raised, and this also placed a *de facto* cap on benefits and hence on the capacity of the system to redistribute risk from the more secure to the less secure groups.[289] As a result, many of those receiving social insurance benefits had their income topped up by recourse to means-tested national assistance (later supplementary benefit), while for those with low pay and incomplete earnings records, even partial access to social insurance remained out of reach.

The flat-rate contribution structure inherited from the 1942 report was also one of the causes of the large deficits run by the National Insurance Fund in the decade after the passage of the National Insurance Act 1946.[290] It was under the impetus of the need to bring the Fund back into balance that the National Insurance Act 1959 introduced a graduated contribution rate for the first time. Expressed as a percentage of earnings between a lower and an upper limit, it was grafted on to the basic flat rate. In return, contributors received a graduated retirement benefit as a supplement to their basic entitlement, but the extra amounts were insignificant and were, moreover, not inflation-proof. The reform was, transparently, a 'money-gathering exercise'.[291] It took a further legislative effort, in 1966, to extend the range of graduated contributions and introduce earnings-related supplements to the short-term unemployment and sickness benefits.

In 1975, following several years of debate, a fully earnings-related scheme for both the long-term and short-term benefits was introduced, and the contribution

---

[287] Cmd. 6404, at para. 273.

[288] Ibid., at p. 6. Beveridge continued to oppose plans for a universal, index-linked state pension as late as the 1960s: see N. Whiteside, 'Historical perspectives and the politics of pension reform: constructing the public-private divide', in G. Clark and N. Whiteside (eds.) *Pension Security in the 21st Century* (Oxford: Oxford University Press).   [289] Ogus, 'Great Britain', op. cit., at p. 197.

[290] D. Williams, *Social Security Taxation* (London: Sweet & Maxwell, 1982), at p. 8.

[291] Ibid., at p. 9.

structure was reorganized accordingly.[292] From this point on, contributors and their employers paid a percentage of all earnings below a specified upper limit; those with earnings below a certain level were not liable to contribute at all and so were placed (in respect of that employment) completely outside the insurance scheme.[293] This system essentially remains in place today, although the structure of contributions was altered on a number of occasions in the 1980s and 1990s with the aim of improving work incentives for workers with low earnings,[294] and the upper limit for employers' contributions was abolished with effect from 1990.[295]

However, rather than instituting a comprehensive, state-run scheme, the reforms of the 1960s and 1970s put in place a hybrid public–private regime. Occupational schemes, provided by employers, were allowed to contract out of the graduated element of the state retirement pension when it was first introduced under the Act of 1959. At that point there were around 8 million members of occupational schemes, up from nearly 2 million in 1936 and over 6 million in 1951; the figure was to rise again to 12 million by 1967.[296] The Conservative government of the early 1970s followed this logic through to its conclusion by proposing that occupational schemes should serve as the principal means for delivering retirement income, with a 'state reserve scheme' providing only for those lower-paid employees whose employers could not afford to provide an occupational scheme.[297] The Labour government which was returned to office in 1974 reversed this emphasis and put in place an extensive state earnings-related pension scheme (SERPS), which provided for the payment, on top of the basic state pension, of an inflation-proofed, earnings-related component.[298] However, the relevant legislation still allowed occupational schemes to continue to contract out of SERPS, while employer-led schemes also benefited from fiscal subsidies of various kinds. The role of the state was shifting from direct provision of benefits, to the subsidization and regulation of private occupational welfare.

5.5 The social insurance rights of married women in the post-1946 scheme

In addition to the structural limitations which were built into the financing of the post-1946 scheme, the notion of social citizenship which guided social insurance was qualified in one particularly significant respect. Consistently with the agenda

[292] The principal Acts were the Social Security Act 1975 and the Social Security Pensions Act 1975.
[293] The 1975 system is described in the early editions of Ogus and Barendt's *Law of Social Security*; see A. Ogus and E. Barendt, *The Law of Social Security* (London: Butterworths, 2nd ed., 1978), ch. 2.
[294] See this chapter below, Section 5.6.   [295] By virtue of the Social Security Act 1989, s. 1.
[296] Ogus, 'Great Britain', op. cit., at p. 198. Substantial incentives for the introduction of company-based pension schemes had already been put in place by virtue of tax law changes introduced in the Finance Act 1956.   [297] See the White Paper, *A Strategy for Pensions*, Cmnd. 4755 (1971).
[298] The Labour government's White Paper was *Better Pensions*, Cmnd. 5713 (1974), and the legislation introducing SERPS was contained in the Social Security Pensions Act 1975.

for the breadwinner wage set out in the Minority Report of 1909, married women, those in Beveridge's Class III, occupied a status entirely distinct from those in his Class I, employed earners. When drafting *Social Insurance and Allied Services*, Beveridge had relied on Census of Population returns for 1931 which showed that only 10 per cent of married women were in regular employment. In the inter-war period, all female employees (and not just those who were married) had paid lower contribution rates than men and received proportionately lower benefits under both the health and unemployment insurance schemes. Unemployment benefits for women were disproportionately low in relation to their contributions, on the assumption that women were at a higher risk than men of losing employment. The Anomalies Act 1931, passed by a Labour government under pressure to cut the liabilities of the Unemployment Fund, excluded married women contributors from access to unemployment benefit if they could not show that they had a reasonable expectation of a quick return to insurable employment.[299] Although subsequent legislation reduced the effects of this and other restrictions on 'anomalous' claims (such as those made by seasonal workers), the result was to disqualify several hundred thousand claims by married female applicants.

Beveridge argued that *single* women should be treated equally with male earners, but that a difference in treatment should continue for women who were married: this was, firstly, because family responsibilities made their participation in the insurance scheme irregular and uncertain, and, secondly, because their earnings were supplementary to those of the male breadwinner and hence, he thought, not vital for family subsistence. Thus the social insurance scheme proposed by Beveridge 'treats married women as a special insurance class of occupied persons, and treats man and wife as a team on the understanding that the great majority of married women must be regarded as occupied on work which is vital though unpaid without which their husbands could not do their paid work and without which the work of the nation could not continue'.[300]

The consequence was that '[m]aternity grant, provision for widowhood and separation and qualification for retirement pensions will be secured to all persons in Class III by virtue of their husband's contributions'.[301] Legislation confirmed this principle of derivative entitlement. Under the 1946 Act, unemployment benefits and retirement pensions were payable at a joint rate for men with dependent spouses, and at a lower, single rate in most other cases.[302] Married women

[299] On the differential contribution rates and benefits set for female contributors in inter-war legislation, and the effects of the Anomalies Act 1931, see Cohen, *Unemployment Insurance and Unemployment Assistance*, op. cit., chs. 2 and 3; for an assessment of the Act, see S. Walby, *Patriarchy at Work* (Cambridge: Polity, 1986), at pp. 172–4. It should also be borne in mind that certain female-dominated employments, such as domestic service, remained outside the social insurance scheme at this time, so that claimants for unemployment relief were required to fall back on the poor law: see Whiteside and Gillespie, 'Deconstructing unemployment', op. cit.   [300] Cmd. 6404, at para. 107.

[301] Ibid., at p. 11.

[302] The principal provision was s. 24 of the National Insurance Act 1946. This allowed a claim to be made by a working wife in respect of a husband whom she 'wholly or mainly' maintained, but only

over pensionable age and widows, but not widowers, were entitled to make derivative claims for pensions based on their spouses' contribution record.[303] In contrast to the practice under the poor law, widowhood in itself conferred the right to a long-term benefit, and not simply to temporary assistance while looking for work. The Widows', Orphans' and Old Age Contributory Pensions Act 1925 conferred the right to a widow's pension for life on the basis of the husband's insurance record, whether or not the applicant had children to look after, in part because of a perception that a contribution-based benefit of this kind should be available as of right and not on the basis of need.[304] This provision was criticized by Beveridge[305] on the grounds that childless widows of working age should be able to find remunerative employment, but his proposal to restrict the long-term benefit to widows with children was rejected. Instead, the 1946 Act made provision for a widow's pension which was payable for life if widowhood occurred after the applicant was 50 years of age, or if she ceased to receive widowed mother's allowance, which was payable in respect of dependent children, after the age of 40.[306]

Following the logic of derivative claims, the legislation gave a married woman the right to elect not to pay contributions at all, or, if she was not in employment, to pay the lower rate applicable to non-employed persons, in which case she would preserve her rights in relation to the long-term benefits.[307] However, a married woman could only qualify for a retirement pension in her own right if she had paid, over a working lifetime, contributions equivalent to half the total contributions which would have been payable had she been continuously employed throughout (the so-called 'half rule').[308] Legislation also allowed married women to be given contribution credits if they re-entered the labour force after an interval looking after other family members.[309] This provision could have assisted married women to build up a substantial contribution record notwithstanding interruptions to their earnings record, but in practice it was confined to those situations, namely widowhood and divorce, in which it was assumed that loss of a male 'breadwinner' would make it necessary for a female contributor to return to regular employment.

The overall effect of these rules was that a majority of married women did not acquire substantial benefit entitlements in their own right. In 1977–78 over

---

if the husband was 'incapable of self-support' (s. 24(2)(a)), a formula which implied a prolonged incapacity resulting from physical or mental infirmity. The equivalent provision for a husband with a dependent wife simply referred to a 'wife who is not engaged in any gainful occupation or occupations' with earnings below a certain, low threshold (initially, £1 a week).

[303] See National Insurance Act 1946, ss. 17–18 (widows' benefits) and 21 (retirement pensions for dependent wives and widows).

[304] See Wikeley, *Law of Social Security* (4th ed.), op. cit., at p. 569.

[305] *Social Insurance and Allied Services*, Cmd. 6404, at para. 346.

[306] National Insurance Act 1946, ss. 17 and 18.

[307] This was the effect of National Insurance Act 1946, s. 59, and the National Insurance (Married Women) Regulations 1948, SI 1948/1470.

[308] National Insurance Act 1946, s. 21(5); Social Security Act 1975, s. 28(2).

[309] SI 1948/1470, reg. 8.

4 million female earners were paying in at the reduced rate, and only 2.25 million at the full rate.[310] In that year legislation passed in 1975 came into effect, repealing the provisions for opting out and for the payment of reduced contributions.[311] Regulations were also passed to allow those who had chosen to opt out to continue to do so, so that only those entering the scheme for the first time after 12 May 1977 were obliged to participate in full.[312] Nevertheless, this was a substantial change, and one which reflected the increased participation of married women in paid employment which had occurred since the 1942 report.

The 1931 Census of Population on which Beveridge had relied in 1942 had reported that only just over 10 per cent of married women were in employment, compared to an activity rate of 34.2 per cent for adult women as a whole and 90.5 per cent for adult men. By 1951 the activity rate for married women had increased to 21.7 per cent; it then increased again to 29.7 per cent and by 1971 it was 42.2 per cent. The increase in the immediate post-war years was brought about in part by the abolition of the marriage bar (the formal or informal bar on women retaining full-time and regular employment following marriage) in the civil service and other occupations, and by the continuation of women's employment in a number of industries which were slow to restore pre-war practices of occupational segregation.[313] However, most of the increased labour market activity of married women took the form of part-time work. Part-time work accounted for just 4 per cent of those in employment in 1951; by 1980 the figure had reached 20 per cent, with married women making up 85 per cent of the part-time labour force.[314]

Women's part-time work 'did not threaten to disrupt the patriarchal status quo in the household, since a married woman working part-time could still perform the full range of domestic tasks'.[315] Conversely, the availability to married women of part-time work did not, in itself, upset the assumption, within social security law, of dependence on a male breadwinner. Part-time earnings supplemented the breadwinner wage. Equal pay and maternity protection legislation had yet to have a major impact on employment practices,[316] most female jobs were concentrated in a few industries as they had been prior to the advent of social security,[317] and a significant gender-pay gap remained.

Nevertheless, the reforms of the mid-1970s recognized the need for married women to have access, in their own right, to social insurance benefits, and attempted to make provision for their need to greater flexibility in contribution

[310] Williams, *Social Security Taxation*, op. cit., at para. 10-04.

[311] Social Security Pensions Act 1975, s. 3(1).

[312] SI 1975/492. For a full account of the transitional arrangements see Williams, *Social Security Taxation*, op. cit., ch. 10.   [313] Walby, *Patriarchy at Work*, op. cit., at pp. 205–6.

[314] See G. Clark, 'Recent developments in working patterns' (1982) 92 *Employment Gazette* 409–416; C. Hakim, 'Trends in the flexible workforce' (1987) 95 *Employment Gazette* 549–60.

[315] Walby, *Patriarchy at Work*, at p. 207.

[316] Equal pay legislation was introduced in 1970 and the first maternity protection legislation in 1975. On the impact of these laws in the 1980s and 1990s, see Section 5.5, below.

[317] Picchio del Mercado, *Social Reproduction of the Labour Market*, op. cit., ch. 4.

conditions. This was recognized in the structure of SERPS when it was introduced in 1975. A particularly important development was the twenty-year rule, according to which pension entitlements were based on the best twenty years of earnings, as opposed to the average of all years in employment. This was introduced in order to avoid indirect discrimination against women contributors, on the basis that they were more likely than men to have spent a number of years outside the labour force on account of domestic responsibilities.[318] The Social Security Pensions Act 1975 also abolished the 'half rule' which had made it difficult for married women with incomplete contribution records to claim the basic retirement pension, and made more generous provision for contribution credits in respect of years spent out of the workforce on account of domestic responsibilities.[319]

The social security legislation of the mid-1970s was intended to mark the culmination of several decades of efforts to implement a fully functioning social insurance system. It addressed many of the structural weaknesses of the post-1946 model and acknowledged the claims of married women to social insurance benefits in their capacity as wage earners rather than as dependants of male bread-winners. However, the new structure was barely in place before it began to fall apart; the twenty-year rule in SERPS was one of the early casualties. The immediate cause of this process was the social security legislation of the Conservative government elected in 1979 but, more fundamentally, it was brought about by the ending of the policy of full employment.

5.6 The erosion of social insurance after 1980

Notwithstanding its shortcomings, social insurance had been one of a set of inter-locking institutions which underpinned post-1945 social and economic policy. The Keynesian notion that unemployment was caused by low levels of effective demand, requiring government intervention, was supported by the political ideal of social citizenship. Because lower-income groups had a higher propensity to spend, a tax-benefit system which was broadly redistributive in their favour (thanks in particular to the progressive element in income tax) helped to maintain aggregate demand for goods and services, as did the growth in the size of the public sector. The achievement of full employment led, in turn, to the integration into the organized sectors of the labour force of those groups which had previously been excluded, and to an upgrading of their incomes and skills. Thus it was no accident that the so-called 'golden age' of Keynesianism, from around 1950 to the mid-1970s, witnessed historically high rates of economic growth along with declining income disparities. When, however, this virtuous cycle was interrupted by the combination of rapidly escalating prices and rising unemployment in the second half of the 1970s, policy makers responded to the crisis by abandoning the core beliefs of full employment policy.

[318] Social Security Pensions Act 1975, s. 6(2).　　[319] Ibid., s. 20.

While the neoliberal policy revolution of the early 1980s had many parts to it, one of its key elements was a reversion to pre-welfare state ideas of the functioning of the labour market. Economists rehabilitated the nineteenth-century theory of the marginal productivity of wages, and its central proposition that if employment was to rise, real wages (money wages deflated by product prices) needed to fall.

Neoclassical economic theory extended the classical political economy notion of the diminishing marginal productivity of land, associated with Ricardo, to capital and labour. But, whereas Ricardo's theory was based on the natural variability of the fertility of land, in neoclassical theory the constraint on labour was technical in nature. Any increase in the employment of equally productive labour relative to the amount of capital caused the output per worker to fall. If therefore, more labour was to be employed profitably, wages had to fall in proportion to the fall in labour productivity. The 'downward sloping' demand curve for labour was confronted by an 'upward sloping' supply curve. Labour supply was upward sloping because of the neoclassical economic assumption that work was inherently distasteful. Moreover, the more work was undertaken, the more distasteful it became, so that as the marginal *disutility* of work increased, ever increasing amounts of offsetting wages were required. With the increase in employment, the decline in the demand price of labour, determined by diminishing productivity, came into equality with the rising supply price, automatically securing full employment in the sense that anyone could secure work (and workers) *if they accepted the equilibrium wage*.

The theory of marginal productivity thereby reinstated the primacy of the market in determining wages and employment. If the market was free, there was no possibility of capitalist exploitation, because excess profits would simply be competed away. At the same time, any worker could enter the market provided they are prepared to accept a wage equivalent to their marginal product. As these ideas were revived in the 1970s and early 1980s, it was a short step to argue that the high unemployment of that period resulted from trade union wage pressure and restrictive practices, statutory labour market regulation, and over-generous social welfare benefits.[320] These institutional interventions were now characterized as labour market *imperfections* which raised the *natural* level of unemployment, that is, the rate which was compatible with stable prices.[321] It followed that any attempt to lower unemployment below its 'natural' or 'non-accelerating inflation' level through the maintenance of aggregate demand would either crowd out existing employment or add to inflationary pressures. The state's contribution to employment policy therefore had to be confined to the maintenance of macroeconomic stability, the elimination of labour market imperfections caused by the influence of trade unions and the effects of employment protection laws, and the restriction of social security benefits paid to the unemployed.

[320] F.A. Hayek, *1980s Unemployment and the Unions* (London: IEA, 2nd ed., 1984).
[321] M. Friedman, 'The role of monetary policy' (1968) 58 *American Economic Review* 1–17.

The implications of the new policy for social insurance were felt almost immediately following the election of the Conservative government which took office in 1979. In 1980 the earnings-related supplements for the short-term benefits (unemployment, sickness, maternity and widowhood) were abolished (with effect from 1982),[322] and allowances for dependent children, previously payable as a supplement to the contributory benefits, were ended following legislative revisions in 1982 and 1984.[323] As a result of these changes, the basic levels of unemployment and sickness benefit were only marginally above those payable, regardless of the claimant's contribution record, through the route of means-tested supplementary benefit. Recipients of unemployment benefit were still better off than those receiving supplementary benefit in one respect, namely that they were not subject to a household means test which could lead to the loss of benefit if another immediate family member was in regular employment. However, the link between contributions and earnings was further eroded by legislation which introduced a new system of benefit uprating, according to which benefits were increased each year by reference to prices rather than, as previously, by reference to whichever of wages or prices was rising most quickly.[324]

Further changes eroded the contributory principle. This was done, firstly, by reforms which tightened the relevant qualifying conditions for the receipt of unemployment benefit. From 1988 it became available only if the claimant had paid the minimum number of national insurance contributions in each of the two preceding tax years, rather than in the last preceding year as before.[325] Provision for 'reduced benefit', payable to a claimant with an incomplete contribution record, was repealed with effect from 1988,[326] at the same time as the rules governing 'requalification' for those with an interrupted earnings record were made more restrictive.[327]

A second step was to increase the grounds for disqualification from unemployment benefit. Thus in the first half of the 1980s the period of disqualification was increased from first six to thirteen and then (in the 1986 Act) to 26 weeks, and the grounds for exclusion were widened to include refusal to take part in a number of government-sponsored training schemes. The Social Security Act 1989 went further in several important respects. Now, for the first time since the inception of the unemployment insurance scheme in 1911, the low level of pay in a job no longer provided good grounds for refusing an offer of work, and claimants for the contributory benefit were required to show not just that they were 'available for work' (the previous formulation) but that they were 'actively seeking employment'.[328] The new

---

[322] Social Security (No. 2) Act 1980, s. 4.

[323] These changes were contained in the Social Security and Housing Benefit Act 1982 and the Health and Social Security Act 1984.

[324] The linking of the long-term benefits to price, rather than wage, inflation was brought about by the Social Security Act 1980, s. 1(1). In 1980–81 the short-term benefits were increased by 5 per cent less than prices (Social Security (No. 2) Act 1980). The duty to uprate benefits with prices is now contained in the Social Security Administration Act 1992, s. 150.

[325] Social Security Act 1988, s. 6.   [326] Social Security Act 1986, s. 42.

[327] Social Security Act 1989, s. 11.   [328] Social Security Act 1989, s. 12.

statutory formula was brought in at the same time as the government initiated a scheme of interviews and questionnaires designed to encourage benefit claimants to look for work, the so-called 'Restart' programme.

The process begun by the 1989 Act reached its culmination in the passage of the Jobseekers Act 1995. This formally abolished unemployment benefit and replaced it with a new benefit entitled the 'jobseeker's allowance'. The distinction between insurance-based and means-tested benefits was retained. However, the period for which the 'contribution-based allowance' could be claimed was reduced from one year to six months. The 'income-based allowance' continued to be payable to those with an inadequate contribution record or who had exhausted their insurance-based benefit. While set at a broadly similar basic level to the contributory benefit, the income-based allowance was (as before) subject to a household means test, thereby depriving claimants of benefit if their spouse or another immediate family member was in regular employment or if the household had substantial savings.

The structure of the jobseeker's allowance differed in several respects from that of unemployment benefit. The former concept of a 'day of unemployment' found no place in the new statutory scheme. Instead, a claim could proceed if the applicant was not 'engaged in remunerative work' for sixteen or more hours in the relevant week.[329] As under the previous law, the claimant had to show that he or she was both 'capable of work' and 'available for work'.[330] The basic criterion of availability was whether the claimant was 'willing and able to take up immediately any paid earner's employment';[331] regulations permitted applicants to set limits on their availability by reference to pay (for up to six months only), other terms and conditions, and locality, but no condition could be imposed unless the claimant could show that he or she had 'reasonable prospects of employment notwithstanding those restrictions'.[332] In addition, a claimant had to show that they were 'actively seeking employment'[333] as required by the 1989 amendments to the rules on unemployment benefit,[334] and that they had entered into a 'jobseeker's agreement' with the relevant employment officer. Under regulations, the jobseeker's agreement was to specify, among other things, 'action that the claimant will take to seek employment and to improve their prospects of finding work'.[335] The grounds for disqualification from receipt of the allowance included refusal to carry

---

[329] Jobseekers Act 1995, s. 1(2)(e); SI 1996/207, reg. 51.

[330] Jobseekers Act 1995, s. 1(2)(f), (a) respectively.   [331] Jobseekers Act 1995, s. 6(1).

[332] SI 1996/207, reg. 8.   [333] Jobseekers Act 1995, s. 1(2)(c).

[334] In one respect, the 1995 Act tightened up on the definition introduced in 1989, by substituting a requirement to take 'such steps as [the claimant] can reasonably be expected to take in order to have the best prospects of securing employment' for the former obligation to take steps to secure '*offers* of employment' (emphasis added): see Wikeley, *Law of Social Security* 5th ed., op. cit., at p. 348.

[335] SI 1996/207, reg. 31. For discussion of the effects of the jobseeker's agreement and other aspects of the Jobseekers Act which affect the autonomy of claimants, see and M. Freedland and D. King, 'Contractual governance and illiberal contracts: some problems of contractualism as an instrument of behaviour management by agencies of government' (2003) 27 *Cambridge Journal of Economics* 465–477.

out a 'jobseeker's direction'[336] (a written direction from an employment officer with a view to 'assisting the claimant to find employment' and/or 'improving the claimant's chances of being employed'[337]) and refusing to apply for or accept a suitable job vacancy; for the purpose of the latter, 'any matter relating to the remuneration in the employment in question' was to be disregarded.[338] By these various means, the Jobseekers Act formalized the kind of close scrutiny of individual cases which had accompanied the Restart programme of the late 1980s. The Act was retained by the New Labour government elected in 1997 and the principle of penalizing those who refused offers of training and/or employment by the withdrawal of benefit was incorporated into its 'new deal' programme of support for the young and long-term unemployed.[339]

These changes to the short-term contributory benefits must be put in the context of a social security system which even at the start of the 1980s was heavily reliant on means-testing. The earnings-related supplement to unemployment benefit had been a late addition to the flat-rate payment. It offered, at best, an imperfect link to previous earnings, and only a minority of workers drew a tangible benefit from its introduction; on the eve of its repeal, only around one quarter of all unemployed were receiving it.[340] The incidence of long-term unemployment would have been a major cause of growing dependence on means-testing during this period in its own right. However, as a result of the changes made to the contributory scheme, less than a fifth of the unemployed (or 'jobseekers') now receive an insurance-related benefit, even at a time of comparatively low unemployment by the standards of the past two decades (see Table 3.1). The value of the means-tested benefits was also reduced as a result of the replacement of supplementary benefit by income support following the Social Security Act 1986.

Table 3.1. Types of benefits paid to claimant unemployed 1978–2002

	1978	1988	1998	2002
Claimant unemployed (000s)	1152	1903	1231	872
Claimant unemployed receiving benefits (000s) % of which received:	938	1566	1113	787
Unemployment benefit only	41.2	24.5	14.1	19.8
Unemployment plus means-tested benefits	8.5	7.3	2.2	2.3
Means-tested benefits only	50.2	68.1	83.7	77.9

Source: Department of Health and Social Security, *Annual Report*, various years.

[336] Jobseekers Act 1995, s. 19(5)(a).   [337] Jobseekers Act 1995, s. 19(1)(b).
[338] Ibid., s. 19(9).   [339] See Section 5.7 of this chapter, below.
[340] J. Micklewright, 'The strange case of British earnings-related unemployment benefit' (1989) 18 *Journal of Social Policy* 527–548. On the salience of means-testing in the post-1945 system, see P. Alcock, '"A better partnership between state and individual provision": social security into the 1990s' (1989) 16 *Journal of Law and Society* 97–111.

The 1980s and 1990s also marked a turning point in the operation of the long-term benefits, most notably the retirement pension. The changes to the benefit uprating system which were introduced in the early 1980s had far-reaching consequences for the basic state pension. Because the 1980s and 1990s were periods of low price inflation and relatively high levels of increases in real wages, the linking of the basic pension to prices meant that it lost much of its value as a replacement for earnings. At its inception it had been pegged at one fifth of male average gross earnings, but by the mid-1990s it had fallen to 15 per cent and by 1998 it had dropped below the level of means-tested income support for the oldest single pensioners.[341] In the same year, 1.7 million pensioners were receiving income support, an additional 1.3 million received council tax benefit, and almost 1 million received assistance with housing costs.[342]

The additional state pension, SERPS, continued at first to be linked to earnings. The earnings formula and contribution requirements put in place for SERPS in the mid-1970s had been designed to provide a pension linked to earnings averaged over the best twenty years of a claimant's working lifetime. As we have seen, this was done in order to ensure that claimants with an irregular and discontinuous employment record of the kind which would previously have made it difficult for them to obtain a substantial retirement pension could now do so; married women had been expected to benefit most from this change. However, the Social Security Act 1986 abolished this 'twenty-year rule' for claims from the year 2000, replacing it with an entitlement equivalent to a fifth of average earnings over an entire working lifetime (to get a full pension, men would normally have to work for 44 years up to the age of 65 and women 39 years to the age of 60). Although the 1986 Act also made it possible to discount years when the claimant 'was precluded from regular employment by responsibilities at home', this statutory formula did not clearly allow for the exclusion of years during which the claimant was in regular *part-time* work, thereby offering little support to the many married women with domestic responsibilities who were in this position. The 1986 Act also implemented a straight cut in SERPS entitlement, so that it was to be calculated using an earnings factor of 20 per cent of earnings between the upper and lower limits for contributions, rather than 25 per cent as before.[343]

In addition, the 1986 Act loosened the conditions upon which occupational schemes could contract out of SERPS.[344] Under the 1975 legislation, employer-based pension schemes could only contract out if they took the form of a 'defined benefit scheme' under which the employer undertook to make a payment calculated as a proportion of either the employee's final salary or their average

341 J. McCormick, 'Prospects for pension reform', in J. McCormick and C. Oppenheim (eds.) *Welfare in Working Order* (London: Institute for Public Policy Research, 1998) 175–249.

342 For details see H. Reed and S. Deakin, 'United Kingdom', in J. van Vugt and J. Peet (eds.) *Social Security and Solidarity in the European Union* (Heidelberg: Physica-Verlag, 1999) 182–222.

343 Social Security Act 1986, s. 18.

344 Social Security Act 1986, Part I.

salary calculated over a certain number of years. The 1986 Act made it possible for employers to offer, as an alternative to defined benefit schemes, 'money-purchase' or 'defined contribution' schemes under which the final payout was dependent on the financial performance of the fund into which the contributions were invested, thereby transferring the investment risk from the employer to the employee. The 1986 Act also made it possible for individual employees to take out personal retirement plans, giving them the right to opt out of SERPS or any relevant employer-based scheme. This led to widespread defection from SERPS and, to a lesser extent, from employer-based schemes. Notwithstanding accusations of pensions 'mis-selling' and some restoration of membership to occupational schemes in the early 1990s, this was an historic shift: by 1998 there were 10 million individuals in personal schemes, 10 million in occupational schemes (down from 12 million in the early 1980s) and only 7 million in SERPS.[345]

Legislation in the 1990s extended the deregulatory agenda of the 1986 Act by altering the minimum contracting out requirements for defined benefit schemes. Under the Social Security Act 1975, occupational schemes had been required to provide a guaranteed minimum pension or GMP which was broadly equivalent to the level of benefit which the employee would have received under SERPS. The Pensions Act 1995 replaced the GMP with a weaker 'requisite benefits test' under which the link with SERPS was removed. Thus the overall effect of these complex changes in pensions law was two-fold: they greatly extended the scope for employer-led and personal pension provision outside the structure of the additional state pension, while reducing the role of SERPS as a *de facto* floor of rights for private pension provision.

Pensions policy since the election of the 'New Labour' government in 1997 has reversed some of the changes made by the Conservative administrations of the 1980s, in particular by improving provision for contributors with irregular earnings records, but in other respects it has confirmed the decline in the role of social insurance as a mechanism for providing retirement income. The 1998 Green Paper, *A New Contract for Welfare: Partnership in Pensions*,[346] set out proposals for the formal abolition of SERPS and its replacement by a new 'second state pension' or S2P which would be introduced in two phases. In the first phase, which was implemented with effect from April 2002 by the Child Support, Pensions and Social Security Act 2000, the earnings-related principle of SERPS was retained, and a pensions formula was introduced which targeted benefit increases on low earners. The assumption behind this policy was that higher earners who were unlikely to benefit from this structure would contract out of SERPS if they had not already done so.

The current government has also taken steps to encourage low and medium earners to make independent provision for retirement by requiring employers

---

[345] See Reed and Deakin, 'United Kingdom', op. cit.   [346] Cm. 4719.

who do not provide an occupational scheme to offer their employees access to a 'stakeholder pension'.[347] This is, in essence, a money-purchase pension or saving scheme which offers, for earners up to a threshold currently in the mid £20,000s, a simpler and more generous tax and regulatory regime than other occupational or personal pension schemes which are contracted out of SERPS. The employer is not under an obligation to *contribute* to a stakeholder pension, merely to ensure that the employee has access to a private pensions provider, and take up has so far been limited. Nevertheless, the second phase of the S2P, if it were implemented, would end the earnings link for the additional state pension, replacing it with a flat-rate pension (but with the preservation of accrued earnings-related benefits under SERPS and the first phase of the S2P). At present, this option is being kept under review. However, a move back to flat-rate benefits would be consistent with other aspects of policy since 1997, in particular the use of means-tested benefits to top-up pensioners' incomes.[348]

There is a sense in which the changes just described for both the short-term and the long-term benefits mark a return to the minimal 'subsistence' model of social insurance which Beveridge himself had advocated in the 1940s, and which had operated prior to the introduction of earnings-related contributions and benefits over the course of the 1960s and 1970s. This development could once have been explained as a response to the particular economic circumstances of the 1980s, and in particular to the steep rise in unemployment from 5 per cent in 1979 to over 12 per cent in 1983. High unemployment, if it continues for a period of time, inevitably threatens the financial stability of social insurance schemes which, because they apply the pay-as-you-go principle, depend on current contributions to pay for outgoings. Measures aimed at dealing with this problem by raising the level of contributions from those still in work and tightening up on claims are not necessarily hostile to the philosophy of social insurance, as long as they are temporary in nature.

This type of justification was indeed offered for the substantial rises in national insurance contribution levels and cuts in benefits which occurred during the 1980s. However, it is instructive, in this respect, to compare the experience of the 1980s with the previous period of mass unemployment in the 1920s and 1930s.[349] Then, high and persistent levels of unemployment delayed but did not fundamentally disrupt the long-term movement towards a mature social insurance system. In the early 1920s, when the unemployment insurance fund was in

---

[347] The relevant legislation here is the Welfare Reform and Pensions Act 1999.

[348] The first step in this process was the introduction in April 1999 of a minimum income guarantee for pensioners, which was in effect a 'rebadging and improvement in benefit levels for pensioners on income support' (Wikeley, *Law of Social Security* 5th ed., op. cit., at p. 596); the second step was the establishment of a new pension credit, designed to top-up pensioner income, under the State Pension Credit Act 2002. The pension credit seeks to avoid some of the disincentive effects of means-testing by means of a new 'savings credit'. See Wikeley, *Law of Social Security* 5th ed., op. cit., at pp. 597–8.

[349] See Section 5.2, above.

deficit, the device of 'uncovenanted benefit' was used to make it possible for benefits to be paid to claimants whose insurance entitlements had been exhausted, on the basis of the useful fiction that these payments would be set against future contributions. In the 1930s, when the numbers in receipt of means-tested unemployment benefits exceeded those receiving insurance-based payments, the response of the Royal Commission of 1930–32 and the Unemployment Act of 1934 was not to dissolve the distinction between the two forms of benefit, but, on the contrary, to formalize it.[350] The 1930s also saw the removal of the controversial 'genuinely seeking employment' test for unemployment benefit, to which the more recent 'actively seeking employment' formula marks something of a return.

A closer look at the financing of the national insurance system during the 1980s and 1990s also casts doubt on the argument that the changes made during this period were simply responses to short-run economic difficulties. While periodic funding crises did occur, and were often the catalysts for legislative change, other factors were at work. As contributions rose (in the early 1980s they were increased from 6.5 to 9 per cent for employees and from 10 to 10.45 per cent for employers) the National Insurance Fund moved quickly back into surplus. However, rather than using this as an occasion to restore the earnings link for the basic state pension, the then Conservative governments took advantage of the opportunity to cut the contribution made by government from general taxation, the 'Treasury supplement'. This had been fixed at 18 per cent in 1975; it was lowered to 13 per cent in 1983 and 5 per cent in 1988 before being abolished in 1989. At the same time, the proportion of national insurance contributions which was paid over to the National Health Service was increased, further removing the pressure on general taxation. By 1988–89, contributions paid into the Fund exceeded outgoings by 18 per cent; at this time, revenue raised from national insurance contributions was over three-quarters of that collected through income tax, whereas in 1949–50, as the post-war national insurance system was being put in place, it had been only one quarter.[351]

National insurance contributions had become, in effect, a substitute for income taxation, during a period when it was a major priority of government to remove the higher income tax bands and to reduce the basic, headline rate of tax. This policy was an inegalitarian one, since income tax rates continued, to some degree, to rise with earnings, whereas national insurance contributions, because of the cap imposed by the upper earnings limit, had a regressive impact (although after 1989 the effect of this was mitigated to some degree by the removal of the upper limit for employers' contributions). It also served further to undermine the contributory principle: during precisely the same period when the link between benefits and earnings was being broken, national insurance contributions not only continued to

350 Ogus, 'Great Britain', op. cit., at p. 189.
351 See S. Deakin and F. Wilkinson, 'Labour law, social security and economic inequality' (1991) 15 *Cambridge Journal of Economics* 125–148.

Table 3.2. National Insurance Fund, benefits and contributions, 1978–2002

	1978	1988	1998	2002
Total National Insurance Fund Benefits (£m.)	10521	26830	44861	53160
Total National Insurance Fund Contributions (£m.)	10078	31394	52968	63372
% contributed by:				
Employers	60.2	52.6	54.2	56.3
Employees	36.6	44.3	42.5	40.3
Self-employed and non-employed	3.2	3.1	3.3	3.4
Contributions as percentages of benefits	95.7	117.0	118.1	119.2

Source: Office of National Statistics, *United Kingdom National Accounts*, various years.

be earnings-related, but represented a growing call on lower and middle income earners. In the late 1980s it was predicted that 'as earnings steadily diverge from prices the gap could become exponential'.[352] In the short run, this windfall for government failed to materialize, in part because of an unexpected consequence of the decision to allow individuals to leave SERPS and set up a personal pension scheme; the numbers opting out after 1988 were so large that the Fund went into deficit again, and the Treasury supplement had to be brought back in 1993, under the name of the Treasury grant. However, the financial position of the Fund was subsequently stabilized and it moved back into surplus, making it possible for the Treasury grant to be reduced once again to zero (see Table 3.2).

The opportunistic use of national insurance finances to cross-subsidize other areas of public expenditure in the 1980s and 1990s highlighted structural weaknesses in the post-war design of social insurance. Although Beveridge had recognized that the principle of state compulsion removed the necessity for pre-funding of benefits, his scheme had attempted to put in place mechanisms for maintaining the integrity of the National Insurance Fund; in particular, contribution rates were to be set according to actuarial calculations of the extent of future claims. One implication of this was that the full retirement pension should not be paid until a number of years had elapsed and the Fund had been stabilized (Beveridge suggested a twenty-year period). In the event, this recommendation was ignored, and provision was made in the National Insurance Act 1946 for immediate payment of pensions at the full rate; a high level of Exchequer contribution was required to make this possible and to introduce a degree of ex-post inflation proofing. However, when graduated contributions were introduced in the course of the 1960s and 1970s, most notably in the context of SERPS, an actuarial element was introduced into the calculation and revaluation (to reflect inflation) of individuals' 'earnings factors', and provision was made to phase in the payment of full earnings-related pensions over a twenty-five year period.

---

[352] W. Keegan, 'Lawson's miracle: is it all done with mirrors?' *The Guardian* (London), 7 November 1988.

Yet the experience of the 1980s and 1990s demonstrated that the Fund's boundaries were porous; according to shifting governmental priorities, revenues could be made to flow out of the Fund to support wider expenditure, with the process being reversed from time to time to meet short-term funding crises. The necessary changes could be made by the normal process of legislative revision and were presented to Parliament as issues of a technical, rather than a constitutional, nature. As a result, efforts to provide the scheme with a firm actuarial basis had no true foundation; benefit payments were dependent, in the final analysis, on decisions taken in the wider context of governments' economic policies and expenditure plans.

The Labour government elected in 1997, rather than taking steps to strengthen the institutional structure of social insurance, continued the policy of using increases in national insurance contributions as a surrogate for income tax rises; in 2002 a one-off rise in contributions was presented as a way of raising funding for the National Health Service. It also confirmed shortly after its election in 1997 that it would not overturn the decision of earlier Conservative administrations to devalue the basic retirement pension by linking it to prices. By now it was clear that the restructuring of social insurance was not a set of temporary or crisis measures, but rather part of a historic shift away from the contributory principle in favour of the 'targeting' of benefits.

5.7 From full employment to activation policy

In Beveridge's notion of full employment it was the responsibility of the state to ensure that work was made available at wages which would support family subsistence and ensure the elimination of poverty. This vision was challenged by the neoliberal turn in economic and social policy at the start of the 1980s; now the state's role was to create the conditions in which the labour market, and other markets, could function. This did not imply any particular commitment to stable employment, nor to the maintenance of a breadwinner wage. On the contrary, government policy sought to encourage alternative forms of employment as a contribution both to labour flexibility and to the opening up of employment opportunities for excluded groups.

This process began in the early 1980s with the adoption of a number of ad hoc measures of so-called active labour market policy. Prior to this point, the payment of temporary subsidies to employers as an emergency response to conditions of economic recession had been arranged in a way which was compatible with the traditional goal of stabilizing employment. In the case of both the Temporary Employment Subsidy and the Temporary Short-Time Working Compensation Scheme, which operated under the Labour government of the late 1970s,[353] subsidies were paid with the aim of preserving full-time, regular employment in

---

[353] See R.M. Lindley, 'Active manpower policy', in G. Bain (ed.) *Industrial Relations in Britain* (Oxford: Blackwell) 339–360; E. Szyszcak, *Partial Unemployment: The Regulation of Short-Time Working in Britain* (London: Mansell, 1990).

industries affected by a fall in demand. By contrast, schemes introduced after 1980 targeted subsidies on to forms of work which were temporary and often, in practice, casual in nature. The Youth Opportunities Programme and its successor, the Youth Training Scheme, created new forms of status which were outside the traditional legal categories. It was unclear whether trainees on these programmes (who were generally young people between the ages of sixteen and eighteen who had recently finished their schooling) had a contract with their employer or 'managing agent'; the balance of legal opinion was that they did not, or that if they did, this was not a contract of employment or apprenticeship unless the employer took steps to make it so.[354] The terms upon which payments were made by the state (through various agencies including the Manpower Services Commission and later the Training Commission) to employers and other managing agents of these programmes imposed only a general obligation to offer training and work experience, which was loosely monitored, and trainees had no expectation of continuing employment once their programme came to an end, which would occur after one or two years. Nevertheless, the principle was established, during this period, that refusal to take part in a YOP or YTS scheme would constitute grounds for the withdrawal of income support. This was later extended to other schemes for the young unemployed, such as the New Workers Scheme which was introduced in the mid-1980s, and remains in place today in the context of the new deal scheme.

A second area of policy to be affected by the targeting of subsidies on to low-paid and irregular work was the interaction of employment taxes and social security benefits. The significance of this area was identified by the 1985 White Paper, *Employment: The Challenge for the Nation*. Having asserted that labour market rigidities, and not the level of aggregate demand, were responsible for unemployment, it identified a role for government in addressing the issue of labour supply: 'the supply-side is crucial, and that needs an efficient labour market'.[355] This meant using the tax-benefit system to improve the incentives of employers to make offers of employment and workers to accept them:

the interaction of the tax and National Insurance systems with the benefit system can mean that the unemployed have little incentive to move into lower paid jobs, and that employers feel bound to pitch wages at a level which reduces the number of jobs which they can offer. The 1985 Budget made a direct and forceful attack on these problems by its action on income tax thresholds and on National Insurance Contributions.[356]

This was a reference to the introduction of 'banded' contribution rates. The idea of using national insurance contributions as a form of employment subsidy initially arose as a result of an unexpected feature of the legislation which had been put in place in the mid-1970s. Under that system, employees with earnings below

---

[354] *Daley* v. *Allied Suppliers Ltd.* [1983] IRLR 14; see S. Deakin and G. Morris, *Labour Law* (London: Butterworths, 3rd ed., 2001), at pp. 168–169.   [355] Cmnd. 9474, at para. 5.4.
[356] Ibid., at para. 7.10.

the lower earnings limit were exempt from paying Class 1 national insurance contributions, as were their employers; as a result, part-time work at low weekly rates of pay did not constitute insurable employment. However, because there was no equivalent to the personal allowance which protected low-paid earners from liability for income tax, once earnings moved above the lower limit, contributions became payable on *all* income from that employment, and not just that part of it which was above the threshold (this effect was later described as a national insurance 'entry fee'). In effect, the structure operated, from the employer's point of view, as a subsidy to low-paid, part-time employment. In line with this effect, there was evidence that part-time work below the threshold was growing quickly in the late 1970s and early 1980s.[357]

From the employee's point of view, the incentive effects were less clear. The contribution structure set a punitive marginal tax rate, in the sense that for every additional pound earned above the lower limit, a high cost had to be met in the form of a deduction (the primary Class 1 national insurance contribution) on all earnings, and not simply the extra amount. The legislation of the mid-1970s had set the lower earnings limit at a level roughly equivalent to one fifth of weekly earnings; formally, it was expressed as a proportion of the basic state pension. When the basic pension was pegged to prices rather than wages after 1981, the level of the lower earnings limit was, like the basic pension, depressed in relation to average wages. However, this did not stop the numbers employed below the threshold from increasing. Between 1982 and 1987, while those employed on part-time work under thirty hours per week grew by a third, those working below sixteen hours per week doubled.[358]

The 1985 Budget sought to take advantage of the implicit national insurance contribution subsidy by providing that for those employees earning above the lower limit, contributions should rise in bands from the lowest rate of 5 per cent to the then top rates of 9 per cent for employees and 10.45 per cent for employers. Once the higher band was reached, the increased rate became payable on all earnings and not just those above the relevant threshold. In the words of the White Paper, these changes, along with related increases in the thresholds for income tax,

will make a substantial difference to job prospects, especially for the young and unskilled on whom unemployment now weighs heaviest. The effect helps in a double way: it cuts the

---

[357] According to O. Robinson and J. Wallace, 'Growth and utilisation of part-time labour in Great Britain' (1984) 92 *Employment Gazette* 391–97, those with earnings below the thresholds constituted 18 per cent of all part-time workers (those working less than 30 hours per week) in 1975 but 33 per cent by 1982. See C. Hakim, 'Workforce restructuring, social insurance coverage and the black economy' (1990) 18 *Journal of Social Policy* 471–503 for discussion of the basis on which these calculations were made, and separate estimates of the numbers affected by the thresholds for the late 1980s.

[358] At this point the 16-hours threshold was a rough proxy for the effect of the lower earnings limit, since employers tended to combine payments below the national insurance threshold with employment for less than the 16 hours normally needed to acquire statutory employment protection: see Deakin and Wilkinson, 'Labour law, social security and economic inequality', op. cit.

cost of employing workers, and by leaving more of their pay in their own pockets, heightens their incentive to work at wages employers can afford.[359]

This reform was a direct application of the theory of the natural or non-accelerating rate of unemployment, whose adherents argued that high unemployment had been caused in part by increases in national insurance contributions and employers' occupational pension payments in the period between 1975 and 1985.[360] As an experiment in the use of supply side incentives to encourage employment, it did not endure; the separate bands were abolished by the New Labour government in 1999 as part of its policy of attempting to reduce the worst effects of high marginal tax rates for the low paid. However, in the sense of establishing a benchmark for policy, it was to prove highly significant.

The most important step in the development of this policy was the introduction of family credit in 1988. This was a key reform to emerge from the comprehensive review of social security launched by the Conservative government in 1984 and which culminated in the Social Security Act 1986. A mechanism for supporting the income of low-paid workers with families, family income supplement (FIS), was already in place. This operated on a relatively small scale and was not intended to influence either the wages offered by employers, or the labour supply decisions of individuals. Family credit was designed as a low-wage supplement replacing FIS; however, rather than being paid as a cash benefit to the household (in practice, to the mother), it was originally to be paid as an addition to the wages of the principal earner (normally the father) and set off against their national insurance and income tax payments.[361] In this way, it would function in the same way as the reforms to national insurance contribution thresholds in the 1985 Budget, namely to provide a subsidy to employers to take on workers at rates of pay which they could 'afford'. This intention was not carried through to the final form of the legislation;[362] the government accepted an argument that the new credit should be directed, as before, to the household as a cash payment. However, the principle that social security payments could be used as a substitute for wages, as a way of topping up low incomes to subsistence level, had been re-established, 150 years after its condemnation by the 1834 poor law report: it was hoped that the new credit would take up expected declines in wages following the abolition, around this time, of minimum wages rates set by the Wages Councils.[363]

---

[359] Cmnd. 9474, at para. 7.10.

[360] R. Layard and S. Nickell, 'The causes of British unemployment' (1985) 111 *National Institute Economic Review* 62–85.

[361] Department of Health and Social Security, *Reform of Social Security: Programme for Change*, Volume 2, Cmnd. 9518 (London: HMSO, 1985), at p. 49.

[362] Family credit was introduced by the Social Security Act 1986, Part II, and SI 1987/1793; the legislation was later consolidated in the Social Security Contributions and Benefits Act 1992.

[363] Department of Employment, *Wages Councils Consultation Document* (London: Department of Employment, 1988).

In the event, the design of family credit was defective and this blunted its potential impact on labour supply. One problem was that other aspects of the social security system continued to respect the principle that benefits should not be paid in partial substitution for wages; the 'earnings disregards' which allowed income support to be combined with wages were set at impractically low levels, while the 'full extent normal' rule prevented unemployment benefit from being combined with regular part-time work.[364] Nor was family credit effectively integrated with these other benefits. The income support rules imposed an absolute bar on combining benefits with wages if the claimant worked more than sixteen hours per week, but family credit, to begin with, was only available if the claimant was in regular employment for more than 24 hours per week. The overall effect was that the Conservative reforms had effects upon labour supply incentives which were often the opposite of those intended; because high marginal tax rates on low earnings just above the basic level of social security support remained in place, there was a significant 'unemployment trap' effect for those moving into paid work and a 'poverty trap' effect for those already in employment.[365]

It was left to the Labour government elected in 1997 to complete the process of aligning the tax and benefit systems begun in the mid-1980s. The incidence of punitive marginal rates of taxation on low incomes was reduced by the abolition of the so-called 'entry fee' for national insurance contributions[366] and by the alignment of the lower earnings limit with the personal allowance for income tax.[367] At the same time, provision was made to extend the attribution of national insurance credits (in lieu of contributions) for those with very low weekly earnings.[368] The original objective of the 1985 social security review, namely that family credit should be paid as an addition to wages and not as a cash benefit, was finally achieved in 2000 under its more comprehensive and generous successor, the working families tax credit (WFTC). A tax credit scheme for disabled workers was put in place at the same time.[369] The rate of increase in the number of claimants and the extent of expenditure since the introduction of WFTC is considerable, while over time it has come to form an increasing proportion of average female low-paid earnings, increasing the substitution effect (see Tables 3.3 and 3.4 and Figure 3.1). In 2003 a similar scheme including single earners, the

[364] On the 'full extent normal' and 'normal idle day' rules in unemployment benefit, see N. Wikeley, *Ogus, Barendt and Wikeley's Law of Social Security* (London: Butterworths, 4th ed., 1995), p. 89 et seq.

[365] Deakin and Wilkinson, 'Labour law, social security and economic inequality', op. cit., at pp. 134–5.   [366] Social Security Act 1998, s. 51.

[367] Welfare Reform and Pensions Act 1999, s. 73 and Sched. 9, amending the Social Security Benefits and Contributions Act 1992, ss. 5–6, 8–9.

[368] Social Security Benefits and Contributions Act 1992, s. 6A, as inserted by the Welfare Reform and Pensions Act 1999. This change was made in order to avoid a situation in which those on earnings above the former lower earnings limit but below the new primary threshold would have been excluded from insurable employment; see Wikeley, *Law of Social Security* 5th ed., op. cit., at p. 107.

[369] The relevant legislation, in both cases, was the Tax Credits Act 1999.

Table 3.3. Family income supplement, 1971–1988

	No of Recipients 000s	Average award £s weekly	Annual cost £000s
1971	55	1.73	4,947
1972	89	2.39	11,060
1973	87	2.61	11,808
1974	76	2.24	8,852
1975	57	2.82	8,358
1976	60	3.47	10,826
1977	84	4.88	21,315
1978	96	5.58	27,855
1979	78	5.17	20,969
1980	88	7.85	35,922
1981	112	9.95	57,949
1982	143	10.54	78,375
1983	186	12	116,064
1984	203	12.2	128,783
1985	199	12.2	126,246
1986	200	13.5	140,400
1987	220	15.2	173,888
1988	213	15.74	174,336

Source: Institute of Fiscal Studies, *Fiscal Facts*, Family Credit Recipients, www.ifs.org.uk/taxsystem/fcclaims.shtmt (2004).

Table 3.4. Family credit and working family tax credit, 1988–2002

	No of Recipients 000s	Average award £s weekly	Annual cost £000s
1988	261	28.31	384,223
1989	303	25.55	402,566
1990	315.2	28.23	462,701
1991	346.6	31.32	564,487
1992	396.7	37.69	777,484
1993	488.3	43.34	1100,472
1994	550.9	47.09	1348,978
1995	607.8	50.17	1585,653
1996	693	55.41	1996,755
1997	747.7	57.85	2249,231
1998	767.1	59.21	2361,839
1999	790.9	62.85	2584,819
2000	1024	73.13	3894,026
2001	1214.8	79.41	5016,298
2002	1302.2	83.75	5671,081

Source: Inland Revenue Analysis and Research, *Working Families' Tax Credit Statistics*, February 2003.

Note: Annual cost = No. of recipients × Average award × 52.

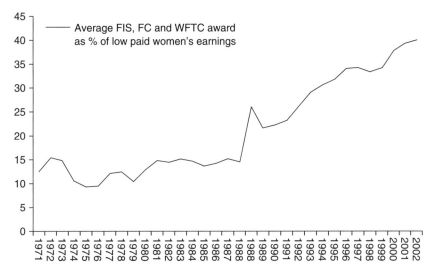

Figure 3.1 Average FIS, FC and WFTC award as % of low paid women's earnings

Sources: Family Credit and Family Income Supplement: 1971 to 1988 Institute of Fiscal Studies, 2000, *Fiscal Facts: Family Credit Recipients*, http://www.ifs.org.uk/taxsystem/fcclaims.shtml; 1988 to 2002 Inland Revenue, 2003, *Working Family Tax Credit Statistics, Summary Statistics*; Office of National Statistics. *New Earnings Survey*, various years.

Note 1: Low-paid women's average earnings were calculated by taking an unweighted average of the weekly earnings for representative low-paid women's occupations derived from the New Earnings Survey (NES) for 1973 to 1999. Estimates for 1971, 1972, and 2000, 2001 and 2002 were calculated by adjusting the low-paid women's earnings for 1973 and 1999 respectively using the official Average Earnings Index.

Occupations used in constructing the index of occupational earnings (the Standard Occupational Classification used for the NES was changed in 1991):

1973–1990:
Sales persons, shop assistants and shelf fillers; chefs/cooks; Barmaids; kitchen hands; home and domestic helps, maids; hospital ward orderlies; sewing machinists (textiles); repetitive assemblers (metal and electric).

1991–1999:
Sales assistants; chefs/cooks; bar staff; kitchen porters, hands; cleaners, domestics; hospital ward assistants; sewing machinists, menders, darners and embroiderers; assemblers and lineworkers (electrical and electronic).

Note 2: Glossary: FIS = Family Income Supplement; FC = Family Credit; WFTC = Working Family Tax Credit.

working tax credit, replaced WFTC.[370] Tax credits are also built into the flagship 'new deal' scheme which offers training, work experience and advice on job search for the long-term unemployed.

The philosophy underlying these changes was summed up in the 2000 Budget Report as follows:

The Government's aim is employment opportunity for all—the modern definition of full employment. Macroeconomic stability is a prerequisite to achieving this aim. But it needs to be backed up by microeconomic policies to ensure that individuals throughout the

---

[370] Under the Tax Credits Act 2002. An additional child tax credit, payable to the principal carer (rather than the main earner) in the household, supplements the working tax credit for families with children. See generally Wikeley, *Law of Social Security* 5th ed., op. cit., ch. 10.

country are able to compete effectively for jobs, that there is a secure transition from welfare to work and that employment is financially rewarding. The Government's long-term employment ambition is that a greater proportion of people should be in work than ever before.[371]

The emphasis on mobilizing the labour supply was coupled with the view that low wages could not be expected, of themselves, to provide access to a subsistence income. The enactment of the statutory national minimum wage (NMW) with effect from 1999[372] did not affect this assessment. The government argued that the NMW prevented employers from simply cutting pay in response to the availability of the various low-income tax credits: '[t]he national minimum wage, by setting a floor for wages, is essential to ensure that low-income workers enjoy the full benefit of the tax credit'.[373] But it was also prepared to accept that the NMW did not represent a living wage: a minimum wage set at a level equivalent to half of the average household income 'could well have adverse consequences for the employment of low-skilled workers, particularly the young'. The advantage of tax credits in this context was that they 'do not raise the direct cost of low-wage workers to employers'.[374]

Beveridge's policy of *regulating* and *stabilizing* the labour supply has thereby been replaced by its opposite, namely a policy aimed at *activating* it. In the same way, the goal of *reducing unemployment* has given way to that of *increasing the employment rate*. These two objectives are not the same. 'Unemployment' is a status defined by reference to a particular type of work relationship, namely stable and well-remunerated employment. A 'high employment rate' by contrast, need not imply that all or even a majority of those who are employed have access to either a living wage or a regular job. It was therefore appropriate that unemployment benefit, and with it the legal status of 'unemployment', were formally abolished in the mid-1990s as this policy shift was taking place; the move to the 'jobseeker's allowance' was significant in both a symbolic and a practical sense.[375]

A similar process has occurred with the concept of retirement. The national insurance legislation of the 1940s, true to Beveridge's intentions, placed a bar on combining receipt of the retirement pension with a significant level of income from waged employment. In 1989, however, the 'retirement' condition and 'earnings rule' which together ensured this result were abolished. At the time the reform was presented as a liberalizing measure which would enable older workers

---

[371] HM Treasury, *Budget Report* (2002), Section 4.

[372] By virtue of the National Minimum Wage Act 1998. See Chapter 4, below.

[373] HM Treasury, *Tackling Poverty and Making Work Pay—Tax Credits for the 21st Century, The Modernisation of Britain's Tax and Benefit System No. 6*, March 2000, at p. 17.

[374] HM Treasury, *Tackling Poverty and Making Work Pay*, at p. 16.

[375] The same point about the distinction between full employment and increasing the employment rate applies to the evolution of the European Employment Strategy since the mid-1990s. See O. De Schutter and S. Deakin (eds.) *Social Rights and Market Forces: Is the Open Coordination of Employment and Social Policies the Future of Social Europe?* (Brussels: Bruylant, 2005).

to continue working up to their full capacity if they chose to do so.[376] It can however also be seen as an important step in the erosion of the practice of treating 'retirement' as a clear-cut event.

In practice, the abolition of the retirement condition had little impact on the numbers continuing to work after they reached state pensionable age. It was estimated that less than 2,500 individuals would be affected by the abolition of the earnings rule, whereas the numbers working after retirement and thereby deferring their pension entitlements numbered some 100,000, although this figure had declined from 250,000 in the early 1970s.[377] Large numbers were already in retirement *before* they reached state pensionable age. This was due to the practice, which began as a response to the recessions and job cuts of the 1980s and 1990s of large numbers accepting redundancy coupled with early retirement. In 2003, only 8 per cent of men and 9 per cent of women were in employment after reaching the state pensionable age (65 for men and 60 for women) and fully one third of those aged between 50 and the state pensionable age were classed as 'economically inactive'.[378] The logic of activation policy operated here too: in the words of the 2003 pensions Green Paper *Simplicity, Security and Choice*:

[i]ncreasing employment among older workers is essential if we are to address the pensions challenge. Working longer can dramatically reduce the rate at which people need to save for their retirement. The Government inherited relatively high inactivity rates among those aged 50 and over in 1997—something we have already done much to tackle. But many people willing to, and capable of, work still do not have the opportunities they need. We cannot allow this waste of older workers' experience and talents to continue. Using these talents is vital both to the economy and to the quality of life of older people. We must remove the cliff edge between work and retirement.[379]

As a result, government policy began to turn to the view that older workers should not just be *permitted* to work, but should be *encouraged* and on occasion *required* to do so. Under the heading 'extending opportunities for older workers', *Simplicity, Security and Choice* set out a range of options. These were not confined to offering enhanced financial incentives for deferred retirement, but also included *mandating* the participation in the new deal of workers between the ages of 50 and 59 once they had been in receipt of the jobseeker's allowance for a period of eighteen months. Proposals to require long-term recipients of incapacity bene-fit to take part in the new deal, announced in the Green Paper *Pathways to Work* in 2002,[380] would also principally affect older workers.

This is just one part of a wider picture. Activation policy involves the mobilization for employment of old and young alike, together with those with disabilities and

---

[376] Wikeley, *Law of Social Security* 4th ed., op. cit., at p. 228.

[377] See Wikeley, ibid., at pp. 227–229.

[378] See H. Desmond, 'The generation game: pensions and retirement' (2003) 32 *Industrial Law Journal* 218–222.   [379] Cm. 5677, at p. 93.

[380] Cm. 5690, November 2002.

long-term incapacities, and those with childcare and other domestic responsibilities. The last of these is perhaps the most telling reversal of the policy of the 1909 Minority Report. The debate over whether women with children were capable of being 'able-bodied' or 'unemployed' has given way to a concern with 'providing more choices for lone parents who are considering work',[381] on the grounds that 'lower labour market participation puts lone parent families at greater risk of low income'.[382] Thus under the new deal for lone parents which was instituted in 2001, single parents who make a claim for jobseeker's allowance or another form of income support are *required* to attend an interview with a personal adviser, and must then choose between a range of options including employment for sixteen hours or more (thereby qualifying for a tax credit), employment for less than sixteen hours, and participation in education and training. Although lone parents have not been subjected to a job search requirement as many other participants in the new deal have been, their refusal to attend an interview with an adviser can lead to loss of benefit.[383]

Thus the switch from full employment to activation policy bears a complex relationship to shifting patterns of labour force participation. Reliance on a sole male breadwinner is now very much the exception; this mirrors the decline in importance of derivative benefits in social security law.[384] Female labour market participation has increased and the gender pay gap has narrowed while the rights of married women to access social insurance and occupational pension benefits in their own right have been recognized. At the same time, for most married women with children, part-time work remains the norm, presupposing a gender-based division of household labour, and continuing dependence of these married women on the earnings of their partners.

The ending of full employment policy means that rather than attempting to stabilize full-time employment, the state now actively encourages the growth of forms of work which, because they are temporary, part-time or simply low paid, do not provide subsistence-level wages. Employment subsidies are needed on an ever-growing scale to make up the gap between wages and the minimum acceptable levels of household income. Thus an unavoidable aspect of activation policy is the increase in the use of means-tested benefits of all kinds, but particularly those focused on the low paid. This is a major factor contributing to the long-term increase in the proportion of GDP devoted to benefit payments (see Table 3.5 and Figure 3.2).

---

[381] HM Treasury, *Budget Report* (London: HM Treasury, 2000), at para. 4.

[382] Ibid., at para. 4.29.

[383] By virtue of the Welfare Reform and Pensions Act 1999, inserting ss. 2A–2C into the Social Security Administration Act 1992; *Law of Social Security* 5th ed., op. cit., at pp. 148–9.

[384] The reduced importance of the derivative principle also helps to explain acceptance of the principle of formal equality between widows and widowers, brought about, in the case of occupational pension schemes, by the Pension Schemes Act 1993, s. 17(3) and in the case of social insurance by the Welfare Reform and Pensions Act 1999 (amending the Social Security Contributions and Benefits Act 1992, ss. 41 and 51). On the background to this process, see Wikeley, *The Law of Social Security* 5th ed., op. cit., at pp. 570–571.

Table 3.5. Expenditure on social security benefits as a percentage of GDP, 1948–2002

	Benefits Expenditure as % of GDP		
1948–49	4.18	1975–76	8.39
1949–50	5.02	1976–77	8.54
1950–51	4.82	1977–78	8.83
1951–52	4.59	1978–79	9.15
1952–53	5.13	1979–80	9.03
1953–54	5.07	1980–81	9.55
1954–55	4.91	1981–82	10.67
1955–56	5.14	1982–83	11.12
1956–57	5.01	1983–84	11.46
1957–58	5.07	1984–85	11.52
1958–59	6.02	1985–86	11.47
1959–60	5.88	1986–87	11.5
1960–61	5.71	1987–88	10.8
1961–62	6.06	1988–89	9.81
1962–63	6.13	1989–90	9.54
1963–64	6.05	1990–91	9.96
1964–65	5.75	1991–92	11.15
1965–66	6.38	1992–93	12.16
1966–67	6.36	1993–94	12.6
1967–68	6.81	1994–95	12.22
1968–69	7.15	1995–96	12.12
1969–70	7.12	1996–97	11.88
1970–71	6.86	1997–98	11.28
1971–72	7.16	1998–99	10.99
1972–73	7.26	1999–00	11.05
1973–74	7.36	2000–01	11.02
1974–75	7.72	2001–02	11.24

Source: Emmerson, C. and Leicester, A., 2001, *A Survey of the UK Benefit System, updated October 2002*, Institute of Fiscal Studies. Published online: http://www.ifs.org.uk/taxsystem/benefitsurvey01. pdf.

6. Conclusion: the Evolution of the Duty to Work

One of the principal functions of social security law, and, before that, the poor law, has been to define the 'duty to work', that is, the obligation of individuals to participate in labour market activity. At various stages in the development of British industrial society, a society characterized from an early stage by near-universal wage dependence, the duty to work has been counterbalanced by a right to subsistence or security. At others, that right has been whittled away almost to vanishing point, to be replaced by a combination of charitable giving and state-organized punishment of the destitute. There is no sense here of any progression within social and economic policy, and little evidence of a capacity for institutional learning; rather, policy has ebbed and flowed as techniques rejected by one generation have been taken up again in a later period.

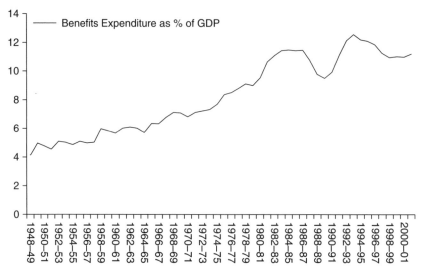

Figure 3.2 Benefits Expenditure as % of GDP

Source: Emmerson, C. and Leicester, A. (2001) *A Survey of the UK Benefit System*, updated October 2002, Institute of Fiscal Studies. Published online: http://www.ifs.org.uk/taxsystem/benefitsurvey01. pdf.

   In the period between the early seventeenth and late eighteenth centuries which was marked by the transition from a fundamentally agrarian and 'corporative' economy to an industrial and commercial one, England was distinctive within western Europe for having a poor relief system which was publicly organized, on the basis of compulsory taxation, and which, although delivered at local level, was national in its coverage. The institution of the poor law settlement provided some protection against the social risks of joblessness, illness and old age at a time of increasing labour mobility. Although narrow in its scope, reflecting the degree to which wage dependence was still partial for most of the population at this point, it was in certain respects a prototype for an integrative model of welfare in which social risks were shared between the state (organized, here, through local parishes), employers (who retained certain obligations to support workers during short-term interruptions to work) and the family unit.

   This model collapsed in the second half of the eighteenth century when grow-ing wage dependence, brought about by the final advance of land enclosure, and a run of harvest failures, brought about an exponential increase in economic insecurity which the system was unable to contain. The Speenhamland system which followed was characterized by the lifting of responsibility from employers, as labour became increasingly casualized, and its displacement on to local ratepay-ers, who were required to make up the difference between low wages and subsist-ence income. When this practice inevitably gave rise to demands for the costs of poor relief to be reduced, the response took the form of the disciplinary regime of the new poor law. Here again there was an active role for the institutions of the state, as legal and bureaucratic mechanisms were put in place with the aim of implementing the principle of 'less eligibility'. Where the old poor law suppressed private giving and, through the institution of the settlement, provided something akin to a legal right, or at least a customary expectation, of relief to which all wage-dependent workers and their dependants could have access, the new poor law focused public intervention on the repression of the 'undeserving poor', and left private charity and the family with the principal responsibility for averting the worst consequences of destitution. Thus the language of entitlements (no matter how loosely expressed, or subjectively interpreted) was replaced by a test of need, with an extreme form of destitution now providing the condition upon which public relief was to be made available.

The core of the Beveridgian model was the inversion of the set of beliefs which sustained the new poor law. Insecurity was now understood to be a result of the way the economy was organized, a 'problem of industry', which outweighed the effects of 'personal character'. The labour market had to be 'publicly organized' and employment regulated. The disintegrative effects of the market upon society, which the poor law had magnified to an extreme degree, would be reversed by institutions designed to collectivize social risk. Social insurance was the result, giving concrete expression to the idea of inter-connected and reciprocal rights and obligations: reciprocity between individual contributions and the benefits received, between the overlapping generations of contributors and beneficiaries, and, most fundamentally of all, between the individual's duty to work and the state's commitment to the maintenance of fair and full employment.

The philosophy which informed the 1942 report and the wider welfare state settlement of the post-war years was predicated upon the stabilization of the employment relationship; it was dependent upon the willingness and ability of the state to run the economy, through macroeconomic management, in such a way as to maintain effective demand, and to regulate basic conditions of employment. In that sense, it could not easily co-exist with the neoliberal economic policy agenda of the 1980s. However, in its most fundamental aspects, the principles underlying the settlement of the 1940s were not incompatible with a market-based economy. The post-war welfare state was not presented as a way of subverting the market order; on the contrary, it was sustained by a belief in the necessity of public regulation if the market system were to be maintained.

The more immediate reasons for the decline of social insurance were outlined earlier in this chapter; they include the financial fragility of the national insurance system, the absence of effective constitutional protections for the insurance fund, and its inability to provide more than a basic level of protection for the recipients of benefits, the consequence of the ill-judged decision to maintain both contributions and benefits at a flat rate for much of the post-war period. Yet many of these weaknesses had been addressed in the legislation of the mid-1970s, when a brief cross-party consensus on the feasibility of an earnings-related state pension system was established. The reforms accompanying the introduction of SERPS also did much to remedy the unequal treatment of married women contributors and to counter the inherent tendency in the system to focus benefits upon male earners.

The neoliberal policy turn of the 1980s was associated with the decline of the notion of the male breadwinner wage in the post-war welfare state. One of the distinguishing features of the part-time and casual forms of work which the realignments of the tax-benefit system sought to promote during the 1980s and 1990s is that they do not provide access to what could be regarded as a subsistence or living wage; or if they do so, it is in conjunction with the earnings of another family member or with the support of one of the number of wage and tax credits paid through the social security system. The growing number of jobs, whether full-time or part-time, which do not provide a living wage, is one of the consequences of the shift away from institutional support for the breadwinner model. The same policy shift is also apparent in the large and growing number of families—approaching a fifth of all households—in which, at the end of the 1990s, there was no wage earner of any kind.

In-work benefits had been out of policy favour between 1834, when the poor law reform put an end to the Speenhamland system, until the supply-side reforms of the 1980s. Attaching welfare benefits to labour market participation has since become a central focus of the New Labour government's welfare to work strategy. There are parallels between current policy and the unravelling of the Speenhamland system. Since the late 1970s, the labour market has been progressively restructured with an increasing polarization of job opportunities, earnings and wealth. This growing divide has been widened by the high levels of joblessness. Meanwhile, the movement of social security away from universal rights towards means testing and the disciplining of the unemployed have removed benefit entitlements. The risk of a Speenhamland effect being triggered now depends upon a number of factors. The more closely social welfare benefits are dependent on labour market activity and the weaker the bargaining power of the recipients of such benefits, the greater the chances are that social welfare will become a factor in determining levels of wages. According to how high unemployment is, there is a greater possibility that workers with subsidized wages will be substituted for those without. In all these respects, the danger is increased by the current vogue for activation policy, which seeks to stimulate an ever greater labour supply under conditions of minimal regulation for lower paid and casual forms of employment.

The effects of activation policy can be seen in the erosion of the categories of 'unemployment' and 'retirement'. This is evident in the introduction of the jobseeker's allowance in 1995 and the blurring of the notion of pensionable age, which is the consequence of the repeal of the retirement condition, the widespread practice of early retirement, and, paradoxically, the formal prohibition on fixed retirement ages which is the likely consequence of EU anti-discrimination legislation.

The demise of Speenhamland was followed by the upheaval of the new poor law. The economic premise underlying the new poor law was that the market, if left alone, would work to produce a 'natural' rate of wages, sufficient in itself to provide access to subsistence; any remaining unemployment was therefore the cause of the 'personal character' of the poor. It followed that the law had a legitimate and necessary role to play in disciplining the workless. Thus it is not surprising to find, in the same way, that the activation policy of today, notwithstanding its rhetoric of enhancing employment opportunities, rests upon the power, under the Jobseekers Act, to impose financial penalties on those who refuse to participate in training and make-work programmes. Current policy faithfully replicates previous experience in the long history of the English poor law: it is in precisely those periods when a belief in the 'natural' properties of the market is at its strongest, that the administration of social welfare is at its most repressive.

4

Collective Bargaining and Social Legislation

1. Introduction

In their analyses of the history and functions of trade unions,[1] Sidney and Beatrice Webb identified labour market regulation as the central purpose of trade union organization. Trade unions were above all associations of wage earners, and the control of wages and terms and conditions within and between trades and occupations was therefore their principal goal. The 'common rule'—a basic set of employment conditions which would bind all employers and workers in a given industry—could be enforced, they thought, in one of three ways: mutual insurance, legal enactment, or collective bargaining. When the Webbs first presented this analysis in the 1890s, they considered the three methods to be potentially equivalent in importance. It was only later that the method of collective bargaining came to occupy a position of pre-eminence in British industrial relations. The result was rationalized by Otto Kahn-Freund, writing in 1959, in terms of 'collective laissez-faire': a system in which the state provided support for the collective self-organization of workers and employers, but without seeking, for the most part, to shape bargaining structures and outcomes.[2]

How did collective laissez-faire become the dominant paradigm for British industrial relations policy during the twentieth century, and what were the consequences of the pre-eminence of this approach for the evolution of the employment relationship? Collective laissez-faire was not synonymous with a complete absence of law governing employment relations. To use terms such as 'voluntarism' or 'abstentionism' in this context may even be actively misleading. In the words of Lord Wedderburn,

Although it has always suited its detractors to paint it as a lawless jungle, collective laissez-faire involved not 'no law', but rather a particular type or quality of law, one which put a premium on protecting autonomous collective bargaining and which necessarily, therefore, demanded areas of liberty for trade unions. Indeed, even at the peak of so-called 'abstention' volumes of regulations about safety at work and hours, for instance on conditions for

---

[1] S. and B. Webb, *The History of Trade Unionism* (London: Longmans, Green and Co., 1894); id., *Industrial Democracy* (London: Longmans, Green and Co., 1897).

[2] O. Kahn-Freund, 'Labour Law', in M. Ginsberg (ed.) *Law and Opinion in England in the 20th Century* (London: Stevens, 1959) 215–263.

women and young workers, sat on the statute book. They gave the lie to the thesis that there was 'no law' in labour relations, while the 'immunities' protecting (barely) basic collective liberties in social conflict after 1906 illustrated the singular character of British labour elsewhere in leaving the pattern and outcome of bargaining very largely to the parties.[3]

The essence of collective laissez-faire, then, was legal support for autonomous collective bargaining. This policy or philosophy implied two additional, structural features which came to characterize the relationship between the state and the system of industrial relations. Firstly, there was no attempt to lay down a general legal model for employee representation. Issues such as the level at which negotiation took place, or the scope and content of collective agreements, remained, essentially, a matter for the collective parties to decide; there was no legislative blueprint. Secondly, the law did not attempt to insert into the employment relationship a universal minimum set of standards. There was no general, legislative or statutory floor to the wages and related terms and conditions set by collective bargaining. As a result, both the definition and enforcement of the 'common rule' depended on union action in particular industries and enterprises. In these respects, British practice fundamentally diverged from that of Continental Europe: collective laissez-faire 'assumes the need for independent trade unions in bargaining with a sufficiently broad band of employers or employers' associations in an autonomous relationship that is not based upon some *Carta del lavoro* or *Chartre du travail'*— that is, it is a system which does not provide the legal guarantees and protections of a labour code or charter of rights.[4]

There were, nevertheless, exceptions to the principle of autonomy for collective bargaining. The laws on factory labour, dating back to the nineteenth century, were one type; another was represented by the legal support provided, initially for minimum terms rates of pay and later for other conditions of employment as well, through the trade boards (from 1909) and wages councils (from 1945). According to Kahn-Freund, these were exceptions which merely confirmed the underlying rule: one of the goals of collective laissez-faire was 'to limit the intervention of the law to those marginal areas in which the disparity of . . . the forces of organized labour and of organized management is so great as

---

[3] Lord Wedderburn, in 'Change, struggle and ideology in British labour law', in Wedderburn, *Labour Law and Freedom* (London: Lawrence and Wishart, 1995) 1–63, at p. 24.

[4] Ibid., at p. 35. On the adoption of general standards governing minimum wage and working time legislation in the continental systems, and the varying degrees to which this reflected the logic of a labour-code model and the notion of fundamental social rights, see T. Ramm, 'Laissez-faire and state protection of workers', in B. Hepple (ed.) *The Making of Labour Law in Europe* (London: Mansell, 1987) 73–113; and for discussion of historical reasons for the divergence of British and continental European practice in this regard, see Lord Wedderburn, 'Industrial relations and the courts' (1980) 19 *Industrial Law Journal* 65–94, reprinted in Lord Wedderburn, *Employment Rights in Britain and Europe: Selected Papers in Labour Law* (London: Lawrence & Wishart, 1991), pp. 41–73, in particular at p. 48: 'The British solution was unique . . . primarily because of the special historical development of its working class movement at a particular phase of its industrial revolution'. We consider the relationship between collective laissez-faire and the distinctive trajectory of British industrialization in more detail in subsequent sections of this chapter.

to prevent the successful operation of what is so very characteristically called "negotiating machinery"'.[5] As Lord McCarthy has more recently pointed out, this view was contested even as it was being advanced: Henry Phelps-Brown's *The Growth of British Industrial Relations*, also published in 1959, argued that a large part of regulatory legislation governing wages and conditions was neither marginal to collective bargaining nor, as Kahn-Freund had suggested, an 'adjunct of, a gloss to' it,[6] but rather 'a way of dealing with fundamental problems affecting groups left out of that system'.[7] Phelps-Brown's analysis represented perhaps more a difference in emphasis than a radically divergent interpretation from that of Kahn-Freund. A more fundamental objection to Kahn-Freund's approach is based upon the prevalence of administrative measures which were designed to shore up collective bargaining. Thus Keith Ewing has argued that 'the state has been a much more active player in the building of collective bargaining and other institutions than a concentration on legal regulation would tend to indicate, thereby reflecting the fact that legal regulation is only one method of intervention, but that there are others—sometimes less formal yet not necessarily less effective'.[8] In his view, trade union freedom was mediated by various forms of administrative action which were the functional equivalent of legal support for trade union recognition; these included government-inspired fair wages resolutions setting minimum rates for government contractors,[9] ad hoc statutory interventions designed to support minimum wages and maintain the force of sector-level collective agreements during the 1930s,[10] and provisions for compulsory arbitration of wage disputes which operated not just during wartime but for a substantial period following the end of the Second World War.[11] However, even this critical perspective accepts that, as a descriptive hypothesis for mid-twentieth century labour law, 'the central tenets of the principle of collective *laissez-faire* cannot be gainsaid', in particular when the pivotal importance of the non-enforceability of collective agreements is taken into account.[12] The most comprehensive analysis of the trajectory of industrial

[5] 'Labour Law', op., cit., at p. 224.   [6] Ibid., at p. 252.

[7] W. McCarthy, 'The rise and fall of collective laissez-faire', in W. McCarthy (ed.) *Legal Intervention in Industrial Relations: Gains and Losses* (Oxford: Blackwell, 1992), pp. 1–78, at p. 11, referring to H. Phelps-Brown, *The Growth of British Industrial Relations: A Study from the Perspective of 1906–14* (London: Macmillan, 1959), at p. 177.

[8] K. Ewing, 'The state and industrial relations: collective *laissez-faire* revisited' (1998) 5 *Historical Studies in Industrial Relations* 1–31, at p. 2.

[9] The first Fair Wages Resolution was adopted by the House of Commons in 1891 and it reached its most developed form in 1946. See below, Section 3.4.

[10] Such as the Cotton Manufacturing (Temporary Provisions) Act 1934 and the Road Haulage Wages Act 1938: see Ewing, 'The state and industrial relations', op. cit.

[11] On Order 1305 (SR&O 1940/1305) see our discussion below; for analysis of its successors, SI 1951/1376 and Schedule 11 of the Employment Act 1975, see Wedderburn, *The Worker and the Law*, op. cit., at pp. 344–347.

[12] Ewing, 'The state and industrial relations', op. cit., at p. 31; on the reasons for non-enforceability, see Wedderburn, *The Worker and the Law*, op. cit., at pp. 318–326; and our discussion below, Section 4.1.

relations policy in the post-Second World War period, that of Paul Davies and Mark Freedland, begins from the starting point that Kahn-Freund's analysis was more or less correct, before proceeding to chronicle the policy shifts which over the following three decades or so 'cumulatively. . . destroyed it'.[13]

The question which we wish to address here is why, at critical junctures in the evolution of British industrial relations, the model of state support for collective bargaining prevailed over the regulatory alternatives outlined by the Webbs, in particular the model of legal enactment, and what the effects of this were for the subsequent development of the industrial relations system. For the Webbs, a comprehensive labour code was needed to address the problem of the 'parasitic' trades, low-paying industries which were, in effect, being cross-subsidized by the wider community. However, the industry-specific form of regulation which emerged out of the protracted debate over the form and function of trade boards and wages councils in the first half of the twentieth century rejected this approach, in effect allowing low pay to continue. Thus adherence to the voluntary principle came at a price, in terms of the ineffective enforcement of the 'common rule'. This had far-reaching implications for the uneven impact of collective bargaining on different industrial sectors and for the instability of wage bargaining mechanisms in the face of external economic shocks.

We develop our analysis in Section 2 below by returning to the roots of the modern industrial relations system in the second half of the nineteenth century, when legal constraints on the growth of collective bargaining were removed and the essentially voluntary and contractual basis of trade union organization was recognized by the state, leading to the emergence of a number of types of industry-level collective bargaining in various trades. Section 3 looks at the response of the state to the rise of collective bargaining in terms of the law relating to conciliation and arbitration, the enforcement of collective agreements, the imposition of minimum statutory standards through the Factory Acts and Trade Board Acts, and statutory support for national collective bargaining. We will see that the principle of legal autonomy for collective bargaining, while deeply rooted in certain labour market institutions at that time, was also highly contested, with significant support being expressed at various points for the alternative, labour code model. Section 4 then examines the economic context and consequences of collective laissez-faire, focusing in particular on the sensitivity of union membership and effectiveness in response to shifts in the wider fiscal and macroeconomic environment. In Sections 5 and 6 we look at the implications for the practice and philosophy of collective laissez-faire of the successive industrial relations policy initiatives of the post-1945 period, namely the incomes policies which were pursued up to 1979, and the policy of labour market deregulation which has been the principal point of reference since then. In Section 7 we conclude by assessing the legacy of collective laissez-faire.

[13] P. Davies and M. Freedland, *Labour Legislation and Public Policy* (Oxford: Clarendon Press, 1993), at p. 59.

2. The Origins of Collective Laissez-faire: Legal Change and Union Growth in the Nineteenth Century

2.1 Wage labour and the transition from corporative regulation to collective bargaining

For the Webbs, the emergence of a developed and stable form of trade union organization in the middle decades of the nineteenth century was associated with the establishment of wage labour as the predominant form of the work relationship. In contrast to the guilds of the 'corporative' system established under the Statute of Artificers,[14] modern trade unions were organizations which were specific to the wage-earning class: 'a trade union, as we understand the term, is a continuous association of wage earners for the purpose of maintaining or improving the conditions of employment'.[15] In labour disputes of the past, 'the "strikers" were not hired wage-workers seeking to improve the conditions of their contract of service into which they had voluntarily entered'.[16] The old journeymen's association was nothing more than 'a subordinate department of the masters' gild'.[17] It was only when wage labour ceased to be just one stage in the life cycle of the artisan that 'ephemeral' trade societies became 'permanent' associations of wage earners. Any link between the guild and the trade union was therefore confined to the desperate and ultimately unsuccessful attempts by early trade unionists to enforce rules which had been designed for the protection of the trade as a whole, just at the point when they stopped being enforced by the regulatory authorities:

We are concerned only with the historical fact that . . . the artisans of the eighteenth century sought to perpetuate those legal or customary regulations of their trade which, as they believed, protected their own interests. When those regulations fell into disuse the workers combined to secure their enforcement. When legal redress was denied, the operatives in many instances, took the matter into their own hands, and endeavoured to maintain, by Trade Union regulations, what had once been prescribed by law. In this respect, and in this respect only, is there any trace of the Gild in the trade union.[18]

The Webbs had their own reasons for wishing to stress the 'modernity' of the 'new model' trade unions which emerged in the 1850s around the objective of organizing workers for the predominantly economic purposes of wage bargaining; but their argument that the institutions of collective bargaining and wage labour evolved alongside each other from the middle decades of the nineteenth century onwards has stood the test of time.[19] This is not the same thing as saying that there

---

[14] 4 Elizabeth c. 5 (1562). See Ch. 2, above.

[15] S. and B. Webb, *The History of Trade Unionism* (London: Longmans, Green and Co., 2nd ed., 1911), at p. 1.   [16] Ibid., at p. 2.

[17] Ibid., at p. 5.   [18] Ibid., at pp. 19–20.

[19] For an assessment of the Webbs' historical analysis of trade unionism which places it in the context of their own intellectual and political programme and also considers the reactions and

were no continuities of any kind in the transition from the corporative regime. The common identity of the guilds had already begun to fracture well before the time of the repeal of the apprenticeship clauses of the Statute of Artificers in 1813, and combination laws had, from the mid-eighteenth century onwards, begun to tighten criminal sanctions for industrial action at the same time as removing protective trade controls.[20] Thus certain features of wage labour were present before the appearance of the first 'permanent' trade unions, as the Webbs were well aware.[21] However, to point out the early growth of wage labour is not to undermine the sense in which wage labour, together with the emergent juridical form of the contract of employment, was *strengthened* and *formalized* from the mid-nineteenth century onwards by the growth of a type of collective bargaining which was distinct from the varieties of corporative regulation which had gone before.

The nature of the legal changes which accompanied the growth of collective bargaining was also far-reaching. Prior to the 1870s, legal constraints on workers' organizations took the form of the common law of conspiracy, the common law doctrine of restraint of trade, and the continuing force of anti-combination laws dating back to the turn of the nineteenth century, only certain parts of which had been abrogated following the Combination Acts of 1824 and 1825.[22] The development of collective bargaining machinery for the regulation of terms and conditions of employment was therefore hindered by the law. Strike action taken with the aim of imposing customary or general rates of wages on recalcitrant employers, or of enforcing union rules which required members to observe agreed rates and refuse to work alongside non-members, was highly likely to constitute a breach of the combination laws and/or of the common law of conspiracy,[23] while picketing, whether or not it involved violence, was likely to constitute one or more of a number of criminal offences.[24] Individual workers taking part in strike action were liable to prosecution under the Master and Servant Acts.[25] The courts proved unwilling to give anything but the most narrow and restrictive of interpretations to statutory measures which had intended to widen the legitimate

critiques of later scholars including E.P. Thompson, Hugh Clegg, H.A. Turner and Vic Allen, see R. Harrison, *The Life and Times of Sidney and Beatrice Webb: 1858–1905: The Formative Years* (London: Macmillan, 2000), ch. 7, in particular at pp. 229–231.

[20] See our analysis in Ch. 2, Section 3.3, above.

[21] See Harrison, *Sidney and Beatrice Webb*, op. cit., at pp. 233–4, concluding, nevertheless, that the Webbs' dismissive explanation of Luddism cannot be reconciled with more recent historiography on that subject.

[22] 5 George IV c. 95 and 6 George IV c. 129 respectively. See W. Cornish and G. de N. Clark, *Law and Society in England 1750–1950* (London: Sweet & Maxwell, 1989), at pp. 299–301, for a full account of these two Acts and their relationship to the common law of conspiracy.

[23] *R. v. Rowlands and Duffield* (1851) 5 Cox 466; *R. v. Hewitt* (1851) 5 Cox 162; *O'Neill* v. *Longman* (1863) 4 B. & S. 376; *Walsby* v. *Anley* (1861) 3 E. & E. 561; Cornish and Clark, *Law and Society in England*, op. cit., 312–313.

[24] *R. v. Druitt* (1867) 10 Cox 592; Cornish and Clark, *Law and Society in England*, op. cit., at pp. 313–314.

[25] See our discussion of the Master and Servant Acts in Ch. 2, above, Section 4.

sphere of union activity.[26] The application of the doctrine of restraint of trade placed union funds, and thus the continuity of union organization, at risk.[27] As long as the law continued to restrict the use of workers' economic sanctions in these ways, while giving full rein to those of employers, collective bargaining arrangements lacked stability and continuity, and on the whole were confined in their effect to particular firms or districts. Union membership, in turn, was highly volatile, with large gains during times of economic prosperity liable to be reversed during periods of slump.[28]

The legal restriction of trade unions found a justification in the prevailing economic ideas of the period. The fixing of a minimum wage above that determined by supply and demand would, it was thought, reduce employment because the 'wage fund' was exogenously fixed. Events, however, progressively weakened the empirical foundations and cast growing doubt on the theoretical basis of the iron law. Thanks to technological progress, additional land was brought into cultivation, lowering the price of food while the size of families fell as a result of growing prosperity. The wage fund theory had constituted a powerful propaganda tool against wage fixing by law or by trade unions: '[o]n the authority of that doctrine, employers and their political spokesmen could argue that trade union action was not simply economic nonsense, but that it also ran against the true interest of an ill-advised and ignorant workforce'.[29] Its refutation lifted the political economy objection to institutional wage determination and this played a part in the campaign by trade unions and their middle-class supporters which eased many of the legal constraints on trade union activities in the 1870s. This was justified by the acceptance of the need for collective action by workers to balance the monopoly power of employers in the labour market.

Thus it was that the reforming legislation of the 1870s, beginning with the Trade Union Act and Criminal Law Amendment Act of 1871[30] and culminating in the Conspiracy and Protection of Property Act and Employers and Workmen

---

[26] Thus the apparent liberalizations of the law brought about by, respectively, the Combination Act 1825 and the Molestation of Workmen Act 1859 (22 Victoria c. 34), made little difference in practice: Cornish and Clark, *Law and Society in England*, op. cit., at pp. 312–314.

[27] This was the effect of *Hornby* v. *Close* (1867) LR 2 QB 153; Cornish and Clark, *Law and Society in England*, op. cit., at p. 315.

[28] See R. Tarling and F. Wilkinson, 'The movement of real wages and the development of collective bargaining in the UK, 1855–1920' (1982) 1 *Contributions to Political Economy* 1–35.

[29] E. Biagini, 'British trade unions and popular political economy 1860–1880' (1987) 30 *Historical Journal* 811–840, at p. 820.

[30] Respectively 34 & 35 Victoria c. 31 and c. 32. The Trade Union Act, among other things, effectively neutralized the doctrine of restraint of trade in so far as it applied to the purposes of trade union organization. The Criminal Law Amendment Act introduced a number of changes to the law governing picketing, not all of which were necessarily liberalizing measures. See Cornish and Clark, *Law and Society in England*, op. cit., at pp. 317–19; D. Brodie, *A History of British Labour Law 1867–1945* (Oxford: Hart, 2003), ch. 1.

Act of 1875,[31] provided a more stable basis for union growth. This philosophy which was to inform the principle of collective laissez-faire was apparent even at this early stage. Even the majority report of the 1874 Royal Commission on Labour Laws, which, although helping to pave the way for the Conspiracy and Protection of Property Act, did not go as far as the unions and their supporters had wished, made a striking confirmation of collective rights of association, using the language of contract:

At all times the natural tendency of . . . [workers'] combinations must be to seek to extend their power by drawing all others belonging to the same trade into their body . . . It is notorious that in some of the more powerful unions the men refuse to work for masters who employ men who do not belong to the union, thus coercing the masters to employ only men belonging to the union, and compelling all who belong to the trade to become members of the union and submit to its dictation. This, though obviously operating in restraint of the freedom of trade, is no more than necessarily flows from the right, now fully admitted, of every man to dispose of his labour as he thinks proper, and to combine with others in order to obtain the best terms he can.[32]

The collective right to combine could thereby be built up out of the individual freedom to contract of the union members. Leaving aside cases of violence or intimidation, the state was not entitled to interfere with their 'liberty to combine for the protection of their common interest', in particular since it was only through combination that 'the working man is enabled to meet the employer on equal terms'.[33]

The same principle of 'non-interference' meant that the Master and Servant Acts required special justification:

The relation of master and servant in every form of it, and not the less in that form which relates to employers of labour and their artificers and workmen, arises out of a contract . . . breach of contract involves no criminality.[34]

Accordingly, the attachment of criminality by statute 'is to a certain extent anomalous. If defensible it can only be so as an exceptional case, on the ground of necessity'.[35]

The crucial step taken by the Conspiracy and Protection of Property Act was to provide an immunity from the law of criminal conspiracy for 'an act or combination by two or more persons to do or procure any act in contemplation or furtherance of a trade dispute between employers and workmen'. Together with the repeal, in the Employers and Workmen Act, of criminal liability for certain breaches of the

[31] 38 & 39 Victoria c. 86 and c. 90, respectively. A significant trigger for the Conspiracy and Protection of Property Act was the decision of *R. v. Bunn* (1872) 12 Cox 316, which appeared to ignore the effects of the 1871 legislation. See Cornish and Clark, *Law and Society in England*, at p. 319; Brodie, *A History of Labour Law*, at p. 16.

[32] Royal Commission on Labour Laws (Cockburn), *Second and Final Report, Parliamentary Papers* (1875) XXX.1, at p. 22.   [33] Ibid., at p. 15.

[34] Ibid., at p. 10.   [35] Ibid.

contract of service,[36] this legislation neutralized much of the previous, restrictive effect of the criminal law. Although the 1890s and early 1900s saw a revival of judicial activism, which used the common law of tort to confine once again the scope of lawful industrial action, the Trade Disputes Act of 1906 extended the immunities first established in 1875 to this new area of civil liability.[37] In certain respects, the 1906 Act surpassed the legislation of the 1870s, in particular by establishing a 'blanket' immunity for trade unions from liability in tort, a reaction to the House of Lords' decision in the *Taff Vale* case.[38] Subsequently (and notwithstanding periodic judicial efforts to 'outflank' the statutory immunities[39]) the 1906 Act served to exclude the courts from the resolution of collective industrial disputes, and thereby protected the growing autonomy of the collective bargaining system. Particularly important was the underpinning which the 1906 formula provided to the institution of the closed shop and to related union efforts to control apprenticeships and entry into particular trades. The definition of 'trade dispute' in section 5(3) of the Act covered:

a dispute between employers and workmen, or between workmen and workmen, which is connected with the employment or non-employment, or the terms of employment, or with the conditions of labour, of any person, and the expression 'workmen' means all persons employed in trade or industry, whether or not in the employment of the employer with whom a trade dispute arises.

The major economic tort cases of the 1890s and 1900s—*Allen* v. *Flood*[40] and *Quinn* v. *Leathem*[41]—had turned on the enforcement of the closed shop and union rules forbidding members from working alongside non-members or members of different unions. The wide terms of section 5(3) ensured that action to support the closed shop, inter-union disputes and attempts to enforce union rules against third party employers would, in principle, fall outside the range of judicial intervention. This line held more or less until another closed shop case, *Rookes* v. *Barnard*,[42] in 1964, and the loophole opened there was quickly closed by legislation.[43] Up to the 1970s the courts also accepted, if rather reluctantly towards the end of this period, a non-interventionist stance in relation to the

---

[36] On the significance of criminal liability under the Master and Servant Acts of the eighteenth and nineteenth centuries, and the effects of the Employers and Workmen Act after 1875, see our analysis in Ch. 2, above.

[37] For a full account of the legal origins of the 1906 Act, its reference back to the model of 1875, and the debate surrounding its adoption, see J. Saville, 'The Trade Disputes Act of 1906' (1996) 1 *Historical Studies in Industrial Relations* 11–45; see also D. Brodie, *A History of British Labour Law*, op. cit., ch. 4.

[38] *Taff Vale Railway Co.* v. *Amalgamated Society of Railway Servants* [1901] AC 426. See Cornish and Clark, *Law and Society in England 1750–1950*, op. cit., at pp. 328–336.

[39] On this, see the full account in Wedderburn, *The Worker and the Law*, op. cit., at pp. 16–47. Judicial 'outflanking manoeuvres' were particularly prevalent in the 1960s and 1970s, but from the 1980s onwards, it was Parliament, rather than the courts, which was responsible for cutting back the scope of the trade dispute immunities.   [40] [1898] AC 1.

[41] [1901] AC 495.   [42] [1964] AC 1129.   [43] By the Trade Disputes Act 1965.

review of the enforcement of internal union rules.[44] Thus the immunity system was the bedrock on which union autonomy and self-regulation were constructed for most of the twentieth century.

2.2 Early forms of industry-level collective bargaining: the hosiery trade

Collective bargaining institutions began to take root as part of attempts to minimize the disruptive effects, for both employers and workers, of fluctuations in business activity across the economic cycle. These attempts pre-dated the legislative reforms of the 1870s. The Midlands hosiery trade, which had been the catalyst for Luddism in the 1810s, also saw the first development of mature institutions for joint conciliation and arbitration in the 1860s. The trajectory of the trade offers a case study in the complex interaction of decaying guild controls, early forms of protective labour legislation, the impact of the poor law, and the beginnings of attempts at self-organization by employers and workers.[45]

Frame knitting had become a trade after the Statute of Artificers of 1562 had become law (the knitting frame was invented in 1589), and therefore fell outside its scope. The Framework Knitters' Company was, however, granted a charter by Charles II which effectively extended the apprenticeship rules of the Statute of Artificers to hosiery. The Charter set the terms for entry into the trade and standards for the quality of products, and conferred upon the Company the 'right of search' for 'fraudulent' goods made in breach of these rules. By the eighteenth century a form of industrial organization based around domestic production had evolved, with frame knitters manufacturing the product in their own home or in small shops under the control of master knitters. Marketing was the responsibility of the hosiers who rented out the frames, supplied yarn, gave out orders for making-up, and finished the products. Some of the operations maintained by the hosiers grew to a considerable size, in some cases providing work for several thousand frames. The hosiers' pressure for unrestricted use of cheap labour and freedom to

---

[44] This case law is analysed by P. Elias and K. Ewing, *Trade Union Democracy, Members' Rights and the Law* (London: Mansell, 1987). An important aspect of union autonomy during this period was the self-regulation of jurisdictional dispute between unions over the right to organize, under the Bridlington Agreement. See Lord Wedderburn, *The Worker and the Law* (Harmondsworth: Penguin, 1986) at pp. 824–834.

[45] The following account draws principally on the contemporary study of William Felkin. See W. Felkin, *Felkin's History of the Machine-wrought Hosiery and Lace Manufactures*, edited with an introduction by S.D. Chapman (Newton Abbot: David & Charles, 1967) (originally published 1845 and 1867). See also F.A. Wells, *The British Hosiery and Knitwear Industry: its History and Organisation* (Newton Abbot: David & Charles, revised edition, 1972); C. Erickson, *British Industrialists: Steel and Hosiery 1850–1950* (Cambridge: Cambridge University Press, 1959); and on Luddism: J.L. and B. Hammond, *The Skilled Labourer*, revised with an introduction by J. Rule (London: Longman, 1979) (originally published 1919); E.J. Hobsbawm, 'The machine breakers', in Hobsbawm, *Labouring Men* (London: Weidenfeld and Nicolson, 1964) 5–22; E.P. Thompson, *The Making of the English Working Class* (Harmondsworth: Penguin, 1968) ch. 14; J. Dinwiddy, *From Luddism to the First Reform Bill: Reform in England, 1810–1832* (Oxford: Blackwell, 1987).

trade came into direct conflict with the frame knitters' attempts to control entry into the labour market through the enforcement of apprenticeship rules and traditional forms of quality control. Employer control over the Framework Knitters' Company revealed itself in an unwillingness to enforce the apprenticeship rules; when in 1710 the journeymen took matters into their own hands and broke the frames of the offending masters, the migration of the trade from London to the Midlands accelerated. In the 1750s the Company's opponents petitioned the House of Commons which found the by-laws 'injurious and vexatious to manufacturers, and discouraging industry and trade', a resolution which effectively neutralized the Charter. Subsequent attempts by the framework knitters to reintroduce legislation protecting the trade from external competition failed in the 1810s. The Luddite protests began in the following year. The main targets of the Nottinghamshire Luddites of 1811 were the makers of 'cut-ups', goods produced in breach of the traditional quality standards, as well as employers accused of paying low wages and 'colting', that is, employing a large number of apprentices as cheap labour. Luddism was finally suppressed only after frame breaking had been made a capital offence and many of the organizers of the protests had been hanged or transported.

Several unsuccessful attempts were subsequently made to introduce legislation requiring the marking of knitted products to indicate their size, quality and method of manufacture and for the frame knitters to be provided with the written terms of their contracts including the type of product, its quality, and the price of labour. Efforts were also made to define frame rent as an illegal form of deduction from wages under the Truck Acts, but these failed despite widespread condemnation of the practice. The decision of the Court of Exchequer Chamber in *Archer* v. *James* (1859)[46] effectively settled the issue by ruling that frame rents were lawful withdrawals from wages if they had been agreed in advance in the contract.

By these means the knitwear trade became characterized by intensive competition in both labour and product markets. In the absence of controls over entry, the labour force expanded rapidly in periods of growth. Large numbers of pauper apprentices were taken on, for whom masters were paid a per capita fee by parish overseers. The semi-skilled nature of frame knitting at the cheaper end of the market also meant that apprentices could quickly be put to productive work, and this opened up frame knitting to the unemployed from other trades. The domestic organization of production led to increasing numbers of women and children being employed on frames. The resulting structure of the industry contributed to its instability. In upturns, frame rents rose, with the effect that investment in knitting frames became an attractive proposition, and

---

[46] (1859) 2 B. & S. 61. The appeal court was evenly split on the interpretation of the statute (the Truck Act 1831, 1 & 2 William IV c. 36) and so the first instance judgment, finding for the employer, was upheld. See Chapter 2, Section 4.3. In the 1870s, specific legislation governing deductions for frame rents, the Hosiery Manufacture Wages Act 1878, finally dealt with the issue, although by this stage outworking was being replaced by factory production.

their numbers multiplied. In recessions, reductions in demand fell initially on middlemen who took the lead in wage cutting, substituting truck for cash wages, and reducing product quality.[47] When demand fell, the hosiers spread the available work over as many frames as possible in order to maximize yields from frame rents. The second-hand price of frames fell, helping to maintain their profitability and thereby preventing them from being scrapped.[48] The effect was to embed overcapacity in the trade. The ability to keep a large number of frames in operation depended, in turn, upon the overstocking of the labour market and the maintenance of intensive competition between frame knitters for work. As a consequence, under-employment and poverty among the frame knitters became widespread during the frequent and extensive recessions.

With these forms of intensified competition came a lowering of quality in the trade which brought its products into disrepute.[49] As early as the middle of the eighteenth century, the overseas penetration of the British market for silk stockings was being attributed to the poor quality of the British products. The manufacturers 'filled their shops with apprentices who made goods of the most wretched description'.[50] Exports markets were lost because 'the competition in the supply had become so urgent' as to 'induce the manufacturers to reduce the size from the standard in length and width', which, 'added to their slighter quality, entirely discredited their character and destroyed their use'. Consequently 'foreign consumption suffered a severe blow'.[51]

The industry also stagnated technically as the large-scale investment which had been made in hand frames and their continued profitability—the result of cheap labour and the practice of frame renting—inhibited mechanization and a switch to factory production. The hosiers had a vested interest in maintaining the putting-out system which resulted from their ownership of the frames. The employment of middlemen also separated the industry leaders from the production process so that they had little practical knowledge upon which to evaluate any technical challenge to the status quo. Consequently, the innovations which eventually led to mechanized production in factories were pioneered by relative newcomers who only gradually displaced the established merchant hosiers.[52]

Trade union activity amongst framework knitters began to revive from the 1830s onwards. From this point, repeated attempts were made to secure agreements with groups of employers and to establish forms of joint control. These attempts received strong support from local communities which felt the effects of poverty among framework knitters in the forms of higher poor rates.[53] But no long-term agreements were achieved. Although hosiery employers could

---

[47] See Erickson, *Steel and Hosiery 1850–1950*, op. cit., at pp. 84–87.
[48] Felkin, *History of Hosiery Manufactures*, op. cit., at p. 455.   [49] Ibid., at p. 230.
[50] Wells, *The British Hosiery and Knitwear Industry*, op. cit., at p. 75.
[51] Felkin, *History of Hosiery Manufactures*, op. cit., at p. 406.
[52] Erickson, *Steel and Hosiery 1850–1950*, op. cit., at pp. 173–8.
[53] Felkin, *History of Hosiery Manufactures*, op. cit., ch. 27.

come together to oppose trade unions, they remained highly individualistic and rivalrous in product markets, and competed on the basis of wage cutting, so that general standards governing employment in the trade could not take hold. Joint organizations of workers and employers were formed but were usually short-lived. In the 1850s, however, a sustained improvement in trading conditions led to the stabilization of prices and wages. As trade unionism recovered again, the prospect of widespread strike action led the three largest employers in Nottingham, led by A.J. Mundella, to convene a conference with representatives of frame knitters and middlemen to propose a conciliatory approach to wage determination. As a consequence, a joint board of conciliation and arbitration, consisting of worker and employer representatives, was established in 1860 to resolve wages disputes. The board proved successful and its membership was extended to include the large majority of employers and workers in Derbyshire and Nottinghamshire. Similar boards were introduced for the Leicester and Hawick regions of the trade.

The conciliation and arbitration boards succeeded in securing a degree of wage uniformity by printing and circulating piecework price lists and by bringing strong pressure upon employers to pay the agreed price. To ensure compliance the hosiers agreed, if necessary, to provide alternative work for frame knitters who refused to work below the agreed price. The board also succeeded in suppressing truck where it still existed by threatening to withdraw frames from middlemen who paid in kind and support prosecutions under the Truck Acts. Frame rents were regulated by the board and middlemen were prevented from adding to the rent set by the hosiers. The success of the boards can in large measure be explained by the discipline which was exercised on the side of the employers, and this was attributable to the dominant position of a relatively small number of large old-established firms which had the power to impose standards throughout the trade.[54] However, this stability was to be disrupted yet again by the process of mechanization and the final shift to factory production, which came late to the hosiery trade.

Although power had been applied to knitting frames in the early nineteenth century it was not until the 1850s that the first mechanized factory was opened. The changeover was at first slow but then accelerated in the third quarter of the nineteenth century and was more or less complete by the turn of the twentieth century. Mechanization had a major impact on the organization of production and marketing. The domination of the product market by the large hosiery employers was broken as mechanization created opportunities for smaller producers to market their products. It became possible for independent producers to produce and market their own goods by renting rooms with power, a few mechanized frames, and sewing machines which could be obtained on easy credit terms. The trade also saw the emergence of independent contract dyers and finishers and final product wholesalers, who further undermined the hosiers' dominance of marketing.

54 Wells, *The British Hosiery and Knitwear Industry*, op. cit., at p. 159.

Consequently, small firms in increasing numbers entered the product market, and the resulting competition was further intensified by growing foreign competition.

Competition between producers put the wholesalers in a strong bargaining position. In contrast to the situation in the domestic system in which the hosiers put out specific orders, the responsibility for initiating designs now rested with the manufacturers who made up samples with which to solicit orders from the wholesalers. Complaints were continually made that the wholesalers submitted the samples produced by one firm to others for a rival quotation and that firms with surplus capacity and yarn stocks took advantage of this by reducing profit margins to a minimum. Orders placed were usually 'for delivery when required' and if, between order and delivery, the price of yarn fell, the wholesalers would insist on a price reduction. Attempts were also made by firms at each stage of the supply chain to set terms of credit in their favour. In the highly competitive state of the market the advantage lay with the buyers so that, for example, the spinners were required to give the manufacturers nine months' credit while having to settle their own debts within thirty days. The danger of the long credit system was that it encouraged over-ordering, especially by small shopkeepers. Dubious business practice therefore became endemic. Resort to law to enforce contractual agreements was possible 'but the manufacturer well knew that such a course meant permanently losing a customer and perhaps being victimised by other dealers'.[55]

Thus the emergence of collective bargaining in hosiery took place in conjunction with mechanization and the move to factory production, and the combined effect of these changes was to displace the domestic system and give rise to the general adoption of direct employment relations. But the stabilization of the trade which the first conciliation and arbitration boards had brought about in the 1860s was only temporary. In the newly competitive environment of the 1870s and 1880s, the arbitration system was continually under pressure. Renewed competition between employers made it difficult for unions to enforce wage agreements. The root of the problem was a lack of solidarity among employers; 'each manufacturer carried out his business in jealous fear of his neighbour while trying to preserve as much secrecy as possible in his own operations'.[56] The experience of the hosiery trade—one of a slow transition away from small-scale and domestic production, a fragmented industrial structure, cut-throat competition among employers, unstable collective bargaining and the continuous threat posed by overseas competition—was to prove characteristic of many sectors of British industry in the following decades.

2.3 Models of collective bargaining after 1875

The hosiery trade was unusual in seeing the establishment of formal mechanisms for joint conciliation and arbitration in the 1860s. In most trades, it was not until the lifting of the restrictive legal regime governing union action and organization

---

[55] Ibid., at p. 146.   [56] Ibid.

in the 1870s that a move to more stable industrial relations took place. Trade union membership grew steadily after 1870. At first growth was not continuous, and early gains were reversed with the onset of industrial depression in 1873 and again between 1889 and 1893. After 1905 the rate of increase once more accelerated, with membership doubling by 1914 and doubling again by 1920, when membership reached the figure of eight and a half million. This was reduced to five and a half million by 1924 in the wake of the post-war slump. Union growth took two main forms during this period: on the one hand the extension of membership to the less skilled, and to white collar and women workers, in the already organized trades; and on the other the unionization of hitherto unorganized industries and firms. Thus whereas in 1897 three-quarters of union members were employed in mining, construction and manufacturing—with over half employed in the mining, engineering, cotton and construction sectors alone—by 1924 the proportion of total membership in transport, public and private services and general labouring occupations had increased from 25 to 40 per cent.[57]

In the absence of a prescriptive legal framework, collective bargaining was shaped by conditions in particular trades and by the strategies of organization and resistance adopted by unions and employers respectively. This can be seen in terms of three models of sectoral organization: firstly, sectors characterized by attempts at unilateral union control of employment conditions, based around craft distinctions, the enforcement of apprenticeships controls and attempts to regulate and limit piecework; secondly, sectors in which collective bargaining took the form of joint control between trade unions and employers' associations, based upon wage and conciliation boards and agreements on sliding scales of wages; and finally sectors of 'no-control' in which trade unions and employers' associations were too weak to establish either controls over the labour supply or forms of joint regulation of minimum terms and conditions—these were known at the time as the 'sweated trades'.

Craft control

Craft control in the sense just indicated was the basis of union strength in engineering, shipbuilding and construction. The apprenticeship system continued intact in a number of trades after the repeal of its statutory supports in 1814; the repeal of the Statute of Artificers offered a stimulus to the formalization of craft rules and their increased enforcement by the associations of skilled journeymen.[58] The Royal Commission on Labour of 1891–94 found that apprenticeship survived especially strongly in small workshops and in trades where large-scale production was still the exception.[59] This was the case in engineering, where the small family firm remained the predominant form of business organization up to

[57] Tarling and Wilkinson, 'The development of collective bargaining in the UK', op. cit.
[58] Webb and Webb, *Industrial Democracy*, op. cit., ch. 10.
[59] Royal Commission on Labour (Devonshire), *Fifth and Final Report*, Part I, 'Majority Report', C. 7421, Parliamentary Papers (1894) XXXV.9, at paras. 24–31.

1900.[60] Employers complained of union attempts to limit labour supply by restricting the numbers of apprentices: 'the trade unions aim at a monopoly of work by the existing number of their members, through establishing such a limitation of apprentices that this number can never increase'.[61] Union control over apprenticeship gave the skilled unions the strength to impose terms and conditions on employers at district and shopfloor level. Irregular hours, including the pre-industrial practice of 'St. Monday', were common up to the 1890s in some areas,[62] while district committees of the Amalgamated Society of Engineers set standard wage rates which were not the subject of formal agreement but depended upon 'the tacit recognition of the employer'.[63]

Union rules were enforced by the practice of withdrawing members from 'illegal' shops and supporting them with unemployment compensation, in an example of what the Webbs termed a 'method of mutual insurance'. These early forms of unemployment insurance were designed not simply to protect members from the consequences of periodic loss of work, but also to ensure that the union regulations on working practices were maintained. As explained by the Webbs,

A member is not only permitted to refuse job after job if these are offered to him below the 'Standard Rate' of remuneration, or otherwise in contravention of the normal term: he is absolutely forbidden to accept work on any but the conditions satisfactory to his branch . . . As understood and administered by all Trade Unions, the Out of Work benefit is not valued exclusively, or even mainly, for its protection of the individual against casualties. In the mind of the thoughtful or experienced Trade Unionist its most important function is to protect the Standard Rate of wages and other normal terms and conditions of employment from being 'eaten away', in bad times, by the competition of members driven by necessity to accept the employer's terms.[64]

The building up by the craft unions such as the Amalgamated Society of Engineeers of large funds for social welfare purposes contributed to the climate of 'moderation' which militated against precipitate strike action, and which was associated with the limited or 'pragmatic' legislative goals of the trade union leadership of the 1860s and 1870s, one of which was to put the holding of union property on a legal footing and protect funds from legal action and other costs arising from strikes. The suspension of benefits for members who broke union rules or who refused to follow central direction was, correspondingly, a powerful mechanism for maintaining internal discipline. It was against this background that the Trade Union Act of 1871 took the first step towards providing unions with immunity from the common law doctrine of restraint of trade, reversing the effect of the judgment in *Hornby* v. *Close*[65] and thereby enabling union branches to protect their collective property.

---

[60] M. Holbrook-Jones, *Supremacy and Subordination of Labour: The Hierarchy of Work in the Early Labour Movement* (London: Heinemann Educational Books, 1982), at p. 18.   [61] Ibid.

[62] Ibid., at p. 57.

[63] H. Clegg, A. Fox and A. Thompson, *A History of British Trade Unions since 1889* Volume I (Oxford: Clarendon Press, 1964), at p. 140.   [64] *Industrial Democracy*, op. cit., at pp. 164–5.

[65] *Hornby* v. *Close* (1867) LR 2 QB 153.

After the onset of the Great Depression in 1873 and the less favourable economic climate which arose from increased international competition, employers became less tolerant of craft controls and sought to organize themselves into associations to impose common terms in resistance to the unions. The introduction of new technology, albeit in a gradual fashion, was increasingly used to undermine apprenticeship regulations from the early 1890s on. In 1896 the Employers' Federation of Engineering Associations was established 'to protect and defend our interests' against the engineering unions and to 'secure mutual support' on issues of apprenticeship, wages and job control.[66] The lock-out of 1897 over the issues of the eight-hour day and the control of working practices was characterized by a high degree of employer solidarity, and led to national agreement between the Employers' Federation and the ASE on the ending of restrictive practices in return for the introduction of a standard scheme of payment by results which incorporated a basic minimum day rate, with bonuses on top. There was also agreement on a limited form of dispute resolution procedure. In addition, the growth of employers' associations at this time led to the establishment of joint conciliation and wage bargaining machinery at a regional level in shipbuilding, printing and construction.

The resulting form of collective bargaining was a variant of 'employer conciliation': workers would take disputes to employers for resolution, and if there was failure to agree, the dispute would be moved away from the shop floor in a series of stages. Failure to reach agreement at the final stage would return the dispute to the shop floor where workers had a choice of abandoning the claim, taking the claim through the procedure again, or going on strike. This became the predominant pattern in the engineering industry and set the pattern for much of the twentieth century for the metal working sectors which subsequently emerged, and for the car industry.

Joint control

The second model is that of 'joint control'. Following the example of the first joint board for arbitration and conciliation in hosiery in 1860, the first joint board in iron and steel, the Board of Conciliation for the Manufactured Iron Trade of the North of England, was set up in 1869, and the second, the Midland Iron and Steel Wages Board, in 1876. As in hosiery the immediate impetus to the establishment of the northern joint board was employers' fear that an upturn in demand would lead to strike activity designed to reverse wage cuts imposed during the previous recession. Each side also had more long-term interests in stabilizing the industry, which was subject to particularly severe cyclical fluctuations in prices. The larger employers wanted to put an end to undercutting and had a vested interest in the rapid adjustment of wages to prices for the finished product. The first union to be actively involved, the National Amalgamated Association of Ironworkers, was

[66] Clegg, Fox and Thompson, *A History of British Trade Unions since 1889*, op. cit., at p. 60.

dominated by contractors who were paid by results and employed their own underhands on time rates; accordingly they had a strong interest in preserving continuity of production and avoiding strikes. The ironworkers' union was not formally represented on the joint boards, which consisted of representatives of employers and operatives elected at each works, but in practice the workers' representatives were usually members of the union and were supported and serviced by it. The unions also played an important role in upholding the policy of the boards.

The iron and steel boards established a sliding scale, under which the tonnage rate paid to the contractors was linked to product prices and in turn determined the rates paid to the underhands. The initial rates were fixed at full meetings of the conciliation boards. From 1889 the sliding scale operated by the northern board automatically linked the general level of wages to changes in the net price of iron, and subsequently only periodic adjustments were made. The board also operated to resolve local disputes over wages, with provision in the event of failure to agree for the matter to be submitted to arbitration, which was understood to be binding on both sides. The system came under pressure with the organization of the underhands in the smelters' and millmen's unions and the effective ending of the internal contract system. The smelters' unions were at first reluctant to participate in arbitration boards, preferring direct negotiations with employers. However there was a gradual move towards centralized bargaining, and in 1905 the British Smelters' Association signed the North of England Sliding Scale Agreement with the newly formed employers' federation, the Steel Ingot Makers Association. The sliding scale remained in force up to 1940. In this way the extension of collective bargaining to the underhands left the basic structure of pay determination more or less unaltered; the sliding scale method of payment and representative system of the joint boards was extended downwards to incorporate the newly organized groups, although with a more directly representative role for the unions.[67]

Sliding scales were also established in the coal industry. The introduction was a step in the process marking the shift away from the 'service' model towards that of 'employment'. Thus the 'pit bond' system of annual hirings, which the unions had resisted as an impediment to collective bargaining over pay and conditions, was finally brought to an end in the Durham coalfield only in 1871, and in 1877 a sliding scale was introduced which was intended to cut the union out again from direct negotiations. This lasted until 1892 when, following a prolonged dispute over pay, a joint wages board was set up on the basis of minimum and maximum general wage levels. In addition, sliding scales were operated in tandem with wages boards in the Midlands coalfields and in South Wales. On the workers' side, these boards normally consisted of representatives of the employees, and it was only

[67] On the experience of the iron and steel joint boards in this period, see generally F. Wilkinson, 'Collective bargaining in the steel industry in the 1920s', in A. Briggs and J. Saville (eds.) *Essays in Labour History 1918–1939* (London: Croom Helm) 102–132.

after 1900 that the national Miners' Federation succeeded in supplanting these employee-dominated committees with regional conciliation boards on which the unions had direct representation.[68]

The pattern of organization in cotton was set by the spinners' unions which, while unable to regulate the trade through apprenticeships in the manner of the traditional craft unions, were nevertheless able to operate rigidly applied policies of exclusion in a way which accorded them a form of craft status.[69] Their ability to do so arose from the particular form of labour contracting, in which the spinners employed their own underhands, the piecers, on time rates, which persisted until the 1930s.[70] The spinners' unions enforced rigid promotion rules based on seniority which restricted entry by the piecers into the spinners' work group. The piecers were organized on a subordinate basis within the Spinners' Amalgamation, and the spinners repeatedly blocked their attempts to form independent unions by enforcing the closed shop against them. A form of centralized bargaining emerged in the 1890s when the cotton employers formed a national federation and organized a lock-out in order to enforce a 5 per cent wage cut. The dispute was ended by the Brooklands agreement which provided for annual adjustments of wages within a band of 5 per cent in either direction, and also established a formalized system of 'vertical' conciliation under which local disputes could be investigated successively by the local secretaries of the union and employers' federation, a committee consisting of their representatives and, finally, a national joint committee of union and federation members. In the weaving section of the industry, which lacked the exclusionary union structure set up by the spinners, a joint conciliation committee was set up in 1881 and progress was made towards the enforcement of a general price list for piecework, culminating in agreement on the Uniform Plain Cloth List in 1892.

The 'disorganized trades'

The third category of sectoral organization which emerged after 1870 was that consisting of the 'irregular', 'unorganized' or 'sweated' trades, industries where joint regulation failed to develop and where, as a result, low pay, insecure employment and degrading employment conditions became established. These included several urban trades offering predominantly male employment, such as dock work, parts of shipbuilding and construction and the various forms of road, rail and river transport; trades such as tailoring in which employment was segmented between a relatively privileged male elite of craft workers and larger groups of women and immigrant workers mainly employed as machinists and assistants; and a number of trades which included dressmaking, nail making and laundry work

[68] On collective bargaining in the coal industry in this period, see Holbrook-Jones, *Supremacy and Subordination of Labour*, op. cit., ch. 4.

[69] H.A. Turner, *Trade Union Growth, Structure and Policy: A Comparative Study of the Cotton Unions* (Toronto: University of Toronto Press, 1962).

[70] Holbrook-Jones, *Supremacy and Subordination of Labour*, op. cit., ch. 5.

which were based around small-scale workshop or domestic production and which were dominated by female labour.[71]

The Royal Commission on Labour of 1891–94 identified a 'vicious circle of interacting causes'[72] as responsible for the persistence of the under-organized trades. Irregularity of employment was the result in the first place of fluctuations in demand, brought about by the volatility of overseas markets and, in the case of the home markets, by seasonal factors such as the weather and changing summer and winter fashions. On the supply side, it was recognized that many of the sweated trades were not necessarily unskilled, but suffered from a chronic over-supply of labour. The use of obsolete technology was a bar to the organization of trades as it meant that start-up costs for employers were low, leading to a proliferation of small units; at the same time, the use of outdated machinery was an incentive to employers to increase the intensity of labour and to attempt to compete on the basis of low wages and subcontracting as a means of cutting costs:

The over-supply of labour renders it difficult to establish effective organisations among the workpeople (a difficulty which is enhanced in the case of occupations scattered through innumerable small workshops or lodgings, especially in the case of an immense and shifting population like that of London), and the absence of organisation, in its turn, deprives them of that protection which is possessed by workmen in trades requiring greater skill or energy.[73]

The casual labour force was understood as a 'residuum' of workers, consisting of those unable to gain entry into a skilled trade and of those displaced from better jobs by unemployment. Under these circumstances of permanent over-supply, it was impossible to establish controls over labour competition:

all unskilled labourers being as it were in possible competition with each other, the most incapable in body or feeble in character (and these include the many who have once belonged to a skilled trade but from helplessness or incompetence or misfortune have been unable to maintain themselves in it) get sifted down, and crowd into certain ill-paid occupations at the bottom of the scale, in which their mere superfluity of numbers renders employment irregular and precarious. Lower still below this class of the casually employed and largely recruited from it, comes that of the unemployable.[74]

Underlying this growth of casual work was the threat of the workhouse; for the unemployed or displaced workers, casual work, even under degrading conditions, was the only alternative to the increasingly rigorous discipline being administered at this time by the urban poor law unions.[75] The docks, wrote Hubert Llewellyn Smith, were 'residual employments which stand as buffers between ordinary productive industry and the poor house'.[76] In addition, the poor law guardians in

[71] See G. Stedman Jones, *Outcast London: A Study in the Relationship between Classes in Victorian Society* (Harmondsworth: Penguin, 1976); J. Morris, *Women Workers and the Sweated Trades* (Aldershot: Gower, 1986).

[72] Royal Commission on Labour, 'Majority Report', op. cit., at para. 39.   [73] Ibid.

[74] Ibid., at para. 221.   [75] See Chapter 3, above.

[76] Stedman Jones, *Outcast London*, op. cit., at p. 73.

some urban districts were ready to supply pauper labour to work at low rates of pay as an alternative to the workhouse, as means of breaking strikes of general labourers and dockers and, in 1897, of undermining the engineers during the lock-out of that year.[77]

The position of women workers was extensively examined by the House of Lords Select Committee on Sweating, which completed its report in 1890,[78] and by the 1891–94 Royal Commission on Labour. Homeworking and subcontracting were identified as major causes of low pay and insanitary and unsafe working conditions and as forms of employment to which women workers were particularly vulnerable. According to the Royal Commission, the expectation that women would undertake the role within the household of carer and secondary earner compelled them to 'accept whatever wages they are able to get' in order to support children or a disabled husband.[79] The difficulties of organizing women homeworkers militated against the establishment of an effective wage floor through union activity. In many cases trade unions were reluctant to admit and organize women workers, and did so only under pressure from the weight of numbers entering the trade once a policy of exclusion proved impossible to maintain. This was the case, for example, in tailoring, where the Amalgamated Society of Tailors in London excluded women from the apprenticeship system and prevented their entry into the union despite seeking their solidarity for strike action over national minimum time rates in 1867. It was only by the late 1890s that 'they were forced to recognise that the threat posed by low paid women machinists was not going to disappear',[80] with the result that a women's section of the union was set up in 1900. Women paid a lower subscription rate and received lower benefits, confirming their subordinate status, and the AST subsequently failed to recruit women workers in sufficient numbers to provide a basis for effective enforcement of minimum wages and conditions in the trade. In the textiles sectors, which offered women operatives the highest wages of any trades, a high proportion of women workers was organized into unions,

but even when they are in a majority they rarely stand on terms of equality with the men. Generally speaking, they pay a lower rate of contributions, receive correspondingly low benefits, and take only a subordinate part, if any, in the government of the society.[81]

The sole exception to this pattern to be identified by the Royal Commission was the female-dominated union of the Dundee jute workers.

The tailoring unions also attempted for a time to exclude Jewish immigrant workers from the trade. The issue was a prominent one throughout the last

[77] Clegg, Fox and Thompson, *A History of British Trade Unions since 1889*, op. cit., at pp. 81 and 165.
[78] House of Lords Select Committee on the Sweating System (Derby), *Fifth Report*, Parliamentary Papers, (1890) (169) XVII.257.
[79] Royal Commission on Labour, 'Majority Report', op. cit., at para. 267.
[80] Morris, *Women Workers and the Sweated Trades*, op. cit., at p. 115.
[81] Royal Commission on Labour, 'Majority Report', op. cit., at para. 284.

quarter of the nineteenth century, and led to calls for restrictions on immigrant numbers which were partially responsible for the passage of the Aliens Act of 1902.[82] Over 200,000 Jewish immigrants from eastern Europe arrived in the country after 1881, and many of them entered the tailoring trade in Manchester, Leeds and London where Jewish communities were already established. At first, separate Jewish unions were set up; the skilled sections amalgamated with the AST in 1886 and general unions for factory machinists and operatives were set up in the 1890s.

Nevertheless, attempts at joint regulation in the under-organized trades were either ineffective or broke down entirely as a result of the inability of unions to control the labour supply and the inability of employers' associations to incorporate smaller firms and sub-contractors into agreed procedures. In London in the aftermath of the docks strike of 1889, a conciliation and arbitration board was set up by the chambers of commerce, but the worst of the sweated trades were not represented within the London Chamber of Commerce and the board was on the whole unable to resolve disputes in those trades. There were unsuccessful attempts to establish common wages and conditions in the tailoring trade, and although the Master Tailors' Association set up an arbitration board, it was not widely used.[83]

3. The Response of the State to the Rise of Collective Bargaining

Although, as we have seen, the growth of collective bargaining pre-dates the reforms of the 1870s, it is unlikely that the sustained development of collective bargaining in the form of joint regulation of wages and conditions at the level of the trade or sector could have been possible without the changes to the laws governing strikes and industrial discipline which took place then. Although certain trades including hosiery and iron and steel largely anticipated the legal changes in their establishment of joint boards, in most of the others it was the increased effectiveness of union organization and the strike weapon after 1875 which prompted the formation and extension of employers' associations, and it was the removal of punitive legal sanctions against strikers which made joint conciliation appear attractive and even necessary to employers as a basis for industrial peace. During this period the state embraced joint control and arbitration within the voluntarist framework with some success, but there were also some notable failures in engineering and the coal industry. The law did not, however, go beyond the point of creating the environment in which joint regulation could develop; statutory measures stopped short of introducing either general legal enforcement of minimum terms and conditions or legal sanctions for the control

---

[82] Morris, *Women Workers and the Sweated Trades*, op. cit., at p. 13.   [83] Ibid., at p. 158.

of industrial disputes. This policy of leaving the enforcement of the 'common rule' to extra-legal forces was most clearly expressed in the Royal Commission on Labour's *Final Report* of 1894, and this document set the tone for much of the subsequent debate over a range of issues: the enforcement of collective agreements, the use of conciliation and arbitration to promote union recognition, the direct statutory regulation of pay, hours of work and other terms and conditions, and the gradual emergence of institutions of national collective bargaining.

3.1 The debate over the enforcement of collective agreements

The final Report of the 1894 Royal Commission contained several declarations of the desirability of strong trade unions and employers' associations as the basis for joint regulation:

strong organisation in any trade is almost a condition precedent to the establishment of permanent and effective joint boards of conciliation and arbitration for the trade generally, because unless most men in a trade belong to the society it is (a) difficult to obtain a satisfactory representation of workmen on such a board, and (b) difficult for the executive or leaders of the men to stop local strikes, or to ensure that disputes shall be carried to the joint board, and that the decisions arrived at by that board should be respected by the workmen.[84]

In the same vein, it was acknowledged that effective trade unionism was a precondition of labour peace:

if peaceable relations are, upon the whole, the result of strong and firmly established trade unionism, it seems no less clear from the evidence that trade unionism in a weak and struggling condition rather . . . tends to increase the number and bitterness of industrial conflicts.[85]

The major causes of industrial disputes were understood to be strikes over union recognition and the use by employers of non-union labour.[86]

Allied to this perception was an acknowledgement of the role played by collective agreements in establishing a floor to wages and conditions. The sliding scale system, based as it was on average commodity prices, was open to the objection that it 'does not provide a minimum below which the wage rate is not to fall'.[87] The Commission made reference to the unions' claim that 'the cost of a certain minimum standard of life for the workers should be the first charge upon the produce of industry, and should be maintained even in times of depression of trade',[88] and without going so far as to criticize sliding scale agreements, argued that they would develop over time into wages boards:

the object of a true wages board is to prevent conflicts by means of periodical and organised meetings of representatives of employers and employed for the purpose of discussing and

[84] Royal Commission on Labour, 'Majority Report', op. cit., at para. 91.
[85] Ibid., at para. 93.   [86] Ibid., at paras. 94–95.   [87] Ibid., at para. 111.   [88] Ibid.

revising general wage rates in accordance with the changing circumstances of the time. Thus a wage board fulfils the same purpose as a sliding scale, but does not pretend to adopt any automatic principle of regulating wages in exact accordance with prices.[89]

Given the absence of direct legal enforceability of joint board awards, however, the *Report* had to accept that 'the sanction to the arrangements, which in many great trades are really the governing contracts made between bodies of employers and workmen, powerful though it very frequently is, is one of a merely moral kind';[90] accordingly, 'the effectiveness of the moral sanction to agreements and awards diminishes as the organisation on each side becomes less perfect'.[91] Enforcement depended on 'a strong and efficient form of internal government'[92] which would enable associations on both sides to keep the membership in line:

It is . . . precisely in those industries where the separation of classes and, therefore, the causes of conflicts are most marked, that we observe the fullest developments of that organization of the respective parties which appears to us to be the most remarkable and important feature of the present industrial situation. Powerful trade unions on the one hand and powerful associations of employers on the other have been the means of bringing together in conference the representatives of both classes, enabling each to appreciate the position of the other, and to understand the conditions subject to which their joint undertaking must be conducted.[93]

In these circumstances, the extra-legal power of custom was enough to ensure the application of agreements: 'custom may become so strong even without assistance from law, as to afford in all such trades an almost certain and practically sufficient guarantee for the carrying out of industrial agreements and awards'.[94]

The implication was that, in the less well-organized trades, spontaneous forces could not necessarily be relied upon. However, a majority of the Commission opposed legal intervention to underpin collectively agreed rates. Existing provisions for giving legal force to arbitration and wage awards—the arbitration clauses of the Masters and Workmen Arbitration Act of 1824[95] (the successor, in this respect, of the Combination Acts), the Conciliation Act of 1867[96] and the Masters and Workmen Arbitration Act of 1872,[97] 'appear to have been complete failures',[98] as no applications had been made to the courts under these Acts for the enforcement of awards. One reason for this, as the Webbs acknowledged, was the hostility of the unions to the involvement of the regular court system in the collective bargaining process, which stemmed from the experience of the courts' administration of the Master and Servant Acts and, after their repeal, the moderated version of disciplinary powers in the Employers and Workmen Act 1875.[99] The majority therefore recommended no change in the legal basis of collective

---

[89] Ibid., para. 112.   [90] Ibid., para. 143.   [91] Ibid., para. 144.
[92] Ibid., at para. 145.   [93] Ibid., para. 364.   [94] Ibid., para. 145.
[95] 5 George IV c. 96.   [96] 30 & 31 Victoria c. 105.
[97] 35 & 36 Victoria c. 46.   [98] 'Majority Report', op. cit., at para. 155.
[99] S. and B. Webb, *History of Trade Unionism*, op. cit., at p. 320.

bargaining, reiterating that 'it would do more harm than good either to invest voluntary boards with legal powers, or to establish rivals to them in the shape of other boards founded on a statutory basis, and having a more or less public and official character'.[100] This view was based on the confident expectation that 'many of the evils to which our attention has been called are such as cannot be remedied by any legislation, but we may look with confidence to their gradual amendment by natural forces now in operation which tend to substitute a state of industrial peace for one of industrial division and conflict'.[101]

3.2 The legal framework for conciliation and arbitration

A segment of the majority opinion in the 1894 Royal Commission wanted to go further in placing collective bargaining on a legal basis. The case for legal enforcement was put by a group consisting of most of the employer members of the Commission and the jurist Sir Frederick Pollock in a note appended to the main report, in which they argued for repeal of section 4 of the Trade Union Act 1871 and provision for registration of trade unions to confer automatic legal personality. Legal personality was seen as the basis for 'securing the means of observance, at least for fixed periods, of the collective agreements' of the two sides.[102] However, even this group did not argue for general legal prohibitions on strikes and lockouts in the event of a failure to arbitrate, only for the possibility of the courts awarding damages for breaches of agreed procedures. Strikes and lock-outs were seen as the basis of collective freedom of contract—'the assertion of . . . essential liberties on the part of employers and workmen'.[103] In the end, this group did not choose to depart from the majority conclusions on enforceability, noting that 'the evidence does not show that public opinion is as yet ripe for the changes in the legal status of Trade Associations which we have suggested'.[104] The minority report of the trade unionist commissioners condemned any amendment of the 1871 Act, predicting that damages claims against unions 'would go far to make Trade Unionism impossible for any but the most prosperous and experienced artisans', and would 'provoke the most embittered resistance from the whole body of Trade Unionists'.[105]

Following on from the majority report, the Conciliation Act of 1896,[106] which was introduced by Mundella in his ministerial capacity as President of the Board of Trade, enabled the Board of Trade to conduct inquiries into trade disputes and, on the application of the parties themselves, to arrange arbitration or conciliation. Registration of joint boards with the Board of Trade was to be voluntary and

---

[100] 'Majority Report', op. cit., at para. 302.   [101] Ibid., para. 363.

[102] Royal Commission on Labour (Devonshire), *Fifth and Final Report*, 'Observations Appended to the Main Report by the Chairman and other Commissioners', Parliamentary Papers, (1894) XXXV.9, at para. 7.   [103] Ibid., para. 16.

[104] Ibid., at para. 29.

[105] Royal Commission on Labour (Devonshire), *Fifth and Final Report*, 'Minority Report', Parliamentary Papers (1894) XXXV.9, at p. 146.   [106] 59 & 60 Victoria c. 30.

primarily for the purposes of collecting information. The Board was given the power to conduct inquiries into the establishment of new, voluntary boards in sectors and districts where joint regulation did not exist, and the earlier conciliation and arbitration legislation was repealed. The Labour Department of the Board of Trade, which Mundella had established in 1893, became the administrative arm by which the government's policy of promoting joint regulation was implemented. Thus although the direct legal impact of the Act was minimal, it confirmed the support of the state for the system of joint regulation while at the same time maintaining the strongly voluntarist ethos which had characterized the legislative settlement of the 1870s. In this respect, the 1896 Act was at least as important in the development of the industrial relations system as the Trade Disputes Act of 1906 a decade later, which adapted an already existing model in extending to the civil law of tort the immunities which the 1871 Act had provided in respect of the criminal law and the law of contract.

With government encouragement, collective bargaining machinery was extended after the 1896 Act so that the number of joint boards increased from 64 to 162 in 1904 and 325 in 1913.[107] The Board of Trade's record in settling industrial disputes was more mixed. In the recession of the late 1890s it met considerable employer opposition to its intervention, notably from Lord Penrhyn during the 1896 dispute in the Penrhyn slate quarries which lasted eleven months and led to the defeat of the union, and from the Engineering Employers' Federation during a lock-out of 1897. With the return to office of the Liberals and the passage of the Trade Disputes Act 1906, the Board of Trade again took a more interventionist line which was instrumental in extending joint regulation in the areas organized by the general unions. The Board sponsored a settlement to the 1907 rail dispute under which joint wage and conciliation boards were established, although without the employers conceding either union recognition or an independent chairman. This procedure proved unsatisfactory to the unions and failed to deliver significant improvements in hours and wages, with the result that the rail unions called a further national strike in 1911. This time a Royal Commission was set up and reported in favour of establishing an independent element in the conciliation system and a more direct role for union representatives. The railway companies agreed to this when faced with the possibility that the government would place the scheme on a statutory footing, but continued to resist recognition up to the outbreak of war.[108] The railway employers were throughout this period among the most determined opponents both of collective bargaining and of statutory regulation of terms and conditions; they were also in the forefront of the use of the law against trade union organization, as exemplified by the *Taff Vale* and *Osborne* cases.[109]

[107] See generally Tarling and Wilkinson, 'The development of collective bargaining in the United Kingdom', op. cit.

[108] H. Clegg, *A History of British Trade Unions since 1889 Volume 2, 1911–1933* (Oxford: Clarendon Press, 1985), at p. 43.

[109] On the economic background to the Taff Vale dispute, see C. Harvey and J. Press, 'Management and the Taff Vale strike of 1900' (2000) 42 *Business History* 63–86.

Major disputes also occurred in coal, cotton and engineering, mostly over the issue of guaranteed minimum wage levels. In coal the South Wales strike of 1911 and the national strike of 1912 over the minimum wage reflected discontent with the calculation of piece work wages and the operation of sliding scales, which had failed to produce increases in pay at a time of general economic upturn. The Liberal government imposed a legislative solution in the form of the Coal Mines Minimum Wages Act 1912[110] which provided, exceptionally, for the establishment of statutory minimum wage boards operating at district level alongside existing voluntary boards. In cotton the Brooklands agreement broke down following a series of disputes over the issue of 'bad material' which reduced piecework earnings, and employer attempts to impose wage reductions which led to a prolonged stoppage in 1908. In 1913 the unions gave notice to cancel the agreement. In engineering the conciliation procedure also came under pressure from local disputes and the authority of the central union leadership was under-mined, particularly in the North-east where a campaign for a 'living wage' led to a prolonged unofficial dispute. A new procedure agreement was drawn up in 1907 but the union, under a new militant leadership, withdrew from it in 1913.

The system of informal state encouragement for joint regulation under the Conciliation Act therefore had its limits. There was no natural or inevitable progress from sliding scales to guaranteed minimum wage rates, nor from systems of representation based on employee elections to ones in which the unions secured recognition in their own right and were represented on joint boards by their full-time, salaried officials. The economic cycle continued to produce sharp swings in the relative bargaining strength of employers and unions, thereby precipitating a series of prolonged industrial disputes as each side would attempt to take advantage of favourable economic conditions while they lasted, and the Board of Trade had limited success in alternately attempting to control employer intransigence and worker militancy. In the face of employer resistance, progress towards more formal union recognition and the enforcement of a common rule in wages and conditions took place only through the threat of legislation, in the case of the railways, or with the establishment of statutory wage-fixing institutions, as in coal.

3.3 Direct statutory regulation of working conditions: the debate over the extension of the Factory Acts

The unwillingness of official opinion to accept the principle of generalized statutory regulation was further confirmed by the debate which occurred in the 1890s and 1900s over the extension of the Factory Acts. At this point, factory legislation only regulated the terms and conditions of children and women, and were confined in their effects to certain kinds of industrial establishments.

[110] 2 & 3 George V c. 2.

The earliest Factory Acts had been concerned with the conditions of employment and working hours of children, and specifically with those of pauper apprentices. As early as 1784 the Manchester magistrates passed a resolution to prohibit indentures of parish apprentices to cotton masters under terms which could require them to work at night or for more than ten hours in the day. An Act of 1793[111] gave the justices power to fine employers for mistreatment of apprentices, and in 1802 the Health and Morals of Apprentices Act[112] set a statutory 12-hour day and prohibited night work for parish apprentices employed in mills and factories. The measure was 'in reality not a Factory Act properly speaking, but merely an extension of the Elizabethan poor law relating to parish apprentices'.[113] A series of Acts between 1819 and 1833 then achieved in gradual stages the exclusion of all children under the age of 9 from factory employment; a maximum 9-hour working day and 48-hour week for the under-13s; a 12-hour working day and 69-hour week for those between 13 and 18; and the abolition of night work for all under 18, although these regulations applied only to textile mills.[114]

The working conditions of women were first the subject of regulation in the early 1840s. The Mines Regulation Act of 1842[115] barred women from underground working and the Factories Act of 1844[116] applied to women textile workers the restrictions on working hours which governed the employment of the under-18s. The fact that early industrial regulation took a legislative rather than a voluntary form reflects the weakness of the factory-based unions during the period prior to 1870 and their inability to achieve agreements through collective bargaining; at the same time, the legislature was reluctant to countenance general interference with the freedom of contract of adult males, rejecting a number of Bills to this effect in the 1850s. Male workers indirectly benefited from the controls over the hours of women and children because the working hours of each

---

[111] 33 George III c. 35.

[112] 42 George III c. 73. See Cornish and Clark, *Law and Society in England 1750–1950*, op. cit., at pp. 301–2.

[113] B.L. Hutchins and A. Harrison, *A History of Factory Legislation* (London: P.S. King, 3rd ed., 1926), at p. 16.

[114] 59 George III c. 66 (1819), 6 George IV c. 63 (1825), 1 & 2 William IV c. 39 (1831) and 3 & 4 William IV c. 103 (1833); see Cornish and Clark, *Law and Society in England 1750–1950*, op. cit., at pp. 302–4.

[115] 5 & 6 Victoria c. 99. There is a substantial literature exploring the implications of the 1842 Act and related strategies of job segregation by gender in the nineteenth century. Jane Humphries has argued that segregation can be understood as a strategy to defend the family against the destabilizing effects of labour market competition. See J. Humphries, 'Class struggle and the persistence of the working class family' (1977) 1 *Cambridge Journal of Economics* 241–258, and ' ". . . The most free from objection. . ." ' The sexual division of labor and women's work in nineteenth century England' (1987) 47 *Journal of Economic History* 929–949; for discussion, highlighting the role of exclusionary strategies in shoring up the mid- to late-nineteenth century notion of the male breadwinner wage, see W. Seccombe, 'Patriarchy stabilised: the construction of the male breadwinner wage norm in nineteenth century Britain' (1986) 11 *Social History* 53–76; J. Mark-Lawson and A. Witz, 'From "family labour" to "family wage"? The case of women's labour in nineteenth century coal mining' (1988) 13 *Social History* 151–174; S. Rose, 'Gender antagonism and class conflict: exclusionary strategies of male trade unionists in nineteenth century Britain' (1988) 13 *Social History* 191–208.

[116] 7 & 8 Victoria c. 15.

group were closely integrated; when employers attempted to defeat this effect through the 'relay system', under which the hours children were permitted to work were spread over a number of separate 'relays' across the different shifts worked by adults, Parliament enacted further legislation in 1850 and 1853[117] to counter this by requiring common starting and finishing times for all workers in a given factory. However, it stopped short of extending the Acts to cover all adult males. Instead, the pattern of regulation in textiles was gradually extended to cover printing, dyeing and bleaching, and lace working. The Factory Acts Extension Act of 1867[118] applied the same principles to all factories of fifty or more employees, and the Workshops Regulation Act[119] of the same year restricted hours of work in smaller manufacturing establishments, although allowing for longer operating hours. Again, these regulations only applied to women and the young. The 1867 Extension Act governed iron foundries and works manufacturing glass and metals, but very few women and children worked in such establishments and so the restraint on their hours did not affect the working hours of men.

After the 1870s, however, the flow of legislation began to dry up. In 1873 Mundella, then a backbench MP, introduced a Bill to establish a 9-hour day and 54-hour week for women and young workers in factories, but this was rejected in favour of a more limited measure passed in 1874 reducing maximum weekly hours in textiles to 55 and a half.[120] By the early 1900s collective bargaining was already beginning to improve upon the hours set by legislation, and women workers covered by the Factory Acts frequently worked longer hours than male workers who had the protection of shop floor or sector-level agreements setting a working day of around 9 hours.[121] From around this time, legislation regulating non-factory employment permitted longer statutory hours than was normal either for core factory employment within the Acts, or for employments regulated by collective bargaining. This was the case for domestic workshops employing family members and 'women-only workshops' under the Factories and Workshops Act of 1878,[122] and for legislation such as the Shops Act 1886,[123] which set a 74-hour maximum week for shop assistants, and the Laundries Act 1907,[124] which set a maximum 68-hour week.

The Royal Commission of 1891–4 came down against introducing statutory compulsion in the hours of adult male workers, but the minority trade union report was more favourable to legislative intervention, as were most of the general unions at this time. Small steps were taken in the direction of more general legislative controls over working time in the Railway Servants (Hours of Labour) Act of 1893,[125] the Factories and Workshops Act of 1895[126] and the Coal Mines Regulation Act of 1908,[127] and, as we have seen, a statutory scheme of minimum

---

[117] 13 & 14 Victoria c. 54 and 16 & 17 Victoria c. 104.   [118] 30 & 31 Victoria c. 103.
[119] 30 & 31 Victoria c. 146.   [120] 37 & 38 Victoria c. 44.
[121] See Hutchins and Harrison, *History of Factory Legislation*, op. cit., at p. 98; Morris, *Women Workers and the Sweated Trades*, op. cit., at p. 79.   [122] 41 & 42 Victoria c. 16.
[123] 49 & 50 Victoria c. 55.   [124] 7 Edward VII c. 39.   [125] 56 & 57 Victoria c. 29.
[126] 58 & 59 Victoria c. 37.   [127] 8 Edward VII c. 57.

wage setting was established for the coal industry in 1912. However, most employment legislation of this period maintained the tradition of partial, as opposed to general, regulation. 'The law', wrote Hutchins and Harrison in 1903, 'is still ostensibly based on the idea of "protection for those who cannot help themselves", instead of openly and avowedly adopting the more fruitful principle of raising the standard of life and health for the common good'.[128]

The increasingly selective and subsidiary character of regulatory legislation was not accepted without opposition. The general unions, in particular, supported the campaign for a statutory eight-hour day at the TUC and in their evidence to the 1894 Royal Commission. The Commission discovered that:

reduction of the normal standard hours of labour has always been one of the leading objects of trade unions; the aim of the modern movement is the attainment of this end by legislation. The working classes are as yet by no means unanimous as to the superiority of legislative over voluntary action in this matter; but to judge by the history of trade union congresses and other indications, the party of legislative intervention has been steadily gaining ground during recent years.[129]

The majority nevertheless rejected a standard set of regulations for all trades as not 'a proposal which bears serious examination',[130] and described the Railway Servants (Hours of Labour) Act of 1893 as an exceptional measure, justified by the threat posed to public safety by the long hours worked by railway employees and to the quasi-public status of the railways as heavily subsidized and regulated concerns: 'the special privileges which the state has given to railways affords a special reason for the regulation of the hours of railway servants'.[131] However, the 1893 Act was not just exceptional; it was also a weak measure which did not purport to lay down any general standard.[132] When it was passed, a normal working week of over 70 hours was common in many of the railway companies. The Act enabled representations concerning excessive hours to be made to the Board of Trade, which then had the power to require a railway company to submit a revised schedule of hours such 'as will in the opinion of the Board bring the actual hours of work within reasonable limits, regard being had to all the circumstances of the traffic and to the nature of the work'.[133] If the company failed to comply, the matter would be considered by the Railway and Canal Commission which, finally, had the power to issue an order enforcing the new schedule, backed up by criminal penalties. There is some evidence that the Act put the railway companies under pressure to reduce hours voluntarily.[134]

[128] *A History of Factory Legislation*, op. cit., at p. 209 (the 3rd edition is identical at this point to the edition of 1903). [129] 'Majority Report', at para. 162.
[130] Ibid., para. 320.   [131] Ibid., para. 326.
[132] See generally, on the background to the Act and its effects, E. Knox, 'Blood on the tracks: railway employers and safety in late-Victorian and Edwardian Britain' (2001) 12 *Historical Studies in Industrial Relations* 1–26.
[133] Railway Servants (Hours of Labour) Act 1893, 56 & 57 Victoria c. 29, s. 1(2).
[134] Clegg, Fox and Thompson, *History of British Trade Unions since 1889*, op. cit., at p. 234.

The minority, trade-union influenced report of the 1894 Royal Commission argued, on the other hand, for statutory controls which would be generally applicable:

for the mass of workers an eight hour day, with the effective suppression of habitual overtime, can be secured only by further legislative enactment. We have been much impressed by the great preponderance of working class witnesses in favour of the legal limitation of hours of labour, and still more by their practical unanimity as to the principle involved. Nothing appears to us more striking than the almost universal acceptance and rapid development of the movement for this explicit extension of the Factory Acts to all classes of labour.[135]

Regulations on a trade by trade basis, in contrast, 'would not only consume much valuable time, but would, in our judgment, result at best in a lopsided regulation of industry'. Legislation should therefore set a universal eight-hour standard, to be brought into effect gradually through orders made by the Board of Trade after consultation.

The majority also considered, but rejected, a 'trade exemption' model, under which standard working hours would be laid down by law, with the possibility of an exemption being granted on the basis of a vote of members of the relevant trade. This was contrasted with the 'trade option', effectively the status quo of regulating working hours by collective agreement. The 'trade exemption' model had received support through TUC resolutions around the time the Commission was hearing evidence; Tom Mann, one of the union-based commissioners, proposed a variation under which statutory controls would come into force if three-fifths of the workers in the trade voted for them. The majority came down against the 'exemption' on the grounds of the difficulties and expense involved in organizing a vote of all the workers concerned.

However, the majority did accept a significant extension of the legal power to regulate working hours. Under the Factories and Workshops Act 1891,[136] the Board of Trade had the power to make rules for employment in dangerous manufacturing processes; the majority suggested extending this power to permit the regulation of male working hours in selected industries. Section 28 of the Factories and Workshops Act 1895[137] was the result. This authorized:

the making of special rules or requirements prohibiting the employment of, or modifying or limiting the period of employment for, all or any classes of persons in any process or particular description of manual labour which is certified by the Secretary of State . . . to be dangerous or injurious to health, or dangerous to life and limb.

---

[135] 'Minority Report', op. cit., at p. 140. The minority report was largely drafted by Sidney and Beatrice Webb and signed by three union leaders (James Mawdsley, of the cotton spinners, Tom Mann of the dockers and William Abraham of the Welsh miners) and Michael Austin, a Liberal MP. See S. Blackburn, ' "The harm that the sweater does lives after him": the Webbs, the responsible employer, and the minimum wage campaign, 1880–1914' (2000) 10 *Historical Studies in Industrial Relations* 5–41, p. 17.   [136] 54 & 55 Victoria c. 75, s. 8.
[137] 58 & 59 Victoria c. 37.

According to Hutchins and Harrison,[138] 'in these apparently unimportant provisions which at first sight read only like a trifling extension of regulations already enacted, the principle is however, implicitly granted that, cause being shown, the protection of the law can be extended to men as well as to women and children'. However, the section was not subsequently used as a basis for general working time regulation. It was confined in its scope to the specific effect of long hours on health and safety. Although the principle of state intervention to provide for safe and sanitary working conditions for all workers gradually took shape in numerous subsequent Acts and regulations governing health and safety,[139] general legislation on hours and wages was not to emerge for another hundred years.[140]

The two Acts of 1908 and 1912 which set an 8-hour maximum underground shift in coal mining and established minimum wage-fixing machinery for the industry conformed to the pattern of selective regulation. The national Miners' Federation was in favour of legislation partly to counter the intransigence of the employers' side and also in order to impose a degree of uniformity on the regional unions. Even then, the 1908 Act did not materially improve on the underground hours established in most districts under collective bargaining. The so-called eight-hour shift was nearer nine hours or even ten in some areas as it was interpreted (apparently incorrectly) as excluding winding time.[141] The Coal Mines (Minimum Wage) Act 1912, which as we have seen established statutory boards at regional level,[142] was overtaken by wartime regulation and subsequently by voluntary machinery in the inter-war period.

3.4 Early minimum wage legislation: the Trade Boards model

The debate for and against regulation to deal with low pay culminated in the campaigns surrounding the passage of the Trade Boards Act in 1909. An initial step had already been taken with the passage in 1891 of a Fair Wages Resolution by the House of Commons, requiring government contractors to observe 'accepted' wage rates for the trades in which they operated.[143] The Resolution did not have statutory force, but it was an indication of the political importance which the campaign against 'sweating' had achieved by that point. The most systematic and reasoned case yet for general legislative standards was put by the

---

[138] *History of Factory Legislation*, op. cit., at p. 203.

[139] See Harrison, *The Life and Times of Sidney and Beatrice Webb*, op. cit., at pp. 143–153, and Blackburn, 'The Webbs and the responsible employer', op. cit., at pp. 7–10, discussing the roles played by Sidney and Beatrice with regard to the work of the House of Lords Select Committee on the Sweating System (on which, see House of Lords Select Committee on the Sweating System, (Derby) *Fifth Report*, op. cit.   [140] See this chapter, below, Section 7.

[141] Clegg, Fox and Thompson, *History of British Trade Unions since 1889*, op. cit., at p. 399.

[142] See Section 3.2, above.

[143] On the background to the Resolutions of 1891 and 1946, their adaptation in a number of different statutory settings, and their repeal in 1982, see B. Bercusson, *Fair Wages Resolutions* (London: Mansell, 1978) and Lord Wedderburn, *The Worker and the Law* (Harmondsworth: Penguin, 1986), at pp. 347–350.

Webbs in *Industrial Democracy* in 1897. Their 'National Minimum' of living and working conditions would, they argued, 'extend the conception of the Common Rule from the trade to whole community'.[144] In this respect, the deficiencies of the Factory Acts were clearly recognized:

> this policy of prescribing minimum conditions, below which no employer is allowed to drive even his most necessitous operatives, has yet been only imperfectly carried out. Factory legislation applies, usually, only to sanitary conditions and, as regards particular classes, to the hours of labour. Even within this limited sphere it is everywhere unsystematic and lop-sided. When any European statesman makes up his mind to grapple seriously with the problem of the 'sweated trades' he will have to expand the Factory Acts of his country into a systematic and comprehensive Labour Code, prescribing the minimum conditions under which the community can afford to allow industry to be carried on; and including not merely definite precautions of sanitation and safety, and maximum hours of toil, but also a minimum of weekly earnings.[145]

There was, from this point of view, 'no logical distinction to be drawn between the various clauses of the wage contract';[146] or as the House of Commons Select Committee on Home Work put it in 1908, 'it is quite as legitimate to establish by legislation a minimum standard of remuneration as it is to establish such a standard of sanitation, cleanliness, ventilation, air space, and hours of work'.[147]

The Webbs were in favour of confining legal regulation to the minimum wage, leaving collective bargaining to set a superior 'living wage' for each trade.[148] The legal minimum would be based on an objective notion of subsistence which would apparently be only a bare improvement on conditions necessary for physical survival—'determined by practical inquiry as to the cost of the food, clothing, and shelter physiologically necessary, according to national habit and custom, to prevent bodily deterioration'.[149] It would be introduced gradually in order to minimize the impact upon those employed in the sweated trades as industrial resources were re-deployed into more efficient areas of production.[150] Yet at the same time, the legal minimum would serve as a means of raising general living standards:

> It will clearly be to the direct advantage of the wage-earning class, and especially to the large majority of self-supporting but comparatively unskilled adult labourers, that the National Minimum should be fixed as high as possible, as this will ensure to them a good wage . . . On the other hand, the employers in trades using low paid labour would resent the dislocation to which a compulsory raising of conditions would subject them, and they would find powerful allies in the whole body of taxpayers, alarmed at the prospect of

---

[144] Webb and Webb, *Industrial Democracy*, op. cit., at p. 767.   [145] Ibid.

[146] Ibid., at p. 773.

[147] Select Committee on Home Work (Whittaker), *Report*, Parliamentary Papers (1908) (246) VIII.1, at p. 38.

[148] The Webbs' conception of the living wage was nevertheless criticized by both J.A. Hobson and R.H. Tawney for being too limited and excessively efficiency-orientated: see S. Blackburn, 'The Webbs and the responsible employer', op. cit., at pp. 38–39.   [149] Ibid., at p. 775.

[150] Ibid., at p. 783.

having to maintain in public institutions an enlarged residuum of the unemployable. The economist would be disinclined to give much weight to any of these arguments, and would rather press upon the statesman the paramount necessity of so fixing and gradually raising the National Minimum as progressively to increase the efficiency of the community as a whole, without casting an undue burden on the present generation of taxpayers.[151]

Closely related to this argument was the claim that the sweated trades were inefficient in the sense of being 'parasitic' upon the community at large; by paying wages below subsistence they received a subsidy from other industries and from the families of the low paid who were required to support them. The House of Commons Select Committee on Home Work, reporting in 1908, defined 'sweating' as work which was 'paid for at a rate which, in the conditions under which many of the workers do it, yields to them an income which is quite insufficient to enable an adult person to obtain anything like proper food, clothing and housing accommodation'.[152] According to the Select Committee,

It is doubtful whether there is any more important condition of individual and general well being than the possibility of obtaining an income sufficient to enable those who earn it to secure, at any rate, the necessaries of life. If a trade will not yield such an income to average industrious workers engaged in it, it is a parasite industry, and it is contrary to the general well being that it should continue.[153]

As the Webbs put it 'the enforcement of a common minimum standard throughout the trade not only stops the degradation, but in every way conduces to efficiency'.[154]

In the event, the Trade Boards Act came to embody a less ambitious model of statutory intervention: joint wage regulation in selected sweated trades was placed on a statutory basis, with independent members sitting with employers' and employees' representatives in order to bring about agreement, but no effort was made to set minimum wage levels at any particular level. The Board of Trade was given the power to establish boards 'if they are satisfied that the rate of wages prevailing in any branch of the trade is exceptionally low as compared with that in other employments, and that the other circumstances of the trade are such as to render the application of this Act to the trade expedient'.[155] Within a short space

---

[151] Ibid., at pp. 778–9.   [152] Select Committee on Home Work, *Report*, at p. 3.
[153] Ibid., at p. 38. See M. Power, 'Parasitic-industries analysis and arguments for a living wage for women in the early twentieth century United States' (1999) 5 *Feminist Economics* 61–78, for a general review of the arguments made in Britain and America around this time on the issue of the 'parasitic' trades, and S. Blackburn, 'The Webbs and the responsible employer', op. cit., for a full account of the evolution of the thinking of the Webbs on the nature of 'sweating', the need for public regulation, and theories of parasitism and under-consumption. For an account of the concept of the 'national minimum' which sets it in the context of Edwardian debates concerning national decline, in particular comparing Britain to Germany, see G. Searle, *The Quest for National Efficiency* (Oxford: Blackwell, 1987). Royden Harrison discusses the relationship between *Industrial Democracy* and the contribution of the Webbs to the debate surrounding the 1891–4 Royal Commission on Labour in chapter 6 of his biography (*The Life and Times of Sidney and Beatrice Webb*, op. cit.); see also pp. 347–8 on the national minimum and 'social imperialism'.   [154] *Industrial Democracy*, op. cit., at p. 773.
[155] 9 Edward VII c. 22, s. 1(2).

of time a case could plausibly be made in favour of the deliberative, trial-and-error approach to wage setting which they embodied, and evidence was produced of tangible improvement in working conditions resulting from their operation.[156] It has also been suggested that the Webbs themselves, notwithstanding their concerns about a measure which was at best 'a modified version of the reform which they recommended', nevertheless 'regarded the first boards as a stepping stone and hoped that a gradual expansion of the system would lead, indirectly, to the attainment of a national minimum wage'.[157]

However, the limited aims of the 1909 Act were all too clear. They stemmed in large part from the desire of the Labour Department of the Board of Trade to incorporate the question of low pay into the larger framework of joint regulation which it was charged with developing, but also from the unwillingness of many of the unions to see the principle of legal intervention in terms and conditions applied on a general basis, for fear that it would lead to legislation for compulsory concili-ation and arbitration in industrial disputes. The workings of the Royal Commission of 1891–4 had demonstrated that the statutory enforcement of minimum terms in collective agreements was seen as inseparable from the issue of the enforcement of agreements to submit disputes to agreed procedures. There was also opposition within Parliament to a generalized breach of the principle of laissez-faire.[158] The Act accordingly made no reference to establishing a minimum subsistence wage, and left it up to the Board of Trade to take the initiative in the establishment of the statutory boards; the Board also had the power to suspend the obligatory effect of trade board rates.[159] The first trades to be regulated in this way, ready-made and bespoke tailoring, paper box making, lace finishing and chain-making, were characterized by extremely low pay. Even then, combating low pay was not the only objective of the Acts. For some supporters of regulation, the suppression of the sweated trades was meant to have the effect of restricting the employment of wives and mothers.[160] As the Royal Commission of 1891–4 had put it, it was through such employment that 'homes are made comfortless, and children and husbands neglected'.[161]

3.5 Wartime legislation and state support for multi-employer collective bargaining

Until the First World War, the coverage of collective bargaining was still effectively confined to skilled workers in a narrow range of industries (principally engineering,

---

[156] This argument, and the evidence to support it, were made by R.H. Tawney, who later became a member of the chain-making boards. See R.H. Tawney, *The Establishment of Minimum Rates in the Chainmaking Industry under the Trade Boards Act of 1909* (London: Bell, 1914) and *The Establishment of Minimum Rates in the Tailoring Industry under the Trade Boards Act of 1909* (London: Bell, 1915).   [157] Blackburn, 'The Webbs and the responsible employer', op. cit., at p. 41.

[158] See generally Morris, *Women Workers in the Sweated Trades*, op. cit.

[159] Trade Boards Act 1909, s. 5.

[160] See Morris, *Women Workers and the Sweated Trades*, passim.

[161] 'Majority Report', op. cit., at para. 276.

iron and steel, coal, cotton, and construction.[162] Moreover, within these sectors, the benefits of collective bargaining were less than evenly spread. The intensity of product market competition even within the better organized trades meant that employers' associations were weakly organized, and this proved a major obstacle to the establishment of industry-wide standards. Where standard rates were set and observed, they had to be sufficiently low to meet the needs of the least profitable firms, so as to prevent them from breaking away and undercutting other members of the association. As a result, standard rates tended to be minima which were improved upon where possible by trade union action, but this proved to be the case only in the relatively more profitable firms.

From the mid-1890s onwards the environment for collective bargaining hardened: the trend in the external terms of trade, which since the 1870s had led to cheaper food and raw materials relative to industrial goods produced within the UK, swung in the opposite direction, putting a downward pressure on real wages and upward pressure on industrial costs.[163] Profits were further squeezed by a slowing down of productivity growth and increasing competition for British goods in international markets. In the years immediately prior to the outbreak of war these pressures led to an increase in union membership and militancy, with widespread strike action and a deterioration in relations between unions and employers.

The war intervened in this process in three important ways: trade unions at national level agreed to cooperate in the war effort by suspending craft controls and strike activity; the government introduced compulsory arbitration for wages and conditions of work; and under the conditions of a wartime economy, with shortages of basic goods and raw materials, price increases accelerated sharply.

Wartime legislation was to prove a major stimulus to the further spread of union membership and to the formalization and centralization of collective bargaining. The Munitions of War Act 1915[164] gave statutory force to the 'Treasury Agreement' under which the trade unions agreed to give up the right to strike in munitions work in favour of binding arbitration, with the government agreeing in return to enforce customary rates of wages (an extension of the fair wages principle which had already been applied to government contractors[165]) and to ensure the restoration of pre-war practices once hostilities were over. Aside from the ban on strikes, this was not seen as amounting to direct government control of wages and conditions. The first serious breach in the voluntary principle

---

[162] See generally Tarling and Wilkinson, 'The development of collective bargaining in the UK', op. cit., which we draw on here.

[163] See further Section 4.1, below, where the significance for collective bargaining of shifts in the external terms of trade is examined in more detail.

[164] 5 & 6 George V c. 54. For an account of the First World War labour legislation, its implementation and its legacy, see G. Rubin, *War, Law and Labour* (Oxford: Clarendon Press, 1987), and see also A. Reid, 'Dilution, trade unionism and the state', in S. Tolliday and J. Zeitlin (eds.) *Shop Floor Bargaining and the State* (Cambridge: Cambridge University Press, 1985).

[165] By virtue of the Fair Wages Resolution of 1891: see above, Section 3.4.

came over calls for the effective enforcement of minimum wage rates for women workers employed on munitions work falling outside the agreement to maintain customary wages and conditions. This led to the establishment under the Munitions Act 1916[166] of a national arbitration tribunal for the specific purpose of dealing with women's wages, the findings of which could be enforced by ministerial order. As before the war, direct legal intervention in wage-fixing was justified for women workers who fell outside the normal scope of collective bargaining.[167]

However, a more significant departure from voluntarism occurred with the onset from 1916 of government efforts to limit general wage increases against a background of increasing union militancy and unofficial strike action aimed at preserving real wages against the effects of inflation. These efforts took the form of legal enforcement of the arbitration decisions of the Committee of Production of the Ministry of Munitions. The Munitions Act 1917[168] made the Committee's awards binding on all employers in the relevant wartime production trades, and trades still subject to voluntary agreements tended to follow the Committee's orders. In this way 'a limited interference with a limited object grew into a system of interference which put the responsibility for all wages in munitions production, and indirectly in much other production, on the shoulders of Government'.[169]

The introduction of compulsory arbitration under wartime conditions provided an institutional framework for the growth of collective bargaining and a means by which a growing number of employers were required to recognize and negotiate with trade unions. However, perhaps the most significant contribution of government policy towards the development of collective bargaining during this period was its advocacy of the findings of the Whitley Committee which was set up in response to the rising industrial militancy in the final years of the war. The Committee reiterated the importance of voluntarism:

We do not . . . regard government assistance as an alternative to the organization of employers and employed. On the contrary, we regard it as a means of furthering the growth and development of such organization.[170]

However, it also recommended the introduction of a generalized system of joint regulation of terms and conditions of employment. Joint representative committees of employers and employees would operate at national, district and workplace level, 'each of the three forms of organization being linked up with the others so as to constitute an organization covering the whole of the trade, capable of considering and advising upon matters affecting the welfare of the

---

[166] 5 & 6 George V c. 99.
[167] H. Clay, *The Problem of Industrial Relations* (London: Macmillan, 1929), at p. 32.
[168] 7 & 8 George V c. 45.   [169] Clay, *The Problem of Industrial Relations*, op. cit., at p. 61.
[170] Ministry of Reconstruction, Committee on Relations between Employers and Employed (Whitley), *Second Report on Joint Standing Industrial Councils*, Cd. 9002, Parliamentary Papers (1918) X.659, at para. 22.

industry, and giving to labour a definite and enlarged share in the discussion and settlement of industrial matters with which employers and employed are jointly concerned'.[171]

Joint Industrial Councils at national level were intended to encourage industrial efficiency and harmonious industrial relations as well as forming the basis for sectoral level bargaining between employers' associations and independent trade unions in the various trades. The Committee came close to recommending legal enforcement of JIC agreements: 'it may be desirable at some later stage for the State to give the sanction of law to agreements made by the Councils, but the initiative in this direction should come from the Councils themselves'.[172] For trades already well organized, the propagation of a standard JIC model and advice from government in setting up JICs would suffice for the time being (a Ministry of Labour, separate from the Board of Trade, had been established in 1917); for less well-organized trades, Interim Reconstruction Committees would be set up as a prelude to the establishment of JICs; and for unorganized trades, the Trade Boards Act 1909 would be amended so as to allow for new sectoral boards to be set up, and to bring about an extension of statutory powers:

The Trade Boards Act was originally intended to secure the establishment of a minimum standard rate of wages in certain unorganised industries, but we consider that the Trade Boards should be regarded as a means of supplying a regular machinery for negotiation and decision on certain groups of questions dealt with in other circumstances by collective bargaining between employers' organisations and trade unions. In order that the Trade Boards Act may be of greater utility in connection with badly organised industries or sections of industries, we consider that certain modifications are needed to enlarge the functions of the Trade Boards. We suggest that they should be empowered to deal not only with minimum rates of wages but hours of labour and questions cognate to wages and hours.[173]

Contrary to the pre-war philosophy, the Whitley Committee did not see the role of legal enforcement as necessarily confined to the worst low paying sectors: 'the general body of employers and employed in any industry should have some means whereby they may bring the whole of the trade up to the standard of minimum conditions which have been agreed upon by a substantial majority of the industry'.[174] In the intermediate category of trades with an uneven pattern of organization, it was suggested that national JICs should be given the option of being converted into trade boards or of setting up partial trade boards with powers of legal enforcement for sections of the relevant industry.

[171] Ministry of Reconstruction, Committee on Relations between Employers and Employed (Whitley), *Final Report*, Cd. 9153, Parliamentary Papers (1918) VIII.629, at para. 2.

[172] Reconstruction Committee, Sub-committee on Relations between Employers and Employed (Whitley), *Interim Report on Joint Industrial Councils*, Cd. 8606, Parliamentary Papers (1917–18) XVIII.415, at para. 21.

[173] Ministry of Reconstruction, *Second Report on Joint Standing Industrial Councils*, op. cit., at para. 11.   [174] Ibid., at para. 15.

The Trade Boards Act 1918[175] incorporated most of the Whitley Committee's recommendations for the trade board sector, and a substantial expansion of the statutory system then took place. Over thirty new boards were set up in 1919 and 1920, and by the end of that year over 3 million workers were covered by the trade boards system; women formed over 70 per cent of them.[176] In addition, between 1918 and 1921 73 JICs were set up and 33 Interim Reconstruction Committees were established in less well-organized trades, fourteen of which were converted into JICs. However, these JICs were placed on an extra-legal basis; Whitley's suggestion of a partial legal underpinning for JICs was not taken up. Nor did the wider remit intended for JICs take hold, as their functions were generally confined to the regulation of terms and conditions. Nevertheless, by 1925 50 JICs remained, covering about 3 million workers.[177] Despite this achievement, further progress towards the formalization of collective bargaining was halted by a combination of industrial depression and employer resistance, which together saw a return to unqualified voluntarism in government policy. The high point of the campaign for statutory intervention was the National Industrial Conference of 1919, which advanced proposals for a universal statutory 48-hour week and minimum wage. This was opposed by the main national employers' organization, the National Confederation of Employers' Organizations, and the government dropped plans to implement the Conference's proposals.[178]

The turning of the tide was further marked by the 1922 Report of the Cave Committee into the functioning of the Trade Boards Acts.[179] Cave saw the trade boards as posing an obstacle to the downwards movement of wages during the recession of the early 1920s, and recommended that the power of statutory compulsion should be reserved for the lowest minimum wage rates set by the boards. This was understood to be a return to the 1909 Act, restricting legal intervention to the enforcement of a bare subsistence wage.[180] A government Bill which would have confined the boards' powers was duly introduced in 1923, only to lapse with the fall of the Conservative government; nevertheless a number of

---

[175] 8 & 9 George V c. 32.

[176] F.R. Bayliss, *British Wages Councils* (Oxford: Blackwell, 1962), at p. 16.

[177] J.H. Richardson, *Industrial Relations in Great Britain* (Geneva: ILO, 2nd ed. 1938), at p. 139.

[178] See R. Lowe, 'The failure of consensus in Britain: the National Industrial Conference, 1919–1921' (1978) 21 *Historical Journal* 649–675, and on the subsequent failure of tripartite negotiations for legislation on working hours, 'Hours of labour: negotiating industrial legislation in Britain, 1919–39' (1982) 35 *Economic History Review* 254–271; A. Fox, *History and Heritage: The Social Origins of the British Industrial Relations System* (London: Allen & Unwin, 1985), at p. 308; D. Brodie, *A History of British Labour Law*, op. cit., ch. 6. For differing interpretations of the roles played by economic changes, trade union militancy, employers' associations and the state in the fluctuating state of national-level collective bargaining during this period, see T. Adams, 'Market and institutional forces in industrial relations; the development of national collective bargaining, 1910–1920' (1997) 50 *Economic History Review* 506–530; H. Gospel, 'Markets, institutions, and the development of national collective bargaining in Britain' (1998) 51 *Economic History Review* 591–596; T. Adams, 'Employers, labour, and the state in industrial relations history: a reply to Gospel' (1998) 51 *Economic History Review* 597–605.

[179] Committee on the Trade Board Acts (Cave), *Report*, Parliamentary Papers (1922) X.669.

[180] Bayliss, *British Wages Councils*, at p. 21.

boards were wound up during this period and the numbers covered by the boards contracted throughout the 1920s.[181]

Subsequently a limited form of minimum wage-fixing through statutory joint boards at county level was applied to agriculture along the line of the Cave formula, and in the 1930s a number of new trade boards were created.[182] By 1939 1.3 million workers were covered by trade board orders, with a further 200,000 within the scope of the Road Haulage Wages Board. The Holidays with Pay Act 1938[183] gave the boards powers to set annual paid leave of up to one week; this Act was passed as a result of concern at the low numbers of workers benefiting from holiday arrangements, with the trade board option being regarded as a means of staving off comprehensive legislation.

However, the condition for the existence of the statutory system was its relative powerlessness. The official position was that the trade boards did not, and should not, operate to close the gap in relative earnings and conditions between the regulated trades and the rest. On the contrary, the Balfour Committee on Industry and Trade of 1929 reported that 'the Trade Boards have generally based their rates not on any theoretic minimum standards of life but on the practical conditions of the industry and on a comparison with the rates arrived at by voluntary agreement in other industries for somewhat similar services'.[184] The Committee concluded that as long as the statutory boards were confined to those sectors which met the twin criteria of exceptionally low pay and inadequate organization, 'there appears to be no grounds for apprehension that the undue extension of the Trade Boards may have serious repercussions for the free working of the normal wage-fixing machinery in the organised trades'.[185]

Outside the trade board sector, there was no single model for multi-employer bargaining during the inter-war period, with legislation playing only a marginal role in selected industries in the enforcement of minimum terms. The Balfour Committee confirmed the established principle of industry-specific regulation, coupled with voluntarism: 'on the whole, the methods of collective negotiation and settlement of wages questions, which have grown up spontaneously in accordance with the varying circumstances of different trades, are vastly preferable to any form of cast-iron system proposed by law'.[186] Within the public sector, national-level bargaining was established through the Whitley Councils and similar representative institutions which served to standardize earnings at national level. In the private sector, national rates were set as a floor to wages, but rates continued to reflect the wide range of interests which were represented in employer

---

[181] See generally R. Lowe, 'The erosion of state intervention in Britain 1917–24' (1978) 31 *Economic History Review* 270–286.

[182] See the Agricultural Wages Act 1921, 11 & 12 George V c. 47, and Road Haulage Wages Act 1938, 1 & 2 George VI c. 44.   [183] 1 & 2 George VI c. 70.

[184] Committee on Industry and Trade (Balfour), *Final Report*, Cmd. 3282, Parliamentary Papers (1928–29) VII.413, at p. 90. For an account and assessment of the Balfour Report see Ewing, 'The state and industrial relations', op. cit.   [185] Ibid., at p. 91.

[186] Ibid., at p. 89.

associations and in particular the needs of the least profitable firms. Moreover, with the rise in unemployment in the 1920s and 1930, many of the remaining JICs ceased to set national wage rates. Defying the confident expectation of the Balfour Committee that the voluntary system could operate without legal support, only 20 JICs remained in operation by 1939.[187] Large areas of industry stayed outside the JIC system altogether, including coal, rail, engineering, shipping, iron and steel, and cotton.[188] In coal the employers refused to engage in national-level bargaining after the strike of 1926. At district level a system of voluntary conciliation boards was in operation and the 1912 Coal Mines Minimum Wage Act continued in force, but in most cases minimum rates were fixed by voluntary machinery and the statutory rates were not kept up to date. The Coal Mines Act 1930[189] established a Coal Mines National Industrial Board consisting of trade union and employer representatives with an independent chairman, with the power to conduct inquiries into wage disputes and make recommendations. The Mining Association of coal employers boycotted the National Board, so depriving it of any general authority. In the railway industry an Act of 1921[190] underpinned a national procedure for resolving wage disputes. The procedure was essentially voluntary and was altered by agreement in 1935 without new legislation being passed.[191]

The economic slump of the early 1930s led to widespread wage-cutting, undermining the rates set by national agreements. An Act of Parliament was passed in 1934 to give statutory effect, on a temporary basis, to minimum rates laid down in the weaving section of the cotton industry, following a joint application from the employers and trade unions.[192] This measure was exceptional for its time, however; in most industries employers continued to resist statutory intervention, and although Bills for the enforcement of collective agreements were introduced in 1924 and 1931, they failed to gain widespread parliamentary support. A further factor was the division of attitudes within the TUC; although unions such as those in the hosiery trade which faced difficulties in enforcing minimum rates consistently favoured statutory intervention, the prevailing view was that this would invite compulsory conciliation and arbitration and the undermining of union autonomy under the Acts of 1871 and 1906.[193]

As Clay pointed out at the time, there was no logical reason for linking the issues of legal enforcement of standard rates and union responsibility; it was possible to draft legislation on the model of the Trade Board Acts to prevent undercutting of minimum terms. The more general objection to giving JICs legal powers was 'that their merits—their spontaneity and adaptability, the spirit of compromise and co-operation they engender' were dependent upon their

---

[187] Fox, *History and Heritage*, op. cit., at p. 297.
[188] See generally Richardson, *Industrial Relations in Great Britain*, op. cit.
[189] 20 & 21 George V c. 34.   [190] V Railways Act, 11 & 12 George 5 c. 55.
[191] See Ewing, 'The state and industrial relations', op. cit.
[192] Cotton Manufacturing Industry (Temporary Provisions) Act 1934, 24 & 25 George V c. 30.
[193] Ewing, 'The state and industrial relations', op. cit.

voluntary status.[194] In rejecting a proposal to make collective agreements drawn up by JICs generally binding by a statutory order, the Balfour Committee argued that 'the situation thus created would probably end in the absorption of all the functions of wage-fixing by the Joint Industrial Council, and the extinction of voluntary methods throughout the industry'.[195] The result was that in conditions of prolonged industrial depression and high unemployment, many trades lacked effective mechanisms for the enforcement of labour standards.

The proposal for works committees also had only limited success. This was the most explicitly cooperative element in the Whitley programme, and yet at the same time the committees were to be firmly based on independent trade unionism. What was envisaged was a division of function between multi-employer bargaining at either district or national level, which would set hours and wages for the trade, and works committees at plant level which would not be involved in wage bargaining but would instead have a consultative role on matters affecting health and safety and work organization—'questions closely affecting daily life and comfort in, and the success of, the business, and affecting in no small degree efficiency of working, which are peculiar to the individual workshop or factory'.[196] The committees should meet fortnightly and 'always keep in the forefront the idea of constructive co-operation in the improvement of the industry to which they belonged'.[197] The membership of the committees was to be agreed between the independent trade unions and employers' association in the trade in question. Again, no legislation was intended, but rather general encouragement from government, with the Ministry of Labour producing a model constitution. By 1922 the Ministry reported that over 1,000 committees had been set up, but in the depression of the early 1920s this early progress was reversed. Agreements for the establishment of committees were made in the engineering and rail transport industries, but in general neither trade unions nor employers' associations pursued the experiment with any great enthusiasm—the unions on the whole displayed an attitude of 'watchful and even suspicious neutrality, while sometimes they have shown definite hostility'.[198]

A move towards a comprehensive system of national-level collective bargaining only took place as a result of the second extension of governmental powers during wartime and the favourable conditions for trade unionism after the war including low unemployment.[199] National collective bargaining was actively fostered by the Conditions of Employment and National Arbitration Order of 1940 (Order 1305) which banned strikes and lock-outs and established compulsory unilateral arbitration. Undercutting was finally prevented by an

---

[194] H. Clay, *The Problem of Industrial Relations*, op. cit., at p. 171.   [195] Ibid., at p. 121.

[196] Ministry of Reconstruction, Committee on Relations between Employers and Employed, *Supplementary Report on Works Committees*, Cd. 9001, Parliamentary Papers (1918) XIV.951, at para. 2.   [197] Ibid., at para. 6.

[198] Richardson, *Industrial Relations in Great Britain*, op. cit., at p. 167.

[199] On the Second World War legislation, see Brodie, *A History of Labour Law*, op. cit., ch. 8.

extension of the fair wages principle to private industry, making agreements 'between organizations or employers and trade unions . . . representative respectively of substantial proportions of the employers in the trade in the district in which the employer is engaged' binding on non-federated employers.[200] The wartime government rejected formal wage controls and concentrated instead on keeping down retail prices and the rationing of essential commodities as means of containing wage inflation. The Wages Councils Act 1945 was the occasion not simply for the expansion of the trade board sectors into a number of service sectors, but for a more general attempt to place institutional wage determination on a secure footing. In addition to strengthening the wages councils, the 1945 Act provided for the continuation of Order 1305 for the enforcement of collectively agreed terms and conditions through unilateral arbitration, and in 1946 the House of Commons passed a strengthened version of the Fair Wages Resolution, requiring government contractors to observe recognized terms and conditions in the relevant trade. By 1946 56 JICs had been either reactivated or newly created, and the Ministry of Labour estimated that almost 90 per cent of workers in industries and services were covered either by joint voluntary collective bargaining or by statutory machinery. By 1960 some 200 JICs were in existence, and union membership had increased to 9.8 million from a figure of 6.1 million in 1938. The war years also saw a revival of shopfloor organization in areas such as mining and engineering where it had been rolled back in the inter-war years, and its establishment for the first time in newer industries such as aircraft and motor production. Factors conducive to the development of shopfloor-level organization and negotiation included the high level of wartime economic activity, low unemployment and the efforts of the Ministry of Labour and Joint Productive Committees to raise plant-level productivity and improve welfare facilities.

The Wages Councils Act 1945[201] was therefore a major step towards putting in place a generalized floor of rights to terms and conditions of employment. Fearing the effects of a post-war depression which did not in fact materialize as expected, Ernest Bevin sought to extend statutory wage regulation well beyond what could have been justified by the traditional criteria of exceptionally low pay and inadequate organization: 'this conception of the function of Wages Councils amounted

---

[200] There is a growing literature on Order 1305. For a sceptical reading, which regards the element of compulsion in the Order as a 'mirage', stresses its 'legal ambiguities' and concludes that it was a 'bluff', see J. Jaffe, 'The ambiguities of compulsory arbitration and the wartime experience of Order 1305' (2003) 15 *Historical Studies in Industrial Relations* 1–25; but see also accounts which stress the significance of Order 1305 as a mechanism for underpinning terms and conditions of employment, and which question the wisdom of its repeal in the early 1950s, in particular N. Fishman, ' "A Vital Element in British Industrial Relations": a Reassessment of Order 1305' (1999) 12 *Historical Studies in Industrial Relations* 109–130; Wedderburn, 'Change, struggle and ideology in British labour law', op. cit., at pp. 8–15.   [201] 8 & 9 George VI c. 17.

to the use of State power to keep collective bargaining going when economic circumstances tended to destroy it, and was quite different from the simpler, ameliorative purpose of abolishing sweating'.[202] The 1945 Act therefore facilitated the setting up of new councils and the scope of wage regulation orders was widened to cover all questions of wages, hours and holidays (the latter now no longer subject to the one-week limit set by the Holidays with Pay Act 1938), so making the councils more like collective bargaining institutions. The principal sectors included within the statutory system for the first time were catering, which had been regulated by an Act of 1943, and the retail trades, where JICs set up at the start of the war had failed to set effective rates and now applied to become wages councils under the new procedure. The result of expansion was to widen the statutory sector to cover one in four of all employees, 3.5 million covered by wages councils and 3.4 million by agricultural wages boards. Around 75 per cent of wages council employees were women workers.[203]

By these means, the 1945 Act implemented a model of wage regulation which departed significantly from the earlier trade boards model. Although the statutory system continued to be confined to low-paying sectors, its scope had been greatly extended. These was still no universal labour code covering all workers. But, in this way a practically comprehensive system of minimum terms and conditions was established without the kind of general legal intervention through a floor of rights which characterized other European countries at this time. The factors which made such a development possible were relatively high employment, which provided a *de facto* floor to wages and conditions, and the indirect support of government for the collective bargaining process, but these very conditions raised basic contradictions within the voluntary system and in its classic form it barely lasted out the 1950s.

4. The Macroeconomic and Fiscal Context of Collective Laissez-faire

4.1 The economic–theoretical underpinnings of full employment policy

The reforms which accompanied the rise of the welfare state and the construction of a comprehensive system of autonomous collective bargaining were targeted not at defects in the 'character' of the poor as nineteenth-century orthodoxies had been, but at the defects in the market system itself: the superior bargaining power of capital over labour was to be redressed by collective bargaining and legally

---

[202] Bayliss, *British Wages Councils*, op. cit., at p. 56.   [203] Ibid., at p. 73.

enforceable minimum labour standards, while income insecurity resulting from the risks of unemployment, sickness and old age was to be countered by national insurance. In its turn, the failure of the economy to generate full employment was to be offset by macroeconomic policy. Of these three, the theoretical justification for state intervention to secure full employment proved to be particularly difficult to establish.

The relief for working-class organization from the strictures of political economy which had been provided by the refutation of the wage fund theory was short-lived. This, along with the threat posed by Marx's exploitation theory of distribution,[204] helped to trigger the development, in the 1880s, of the *neo*classical theory of wages which was developed out of the 'marginalist' analysis of W.S. Jevons and Alfred Marshall.[205] Neoclassical economics extended the Ricardian theory of the diminishing marginal productivity of land to labour. But, whereas Ricardo's theory was based on the natural variability of the fertility of land, there was an inherent restraint on the productivity of labour in the new theory. The idea was that labour productivity declined as the labour employed increased relative to capital and/or other factors of production. From the supply side, the acceptance of a job would depend on whether the wage it offered compensated for the marginal disutility of work. And, as the onerousness of work was assumed to increase as more of it was done, its marginal disutility rose and with it the wage necessary for its compensation. The supply curve of labour, therefore, sloped upwards. The intersection of the aggregate demand and supply curves of labour determined the wage which firms can afford to pay *and* which cleared the market of all workers willing to work and capable of working for that wage. In such a world there could be no involuntary unemployment.

Thus neoclassical economics rehabilitated the conclusions of the wage fund theory, namely that wages needed to fall if employment was to rise, with one major difference. Wages were now directly linked to the productivity of labour, which determined what employers could pay, and which declined as employment grew. Any institutional impediment to the downward movement of wages to this level created unemployment, as would any social welfare benefits which provided a credible alternative to wage income. Thus at the end of the nineteenth century, marginal productivity theory again under-scored the principle of less eligibility in the administration of social welfare and put laissez-faire on a more 'scientific' basis. Unemployment and poverty could be safely blamed on trade unions, misguided

---

[204] The Austrian economist Bohm-Bawerk, one of the pioneers of the marginal productivity theory of wages, argued that the Marxist theory of distribution constituted 'the focal point about which attack and defence rally in the war in which the issue is the system under which human society shall be organised': A. Campus, 'Marginalist economics', in J. Eatwell, M. Milgate and P. Newman (eds.) *The New Palgrave: A Dictionary of Economics*, Vol. 3 (London, Macmillan, 1987), at p. 320.

[205] See P.S. Atiyah, *The Rise and Fall of Freedom of Contract* (Oxford: Clarendon Press, 1979), at pp. 607–611. As Atiyah explains, 'marginalism' was used in the 1870s to attack inequalities between rich and poor, but this strand of neoclassical thought was increasingly discarded in the effort to discredit Marxist theory. See also Ch. 3, Section 5.6, above.

charity, wrong-headed protective legislation, and the poor and unemployed themselves.

The key to progress was a theoretical explanation for the possibility of involuntary unemployment, understood as a situation in which workers are jobless because there is no work for them to do even if they are prepared to work and to accept lower wages. The very possibility of involuntary unemployment ran counter to one of the most firmly held views of the classical economists, namely that supply created its own demand (Say's Law). The neoclassical elaboration of this idea was the notion that individuals only worked for the utility from consumption provided by wages. Workers might be persuaded to postpone consumption if the return on their savings was high enough to compensate them for that delay. Investors would provide this in the form of interest if it was no higher than their expected returns on capital investment. By these means, the market for savings (the capital market) would clear, guaranteeing that any surplus resources would be taken up and invested. Any attempts by government to increase employment would merely squeeze out private expenditure.

Unorthodox theoretical support for the grievance of the unemployed came from the work of J.A. Hobson. Hobson followed Malthus in arguing that the relatively slow growth of effective demand resulting from the conservatism of consumers led to the unemployment of both labour and capital. But he also attributed under-consumption to inequalities in the distribution of income, and to the satiation of the consumption demands of the rich, which automatically generated over-saving and over-capitalization. Thus:

... a natural conservatism in the arts of consumption in part [explains] the failure of consumption to keep full pace with the more progressive arts of production. But this natural tendency is strongly reinforced by inequalities in the distribution of income, which places a larger proportion of the aggregate incomes in the possession of comparatively small classes who, after satisfying all their economic desires, have large surpluses for automatic saving and investment.[206]

Hobson identified *unearned income*, which accrued to the rich in the form of rents from land, speculation and high profits from monopolies, as a major source of over-saving. The solution was to redistribute consuming power by taxing unearned income and increasing wages, the incidence of which he argued would fall on unearned income. The parasitic nature of unearned income meant that it could be depleted without any disincentive to productive activity.

The supply side explanations for unemployment offered by Beveridge and the Webbs, which stressed the role of the poor law and ineffective labour regulation in perpetuating a cycle of casualization,[207] received more policy attention than Hobson's demand side analysis prior to the 1930s. However, the high levels of unemployment and poverty of inter-war years, and the social and political

[206] J.A. Hobson, *Economics of Unemployment* (London: Allen & Unwin, 1922), at p. 35.
[207] See Chapter 3, Section 5, above.

response to them, set the context for a successful challenge to laissez-faire orthodoxy on the aggregate level of employment, which was set out by Keynes in the *General Theory*.[208]

Keynes' main attack on neoclassical employment theory came in his refutation of Say's Law. He argued that as incomes rose the proportions saved by individuals increased. He refuted the neoclassical claim that the capital market functioned so as to ensure that savings were invested by arguing that the interest rate was determined by the supply and demand for money rather than by savings, and that speculative demand for money played a decisive role in determining interest rate fluctuations. As no mechanism existed whereby the income which was saved was automatically taken up and invested, an increased propensity to save progressively lowered consumption demand and employment, until the reduction in aggregate income squeezed out excess saving. Thus, saving was brought into line with invest-ment not by the working of the capital market but by changes in the level of income and employment. The result was *involuntary* unemployment: workers were unable to find jobs at, or even below, the going wage because of a shortage of demand for the products or services which they could produce.

Keynes also integrated the *real* and *money* worlds and argued for an alternative role for money to that of simply regulating the general level of prices. He reasoned that the money supply influences the level of economic activity through its effect on the interest rate, which is one of the determinants of the level of investments. An increase in the money supply by lowering the rate of interest leads to an increase in investment and an increase in employment, opening the way for the use of monetary policy to increase effective demand and employment. The other policy possibility for increasing employment opened up by Keynes was an increase in government expenditure relative to taxation, a use of fiscal policy for macro-economic purposes which made budget deficit financing respectable.

In his critique of the neoclassical theory of employment, Keynes retained a marginalist explanation for the demand for labour but rejected the marginal disutility explanation of labour supply.[209] This rejection was on two grounds. The first related '. . . to the actual behaviour of labour'. 'A fall in real wages due to a rise in prices, with money wages unaltered, does not as a rule, cause the supply of available labour on offer at the current wage to fall below the amount actually employed prior to the rise in prices.'[210] The second objection, which Keynes regarded as more fundamental, was to the assumption that bargaining between workers and their employers determined the level of *real* wages.

For there may be *no* method available to labour as a whole whereby it can bring the wage-goods equivalent of the general level of money wages into conformity with the

---

[208] J.M. Keynes, *The General Theory of Employment, Interest and Money* (London: Macmillan, 1936), reprinted as *The Collected Writings of John Maynard Keynes Volume 7* (London: Macmillan, 1973) (subsequent references are to this edition).   [209] Ibid., at p. 5.
[210] Ibid., at pp. 12–13.

marginal disutility of the current volume of employment. There may exist no expediency by which labour as a whole can reduce its *real* wage to a given figure by making revised *money* bargains with the entrepreneurs. This will be our contention. We shall endeavour to show that primarily it is certain other forces which determine the general level of real wages.[211]

For Keynes then, neoclassical theory was invalid because workers had no way of determining their real wages and did not operate as if real wages (as opposed to money wages) were of crucial importance in their employment decisions.

Keynes admitted that his continued adherence to the theory of the diminishing marginal productivity of labour seriously complicated his analysis.[212] In effect, it left him with two distinct theories of employment. At the macro level, employment depended on aggregate demand, which, in turn, was *positively* related to the real wage. This was because of the effect of the real wage on consumption. At the level of the firm—the micro-level—employment was *inversely* related to the real wage because of diminishing marginal productivity. To rescue himself from this dilemma, Keynes argued that an external stimulus to aggregate demand would create the conditions for an increase in employment. This would be realized at micro-level because workers either would not, or would simply be unable to, resist a reduction in the real wage as prices responded to the increase in demand.

The need for this convoluted argument was challenged by Dunlop[213] and Tarshis[214] who demonstrated that the historical record showed no tendency either for real wages to fall as employment increased, or for them to rise as employment fell, as neo-classical theory predicted. Rather, it was more usual for real wages to move pro-cyclically. In responding to this criticism Keynes admitted that Dunlop and Tarshis had: 'seriously shaken the fundamental assumptions on which the short-period theory of distribution had been based hitherto'.[215] Once free of marginal productivity theory, Keynesian policy makers could concentrate on developing macroeconomic solutions to unemployment in the knowledge that a real wage reduction was not a necessary condition for their success. Keynes' reluctance to abandon the wage theory of his Marshallian forebears left a way open for the neoclassical revival, but that was another forty years away.[216]

4.2 The dynamics of inflation, union growth, and state intervention in industrial relations

The adoption by government of the goal of full employment policy was defined by Beveridge as a situation in which there was a decisive shift in power from the

[211] Ibid., at p. 13.   [212] Ibid., at p. 40.
[213] J.T. Dunlop, 'The movement of real and money wage rates' (1938) 48 *Economic Journal* 413–434.
[214] L. Tarshis, 'Changes in real and money wages' (1939) 49 *Economic Journal* 150–7.
[215] J.M. Keynes, 'Relative movement of real wages and output' (1939) 49 *Economic Journal* 34–51, at p. 50.   [216] See below, Section 6.

buyers of labour to the sellers.[217] In *Full Employment in a Free Society*, written in 1944, Beveridge anticipated that if the state took steps to guarantee access to regular and stable employment, through the active management of demand and the expansion of the public sector, the result might well be to strengthen collective bargaining, but at the same time to create new pressures for state control over the outcome of wage negotiations. This proved to be a prophetic observation.

Two further institutional changes helped to place inflation at the top of the policy agenda in the post-war period. After 1945, the emphasis on centralized bargaining increased the proportion of earnings accounted for by nationally-agreed wage rates. Again, national agreements were supplemented by local negotiations, so that a two-tier system emerged. In the boom which occurred after the end of the war, local union organizations were well placed to exploit shortages of labour and the enhanced ability of newly profitable firms to meet their claims, so that earnings as a whole grew at a faster rate than nationally-agreed rates. This helped offset the otherwise equalizing effect of national bargaining, and it also added to a new problem: controlling wage inflation.

The second element also came to the fore after 1945. Thanks to the expansion of the welfare state, public expenditure rose together with levels of taxation. Income tax, previously confined to higher earners, was extended to most of the workforce over the next twenty years, and national insurance contributions increased in scale and significance, in particular for lower earners. The result of this process was to place new strains on the capacity of the collective bargaining system to maintain real wage levels, in particular during periods of rapidly rising inflation. For these various reasons, the external policy environment became highly unfavourable to the goal of autonomous collective bargaining, precisely at the point when it appeared to be enjoying the support of an unprecedented political consensus. When these stresses were brought to bear on collective bargaining in the 1960s and 1970s, what had once been thought to be strengths of the system, in particular its decentralized nature and industry-specific focus, turned out to be serious weaknesses.

Thus the course of the twentieth century was marked by a series of inflationary cycles which arose from the interaction of collective bargaining, increased employment taxation and full employment policy. The process began as a consequence of the growing institutionalization of collective bargaining in the early twentieth century. As collective bargaining was put into place at the end of the nineteenth century and gradually extended downwards to increased numbers of workers in the course of the twentieth, earnings differentials significantly narrowed. Between 1913/14 and 1978, the percentage pay differential separating higher professionals from the lower skilled occupations more than halved (see Table 4.1). However, the erosion of the pay gap was not a steady, continuous progress. The narrowing effect was mainly confined to periods of high inflation: 1913/14–24, 1935/6–55/6, and

---

[217] In *Full Employment in a Free Society* (London: Liberal Party Publications, 1944). See our discussion in Chapter 3, Section 5, above.

Table 4.1. Skill differentials 1913/14 to 1978: percentage of earnings of lower skilled manual worker (male workers)

	1913/4	1922/4	1935/6	1955/6	1960	1970	1978
Higher professionals	521	455	492	354	380	254	244
Higher skilled manual worker	168	141	151	143	149	125	128
Lower skilled manual worker	100	100	100	100	100	100	100

Source: G. Routh, *Occupation and Pay in Great Britain* (2nd edition, Macmillan, 1980).

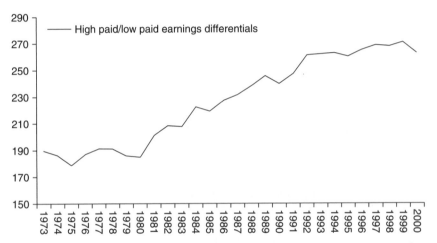

Figure 4.1. Earnings differentials: earnings of high paid occupations as a percentage of the earnings of low paid occupations.

Notes: Occupations used in constructing the index of occupational earnings:

1973–1990

a. High paid men: accountants; finance, insurance tax etc. specialists; marketing and sales managers and executives; secondary school teachers; medical practitioners; journalists; scientists and mathematicians; and, engineers—electrical, electronic.

b. Low paid men: sales persons, shop assistants and shelf fillers; security guards and patrolmen; chefs/cooks; caretakers; hospital porters; general farm workers; butchers, meat cutters; and goods porters—warehouse, markets etc.

1991–2000

a. High paid men: marketing and sales managers; biological scientists and biochemists; electrical engineers; medical practitioners; secondary school teachers; chartered and certificate accountants; underwriters, claims assessors, brokers, investment analysts; and, artists, commercial artists, graphic designers.

b. Low paid men: sales assistants; security guards and related occupations; chefs/cooks; caretakers; hospital porters; farm workers; butchers, meat cutters; and, goods porters.

Source: Office of National Statistics, *New Earnings Survey, Part D, Analysis by Occupation*, various years.

1960–78. In periods when prices were growing more slowly, the process of equalization was reversed: this was the case between 1922 and 1936 and 1956 and 1960. Since 1980, the process has been even more marked. Figure 4.1 reports the changing differential in the average of the median earnings of male employees for representative high and low paid occupations, drawn from the New Earnings Survey. Between 1979 and 1989 the gap between high and low paid occupations widened from 85 per cent to 146 per cent, and by 2000 it had widened further to 163 per cent.

The narrowing of differentials during periods of inflation occurred in large part as a result of the widespread practice of making flat-rate wage settlements, which prevailed for much of the twentieth century; the effect was that lower paid workers caught up, in real terms, with groups above them in the pay hierarchy.[218] By contrast, during recessions, differentials tended to widen because the least well paid, and the least well organized, suffered a disproportionate loss of bargaining power at times of low demand for labour, thanks to competition from the unemployed and the general increase in economic insecurity for these groups. This effect was particularly strong in the first few decades of the twentieth century when, as we have seen, competitive pressures in the disorganized trades were particularly intense.

A major external factor affecting the extent and duration of inflationary episodes was provided by shifts in the prices of imported goods relative to home-produced goods. Rising import prices played a significant role in triggering each of the turning points in the long inflationary cycles of the twentieth century (see Figure 4.2). Again, the system of wage determination was a major determinant in the process whereby import prices were transmitted into domestic inflation. Throughout the twentieth century the intensity of wage demands and the degree of worker militancy were linked to shifts in the cost of living, so that when prices increased, so did wage claims.[219] Employers would respond to increased wage demands by increasing prices so as to maintain profitability. Under these circumstances, a fall in the price of imported goods, relative to those produced domestically, would exert a downward pressure on prices and so reduce the cost of living element in wage claims. When, on the other hand, import prices were rising relative to domestic prices, the downward pressure on both the cost of living and profits would be intensified, thereby building an upward pressure on wages and prices.

Table 4.2 illustrates how the main constituents in the inflationary process operated in each of the main inflationary episodes of the twentieth century. The importance of the external terms of trade is indicated by the increase in import prices relative to domestic costs in each inflationary upswing, and by the relative fall in import prices by comparison to home costs in the subsequent periods of decelerating prices. Table 4.2 also indicates that there was no clear relationship between the inflation cycle and growth in labour productivity, which was

---

[218] H.A. Turner, 'Inflation and wage differentials in Great Britain', in J.T. Dunlop (ed.) *The Theory of Wage Determination* (London: Macmillan, 1957).
[219] W.W. Daniel, *Wage Determination in Industry* (London: PEP, 1976).

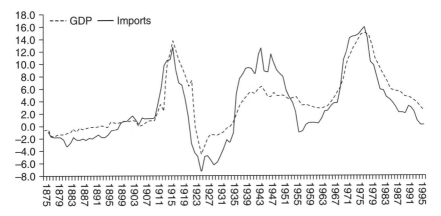

Figure 4.2. Trends in home costs and import prices: (9 year moving average)

Sources: C.H. Feinstein (1972) *National Income, Expenditure and Output of the United Kingdom, 1855–1965,* Cambridge University Press, Office of National Statistics, *Economic Trends Annual Supplement*, various years.

Table 4.2. Average annual increases in prices, productivity and earnings in the inflationary episodes

Inflationary Episode	Home costs	Import prices	Labour productivity	Average earnings	Retail prices	Real take-home pay
1895–1920	4.7	5.1	0	4.9	4.5	0.4
1920–1933	−3.9	−8.8	1.6	−3.1	−4.3	1.3
1933–1952	4.6	9.0	1.1	6.2	4.9	1.4
1952–1960	3.3	−1.0	2.3	5.8	2.8	2.2[a]
1960–1979	8.4	8.1	2.3	10.6	8.3	1.2[a]
1979–2000	5.1	2.5	1.9	7.4	5.4	2.3[a]

[a] including the direct tax effect.

Sources: C.H. Feinstein, *National Income, Expenditure and Output of the United Kingdom, 1855–1965,* Cambridge University Press, 1972; Office of National Statistics, *Economic Trends Annual Supplement*, HMSO (various years); Office of National Statistics, *Labour Market Trends*, HMSO (various years).

generally slower before the mid-point of the century than after, and particularly slow in the period up to and during the First World War.

The final three columns of Table 4.2 summarize the effects of changes in earnings and prices: earnings grew more slowly relative to prices in periods of accelerating inflation so that real take-home pay increased more quickly during the deflationary part of the cycle. This is particularly the case for the period between 1895 and 1920, which followed a period from the early 1870s (the 'Great Depression') when falling import prices had exerted a strong downwards pressure on domestic prices relative to wages, and real take-home pay had risen, as a result, by around 2 per cent per annum. The period between 1933 and 1952 is an exception to the regular pattern since real wages grew even when price inflation was accelerating; however, this can be explained by the effect of price controls and subsidies which were in operation during the Second World War.

Table 4.2 also illustrates the growing role of taxation. Until the Second World War, real take-home pay consisted of money wages adjusted for retail prices. From 1940, income tax and, in the post-war period, rising national insurance contributions, increasingly eroded real take-home pay, as the last three rows of the final column indicate. On average, these employment taxes reduced the annual increase in real take-home pay by 0.7 per cent between 1952 and 1960 and 0.9 per cent between 1960 and 1979, whereas tax reductions added 0.4 per cent to the average annual increase in real take-home pay after 1979.

The ability of workers to maintain and enhance earnings levels can therefore be seen to have been dependent on a range of factors. Some of these would have been internal to the structure of particular unions or were influenced by labour history and culture, such as the degree of militancy or the capacity for self-organization in a particular industry or occupation, but others were the consequence of wider economic factors: changes in price inflation, the incidence of taxation, and the extent of unemployment. As the bargaining environment changed, this affected the bargaining strength of workers, with further effects upon bargaining outcomes in terms of real take-home pay, the extent of pay inequality, and price inflation. However, particular factors were more strongly linked than others.

Figure 4.3 suggests that there was a strong relationship between the inflationary cycle and changes in trade union membership and density (the proportion of the employed labour force in trade unions). Membership and density increased slowly between 1895 and 1905 but then increased rapidly to reach a peak of 8.2 million and 48 per cent respectively by 1920. Membership then fell precipitously to a low

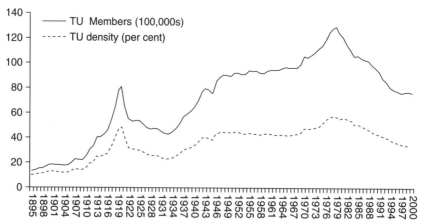

Figure 4.3. Trade union membership and trade union density.

Source: G.S. Bain and R. Price (1980) *Profiles of Union Growth: A Comparative Statistical Portrait of Eight Countries,* Oxford, Basil Blackwell, Certification Officers Annual Reports.

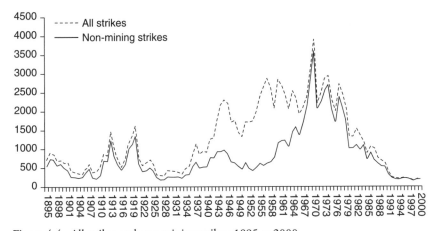

Figure 4.4. All strikes and non-mining strikes, 1895 to 2000.

Source: Department of Employment and Productivity (1971) *British Labour Statistics: Historical Abstract 1886–1968*, HMSO, Office of National Statistics, *Labour Market Trends*, various years.

of 4.2 million in 1933 when density stood at 23 per cent, but then began to recover. By 1952, membership had risen to 9.3 million and density to 45 per cent. During the 1950s growth in membership slowed and density was static, but it then rose again in the 1960s. From 9.5 million in 1960, membership reached 10.6 million in 1970 and 12.6 million in 1979, by which time density was 53 per cent. After 1979 membership fell and by 2000 stood at 7.9 million, while density was only 30 per cent.

The pattern of strikes also closely reflects trends in inflation. This relationship is partly obscured between 1940 and 1960 by the large number of small strikes in the coal industry. The solid line in Figure 4.4 indicates the level of non-mining strikes, which reached high levels between 1910 and 1920, in the 1940s and again in the 1970s when inflation was high and rising.

Thus inflationary upswings saw rising union membership and militancy in response to falling take-home pay, with the overall result tending towards greater equality in the earnings distribution. During these periods, increases in trade union membership were accompanied by the extension of trade unionism into less well-organized sectors and industries.

Figure 4.5 indicates the movement in annual percentage rates of unemployment. Between 1895 and 1920, unemployment was substantially lower than during most of the inter-war years (although, since unemployment figures before 1912 come from the records of skilled craft unions whose members received unemployment compensation, the data for these periods are probably underestimates). Between the wars, unemployment remained high until 1940, but then fell rapidly away and remained below (for long periods, well below) 5 per cent until 1976. Thus in two periods of low inflation, the 1920s and the period between 1980 and

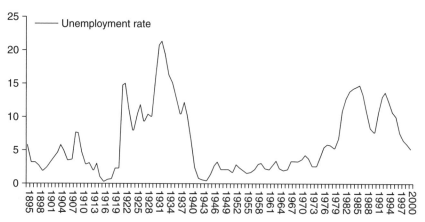

Figure 4.5. Rates of unemployment, 1895 to 2000.

Source: C.H. Feinstein (1972) *National Income, Expenditure and Output of the United Kingdom, 1855–1965*, Cambridge University Press, Office of National Statistics, *Economic Trends Annual Supplement*, various years.

the present day, unemployment was high, but in another, for most of the 1950s, it was very low. The picture is repeated for the inflationary periods: between 1960 and 1979, when inflation was accelerating, unemployment was low by historical standards, but between 1895 and 1920 and 1933 to 1952 wages and prices began to rise when unemployment was also rising. There was therefore no simple relationship between unemployment and inflation.

Table 4.3 sums up the trajectory, over the course of six inflationary episodes, of the factors making up respectively the bargaining environment, the bargaining strength of workers, and bargaining outcomes. From this it can be seen that the 1950s was a period when the economic environment was particularly favourable to orderly and stable collective bargaining: labour productivity was rising rapidly, import prices were falling and unemployment was low. Inflation was low, allowing real incomes to rise, but in contrast to other periods when low inflation saw a sharp decline in union membership (from the 1920s to the mid-1930s and the period from 1979 to 2000), union density was steady and membership was slowly increasing. This was reflected in rapidly rising real incomes. By contrast, in each of the periods of high inflation—1895–1920, 1933–52 and in particular 1960–79—the bargaining environment hardened, with the impact, in the last of these, of direct taxes on earnings, adding to the effect. The effect, in each case, was an increase in union membership and also in union militancy, measured in terms of the level of strike activity.

Thus across the twentieth century as a whole, the growth of collective bargaining and trade union membership has been a discontinuous process, with numerous, partial reversals. The policy preference for collective laissez-faire set the general context in which this process unfolded. From an early stage in its development, the British system was characterized by the absence of a general statutory floor to

Table 4.3. Bargaining environment, bargaining strength and bargaining outcomes in inflationary episodes

Inflationary episode	Bargaining environment				Bargaining strength			Outcomes		
	Import prices relative to home costs	Productivity growth	Unemployment	Direct taxes on wages	Trade union membership	Trade union density	Strikes (non-mining)	Real take-home pay	High pay/low pay	Price inflation
1895 to 1920	Rising	Slow	Moderate then low	None	Rising rapidly	Rising rapidly	Rising rapidly	Falling then recovering	Narrowing	Rising
1920 to 1933	Falling	Moderate	High	None	Falling rapidly	Falling rapidly	Falling rapidly	Rising moderately	Widening	Falling
1933 to 1952	Rising	Moderate	High then low	None	Rising rapidly	Rising rapidly	Rising rapidly	Rising moderately	Narrowing	Rising
1952 to 1960	Falling	Fast	Low	Rising	Rising slowly	Stable	Falling	Rising rapidly	Widening	Falling
1960 to 1979	Rising	Fast	Low then moderate	Rising	Rising rapidly	Rising	Rising rapidly	Rising rapidly then slowing down	Narrowing	Rising
1979 to 2000	Falling	Moderate	High	Falling	Falling rapidly	Falling rapidly	Falling	Rising rapidly	Widening	Falling

wages and conditions and by industry-specific bargaining which reflected the negotiating power of particular occupational groups. Under these circumstances, shifts in real wages over time, brought about by price inflation and, latterly, by employment taxation, were reflected in sharp cyclical fluctuations in union membership and militancy. It is difficult to provide a general answer to the question of whether trade unions caused inflation or inflation caused trade unions, since the relationship between them was one of mutual reinforcement. What we can say is that because of the policy preference for leaving wage determination to the free play of collective forces, the industrial relations system was left highly vulnerable to the destabilizing shifts in the wider economic environment.

In this respect, the particular conjunctions of economic and institutional forces which operated at different points in the inflationary cycle proved to be decisive turning points. Just as the 1950s were a particularly benign period for collective bargaining, the 1960s and 1970s, for a combination of reasons, presented a completely different bargaining environment, one in which the fundamental tenets of the voluntary system would be tested to breaking point.[220]

5. Incomes Policies: Their Forms, Economic Effects, and Consequences for Collective Bargaining

5.1 Form

The incomes policies which operated in various forms after 1945 could have been an extension of full employment policy, as Beveridge had recognized. The view that they were there to 'facilitate socialist economic planning by the Government'[221]— government intervention to regulate prices and incomes in the interests of achieving full employment and sustained economic growth—found expression in policy circles from time to time. In practice, however, incomes policies were almost invariably introduced as ad hoc measures to deal with economic crises, and their aim was the severely practical one of slowing the growth of wage increases relative to price increases.

The first experiment in the use of incomes policies occurred during the period of office of the post-war Labour government, which put in place a zero-increase pay policy between 1948 and 1950. However, no legal or other institutional measures were taken to enforce the norm. With the TUC's encouragement, exceptions to the norm were made if an increase was justified by the need to improve pockets of low pay, maintain established differentials, or recognize improvements in productivity. The next use of an incomes policy was in 1956–57 when the

---

[220] See Davies and Freedland, *Labour Legislation and Public Policy*, op. cit., contrasting 'the easy decade' (Ch. 3) of the 1950s with 'the end of agreement' (Ch. 6) in the 1960s.

[221] See L. Panitch, *Social Democracy and Industrial Militancy: The Labour Party, the Trade Unions and Incomes Policy, 1945–1974* (Cambridge: Cambridge University Press, 1976), at p. 17.

then Conservative government established the Council on Prices, Productivity and Incomes (the 'Three Wise Men') to report on movements of prices, wages and profits. A degree of voluntary pay restraint was encouraged in the light of the Council's findings. The Council was empowered to examine particular pay settlements but it had no legal power to intervene in the collective bargaining process and no mechanism by which to enforce its recommendations. Then in 1961–2 the Conservative government adopted a zero-increase norm which it sought to implement via its control over public sector pay settlements and through the decisions of wages councils, whose orders were, at this point, subject to ministerial approval. It subsequently set a 'guiding light' or upper limit of 2–2.5 per cent for pay increases, later raised to 3–3.5 per cent, with exceptions for increases representing outstanding gains in productivity or designed to attract scarce labour.

The Labour government of 1964–70 took more direct powers in the area of pay restraint. In 1965 the government signed a 'Statement of Intent' with the TUC and the CBI based on a maximum norm of 3–3.5 per cent with certain exceptions, but when this did not have the desired effect of limiting increases the TUC was persuaded to introduce its own 'wage-vetting scheme'. In 1966 a statutory wage freeze was introduced for the first time via the Prices and Incomes Act[222] which set criminal sanctions for firms disobeying the law. Although the freeze was lifted the following year and the policy of voluntary adherence was formally resumed, certain statutory powers were retained for the purpose of referring wage settlements to the National Board for Prices and Incomes, which could delay their implementation for a period of six months. This period was later extended to a year. The Conservative government of 1970–74 also took statutory powers to enforce wage freezes and limits on pay during its term of office.[223]

In a reaction against the use of coercive powers the Labour government of 1974 to 1979 left the enforcement of pay norm to the TUC which in effect became responsible for 'policing' settlements on the government's behalf. The 'Social Contract' originated in discussions between the TUC and the Labour Party in 1973, when Labour was in opposition. In essence, the agreement committed the Labour Party to introducing a series of statutory measures (including price and rent controls, improved social welfare and employment legislation, industrial democracy legislation, public control of investment, and measures for the redistribution of income and wealth through the tax and social security system), in return for voluntary pay restraint on the part of the unions. Phase 1 of the policy aimed to peg wage increases to increases in prices which had occurred since the last annual settlement. This continued the practice begun by the previous Conservative government of setting a twelve-month interval between wage agreements. At this point the aim was to limit price increases through the Price Commission and let wages follow prices down, but faced with price and wage

---

[222] 15 Elizabeth II c. 33.
[223] See Davies and Freedland, *Labour Legislation and Public Policy*, op. cit., at pp. 328–333.

inflation of over 20 per cent this approach was abandoned in mid-1975. This led on to Phase 2 under which a £6 maximum increase was agreed with the TUC, with no rises for those on annual incomes over £8,500. In 1976–77 a maximum percentage rate of 5 per cent was set, with a flat rate minimum of £2.50 and a maximum of £4; the following year, the government and the TUC agreed a 10 per cent maximum across the board, with greater increases for 'self-financing' productivity deals. However, at its 1977 Congress the TUC voted for a return to free collective bargaining, to take effect upon the expiry of the twelve-month settlements then in force.

This signified the effective end of the Social Contract. In its final year in office the Labour government proposed a 5 per cent pay norm but took no direct legal measures to enforce it. In the public sector direct government influence was brought to bear, at the cost of provoking widespread strike action by local authority and health service employees during the 'winter of discontent'. In May 1979 the Conservative government of Mrs. Thatcher took office, committed to an economic policy which avoided formal pay norms and direct interference with collective bargaining, but made the reduction of the 'monopoly power' of the trade unions through changes in labour law a major plank of its economic policy.

5.2 Economic consequences

The incomes policies of the 1960s and 1970s were markedly unsuccessful from the point of view of repressing inflation. Pay restraint was only effective for short periods. The ending of phases of restraint was normally accompanied by an inflationary wage 'explosion' coupled with high levels of strike action and worker militancy. Between 1948 and 1972 the average annual rate of increase of gross weekly earnings for manual workers was 2.3 per cent; however, this figure conceals growth of only 1 per cent in 'policy-on' periods, in contrast to growth of around 3.5 per cent in the 'policy-off' periods.[224] When the effects of direct taxation are taken into account together with pay restraint, the result was considerable falls in real disposable income during the policy-on periods; between 1972 and 1976, as much as 10 per cent, on average, for manual workers.

Incomes policies also had uneven effects across different groups of workers which contributed to their lack of legitimacy. Most incomes policies allowed exceptions for productivity bargaining which would best be exploited by unions which were well-organized at local level and whose firms were able to meet their demands. Incomes policies were also more easily implemented in some sectors. In the public sector, wage determination was highly centralized and the government was directly involved in the bargaining process, either as the employer or the

---

[224] See R. Tarling and F. Wilkinson, 'The Social Contract: post-war incomes policies and their inflationary impact' (1977) 1 *Cambridge Journal of Economics* 395–414.

paymaster, and sometimes as both. As a consequence, certain groups suffered particularly large wage reductions during policy-on periods, and pressure from them for the restoration of differentials was a major factor in strike action which led to the periodic break-up of incomes policies.

In addition, incomes policies failed in the wider sense of providing a framework for economic planning. In particular, they made little contribution to improving levels of investment and productivity. As we noted above, independently from the claims that pay restraint was necessary in order to curb the 'inflationary' tendencies of collective bargaining, incomes policies were at various times advocated as means of diverting resources from wages and consumption into investment, as a part of strategies for securing national competitive advantage. In practice this did not happen in the 1960s and 1970s, largely because the private sector not only did not respond by increasing investment as expected, but also used the surpluses from wage restraint for other purposes, returning much of it to shareholders in the form of dividends.[225]

A principal reason for the failure of incomes policies to achieve their stated economic outcomes is related to developments within the wider collective bargaining system during this period. Incomes policies were highly dependent for their success on the maintenance of stability in collective bargaining arrangements, and in particular upon the effectiveness of multi-employer agreements in keeping individual firms to a common norm. However, the predominant trend from the mid-1950s was towards a reduction in the significance of national bargaining. This was reinforced by state policy including, paradoxically, some unintended effects of income policies themselves.

In conditions of near full employment and historically high levels of productivity growth after 1950, national bargaining procedures in the private sector proved incapable of containing either workers' ability to press for higher pay claims or employers' capacity to concede them at the local level. The result was 'wage drift' based on a growing 'earnings gap' between nationally-agreed wage rates and actual earnings, together with a high incidence of unofficial 'wildcat' strikes over pay and conditions at plant level. From the early 1960s, plant and company-level bargaining, although still largely informal, began to become more formal and systematic. The growth of organized local bargaining was encouraged by government sponsorship of productivity deals as part of the early incomes policies. Incomes policies made it increasingly necessary for organized workers to make concessions on manning, working practices and other forms of job control in return for securing wages above the norms set by government policy. Such changes could only be effectively achieved at local level; at the same time, it was at the local level that wage bargaining was most effectively hidden from government surveillance.

Plant and company-level bargaining began to be more formalized and systematic from the early 1960s for a variety of other reasons. Firstly, British industry was

[225] Ibid.

becoming increasingly concentrated, and a number of firms began to develop their own industrial relations policies. Secondly, as the competitive pressure on British firms increased again after the respite of the war and its immediate aftermath, firms used local-level bargaining as a means to keep wage costs more firmly under control. The impact of the growth in more formalized plant-level and company-level bargaining was to turn national agreements into 'safety-nets', setting basic or minimum terms and conditions which few firms in the industry actually observed in practice. In this way, national bargaining gradually ceased to function as a means of co-ordinating pay and conditions across whole sectors. The effect of revisions made to the national engineering agreement in 1964, for example, was to replace national *wage rates* with national minimum *earnings levels*; it was only those workers with wages below the minimum earnings levels who received increases based on national negotiations. In other cases, plant or company level bargaining set the rate of pay. A similar pattern of single firm bargaining coupled with national minimum earnings levels was adopted in chemicals and in a number of other sectors at this time. The fact that national bargaining still set a floor to earnings was important, in particular for combating low pay. However, the floor tended to be low in relation to average earnings within sectors.

Collective bargaining in the public sector, by contrast, remained more highly centralized. However, comparability of public sector and private sector pay emerged as a major problem in the 1950s, as private sector earnings drew steadily ahead. Under the Whitley Council system, ministers had the power to confirm the decisions of the joint boards of union and employer representatives, but with increasing concerns over public expenditure and the application of pay restraint, the role of the government went beyond mere confirmation and became one of entering directly into negotiations, even where it was not, formally, the employer, as in the case of education. In 1965 the Ministry of Education refused to confirm the agreement of the Burnham Committee on teachers' pay (consisting of representatives of the local authority employers and the teachers' unions) and imposed its own salary scales. The Committee's constitution was later amended to give Ministry (later Department) of Education representatives a formal role. During periods of active incomes policies, public sector pay was held back, but when the restraints were taken off, governments came under pressure to re-establish parity with the private sector. The 'catch up' required was a major factor in the instability of wage inflation in the late 1960s and 1970s, and contributed to the growth of local-level union organization in the public sector. Dissatisfaction with pay and with the undermining of the Whitley principle of joint control led to a strengthening of the role of shop stewards and to local militancy over pay.

Thus the result of a combination of factors, some of them the effect of government intervention including income policies themselves, was that national-level bargaining was weakening as a source of regulation at the expense of plant-level procedures, while union density and shop-floor militancy were on the increase. These were perhaps the least favourable circumstances there could have been for the operation of an anti-inflation strategy based on nation-wide pay norms. The Social Contract failed, in particular, because it gave the TUC the implausible role of 'policing' the implementation of pay restraint. The TUC was unsuited for this role since, in a system which remained essentially based on voluntarism, it had few compulsory powers over its own members; at best, the General Council of leading union representatives which negotiated directly with government could only deliver its side of the deal if it continued to have majority support in the constituent unions. The problem was evident early on in the life of the Social Contract when there was high-level opposition within the TUC to Phase 1, which pegged wage increases to increases in prices which had occurred since the last pay settlement for the workers concerned. By the time the final phase was reached with the announcement of the 5 per cent limit in July 1978, TUC support had already been withdrawn, and as a result there was no realistic possibility that the government could impose the 5 per cent norm on a general basis, short of taking compulsory legal powers which it declined to do.

5.3 The impact on collective laissez-faire

But despite failing on their own terms, incomes policies had profound implications for the voluntary system. This was not particularly visible at the level of legal form, where the impact of incomes policies was marginal; even when statutory powers were taken, every effort was made to separate the legislation governing incomes policies from the normal working of collective labour law and the trade dispute immunities in particular.[226] Thus as far as the conceptual structure of labour law was concerned, incomes policy legislation left no lasting mark.

However, at the structural level of the relationship between state intervention and the voluntary process of wage determination, incomes policies marked a turning point as part of a wider move towards more intrusive governmental interference in the outcomes of wage bargaining.[227] The theme of the modernization of industrial relations procedures, together with a new emphasis on plant and enterprise level relations at the expense of the industry or trade, was validated by the Royal Commission on Trade Unions and Employers' Associations, which was completed in 1968 (the 'Donovan Report').[228] Donovan appeared to confirm the continuing relevance of the principles of collective laissez-faire: the Commission rejected proposals for the legal enforcement of collective agreements containing

[226] Lord Wedderburn, 'Labour law now: a hold and a nudge?' (1985) 13 *Industrial Law Journal* 73–85.
[227] P. Davies and M. Freedland, 'Introduction', in Davies and Freedland (eds.) *Kahn-Freund's Labour and the Law* (London: Stevens, 1983), and *Labour Legislation and Public Policy*, op. cit., ch. 4.3.
[228] Royal Commission on Trade Unions and Employers' Associations (Donovan), *Report*, Cmnd. 3623 (1968); see R. Lewis, 'The role of law in employment relations' in Lewis (ed.) *Labour Law in Britain* (Oxford: Blackwell, 1986); W.E.J. McCarthy, 'The rise and fall of collective bargaining', op. cit.; Davies and Freedland, *Labour Legislation and Public Policy*, op. cit., ch. 6.

'peace obligations' taking the form of commitments not to strike until certain procedures were exhausted. On the other hand, the Commission marked a turning point in attitudes towards the voluntary system of collective bargaining, by criticizing both employers and trade unions for 'sustaining the facade of industry-wide bargaining'.[229] It favoured the development of greater formality of procedures and processes at plant level as a means of combating what was seen as the 'disorder' of the 'informal system' of industrial relations within individual firms and establishments. Employment protection legislation was to be an important part of this. The Commission recommended the enactment of unfair dismissal legislation, to be administered through a system of 'labour tribunals', one of the functions of which would be to reduce the incidence of wildcat strikes by providing a forum within which disputes over dismissal and discipline could be resolved without resort to industrial action. This proposal was later enacted as part of the Industrial Relations Act 1971,[230] which adopted for this purpose the existing system of industrial tribunals, which already had jurisdiction to resolve issues arising out of legislation on training levies and redundancy compensation.

Donovan's endorsement of abstentionism in the collective sphere was qualified not just by this specific recommendation for legislation in the individual field, but also by its more general call for reform of voluntary processes. As Roy Lewis has suggested, 'Donovan's reform strategy . . . departed from traditional non-intervention by advocating a series of legislative measures and by strongly emphasising the need for managerial and economic efficiency, a strand of industrial relations policy which was closely linked with the requirements of incomes policy'. However, 'the central issue for Donovan was how to restore order, peace and efficiency to industrial relations and yet to preserve and even extend the voluntarist tradition of collective bargaining'.[231]

Donovan's rejection of greater legal compulsion in the field of collective relation was itself rejected by the Conservative government of 1971–74, whose Industrial Relations Act introduced a completely new system of collective labour law. The traditional combination of common law liability coupled with statutory immunities for industrial action was replaced by a system of unfair labour practices loosely modelled on the American Taft-Hartley Act of 1947; provision was made for pre-strike ballots and 'cooling-off periods' and for compulsory arbitration and conciliation to settle disputes, with a prominent role for a new labour court, the National Industrial Relations Court. Statutory controls over the closed shop were introduced for the first time. Protection for trade unions against the large part of civil liabilities was made conditional upon unions re-registering under the Act, but virtually all refused to do so as this would have exposed union rulebooks to substantive powers of legal review.

The 1971 Act proved to be a failure, largely thanks to the strength of union resistance; it did nothing to reduce levels of strike activity, and the National

---

[229] *Donovan Report*, para. 111.   [230] 18 Elizabeth II c. 72.
[231] 'The role of law in employment relations', op. cit., at p. 32.

Industrial Relations Court was faced with repeated embarrassments in attempting to enforce its orders.[232] But even this measure, which contained what were then unprecedented powers of direct legal compulsion, was not necessarily hostile to the Donovan Report's underlying goal of preserving collective bargaining by reforming it. Unions were offered a range of positive rights, in particular a right to recognition in certain circumstances, in return for submitting themselves to the controls which would stem from registration under the Act. It was 'a package under which the unions were offered integration into a corporatist framework of economic management'.[233] As it was, although the unions declined this offer, the supporters of the 1971 Act 'always refused to accept that it was an anti-union measure . . . it was sometimes argued to be compatible with the underlying intentions of [collective laissez-faire]—if not with its outward form'.[234]

The Labour government of 1974–1979 formally repealed the Industrial Relations Act and restored the 1906 pattern of statutory immunities in a strengthened form in the Trade Union and Labour Relations Act 1974.[235] Nonetheless, certain parts of the 1971 Act were subsequently revived. The unfair dismissal jurisdiction was re-enacted in the Act of 1974, and the Employment Protection Act 1975[236] contained a modified recognition procedure, under which a union with substantial support in a given workplace could obtain the right to recognition through a procedure operated by the Advisory, Conciliation and Arbitration Service. This procedure, although successful in achieving advances in recognition in areas of professional and managerial employment where it had previously been resisted, was dogged by the intervention of the courts through judicial review,[237] and was repealed in 1980. However, the unfair dismissal legislation, together with the other elements of employment protection law which were significantly strengthened by the Act of 1975, has largely remained in place to this day, and has had a considerable influence in leading management to adopt more formal procedures at plant level,[238] much as the Donovan Report had intended.

Although the more ambitious corporatist experiments of the 1960s and 1970s did not survive into the very different climate of the 1980s, they nevertheless marked a new phase for the voluntary system. Henceforth, the role of the state would not be confined, as it had been, to supporting voluntary collective bargaining, and intervening only occasionally in areas which the voluntary system had failed to take root. This development was epitomized by the changing

---

[232] See B. Weekes, M. Mellish, L. Dickens and J. Lloyd, *Industrial Relations and the Limits of the Law: The Industrial Effects of the Industrial Relations Act 1971* (Oxford: Blackwell, 1975).

[233] Lord Wedderburn, 'The new politics of labour law', in Wedderburn (ed.) *Employment Rights in Britain and Europe*, op. cit., pp. 74–105, at p. 80.

[234] McCarthy, 'The rise and fall of collective *laissez-faire*'; op. cit., at p. 21.

[235] 21 Elizabeth II c. 52.   [236] 22 Elizabeth II c. 71.

[237] See B. Simpson, 'Judicial review of ACAS' (1979) 8 *Industrial Law Journal* 420–426.

[238] See L. Dickens, M. Jones, B. Weekes and M. Hart, *Dismissed: A Study of Unfair Dismissal and the Unfair Tribunal System* (Oxford: Blackwell, 1985).

functions of the Ministry of Labour in the twenty years after 1960. What had been, in effect, the 'ministry of free collective bargaining' in the 1950s[239] assumed wider responsibilities for managing the process of reducing inflation and enhancing productivity in the 1960s, when it changed its name to the Department of Employment and Productivity. During this period, 'governments required the Department to pursue policies for industrial society very much at variance with its collective *laissez-faire* tradition'; whereas the Ministry of the 1950s had embodied the commitment of successive governments to free collective bargaining, 'this symbiosis between government and the voluntary collective bargaining system broke down . . . under the stress of incomes policies and interventionist labour legislation in the late sixties and early seventies'.[240]

6. Collective Laissez-faire and Labour Market 'Deregulation'

6.1 The neoliberal counter-revolution and the end of full employment policy

The arrival of a new Conservative administration in 1979 was a turning point for the system of collective laissez-faire, marking a fundamental change in the philosophical underpinnings of industrial relations policy and the direction of legislative change. Collective bargaining was now viewed sceptically, as a potential impediment to the efficient allocation of labour and a contributing factor in high inflation. The economic arguments which were advanced at this time all pointed in the same direction: the need to change the law so as to limit the power and influence of trade unions, at the same time as removing what the government called 'obstacles' to the creation of jobs in the form of statutory regulation of terms and conditions of employment. Labour law was to feel the effects of a neoliberal 'counter-revolution' which, both in intellectual and policy terms, predated 1979.

The challenge to Keynesian orthodoxy came as the consequence of the growing crisis which culminated in the inflationary explosion of the 1970s, which was led by a sharp increase in primary product prices, in particular that of oil. Prior to this, from the mid-1960s, prices and unemployment had begun to rise together, a tendency which appeared to refute the conventional post-war understanding of the relationship between inflation and employment, which was based on the trade-off between them expressed in the 'Phillips curve'.[241] As we have just

---

[239] M.R. Freedland, 'The role of the Department of Employment—twenty years of industrial change', in W.E.J. McCarthy (ed.) *Legal Intervention in Industrial Relations: Gains and Losses* (Oxford: Blackwell, 1992) 274–295, at p. 276.

[240] Ibid., at pp. 281, 290. After various further changes of name and remit, the Department was abolished in 1995 and its functions split between the Department of Trade and Industry and a number of other government departments with responsibilities for education, training and aspects of social security.

[241] See D. Deaton, 'Unemployment' in G.S. Bain (ed.) *Industrial Relations in Britain* (Oxford: Blackwell, 1983) 237–262.

seen, incomes policies failed to control inflation over the medium to long term. To provide an explanation for the persistence of rising prices in the face of counter-inflationary measures, Friedman argued that inflation was a purely monetary phenomenon, that is to say, one caused by an increase in the money supply. The level of unemployment, he argued, was determined by supply and demand in the labour market and that a level of unemployment existed at which inflation was stable: a *natural level* determined by labour market inflexibility and imperfections such as regulation. Friedman accepted that an increase in the money supply could cause employment to rise beyond the natural level, but only temporarily whilst inflationary expectations expressed in wage claims were adjusted upwards to the higher level of price increases.[242] This 'adaptive expectations' view was subsequently challenged by the rational expectations theorists who argued that by experiencing inflation, individuals come to understand the inflationary process and what triggers it.[243] This ruled out unanticipated inflation and also the possibility of any deviation of unemployment from the natural rate. The rational expectations school of monetarists thus fully restored the pre-Keynesian orthodoxy of the primacy of the money supply in determining the overall price level and of conditions in the labour market in determining the level of unemployment. It followed from this stance that the cure for inflation took the form of monetary control while the cure for unemployment consisted of supply side measures including labour market 'deregulation', or the removal of protective standards and legal support for the autonomy of collective bargaining. This was therefore a policy prescription which went to the very essence of the philosophy of collective laissez-faire.

Similar policy conclusions were arrived at by the so-called *neo-Keynesians* using a different theoretical route. Meade[244] claimed that for any given increase in total monetary expenditure, the balance between inflation and unemployment was determined by the degree of wage pressure generated by trade unions. Meade took the wages which firms could afford to pay as determined by the diminishing marginal productivity of labour. Therefore, the level of unemployment at which inflation stabilized, the so-called non-accelerating inflation rate of unemployment (NAIRU), was a function of the excess of wages negotiated by trade unions over the level of marginal labour product which was necessary to deliver full employment. The lowering of NAIRU therefore required a moderation of wage increases: 'first, because less and less output may be added to production as more and more men have to work with the given equipment and other resources of the firm: and, second, because the employer may be selling his product in an imperfect market so that if he produces and sells more he may have to lower his selling price (or incur greater selling costs) in order to dispose of the

---

[242] See M. Friedman, *Unemployment and Inflation* (London: Institute of Economic Affairs, 1977).
[243] R. Lucas and T. Sargent, *Rational Expectations* (London: Macmillan, 1981).
[244] J.E. Meade, *Stagflation Volume 1: Wage Fixing* (London: Allen & Unwin, 1982).

increased output'.[245] Imperfect competition in product markets had previously been viewed as driving a wedge between wages and marginal productivity, and thereby giving rise to the *exploitation* of workers by capitalists.[246] The neo-Keynesians argued further that this wedge was widened by employers' taxes, excise tax, real import prices and other non-labour costs.[247]

Whatever the precise justification offered, the response of the economic orthodoxy to the inflationary crisis was the abandonment of the core Keynesian belief that without intervention the labour market could not be relied upon to guarantee full employment. This retreat to neoclassical orthodoxy rehabilitated the marginal productivity theory of wages and its central proposition that if employment was to rise, real wages (money wages deflated by product prices) had to fall. Unemployment, the neo-liberals reasserted, resulted from trade union wage pressure and restrictive practices, government labour market regulation and excessively high social welfare benefits. These labour market imperfections created a *natural* or, less pejoratively, a non-accelerating inflation level of unemployment (the 'NAIRU'), and any attempt to lower unemployment below this level by stimulating demand would merely crowd out existing employment or add to inflationary pressures. The state's contribution to full employment was therefore confined to the creation of a stable or 'prudent' macro-economic framework, coupled with deregulation to eliminate labour market imperfections and parsimony in the provision of out-of-work benefits. This paradigm shift in economic perspective has been maintained by both Conservative and Labour governments since the late 1970s.[248]

6.2 The legislative programme of 'deregulation'

The extent of legislative change prompted by this shift in economic policy was substantial: in a reversal of the policy of the Trade Disputes Act 1906 and its successors, including the Trade Union and Labour Relations Act 1974, the trade dispute immunities were cut back, thereby inviting the courts back into the control of industrial disputes; new statutory procedures were put in place to govern the conduct of strikes and legal support for the closed shop was

---

[245] J.E. Meade, *Stagflation Volume 1: Wage Fixing* (London: Allen & Unwin, 1982), at p. 49.

[246] Joan Robinson had written: 'we shall say that a group of workers are being exploited when their wage is less than the marginal physical product that they are producing valued at the price at which it is being sold': *The Economics of Imperfect Competition* (London: Macmillan, 1933) at p. 283. She had also spelled out in detail the conditions under which a reduction in the degree of monopoly, and hence the exploitation of workers, would or would not increase employment (ibid., ch. 8).

[247] S. Nickell, 'The government's policy for jobs, an analysis' (1985) *Oxford Review of Economic Policy* 98–115.

[248] On the degree to which it continues to inform the labour law and industrial relations policy of the present 'New Labour' administration, see A. Charlwood, 'Annual review: the new generation of union leaders and the prospects for union revival' (2004) 42 *British Journal of Industrial Relations* 379–397.

removed.[249] Alongside these general changes to collective labour law, the Fair Wages Resolution was rescinded; fair labour clauses in local government contracts prohibited; collective bargaining rights removed from parts of the public sector, such as school-age education; statutory working time controls in factories removed; and minimum wage fixing through the wages councils abolished.[250]

As these legal changes were being made, the wider bargaining environment was also being transformed. The 1980s and 1990s were a period of low inflation. There was a decisive shift in the external terms of trade at the start of the 1980s which has been maintained up to the present day.[251] In addition, government policy since the 1980s has aimed at reducing the headline rate of income tax and this has had the effect of reversing the post-war trend of increases in employment taxation. Although higher income groups have benefited most, middle income earners and the better off groups of manual workers have also gained from this policy, and the overall effect has been to reduce the pressure on the wage bargaining system to maintain real take-home pay.[252] The 1980s and 1990s have also seen high unemployment by historical standards. Unemployment reached a post-war peak of 12 per cent of the labour force in the early 1980s, and although it has since fallen back to around 5 per cent on the standard ILO definition, a large proportion of the labour force is without work but no longer counted as unemployed because of their receipt of long-term disablement and incapacity benefits.[253]

As in previous such periods in the inflationary cycle, trade union membership and militancy have both declined precipitously since the late 1970s. By 2000 union density was just below 30 per cent and the coverage of collective agreements had fallen to around 40 per cent, and was increasingly concentrated in public

---

[249] The principal measures were the major Conservative employment laws of the 1980s and 1990s: the Employment Acts of 1980 and 1982, the Trade Union Act 1984, the Employment Acts of 1988 and 1990, and the Trade Union Reform and Employment Rights Act 1993. For a full account of these changes see S. Deakin and G. Morris, *Labour Law* (3rd ed., Butterworths, 2001), at pp. 32–46, and for assessments of their impact on the philosophy and practice of collective laissez-faire, see Wedderburn, *The Worker and the Law*, op. cit., at pp. 68–96; S. Fredman, 'The new rights: labour law and ideology in the Thatcher years' (1992) 12 *Oxford Journal of Legal Studies* 24–44; McCarthy, 'The rise and fall of collective laissez-faire', op. cit., at pp. 48–57, Davies and Freedland, *Labour Legislation and Public Policy*, op. cit., ch. 10.
[250] Major deregulatory initiatives taking the form of the abrogation of laws, as opposed to the creation of new layers of regulation or the revival of common law constraints in the form of the economic torts, were rare in this period, but examples include the abolition of remnants of Factory Act legislation controlling the employment of women (Sex Discrimination Act 1986) and young people (Employment Act 1989) as well as the abolition of wages councils in the Trade Union Reform and Employment Rights Act 1993.   [251] See our discussion, above, Section 4.2.
[252] On this aspect of tax policy, see S. Deakin and F. Wilkinson, 'Labour law, social security and economic inequality' (1991) 15 *Cambridge Journal of Economics* 125–148.
[253] See S. Nickell, 'Unemployment in Britain', in P. Gregg and J. Wadsworth (eds.) *The State of Working Britain* (Manchester: Manchester University Press, 1999), for an account of UK unemployment in the 1980s and 1990s which contains a full explanation of the different methods for measuring unemployment, noting the difference between the claimant count and the ILO measure, and offering instructive comparisons of the stated UK unemployment count with those of other European countries.

sector employment. The proportion of union members in workplaces with more than 25 workers, which stood at 65 per cent in 1980, had fallen to 47 per cent by 1990 and 36 per cent by 1998. Strike activity has also fallen; in most years in the mid-1990s, less than one million working days were lost to strikes across the whole economy, as opposed to an average of 3.5 million in the 1960s, 12.9 million in the 1970s and 7.2 million in the 1980s. In a further echo of the 1920s, national-level collective agreements have begun to break up, with the demise of the national agreement in engineering leading the way following the ending of a dispute over working time in the late 1980s. These shifts have been reflected, in turn, in bargaining outcomes. As already noted, differentials between groups at various points in the pay hierarchy have widened considerably, at the same time as real wages have been increasing, in particular for those in regular employment and in those parts of the labour market which continue to be subject to institutionalized pay bargaining of one kind or another.

A radical individualism characterized many of the official policy documents of the 1980s and early 1990s:

Many existing approaches to pay bargaining, beloved of trade unions and employers alike, will need to change if we are to secure the flexibility essential to employment growth. In particular, the 'going rate', 'comparability' and 'cost of living increases' are all outmoded concepts—they take no account of differences in performance, ability to pay or difficulties of recruitment, retention or motivation. Pay structures too have to change. National agreements which affect the pay of half the workforce all too often give scant regard to differences in individual circumstances or performance.[254]

It seems a short step from this statement in the 1988 *Employment* White Paper to the subsequent dismantling of many national level agreements. However, the relationship between legal change and collective bargaining outcomes is, in this respect, far from straightforward.[255] At the start of the 1980s, as part of the legacy of collective laissez-faire, there was little direct legal underpinning of collective agreements. Some legal changes introduced in the 1980s may have contributed to the weakening of national bargaining; these include the amendments to strike law in the Employment Acts of 1980 and 1982, which limited the scope for legitimate trade disputes involving multiple employers and narrowed down the range of lawful solidarity and sympathy action. The abolition of the fair wages resolution with effect from 1982 and the ban on local authorities using contract compliance to enforce labour standards on contractors, following the Local Government Act 1988, removed significant powers to extend the effects of collective agreements from stronger areas of organization to more weakly organized firms. However, precisely because direct legal regulation of this kind only played a marginal role to begin with

[254] White Paper, *Employment for the 1990s*, Cm. 540, 1988, at pp. 23–24.
[255] See W. Brown and S. Wadwhani, 'The economic effects of industrial relations legislation since 1979' (1990) 131 *National Institute Economic Review* 57–70; W. Brown, S. Deakin and P. Ryan, 'The effects of British industrial relations legislation 1979–1997' (1997) 161 *National Institute Economic Review* 69–83.

in supporting collective bargaining, the decline of national agreements during the 1990s cannot be attributed solely or even principally to these legal changes.

A similar disjunction between the rhetoric of 'deregulation' and the practical effect of legislative change can be seen in relation to the removal of statutory supports for the regulation of working time and minimum wages. The major working time reform occurred through the passage of the Sex Discrimination Act 1986, a measure devoted in part to belatedly implementing the European Community Directive of 1976[256] requiring equal treatment between men and women in employment. In the name of gender equality, provisions which were in the spirit of nineteenth-century factory legislation, setting maximum limits to the working time of women in certain manual employments, were removed. Although the 1986 Act repealed, in this respect, parts of an Act of 1961, this Act was a consolidating measure, and the provisions in question dated back to laws of the 1930s (and before). These provisions, in their turn, had set weekly maximum limits of around 48 hours with a maximum of six further hours of overtime; by the time of their effective repeal in the 1990s, the normal working week was around 39 hours for most industrial employments. Although these laws could have imposed real restraints on overtime working by women which would have taken them above the statutory limit, no evidence was presented to Parliament at the time of the Act's passage to indicate that this was a common problem in practice. It was, moreover, the case that many of the restrictions in the Act could lawfully have been the subject of a derogation by agreement with the health and safety inspectorate. Thus the repeal was very largely symbolic.[257]

This is not to say that there was not a serious problem of long-hours working in the British economy during the 1980s and 1990s. The absence of a general set of standards governing working time, along the pattern already well established by that stage in most continental countries, meant that working time patterns in the UK were highly dispersed according to occupation, reflecting differentials in bargaining power across sectors and occupations. Thus whereas 72 per cent of workers, on average, in the other then eleven member states worked between 36 and 40 hours each week, the corresponding figure for the UK was 36 per cent. In the UK, over 41 per cent of male workers were employed on average for more than 46 hours per week, compared to 23 per cent for the EU as a whole.[258]

---

[256] Directive 76/206/EC.

[257] See generally S. Deakin, 'Equality under a market order: the Employment Act 1989' (1990) 19 *Industrial Law Journal* 1–23. The 1989 Act completed the process begun in the Act of 1986 by removing regulations governing the employment of young people above school leaving age, and removing restrictions on the employment of both women and young persons in certain industrial employments (including mining, thereby abrogating the Mines Regulation Act 1842, although the rapid decline of the mining industry which followed shortly afterwards meant that this change in the law had few effects).

[258] See M. Wareing, 'Working arrangements and patterns of working hours in Britain' (1992) 100 *Employment Gazette* 88–100; C. Marsh, *Hours of Work of Women and Men in Great Britain* (London: DTI, 1991).

However, this pattern of long hours working had little or nothing to do with the deregulatory reforms of the 1980s; it mostly occurred in sectors which were unaffected by any legal change during that period. Rather, it was part of the legacy of collective laissez-faire, in particular the focus on industry-specific regulation and the absence of a general statutory floor to basic working conditions. Historically, working time reductions were the achievement not of legislation, but of collective bargaining. The national engineering agreement led the way, with normal weekly hours going down in steps from 48 in the 1920s to 44 in 1947, 42 in 1960, 40 in 1965 and 39 in 1979. In each case, other sectors followed, often catching up only several years later; thus the 39-hour norm was still the subject of negotiation in a number of less well-organized sectors, such as cleaning services and hotels and catering, a decade later.[259] Nor was the model established in this way by collective bargaining an effective constraint on long hours working. No upper limit on overtime was set, and because national agreements calculated overtime rates as a proportion of the basic national rates for normal weekly hours, rather than the higher basic rates which were generally set at local level, it was not even clear, in all cases, that overtime was more expensive for the employer.[260] The failure of the collective bargaining system to deal with the over-reliance of both employers and workers alike on high levels of overtime working was noted at the time of the Royal Commission of Labour 1891–4;[261] it was repeated in the early 1960s at the time of attempts to modernize plant-level industrial relations,[262] and the same issue has emerged again more recently as part of the debate over the implementation in the UK of the EU Working Time Directive.[263]

A similar picture emerges with regard to minimum wage legislation: the effects of deregulation may have been more tangible here than in the case of working time, but the problem of low pay long predated the neoliberal policy reforms of the 1980s. Notwithstanding the expansion of minimum wage fixing powers which occurred in the Wages Councils Act 1945, the wages councils system remained highly fragmented with, at one stage, over 60 sectoral bodies. During this period, most wages councils set rates not just well below those in comparable industries with collective agreements, but also below those which a majority of workers in the regulated sectors were receiving.[264] From 1960 there was a

[259] See J. Rubery, S. Deakin and S. Horrell, 'Great Britain', in G. Bosch, P. Dawkins and F. Michon (eds.) *Times are Changing* (Geneva: IILS, 1992); J. Arrowsmith, 'The struggle over working time in nineteenth and twentieth century Britain' (2002) 13 *Historical Studies in Industrial Relations* 83–117.   [260] Ibid.

[261] One of the objectives of the eight-hour day reform proposed by the union-based members of the Royal Commission was the 'suppression of habitual overtime': 'Minority Report', op. cit., at p. 140; see our discussion, above, Section 3.3.

[262] See A. Flanders, *The Fawley Productivity Agreements: A Case Study of Management and Collective Bargaining* (London: Faber, 1964), at p. 227.

[263] Directive 93/104/EC; see C. Barnard, S. Deakin and R. Hobbs, 'Opting out of the 48 hour week: employer necessity or individual choice? An empirical study of the operation of Article 18(1)(b) of the Working Time Directive in the UK' (2003) 32 *Industrial Law Journal* 223–252.

[264] C. Craig, J. Rubery, R. Tarling and F. Wilkinson, *Labour Market Structure, Industrial Organization and Low Pay* (Cambridge: Cambridge University Press, 1982), at p. 19.

significant reduction in the scope of the statutory system, as 27 wages councils covering over half a million workers were abolished. This was done out of the belief that the presence of statutory regulation was holding back collective bargaining, and that following abolition, voluntary arrangements would be established and wages would rise. However, following abolition, there was no general rise in wages in most of the deregulated sectors, and collective bargaining failed to take root for reasons which would have been entirely familiar in the context of the early twentieth-century discussion of low pay: the difficulties of organizing both workers and employers in trades with ease of entry, tight profit margins, intense competition on price, and reliance on casual labour.[265]

The reforms of the 1980s and 1990s were inspired by an entirely different philosophy, one which saw the remaining powers of the wages councils as an impediment to employment growth and competitive labour markets: in the words of a government economic adviser, deregulation would 'serve to expand employment [and] offer competitive wages for the socially disadvantaged'.[266] In this vein, Part II of the Wages Act 1986 excluded workers under the age of 21 from the scope of coverage and restricted the powers of wages councils to setting single minimum wage rates for each sector as a whole, removing their powers to set a range of rates for workers of different grades. Powers to set paid holiday entitlements, dating back to the Act of 1938, were repealed, and wages councils were required to consider the effect that minimum rates would have 'on the level of employment among the workers to whom it will apply, and in particular in those areas where the remuneration received by such workers is generally less than the national average for such workers'.[267] Thanks to the growing weakness of regulation brought about by these provisions, increased numbers of workers found themselves receiving the bare minimum rate set by the relevant wages order. This effect was taken by the government to be evidence of the anti-competitive impact of this one remaining power of the wages councils,[268] and used to justify their complete abolition, which finally arrived in 1993. At this point, the wages councils sector still covered 2.5 million workers, equivalent to 10 per cent of the workforce. Within five years, following the return to office of a Labour government, Parliament was to pass the National Minimum Wage Act 1998, establishing a legal floor to wages, and adopted legislation implementing the EC Working Time Directive, which went further than any previous UK legislation had done to recognizing a general limit on working hours, but, as we shall see in more detail in the final chapter,[269] even these attempts at comprehensive regulation could not entirely escape the tradition of partial and selective regulation.

---

[265] For a full account of the aftermath of abolition, see Craig et al., *Labour Market Structure*, op. cit.   [266] P. Minford, *Unemployment: Cause and Cure* (Oxford: Blackwell, 1986), at p. 122.
[267] Wages Act 1986, s. 14(6)(a).
[268] See Department of Employment, *Wages Councils Consultation Document* (London: Department of Employment, 1988).   [269] See Chapter 5, Section 4.6, below.

7. Conclusion: The Legacy of Collective Laissez-faire

The system of collective laissez-faire of the middle years of the twentieth century may have offered, as Kahn-Freund suggested, a distinctively British solution to the problem of how to locate and legitimize the institutions of collective bargaining in a market economy, but it was in no sense the inevitable outcome of the preceding decades. On the one hand, the principle of state support for voluntary collective bargaining was vigorously contested at various points by employers hostile to worker organization, only for this opposition to be neutralized by a combination of strike action and state intervention to settle industrial disputes on terms which included union recognition. On the other, there were periods during which unions pressed strongly for legislative limits on hours of work and a generalized minimum wage, only to see these efforts rebuffed by employer interests opposed to statutory regulation of industry. Thus although the voluntary system was supported, from an early stage, by a well articulated philosophy and by well entrenched interests on both the employer and union side, there is also a sense in which it was a default option which triumphed only because various alternatives—individual laissez-faire, on the one hand, and a comprehensive labour code, on the other—failed to gain a sufficiently broad consensus.

The features which defined the British 'compromise' of collective laissez-faire by comparison with systems of labour law in continental Europe during this formative period were the partial and uneven quality of regulation through collective bargaining and the absence of a comprehensive statutory floor of rights to terms and conditions of employment. Working time controls and minimum wages, which in France, Germany and Italy became the subject of either national legislation or sectoral collective agreements which could be extended by statutory order,[270] were regulated in Britain via the selective statutory regulation of under-organized trades; but even in well organized industries, arrangements for national bargaining were often fragile and incomplete in their coverage. This was a reflection of the structure of British industry and on the nature and orientation of British trade unions. Trade unions and employers' associations alike were highly local in character, with limited control from the centre over wage determination. As a result there were wide variations in terms and conditions of employment across otherwise comparable firms and occupations. These differentials were largely the effect of variations in the ability of firms to pay, based upon differences in their product market strategies, the productivity of capital equipment, managerial efficiency and other non-labour influences, rather than the result of differences in the skill and productivity of workers. The ability of less well-performing firms

---

[270] For a review of minimum wage and working time floors, see S. Deakin, 'The floor of rights in European labour law' (1990) 15 *New Zealand Journal of Industrial Relations* 219–240, and for the historical process which led to the growing adoption of these measures up to 1945, see the various contributions to B. Hepple (ed.) *The Making of Labour Law in Europe* (London: Mansell, 1986).

to withstand the pressure to pay higher wages provided them with an alternative to improvements through managerial efficiency and investment in new technology, while, conversely, the ability of well-organized groups of workers to extract rents from improved profitability which were unrelated to labour input acted as a brake on industrial progress.[271]

As the basis for a settlement between labour and capital, collective laissez-faire proved to be precarious. It was relatively stable and uncontested for only a short period in the 1950s, but its influence did not cease after that point. For most of the 1960s and 1970s there was a fundamental tension between state support for voluntary collective bargaining and the aim of reducing wage and price inflation through incomes policies. However, in the end incomes policies failed because they were incompatible with the decentralized and sectional nature of the voluntary system: the long-term trade-offs between sectional interests which had to be made if the goals of national economic policy were to be met could not be sustained. The period of neoliberalism which followed reduced the scale of the trade-offs needed by reverting to an even more selective approach to regulation: basic labour standards became non-existent in those areas of employment upon which the effects of economic change and structural reform were concentrated. Thus notwithstanding the neoliberal rhetoric of complete deregulation and individualization, these reforms too continued in a long tradition of partial and selective regulation of the labour market.

The legacy of collective laissez-faire has been particularly negative for British trade unions. In the majority of sectors in which national bargaining has ceased to function, union power is increasingly restricted to islands of organized firms and establishments. This is proving a remarkably hostile environment in which to try to reverse the decline in trade union membership and influence which began in 1979. Decentralization and the absence of a meaningful statutory wages floor threaten the long-term viability of collective bargaining: as the coverage of collective bargaining falls and becomes increasingly concentrated on pockets of strong unionization, even those firms which see an advantage from trade union recognition in terms of labour peace and cooperation over productivity improvements will be deterred by the greater cost of employing unionized labour, a pattern which has led to a catastrophic decline in union density in the United States. These trends may be reversed by a shift in the bargaining environment of the kind which has occurred in the past; as we have seen, union membership in Britain appears to be highly volatile, rising and falling according to wider changes in the economy. If, however, such a shift were to occur, it would not

---

[271] See more generally F. Wilkinson, 'Industrial organization, collective bargaining and economic efficiency' (1991) 1 *International Contributions to Labour Studies* 1–25 and 'Inflation and employment: is there a Third Way?' (2000) 24 *Cambridge Journal of Economics* 643–670, and on the links between industrial structure and economic decline in twentieth-century Britain, see E.J. Hobsbawm, *Industry and Empire* (Harmondsworth: Penguin, 1969), ch. 9, and the contributions to B. Elbaum and W. Lazonick (eds.) *The Decline of the British Economy* (Oxford: Clarendon Press, 1987).

guarantee a return to high levels of union influence, merely present the British union movement with an opportunity to turn the tide in its favour. It seems unlikely that such an opportunity could be fully grasped by an exclusive focus on the method of collective bargaining. It was once recognized that, as the Webbs put in 1911, 'the getting and enforcing of legislation is as historically as much a part of the Trade Union function as maintaining a strike'.[272] Is it possible that a neo-Fabian agenda for labour market regulation will re-emerge in the early decades of the twenty-first century? We will consider that possibility in the final chapter.

---

[272] In the preface to the 1911 edition of the *History of Trade Unionism* (London: Longmans, Green and Co.), at pp. xiii–xiv.

5

Competition, Capabilities and Rights

1. Introduction

In preceding chapters we examined, from an historical perspective, forms of regulation which have sought in different ways to govern or control employment relations and to influence labour market outcomes. Our aim in this final chapter is explore the question of what an effective rationale might be for the present state of labour market regulation, and for its future development. We do not set out to provide a blueprint or checklist for labour law reform. Rather, our intention is to offer a framework for analysis and evaluation of the existing law and of proposals for legal change. The question which is above all facing labour lawyers today is whether a means can be found for expressing the enduring values of labour law—including protection for the person and security of the individual worker and respect for the autonomy of collective organizations—within the framework of a market-based economic system. To address this question it will be necessary not simply to look at evidence relating to the economic impact of particular aspects of labour legislation, but also to consider, at a fundamental theoretical level, the nature of the relationship between labour law and the labour market, and, more generally, between the legal and economic systems.

Over the course of the past three decades, the neoliberal discourse of deregulation and flexibility has gradually come to dominate the debate over labour law and labour market regulation in advanced economies. The premise of policies of labour market 'deregulation' was that the removal of regulatory 'rigidities' would free up the labour market to operate in such a way as to maximize efficiency. In the case of the economies to which these policies were addressed, the results have, from one point of view, been disappointing. High unemployment (by historical standards) persists at the same time as inequality has increased and levels of growth remain below those of the so-called 'golden age' between 1945 and 1970.[1] However, for proponents of deregulation, there is a ready answer to this apparent failure: the deregulatory agenda has simply not gone far enough. The goal of a

---

[1] See S. Marglin and J. Schorr (eds.) *The Golden Age of Capitalism: Reinterpreting the Postwar Experience* (Oxford: Clarendon Press, 1990).

fully flexible labour market will finally be realized once systems 'cross the river' to complete liberalization.[2]

Perceptive critics argued, early on in the flexibility debate, that so-called deregulation would not put an end to the role of the state. Rather, the task of putting in place the conditions for a well-functioning labour market would require the state to assume new and potentially far-reaching forms of intervention.[3] The British experience since 1980 certainly suggests that the promise of a lighter regulatory burden has not been met. New types of labour law have arisen, including far-reaching powers over the internal constitution and governance of trade unions and the conduct of industrial action,[4] and the use of techniques borrowed from competition policy to control standard setting in labour and product markets.[5] These interventions are justified in the name of preserving effective competition. Controls over the unemployed have also increased, a policy supported by the need to heighten individual work incentives.[6]

But there have been other, perhaps less predictable, changes. As collective institutions have lost a certain amount of their influence, the law governing the individual employment relationship has grown considerably, not simply in terms of its volume and complexity, but also in terms of its social and economic impact. In the process, an active debate has been triggered about the regulatory 'burden' of employment tribunal hearings and judgments, and employment law has been amended (and made even more complex) as a result.[7] Yet it is also clear that many of the new laws which have been introduced to regulate the employment relationship, in particular since the early 1990s, cannot be easily categorized as 'burdens' on employment. On the contrary, many of them have been justified by reference to a logic of 'correcting market failures' which sees regulation as a necessary part of a market order.[8]

Thus the terms of the debate over labour market regulation are slowly but surely shifting. Our aim in this final chapter is to try to assess the nature of the

---

[2] G. Bertola and A. Ichino, 'Crossing the river: a comparative perspective on Italian employment dynamics' (1995) 21 *Economic Policy: A European Forum* 359–415.

[3] N. McCormick, 'Spontaneous order and the rule of law: some problems' (1986) 35 *Jahrbuch des Öffentlichen Rechts der Gegenwart* 1–13; S. Simitis, 'Juridification of labour relations', in G. Teubner (ed.) *Juridification of Social Spheres* (Berlin: De Gruyter, 1987) 113–161.

[4] See S. Deakin and G. Morris, *Labour Law* (London: Butterworths, 3rd ed., 2001), chs. 10 (on trade union governance) and 11 (on industrial action) respectively, and our discussion in Chapter 4, above.

[5] Particularly in the context of the contracting out of public sector services, under the Local Government Act 1988 and related legislation. On the implications for contract compliance and the enforcement of fair wages standards, see Deakin and Morris, *Labour Law*, op. cit., at pp. 790–91.

[6] See Chapter 3, above.

[7] The result was the Employment Act 2002. See B. Hepple and G. Morris, 'The Employment Act 2002 and the crisis of individual employment rights' (2002) 31 *Industrial Law Journal* 245–269.

[8] See H. Collins, 'Justifications and techniques of legal regulation of the employment relation', in H. Collins, P. Davies and R. Rideout (eds.) *Legal Regulation of the Employment Relation* (Deventer: Kluwer, 1999) 3–27, at pp. 7–11, and *Employment Law* (Oxford: Oxford University Press, 2003), ch. 2.

shift that is taking place. Our analysis is partly descriptive in the sense of pointing to certain emergent features of contemporary labour market regulation, and partly normative in the sense of charting a path for reform.

The question which we wish to address is: *what kind of normative or regulatory framework is needed in order for labour markets to function in the interests of a range of societal goals, of which efficiency is one?* Our way into this debate is to consider more closely the nature of market processes and the role within them of norms, conventions and legal rules. We explore the idea that the labour market, like other markets, is a spontaneous order or self-organizing system which ultimately rests on a set of mutually-reinforcing conventions which are themselves the outcome of an evolutionary process. In contrast, however, to adherents of a completely voluntarist conception of norms, we argue below that the role of self-enforcing norms and conventions cannot be separated from that of more formal mechanisms of legal regulation and intervention (judicial decisions, legislation, collective self-regulation). These formal mechanisms can operate to change the 'architecture' or parameters within which the conventions of the market evolve, and in so doing can influence the path of social and economic development.

In this vein, we will also argue that social rights, far from being inimical to the effective functioning of the labour market, are actually at the core of a labour market order in which the resources available to society are fully realized. For this to happen, certain institutional conditions which are prior to the process of market exchange must be satisfied. In particular, individuals should be provided with the means to achieve economic self-sufficiency. The social rights which we have in mind are therefore those which would empower individuals with the means needed to realize their potential in a sustainable way, thereby enhancing the wealth of well-being of society as a whole. Our analysis here builds on the capability approach of Amartya Sen[9] and the uses to which it has been put in the context of the *Supiot Report* to the European Commission.[10]

We will proceed as follows. Section 2 below considers the nature of competition in the labour market and its relationship to the constitutive role played by legal institutions in shaping the market order. In Section 3 we outline the nature of a capability-based approach to labour market regulation and the link to reflexive law and social rights. In Section 4, we look at a number of concrete instances in which new solutions to the issues of labour market regulation could be said to be emerging. Section 5 concludes by arguing for a particular conception of 'labour market law', one in which social rights play a central, constitutive role in the formation of labour market relations.

---

[9] A. Sen, *Commodities and Capabilities* (Deventer: North-Holland, 1985) and *Development as Freedom* (Oxford: OUP, 1999).

[10] A. Supiot (ed.) *Au delà de l'emploi. Transformations du travail et devenir du droit du travail en Europe* (Paris: Flammarion, 1999); R. Salais, 'Libertés du travail et capacités: une perspective pour une construction européenne?' (1999) *Droit Social* 467–471.

2. Competition and the Labour Market

2.1 The market as a spontaneous order

For many neoclassical critics of labour law, the search for labour market efficiency involves an attempt to recreate the general equilibrium framework of neoclassical labour economics. Under conditions of perfect competition, the fundamental theorems of welfare economics dictate that resources will necessarily gravitate, through voluntary exchange, to their most efficient use. Specifying the role of law in the general equilibrium model, therefore, is inherently problematic. In a world of zero transaction costs, there is, strictly speaking, no *economic* function for law to perform, although it may well operate for other purposes such as redistribution.[11] This, however, obscures the relationship between law and the market system. The absence of law from general equilibrium models is above all a reflection of the limited capacity of those models to explain social reality.

Some progress is made by approaches which accept the existence, in the real world, of positive transaction costs, and see a role for the law in seeking to reproduce the outcomes which a competitive market would have achieved, had it been able to operate as the model predicts. This 'market perfecting' agenda is superficially attractive since it holds out the promise that the legal system can enhance efficiency by selective interventions which address particular issues of market failure. However, it faces a formidable theoretical and practical objection which was made by Hayek, namely that courts and legislators alike are unlikely to have the information which they require to make these interventions effective. Economic systems are too complex to be easily amenable to centralized legal direction.[12] The power of this critique, and the problem which it poses for those who wish to defend market regulation, cannot easily be brushed aside.[13] As the most articulate and influential theoretical critic of labour law and the modern welfare state, Hayek demands our attention.

The theory of the market as a spontaneous order seeks to address the issue of complexity. Information and knowledge (understood as *applied* information) are individually held by private agents, and cannot straightforwardly be mobilized through centralized direction or command. Under these circumstances, the contribution of the market is to operate as a mode of coordination which enables each individual to benefit from the possession and use of information *by others*.[14]

---

[11] See R.H. Coase, 'The firm, the market and the law', in Coase, *The Firm, the Market and the Law* (Chicago: University of Chicago Press, 1988) 1–31.

[12] F.A. Hayek, *Law, Legislation and Liberty. A New Statement of the Liberal Principles of Justice and Political Economy* (London: Routledge, 1982). This consolidated volume contains reprints of the three volumes which make up the work, namely *Rules and Order* (1973), *The Mirage of Social Justice* (1976) and *The Political Order of a Free People* (1979).

[13] See generally G. Hodgson, *Economics and Utopia* (London: Routledge, 1998).

[14] F.A. Hayek, *Rules and Order* (London: Routledge, 1973).

Competition operates as *a process of discovery*, generating information which is transmitted through the price mechanism. By mobilizing the resources available to a society in this way, the market enhances the total well-being of its members. This is a key point: for Hayek, individualism does not detract from the sense in which the market is a social institution, which, in the final analysis, serves social goals.

Hayek's definition of a system or 'order' is 'a state of affairs in which a multiplicity of elements of various kinds are so related to each other that we may learn from our acquaintance with some spatial or temporal part of the whole to form correct expectations concerning the rest, or at least expectations which have a good chance of proving correct'.[15] Hayek's definition implies a certain type of relationship between the overall properties of the system and its constituent parts. Robert Sugden offers the following account:

[a]n order is a regularity among a set of elements. To say that the order is spontaneous is to say that in some sense the elements have *arranged themselves* into that order . . . For the elements to be able to arrange themselves, each must act on its own principles of behaviour or laws of motion; the regularity among the set of elements must be capable of being explained by the individual actions of the elements. This requires that each element have its own motive power, or be acted on by its own set of forces.[16]

A spontaneous order therefore rests on the symbiotic relationship between what Sugden calls 'general' and 'particular' mechanisms. In the case of the market, it is through *general mechanisms*, such as the price mechanism, that the transmission of detailed knowledge from one part of the system to another takes place. The price system is itself the product of interactions among a large number of individual economic actors. It both results from, and operates through, the *particular mechanism* of the self-interested behaviour of each actor.

The price mechanism is just one of the means by which coordination problems are overcome through the operation of the market understood as a social institution. The market rests on numerous inter-locking *conventions* which guarantee the conditions under which it operates. As we saw in our earlier analysis,[17] conventions or social norms can be thought of as forms of shared information which enable parties to coordinate their behaviour on the basis of mutual expectations of each other's conduct.[18] Another way of putting this is to say that the value of the information contained in conventions and norms is equivalent to the sum total of the transaction costs which prevent actors from knowing what the strategies of others are going to be.[19] The price mechanism, for example, encodes knowledge about scarcity in a way that saves on transaction costs, in the sense that consumers do not need to know the reason for a particular shift in prices (such as a disruption

[15] Ibid., at p. 36.

[16] R. Sugden, 'Spontaneous order', in P. Newman (ed.) *The New Palgrave Dictionary of Economics and the Law* (London: Macmillan, 1998) Vol. 3, 485–495, at p. 487.   [17] See Ch. 1, above.

[18] D. Lewis, *Convention: A Philosophical Study* (Cambridge, MA: Harvard University Press, 1969).

[19] K. Warneryd, 'Conventions and transaction costs', in P. Newman (ed.) *The New Palgrave Dictionary of Economics and the Law* (London: Macmillan, 1998) Vol. 1, 461–5.

to supply); the price signal is enough for them to adjust their behaviour. Thus not only the price system but also social norms and the legal system operate as 'information transmission systems' which aid agents to overcome coordination problems.

Other norms which operate to sustain market activity include property rights which serve to identify the subject-matter of exchange. Property rights can be thought of as conventions which, in the terminology of evolutionary game theory, solve coordination failures which would otherwise arise from individually self-interested behaviour.[20] Repeated disputes over ownership result in socially wasteful conflicts. The emergence of rules for settling these disputes is therefore a precondition of an extended system of exchange. Norms favouring the enforcement of contracts and respect for the security of commercial undertakings can be seen in the same light. In Hayek's terms, the function of these 'abstract rules of just conduct' is that 'by defining a protected domain of each [individual], [they] enable an order of actions to form itself wherein the individuals can make feasible plans'.[21] In other words, these norms supply institutional support for the 'motive power' of individual economic actors, without which there would be no basis for the decentralized action upon which the spontaneous order depends for its effectiveness.

So far, so good; but are we simply back, yet again, with the idea of self-enforcing conventions which appear to operate independently of any centralized enforcement mechanism? Sugden[22] suggests that '[m]any of the institutions of a market economy are conventions that no one has designed, but that have simply evolved', and that '[a]lthough markets may work more smoothly when property rights are defined by formal laws and enforced by the state, they can come into existence and persist without any such external support'. The basis for this claim is the argument that self-enforcing conventions emerge through a process of social learning. In a world characterized by complexity and 'bounded rationality', actors have an interest in following those strategies which have proved to be successful in overcoming coordination problems. Norms, in the sense of regularities, can therefore emerge on the basis of repeated interactions between individuals.[23]

But many of those who argue for the spontaneous character of many of the conventions which are characteristic of market exchange also accept, for good reasons, that, in a wide range of contexts, these norms are supported by legal mechanisms of various kinds. This is not just a concession to the social reality of legal institutions; it is a recognition, at a basic theoretical level, of their necessity in a market order. In suggesting that markets may work 'more smoothly' when legal

---

[20] R. Sugden, 'Spontaneous order' (1989) 3 *Journal of Economic Perspectives* 85–97, at p. 85; L. Costabile, 'Ordine spontaneo o ordine negoziato? Conflitti e resoluzione dei onflitti nella nuova teoria economica delle istituzione', in A. Amendola (ed.) *Istituzione e mercato del lavoro* (Rome: Edizione Scientifiche Italiane, 1998) 1–66, at pp. 12–14, 24–27.

[21] *Rules and Order*, op. cit., at pp. 85–86.   [22] 'Spontaneous order' (1989), op. cit., at p. 86.

[23] See Costabile, 'Ordine spontaneo o ordine negoziato', op. cit.

enforcement is present, Sugden echoes Hayek, who argues that social norms are not sufficient for the preservation of the spontaneous order of the market: 'in most circumstances the organization which we call government becomes indispensable to assure that those rules are obeyed'.[24] Hence, for Hayek, the exercise of 'coercion' or legal enforcement of norms is justified within a spontaneous order 'where this is necessary to secure the private domain of the individual against interference by others'.[25] While a given rule of just conduct may have had a spontaneous origin, in the sense that 'individuals followed rules which had not been deliberately made but had arisen spontaneously',[26] such rules do not lose their essential character merely by virtue of being put into legal form: '[t]he spontaneous character of the resulting order must therefore be distinguished from the spontaneous origin of the rules on which it rests, and it is possible that an order which would still have to be described as spontaneous rests on rules which are entirely the result of deliberate design'.[27] In this perspective, it is the particular function of private law to underpin the spontaneous order of the market.

2.2 Regulation and efficiency in a market order

Legal norms may therefore have a role to play in establishing the conditions for the effective operation of the market. Neither Hayek nor Sugden go into much detail on why this might be so. One reason could be the fragility of many social norms, that is to say, their tendency to be destabilized by changing environmental conditions. Legal enforcement of social norms could provide some degree of protection against this kind of effect. If this were the case, legal enforcement would have the important but somewhat limited role of crystallizing in juridical form practices which were widely followed in practice.

A much broader role for law as an instrument for *changing*, rather than *confirming*, norms arises from the tendency for spontaneously-emerging norms to give rise to inefficient solutions over time through lock-in effects and other features of path dependence.[28] Although, as we have seen, a normative foundation of some kind is essential if a market order is to operate at all, it does not follow that norms evolve and adapt in such a way as to supply solutions which are optimal. As we have seen, in the case of conventions which emerge on the basis of social learning, the usefulness of a particular norm is a function of its adaptiveness in the *past*; hence 'evolution will tend to favour versatile but inefficient conventions relative to ones that are less versatile but more efficient'.[29] The adaptation of existing concepts and ideas to new ends means that 'features of existing conventions and institutions may often have arisen for one reason, but now serve very different functions and purposes'.[30]

---

[24] *Rules and Order*, op. cit., at p. 47.   [25] Ibid., at p. 57.   [26] Ibid., at p. 45.

[27] Ibid., at pp. 45–46.   [28] See Ch. 1, above.

[29] R. Sugden, 'Spontaneous order' (1989), op. cit., at p. 94.

[30] J. Balkin, *Cultural Software: A Theory of Ideology* (New Haven, CT: Yale University Press, 1998), at p. 72.

The notion of efficiency in a spontaneous order is therefore a highly *qualified* one. Norms which emerge spontaneously are unlikely to be ideal in the sense of being Pareto-optimal, that is, of producing situations in which no further gains from trade can be made except by making at least one party worse off.[31] However, the configuration of incentives which emerges from the accumulation of conventions may be the best that is available. The costs of attempting to shift the system to a notional optimum through 'market perfecting' laws may outweigh the resulting gains (the so-called 'irremediability' principle[32]).

The use of intervention to achieve Pareto improvements may be undesirable for other reasons. This is because spontaneous orders may be *self-correcting*. It is precisely because of so-called imperfections—such as imperfect transmission of information—that opportunities for profit from entrepreneurial activity or, more generally, from innovation in organization and design of goods and services, exist. In the general-equilibrium world of pure competition, in which information and resources move perfectly freely in response to the price mechanism, such opportunities would be instantly competed away. In the real world of positive transaction costs, by contrast, it is the possibility of capturing 'supra-competitive rents' or surpluses representing a competitive advantage over their rivals which motivates potential entrepreneurs or innovators and which, as a result, ensures long-run technological and organizational progress.[33]

In this account, the appropriate role for the law, then, is to support private property rights, ensure that returns accrue to those who make investments in the process of discovery, and guarantee freedom of access to markets. The inequalities and concentrations of power and wealth which arise from the unbridled operation of market forces produce their own solution by incentivizing those who, by misfortune or otherwise, fail to profit from the system. Even if certain gains and losses accrue by chance, leaving some with 'undeserved disappointments',[34] ex-post redistribution of resources blunts incentives for individuals to invest in their own skills and efforts. This and similar interventions which might be justified from a 'market perfecting' point of view merely block the *process* of competition as discovery which provides the means by which dispersed knowledge and information are put to use: hence, 'attempts to "correct" the order of the market lead to its destruction'.[35]

The precise claim being made here by Hayek and his followers needs to be carefully identified. It should not be read as suggesting that markets, if left to their own devices, will tend towards an optimally efficient state. The market never 'clears' in the sense used by the neoclassical theory of general equilibrium. Rather, the market is useful because it generates a process of discovery which makes the

---

[31] Costabile, 'Ordine spontaneo o ordine negoziato', op. cit., at pp. 27–30.

[32] See O. Williamson, *The Mechanisms of Governance* (Oxford: Oxford University Press, 1996), ch. 9.

[33] I. Kirzner, *How Markets Work: Disequilibrium, Entrepreneurship and Discovery*, IEA Paper No. 133 (London: Institute of Economic Affairs, 1997).

[34] *The Mirage of Social Justice* (London: Routledge, 1976), at p. 127.   [35] Ibid., at p. 142.

best available use of society's resources. It is accepted that the process of economic change which this account implies is one which is dynamic and non-linear. It is therefore the *dynamic efficiency* of the market system—in other words, its capacity to generate new knowledge and information in a way which will ensure the system's long-run survival in a changing environment—which justifies institutional support for individual property and contract rights, but which, at the same time, allows for only a very limited degree of market regulation, and rules out redistribution carried out in the name of those values of 'social justice' which were the traditional foundation of labour law.[36]

2.3 The limits of spontaneous order

On closer inspection, this 'minimalist' approach to the regulation of the market is hard to sustain, even if we take as given the assumptions underlying the spontaneous order approach. Our approach here will be to do precisely that. Indeed, one of the virtues of the theory of spontaneous order is that, in addition to explaining the many benefits of markets, it also helps us to understand their limits. Thus Sugden[37] acknowledges the limits of market ordering when he accepts that the market is good at meeting one particular type of objective, namely satisfying those wants or preferences which can be encapsulated in property rights. The market will not provide well in relation to those wants or preferences for goods for which no property rights exist. It therefore fails to work well in relation to so-called 'non-excludable' public goods or 'indivisible' commodities.[38]

Moreover, the spontaneous order argument for markets is based on the power of individuals to make mutually-agreed exchanges with others; but this only satisfies wants *in general* if each transaction affects only those who are party to it. If there are externalities, then transactions between some parties affect the opportunities of others to satisfy their wants. As the 'Coase theorem' recognizes,[39] the state has a role in dealing with externalities in situations where negotiation is unduly costly. But this opens up another arena for policy intervention in an area where the market is not self-correcting.

Nor is this point simply related to limits to the spill-over effects of exchange. Sugden argues that for the market to operate effectively, it is necessary not simply to have a system of property rights, but for individuals to have *endowments* in the sense of items of value which are tradable—'the market has a strong tendency to supply each person with those things he wants, *provided that he owns things that other people want, and provided that the things he wants are things that other people own*'.[40] Another way of putting this is to say that the market has no inbuilt tendency to satisfy the wants of those who do not have things that other people want.

---

[36] *Rules and Order*, op. cit., at pp. 140–142.   [37] 'Spontaneous order' (1998), op. cit.

[38] See also A. Sen, *Development as Freedom*, op. cit., at pp. 127–9.

[39] See Coase, 'The firm, the market and the law', op. cit.

[40] Sugden, 'Spontaneous order' (1998), at p. 492.

This leads us to pose the question: can a market order function effectively in a situation in which there are large and enduring disparities in the wealth and resources of market participants? For certain supporters of a neoclassical approach to the economics of law, such as Richard Posner, the answer is clearly that it can; supply and demand can still be brought into equilibrium and resources will flow to their most highly valued use, value being measured by willingness to pay.[41] From the point of view of the theory of spontaneous order, however, the answer is not so clear. Extremes of inequality exclude certain groups from the market altogether. The result is not just that these individuals no longer have access to the goods which the market can supply; the rest of society also suffers a loss from their inability to take part in the system of exchange. Resources remain unutilized. The logic of this position, as Sugden makes clear,[42] is that redistribution is needed not to reverse the unpleasant results of the market, but rather to provide the preconditions for the market working in the first place. From this perspective, we would suggest, many of the redistributive and protective rules of labour law have a *market-creating* function.

The argument for redistribution, and for regulation, can be taken a step further. The market itself may be a cause of inequality; inequality, in other words, may be *endogenous*. Neoclassical theory simply denies this on *a priori* grounds; the causes of inequality are assumed to be *exogenous*, in the sense that different individuals have different capacities and propensities to work. The market itself tends towards proportionality of effort and reward, by setting wages in proportion to the contribution which particular individuals bring to the employment relationship.

However, an implication of the path-dependent nature of norms and conventions within labour markets is that forces are at work which disrupt this assumed correspondence of efforts and rewards. Unregulated markets contain within them the seeds of their own destruction. In the terms of spontaneous order, the symbiotic relationship between the general and particular mechanisms can break down. The market loses its capacity for self-correction. Externalities causing losses beyond the exchange, which cannot be internalized because of high transaction costs, reduce aggregate well-being. Persistent inequalities mean that groups and individuals lack the resource endowments to enter the market in a meaningful way. In an extreme case, the market will destroy itself unless these negative effects are counter-acted by non-market institutions in the form of regulation and redistribution. In a less extreme case, the market order will continue to function, but will fail to provide adequate economic opportunities for an increasingly large segment of the population.

2.4 The sources of inequality in labour markets

The suggestion that labour markets tend towards a fundamental lack of correspondence between endowments and efforts, on the one hand, and rewards on the other, can be understood by considering the role of norms, conventions and more formal

---

[41] See R. Posner, *Economic Analysis of Law* (New York: Aspen Law and Business, 5th ed., 1999), ch. 1.
[42] 'Spontaneous order' (1998), op. cit., at 493.

laws in constituting and structuring both the demand-side and supply-side of the exchange.[43] The result of this process is that *conventions operate to structure the capabilities and hence the opportunities of individuals within the labour market.* These conventions are the product of the strategies of labour market actors, and may be more or less institutionalized in legal and/or contractual form. Their cumulative effect is to induce dynamic processes which lead to the segmentation of the labour market and, as a result, to mismatches (or imperfections) in the process of pricing of labour power. As a result, inequality becomes endogenous to the economic system.[44]

An initial distinction may be drawn between the *resource endowments* of individuals, their *capabilities*, and their economic *functioning*. The *resource endowments* of individuals include their labour power, their accumulated assets, and their entitlements (net of contributions) to private and public transfers. Resource endowments vary widely in both levels and composition between individuals and over an individual's lifetime. For example, the resource endowments of children consist mainly of their claim to intra-household transfers based on their family affiliation and public transfers in the form of child benefits, education, health and other social provisions. In early adult life the most important part of individuals' resource endowment is usually their labour power and they have probably become net contributors, at this stage, to the tax/benefit system and possibly to private transfers. The importance of labour power and net contributions to public and private transfers increase with cohabitation and the formation of families but as individuals grow older their net contribution to private transfers can be expected to decline as their children leave the household, and when they retire their resource endowments become mainly state transfers, accumulated private assets (including private pension rights) and, possibly, private transfers.

There are, however, wide variations between individuals around this stylized life-time profile of resource endowment. These variations are related to time spent in education, age at cohabitation and family formation, types of household, participation in the labour market, and other socially and economically determined factors.

Given their resource endowments, the *economic functioning* of individuals is determined by their *capabilities*. For present purposes, the concepts of capability and functioning will be developed within the framework of a discussion of the effective mobilization by individuals of the resources at their disposal as the means of becoming and remaining self-sufficient. According to Sen,[45]

the concept of 'functionings' . . . reflects the various things a person may value doing or being. The valued functionings may vary from elementary ones, such as being adequately

---

[43] See generally Ch. 1, above.

[44] See generally C. Craig, J. Rubery, R. Tarling and F. Wilkinson, 'Economic, social and political factors in the operation of the labour market', in B. Roberts, R. Finnegan and D. Gallie (eds.) *New Approaches to Economic Life* (Manchester: University of Manchester Press, 1985) 105–123. Our argument here also builds on S. Deakin and F. Wilkinson, '"Capabilities", ordineo spontaneo del mercato, e diritti sociali' (2000) 2 *Il diritto del mercato del lavoro* 317–344.

[45] *Development as Freedom*, op. cit., at p. 75.

nourished and being free from avoidable disease, to very complex activities or personal states, such as being able to take part in the life of the community and having self-respect.

Within this context, a 'capability' is 'a kind of freedom: the substantive freedom to achieve alternative functioning combinations'.[46]

However, capabilities are a consequence not simply of the endowments and motivations of individuals but also of the access they have to the processes of socialization, education and training which enable them to exploit their resource endowments. Inter-community and inter-family differences in wealth, expectations and information provide individuals with variable degrees of access to these processes and hence to opportunities for more highly rewarded employment. The 'traditional' division of labour and household organization, on the other hand, serves to reduce the capabilities of women in the labour market. Unequally distributed responsibility for domestic labour inhibits the labour market activities of women in varying degrees, depending on the collective resource endowment of household members and the willingness of other members to use their resources (either labour or capital) to provide substitutes for the cooking, cleaning, child care and other domestic services traditionally provided by women. The greater the domestic responsibility of a woman (and hence the greater her transfer to others in her household) the less favourable are likely to be her labour market opportunities. At one extreme, in resource-poor households which are highly dependent on the domestic services of female members (female-headed, single-parent households for example), women will find it extremely difficult to realize their full capability on the labour market whatever skills they might have. At the other extreme, in households with access to ample resources to replace female domestic labour, women members will be strongly placed to exploit fully their labour market assets.

The norms associated with the division of labour are affected by the state in a number of ways. The state influences the economic functioning of individuals by reference to social security and labour legislation and through direct provision of health and education services. The growth of the welfare state can therefore be regarded as counteracting social, economic and other disadvantages and therefore breaking down the barriers to effective labour market participation. However, the extent to which individuals can take advantage of education and training to enhance their resource endowment will still depend on the willingness and ability of households to support non-economically functioning members and their experience, expectations and information about education, training and labour market opportunities.

At the same time, the impact of state intervention may be ambivalent in its effects. The resource endowments of the better-off may be enhanced by many forms of state provision of education and training as well as through access to health care and social security (state subsidies for occupational social security are

---

[46] *Development as Freedom*, op. cit., at p. 75.

a major source of wealth for higher-income groups). Those elements of state expenditure to which the worse-off have greatest recourse, on the other hand, often work to impair their economic functioning. For example, the capabilities of social welfare recipients are *reduced* by social security systems which rely on means-tested benefits which are cut as incomes rise. This effectively imposes high marginal taxes on the low income households who find themselves in the 'poverty trap'.[47]

Within the labour market, professional associations, sectionally-based trade unions and other formal and informal organizations and networks exercise control over entry to particular labour market segments and to training, as well as to other forms of in-market advancement. In this way, they restrict access to and use of human capital. Labour market disadvantages associated with sex, race, age, low social status and poor educational achievement are exacerbated by the difficulties particular groups experience in forming or joining effective in-market organizations. The hiring, training and labour management policies of firms interrelate with supply side factors in further differentiating job opportunities. Hiring rules adopted by firms rest on signals transmitted by social characteristics (age, sex, race, education and training qualification, dress, deportment and so on) which are only partially objectively based if at all, but which are taken to measure the relative worth of job applicants.

The technical and organizational structure of the firm, the related systems of labour management, and collective bargaining (or its absence) all structure job opportunities within firms, while training and promotion policies regulate the allocation of workers within internal labour markets. Firms with a range of abilities to pay offer widely different levels of wages for comparable jobs so that differential promotion prospects—in terms of job content and/or pay—exist both within and between firms. Successful progression within job structures enhances the labour market status of individuals whereas redundancy and other involuntary quits, periods out of the labour market for domestic reasons, and spells of unemployment have the opposite effect. Thus job prospects of individuals can be continuously modified from the supply side by their own employment experience and from the demand side by such factors as plant closures, industrial restructuring and changes in hiring and training rules adopted by employers.[48]

The structuring of job opportunities and related differences in the terms and conditions of employment are further reinforced by variations in the incidence and effectiveness of collective bargaining and protection afforded by the law. Collective agreements reflect the bargaining power of labour and the ability of firms and industries to pay and so their benefits can vary widely. The employees of small firms, part-timers, workers on temporary and other non-standard contracts

---

[47] See Chapter 3, Section 5.7.

[48] For detailed analyses of the dynamic effects of industrial restructuring and changes in hiring, training and other aspects of labour management on the supply and demand side structuring of the labour market, see the collection of articles in *Labour and Society*, October 1988.

and others whose employment status is ambiguous are frequently excluded from the scope of both collective bargaining and protective legislation.

One of the most pervasive characteristics of labour markets is, therefore, that access to jobs is carefully controlled, and that the higher the pay and status of a particular occupation, the more obstructive are the rules of entry. Rules of exclusion operate on all groups at all levels and are mutually reinforcing in the sense that workers in each labour market group, excluded from better jobs, more carefully protect those within their control. However, the ability to exclude others can be expected to decline at successively lower levels in the labour market hierarchy. At the bottom end of the labour market, jobs tend to be classified as unskilled whatever their job content, trade unionism is weak or non-existent, and the law offers little, if any, protection. As a result, terms and conditions of employment are poor, work is often casualized and non-standard forms of employment contracts are common. Individuals are often unable to move out of this segment by their lack of transferable and/or socially recognized and credentialized skills, by the many forms discrimination takes, and by the priority which they are obliged to give to domestic and other responsibilities. At this level, jobs tend to be much more open to anyone, and therefore regular employees are thrown into competition with students and others who want temporary jobs to top up their income from other sources, and who are therefore prepared to accept wages below that necessary for self-sufficiency.

Cumulative effects are thereby built into the interaction between the resource endowments of individuals, their capabilities and their economic functioning. A virtuous cycle is in operation through which ample resource endowment leads to labour market advantage which enhances capability and economic functioning, which in turn enables increases in resource endowment. By contrast, paucity of resource endowment interacts with reduced capabilities in reinforcing poor economic functioning, leading to a vicious cycle of disadvantage. This defines what we may refer to as the *out-market* undervaluation of the labour. This is compounded by *in-market* undervaluation which results from the structuring of labour markets by social, organizational and legal forces which relegate the socially disadvantaged to labour market segments where their capabilities are further reduced because wages are low relative to the real value of labour input.

The segmentation of labour markets and the social and economic deprivation which it engenders therefore have significant macroeconomic and microeconomic implications. The *out-market* undervaluation of labour reduces the overall productive potential of an economy, while *in-market* undervaluation leads to further waste to the extent that it permits the continued existence of outmoded techniques and inefficient managerial practices. *In-market* undervaluation of labour also leads to a more unequal distribution of income than would be warranted by the distribution of what Alfred Marshall called *efficiency* earnings— 'earnings measured with reference to the exertion of ability and efficiency required of the workers'.[49] The beneficiaries of this unequal distribution of income may be either those in receipt of profits or more advantaged groups in the labour market depending on whether, and the extent to which, the cost advantage of employing undervalued labour is passed on to the customer. There are a wide range of direct and indirect ways by which the wage share is distributed unequally in which both relative wages, prices and the system of taxation act together to enhance the resources, endowments and capabilities of some while reducing those of others.

The process of market structuring, as we have seen throughout our analysis in the preceding chapters, is an historical one. Competition in labour markets is historically situated, in the sense of being the outcome of a particular process of interaction between the business enterprise, worker organization, the family and the welfare state. Both informal or social norms, on the one hand, and the more formal elements of the legal system or contractual agreements, on the other, play a key role in shaping competition. As Mark Harvey explains:

> The social organization of the parties to the exchange, the mode of exchange (e.g. transparency, repeatability, integration), the constitution of the 'objects' of exchange (e.g. extent of standardization, regulation and control of quality), the pricing mechanisms (e.g. centralised auction, bartering, price-taking, or price-setting), are each open to variation, as a consequence of which *whom* competition is between, *what* competition is about, and *how* competition is pursued will also vary.[50]

It is because competition is, in this sense, the outcome of an evolutionary process, rather than being a 'natural' presence in markets, that its form will differ over time and from one context to another. Competition in the labour market is competition of a very particular kind. It depends upon the historical process by which wage dependence comes into being in a given society and on the degree to which it is counterbalanced by the institutions of the family and the welfare state. It also rests on the way in which the employment relationship defines not simply the mutual obligations of the parties, but also, at an even more basic level, the object of the exchange itself. The idea that the contract of employment is founded on an agreement to serve, whereby one party is placed, for a certain time and space, at the disposal of another, is the product of a particular historical development, which is sensitive to the initial conditions under which industrialization occurred. Thus in the British context, as we have seen in preceding chapters, the particular historical conditions surrounding the trajectory of the poor law, the emergence of the master–servant model, the growth of collective bargaining and the formalization of the breadwinner wage have all been influential in determining the nature of labour market relations and the extent of inequality within and between social groups.

[49] A. Marshall, *Principles of Economics: An Introductory Volume* (London: Macmillan, 8th ed., 1949), at p. 549.
[50] M. Harvey, 'Productive systems, markets and competition as "instituted economic process"', in B. Burchell, S. Deakin, J. Michie and J. Rubery (eds.) *Systems of Production: Markets, Organisations and Performance* (London: Routledge, 2003) 40–59, at p. 45.

To sum up this part of the argument: the operation of spontaneous order within labour markets is a complex process, involving the interaction of a number of forces on the supply-side and demand-sides of the exchange. Conventions, norms and laws structure both the demand and supply for labour. Because of the path-dependent nature of conventions, these effects become locked in, with the result that they influence the direction of economic change. The trajectory of economic development is determined by cumulative, feedback effects, which, while capable of producing the conditions for economic coordination and a more general societal cooperation, are not bound to do so; they can also give rise to a 'pathology of the labour market' in which inefficiencies, and hence inequalities, become embedded in the system.

Under such circumstances, there can be no assumption that a self-correcting mechanism will undo these effects. A role for policy is opened up, in terms of redressing what may be seen as effects which are undesirable not just for particular groups, but for society as a whole, given the waste and under-utilization of resources which they produce. But at the same time, there is a limit to what law can achieve as an instrument of social and economic policy. The law is a part of, and reflects, the society of which it forms a part. The extent to which the law can be mobilized to fulfil the objectives of policy depends upon its own regulatory capability, which is a function of its history and evolution. Thus to respond fully to Hayek's critique it is necessary not simply to point to a space which regulation can occupy thanks to the limits of self-ordering, but also to conceptualize a form of legal order which can co-exist with the multiple, complex forms of the modern economy.

We now turn to consider the nature of the policy responses which this perspective implies.

3. A Capability-based Approach to Labour Market Regulation

3.1 Labour standards as institutionalized capabilities

Sen's 'capability approach' envisages a central role for what he calls *conversion factors*. A person's capability to achieve a particular range of functionings is determined by characteristics not just of their *person* (such as their metabolism or biological sex) and of their *environment* (which could include climate, physical surroundings, and technological infrastructure) but also of the institutional structure of the *society* in which they live. Thus social norms, legal rules and legal-political institutions play a vital role in either extending, or diminishing, individual capability sets. In this respect, an individual's capability to make use of a particular commodity may depend not just upon the ability to deploy a legal system which recognizes and guarantees protection of contract and property rights, but also upon access to health care, education and other resources which equip them to enter into relations of exchange with others.[51]

If capabilities are a consequence not simply of the endowments and motivations of individuals but also of the access they have to the processes of socialization, education and training which enable them to exploit their resource endowments, then by providing the conditions under which access to these processes is made generally available, mechanisms of redistribution may be not just compatible with, but become a precondition to, the operation of the labour market. In this way, social rights may play a pivotal role in providing an institutional foundation for individual capabilities.

It is relevant to consider, in this context, laws protecting workers against dismissal on the grounds of pregnancy. A conventional economic view of such laws would be as follows. From the viewpoint of enterprises which would otherwise dismiss pregnant employees once they become unable to carry on working as normally, such laws impose a private cost. These enterprises may respond by declining to hire women of child-bearing age who will, as a result, find it more difficult to get jobs. If this happens, there may be an overall loss to society in terms of efficiency, because resources are misallocated and under-utilized, as well as a disadvantage to the women who are unemployed as a result.

An alternative way of thinking about discrimination against pregnant workers is as follows. In the absence of legal protection against this type of discrimination, women of child-bearing age will not expect to continue in employment once (or shortly after) they become pregnant. It is not necessary for all market participants to make a precise calculation along these lines; rather, a norm or convention will emerge, according to which pregnant women expect to lose their jobs and their employers expect to be able to dismiss them without any harm attaching to their reputation. The overall effect is that investments in skills and training are not undertaken, making society worse off as a result. Women workers will have an incentive not to make relation-specific investments in the jobs which they undertake. In an extreme situation, they may withdraw from active participation from the labour market altogether, and norms may encourage this too—as in the case of the 'marriage bar' norm, according to which any woman who married was expected thereupon to resign her position. This norm was widely observed in the British public sector up to the 1950s and, in the case of some local authorities, was actually enshrined in regulations.[52]

What is the effect of the introduction of a prohibition on the dismissal of pregnant women under these circumstances? In addition to remedying the injustice which would otherwise affect individuals who are dismissed for this reason, a law

[51] See S. Deakin and J. Browne, 'Social rights and the market order: adapting the capability approach', in T. Hervey and J. Kenner (eds.) *Economic and Socail Rights under the European Charter of Fundamental Rights* (Oxford: Hart, 2003), 28–43. J. Browne, S. Deakin and F. Wilkinson, 'Capabilities, social rights, and European integration' in Salais, R. and Villeneuve, R. (eds.) *Towards a European Politics of Capabilities* (Cambridge: CUP, 2005). We are grateful to Jude Browne for permission to draw on our joint work on this aspect of Sen's capability approach.

[52] S. Walby, *Patriarchy at Work* (Cambridge: Polity, 1985); see Chapter 3, Section 5.5, above.

of this kind has the potential to alter incentive structures in such a way as to encourage women employees to seek out, and employers to provide training for, jobs involving relation-specific skills. The demonstration effect of damages awards against employers may over time lead to a situation in which the norm of automatic dismissal is replaced by its opposite. Stigma attaches to those employers who flout the law. As more employers observe the new norm as a matter of course, it will tend to become self-enforcing, in a way which is independent of the law itself. Conversely, more women will expect, as a matter of course, to carry on working while raising families, in a way which may have a wider destabilizing effect on the set of conventions which together make up the 'traditional' household division of labour between men and women.

Recent empirical research casts light on this claim. In the United Kingdom, pregnancy protection laws were significantly strengthened in the mid-1990s, as a result of the combined effect of a number of rulings of the European Court of Justice,[53] extending the scope of the (then) Equal Treatment Directive to pregnancy cases, and the implementation of the Pregnant Workers' Directive of 1992.[54] These changes meant that both protection against dismissal and the right to return to work after pregnancy were more effectively guaranteed. The result has been a lengthening of the average job tenure of full-time women workers which has contributed to a more general rise in labour market participation by women of working age.[55]

Pregnancy protection laws, therefore, can be seen as a form of institutionalized conversion factor. In other words, they provide the conditions under which, for women workers, the freedom to enter the labour market becomes more than merely formal; it becomes a substantive freedom. This effect is not confined to laws in the area of equality of treatment. Laws which set minimum wages or which otherwise establish legally-binding wage floors (such as the principle of 'inderogability' in Italian labour law[56]) may have a similar effect. These laws have been the subject of severe criticisms from economic and legal commentators.[57]

---

[53] In particular Case C-177/88 *Dekker* v. *VJV Centrum* [1991] IRLR 27 and Case C-32/93, *Webb* v. *EMO Air Cargo (UK) Ltd.* [1994] IRLR 482.

[54] Council Directive 92/85/EEC on the introduction of measures to encourage improvements in the safety and health of pregnant workers and workers who have recently given birth or are breast-feeding, OJ 1992 L348, 28.11.92. The relevant domestic legislation is now to be found in various provisions of the Employment Rights Act 1996 (as amended) and in the Maternity and Parental Leave etc. Regulations, SI 1999/3312. See S. Deakin and G. Morris, *Labour Law* (3rd ed., London: Butterworths, 2001), at 645–655.

[55] See H. Robinson, 'Gender and labour market performance in the recovery', in R. Dickens, P. Gregg and J. Wadsworth (eds.) *The Labour Market Under New Labour. The State of Working Britain 2003* (London: Palgrave, 2003) 232–247 at p. 237.

[56] See Lord Wedderburn, 'Inderogability, collective agreements and Community law' (1992) 21 *Industrial Law Journal* 245–264.

[57] See A. Ichino and P. Ichino, 'A chi serve il diritto del lavoro? Riflessioni interdisciplinari sulla funzione economica e la giustificazione costituzionale dell'inderogabilità delle norme giuslavoristiche', in A. Amendola (ed.) *Istituzione e mercato del lavoro* (Rome: Edizione Scientifiche Italiane, 1998) 67–102.

The objection made against them is that they artificially raise wages above the market clearing level, thereby reducing demand for labour and excluding the less able from access to the labour market. By doing so, they potentially infringe the basic constitutional right to work in systems which recognize that concept.

This argument assumes that a 'free' labour market more or less accurately allocates wages to workers according to their relative productivity. As explained above, there are spontaneous forces at work in the labour market which make this unlikely. In an unregulated or 'free' labour market without effective labour standards, wage rates are only weakly linked, at best, to the comparative productivity of workers.[58] The effect of segmentation is that workers with comparable skills and efficiencies are undervalued to varying degrees because they receive different wages per 'efficiency unit'. The persistence of structural inequality opens up the possibility of 'predatory' strategies by firms which seek to tap sources of undervalued labour. Individual employers adjust their wage costs to their ability to pay by either shifting their demand for labour to a more disadvantaged segment or because their workers, trapped in their respective segment, are unable to resist a decline in their relative wage. By being in a position to increase the degree of undervaluation of the workers they employ, firms can avoid more radical remedies such as the restructuring of production, managerial reorganization and the replacing of obsolete equipment with new technology. The direct relationship between wage rates and the ability of the firm to pay in a structured labour market also has the effect of discouraging innovation by more creative entrepreneurs, who find it difficult to expand their share of the market because of the difficulties of dislodging technically and managerially inefficient firms which can remain profitable in the short term by employing undervalued labour. The overall result is a lower average level of productivity in the economy, both because managerial practices and obsolete equipment which should be scrapped remain in existence, and because of slow rate of introduction of new techniques.[59]

By contrast, legislation setting a floor to wages and terms and conditions of employment in effect requires firms to adopt strategies based on enhancing the quality of labour inputs through improvements to health and safety protection, training, and skills development. This form of labour regulation may therefore be expected to have a positive impact on incentives or training. Minimum wage laws are therefore another form of institutional conversion factor, improving the substantive labour market freedoms of workers.

By removing protective legislation which has a general or 'universal' effect, protecting all labour market entrants, deregulation directly undermines the capabilities of those individuals who are at most risk of social exclusion through discrimination and the undervaluation of their labour. The de-motivation of those who find themselves excluded from access to productive employment is met by

---

[58] See Craig et al., 'Economic, social and political factors', op. cit.

[59] F. Wilkinson, 'Industrial organization, collective bargaining and economic efficiency' (1991) 1 *International Contributions to Labour Studies* 1–25.

ever-increasing pressure on them to take jobs at any cost. This takes the form of measures within social security law which discipline the 'voluntarily' unemployed by, for example, withdrawing benefits from individuals who refuse to accept jobs offering low-standard terms and conditions of employment. On the demand side, employers are encouraged to take on the unemployed by subsidy schemes which top up low wages. This exacerbates the effect of removing the incentives for training and investment in human capital which flow from a legal requirement for employers to pay a minimum wage. All these developments are well documented in the case of the British experience of deregulation which reached its high point in the early 1990s,[60] just as an earlier generation recorded the adverse social and economic effects of the 'parasitic' trades to which the lop-sided regulation of the nineteenth century had given rise.[61]

3.2 Legal form as the basis for a critique of labour market regulation

The general case for labour regulation which we have just made should not be translated into uncritical support for all aspects of existing labour law systems. In particular, it raises issues of the capacity of legal regulation to deliver solutions which are compatible with the preservation of a market order. Here, again, the main critique of the existing forms of labour regulation is that of Hayek.

Hayek's antipathy to labour law was rooted in part in his analysis of the role of legislation within the legal order of a market society. The market order, or *catallaxy*, rests on rules of a particular kind, the 'abstract rules of just conduct', which as we have seen, Hayek associates with private law. Private law and the market order are, according to Hayek, mutually supportive elements of a wider, societal spontaneous order which is both the foundation of a society's well-being and also the necessary condition for the freedom of its individual members. For Hayek, the opposite of a 'spontaneous order' or (in Hayek's terminology) *cosmos*, is a made or imposed order, or *taxis*. The term *taxis* describes an order which is purpose-orientated and is the result of conscious planning or organization. As such, there is a limit to the degree of complexity which it can achieve: 'very complex orders, comprising more particular facts than any brain could ascertain or manipulate, can be brought about only through forces inducing the formation of spontaneous orders'.[62] The distinction between *cosmos* and *taxis* further corresponds to a distinction between types of norms, that is, between the abstract rules of just conduct (*nomos*) and the rules of organization (*thesis*). Although a spontaneous order cannot be consciously planned, it nevertheless rests on the abstract rules of just conduct in the sense that 'the formation of spontaneous orders is the result of their elements following

---

[60] See S. Deakin and F. Wilkinson, 'Labour law, social security and economic inequality', op. cit., and Chapter 4, Section 6, above.

[61] See Chapter 4, above, discussing the analysis of the Webbs and of Hutchins and Harrison.

[62] *Rules and Order*, op. cit., at p. 38.

certain rules in their responses to their immediate environment'.[63] The principal features of the rules of just conduct are firstly, that they are purpose-independent; secondly, that they apply generally across a large range of cases and situations whose nature cannot be known in advance; and thirdly, that 'by defining a protected domain of each, [they] enable an order of actions to form itself wherein the individuals can make feasible plans'.[64] By contrast, the rules of organization are concerned with the internal ordering of governmental and similar bodies; they are 'designed to achieve particular ends, to supplement positive orders that something should be done or that particular results should be achieved, and to set up for these purposes the various agencies through which government operates'.[65] Here 'the distinction between the rules of just conduct and the rules of organisation is closely related to, and sometimes explicitly equated with, the distinction between private and public law'.[66]

This distinction is important because in Hayek's view, public law cannot substitute for private law as the basis for a spontaneous order; nor can the two forms be combined. This is because private law respects, where public law does not, the autonomy and capacity for action of individuals:

It would . . . seem that wherever a Great Society has arisen, it has been made possible by a system of rules of just conduct which included what David Hume called 'the three fundamental laws of nature, *that of stability of possession, of its transference by consent*, and *of the performance of promises*', or . . . the essential content of all contemporary systems of private law . . . [67]

Although he does not undertake a detailed examination of juridical structures, Hayek implies that the relationship between contract, property and tort is determined by their respective roles in defining and protecting the autonomy of individual agents. Private law is the precondition of the market order in the sense that without it, individuals would not be free to use their own information and knowledge for their own purposes. The imposition of specific duties of affirmative action, of the kind which blur the tort-contract boundary and place restrictions on freedom of disposition, should therefore be opposed, and tortious liabilities should be limited to situations of active harm (misfeasance, as opposed to nonfeasance).[68]

Thus the existence of a coherent classificatory scheme *within* private law helps to explain the distinctiveness of private law as a form of normative ordering. But equally, as we have seen, Hayek was clear that social norms were not sufficient for the preservation of the spontaneous order of the market. Private law has a wider 'purpose' in relation to society, even if the individual rules of private law are not themselves purpose-orientated in the sense of being designed to bring about particular distributive or regulatory goals: 'only when it is understood that the

---

[63] Ibid., at p. 43.   [64] Ibid., at p. 86.   [65] Ibid., at p. 125.
[66] Ibid., at pp. 131–132.   [67] *The Mirage of Social Justice*, op. cit., at p. 40.
[68] *Rules and Order*, op. cit., at p. 37; see also, on contract, ibid., at p. 110 and on property rights, ibid., at pp. 106–7.

order of actions is a factual state of affairs distinct from the rules which contribute to its formation can it be understood that such *an abstract order can be the aim of the rules of conduct*.[69]

The final step in this part of Hayek's argument was to identify the legitimate domain of public law, or the 'law of organisation'. The existence of organizations is not denied; thus 'the family, the farm, the plant, the firm, the corporation and the various associations, and all the public institutions including government, are organisations which in turn are integrated into a more comprehensive spontaneous order', that is to say, the spontaneous order of society.[70] Equally, there is a need for a form of public law which underpins the internal relations of hierarchy and command within organizations, and in particular those of the state. What is illegitimate, in Hayek's view, is to apply this form of legal ordering to the regulation of spontaneous orders, such as the market. 'Specific commands ("interference") in a catallaxy create disorder and can never be just';[71] equally, 'attempts to "correct" the order of the market lead to its destruction'.[72] This is because regulations which seek to correct for 'market failure', in an attempt to bring about a more allocatively efficient state of the world, merely block the *process* of competition as discovery which provides the means by which dispersed knowledge and information are put to use. The information which is in the hands of individual economic agents cannot, by definition, be possessed by the authority responsible for the conscious design of a regulation:

This is the gist of the argument against 'interference' or 'intervention' in the market order. The reason why such isolated commands requiring specific actions by members of the spontaneous order can never improve but must disrupt that order is that they will refer to a part of a system of interdependent actions determined by information and guided by purposes known only to the several acting persons but not to the directing authority. The spontaneous order arises from each element balancing all the various factors operating on it and by adjusting all its various actions to each other, a balance which will be destroyed if some of the actions are determined by another agency on the basis of different knowledge and in the service of different ends ... What the general argument against 'interference' thus amounts to is that, although we can endeavour to improve a spontaneous order by revising the general rules on which it rests, and can supplement its results by the efforts of various organisations, we cannot improve the results by specific commands that deprive its members of the possibility of using their knowledge for their own purposes.[73]

It is important, again, to be clear about the claim being made. As we have seen, Hayek does not suggest that legal intervention, for example for the enforcement of property and contract rights, is unnecessary and illegitimate. On the contrary, he accepts the occasionally 'coercive' character of private law. Nor does he claim

[69] *Rules and Order*, op. cit., at pp. 113–114.   [70] Ibid., at p. 46.
[71] *The Mirage of Social Justice*, at p. 128.   [72] Ibid., at p. 142.
[73] *Rules and Order*, op. cit., at p. 51.

that the techniques of public law can never be legitimately deployed (although it is not altogether clear how far they should apply to the internal governance of *private-sector* organizations). Nor, even, are all forms of legislative intervention in market activity deemed to be inappropriate. Hayek excludes from condemnation legislation which involves 'the removal of discriminations by law which had crept in as a result of the greater influence that certain groups like landlords, employers, creditors, etc., had wielded on the formation of law';[74] he also accepts a role for 'the provision by government of certain services which are of special importance to some unfortunate minorities, the weak or those unable to provide for themselves'.[75] He draws the line at a 'third kind of "social" legislation', whose aim is 'to direct private activity towards particular ends and to the benefit of particular groups', and refers in this context to the Trade Disputes Act 1906 and to legislation of the New Deal; and in this context, what is singled out for condemnation is precisely the 'progressive replacement of private law by public law'.[76]

In short, Hayek's theory of private law is one which accepts and builds on the internal classifications of the law of obligations, and which asserts the autonomy and coherence of private law as a whole. The internal features of private law are linked to a broader theory of the relationship between legal norms and the market order. Here, Hayek insists on the need for a *positive* account of private law in which its relationship to the economic system is central to the analysis of legal concepts: '[a]n important consequence of this relation between the system of rules of conduct and the factual order of actions is that there can never be a science of law that is purely a science of norms and takes no account of the factual order at which it aims'.[77]

The *normative* implications of this approach are not confined to a broad affirmation of the values of corrective justice; encroachments by legislation on the sphere traditionally occupied by private law are opposed on the grounds of the coercion and injustice which they engender. Hence, the general classification of legal rules into norms of private law and norms of public law is the basis for a normative argument to the effect that the large part of modern regulatory legislation lacks legitimacy. In Hayek's view, such regulation even lacks the inherent normative force of the rule of law:

[o]nly if one understands by law not the general rules of just conduct only but any command issued by authority (or any authorisation of such commands by a legislature), can the measures aimed at distributive justice be represented as compatible with the rule of law. But this concept is thereby made to mean mere legality and ceases to offer the protection of individual freedom which it was originally intended to serve.[78]

At this level, the internal conceptual structure of the law is concerned with nothing less than the political legitimacy and legal identity of the modern regulatory state.

[74] Ibid., at p. 141.   [75] Ibid., at pp. 141–2.   [76] Ibid., at pp. 142–143.
[77] Ibid., at p. 105.   [78] *The Mirage of Social Justice*, at p. 87.

3.3 The evolutionary character of modern labour law

Hayek's critique was carried out in isolation from the concrete experience of labour law systems. Even a cursory examination of such systems is enough to indicate that elements of private law are present, indeed widespread, within modern labour law. While this phenomenon is widely acknowledged, private lawyers have argued that it in no way compromises the doctrinal unity of private law as a coherent whole nor that of its particular, component parts, such as the law of contract or of restitution. This is because 'contextual subjects' such as labour law are precisely lacking in the kind of conceptual unity which can be observed in private law. As Peter Birks has put it, such subjects

> have no unity of concept or event . . . There is nothing wrong with categories of that kind. They tell you all the law there is about the particular aspect of life which interests you. It is the function and virtue of these contextual categories that they collect together bits and pieces which are kept apart in other ways of dividing up the law.[79]

Similarly, Ernest Weinrib suggests that there is an important contrast between the body of private law, which expresses 'an inwardly organising normative principle', and an area such as labour law which is the result of 'social concern'.[80] This is because contextual bodies of law are 'regulated by various principles (as environmental law and accident law are by private law) and by administrative regulation'.[81] At best, it seems, common law and legislation can co-exist, or operate alongside each other, within the relevant 'contextual area'; but by their nature, they cannot be effectively integrated into a single, coherent body of doctrine.

The view that labour law is characterized by an unresolved tension between the techniques of private law and public law is by no means confined to theorists of the law of obligations. Kahn-Freund himself suggested that the English courts had tended to regard social legislation which protected the individual worker or employee as giving rise to 'extra-contractual impositions', that is to say, obligations which are *superimposed* on the contract of employment, rather than forming part of it.[82] There are many examples of this effect: notoriously, courts held in the 1940s that an employee had no cause of action in breach of contract for the employer's failure to pay the agreed wage without deduction, as required by legislation. The action was statutory in nature, and subject, as a result, to a statutory period of limitation.[83] This result had to be reversed by statute. And it is still the case that legislation sometimes specifically states the instances in which the employer's statutory obligations take effect as terms in the contract of employment. The employer's obligations under the Equal Pay Act 1970 take effect

---

[79] P.B.H. Birks, *Introduction to the Law of Restitution* (Oxford: Clarendon Press, 1985), at pp. 73–74.

[80] E. Weinrib, 'The juridical classification of obligations' in P.B.H. Birks (ed.) *The Classification of Obligations* (Oxford: Clarendon Press, 1997) 37–55, at p. 40.   [81] Ibid.

[82] O. Kahn-Freund, 'A note on contract and status in modern labour law' (1967) 30 *Modern Law Review* 635–644.   [83] *Pratt* v. *Cook* [1940] AC 437.

through an 'equality clause' which operates within the contract of employment to align the terms and conditions of the applicant with his or her comparator.[84] This is perhaps best thought of not so much as some kind of compulsory contract term, as a mechanism for altering contract terms for a particular purpose. Nor is the effect completely analogous to a variation of those contract terms, as a shorter, statutory limitation period applies to any claim for back pay than would apply at common law.[85] By contrast, in the case of the employer's obligation to give minimum statutory notice of termination of employment,[86] no mention is made of any 'term' being imported into the contract of employment. Nevertheless, the relevant statute stipulates that any failure by the employer 'shall be taken into account in assessing his liability for breach of contract'.[87] As in the case of a contract term, the employee may waive the right to actual notice and accept payment of wages in lieu. However, the statute is silent on the effect of the failure of the *employee* to give the minimum notice of termination set by the same provision of the Act. As a result, it is not clear if the common law would recognize a cause of action by the employer in respect of the employee's breach of the Act.[88]

But is it really the case that private law and social legislation, like law and equity after the Judicature Acts, 'run side by side, and do not mingle their waters'?[89] In practice, 'intermingling' has taken place increasingly over time. It is not simply that modern social legislation builds directly on contractual foundations, in the sense that the scope of such legislation is very largely set, as we have seen, by reference to the common law concept of the contract of employment.[90] It is also generally agreed that contractual concepts *permeate* the structure of statutory employment law, since the central statutory concepts (such as 'continuity of employment', or 'dismissal') rely heavily on contractual language, albeit with varying degrees of modification. This is why 'the contract of employment has emerged more resilient, and has proved to be infinitely more relevant than could possibly have been foreseen'[91] when the legislation was first enacted. In particular, the emergence of the reciprocal duty of cooperation as the 'core' of the employment relationship,[92] which we examined earlier, is a powerful illustration of the evolutionary potential of the law. It exemplifies the kind of 'blind legal evolution' which may occur as a result of the interaction of statute and the common law, in an area where statute draws heavily on the common law for its own conceptual

---

[84] Equal Pay Act 1970, s. 1(1).   [85] Deakin and Morris, *Labour Law*, op. cit., at p. 246.

[86] Now contained in the Employment Rights Act 1996, ss. 86–87.

[87] Employment Rights Act 1996, s. 91(5).

[88] The Act does nevertheless state that the employer is relieved from the obligation to make certain payments in respect of the notice period if the employee breaks the contract during that period: Employment Rights Act 1996, s. 91(5).

[89] W. Ashburner, *Principles of Equity* (London: Butterworths, 1933), 2nd ed. by D. Brown, at p. 18.

[90] See Chapter 2, above.

[91] P. Elias, 'The structure of the employment contract' (1982) 35 *Current Legal Problems* 95–116, at p. 95.   [92] See our discussion in Chapter 2, Section 7.

structure. Through a series of 'loops', the philosophy and perspectives of the legislation have fed back into the common law, and *vice versa*. To that extent, it is no longer possible to talk about two separate systems operating side by side, but, to an ever greater extent, of an integrated, single body of law. What occurs, then, is the dynamic *transformation* of the common law through its encounter with social legislation. An important aspect of this transformative process lies in the increasing adoption by the courts of a purposive approach to statutory interpretation, which assists the search for statutory principle.[93]

A further example of this may be found in the law of discrimination. Under the Sex Discrimination Act 1975 and the Race Relations Act 1976, the victim of discrimination may bring a complaint before an employment tribunal, which under the circumstances has the power to award compensation. The statutory cause of action adopts, for this purpose, the conceptual structure of the common law of tort.[94] Among these are the concept of vicarious liability, which in this context has the effect that 'anything done by a person in the course of his employment shall be treated for the purposes of this Act as if done by his employer as well as by him, whether or not it was done with the employer's knowledge or approval'.[95] In *Jones* v. *Tower Boot Ltd*.[96] the Court of Appeal had to consider the meaning of this provision in the context of a case of racial harassment. The complainant, a young man of sixteen, was subjected while at work to racially motivated insults and assaults. His employer took no action, despite representations from the complainant himself and from his mother. This failure to act was also a breach of the employer's own code concerning racial harassment. However, the Employment Appeal Tribunal[97] (overturning the Industrial Tribunal), found that the employer was not vicariously liable for the acts of its employees who had been carrying out the harassment: by analogy with common law cases concerning 'practical jokes' against employees, the insults and assaults suffered by the complainant could not be regarded as acts in any sense done 'in the course of employment' of his fellow employees. The Court of Appeal reversed, on the basis that the relevant provision of the Act should be given a purposive interpretation, one which reflected the educative function of the Act. Parliament's aim of deterring racial and sexual discrimination meant that it would be inappropriate to apply to the Act the meaning attributed to 'course of employment' at common law. It is possible to see here an approach which results in the modification of a private law concept in a particular statutory context. At the same time, it is not inconceivable that a decision such as *Tower Boot* might also have some influence, in time, on the excessively rigid conception of the employer's vicarious liability which operates in

[93] See J. Beatson, 'Public law influences in contract law', in J. Beatson and D. Friedmann (eds.) *Good Faith and Fault in Contract Law* (Oxford: Clarendon Press, 1995) 263–288, at p. 288.
[94] Sex Discrimination Act 1975, ss. 65(1)(b), 66(1); Race Relations Act 1976, ss. 56(1)(b), 57(1); see *Ministry of Defence* v. *Cannock* [1994] IRLR 509.
[95] Sex Discrimination Act 1975, s.41; Race Relations Act 1976, s. 32.   [96] [1997] IRLR 168.
[97] [1995] IRLR 529.

the common law.[98] That will depend on the capacity of the courts to recognize the wider, analogical value of a decision of this kind.

It is precisely this 'transformation' of private law through social legislation which Hayek argued against. His claim that the passage of far-reaching social legislation was contrary to both efficiency and justice was echoed in his theory of private law. The claim that statutory 'interference' in the rules of private law produces conceptual confusion has, as we have seen, been advanced by private law jurists and has perhaps been believed at various times by some judges. Hayek's concept of 'interference' refers to the creation of those 'specific orders which, unlike the rules of just conduct, do not serve merely the formation of a spontaneous order but aim at particular results'.[99] So defined, interference is necessarily 'an isolated act of coercion, undertaken for the purpose of achieving a particular result, and without committing oneself to do the same in all instances where some circumstances defined by a rule are the same'.[100] On the face of it, this description might seem to apply more to the case of a discrete administrative order, than to the composite body of rules and principles which go to make up a 'contextual subject' such as labour law. However, this would be to give Hayek's notion of interference an excessively narrow interpretation. What he was criticizing was the tendency for regulatory legislation to carve out exceptions from the general, abstract rules of private law. In that sense, regulatory interferences are 'isolated'. A 'contextual area' such as labour law upsets the traditional system of conceptual classification in two ways. Firstly, it creates new classificatory schemes based on purpose-orientated norms. Thus the contract of employment is separated out from the general law of contract, with the aim of subjecting it to special rules whose principal purposes include the protection of the employee. Secondly, within the contextual subject, the traditional classifications which operate within private law—the division between property, contract and tort which represents 'Hume's three laws'—no longer apply.

The establishment of a new classificatory scheme, based on the distinctive characteristics of the contract of employment, is, as we have seen in preceding chapters, the central, defining feature of labour law. It was viewed that way by the German jurists who, at the turn of the century, first identified the emergence of labour law as a discipline in its own right, and their perspective influenced British labour law, above all through the contribution of Kahn-Freund. Labour law, overcame, or spanned, the divide between, public law and private law.[101] The separation of the contract of employment from the general law of contracts involved a recognition that the employment relationship was, in some sense, unequal or asymmetrical. This was a recognition of a potential for injustice (and, arguably, for

---

[98] It was this highly rigid conception which led the common law courts to seek a solution in the personal liability of the employer: *Hudson* v. *Ridge Manufacturing Co. Ltd.* [1957] 2 QB 348. For the view, however, that *Tower Boot* has no authority in relation to the common law definition of vicarious liability, see the judgment of Lord Clyde in *Lister* v. *Helsey Hall Ltd.* [2002] 1 AC 215, 234.

[99] *The Mirage of Social Justice*, at p. 128.   [100] Ibid., at p. 129.

[101] B.A. Hepple, 'Introduction', in Hepple (ed.) *The Making of Labour Law in Europe* (London: Mansell, 1986) 1–30.

inefficiency) which private law, with its abstract categorizations, was and is unable to make. Labour law will, as a result, tend to dissolve certain distinctions within private law which are said to represent a conception of corrective justice—in particular, the distinction between misfeasance and nonfeasance which is related to the tort–contract divide. The evolution of the employer's affirmative duty of good faith, the 'core' of the modern employment relationship, very well exemplifies this process.

Thus the substitution of distributive or social justice for corrective justice has important implications for the form of law; the legal order incorporates and reflects the *social* fact of inequality, or asymmetry, between employer and employee. Labour law reorientates the 'cognitive map' of the law:

it is a characteristic of social law to seek to reverse legal reasoning: to think about a situation no longer in terms of the abstract legal categories of civil law, but in terms of its concrete characteristics. This is, in a sense, the extraction of law from the fact. The legal subject gives way to the wage earner, the consumer, the professional; the notion of contract breaks down into a multiplicity of types of contract, each capable, like the labour contract, of being governed by a special regulation.[102]

From a systems theory perspective, the conceptual maturity of labour law is a precondition of its effectiveness as an instrument of social policy. A body of legal doctrine must possess a high degree of internal conceptual ordering, and hence a high degree of autonomy with regard to the external subject-matter of regulation and to the policy-making process, in order to 'process the complexity' of the external environment to which it relates.[103] Mutual influences between system and environment may be indirect and uncertain in their effects. Above all, the relationship between them cannot be thought of as a smooth process of evolutionary adaptation.[104] But contrary to Hayek's rejection of social legislation, the possibility of regulation through 'reflexive law', which would be sensitive to the self-regulating aspects of social orders, remains open. An important step in realizing that possibility is the systematization of legal concepts which are capable not simply of 'translating' social and economic phenomena into the categories of juridical thought but of recognizing, at the same time, the limits of the law itself as a regulatory technique.[105] In that sense, the highly complex and contested jurisprudence of the contemporary law of the individual employment relationship (under both common law and statutory jurisdictions) is a reflection of the modern enterprise, which has been aptly described as 'a mini-society with a vast array of norms centred on exchange and its immediate processes'.[106]

---

[102] F. Ewald, 'Justice, equality, judgement: on "social justice"', in G. Teubner (ed.) *Juridification of Social Spheres* (Berlin: de Gruyter, 1987) 91–110, at p. 109.

[103] On the role of legal autonomy as a precondition of law's capacity to process the complexity of its external environment, see N. Luhmann, *Social Systems* (Stanford, CA: Stanford University Press, 1995), at p. 37.   [104] See Chapter 1, Section 4, above.

[105] See generally, G. Teubner, *Law as an Autopoietic System* (Oxford: Blackwell, 1993); R. Rogowski and T. Wilthagen (eds.) *Reflexive Labour Law* (Deventer: Kluwer, 1994).

[106] I. Macneil, 'The many futures of contracts' (1974) *Southern California Law Review* 691–816, at p. 801.

The evolutionary quality of modern labour law suggests that it has the capacity to express a series of complex regulatory mechanisms and functions. In the next section we will look more closely at ways in which labour law is perhaps already in the process of reorienting its conceptual language and processes towards the goal of coordinating labour market relations.

4. Labour Law in Transition

4.1 The historical legacy of the employment model

The recent trend towards deregulation within labour law raises two sets of questions which bear upon the idea of a 'return to contract' via the liberalization of the labour market. The first is a set of questions about the origins of the employment contract: at what point did the legal concept of the contract of employment emerge, and how was its evolution subsequently linked to changes in economic organization and social structure which have taken place since the industrial revolution? The second is a set of questions which are concerned with the specification of the relationship between the common law of contract on the one hand and social legislation on the other. Are contract and regulation mutually incompatible forms of governance and incompatible forms of regulation as neoliberal arguments for deregulation suggest? From the analysis of the preceding chapters we can see that the answers to these two questions are related. An historical perspective demonstrates both the modernity of the contract of employment, and the way it has been shaped by changes in the form of the business enterprise, collective bargaining and the welfare state.

Neither the judges nor the drafters of legislation had a consistent conception of the contract of employment in the nineteenth century. Although formal freedom of contract in the hiring of labour was established in the early nineteenth century, the contents of the employment relationship were not rationalized in terms of bipolar contractual relations, but in terms of the subordinate status of the industrial worker or 'servant'. This specialized status was a creation of the legislation of the period in question, the Master and Servant Acts, and not a leftover of pre-modern, household or guild forms of production. This form of status was, in turn, differentiated, so that higher-level workers such as clerks and commercial agents were not covered by the Master and Servant Acts, and for these workers a particular contractual model, based on 'relational' conceptions of reciprocity between employer and employee, began to emerge.

When we compare modern labour law with its nineteenth-century antecedents, it is clear that there was no general movement from status to contract during the period of the industrial revolution, so there has been no straightforward movement from contract back to status of the kind sometimes associated with the rise of the welfare state. There is still an 'overlapping' of contract and status as forms of governance or regulation of the employment relationship, and work relations continue to be categorized and differentiated along lines which determine access to security of work and income. Thus today's boundaries are no longer drawn between white collar and blue collar workers, but between those in the core or 'standard employment relationship' on the one hand and those, on the other, who are employed in forms variously described as 'marginal', 'flexible' or 'non-standard'.

The movement of labour law between the two points just described has been neither smooth nor continuous. Rather, it has been shaped by the uneven development of the law alongside wider changes in society. Three distinct periods can be identified: from the industrial revolution up to the legislative settlement of the 1870s and the associated lifting of restrictions on trade union organization and activity; the period of the gestation of the modern welfare state, from the 1870s to the 1940s; and the period of the mature welfare state from the 1940s to the present day, a period increasingly marked, from the 1980s onwards, by policies of deregulation.

Thus in the early nineteenth century the legal pre-conditions of a system of 'free labour' consisted, on the one hand, of the dismantling of the 'corporative' system of apprenticeship and trade regulation, and the repeal of the old poor law, which together removed access to sources of subsistence which had previously supported the emerging institution of wage labour. The 'free market' order was complemented, in its turn, by the master–servant model with its emphasis on 'exclusive service' as the principal criterion of classification.

The reforming legislation of the 1870s, which, through the 'immunities' system granted legitimacy to trade unions, was then followed by social legislation providing protection against work-related risks, including personal injury and the risk of loss of income through unemployment and old age. The concept of 'workman' replaced that of servant, but the 'relational' model of employment still did not apply uniformly to all wage-dependent workers; what succeeded the 'service' model was, to begin with, employment at will, a form which reflected the claim for autonomy from both employers and the state which was made by trade unions at the turn of the twentieth century. During this period, the limited liability company replaced the partnership and the family-based firm as the typical employer, but even as mass production techniques became more widely used, the vertically-integrated form of the enterprise was slow to develop. The question of the ultimate employer's responsibility for contract workers who were hired by intermediaries remained unclear in both law and practice. The courts, in adopting the 'control' test as a new paradigm of subordinated labour, excluded casual workers from protection and separated industrial and managerial ranks. The judges' attitude was one of hostility to the goals of social legislation, which reflected their continuing opposition, for much of this period, to the values of collective self-organization by workers.

The new tests of 'employee' status which developed after 1945, were a function, in part, of greater vertical integration, which itself was a product, to a large degree, of government-inspired corporate consolidation and of nationalization. In addition, social legislation, in particular social insurance legislation, formalized the distinction between employment and self-employment, and regularized the contract of employment as a relation between the company limited by share capital, or its public sector counterpart, and the individual employee. The post-war welfare state provided the framework within which all wage-dependent workers could be afforded protection, and the 'control' test gave way to the new criteria of 'integration' and 'economic reality'.

The post-war welfare state was, nevertheless, built on selectivity, just as its predecessors had been. The growth of so-called flexible or marginal forms of employment since the 1980s has thrown this into sharp relief. The emergence of these types of work can be seen as a development 'outside' the law to which the law must now 'respond'. Yet, in another sense, the law created a paradigm form— the so-called 'standard' employment relationship—to which the marginal forms of employment came to be compared.[107] The 'standard' employment relationship is just as much an institutional creation of the legal system as its predecessors were; like them, it is a normative form, that is to say, one which reflects certain values, and not simply a technical 'description' of an external social reality. The form of the 'standard' model presupposes a particular structure of the enterprise, one in which stable employment is the principal source of income security, and a certain structure of the family, one in which continuity of waged income is reserved for a typically male 'breadwinner' on whom other family members are dependent. Deregulation is now eroding away the foundations of this particular model of employment, but without as yet offering any replacement for it, other than the generalized form of insecurity which would flow from the complete 'abolition' of labour law. But 'abolition' is unlikely if only because labour law continues to be deeply implicated in the project of regulating, and in a still more fundamental sense constituting, the labour market order.

Given that labour law has reached this hiatus, or possibly interregnum,[108] what are the future prospects for the employment model? We will consider a number of recent developments in law and practice, beginning with statutory and judicial attempts to redefine the employment relationship, then moving on to the role of the law in shaping labour supply decisions, and further including an assessment of recent changes in the law regulating workplace relations and the governance of the enterprise. We conclude with a look at the new laws making up the statutory floor of rights in respect of the minimum wage and maximum working week.

[107] See U. Mückenburger and S. Deakin, 'From deregulation to a European floor of rights: labour law, flexibilisation and the European single market' (1989) 3 *Zeitschrift für ausländisches und internationales Arbeits- und Sozialrecht* 153–207, in particular at pp. 157–162 and 191–2. The 'standard' model, as described here, is an ideal type which is narrower than the juridical notion of the 'contract of employment' in British labour law, since there are certain categories of employee who will not qualify for employment protection rights of any significance because they lack continuity of employment. See further our discussion in Section 4.2, below.

[108] See B. Hepple, 'The Future of Labour Law' (1995) 24 *Industrial Law Journal* 303–322.

4.2 Redefining the scope of employment law

A starting point is provided by current debates on the definition of the contract of employment. The development of a relational model of the employment contract under the influence of collective bargaining and protective legislation created its own reaction: the greater the emphasis placed by the courts upon reciprocity between employer and employee, the more problematic it became to apply the employment model to casual or irregular forms of work. The result was the 'mutuality of obligation' test for determining employee status: according to this test, in order for the court to find a contract of employment, it is necessary not just to show that there has been an exchange of work for wages, but that, in addition, there has been an exchange of mutual undertakings to be available for work over a period of time, on the employee's part, and to make work available, on the employer's.[109]

The background to the rise of the mutuality test is the now near-universal adoption of the contract of employment as the gateway to statutory rights. In the context of employment protection legislation, an employee means 'an individual who has entered into or works under (or, where the employment has ceased, worked under) a contract of employment',[110] and a contract of employment means 'a contract of service or apprenticeship, whether express or implied, and (if it is express) whether oral or in writing'.[111] The substantive meaning of the contract of employment is not made clear by statute; it has been left up to the courts to decide this question, applying common law tests. The result of the process of historical evolution outlined earlier in this chapter is that four tests are now in use: 'control', 'integration', 'business reality', and 'mutuality of obligation'. As we have seen,[112] each of these tests reflects the institutional pressures which were brought to bear on the process of classification of employment relationships at particular points in the historical development of labour law.

It is arguable that the mutuality of obligation test only has a tenuous connection to mainstream contract law. Although the test has antecedents in nineteenth-century decisions on mutuality and the definition, for master and servant purposes, of 'exclusive service',[113] its modern use appears to date from the period in the 1970s[114] when the courts first undertook the task of interpreting and applying the newly created body of statutory employment protection rights. In so far as the new legislation provided employees with legal expectations of continuing income and employment in the event of interruptions to work on the grounds of lay-off, illness and maternity, as well as compensation for redundancy for unfair dismissal, it assumed a normal pattern of continuous and regular employment. The rise of the mutuality test reflects the difficulty which the courts have had in applying these

---

[109] See generally M.R. Freedland, *The Personal Employment Contract* (Oxford: Clarendon Press, 2003) ch. 1, section 2; Deakin and Morris, *Labour Law*, op. cit., at pp. 161–165.
[110] Employment Rights Act 1996, s. 230(1).   [111] Ibid., s. 230(3).
[112] See Chapter 2, above.   [113] See Chapter 2, Section 4.1.
[114] See, in particular, the discussion in *Airfix Footwear Ltd.* v. *Cope* [1978] ICR 1210.

Table 5.1. The genealogy of tests for identifying the contract of employment

Test	Period of pre-eminence	Initial statutory context	Function
Control	1890s to 1920s	Early workmen's compensation and social insurance legislation	Enabling the courts to draw a distinction between manual and non-manual or managerial labour in the application of social legislation
Integration	1930s to 1940s	Advanced workmen's compensation and social insurance legislation	Providing an explanation for the inclusion in the 'employee' category of middle-class and managerial employees
Economic reality	1940s to 1970s	Advanced social insurance and income taxation legislation	Applying a purposive test to the binary divide between employees and the self-employed
Mutuality of obligation	1980s to 2000s	Employment protection legislation	Reflecting judicial scepticism concerning the application of employee status to casual, agency and freelance workers

rights to the growing number of employment relationships which were, by their nature, discontinuous and irregular, in particular those involving outworking, task contracts, and frequent re-hirings. Like control, integration and economic reality before it, it emerged in a particular statutory and social context of employment law (see Table 5.1).

Within this context, the principal significance of the mutuality test has been to revive old notions of subordination and control in a new form. The essence of the test is that unless the worker agrees to be available for work on a continuing basis, and in this extended sense *at the disposal of the employer*, the agreement is said to lack the necessary mutuality of obligation. What counts here is not reciprocity in exchange as such, but a particular form of mutuality under which the worker must cede autonomy to the employer over the timing and physical location of the work in order to count as an employee. Thus in the employment sphere, 'mutuality of obligation' does not bear its normal meaning in contract law. A contract to work in return for pay will not lack 'mutuality' in the sense of the reciprocal promises needed for consideration as one of the elements in the formation of a contract. However, if the judgments of the Court of Appeal in *O'Kelly* v. *Trusthouse Forte plc*[115] are to be believed, such an arrangement, without more, will not be a contract *of employment*.

[115] [1983] IRLR 369; although for a different view of the nature of the mutuality test, arguing that it is indeed simply an application of general contract law, see *Stephenson* v. *Delphi Systems Ltd.* [2003] ICR 471 at para. 11, Elias J.

The emphasis within the mutuality test upon the form of the contract has further consequences. In particular, it has opened up the possibility that employers can avoid employee status through the use of contractual 'boilerplate'. In principle the courts will disregard a 'label' attached to the relationship by the parties. However, they will also look to the underlying agreement when determining the nature of that relationship. Contractual waivers and exclusions aimed at denying employee status or, in situations where this status is not in doubt, placing obstacles in the way of employees achieving the necessary continuity of employment to qualify for protective rights, are now in common use. However, they can only work if the courts take a particular approach towards the interpretation of employment agreements. This is that contracts made between workers and employers are agreements made by the individual parties at arms' length, and which therefore fall to be interpreted according to normal canons of contractual construction. A clause which purports to grant the worker the right to appoint a substitute to take their place if they are unable to work (a 'substitution clause'), if read literally, would amount to a denial not just of employee status (since mutuality of obligation would be lacking) but, going further, of the essential element of a personal commitment to provide labour which is also present in the contract for services. Another technique is to assert that the employer is under no obligation to provide work, nor does the employee have to accept it (a 'no mutuality clause'). If, in practice, there is evidence that work is carried out continuously, and that the worker does not regard him- or herself as having discretion to take time off or to appoint a substitute whenever they feel like it, it should be open to a court to treat the clause as nothing more than the boilerplate which it so clearly is.

However, in a number of decisions, courts have taken these clauses at face value. A 'substitution clause' was given effect in *Express and Echo Publications Ltd. v. Tanton*[116] and a 'no mutuality clause' received similar treatment in *Stevedoring & Haulage Services Ltd. v. Fuller*.[117] There, the employment tribunal had taken the view that it could look to the practice of employment in order to establish what the parties must have intended the terms of the contract to be. On that basis, it implied an agreement between the two parties which would have satisfied the mutuality test. This approach, while admittedly heterodox from the viewpoint of general contractual construction, has highly respectable antecedents in employment law.[118] However, the tribunal's decision was reversed, the Employment Appeal Tribunal ruling that it was not possible to have regard to the practice or conduct of the employment relationship where the wording of the express contract was clear. Behind the mutuality test, then, is the assumption that an express

[116] [1999] IRLR 367; cf. *McFarlane* v. *Glasgow City Council* [2001] IRLR 7, *Byrne Bros.* v. *Baird* [2002] IRLR 96 and *Staffordshire Sentinel Newspapers* v. *Potter* [2004] IRLR 752; *Redrow Homes (Yorkshire Ltd.)* v. *Wright* [2004] IRLR 720.

[117] [2001] IRLR 267; *Dacas* v. *Brook Street Bureau* [2004] IRLR 358.

[118] See in particular the judgments of Browne-Wilkinson J. in *Jones* v. *Associated Tunnelling Ltd.* [1981] IRLR 477 and Lord Hoffmann in *Carmichael* v. *National Power plc* [2000] IRLR 43.

agreement, even one which is plainly based on a standard form proffered by the employer, represents a *consensus ad idem* between the two parties.[119]

A further assumption behind the mutuality test, which is related to the idea of bargaining over employment status, is that the decision to opt for employee status as opposed to self-employment involves a trade-off between risk and security. Thus in entering into a contract of employment, the employee trades off 'subordination' or acceptance of the employer's right to give instructions and to organize the carrying out of the work, in return for certain protections: at a basic level, a regular wage which a self-employed person would not expect to receive; at a more extended level, the full set of income and job security rights which go with continuous service under the current provisions of employment protection legislation. By contrast, an independent or autonomous worker employed under a contract for services cannot look to the employer for security of income or employment, but is able to take advantage of a more favourable tax and social security regime (in the sense that income tax is paid net of work-related expenses and National Insurance contributions are paid at a lower rate), as well as the autonomy of being able to decide when, where and how to work. The Employment Appeal Tribunal expressed the idea in the following way in *Byrne Bros.* v. *Baird* when attempting to determine the scope of the Working Time Regulations 1998, which impose maximum limits on weekly working hours:

The reason why employees are thought to need such protection is that they are in a subordinate and dependent position vis-à-vis their employers: the purpose of the Regulations is to extend protection to workers who are, substantively and economically, in the same position. Thus the essence of the intended distinction must be between, on the one hand, workers whose degree of dependence is essentially the same as that of employees and, on the other, contractors who have a sufficiently arm's-length and independent position to be treated as being able to look after themselves in the relevant respects.[120]

The practical effect of the rise of the mutuality test is substantial. Where the existence of mutual obligations to provide work (in the case of the employer) and to accept any work which is offered (in the case of the worker) is in doubt, the relationship may be classified as one of self-employment, or otherwise outside the scope of the 'employee' concept. These exclusionary aspects of the mutuality test adversely affect homeworkers,[121] agency workers,[122] 'zero-hours' contract workers[123] and workers in casualized trades or occupations.[124]

[119] Our argument here draws on and updates S. Deakin, 'Interpreting employment contracts: judges, employers and workers' in S. Worthington (ed.) *Commercial Law and Commercial Practice* (Oxford: Hart, 2003) 433–55 in which there is a more extended discussion of the possibility of the courts subjecting standard form employment agreements to the kind of review which applies to certain consumer and commercial contracts. [120] [2002] IRLR 96.
[121] *Airfix Footwear Ltd* v. *Cope* [1978] ICR 1210; *Nethermere (St Neots) Ltd* v. *Taverna and Gardiner* [1984] IRLR 240.
[122] *Wickens* v. *Champion Employment Agency* [1984] ICR 365; *Ironmonger* v. *Movefield Ltd* [1988] IRLR 461; *Pertemps Group plc* v. *Nixon*, 1 July 1993, unreported, EAT/496/91; *Dacas* v. *Brook Street Bureau* [2004] IRLR 358. [123] *Clark* v. *Oxfordshire Health Authority* [1998] IRLR 125.
[124] *O'Kelly* v. *Trusthouse Forte plc* [1983] IRLR 369; *Carmichael* v. *National Power plc* [1998] IRLR 301, [2000] IRLR 43.

The mutuality test also has negative implications for workers who fall into the employee category. This is because the statutory rules of continuity of employment operate so as to require an individual to establish not simply that they were employed under a contract of employment at some point, but that the contract remained in force for a sufficient period of time for them to acquire the necessary statutory length of service.[125] Although the continuity rules became more straightforward following the abolition of the eight-hour and sixteen-hour thresholds in the mid-1990s,[126] establishing that a contract of employment existed during periods in-between separate jobs remains problematic. Statute itself only allows for a few exceptional periods of non-employment to be counted towards continuity.[127]

For 'zero hours contract' workers and others whose working patterns are irregular or interrupted, this is a particular problem. For example, in *Carmichael* v. *National Power plc*,[128] the issue was whether the applicants, who worked periodically as tour guides at a power station, had contracts of employment not while they were at work, but *between* ad hoc hirings; the House of Lords, restoring the ruling of the employment tribunal, ruled that they did not. This meant that they could not claim the right to receive a written statement of particulars of employment from their employer, for which one month of continuous employment was required.

As the mutuality test has grown in importance, so the numbers employed in the casualized forms of work affected by this potential exclusion have increased, thereby giving rise to concerns that the concept of the contract of employment is no longer able to deal effectively with the task of defining the scope of protective legislation. However, the increase in numbers excluded from employment protection does not take the form of an increase in self-employment as such. The Labour Force Survey (LFS), which records numbers in different types of work, records that while self-employment rose in the 1980s from 9 per cent to 13 per cent of the employed population, it has since fallen back to around 11 per cent. Employee status is still, it seems, the norm for the vast majority of the working population of the United Kingdom.

The LFS nevertheless gives, in this respect, a potentially misleading picture of the interaction of the rules defining employment status with the practice of casual work. The LFS data are based on self-reporting of employment status by individual respondents. The 1999 Cambridge-DTI survey used a different methodology which aimed to present a more objective estimate of the numbers in different categories of employment. It was also designed to capture the degree of uncertainty in the application of the tests of employment status. Respondents were regarded as 'clearly employees' if they defined themselves as such; were paid a salary or wage;

---

[125] For the source of the rules governing continuity of employment, see ERA 1996, Part XIV, Ch. 1; and for discussion of the relationship between contract and continuity, Deakin and Morris, *Labour Law*, op. cit., at pp. 203–208.　　　　[126] Ibid., at pp. 193–198.
[127] See Deakin and Morris, ibid.　　　[128] [2000] IRLR 46.

held what they regarded as a permanent job; *and* had no non-standard working patterns (such as fixed-term, casual or part-time work). Conversely, they were 'clearly self-employed' if they were either a director or partner in their own business, *and/or* employed others. On this basis, 64 per cent of all respondents were classified as clearly employees, and 5 per cent were clearly self-employed. This compares to the 86 per cent of the sample who saw themselves as employees, and 13 per cent who saw themselves as self-employed (a result which corresponds to that of the LFS for the same period). Thus a large proportion of the national labour force, 30 per cent on this estimate, was employed under terms and conditions which created some degree of uncertainty over their employment status.[129]

In addition, the survey reported a much higher degree of fixed-term employment than the LFS had indicated: where the equivalent LFS (for 1997–98) gave a figure of around 3 per cent of the workforce for this form of work, the Cambridge-DTI survey reported a figure closer to 19 per cent. The discrepancy arises from the large numbers of those who regarded themselves as having a permanent job, but who, on further questioning, said that they were employed under a fixed-term contract. In the LFS survey, this additional question was not put, and all those who reported themselves as working permanently were recorded as employed for an indeterminate duration.[130]

The problem arises, therefore, not from an increase in self-employment at the expense of employment, but from a blurring of the 'binary divide' itself. This can be seen from the qualitative wave of the Cambridge-DTI study. This wave of data collection involved re-visiting a small proportion of that part of the original sample whose employment status was uncertain or ambiguous in order to gather more in-depth information in less structured discussions, and to analyse their written contracts of employment or terms and conditions of employment. The case studies suggest that, in practice, perceptions of control and accountability are more complex than the binary divide implies. Self-employed respondents commented that they came under pressure to accept work from particular clients and had to operate to very tight deadlines. Similarly, respondents employed on zero-hours or on-call contracts saw themselves as being required to respond to the employer's demands, even if their contracts suggested that they had the right to turn down work offered to them. Nor was there a clear perception that respondents, by choosing one form of employment status as against another, could trade off security against autonomy. Self-employment could result in a considerable restriction of personal autonomy in practice and to long and intense working hours, thanks to the need to meet tight deadlines and maintain reputation with

---

[129] The findings of the survey are reported in B. Burchell, S. Deakin and S. Honey, *The Employment Status of Individuals in Non-standard Employment* EMAR Research Series no. 6 (London: Department of Trade and Industry, 1999), which explains in greater detail the objectives of the study (carried out jointly by researchers at the University of Cambridge, including the present authors, and at the Department of Trade and Industry), the methodology used, and the significance of the findings.

[130] See further Burchell, Deakin and Honey, *Employment Status*, op. cit., ch. 3, where this issue is discussed.

clients. Employees in non-standard employment, conversely, commented on growing insecurity and stress caused by uncertainty over job prospects.

Dissatisfaction with the mutuality test has been one of the moving forces behind the recent attempt to extend the scope of employment legislation through the use of the concept of the *worker*. Under the Employment Rights Act 1996, section 230(3), a worker is defined as 'an individual who has entered into or works under (or, where the employment has ceased, worked under)—(a) a contract of employment, or (b) any other contract, whether express or implied and (if express) whether oral or in writing, whereby the individual undertakes to do or perform personally any work or services for another party to the contract whose status is not by virtue of the contract that of a client or customer of any profession or business carried on by the individual'.[131] Similar definitions have been used in the context of recent legislation on the national minimum wage[132] and the organization of working time.[133]

In *Byrne Bros.* v. *Baird*,[134] an early leading case on the 'worker' definition, the Employment Appeal Tribunal took a policy-orientated view of the statutory concept, holding that it was intended 'to create an intermediate class of protected worker, who is on the one hand not an employee but on the other hand cannot in some narrower sense be regarded as carrying on a business'. At the same time, the Court recognized that the 'wording of limb (b) [that is, the extended 'worker' definition] gives no real help on what are the criteria for carrying on a business undertaking in the sense intended by the Regulations—given that they cannot be the same as the criteria for distinguishing employment from self-employment'. The EAT then went on to say this about the distinction between a worker and an independent contractor falling outside the scope of protection altogether:

Drawing that distinction in any particular case will involve all or most of the same considerations as arise in drawing the distinction between a contract of service and a contract for services—but with the boundary pushed further in the putative worker's favour. It may, for example, be relevant to assess the degree of control exercised by the putative employer, the exclusivity of the engagement and its typical duration, the method of payment, what equipment the putative worker supplies, the level of risk undertaken etc. The basic effect of limb (b) is, so to speak, to lower the pass-mark, so that cases which failed to reach the mark necessary to qualify for protection as employees might nevertheless do so as workers.

This is a frank acknowledgement that the test for determining 'worker' status may well not be fundamentally different from that which is applied to the 'employee'—if there is a difference it is one of degree, not kind. The outcome in this case, in which the court found that the applicants were 'workers' and rejected

[131] See also TULRCA 1992, s. 296(1).   [132] National Minimum Wage Act 1998, s. 54.
[133] Working Time Regulations 1998, reg. 2.
[134] [2002] IRLR 96. Cases decided since *Byrne Bros.* suggest that the policy-orientated approach taken by the Court of Appeal in that case will not necessarily be followed on all occasions, and that the restrictive 'mutuality' test is likely to reappear in the context of the 'worker' definition: see the decision of the Court of Appeal in *Mingeley* v. *Pennock* [2004] IRLR 373.

an argument that a 'substitution clause' in their contracts prevented this outcome, suggests that the introduction of the 'worker' concept may just tip the balance in certain cases. But if the dictum just quoted is any guide, it is highly likely that the same assumptions concerning the trade-off between security and autonomy which underlie the court's approach to the 'employee' issue will continue to be relevant in the changed statutory context of the 'worker' test.

The Cambridge-DTI study attempted to arrive at an estimate of how many individuals could be classified as 'workers' under the extended definition of that concept. For this purpose, the analysis focused on the group of individuals which would remain outside the 'worker' definition, that is to say, the 'independent self-employed'. These were identified as those respondents who had worked for more than one employer in the six months prior to the questionnaire, and who 'passed' the tests of 'economic reality' for autonomous work: in other words, they were able to sub-contract, they were not paid a wage or salary, they paid their own income tax and national insurance contributions, and they were not entitled to receive either sick pay or paid holidays. This group constituted 8 per cent of the total sample, leaving a figure of 92 per cent of the labour force as 'workers'. But of this 92 per cent, many would be affected by uncertainty as to their status, because they, in turn, would only 'fail' perhaps one or two of the economic reality tests. When this factor was taken into account, the proportion of the total labour force which could be classified as *clearly* in the 'worker' category fell to only 80 per cent.[135]

It would therefore seem that whichever concept is used, 'employee' or 'worker', the nature of modern employment relations is such that there will inevitably be a large group of individuals whose employment status is in an unclear 'grey zone' between employment and self-employment. The 'worker' concept, in so far as it can be assumed to map reasonably closely on to the test of 'economic reality', reduces the size of the 'grey zone', but does not eliminate it.

4.3 The challenge of the vertical disintegration of the enterprise and the response of employment law

The contemporary 'crisis' affecting the concept of the contract of employment is only partially addressed by measures aimed at extending the definition of employment status. As Hugh Collins has suggested,[136] a distinct set of issues arises from the 'vertical disintegration' of the enterprise. This is the result, in part, of policies of privatization, which have reversed the post-1945 policy of state support for public enterprise. In addition, the century-long trend towards concentration of ownership in the private sector has gone into reverse. There are many, overlapping causes

---

135 For the precise basis of this calculation, and an explanation and justification of the methodology used to arrive at it, see Burchell, Deakin and Honey, *Employment Status*, op. cit., at pp. 43–46.

136 H. Collins, 'Independent contractors and the challenge of vertical disintegration to employment protection laws' (1990) 10 *Oxford Journal of Legal Studies* 353–80.

of this development, which include growing pressure from capital markets for regular restructurings to release value for shareholders, to the impact of product market deregulation in terms of breaking up quasi-monopolistic forms of organization and encouraging new entrants. Government policy has also sought in various ways to encourage the growth of small- and medium-sized enterprises. The net effect is that employment growth is no longer viewed, in itself, as a sign of strength or success for the firm, but rather as a source of fixed costs, which should as far as possible be minimized. From this perspective, flexibility of costs, from the firm's point of view, can be achieved not simply by demanding greater leeway in the application of job definitions for core staff ('functional' flexibility), but also by outsourcing to external suppliers, thereby enhancing both 'numerical' flexibility (variability in labour inputs) and 'financial flexibility' (variability of pay).[137]

Vertical disintegration poses new issues for labour law in two particular senses. First, the fragmentation of previously integrated production processes among a number of enterprises may reduce the scope for employers in a given sector to offer direct employment. This is the case in industries such as film and television production, for example. The growth, with regulatory encouragement, of an independent television production sector has meant that technicians who once worked for a single employer now have a series of clients to whom they offer their services. Even if the relationships thereby established are regular and stable, it is unlikely that any single one of them could give rise to an employer–employee relationship; the status of the supplier thereby becomes that of a self-employed or 'freelance' worker.[138] Extending the 'worker' definition to these individuals is not necessarily feasible, since it is far from clear that they would pass a test of economic dependence in relation to any one of their clients. This extreme form of disintegration is, however, relatively rare. It is much more commonly the case that, as a result of outsourcing, the identity of the employer changes, without affecting the employment status of the worker, who remains an employee. However, this second type of vertical disintegration, in addition to being far more common than the first, poses, if anything, a more significant structural problem for the application of employment standards. This arises from the splitting, between one or more entities, of the 'risk' and 'coordination' functions which were previously united in the person of the 'employer'.

Thus in the case of the subcontracting or outsourcing of production from one employer to another, although the subcontractor now assumes the task of

---

[137] Since the mid-1980s there has been a very large literature on the model of the 'flexible firm', its links to changes in regulation and market structure, and its implications for industrial relations and labour law. Among the most important of the original contributions are J. Atkinson, *Flexibility, Uncertainty and Manpower Management* IMS Report no. 89 (Brighton: Institute of Manpower Studies, 1985) and J. Atkinson and N. Meager, *Changing Working Patterns and Practices* (London and Brighton: National Economic Development Office/Institute for Manpower Studies).

[138] See *Hall* v. *Lorimer* [1994] IRLR 171. The legislation which has prompted the growth in the independent television sector dates back to the Broadcasting Act 1990 and is now contained in the Communications Act 2003.

coordination from the end user, it is often the user which sets the parameters within which the work is to be carried out, and which also retains the resources necessary to ensure an effective protection of the worker against the social and economic risks of employment. Here, the search for a solution has turned on the interpretation of the Acquired Rights Directive and the Transfer of Undertakings (Protection of Employment) Regulations (TUPE), which provide for the compulsory novation of contracts of employment when a 'relevant transfer' takes place in the delegation of responsibilities from user to subcontractor. The decision of the House of Lords in *Litster*[139] is a strong affirmation of this idea: the transferee, when it assumes the managerial function which goes with the ownership of the business as a going concern, cannot at the same time displace the economic risks of the resulting reorganization on to the workforce by leaving them with limited claims against an insolvent transferor. The limits of TUPE are set by a further juridical attempt to define the boundaries of managerial coordination. The concept, now contained in the revised version of the Acquired Rights Directive, of 'an economic entity which retains its identity' following the transfer in effect requires the court to identify the *smallest* unit within which it is compatible with the exercise of managerial control; in that sense, it seeks to reinstate the unity of risk and coordination.

The same set of issues arises in an even clearer form in the case of agency work and the supply of labour through intermediaries: the 'coordination' function vests in the end user of labour, while the residual 'risk' function is left either with the agency or with the individual worker. The worker's rights against the agency are likely to be insubstantial in practice, thanks to the presumption that agency workers lack the necessary mutuality of obligation to establish a contract of employment.[140] Although there are decisions in which the courts have held that a contract of employment between the worker and the user may be implied in an appropriate case,[141] for a court to do this *solely* by reference to the exercise of managerial control by the user would involve a fundamental rejection of the contractual basis of the employment relationship. In other contexts, the courts have been shown to be unlikely to upset, after the event, the contractual allocation of risks which they understand the parties to have made. On this basis, they have upheld formal distinctions between 'sponsor' and 'user' organizations for disabled workers,[142] and upheld the use by employers of separate employing entities within a single corporate group, in circumstances where the statutory notion of 'associated employers' has no application.[143] However, there are situations in

---

[139] *Litster* v. *Forth Dry Dock & Engineering Co. Ltd.* [1989] IRLR 161.

[140] See e.g. *Wickens* v. *Champion Employment Agency* [1984] ICR 365, although cf. *McMeechan* v. *Secretary of State for Employment* [1997] IRLR 353.

[141] See, in particular, the judgment of Mummery LJ in *Dacas* v. *Brook Street Bureau* [2004] IRLR 358, using an agency-based analysis.

[142] *Secretary of State for Education and Employment* v. *Bearman* [1998] IRLR 431.

[143] *Hardie* v. *C.D. Northern* [2000] ICR 207. On 'associated employers' and related techniques for ascribing responsibility to groups or networks of employers, see H. Collins, 'Ascription of legal responsibility to groups in complex patterns of economic integration' (1990) 53 *Modern Law Review* 731–744;

which the courts have taken advantage of particular statutory provisions to allow employment law claims to be brought against the final user or beneficiary of labour services, even in the absence of a contractual nexus.

Legislation deems the worker to be an employee of the agency for tax and social security purposes,[144] but this is a device aimed above all at protecting the integrity of the tax base, rather than ensuring that agency workers have access to social security rights. More helpfully, agency workers have been brought under the scope of minimum wage and working time legislation by imposing the relevant obligation on either the agency or the user, depending, firstly, on which of the two of them is contracted to pay them and, failing that, on which one actually does pay them.[145] In addition, both the user and the agency may be required to treat agency workers equally with respect to sex, race and disability discrimination.[146]

In *Abbey Life Assurance Co. Ltd.* v. *Tansell*[147] the court took advantage of the ban on discrimination against contract labour contained in the Disability Discrimination Act to extend an obligation of equal treatment to the ultimate user. In this case the complainant's personal service company contracted with an employment agency to supply his services to the end user, Abbey Life, which later terminated its use of his services, on grounds alleged to be discriminatory. The EAT and the Court of Appeal held that the user, and not the agency, owed the complainant obligations of non-discrimination under section 12 of the Disability Discrimination Act. This provision, which mirrors similar provisions in the Sex Discrimination Act 1975 and the Race Relations Act 1976, imposes the equal treatment obligation on a 'principal' to whom the labour of a 'contract worker' is supplied under the terms of a contract entered into between the principal and another person. The court adopted a purposive interpretation of the Act in order to avoid a result that would 'make it easy to evade the wide coverage which the Act was intended to achieve'; the correct approach was to have regard to 'the general principle which applies in social legislation of this kind, namely that the statute should be construed purposively, and with a bias towards conferring statutory protection rather than excluding it'.[148]

Tansell follows a line of earlier decisions[149] in which versions of the equal treatment principle were applied to the end user of labour. The justification for doing

Deakin and Morris, *Labour Law*, op. cit., at pp. 212–216; P. Davies and M. Freedland, 'Changing perspectives on the employment relationship in British labour law' in C. Barnard, S. Deakin and G. Morris (eds.) *The Future of Labour Law: Liber Amicorum Bob Hepple* (Oxford: Hart, 2004) 129–148.

[144] See Income and Corporation Taxes Act 1988, s. 134; SI 1978/1689.

[145] National Minimum Wage Act 1998, s. 34; Working Time Regulations 1998, reg. 36.

[146] See, in the case of the user or 'principal', Sex Discrimination Act 1976, s. 5, Race Relations Act 1976, s. 7, Disability Discrimination Act 1995, s. 12, and *Abbey Life Assurance Co. Ltd.* v. *Tansell* [2000] IRLR 387; in relation to the agency, see Sex Discrimination Act 1975, s. 15, Race Relations Act 1976, s. 14, and Disability Discrimination Act 1995, s. 68(1).

[147] [2000] IRLR 387; see also the judgment of the EAT sub. nom. *MHC Consulting Ltd.* v. *Tansell* [1999] IRLR 677.   [148] [1999] IRLR 677, 679.

[149] *BP Chemicals Ltd.* v. *Gillick* [1995] IRLR 128; *Harrods Ltd.* v. *Remick* [1997] IRLR 9 (EAT), 583 (CA); *Patefield* v. *Belfast City Council* [2000] IRLR 264; see also *Jones* v. *Friends Provident Life Office* [2004] IRLR 783.

so seems to lie in the priority accorded to the principle of equality of treatment: the legislation rests on the assumption that this principle is so fundamental as to override considerations derived from the contractual allocation of the rights and duties of the parties. However, in the absence of specific statutory support, the courts have more limited scope for manoeuvre. The exceptional nature of the *Tansell* judgment is apparent if it is compared with other decisions testing the scope of the Disability Discrimination Act. The Act contains a significant exclusion, in that it does not apply to any employment in which the employer has fewer than fifteen employees. In *Colt Group Ltd.* v. *Couchman*[150] the complainant was employed by the parent company of a group which had 40 subsidiary companies operating worldwide. The parent company, however, employed only seven persons. The EAT ruled out the claim on these grounds (at that time, the relevant threshold was twenty employees), noting that, as a matter of company law, a corporate group has no legal identity as such: '[t]he legal persons or bodies are the individual companies that make up that group'.[151] *Tansell* is also exceptional from the point of view of other cases concerning agency labour. In *Costain Building & Civil Engineering Ltd.* v. *Smith*[152] the EAT ruled that an agency-supplied worker who was appointed by his trade union to be a safety representative on the site at which he worked had no basis for claiming unfair dismissal under section 100(1) of the Employment Rights Act when his employment was terminated at the behest of the user, since his only contract was with his agency.

The principle of equal treatment has nevertheless created additional possibilities for judicial innovation, in particular in the context of transfers of employment. The House of Lords' decision in *North Yorkshire CC* v. *Ratcliffe*[153] established that workers whose terms and conditions are reduced in order to ensure that their employer succeeds against a lower-paying rival, in order to win a round of competitive tendering, can then seek to restore their pay by bringing an equal pay claim using fellow workers in the same employment as comparators. In *Lawrence* v. *Regent Office Care Ltd.*,[154] the EAT held that in the converse situation, where it is the external competitor which succeeds in the tendering process, the workers, once transferred to the employment of the competitor as a result of TUPE, lose the right to equality with their former colleagues in the transferor: 'there is nothing about this case which would distinguish it from any other case where an applicant claimed equal pay with a comparator employed by another company'.[155] This apparently clear-cut conclusion was then challenged under Article 141 of the EC Treaty: on appeal in *Lawrence*,[156] the Court of Appeal decided that it could not rule out the application of Article 141 to the transfer of employment in that case, and referred the matter on a preliminary reference to the ECJ. This argument was later rejected by the Court,[157] which has also held, in *Allonby* v. *Accrington and*

---

[150] [2000] ICR 327.   [151] [2000] IRLR 327, 331.   [152] [2000] ICR 215.
[153] [1995] ICR 839.   [154] [1999] IRLR 149.   [155] [1999] IRLR 149, 154.
[156] [2000] IRLR 608.
[157] Case C-320/00 *Lawrence* v. *Regent Office Care* [2002] ECR I-7325.

Rossendale DC,[158] that a worker who was dismissed and re-employed through an agency could not compare her pay and conditions with those of her former colleagues still employed by the end user.

Thus the default position taken by the courts, it seems, is one of respect for the pre-existing arrangements made by the parties, whether these relate to supply through intermediaries or the use of corporate group structures. It is only in those few instances where a specific statutory provision extends employment rights across contractual or capital boundaries—as in the case of the statutory provision relied on in *Tansell*—that they will depart from this approach. However, it could be argued that the case law on the definition of the employer is beginning to reveal a solution through which the law can respond to vertical disintegration.

This is a legal conception of the enterprise which is based on three overlapping and complementary criteria for identifying the employer: coordination, risk and equity. An emergent notion of the 'employer' could therefore be said to be one which corresponded to an entity in which these functions were *united*.[159] Thus the criterion of 'coordination', which to some extent mirrors the traditional tests of employee status based on 'control' and 'integration', associates the concept of the employer with the exercise of powers of centralized management. On this basis, the scope of employer liability should be determined by reference to the presence of managerial control. The criterion of 'risk' forms a complementary basis for identifying the enterprise. The underlying idea here, which is close to the 'economic reality' test, is that the enterprise operates as a mechanism for absorbing and spreading certain economic and social risks, including the risks of unemployment, interruption to income, and work-related injury and disease. As we have seen, the mechanisms for spreading risks in this way include the welfare state institutions of income taxation and social insurance. A third way of defining the employer in respect of the scope of the enterprise is by reference to the idea of 'equity'. Equity refers here to the identification of the enterprise with a space within which the principle of equal treatment must be observed. In the same way as the employer assumes the responsibility for pooling and spreading economic risks, the obligation to respect the equality principle is imposed as a counterpart to, and is coterminous with, the power of managerial coordination. This supplies the justification for imposing the equal treatment requirement on the end user in the case of agency labour. In each case, it is the *organizational* unity of the enterprise which makes it legitimate for the court to go beyond an analysis based on the traditional employment model.[160]

---

[158] Case C-256/01, decision of 13 January 2004.

[159] See generally S. Deakin, 'The changing concept of the employer in labour law' (2001) 30 *Industrial Law Journal* 72–84.

[160] A broadly similar argument, making the case for a renewal of the employment model by reference to a third axis based on the social-psychological dependence of the employee on the enterprise, is made by Guy Davidov, 'The three axes of employment relationships. A characterisation of workers in need of protection', SJD Thesis, University of Toronto, 2001.

4.4 Changing patterns of labour supply, household structure, and the redistribution of employment opportunities

Rising levels of female labour market participation, and the diffusion of the principle of equal treatment in employment and social security, have necessitated a radical rethink of the post-war model in which full employment and social insurance were constructed on the foundations of the male 'breadwinner' wage.[161] The background to the decline of the breadwinner model is increasing inequality resulting from the polarization of employment opportunities. As long as near-full employment persisted, into the 1970s, nearly all households had access to waged income. In 1975, only around 6 per cent of households had neither partner in waged employment. By the mid-1990s, the same figure had almost reached 20 per cent, and although it subsequently fell back slightly, in 2002 it was still above 15 per cent. During the period between the mid-1970s and the mid-1980s, the number of individuals without employment remained roughly the same.[162] What has occurred, therefore, is a far-reaching redistribution of employment, with a segment of households losing all contact with the labour market at the same time as the number of two-earner households has been increasing.

This trend is reflected in the declining rates of labour market participation by adult males. Male activity rates began to fall, and female rates to rise, in the 1950s, but these trends have since accelerated, so that by the early 2000s the participation rates for men and women had almost converged. The effect has been to reduce considerably the number of households dependent on a male breadwinner. In 2002, of those households with married or cohabiting couples between the ages of 25 and 49, around one third had two full-time earners and a further third had a full-time male earner and a part-time female earner. Less than 20 per cent had a sole male breadwinner, around 4 per cent had a sole female breadwinner, and around 6 per cent of this age group had neither partner in work.[163] At the same time there was a falling-off in the participation rates for older male workers, reflecting the numbers of workers displaced by redundancy coupled with early retirement (see Table 5.2 and Tables 5.3a–5.3e). One of the consequences of this shift in household structure is greater inequality: well over half of those living in workless households with at least one unemployed member of the family have an income which is less than 60 per cent of the median (see Table 5.4.). Fully one-fifth of all children have incomes below this level (Table 5.5). Poverty and inequality are increasingly concentrated on a particular segment of households without access to a living wage.

[161] See Chapter 3, Section 5, above.

[162] P. Gregg and J. Wadsworth, 'Workless households and the recovery', in R. Dickens, P. Gregg and J. Wadsworth (eds.) *The Labour Market under New Labour: The State of Working Britain* (London: Palgrave, 2003) 32–39, at p. 33.

[163] S. Harkness, 'The household division of labour: changes in families' allocation of paid and unpaid work, 1992–2002', in R. Dickens, P. Gregg and J. Wadsworth (eds.) *The Labour Market under New Labour: The State of Working Britain* (London: Palgrave, 2003) 150–169, at p. 153.

Table 5.2. Individuals occupied in employment as a proportion of the total population, 1841–1991

	Women			Men			Men and women		
	Occupied for pay or profit	Population	Economic activity rate	Occupied for pay or profit	Population	Economic activity rate	Occupied for pay or profit	Population	Economic activity rate
1841	1815	9515	19.1	5093	9020	56.5	6908	18535	37.3
1851	2819	10659	26.4	6554	10156	64.5	9373	20815	45.0
1861	3252	11902	27.3	7271	11226	64.8	10523	23128	45.5
1871	3570	13410	26.6	8182	12662	64.6	11752	26072	45.1
1881	3887	15271	25.5	8844	14439	61.3	12731	29710	42.9
1891	4489	17025	26.4	10010	16003	62.6	14499	33028	43.9
1901	4732	19097	24.8	11548	17903	64.5	16280	37000	44.0
1911	5356	21077	25.4	12930	19755	65.5	18286	40832	44.8
1921	5684	22346	25.4	13670	20423	66.9	19354	42769	45.3
1931	6265	23336	26.8	14790	21459	68.9	21055	44795	47.0
1941									
1951	6961	25404	27.4	15649	23450	66.7	22610	48854	46.3
1961	7782	26498	29.4	16232	24787	65.5	24014	51285	46.8
1971	9186	27781	33.1	15917	26198	60.8	25103	53978	46.5
1981	9878	27875	35.4	15499	26273	59.0	25377	54147	46.9
1991	11437	26198	43.7	15340	27958	54.9	26776	54156	49.4

Sources: Department of Employment and Productivity, *British Labour Statistics, Historical Abstract 1886–1968* (London: HMSO, 1971); Office of Population *Census and Surveys, Report for Great Britain*, various years.

Note: In the Censuses of Population from 1841 onwards respondents were asked whether they were normally occupied for pay or profit. The economic activity rate is the number normally occupied for pay or profit (that is, economically active) in each group as a percentage of the population in that age. For 1841 the response to the occupation for pay of profit question is not regarded as reliable. For the 1961 Census the definition of economically active was made more precise by defining it as either in employment or seeking work in the particular week before the Census (Department of Employment, *British Labour Statistics, 1886–1968* (London: HMSO, 1971)).

Table 5.3. Economic activity rates by age, sex and marital status, 1891–1991

(a) Activity rates: all males and all females

Age	Under 20	20–24	25–44	45–64	65 and over	All ages
1891		77.2	62.3	57.1	37.6	
1901		76.0	61.1	55.6	34.1	
1911		78.7	62.4	56.2	30.9	
1921	55.8	78.3	60.4	56.0	30.9	58.1
1931	77.6	80.7	62.5	54.7	25.3	60.7
1951	81.3	79.7	66.7	59.5	15.9	59.6
1961	72.9	76.8	69.4	66.0	12.7	60.5
1971	58.5	75.1	74.4	71.5	11.3	61.2
1981	60.6	79.3	78.6	70.6	6.5	61.0
1991	58.5	80.1	82.5	67.6	5.1	61.0

(b) Economic activity rates: all males

Age	Under 20	20–24	25–44	45–64	65 and over	All ages
1891		98.1	97.9	93.7	65.4	
1901		97.4	98.1	93.6	61.4	
1911		97.3	98.5	94.1	56.8	
1921	63.2	97.0	97.9	94.9	58.9	87.1
1931	84.7	97.2	98.3	94.3	47.9	90.5
1951	83.8	94.9	98.3	95.2	31.1	87.6
1961	74.6	91.9	98.2	97.6	24.4	86.0
1971	60.9	89.9	97.9	94.5	19.4	81.4
1981	64.6	89.1	97.5	90.2	10.8	77.8
1991	61.7	87.5	95.3	80.7	8.0	73.3

(c) Economic activity rates: all females

Age	Under 20	20–24	25–44	45–64	65 and over	All ages
1891		58.4	29.5	24.6	15.9	
1901		56.7	27.2	21.1	13.4	
1911		61.9	29.3	21.6	11.5	
1921	48.4	62.4	28.4	20.1	10.0	32.3
1931	70.5	65.1	30.9	19.6	8.2	34.2
1951	78.9	65.4	36.1	28.7	6.3	34.7
1961	71.1	62.0	40.8	37.1	5.4	37.4
1971	55.9	60.1	50.6	50.2	6.4	42.7
1981	56.5	69.2	59.5	51.9	3.7	45.5
1991	55.0	72.8	69.9	54.7	3.1	49.9

(d) Economic activity rates: married females

Age	Under 20	20–24	25–44	45–64	65 and over	All ages
1891						
1901						
1911	12.6	12.1	9.9	9.3	4.9	9.6
1921	14.6	12.5	9.1	8.0	4.2	8.7
1931	18.7	18.5	11.7	7.7	2.9	10.0
1951	38.1	36.5	25.1	19.0	2.7	21.7
1961	41.0	41.3	33.6	29.6	3.3	29.7
1971	41.6	45.7	46.4	47.5	6.5	42.2
1981	45.2	54.7	55.8	51.7	4.2	47.2
1991	47.4	62.6	67.9	55.7	4.0	53.1

(e) Economic activity rates: single, widowed and divorced females

Age	Under 20	20–24	25–44	45–64	65 and over	All ages
1891						
1901						
1911		77.6	70.3	44.7	14.4	
1921	48.8	80.5	69.3	44.3	12.7	53.8
1931	72.1	84.0	74.5	43.9	10.9	60.2
1951	80.7	91.0	81.2	50.5	6.6	55.0
1961	73.2	89.4	84.2	57.4	6.5	50.6
1971	57.2	81.2	80.4	58.7	6.3	43.7
1981	57.1	80.9	77.0	52.5	3.4	42.9
1991	55.1	75.8	75.4	51.8	2.5	45.8

Note: For sources and definitions see Table 5.2.

Table 5.4. Individuals living in households with less than 60 per cent of median earnings by economic status of benefit unit: percentages

Economic Status	1996/7	2002/03
Single/couple one or more self-employed	22	18
Single/couple all in FT work	2	3
Couple, one FT, one PT work	2	3
Couple, one FT, one not working	14	12
Single/couple, no FT one or more part-time work	24	24
Workless, head or spouse age 60 and over	24	23
Workless, head or spouse unemployed	62	64
Workless, other inactive	42	42
All individuals	24	22

Source: Department of Work and Pensions, *Households below Average Income, 1994/5–2002/3*, National Statistics, HBAI, Supplementary Tables.

Table 5.5. Individuals falling below 60 per cent of median income

	1979	1996/7	2002/03
All	12	18	17
Children	12	25	21
Working-age adults	7	15	14
Pensioners	28	21	21

Source: Department of Work and Pensions, *Households below Average Income, 1994/5–2002/3*, National Statistics, HBAI, Supplementary Tables.

Table 5.6. Composition of employment: self-employed and full-time and part-time male and female employees, 1971–2001

	Self-employed	Employees in employment						Total in employment
		Males			Females			
	%	Full-time %	Part-time %	All %	Full-time %	Part-time %	All %	
1971	8.8	54.1	2.5	56.6	23.0	11.6	34.6	23737
1981	9.3	49.0	3.0	52.1	22.6	16.0	38.6	23586
1991	13.2	40.5	4.2	44.6	23.6	18.7	42.2	25216
2001	11.7	38.9	6.0	44.9	22.9	20.5	43.3	28384

Source: Office of National Statistics, *Department of Employment Gazette, Labour Market Trends*, various years.

At the same time, most of the increase in female labour market participation since the early 1970s has taken the form of part-time work. Although part-time work by men has also been increasing, married women continue to make up the large majority of part-time workers (see Table 5.6). There has been a narrowing of the gender pay gap and average job tenure rates for women have been lengthening at the same time as those of men have been falling. Equal pay legislation, beginning in the 1970s, contributed significantly to the substantial reduction in wage inequality between men and women, and the longer job tenure of women was the result in part of the passage of maternity protection legislation, mandating a period of maternity leave and providing for the right to return to employment. However, these gains are largely concentrated on full-time working women; in the 1990s, while the gender pay gap was falling in overall terms, it remained constant for part-time work. Notwithstanding the elimination of discrimination against part-time workers in relation to terms and conditions of employment and access to occupational pension schemes, part-time work remains poorly paid in relation to full-time employment. In addition, the division of household tasks between men and women remains unequal. This is so across all households, including those with two full-time earners and even those with sole female breadwinners, but it is particularly marked for households with part-time female earners and for those solely dependent on a male breadwinner.[164]

Thus it has not been possible to move straightforwardly from an insurance system based on the single male earner, to one incorporating a dual-earner system in which men and women acquire effective earnings-replacement rights on the basis of their individual employment records. The household continues to be the site for extensive cross-subsidization of economic activity between family members, on the basis of an uneven division of labour. Few married women have earnings records based on continuous full-time employment across the life cycle. Such households accordingly operate on the basis of a 'one and half times earner' model.[165]

This means that, notwithstanding the removal of the more obvious forms of discrimination against part-time workers both in respect of terms and conditions of employment and the fiscal system, women who work part-time remain significantly dependent on male earnings for security of income. More flexible working patterns for men, of the kind envisaged by laws on parental leave, have, as yet, barely made an impact. The uneven division of household labour is evident from the reasons given by women for seeking out casual and precarious forms of employment which, while providing little or no income security, nevertheless give them the opportunity to strike a better balance between family commitments and working time than they could achieve if they were employed under an open-ended contract of employment.[166] From this point of view, many of the reforms initiated in the course of the 1990s to the regulation of so-called non-standard work are potentially deeply paradoxical. By requiring greater equality of treatment between, for example, part-time work and fixed-term work,[167] on the one hand, and full-time work on the other, against the background of an uneven division of household labour between men and women, they may be making it more acceptable for women to undertake non-standard work which still does not provide access to economic security. In this vein it has been suggested that new

[164] See H. Robinson, 'Gender and labour market performance in the recovery', op. cit.

[165] J. Lewis, 'Reforming social insurance and social protection', presentation to SASE seminar on *The Transformation of Work and the Future of the Employment Relationship*, LSE, 8 July 2000.

[166] See Burchell, Deakin and Honey, *Employment Status*, op. cit., ch. 7.

[167] This process began with the judgment of the House of Lords in *R. v. Secretary of State for Employment, ex parte Equal Opportunities Commission* [1994] IRLR 176 and was continued by the implementation in the UK of the Framework Directives requiring equal treatment for part-time and fixed-term workers, respectively, with full-time workers (Directives 97/81/EC, implemented by SI 2000/1551, and 99/70/EC, implemented by SI 2002/2034). The manner in which the Directives have been implemented has, even so, been the subject of much critical discussion: see A. McColgan, 'Missing the point: the Part-Time Workers (Prevention of Less Favourable Treatment) Regulations 2000 (SI 2000 No. 1551)' (2000) 29 *Industrial Law Journal* 260–267. See generally Deakin and Morris, *Labour Law*, op. cit., at pp. 191–203 for an account of the principles governing equality of treatment between part-time work, fixed-term work and full-time work.

laws supporting the rights of full-time carers to request time off work for family commitments may, since most carers are women, simply 'reinforce the gendered division of household labour'.[168]

The overall effect of these changes is that 'the erosion of the [male breadwinner family wage] has been only partial and has been accompanied by a number of interrelated problems, including increasing polarization between households, greater poverty, an uneven distribution of opportunities between households and difficulties in combining paid work with childcare'.[169] The law is more effective than it has been in the past in ensuring access to the labour market for groups falling outside the 'core' of working age adult males, and in ensuring greater equality of treatment across groups within employment, but it has not yet arrived at a viable post-breadwinner model of employment. The effect is that the career pathways of men and women continue to reflect different priorities, and that married women, in particular, remain vulnerable to economic insecurity in the event of marriage break-up, as Jean Gardiner explains:

In most households, outside the professional and managerial occupational groups, men continue to act as the primary earners and women as primary carers and secondary earners. This 'gendered employment and care pathway' enhances men's self-sufficiency through paid employment, as long as well-paid jobs are available. Women are unlikely to achieve individual self-sufficiency or to access opportunities for training and career development. They are therefore vulnerable if marriages break up. Men tend to be excluded from family care because of long working hours. Labour markets locked into this gendered pattern place lone mothers at a particular disadvantage, as they are unable to earn enough to make employment a feasible alternative to dependence on state support. This pathway discourages the development of affordable substitutes for family care.[170]

As Gardiner suggests, the conditions which need to be met if households are to achieve self-sufficiency include not simply affordable access to care services for needs which cannot be met within the household, but also access to paid employment which meets customary expectations of living standards, and adequate, shared time to meet the care needs of family members which are not met by the state or third parties. In other European systems, these objectives are being met by a combination of laws regulating family leave and working time, and the public provision of care services. These initiatives include legislation in the Netherlands which permits parents to reduce their working time to a limited proportion of the normal duration in order to fulfil child care commitments, the object of which is

---

[168] S. Harkness, 'The household division of labour: changes in families' allocation of paid and unpaid work, 1992–2002', op. cit., at p. 168. On the right to request flexible working, see Employment Rights Act 1996, ss. 80F–80I, as inserted by the Employment Act 2002, and SIs 2002/3207 and 3236.

[169] C. Creighton, 'The rise and decline of the "male breadwinner family" in Britain' (1999) 23 *Cambridge Journal of Economics* 519–541, at p. 519.

[170] J. Gardiner, 'Alternative pathways to full employment' (2000) 51 *Federation News* 25–6, at p. 26; see also her 'Rethinking self-sufficiency: employment, families and welfare' (2000) 24 *Cambridge Journal of Economics* 671–689.

to encourage a more even division of household responsibilities between women and men. Even this type of provision will only be effective in supporting self-sufficiency for both men and women 'if men's and women's earnings were more equal, if the income of people in lower paid jobs were raised and if there was a significant improvement in the quality of part-time work'.[171] In the UK, similar initiatives are so far limited: the principal relevant measure is the right to take unpaid parental leave of up to thirteen weeks over the course of the first five years of a child's life, a right which is equally available to mothers and fathers, and which in any case simply implements an EU Directive.[172] In addition, a limited right to paid paternal leave for two weeks following the birth of a child came into effect from April 2003.

4.5 Cooperation in production, partnership at work and the governance of the enterprise

The Labour Government which was elected in 1997 endorsed labour-management cooperation and 'partnership' as an effective approach for improving economic performance. The government's position was summed up by Tony Blair, the Prime Minister, when he laid out the Labour government's primary industrial relations objectives in the foreword to the White Paper, *Fairness at Work*. These objectives required 'nothing less than to change the culture of relations in and at work'.[173] He stressed the need for the new culture to be 'one of voluntary understanding and cooperation because it has been recognised that the prosperity of each (employer and employee) is bound up in the prosperity of all;'[174] and he emphasized that 'partnership works best when it is about real goals—part of a strategy for instance for doubling business. Or bringing employee relations in line with market re-positioning. Or ending the often-meaningless ritual of annual wage squabbling'. In interpreting the Labour government's conception of partnership, Stephen Wood identifies the requirements of the new system as 'one of partnership at work . . . associated with the kind of model of HRM [human resource management] . . . focused on the achievement of a particular role orientation on the part of employees so that they are flexible, expansive in their perceptions and willing contributors to

[171] J. Gardiner, 'Rethinking self-sufficiency: employment, families and welfare' (2000) 24 *Cambridge Journal of Economics*, 671–689, at p. 680, linking this point to a capability-based agenda for reform. See also, on strategies for achieving a more even division of family-related responsibilities between men and women, S. Fredman, 'Reversing discrimination' (1997) 113 *Law Quarterly Review* 575–600 and *Women and the Law* (Oxford: Clarendon Press, 1997) passim.

[172] The relevant EU measure is Directive 96/34/EC and the legislation is contained in the Employment Rights Act 1996, ss. 76–80, as inserted by the Employment Relations Act 1999, and SI 1999/3312. The provisions on paternal leave are contained in the Employment Rights Act 1996, ss. 80A–80E (see also ss. 75A–75D on adoption leave), and SI 2002/2788.

[173] Cm 3968 (1998), at p. 3.

[174] Speech by T. Blair to the TUC partnership conference, May 1999, quoted in S. Wood, 'From voluntarism to partnership: a third way overview of the public policy debate in British industrial relations', in H. Collins, P. Davies and R. Rideout (eds.) *Legal Regulation of the Employment Relation* (Deventer: Kluwer, 2000) 111–135, at p. 133.

innovation.'[175] He suggests that partnership, so conceived, 'is a matter of employers having the right to ask employees to develop themselves in order to accept fresh responsibilities whilst they themselves must take responsibility for providing the context in which this can happen'. In this formulation of partnership, then, the strong emphasis is on the need for workers to make far-reaching commitments to their employer's business interests and objectives, and to mould themselves to its needs. In this way, workers provide additional and improved resources for management to perform its function of coordination more effectively.

Human resource management is the latest in a line of organizational theories which have sought to rationalize and justify managerial practices. In the early industrial revolution, the disciplinary intervention of the master–servant code was matched by a similarly harsh application of hierarchical managerial power. In exceptional cases, factory owners, such as Robert Owen, believed that concern for the welfare, education and social development of their workforce offered the best way forward; but the vast majority used close supervision and discipline to 'force human character into a mechanical mode'.[176] The position of workers in the workplace was further weakened as the finer division of labour progressively simplified tasks, with mechanization and with the growth of employers' scientific, engineering and managerial knowledge. And, it was from this cumulative process that scientific management evolved.[177] At the turn of the twentieth century, the American pioneers of scientific management proposed that managers should acquire workers' craft knowledge, plan production in detail, precisely define each worker's tasks and carefully control every stage of production. The need to achieve these objectives, Frederick Winslow Taylor claimed,[178] rested on the discovery and development of the scientific laws governing production.

Taylor made far-reaching claims for scientific management. He argued that it provided a rational basis for designing and standardizing factory lay-out, equipment and industrial organization, and for codifying worker knowledge. It offered a scientific basis for worker selection, vocational guidance, training, planning work to individual capabilities, ensuring workers' physical and psychological well-being, and designing wage payment systems to reward efficiency. In doing this, it raised workers' skill levels, stimulated them intellectually, promoted individuality and self-reliance, while at the same time increasing pay, cutting hours of work and improving employment security. Taylor also claimed that his methods improved the management of labour by creating a cadre of specialists to instruct, train and advise workers, and encourage involvement. Of particular importance was the assertion that replacing a system of arbitrary managerial decisions by one in which managerial control of worker activity was governed by

[175] Ibid., at p. 130.
[176] S. Pollard, *The Genesis of Modern Management: A Study of the Industrial Revolution in Great Britain* (Cambridge, MA: Harvard University Press, 1965), at p. 256.
[177] See W. Hollway, *Work Psychology and Work Organisation* (London: Sage, 1991).
[178] F.W. Taylor, *Principles of Scientific Management* (New York: Harper, 1911).

scientific laws would improve management/worker relationships, democratize industry and eliminate the need for trade unions and collective bargaining. Taylor claimed that:

No such democracy has ever existed in industry before. Every protest of every workman must be handled by those on management's side, and the right or wrong of the complaint must be settled not by the opinion, either of the management or the workman, but by the great code of laws which has been developed and which must satisfy both sides. It gives the worker in the end equal voice with the employer; both can refer only to the arbitrament of science and fact.[179]

If his blueprints were followed, Taylor claimed, combining managerial authority with science would remove the conflict resulting from the exercise of, and resistance to, arbitrary managerial power and clear the way for full cooperation.

However, the practice of scientific management proved different from its theory. In his detailed study of the practical application of scientific management, Robert Franklin Hoxie came to quite the opposite view of its effects to those anticipated by Taylor.[180] He found that scientific management mainly served to concentrate into management's hands the power to deskill, control and speed up work and to justify this in the name of science. The main problem, Hoxie argued, was managerial emphasis on short-term increases in production and profit by task and rate setting, without concern for the longer-term reform of technical and organizational structures required for full-blown scientific management. As a result, the weight of change fell on workers who experienced it as the degradation of skills, increased alienation from the work process, and loss of power.

While recognizing this, neither Hoxie, nor the unions he consulted, opposed the principle of the application of science to industry. The problem, as they saw it, was not so much with the *application* of science as with the *way* it was applied. On the democratization of industry, Hoxie wrote:

It is a noble ideal, as old at least as Saint Simon, and the time may come when it is capable of realisation. Before this however, the science of psychology must make long strides, industry must attain a much greater degree of regularity and stability than at present exists, and the type of man who is supposed to discover and voice the dictates of science—and stand thus as the just judge between employers and workers—must be very different from the present general run of time study men and task setters.[181]

As it turned out, the first half of the twentieth century was characterized by a rapid growth in employers' interest in the role of human relations in industry and the potential to improve such relations by applying psychological and sociological research findings to work organization. Increasing attention was paid to matching workers to jobs by means of psychological methods in selection and training, the

[179] F.W. Taylor, *Principles of Scientific Management* (New York: Harper, 1911), at p. 22.
[180] R.F. Hoxie, *Scientific Management and Labour* (New York: Appleton, 1915).
[181] See Hollway, *Work Psychology and Work Organisation*, op. cit., at p. 103.

use of such techniques as ergonomics to fit jobs to workers, and of counselling to improve their mental well-being. Reflecting on his combined experience of management and social research, Seebohm Rowntree wrote in 1921:

The attempt to establish an ideal working environment is not the fad of a sentimentalist, nor is it a counsel of perfection, which can only be operated by a wealthy firm. If workers are to cooperate in producing a high output of goods, which will compete successfully in world markets, they rightly demand, in their working lives, conditions which will enable and encourage them to give of their best.[182]

The benefits of collective employee involvement and the negative effects of unrestricted managerial prerogative were also underlined in the so-called Hawthorne Experiments of the 1930s, as well as by the Tavistock Institute's war-time experiments and their peacetime industrial applications.[183] These developments in human relations were designed to improve management rather than to challenge its authority or the extent and definition of managerial responsibility. They were largely remedial and targeted at increasing efficiency by making the employment systems more worker-friendly, by fitting workers better into work systems and by providing treatment for their physical and psychological defects. In this process:

A new conception and practice of the worker emerged. This had as its objective to ensure that the bond linking the individual and the enterprise and also the individual to society would hence forth not be solely economic. The wage relationship and the power of the boss would be supplemented by a personal bond that would attach individuals to the lives they lived in the world of work, to their co-workers and bosses, and to society as a whole. It would be possible to conceive of administering the working environment in such a way as to ensure simultaneously the contentment and health of the worker and the profitability and efficiency of the enterprise.[184]

The increasing weight given to this perspective shifted the focus in labour management from labour as a *factor of production* to be directed and cajoled by hierarchical management, to labour as a *productive resource* with creative capabilities to be developed by inter-active management. The expectation was that employers would reap the rewards of greater worker motivation, increased job satisfaction and improved job performance by greater operational and dynamic efficiency and higher profitability. These objectives are seen as requiring the enlarging and enriching of jobs, more challenges and opportunities, new skills and more effective incentives. With this change in management objectives and

---

[182] Quoted in A. Briggs, *A Study of the Work of Seebohm Rowntree, 1871–1954* (London: Longmans, 1961), at p. 87.

[183] See G. Slinger, 'Spanning the gap: the theoretical principles that connect stakeholder policies to business performance' (1999) 11 *Corporate Governance: an International Review* 136–151.

[184] P. Miller and N. Rose, 'Governing economic life', in G. Mabey, G. Salaman and J. Storey (eds.) *Strategic Human Resource Management: A Reader* (London: Sage) 46–57, at p. 53.

style came a modification in nomenclature from 'personnel and industrial relations management' to 'human resource management'.[185]

HRM has been defined 'as a set of policies designed to maximize organizational integration, employee commitment, flexibility and the quality of work',[186] and variants of the basic model have been identified. So-called *soft HRM* is 'a method of releasing untapped reserves of "human resourcefulness" by increasing employee commitment, participation and involvement',[187] and has a greater emphasis on human relations. *Hard HRM* is designed to maximize the economic return from labour resources by integrating HRM into business strategy. Although it usually incorporates soft HRM practices, hard HRM is more strongly oriented towards meeting market requirements by means of greater production flexibility and product improvement.[188] Key objectives in hard HRM, which have a clear affinity with Taylor's vision of scientific management, include continuous improvement in quality and performance, just-in-time inventory systems, and statistical process control designed to iron out variation in quality, create consistency in meeting standards, locate inventory savings and eliminate waste. Broadly speaking, the purpose of HRM is to foster a pre-emptive rather than re-active approach to operational efficiency, quality control, and innovation by shifting responsibility and accountability for decision making towards the shop floor. Its adoption testifies to a shift in labour management practice 'from coercion to the attempted production of self-regulated individuals'.[189]

However, despite recognizing the psychological needs of workers, the importance of democratic management and the central role of worker self-regulation and involvement in management as mechanisms for securing full cooperation, the human resources school is deep down no more sympathetic to the idea of workers' independent representation than liberal economists or the scientific management school. The idea of democratizing industry goes no further than F.W. Taylor's view that this purpose is served by the enlightenment of management through knowledge of scientific laws, except that the science needed now extends beyond that of production to include the psychology and sociology of the producers. Even

---

[185] For reviews of the literature on HRM see P. Blyton and P. Turnbull, 'Debates, dilemmas and contradictions', in P. Blyton and P. Turnbull (eds.) *Reassessing Human Resource Management* (London: Sage Publications, 1992) 1–15, and E. Appelbaum and R. Batt, *The New American Workplace: Transforming Work Systems in the United States* (New York: ILR Press, 1994); for surveys of the extent of HRM practices in Britain, see S. Wood and L. De Menezes, 'High commitment management in the UK: evidence from the Workplace Industrial Relations Survey and Employers' Manpower and Skill Practice Survey' (1992) 51 *Human Relations* 485–515, and M. Cully, S. Woodland, A. O'Reilly and G. Dix, *Britain at Work, as Revealed by the 1998 Workplace Employee Relations Survey* (London: Routledge, 1999), passim.

[186] D. Guest, 'Human resource management and industrial relations' (1987) 24 *Journal of Management Studies* 503–21, at p. 503.

[187] Blyton and Turnbull, 'Debates, dilemmas and contradictions', op. cit., at p. 4.

[188] Appelbaum and Batt, *The New American Workplace*, op. cit.

[189] Hollway, *Work Psychology and Work Organisation*, op. cit., at p. 20.

Elton Mayo, who was responsible for the Hawthorne experiments in worker participation, believed that:

Conflict was neither inevitable nor economic. It was the result of the maladjustment of a few men on the labour side of industry. Even after Hawthorne forced Mayo to grow, he remained firm in his conviction that conflict was an evil, a symptom of the lack of social skills. Cooperation, for him, was symptomatic of health; and, since there was no alternative in the modern world, cooperation must mean obedience to managerial authority. Thus collective bargaining was not really cooperation, but merely a flimsy substitute for the real thing.[190]

More recently, advocates of human resource management have stressed the importance of unity of purpose and values. Total quality management (TQM) has been characterized as an organizational form in which 'employees can be trusted and empowered to take on more responsibility in a context of HRM practices which ensure a homogeneity of values'.[191] Traditional 'pluralistic' industrial relations (where a diversity of interests is recognized) are effectively ruled out and collective bargaining becomes 'integrative' rather than 'distributive'.[192]

Even so, there is now a considerable body of literature suggesting a positive link between the use of HRM practices and performance, particularly when such methods as flexible work assignments, work teams, skill training, effective communications, and incentive pay schemes are used in combination.[193] The superior performance of close worker involvement and cooperation compared with arm's-length market relations and hierarchical management has also been demonstrated by the product market success of what Michael Best described as the *new competition*.[194] This brought to the market improved design, greater variety, high quality, more rapid product innovation as well as keener prices.

The 'new competition' originated with mainland European and Japanese producers, many of whom combined leading edge HRM and close cooperation within networks of firms.[195] Within these more competitive and highly successful

---

[190] L. Baritz, 'The servants of power', in G. Esland, G. Speakman and M.A. Speakman (eds.) *People and Work* (Edinburgh: Holmes-McDougall, 1975), at pp. 332–333.

[191] G. Sewell and B. Wilkinson, 'Empowerment or emasculation? Shopfloor surveillances in a total quality organisation', in P. Blyton and P. Turnbull (eds.) *Reassessing Human Resource Management*, op. cit., 97–115.

[192] On this distinction, see R. Walton and R. McKersie, *A Behavioural Theory of Labour Negotiations* (New York: McGraw-Hill, 1965).

[193] See, in particular, C. Ichniowski, K. Shaw, and G. Prennushi, 'The effects of human resource management practices on productivity: a study of steel finishing lines' (1997) 87 *American Economic Review* 291–312.

[194] M. Best, *The New Competition: Institutions of Industrial Restructuring* (Cambridge: Polity, 1990).

[195] Appelbaum and Batt, *The New American Workplace*, op. cit., in their extremely valuable study, identified four main systems of cooperative production: Japanese lean production; Italian flexible specialization; German diversified quality production; and Swedish socio-technical systems. The Japanese and Swedish systems are more firmly rooted in Taylorist mass production than the German or, particularly, the Italian. But what the four systems have in common is the importance given to high levels of worker training and the success they have achieved in closely involving workers at all levels in the organization and management of production, in product and process innovation and in the development of organizations and institutions designed to facilitate cooperative working relationships.

productive systems, work organization was participatory and non-hierarchical and inter-firm links were close and cooperative rather than arm's-length and antagonistic. The result was a more effective mobilization of the commitment, skills and knowledge of workers and trading partners, serving to raise efficiency, improve quality, and generate a faster rate of product, process and organizational innovation.

But such organizational redesign has proved very difficult in Anglo-American systems. Rather than radically reforming their work systems, employers in the US and UK have generally attempted to incorporate degrees of worker involvement and other HRM practices into existing managerial structures. Moreover, even when these changes have been successfully implemented to begin with, they have proved difficult to sustain over time.[196] Consequently, little has been done to change 'the fundamental nature of the production system or threaten the basic organization or power structure of the firms'.[197]

Concurrently, neoliberal macro-economic policies and globalization have intensified competition in buyers' markets to the advantage of consumers; whilst deregulation has shifted the balance of power in the labour market in favour of capital and, in the capital market, in favour of shareholders. Firms have responded to growing product and capital market pressures by passing on costs to suppliers, sub-contracting, cutting jobs and increasing the use of temporary and casual workers. But the main burden of securing higher performance at lower costs has fallen on the core workforce. This has been driven by the changing market demands and the additional burdens imposed on the survivors by downsizing and the delayering of management. Workers are required to be more responsive and cooperative, to acquire greater skills, to intensify effort, to accept greater responsibilities, and become more flexible. But, while employees have generally welcomed opportunities to take more control over the planning and execution of their work, distrust of management is widespread and the perception is that pay levels have failed to adequately compensate for the extra responsibility, accountability, work-load, working hours and effort that workers are expected to bear.[198]

In what ways have these developments been affected by the development of the law and practice relating to employee representation over the course of the 1980s and 1990s? The transformation in the influence of collective bargaining in Britain since the early 1980s has been three-fold: firstly, a reduction in the influence of multi-employer, sectoral bargaining, which while traceable to the 1960s, accelerated rapidly in the mid-1980s; secondly, a fall in the coverage of collective agreements and other forms of wage determination from over 80 per cent of the employed labour force at the start of the 1980s to around a third of the workforce

---

[196] S. Konzelmann and R. Forrant and F. Wilkinson, 'Work systems, corporate strategy and global markets: creative shop floors or a "barge mentality"?' (2004) 35 *Industrial Relations Journal* 216–232.

[197] Appelbaum and Batt, *The New American Workplace*, op. cit., at p. 22.

[198] See generally B. Burchell, D. Ladipo and F. Wilkinson (eds.) *Job Insecurity and Work Intensification* (London: Routledge, 2002).

twenty years later; and, even with organizations where trade unions continued to be recognized for the purposes of collective bargaining, a loss of union influence over traditional areas of negotiation, in particular pay.[199]

The decline of collective bargaining would seem, in principle, to be one aspect of the process by which greater priority was placed on the relationship of the individual worker to the firm, within the framework of the theory and practice of human resource management. But empirical research, comparing the experience of firms which derecognized trade unions with those in which union recognition was retained in the early and mid-1990s, suggests otherwise.[200]

The employment contract, if anything, became *more* standardized at enterprise level, not less, as a result of the diminution of union influence. There was only limited evidence of greater individual differentiation of contract terms. In both unionized and de-unionized firms, the contractual terms of the employment relationship, in terms of job definition, working time and the composition of the wage, took the form of a standard form agreement which was largely set by the employer. In many cases, job definitions were widened and controls on working time removed. The process went further in the de-unionized firms, but the difference was one of degree. Individual *bargaining* was exceptionally rare, and the influence of contract over the performance appraisal systems which were now widely used to set individual pay, replacing the annual pay round, tended not to take a contractual form. Instead, they were administered under terms which give employers a very wide, extra-contractual discretion. In so far as the role of contract law within the open-ended employment relationship was, however imperfectly, to set limits to managerial prerogative,[201] these developments signified a retreat from the relational contract model of employment, and, in that sense, a '*de*-contractualization' of employment.[202]

This process was partially offset by the formalization of contract terms and conditions which took place under the influence of employment protection legislation, and by the growing recourse of individual employees, with union assistance, to employment tribunals as a source of protection. Rather than seeing regulation give way completely, then, there has been a shift in the *level* of regulation from the collective sphere to that of the individual relationship. This has been accompanied by a certain change of emphasis in the role of unions, from co-regulators of terms and conditions of employment, to monitors and enforcers of employees' legal rights.[203] In short, the open-ended employment contract

---

[199] See generally Chapter 4, Section 6, above.

[200] See W. Brown, S. Deakin, M. Hudson, C. Pratten and P. Ryan, *The Individualisation of Employment Contracts in Britain* EMAR Research Series no. 4 (London: Department of Trade and Industry, 1998). [201] See above, Chapter 1, Section 2.

[202] S. Deakin, 'Organisational change, labour flexibility and the contract of employment in Britain', in S. Deery and R. Mitchell (eds.) *Employment Relations, Individualisation and Union Exclusion: An International Study* (Annandale, NSW: Federation Press, 1999), 130–152.

[203] W. Brown, S. Deakin, D. Nash and S. Oxenbridge, 'The employment contract: from collective procedures to individual rights' (2000) 38 *British Journal of Industrial Relations* 611–629.

continues to a principal focus of regulation of enterprise-level relations, albeit under conditions where the weakening of union power has exposed even 'core' employees to the dangers of unfettered managerial prerogative and growing work intensification.

A major shift in legal policy occurred with the enactment, as part of the Employment Relations Act 1999, of a statutory procedure under which an independent union may establish a legal right to recognition for the purposes of collective bargaining, in respect of a particular bargaining unit.[204] In principle, the union will be entitled to recognition if a majority of the workers in the relevant unit are members of that union, or if, in a recognition ballot, a majority of those voting and 40 per cent of those entitled to vote support recognition.[205] If the employer still resists, the Central Arbitration Committee has the power to impose a 'default procedure agreement'[206] which is a method for conducting negotiations,[207] *not* a collective agreement laying down terms and conditions of employment; the default agreement can if necessary be implemented through a court order for specific performance.[208]

The adoption of the new statutory recognition procedure was a major part of the Labour government's commitment to legislate to encourage the growth of partnership at work. The new recognition procedure is administered by the Central Arbitration Committee, and a substantial body of practice has built up since the law came into force in 2001. Although the statutory recognition procedure is open to criticism for providing inadequate protection for unions engaged in recognition drives and for providing employers with continuing opportunities to resist and obstruct the recognition process, it has already had an effect in terms of encouraging the growth of voluntary recognition agreements; this 'shadow effect' arises from the way in which both sides are provided with strong incentives to reach agreement on recognition before having recourse to the procedures administered by the Central Arbitration Committee. More generally, the announcement of the Labour government's intention to legislate for recognition upon taking office in 1997 has had an encouraging effect. Thus between 1995 and 2002, recognition agreements were struck covering around one million workers, against decisions to derecognize covering just over 60,000 workers.[209]

---

[204] Employment Relations Act 1999, s. 1 and Sch. 1. See Deakin and Morris, *Labour Law*, op. cit., at pp. 766–781.

[205] Trade Union and Labour Relations (Consolidation) Act 1992 (as amended by the Employment Relations Act 1999, s. 1 and Sch. 1), Sch. AI, para. 29.

[206] *Fairness at Work*, Cm. 3968 (1998), Annex 1.

[207] Trade Union and Labour Relations (Consolidation) Act 1992, Sch. A1, para. 31(3).

[208] Ibid., para. 31(6).

[209] G. Gall, 'Trade union recognition in Britain, 1995–2002: turning a corner?' (2004) 35 *Industrial Relations Journal* 249–270; and see also S. Oxenbridge, W. Brown, S. Deakin and C. Pratten, 'Initial responses to the statutory recognition procedures of the Employment Relations Act 1999' (2003) 41 *British Journal of Industrial Relations* 315–334; S. Moore, S. Wood and K. Ewing, 'The impact of the trade union recognition procedure under the Employment Relations Act 1999' in H. Gospel and S. Wood (eds.) *Representing Workers: Trade Union Membership and*

Prior to the Act's implementation there had been a growth, from the mid-1990s onwards, of so-called 'partnership agreements'.[210] Some companies pursuing a partnership agenda re-recognized unions at workplaces which had undergone derecognition a few years before as part of an effort to build up a cooperative relationship with the workforce. Partnership agreements are difficult to define and hence somewhat hard to identify, but most of them are characterized by union agreement to support and encourage flexible working arrangements aimed at enhancing the competitive position of the firm, in return for the renewal or extension of rights of collective representation. In its May 1999 *Partners for Progress—New Unionism at the Workplace*,[211] the TUC advocated enterprise-level industrial partnership and identified six underlying principles:

(1) a shared commitment to the success of the organisation; (2) a commitment by the employer to employment security in return for which the union agrees to a higher level of functional flexibility in the work place; (3) a renewed focus on the quality of working life, giving workers access to opportunities to improve their skills, focusing attention on improving job content and enriching the quality of work; (4) openness and a willingness to share information; (5) adding value—unions, workers and employers must see that partnership is delivering measurable improvements; and (6) a recognition by both the union and employer that they each have different and legitimate interests.

The full impact of the new statutory procedure on the growth of a partnership model based on bilateral relations of mutual interest remains to be seen. The procedure has helped, along with other institutional factors such as an increased role in collective conciliation for the Advisory, Conciliation and Arbitration Service (ACAS),[212] in reversing the trend towards derecognition. However, the mere reinstatement of recognition does not in itself guarantee that the conditions for effective and genuine partnership are being met. Thus 'partnership agreements in contemporary Britain range from some that do indeed seek to nurture trade unions as genuinely representative and independent, albeit on a cooperative basis, through to some that are thinly veiled devices to limit and constrain union influence'.[213] Some employers responded to the new procedure by taking active steps to minimize and exclude union influence; others proactively courted unions which they thought they more easily work with than others; and in other cases, recognition has taken a form more akin to consultation rather than negotiation over terms and conditions of employment.[214]

Recognition in Britain (London: Routledge, 2003) 119–143; S. Moore and H. Bewley, *The Content of New Voluntary Trade Union Recognition Agreements 1998–2002: Report of Preliminary Findings* EMAR Research Series no. 26 (London: DTI, 2004).

[210] See J. Knell, *Partnership at Work* EMAR Research Series no. 7 (London: Department of Trade and Industry, 1999). [211] London: TUC, 1999.

[212] On this see W. Brown and S. Oxenbridge, 'Trade unions and collective bargaining: laws and the future of collectivism', in C. Barnard, S. Deakin and G. Morris (eds.) *The Future of Labour Law: Liber Amicorum Bob Hepple* (Oxford: Hart, 2004) 64–77, at p. 73. [213] Ibid.

[214] Ibid.

The recognition procedure is a relatively weak influence on the development of cooperative work relations when set against the context of wider constraints on partnership at work. Thanks in large part to the changes made to industrial structure following privatization in the 1980s and 1990s, a large proportion of UK productive capacity, in relative terms, is held in the form of publicly-listed companies. The predominant type of ownership in UK publicly-listed companies may be described as *dispersed-share ownership*. The principal shareholders are institutions—insurance companies and pension funds—who invest on behalf of their policy-holders and beneficiaries respectively. They vest the day-to-day control and management of their shareholdings in fund managers—investment banks and other specialist investors—who act as their agents. Typically, the share structure of a listed company will consist of several blocks (of between 5 and 10 per cent) that are controlled by fund managers on behalf of a number of clients. By contrast, the *dominant block-holding* model, in which one shareholder holds a majority or near-majority stake, is rare in UK-listed companies. In general, dispersed share-holder ownership strongly privileges exit over voice as the mechanism by which shareholders can exercise control over management. The deep liquidity of the London stock exchange means that there is a highly active market for the shares of UK-listed companies.

A specific mechanism for overcoming costs of dispersed shareholder voting is the hostile takeover. A hostile takeover is, in effect, an appeal to the shareholders of a listed company to sell out en masse to an external bidder. The shareholders are induced to exit the company by the offer of a premium on top of the current value of their shares, the cost of which the new owner will aim to recover by restructuring the company. The collective action costs of voting in response to a 'tender offer' of this kind are reduced by regulation—a combination of provisions of the Companies Acts and the City Code on Takeovers and Mergers—that enables minority shareholders, who would otherwise 'hold out' against the offer in the hope of getting a better deal, to be compulsorily bought out. Conversely, minority shareholders receive strong protection against expropriation by majorities during a bid. Two-tier offers, partial bids and other techniques that seek to lever a bid by offering differential terms to particular shareholders are, in effect, banned. Other rules of UK securities law and practice make it nearly impossible for the managers of a listed company to put in place advance protection against hostile bids. Such protection might include the issuing of non-voting stock or the implementation of various 'poison pill' defences that are much more regularly observed in the USA.

Thus during a hostile takeover bid, the boards of target companies are required to assume a neutral stance and offer disinterested advice to shareholders on the financial merits of the bid. Although the rules of the Code require bidders to state their intentions with regard to the future treatment of employees, this results in little more than the insertion of a standard-form legal 'boilerplate' in offer documents. There is no obligation on the part of either the target board or the board of the bidder to consult employee representatives during a bid; this only occurs after a bid has gone through when large-scale redundancies are announced. There is even some doubt as to how far either board may go in providing information to employee representatives without contravening the provisions of the Code and the listing rules on the disclosure of price-sensitive information. These rules, together with the doctrine of 'pre-emption' (which makes it impractical for most listed companies to issue non-voting stock as a way of beating off a takeover bid), create particular incentives for boards to prioritize short-term shareholder interests over other interests during a bid.[215]

By international standards, there is a high level of hostile takeover activity in the UK. Even so, the numbers of hostile bids in a given year will be in the tens rather than the hundreds, whereas the number of listed companies runs into the thousands.[216] More significant is the long shadow cast over corporate governance by the Code and by the listing rules. No listed company is immune from the possibility of a hostile bid. To varying degrees, companies can insulate themselves against short-term fluctuations in their share price relative to the market by cultivating a culture of long-term investment. But this is not an option open to all; and there is a question as to whether it is continuously available for any. In practice, the takeover mechanism has been the principal catalyst for corporate restructuring in the UK during the last decade; and virtually no industrial or services sector has escaped the changes induced by takeover activity. The corporate governance rules clearly have a wider effect on the economy and industrial structure of the UK.

There is therefore a serious issue of whether the dispersed shareholder model constrains the development of a 'partnership' approach in employment relations in the UK. The hallmark of effective partnership is that parties give open-ended commitment to cooperate based on their expectation that significant benefits will result for them. Important factors for creating such expectations can be expected to include: fairness of treatment, job satisfaction, high quality of work environment and, particularly, income and job security. However, the decision to cooperate and form a productive partnership also means giving a hostage to fortune because the benefits are unlikely to accrue immediately. When deciding to cooperate, it must be taken on trust by individuals that their action will be reciprocated. This depends on the reliability of the person or persons with whom the agreement is made as well as upon the commitment parties have from each other and the priority they are required to give to the latter. Because managers, through the combined effect of convention and law, are required to prioritize

---

[215] See generally S. Deakin and G. Slinger, 'Hostile takeovers, corporate law and the theory of the firm' (1997) 24 *Journal of Law and Society* 124–150; S. Deakin, R. Hobbs, D. Nash and G. Slinger, 'Implicit contracts, takeovers and corporate governance: in the shadow of the City Code', in D. Campbell, H. Collins and J. Wightman (eds.) *Implicit Dimensions of Contract* (Oxford: Hart, 2003) 289–331.

[216] See Deakin, Hobbs, Nash and Slinger, 'Takeovers and corporate governance', op. cit., for details.

shareholder value over other interests when decisions regarding corporate structure are made, they are to that extent correspondingly less able to make 'credible
commitments' to respect the long-term interests of other stakeholders, in particular, employees. As a result, employees have no meaningful guarantee of economic
security and therefore a reduced incentive to engage in the sharing of information
and reciprocal learning. The prevailing system of corporate governance would
then represent a major constraint on the possibilities for effective partnership in
UK employment relations.

Empirical evidence based on a small sample of partnership-orientated companies
over the course of the 1990s nevertheless suggests that partnership agreements can
develop notwithstanding the operation of the market for corporate control.[217]
While the UK system of corporate governance may sometimes operate as a
constraint on cooperation between workers and managers, it may also provide an
opportunity for publicly traded firms to pursue partnership with their various
stakeholder groups, in particular with employees. As a constraint, the nature of
shareholder pressure varies depending upon how companies choose to manage
investor expectations. Companies that succeed in building a long-term orientation into relations with shareholders have an important degree of flexibility in
managing their way through the other pressures to which they are subject (that is,
product market pressures and regulatory pressures). For these firms, the corporate
governance system offers an opportunity to gain an important competitive edge
by demonstrating their ability to better handle conflicting pressures than rivals.
Other cases suggest that when confronted with a range of unfavourable conditions (that is, corporate governance prioritizes short-term shareholder returns;
product markets are volatile and have turned against the UK-based operations;
and regulation supports open transnational competition), partnership may be very
difficult to construct and maintain, even if the different corporate constituencies
would prefer to choose partnership in order to support the competitive survival of
the firm.

The law and practice relating to the governance of the enterprise in Britain is
therefore at a crossroads. The economic advantages which flow from cooperation
between labour and management are now generally accepted and understood.
However, there is a lack of consensus on the institutional means by which this
type of cooperation should be encouraged. Because of the organizational changes
which are associated with the intensification of competition in both national and
global markets, and with the pressure upon accountability and audit in the public
sector,[218] employees are being called on to make unconditional commitments to
the competitive success of the enterprise, under circumstances where no reciprocal
set of undertakings is made by the employer. The institutional framework is not, on
the whole, favourable to the making of credible commitments by management, in

[217] S. Deakin, R. Hobbs, S. Konzelmann and F. Wilkinson, 'Partnership, ownership and control:
the impact of corporate governance on employment relations' (2002) 24 *Employee Relations*
335–352.   [218] See Burchell, Ladipo and Wilkinson, *Work Intensification*, op. cit.

large part because of the pressure for short-term returns which is a feature of the system of ownership and governance in the private sector, and to some degree, thanks to financial controls, in the public sector too. Until this institutional deficit is addressed,[219] there is only limited scope for the development in Britain of those complex forms of cooperation in production which characterized other advanced economies which, in the course of the 1980s and 1990s, were arguably more successful in maintaining competitive advantage without abandoning social cohesion.

4.6 Return to the floor of rights?

The late 1990s saw the adoption for the first time in the UK of comprehensive minimum wage and working time legislation. Up to that point, as we saw earlier, selective and partial regulation of basic terms and conditions was the rule. Parliament passed the National Minimum Wage Act 1998, establishing a legal floor to wages, and adopted legislation implementing the EC Working Time Directive, which went further than any previous UK legislation had done to recognizing a general limit on working hours. The final removal of the last remnants of the traditional form of working time and minimum wage legislation by the preceding Conservative governments, together with the clear impossibility of voluntary collective bargaining filling the void, had prompted the legislature to act, although it is unclear whether the relevant steps would have been taken in the field of working time had it not been for pressure from the European Community. However, neither of these measures represents a complete departure from the tradition of collective laissez-faire.

The Working Time Directive[220] has been implemented[221] in a way which takes full advantage of a number of derogations which severely limit the effect of the standards which it lays down including, crucially, the maximum 48-hour limit to working time. Thanks to the insistence of the UK government (then under a Conservative administration) at the time the Directive was negotiated in the early 1990s, a member state may make provision for individual derogation from this standard, by an agreement in writing to this effect between worker and employer.[222] The UK is the only member state to have done so by way of a *general* derogation, applying to all the sectors and occupations covered by the Directive. The UK has also given a broad (and contentious) reading to a further derogation, which allows member states to exclude from the scope of the 48-hour week workers whose duties involve them in 'autonomous decision-making powers';[223] in the

---

[219] On the possible role of the implementation of Directive 2002/14/EC establishing a general framework for informing and consulting employees in the European Community, see H. Gospel and P. Willman, 'High performance workplaces: the role of employee involvement in a modern economy. Evidence on the EU Directive establishing a general framework for informing and consulting employees' CEP Discussion Paper no. 562, February 2003 (London: LSE).

[220] Directive 93/104/EC.

[221] By the Working Time Regulations 1998 (1998/1833) and 1999 (SI 1999/3372).

[222] Directive 93/104/EC, Art. 18(1)(b)(i).   [223] Ibid., Art. 17(1).

UK Regulations this has become a reference to 'unmeasured working time'.[224]
Under the Working Time Regulations, the 48-hour week limit applies only to that
part of the working week which is not 'unmeasured'.[225] The alternative interpretation would have allowed the derogation to apply only if the worker's employment,
as a whole, constituted 'unmeasured work'. In addition, the conditions imposed
by the Directive upon the employer in return for applying the derogation, in
terms of record keeping and health and safety checks for workers, were watered
down shortly after the first set of implementing regulations were issued, in
response to employer lobbying.[226]

Together these derogations have had a chilling effect on the application, in
practice, of the Directive and implementing regulations; the individual opt-out is
in widespread use in a wide range of sectors, and the unmeasured work exception
is widely relied on in professional and managerial occupations. It is against this
background that the Directive has so far had a minimal effect on the prevalent
culture of long-hours working in the UK, and in particular has done little to
discourage the systematic use of overtime working, which remains popular with
some workers as a way of boosting earnings and with employers as tried and tested
mechanisms for varying labour inputs. Because of the width and simplicity of
application of the individual derogation, collective agreements combining the
annualization and reduction of working hours, common in a number of continental systems, have been rare in the UK.[227] By contrast, the implementation of
the right to paid annual leave, a provision of the Directive which is not subject to
a derogation of any kind,[228] has had, in a short time, an appreciable effect in
extending paid holidays and in reducing total yearly hours worked.[229]

Nor has the Directive been used, as it might have been, to promote more effective employee representation. The Directive, using a continental European model
of regulation, makes extensive provision for the basic standards on working hours,
shift work and night work to be varied by collective agreement at sector level or by
agreement between the employer and trade unions or enterprise committees at
workplace or company level. In the absence of collective agreement, the 'default'
standards apply; thus the employer has a powerful incentive to engage in joint
regulation with the employee representatives. In the UK this option for achieving
greater flexibility in the application of labour standards via collective bargaining
has not been taken up to any significant degree. There have been no sectoral

---

[224] SI 1998/1833, reg. 20.

[225] This aspect of the provision was introduced by the 1999 Regulations.

[226] For an account of the Directive and the implementing regulations of 1998, as amended in
1999, see S. Deakin and G. Morris, *Labour Law*, op. cit., at pp. 306–315; C. Barnard, 'Working time
in the UK' (1999) 28 *Industrial Law Journal* 61–75, and 'The Working Time Regulations 1999'
(2000) 29 *Industrial Law Journal* 167–171.

[227] See Barnard, Deakin and Hobbs, 'Opting out of the 48-hour week' (2003) 32 *Industrial Law
Journal* 223–252, for a full account.

[228] Directive 93/104/EC, Art. 7; Working Time Regulations, SI 1998/1833, regs. 13–14.

[229] F. Green, 'The demands of work', in R. Dickens, P. Gregg and J. Wadsworth (eds.) *The Labour
Market Under New Labour. The State of Working Britain* (London: Palgrave Macmillan, 2003) 137–149.

collective agreements varying working hours across a whole trade or industry, reflecting the long-term decline and current ineffectiveness of sectoral arrangements; but, more surprisingly perhaps, there are only isolated examples of collective agreements at enterprise level playing this role, and very few instances of the same effect being achieved through workforce agreements of the kind which may be agreed in workplaces where there is no recognized trade union. To a large extent this is because, in the UK context, the employer has the straightforward option of using the individual derogation to vary the length of the basic working week, bypassing the collective route.[230]

This aspect of the failure of the Working Time Directive demonstrates the degree to which, in industrial relations practice, collective bargaining and social legislation are still seen as separate forms of labour market regulation, rather than as being potentially complementary. The idea that self-regulation might be used to vary a legislative standard in this way is not new. As we saw in our discussion of the late nineteenth-century debate on the statutory control of working hours, a 'trade exemption' model was discussed by the Royal Commission on Labour of 1891–94 under which a vote of the trade would decide whether to opt in, or in some versions to opt out, of statutory regulations. The proposal was rejected on the grounds that a vote of all the workers in a given trade would be a complex and expensive undertaking.[231] Just over a century later, the more pragmatic route of varying legislative standards through an agreement of employers and employee representatives has been enacted, only to meet a similar degree of indifference.

The National Minimum Wage Act 1998 empowered the Secretary of State for Trade and Industry to set a basic hourly rate covering (with very few exceptions) the entire employed labour force; to this end he was required, when setting the initial rate, to take advice from the Low Pay Commission, a tripartite body endowed with a number of statutory functions under the Act.[232] Contrary to the practice in some other European countries,[233] the 1998 Act does not contain a mechanism for the automatic annual uprating of the minimum wage by reference to wages or prices. The initial rate was set in at £3.60 an hour from April 1999 for those aged 22 or over; by March 2004 it had risen to £4.50. A separate rate for 18–21 year-olds was initially set at £3.00 an hour, and had risen to £3.80 an hour by March 2004. In its *First Report*, the Low Pay Commission took the view that in setting a national minimum wage rate it should act 'without risking damage to the

[230] See Barnard, Deakin and Hobbs, 'Opting out of the 48-hour week', op. cit.

[231] See our discussion in Chapter 4, Section 3.3, above.

[232] For a full account of the National Minimum Wage Act 1998 and the National Minimum Wage Regulations 1999 (SI 1999/584), see S. Deakin and G. Morris, *Labour Law*, op. cit., at pp. 279–288; B. Simpson, 'A milestone in the legal regulation of pay: the National Minimum Wage Act 1998' (1999) 28 *Industrial Law Journal* 1–32, and 'Implementing the national minimum wage—the 1999 Regulations' (1999) 28 *Industrial Law Journal* 171–182.

[233] For a comparative survey of minimum wage laws and other basic labour standards, see S. Deakin, (1990) 15 'The floor of rights in European labour law' *New Zealand Journal of Industrial Relations* 219–240.

economy'[234] and that the rate should be 'manageable to a wide range of business interests'.[235] The Commission accepted an argument that 'one way to secure a sustainable reduction in earnings inequality without damaging economic performance is to improve the productivity of those working in low paying industries'[236] and noted that 'many employers currently pursuing a high productivity strategy thought they were being undermined by competitors' reliance on low-paid employment',[237] but concluded that it should be guided in its approach by the need to 'avoid putting jobs or prices at longer-term risk'.[238]

The initial rate recommended by the Commission was below an employment-weighted average of the rates last set by wages councils in the early 1990s.[239] Moreover, a precondition for setting even this rate was, in the view of the Commission, the weakness of collective bargaining in the sectors concerned, which would have the effect of nullifying any knock-on effect upon wage differentials. Because of the decline of national level collective bargaining and the absence of enterprise-level collective bargaining in most low-paying firms, 'for the majority of enterprises there will be no employees likely to be directly touched by the National Minimum Wage, and therefore the question of the restoration of differentials should not be a major issue'.[240] In the event, the Secretary of State set an even lower rate, the economic impact of which has so far been slight. In its *Fourth Report*, published in 2003, the Commission reported that 'we found no significant impact, positive or negative, of the National Minimum Wage on productivity . . . the introduction of the National Minimum Wage had not provided a boost to productivity, but neither had it led to a general increase in unit labour costs'.[241] An independent assessment of the impact of the minimum wage, published in 2003, likewise concluded that it had had little effect on either business practice or productivity, and, conversely, had not made a significant contribution to poverty reduction.[242] Thus as in the case of working time regulation, the evidence, to date, is that the statutory minimum wage is not acting as a Fabian 'national minimum', capable of guaranteeing subsistence while also promoting societal efficiency.

5. Conclusion: Social Rights as the Juridical Expression of Capabilities

The overview of contemporary developments in British labour which we have just provided suggests that a clear alternative to the neoliberal agenda has yet to emerge, but that there are many signs of renewal and of innovation in the forms of

[234] Low Pay Commission, *The National Minimum Wage. First Report of the Low Pay Commission* (London: LPC, 1998), at para. 6.1.   [235] Ibid., para. 6.3.
[236] Ibid., para. 6.43.   [237] Ibid., para. 6.44.   [238] Ibid., para. 6.52.
[239] See ibid., para. 6.108.   [240] Ibid., para. 6.23.
[241] Low Pay Commission, *The National Minimum Wage. Fourth Report of the Low Pay Commission, Building on Success* (London: LPC, 2003), at para. 2.128.
[242] R. Dickens and A. Manning, 'Minimum wage, minimum impact', in R. Dickens et al. (eds.) *The Labour Market Under New Labour* (London: Palgrave, 2003) 201–213.

labour market regulation. The aim of this final section is to see whether a common, unifying thread can be found for these emergent developments, building on the analysis of capabilities in the *Supiot Report*.

As we have seen, the social legislation which emerged from the mid-twentieth century welfare state embodied a particular notion of citizenship centred on the concept of employment. Social security legislation—social insurance and social assistance—addressed the risks which arose from the dependence of the vast majority of the population on wages for subsistence. The aim of stabilizing employment through collective bargaining and employment policy was to avoid a situation in which the costs of dealing with insecurity then fell entirely on the social security system. The catastrophic experience of Speenhamland was now reinterpreted as the inevitable consequence of the de-institutionalization of the labour market which occurred at the turn of the nineteenth century. Karl Polanyi's *The Great Transformation*, the first version of which appeared in 1944, saw the old poor law as having 'sheltered' the rural poor 'from the full force of the market mechanism'. However, a policy 'which proclaimed the "right to live" whether a man earned a living wage or not' was bound to fail, in the process discrediting the traditional objectives of the poor relief system.[243] The solution, for Polanyi and others, lay in the institutional re-regulation of the labour market which accompanied the construction of the welfare state. As a result, the first social rights were instituted as part of a wider effort to regulate the market mechanism.

But these were not rights which bore the character of claims in the manner of private law. A striking feature of British social legislation of this period was how few justiciable legal rights it conferred upon individuals, either as workers or as recipients of social security benefits. This was no accident. Writing in the late 1940s,[244] T.H. Marshall argued that the concept of citizenship consisted of three parts: the civil, the political and the social. The civil element 'is composed of the rights necessary for individual freedom—liberty of the person, freedom of speech, thought and faith, the right to own property and to conclude valid contracts, and the right to justice',[245] and was associated above all with the courts. Political rights were 'the right to participate in the exercise of political power, as a member of a body invested with political authority or as an elector of the members of such a body';[246] these rights were the province of the national legislature and local government. Finally, the social element 'covered the whole range from the right to a modicum of economic welfare and security to the right to share in the full in the social heritage and to live the life of a civilized being according to the standards prevailing in society', rights which were expressed through 'the educational system and the social services'.[247] Marshall caught the spirit of the time in arguing that social rights occupied a sphere largely beyond the reach of juridical mechanisms.

---

[243] K. Polanyi, *The Great Transformation: The Political and Economic Origins of our Time* (Boston, MA: Beacon Press, 1957) at 80.

[244] T.H. Marshall, 'Citizenship and social class', reprinted in T.H. Marshall and T. Bottomore, *Citizenship and Social Class* (London: Pluto Press, 1992) (originally published 1949).

[245] Ibid., at p. 8.   [246] Ibid.   [247] Ibid.

Part of Marshall's thinking was the claim that the three components of citizen-ship—the civil, the political and the social—were not only conceptually discrete; they were subject to distinct phases in the evolution of the law. Thus 'it is possible, without doing too much violence to historical accuracy, to assign the formative period in the life of each to a different century—civil rights to the eighteenth, political to the nineteenth and social to the twentieth'.[248] In Marshall's view, there had been a time when 'these three strands were woven into a single thread'. Although, in feudal society, 'status was the hallmark of class and the measure of inequality', institutions had nevertheless existed to give expression to 'social rights which had been rooted in membership of the village community, the town and the guild'.[249] It was the process of economic development, beginning in the late Middle Ages and accelerating during the seventeenth and eighteenth centuries, which eroded these institutions and led to the eclipse of social rights during the period of industrialization.

Marshall supported the absence of a clear legal framework for many of the social welfare provisions created at that time. The legal form of social rights differed, he argued, from that of civil and political rights: in relation to the receipt of welfare services, 'the rights of the citizen cannot be precisely defined . . . A modicum of legally enforceable rights may be granted, but what matters to the citizen is the superstructure of legitimate expectations'.[250] In particular the principle of universal access to health and education services took the concrete form of state provision funded by general taxation and delivered through public employ-ment—so-called 'collective consumption'. This was in contrast to individual civil rights which Marshall saw as 'an eighteenth century achievement . . . in large measure the work of the courts'. Civil rights, Marshall thought, were 'intensely individual, and that is why they harmonized with the individualistic phase of capitalism'.[251] The social rights of the twentieth century, by contrast, *displaced* market relations: the process of 'incorporating social rights in the status of citizenship' involved 'creating a universal right to real income which is not proportionate to the market value of the claimant'.[252]

Marshall was also aware that social rights could be seen quite differently, that is to say, as a mechanism for instituting the market order:

Social rights in their modern form imply an invasion of contract by status, the subordination of market price to social justice, the replacement of the free bargain by the declaration of rights. But are these principles quite foreign to the practice of the market today, or are they there already, entrenched within the contract system itself? I think it is clear that they are.[253]

This was true, for example, of collective bargaining, which had a dual nature as 'a normal peaceful market operation' which also gave expression to 'the right of the

---

[248] T.H. Marshall, 'Citizenship and social class', reprinted in T.H. Marshall and T. Bottomore, *Citizenship and Social Class* (London: Pluto Press, 1992) (originally published 1949), at p. 10.
[249] Ibid., at p. 9.   [250] Ibid., at p. 34.   [251] Ibid., at p. 26.
[252] Ibid., at p. 28.   [253] Ibid., at p. 40.

citizen to a minimum standard of civilized living'.[254] But in this respect, collective bargaining was something of an exception; in most respects, the legislation of the welfare state was characterized by 'a basic conflict between social rights and market value'.[255]

Since Marshall wrote his Cambridge lectures, many of the institutions of the welfare state which he described, including collective bargaining, have been weakened in the name of greater 'flexibility' or the application of 'market forces'. But the very same individualization which this process has engendered has now given rise to a need for a new form of social rights to guarantee the effective conditions for the functioning of the modern labour market. These are social rights of the type which have been articulated in the context of the continuing debate over the constitutional structure of the European Union. It is no accident that one of the guiding principles of the European Union is the creation of an integrated, transnational economic space in Europe. The social rights contained in the Charter of Fundamental Rights agreed at the Nice Summit in 2001, even if, as yet, they are not fully justiciable,[256] are perhaps the most concrete expression of the idea that economic integration and social regulation are mutually complementary aspects of a process of market construction. The adoption of the Charter is not an isolated event in the development of the EU. In contrast to the priority long granted by the English common law to civil and political rights, the European Court of Justice has consistently found that social rights do not have to yield to the economic policy goal of an integrated market; the two are conjoined.[257] Thus it could be said that the emerging European market order incorporates a set of core social rights.

More precisely, constitutionalized social rights can be thought of as the juridical instantiation of the concept of capability. The attempt to link the concept of capability to social rights originates in the report on the *Transformation of Work and the Future of Labour Law in Europe* which was prepared for the European Commission by a group led by Alain Supiot.[258] The *Supiot Report* argued that a capability-based approach would help to overcome the opposition between

---

[254] Ibid.   [255] Ibid., at p. 42.

[256] On the Charter of Nice, see generally T. Hervey and J. Kenner (eds.) *Economic and Social Rights under the EU Charter of Fundamental Rights* (Oxford: Hart, 2003) and for a discussion of the position of the rights contained in the Charter in the light of the institutional changes proposed in the course of 2004 by the Convention set up to design a constitution for the EU, see B. Bercusson, 'Episodes on the path towards the European social model: the EU Charter of Fundamental Rights and the Convention on the Future of Europe', in C. Barnard, S. Deakin and G. Morris (eds.) *The Future of Labour Law: Liber Amicorum Bob Hepple* (Oxford: Hart, 2004) 179–199.

[257] This is a theme running through the case law of the ECJ from Case 43/75 *Defrenne* v. *Sabena (No. 2)* [1976] ECR 455 to Case C-67/96 *Albany International* v. *Stichting Bedrijfspensioenfonds Textielindustrie* [1999] ECR-I 5751. See generally S. Deakin, 'Labour law as market regulation: the economic foundations of European social policy' in P. Davies, S. Sciarra, S. Simitis and M. Weiss (eds.) *European Community Labour Law: Principles and Perspectives. Liber Amicorum Lord Wedderburn* (Oxford: Clarendon Press, 1997) 63–93.

[258] A. Supiot (ed.) *Au delà de l'emploi*, op. cit.

'security' and 'flexibility' which had been established in neoliberal critiques of labour law and the welfare state, and provide a basis for 'real freedom of choice' in relation to labour market participation. This analysis was further developed in a paper published in *Droit Social* by the economist Robert Salais, one of the members of the Supiot group.[259]

At the heart of the *Supiot Report's* analysis is the claim that the increasing flexibilization and individualization of work necessitate the establishment of a 'convention of trust' as the basis for the governance of the employment relationship.[260] The importance of trust in this context lies in the growing influence of flexibility both in production and in the movement of individuals between jobs and careers across the life cycle. Radical uncertainty creates a set of conditions in which the effectiveness of the employment relationship depends upon the presence of goodwill trust, in the sense of both parties being willing to perform over and above the express terms of their contract.[261] At the same time, this is a high-risk strategy which exposes each side to the risk of non-cooperation or 'opportunism'. The question is, given the high-risk strategy which is implicit in the pursuit of goodwill trust, how is it achieved? The role of goodwill trust extends, in Alan Fox's seminal analysis, 'beyond contract',[262] to encompass a degree of open-ended cooperation with expected returns only being realized over a long period. As a result, 'in the context of flexibility, the governance of employment amounts to more than just the management of opportunism; it must provide room for creative action on the part of the social partners, a space for the exercise of freedom'.[263]

Factors which are important in creating positive expectations of future performance may be expected to include fairness of treatment, job satisfaction, high quality of work environment and, particularly, income and job security. The scope for determining these factors depends both on the conditions within a given enterprise, but also on those within the wider environment consisting of the firm, its supply chains, the markets in which the firm operates, and the wider economy of which it forms a part. From this perspective, the issue is not simply whether regulatory intervention can cure particular market failures, but rather, how successful the regulatory framework is in creating an environment which is favourable to the emergence of high-trust employment relationships. More specifically, the question is how far labour standards and social rights, by providing the conditions for investments in labour quality, may contribute to dynamic efficiency in the sense of the capacity of a firm or other productive system, such as a network or district of linked enterprises, to respond effectively to changes in its trading environment, and in particular in the sense of its capacity for innovation.

---

[259] R. Salais, 'Libertés du travail et capacités: pour une construction européenne?', op. cit.

[260] A. Supiot, *Au delà de l'emploi*, op. cit., at p. 271.

[261] D. Marsden, 'Employment policy implications of new management systems' (1996) 9 *Labour* 17–61.

[262] A. Fox, *Beyond Contract: Work, Power and Trust Relations* (London: Allen & Unwin, 1974).

[263] Supiot, *Au delà de l'emploi*, op. cit., at pp. 270–271.

The idea of capabilities as substantive economic freedoms provides the foundation for this new conceptualization of social rights. Social rights should be understood as *institutionalized forms of capabilities which provide individuals with the means to realize the potential of their resource endowments and thereby achieve a higher level of economic functioning*. Social rights are therefore part of a wider set of institutional preconditions for individual economic self-sufficiency and for the sustainability of the flexible forms of production which increasingly characterize modern economies.

Amartya Sen has not sought to develop a juridical theory which might give some institutional shape to the capability concept, beyond insisting that his 'capability approach' does not prescribe any particular set of outcomes for a given society or group of societies. The high level of generality and theoretical abstraction of the capability approach lends itself to adaptations which may be far from Sen's initial formulation; the *Supiot Report* is perhaps one example. In the *Supiot Report*, the capability concept appears in the context of a discussion of the meaning of labour market flexibility.[264] The *Report* notes that 'flexibility' is frequently associated with greater variability in the application of social protection and labour standards, and thereby appears to be opposed to 'security'. However, this view, it is argued, overlooks the degree to which the capabilities of an individual depend on them having access to the means they need to realize their life goals. These include guarantees of a certain minimum standard of living and the resources needed to maintain an 'active security' in the face of economic and social risks, such as those arising from technological change and uncertainty in labour and product markets. Thus 'real freedom of action' for entrepreneurs, in the form of protection of property rights and recognition of managerial prerogative, has its equivalent in guarantees for the development of human resources for workers. However, these, the *Report* suggests, would not necessarily take the same form as the 'passive protections' traditionally provided, in twentieth-century welfare states, against unemployment and other interruptions to earnings. 'Protection against' social risks is not the same as mechanisms aimed to maintain 'security in the face of' risks:

We can understand the fundamental difference between protection, on the one hand, and security in the face of risks, on the other, by seeing that the latter includes but goes beyond the former. The capacity to work flexibly is conditional upon being able to deal with the consequences of risks. Protective regulations, because of the essentially negative way in which they are formulated, go against this kind of learning process. Security in the face of risk, on the other hand, is about providing the individual with the means to anticipate, at any given moment, long-term needs . . . Thus guarantees of minimum living standards (for example, that each person should have an effective right to housing, and not just to a minimum income), far from being undermined by the need for flexibility, should be reinforced by virtue of this need, and, if anything, more clearly and concretely defined as a result.[265]

---

[264] See Supiot, *Au delà de l'emploi*, op. cit., ch. 7, in particular at pp. 267–291: 'Flexibilité du travail et capacités des personnes'.   [265] Ibid., at p. 278.

Phrased in this way, the capability concept can be understood as an answer, or perhaps the beginning of an answer, to the neoliberal critique of labour and social security law. That holds, among other things, that regulation which interferes with freedom of contract upsets the process of mutual learning and adjustment which is implicit in market relations. As we have seen, as Hayek put it, private law is the precondition of the market order in the sense that without the guarantees which private law provides, individuals are not free to use their own information and knowledge for their own purposes. By contrast, public or regulatory law, which Hayek regarded as consisting of specific commands and directions aimed at the substantive redistribution of resources, introduces an illegitimate form of interference *by the state*. Where this occurs, the 'spontaneous order' of the market is upset, and a certain part of the advantages to individuals and society alike of a market order, in terms of a higher degree of specialization and a more extensive division of labour, are lost.

The version of the capability approach which we are outlining here offers a response which is based on the *market-creating* function of the rules of social law. In order to participate effectively in a market order, individuals require more than formal access to the institutions of property and contract. They need to be provided with the economic means to realize their potential: these include social guarantees of housing, education and training, as well as legal institutions which prescribe institutionalized discrimination. Mechanisms of this kind, by extending labour market participation on the part of otherwise excluded or disadvantaged groups, widen the scope of the market and thereby benefit all those who participate in it—in the sense used by Hayek, through participation in the market, economic agents benefit not simply from the use and exercise of their own knowledge, but from *that of others*.

Contrary to the prescription advanced by Hayek, social rights are crucial for both economic efficiency and social justice. Properly constituted, such rights create a balance of power in the workplace, in organizations and in the wider society. This in turn improves the creation, development and use of productive resources, and prevents their dissipation in unemployment and poverty. For these reasons it is necessary to have laws which legitimize and promote the role of trade unions and collective bargaining, on the one hand, and establish legally binding minimum terms and conditions of employment, the provision of health care, education and social support, and full employment as a primary policy objective, on the other.

As we have seen, this is not the same thing as saying that all extant forms of labour law are, necessarily, efficient. But it is to argue for a role for social rights which are understood as legal entitlements and not simply as technical rules of economic coordination. The need for laws and institutions guaranteeing workers' rights is denied by neo-liberals who claim that unconstrained markets deliver economic justice. But for some labour lawyers, too, the role of legal regulation should be confined so as to avoid the creation of unnecessary 'rigidities'. Hugh Collins writes:

The tasks of facilitating and channeling the flexible employment model appear in some respects to be more complex and demanding than traditional objectives for labour law. In the past, labour law aimed to protect employees from particular market outcomes either by granting inalienable legal rights, such as a minimum wage, maximum hours, and protection from unfair dismissal, or by promoting collective bargaining in order to adjust market outcomes. But regulating for competitiveness has the bolder objective of facilitating changes in the organization of the workplace that entail a transformation in the nature of the employment relation.[266]

There can be little disagreement with Collins regarding the benefits to be derived from close cooperation in production. Not only does it allow for the close working together which is needed to raise and maintain productivity, but it also fuels learning within organizations by which new information is generated, new knowledge is created and diffused, and product, process and organizational innovations are encouraged. The resulting operational and dynamic efficiencies are crucial determinants of competitive success, and the ability to create new opportunities and respond quickly and flexibly to changing circumstances. In turn, these fuel the prosperity which forms the basis for long-term income and employment security. Close cooperation between workers and management is therefore a potent force for improving industrial performance.

However, it is essential to recall the lessons of labour law's pluralist heritage: it does not follow from the requirement of cooperation that the interests of managers and workers are *identical*.[267] No doubt, managers and workers have common interests in the present and future prosperity of their organization because it determines both parties' income and job security. But this mutuality cannot extend to the distribution of the income generated by the organization because what one gets the others cannot have. Further, as value added is a joint product of the activity of all those involved in production, there is no objective method by which the contribution of any individual can be identified and suitably rewarded. In these circumstances, it is unlikely that workers will willingly accept the argument that the terms and conditions of their employment should be *unilaterally* determined by management or by an abstract appeal to market forces.

---

[266] H. Collins, 'Regulating the employment relation for competitiveness' (2001) 30 *Industrial Law Journal* 17–47. See also ibid. at 47: 'regulation on distributive grounds, such as family-friendly policies and the National Minimum Wage can only be pursued . . . to the extent that they do not obstruct the development of flexible employment relations or undermine their stability'; and see also H. Collins, 'Is there a third way in labour law?' in J. Conaghan, R.M. Fischl and K. Klare (eds.) *Labour Law in an Era of Globalisation: Transformative Practices and Possibilities* (Oxford: Oxford University Press, 2002) 449–469.

[267] On 'pluralism' in labour law and industrial relations law, see Lord Wedderburn, 'The new policies in industrial relations law', in P. Fosh and C. Littler (eds.) *Industrial Relations and the Law in the 1980s: Issues and Future Trends* (Aldershot: Gower, 1985) 22–63, in particular at 32–4.

In an economy characterized by wage dependence and 'formal' freedom for labour, it is inevitable that the standard of living of workers and their families is a primary consideration in workers' decisions regarding the acceptance of the terms and conditions of employment offered by employers.

Nor can the wider role of social rights in underpinning the operation of labour markets be neglected. Here, it is instructive to consider what a capability approach might look like in the absence of social rights and guarantees. The 'prehistory' of the concept of capability suggests the need for extreme care here. For most of the period of the poor law, notions of 'able-bodiedness' were derived from the existence of a duty to work which the law imposed on those without property. Social insurance carved out a limited series of exceptions to this principle, based on a model of the breadwinner wage which now increasingly lacks legitimacy even if, at the same time, there seems to be no clear alternative to it. As social insurance has declined, there has been a revival of laws imposing draconian work incentives on the unemployed. The withdrawal of benefits from the unemployed, now termed 'jobseekers', who refuse work on the grounds of its unsuitability or low level of remuneration is a policy which successive governments, Conservative and Labour, have followed during the 1990s. This is the background, at least in the UK, against which the capability debate is currently being played out: a neoliberal-inspired *activation policy*, which is in many respects the polar opposite of the policy of full employment which it has replaced. Full employment, in its classic, Beveridgian sense, implied a set of measures to control and stabilize the labour supply. The policy of 'a high employment rate', by contrast, aims to increase numbers in employment even if this is carried out at the cost of creating categories of low paid and 'flexible' work which do not provide access to a living wage. Deregulation of terms and conditions of employment goes hand in hand with the restriction of the conditions under which social security benefits are made available. For the time being, contemporary policy is closer to the old, pre-1834 poor law, in the use being made of tax credits and other forms of wage subsidization which echo Speenhamland, than it is to the late Victorian institutionalization of the workhouse and labour yard. Yet it was precisely the same combination of rising expenditure and the use of poor relief to subsidize low wages which prompted the 1834 reforms, the last vestiges of which were swept away as recently as the 1940s.[268]

Is it possible to see in the concept of capability a basis for reversing the logic of the poor law and reinventing the welfare state, so that the duty to work is *only* imposed under circumstances where the state has provided the conditions under which individuals are equipped for *effective* labour market participation? Simply to state this proposition in such terms is to see how far removed

---

[268] The last workhouses were converted into hospitals with the creation of the National Health Service in 1946 and poor relief for the sick and aged was replaced by national assistance in 1948. See Chapter 3, above.

today's mainstream debate is from any such conception of capability, at least in Britain.[269]

The capability approach may nevertheless provide us with an essential first step in a particular way of thinking about social rights with respect to market processes. The purpose of the capability approach is not to provide a blueprint for social reform; as Sen has put it, '[i]t is not clear that there is any royal road to evaluation of economic or social policies'.[270] This insistence that there is no universally-applicable, prescriptive list of functionings and capabilities means that attention is focused instead on social choice procedures by which the content of capability sets can be collectively determined in particular contexts. In that sense, a capability-based approach to labour market regulation is compatible with the aims of the kind of 'reflexive' labour law which seeks to reconcile social protection with the requirements of a market order.

A capability approach to labour market regulation could justify a wide range of legal relations or 'social rights' requiring substantial policy intervention in the labour market and elsewhere, in order to guarantee that individuals are equipped with what a given polity regards as the minimum necessary capability set to participate in society. This stands in contrast to a pure market mechanism which is based exclusively upon a process of resource allocation according to voluntary transactions between (often competing) individuals, without specific reference to the resulting 'quality of life' either of those engaged in the transaction or of third parties. In this way, the capability approach may provide a basis for resolving the uncomfortable relationship between on the one hand, social rights, and on the other, a dynamic market economy—thus transcending rather than reinforcing the dilemma famously identified by T.H. Marshall.

More precisely, there are several ways in which a capability approach might be helpful in this regard. In thinking about social rights in a manner influenced by Sen, we can discern two categories of such rights: (1) social rights as immediate claims to *resources* (financial benefits such as welfare payments) and (2) social rights as particular forms of *procedural* or institutionalized interaction (such as rules governing workplace relations, collective bargaining and corporate governance). In relating to the first of these categories, we can think of social rights simply as claims to commodities which can then be converted by individuals into functionings or potential functionings (capabilities). The provision of sick pay, maternity pay, or social welfare benefits are social rights in a quite traditional, well-recognized sense.

---

[269] But not, for example, in the Nordic systems, which operate according to a version of the duty to work which is very similar to that just stated in the text. On the possible contribution which this model could made to the development of the wider EU employment strategy, see A. Lyon-Caen and J. Affichard, 'From legal norms to statistical norms: employment policies put to the test of coordination' in O. De Schutter and S. Deakin (eds.) *Social Rights and Market Forces: Is the Open Coordination of Employment and Social Policies the Future of Social Europe?* (Brussels: Bruylant, 2005).

[270] *Development as Freedom*, op. cit., at p. 84.

The second category of social rights, however, links more closely to Sen's idea of 'social conversion factors'. Sen suggests that social or institutional settings shape individuals' possibilities of achieving their goals. Resources must be filtered through such frameworks as part of the process of enhancing functionings and potential functionings. Social rights, seen in this way as procedural rights, are the means by which to shape those institutional environments to ensure that all individuals are able to convert their assets—skills, capital—into positive outcomes. This works in both a direct and an indirect way. Directly, such rights can range from the provisions of anti-discrimination laws (which might aim, for example, at enabling excluded workers, such as those in ethnic or religious minorities, to engage effectively in the labour market) to more indirect forms of intervention (such as the provision of social security assistance to women with children to enable them more successfully to strike a satisfactory work–life balance.) More indirectly, the very existence of social rights can contribute to the development of a different social ethos or set of norms which may enhance individuals' functionings or potential functionings. A society which recognizes a wide range of social rights is unlikely to be a society which possesses norms and expectations which create obstacles for particular groups of individuals to engage in lives that they have reason to value. At this level, the objective of public intervention through the legal-political system is to 'seed' social conventions to the extent that they are 'taken for granted' in the way that conventions of property and contract currently are.

Given that social rights can work in this variety of ways, they should be viewed as providing a central normative goal—the enhancement of capabilities—which can structure a discourse about social and economic policy, *without presupposing* any particular outcome. This leaves open to further argument the particular form of social rights recommended by the capability approach, and the appropriate balance between mandatory rights, 'default rules', soft law, and other aspects of modern regulatory technique.[271] The capability approach is not in itself prescriptive about the mechanisms that should be employed to realize its goal and thus can be sympathetically disposed to a variety of *means* of ensuring equality of capability, including direct state provision of resources, compulsory reshaping of institutions, or voluntary action to refashion widely held norms. The relative efficiency of the systems is assessed through a context-dependent process of social learning, rather than being theoretically or dogmatically asserted. The capability approach is inherently non-dogmatic in asserting what rights individuals should possess at particular times and places. It encourages and enables a debate over the precise meaning of 'capabilities' in different circumstances, thus enabling a reflexive approach to the content of social rights in different circumstances, including in different economic and social situations.

This flexibility, of course, ensures that the capability approach may be more easily rendered compatible with a market model than other forms of social rights

---

[271] See Collins, 'Justifications and techniques', op. cit.

theory. In this way the capability approach and its form of social rights should not be seen as replacing or stifling market mechanisms. This is because the capability approach concentrates not on guaranteeing a particular, final distribution of resources in society, but rather upon aiming to enable individuals to develop their capacity to make substantive choices from a range of economic functionings, thereby making possible their productive interaction in the market. The capability concept could provide us with a guiding principle for a neo-Fabian agenda of labour market reform, one which would seek to recreate, under modern conditions, the institutional basis for reconciling individual freedom with the market order. Its incorporation into legal and institutional forms would therefore mark the beginning of a new stage in the history of labour market regulation, namely the emergence of a *law of the labour market*.

Bibliography

Adams, T. (1997) 'Market and institutional forces in industrial relations; the development of national collective bargaining, 1910–1920' *Economic History Review*, 50: 506–530.

Adams, T. (1998) 'Employers, labour, and the state in industrial relations history: a reply to Gospel' *Economic History Review*, 51: 597–605.

Alcock, P. (1989) ' "A better partnership between state and individual provision": social security into the 1990s' *Journal of Law and Society*, 16: 97–111.

Aoki, M. (2001) *Toward a Comparative Institutional Analysis* (Cambridge, MA: MIT Press).

Appelbaum, E. and Batt, R. (1994) *The New American Workplace: Transforming Work Systems in the United States* (Ithaca, NY: ILR Press).

Archbold, J.F. (1842) *The New Poor Law Amendment Act etc.* (London: Shaw).

Arkell, T. (1987) 'The incidence of poverty in England in the later seventeenth century' *Social History*, 12: 23–47.

Arrowsmith, J. (2002) 'The struggle over working time in nineteenth and twentieth century Britain' *Historical Studies in Industrial Relations*, 13: 83–117.

Ashburner, W. (1933) *Principles of Equity*, 2nd ed. by D. Browne (London: Butterworths).

Ashworth, D. (1976) 'The urban poor law', in D. Fraser (ed.) *The New Poor Law in the Nineteenth Century* (London: Macmillan), 128–148.

Atiyah, P.S. (1979) *The Rise and Fall of Freedom of Contract* (Oxford: Clarendon Press).

Atkinson, J. (1985) *Flexibility, Uncertainty and Manpower Management* IMS Report no. 89 (Brighton: Institute of Manpower Studies).

Atkinson, J. and Meager, N. (1986) *Changing Working Patterns and Practices* (London and Brighton: National Economic Development Office/Institute for Manpower Studies).

Atleson, J. (1984) *Values and Assumptions in American Labor Law* (Amherst, MA: University of Massachusetts Press).

Balkin, J. (1998) *Cultural Software: A Theory of Ideology* (New Haven, CT: Yale University Press).

Baritz, L. (1975) 'The servants of power', in G. Esland, G. Speakman and M.-A. Speakman (eds.) *People and Work* (Edinburgh: Holmes-McDougall).

Barnard, C. (1999) 'Working time in the UK' *Industrial Law Journal*, 28: 61–75.

Barnard, C. (2000) 'The Working Time Regulations 1999' *Industrial Law Journal*, 29: 167–171.

Barnard, C., Deakin, S. and Hobbs, R. (2003) 'Opting out of the 48 hour week: Employer necessity or individual choice? An empirical study of the operation of Article 18(1)(b) of the Working Time Directive in the UK' *Industrial Law Journal*, 32: 223–252.

Batt, F.R. (1929) *The Law of Master and Servant* (London: Pitman).

Bayliss, F.R. (1962) *British Wages Councils* (Oxford: Blackwell).

Beatson, J. (1995) 'Public law influences in contract law', in J. Beatson and D. Friedmann (eds.) *Good Faith and Fault in Contract Law* (Oxford: Clarendon Press), 263–288.

Beier, A. (1985) *Masterless Men. The Vagrancy Problem in England 1560–1640* (London: Methuen).

Bentham, J. (2001) 'Essay II. Fundamental Positions in Regard to the Making of Provision for the Indigent Poor', in *Essays on the Subject of the Poor Laws* (1796), reproduced in M. Quinn (ed.) *The Collected Works of Jeremy Bentham. Writings on the Poor Laws*, Vol. I (Oxford: Clarendon Press).

Bercusson, B. (1978) *Fair Wages Resolutions* (London: Mansell).

Bercusson, B. (2004) 'Episodes on the path towards the European social model: the EU Charter of Fundamental Rights and the Convention on the Future of Europe', in C. Barnard, S. Deakin and G. Morris (eds.) *The Future of Labour Law: Liber Amicorum Bob Hepple* (Oxford: Hart), 179–199.

Berg, M. (1985) *The Age of Manufactures: Industry, Innovation and Work in Britain 1700–1820* (London: Fontana).

Bertola, G. and Ichino, A. (1995) 'Crossing the river: a comparative perspective on Italian employment dynamics' *Economic Policy: A European Forum*, 21: 359–415.

Best, M. (1990) *The New Competition: Institutions of Industrial Restructuring* (Cambridge: Polity).

Beveridge, W. (1909) *Unemployment: A Problem of Industry* (London: Longmans, Green & Co.).

Beveridge, W. (1944) *Full Employment in a Free Society* (London: Liberal Publications Department) 2nd ed., 1967 (London: Allen and Unwin).

Biagini, E. (1987) 'British trade unions and popular political economy 1860–1880' *Historical Journal*, 30: 811–840.

Biernacki, R. (1995) *The Fabrication of Labour: Britain and Germany, 1640–1914* (Berkeley, CA: University of California Press).

Birks, P.B.H. (1985) *Introduction to the Law of Restitution* (Oxford: Clarendon Press).

Blackburn, S. (2000) ' "The harm that the sweater does lives after him": the Webbs, the responsible employer, and the minimum wage campaign, 1880–1914' *Historical Studies in Industrial Relations*, 10: 5–41.

Blackstone, W. (1979) *Commentaries on the Laws of England. A Facsimile of the First Edition of 1765–69*, edited with an introduction by S.N. Katz (Chicago, IL: University of Chicago Press).

Blaug, M. (1963) 'The myth of the old poor law and the making of the new' *Journal of Economic History*, 23: 151–184.

Blaug, M. (1964) 'The poor law Report reexamined' *Journal of Economic History*, 24: 228–245.

Blyton, P. and Turnbull, P. (1992) 'Debates, dilemmas and contradictions', in P. Blyton and P. Turnbull (eds.) *Reassessing Human Resource Management* (London: Sage Publications), 1–15.

Boyer, G. (1990) *An Economic History of the English Poor Law 1750–1850* (Cambridge: Cambridge University Press).

Boyer, G. (2004) 'The evolution of unemployment relief in Great Britain' *Journal of Interdisciplinary History*, 34: 393–433.

Brand, P. (1992) *The Making of the Common Law* (London: Hambledon).

Briggs, A. (1961) *Social Thought and Social Action: A Study of the Work of Seebohm Rowntree 1871–1954* (London: Longmans).

Brodie, D. (1996) 'The heart of the matter: mutual trust and confidence' *Industrial Law Journal*, 25: 121–136.

Brodie, D. (1998) 'Beyond exchange: the new contract of employment' *Industrial Law Journal*, 27: 79–102.

Brodie, D. (2001) 'Mutual trust and the values of the employment contract' *Industrial Law Journal*, 30: 84–100.

Brodie, D. (2002) 'Legal coherence and the employment revolution' *Law Quarterly Review*, 117: 604–625.

Brodie, D. (2003) *A History of British Labour Law 1867–1945* (Oxford: Hart).

Brown, W. and Oxenbridge, S. (2004) 'Trade unions and collective bargaining: laws and the future of collectivism', in C. Barnard, S. Deakin and G. Morris (eds.) *The Future of Labour Law: Liber Amicorum Bob Hepple* (Oxford: Hart), 63–77.

Brown, W. and Wadwhani, S. (1990) 'The economic effects of industrial relations legislation since 1979' *National Institute Economic Review*, 131: 57–70.

Brown, W., Deakin, S. and Ryan, P. (1997) 'The effects of British industrial relations legislation 1979–1997' *National Institute Economic Review*, 161: 69–83.

Brown, W., Deakin, S., Hudson, M., Pratten, C. and Ryan, P. (1998) *The Individualisation of Employment Contracts in Britain* EMAR Research Series no. 4 (London: Department of Trade and Industry).

Brown, W., Deakin, S., Nash, D. and Oxenbridge, S. (2000) 'The employment contract: from collective procedures to individual rights' *British Journal of Industrial Relations*, 38: 611–629.

Browne, J., Deakin, S. and Wilkinson, F. (2004) 'Capabilities, social rights, and European integration' in R. Salais and R. Villeneuve (eds.) *Towards a European Politics of Capabilities* (Cambridge: Cambridge University Press).

Buckley, F.H. (ed.) (1999) *The Fall and Rise of Freedom of Contract* (Durham, NC: Duke University Press).

Burchell, B., Deakin, S. and Honey, S. (1999) *The Employment Status of Individuals in Non-standard Employment* EMAR Research Series no. 6 (London: Department of Trade and Industry).

Burchell, B., Ladipo, D. and Wilkinson, F. (2002) (eds.) *Job Insecurity and Work Intensification* (London: Routledge).

Burn, R. (1762) *The Justice of the Peace and Parish Officer*, 7th ed. (London: Millar).

Burnett, J. (1994) *Idle Hands. The Experience of Unemployment 1790–1990* (London: Routledge).

Cairns, J. (1989) 'Blackstone, Kahn-Freund and the contract of employment' *Law Quarterly Review*, 105: 300–314.

Campus, A. (1987) 'Marginalist economics', in J. Eatwell, M. Milgate and P. Newman (eds.) *The New Palgrave: A Dictionary of Economics*, Vol. 3 (London, Macmillan).

Cappelli, P. (2000) 'Market-mediated employment: the historical context', in M. Blair and T. Kochan (eds.) *The New Relationship. Human Capital in the American Corporation* (Washington DC: Brookings Institution), 66–90.

Charlwood, A. (2004) 'Annual review: the new generation of union leaders and the prospects for union revival' *British Journal of Industrial Relations*, 42: 379–397.

Chitty, J. (1812) *A Practical Treatise on the Law Relating to Apprentices and Journeymen, and to Exercising Trades* (London: W. Clarke & Sons).

Church, R. (1986) *The History of the British Coal Industry*. Vol. 3, *1830–1913: Victorian Pre-eminence* (Oxford: Clarendon Press).

Clark, A. (2000) 'The new poor law and the breadwinner wage: contrasting assumptions' *Journal of Social History*, 34: 262–281.

Clark, G. (1982) 'Recent developments in working patterns' *Employment Gazette*, 92: 409–416.

Clark, J. and Wedderburn, Lord (1983) 'Modern labour law: problems, functions and policies', in Lord Wedderburn, R. Lewis and J. Clark (eds.) *Labour Law and Industrial Relations: Building on Kahn-Freund* (Oxford: Clarendon Press), 147–242.

Clarke, L. (1992) *Building Capitalism: Historical Change and the Labour Process in the Production of the Built Environment* (London: Routledge).

Clarkson, L. (1982) 'Wage labour 1500–1800', in K. Brown (ed.) *The English Labour Movement 1700–1951* (Dublin: Gill and Macmillan), 1–27.

Clay, H. (1929) *The Problem of Industrial Relations* (London: Macmillan).

Clegg, H. (1985) *A History of British Trade Unions since 1889*. Vol. 2, *1911–1933* (Oxford: Clarendon Press).

Clegg, H., Fox, A. and Thompson, A. (1964) *A History of British Trade Unions since 1889* Vol. I (Oxford: Clarendon Press).

Coase, R.H. (1937) 'The nature of the firm' *Economica* (NS), 4: 386–405.

Coase, R.H. (1988) 'The firm, the market and the law', in R.H. Coase, *The Firm, the Market and the Law* (Chicago: University of Chicago Press), 1–31.

Cohen, P. (1938) *Unemployment Insurance and Assistance in Britain* (London: Harrap).

Collins, H. (1986) 'Market power, bureaucratic power and the contract of employment' *Industrial Law Journal*, 15: 1–15.

Collins, H. (1990) 'Ascription of legal responsibility to groups in complex patterns of economic integration' *Modern Law Review*, 53: 731–744.

Collins, H. (1990) 'Independent contractors and the challenge of vertical disintegration to employment protection law' *Oxford Journal of Legal Studies*, 10: 353–380.

Collins, H. (1997) 'The productive disintegration of labour law' *Industrial Law Journal*, 26: 295–309.

Collins, H. (2000) 'Employment rights of casual workers' *Industrial Law Journal*, 29: 73–78.

Collins, H. (2000) 'Justifications and techniques of legal regulation of the employment relation', in H. Collins, P. Davies and R. Rideout (eds.) *Legal Regulation of the Employment Relation* (Deventer: Kluwer), 3–27.

Collins, H. (2001) 'Regulating the employment relation for competitiveness' *Industrial Law Journal*, 30: 17–47.

Collins, H. (2002) 'Is there a third way in labour law?' in J. Conaghan, R.M. Fischl and K. Klare (eds.) *Labour Law in an Era of Globalisation: Transformative Practices and Possibilities* (Oxford: Oxford University Press), 449–469.

Collins, H. (2003) *Employment Law* (Oxford: Oxford University Press).

Colquhoun, P. (1799) *The State of Indigence, and the Situation of the Casual Poor in the Metropolis, Explained* (London: Baldwin).

Comyns Carr, A.S., Garnett, G.H.S. and Taylor, J.H. (1912) *National Insurance*, 3rd ed. (London: Macmillan).

Cornish, W.R. and Clark, G. de N. (1989) *Law and Society in England 1750–1950* (London: Sweet & Maxwell).

Costabile, L. (1998) 'Ordine spontaneo o ordine negoziato? Conflitti e resoluzione dei conflitti nella nuova teoria economica delle istituzione', in A. Amendola (ed.) *Istituzione e mercato del lavoro* (Rome: Edizione Scientifiche Italiane), 1–66.

Crafts, N.F.R. (1985) *British Economic Growth During the Industrial Revolution* (Oxford: Clarendon Press).

Craig, C., Rubery, J., Tarling, R. and Wilkinson, F. (1982) *Labour Market Structure, Industrial Organization and Low Pay* (Cambridge: Cambridge University Press).

Craig, C., Rubery, J., Tarling, R. and Wilkinson, F. (1985) 'Economic, social and political factors in the operation of the labour market', in B. Roberts, R. Finnegan and D. Gallie (eds.) *New Approaches to Economic Life* (Manchester: University of Manchester Press), 105–123.

Cranston, R. (1985) *Legal Foundations of the Welfare State* (London: Weidenfeld and Nicolson).

Creighton, C. (1999) 'The rise and decline of the "male breadwinner family" in Britain' *Cambridge Journal of Economics*, 23: 519–541.

Cully, M., Woodland, S., O'Reilly, A. and Dix, G. (1999) *Britain at Work, as Revealed by the 1998 Workplace Employee Relations Survey* (London: Routledge).

Dalton, M. (1618 onwards) *The Country Justice: Containing the Practice, Duty and Power of the Justices of the Peace, as Well In as Out of their Sessions* (London: various editions).

Daniel, W.W. (1976) *Wage Determination in Industry* (London: PEP).

Daunton, M. (1995) *Progress and Poverty: An Economic and Social History of Britain 1700–1850* (Oxford: Oxford University Press).

David, P. (1985) 'Clio and the economics of QWERTY' *American Economic Review*, 75: 332–337.

David, P. (1994) 'Why are institutions the "carriers of history"? Path dependence and the evolution of conventions, organizations and institutions' *Structural Change and Economic Dynamics*, 5: 205–220.

Davidov, G. (2001) 'The three axes of employment relationships. A characterisation of workers in need of protection', SJD Thesis, University of Toronto.

Davies, P. and Freedland, M. (1980) *Labour Law: Text and Materials* (London: Weidenfeld and Nicolson); 2nd ed., 1984.

Davies, P. and Freedland, M. (1983) 'Introduction', in P. Davies and M. Freedland (eds.) *Kahn-Freund's Labour and the Law* (London: Stevens).

Davies, P. and Freedland, M. (1993) *Labour Legislation and Public Policy* (Oxford: Clarendon Press).

Davies, P. and Freedland, M. (2004) 'Changing perspectives on the employment relationship in British labour law', in C. Barnard, S. Deakin and G. Morris (eds.) *The Future of Labour Law: Liber Amicorum Bob Hepple* (Oxford: Hart), 129–158.

Davis, J.E. (1868) *The Master and Servant Act 1867* (London: Butterworths).

De Schweinitz, K. (1961) *England's Road to Social Security. From the Statute of Labourers in 1349 to the Beveridge Report of 1942* (New York: A.S. Barnes & Co.).

De Schutter, O. and Deakin, S. (eds.) (2005) *Social Rights and Market Forces: Is the Open Coordination of Employment and Social Policies the Future of Social Europe?* (Brussels: Bruylant).

Deacon, A. (1977) 'Concession and coercion: the politics of unemployment insurance in the twenties', in A. Briggs and J. Saville (eds.) *Essays in Labour History 1918–1939* (London: Croom Helm), 9–35.

Deakin, S. (1990) 'Equality under a market order: the Employment Act 1989' *Industrial Law Journal*, 19: 1–23.

Deakin, S. (1990) 'The floor of rights in European labour law' *New Zealand Journal of Industrial Relations*, 15: 219–240.

Deakin, S. (1997) 'Labour law as market regulation; the economic foundations of European social policy', in P. Davies, S. Sciarra, S. Simitis and M. Weiss (eds.) *European Community Labour Law: Principles and Perspectives. Liber Amicorum Lord Wedderburn* (Oxford: Clarendon Press), 63–93.

Deakin, S. (1999) 'Organisational change, labour flexibility and the contract of employment in Britain', in S. Deery and R. Mitchell (eds.) *Employment Relations, Individualisation and Union Exclusion: An International Study* (Annandale, NSW: Federation Press, 1999), 130–152.

Deakin, S. (2001) 'The changing concept of the employer in labour law' *Industrial Law Journal*, 30: 72–84.

Deakin, S. (2002) 'Evolution for our time: a theory of legal memetics' *Current Legal Problems*, 55: 1–42.

Deakin, S. (2003) 'Interpreting employment contracts: judges, employers and workers', in S. Worthington (ed.) *Commercial Law and Commercial Practice* (Oxford: Hart), 433–455.

Deakin, S. and Browne, J. (2003) 'Social rights and the market order: adapting the capability approach', in T. Hervey and J. Kenner (eds.) *Economic and Social Rights in the European Charter of Fundamental Rights* (Oxford: Hart).

Deakin, S. and Morris, G. (2001) *Labour Law*, 3rd ed. (London: Butterworths).

Deakin, S. and Slinger, G. (1997) 'Hostile takeovers, corporate law and the theory of the firm' *Journal of Law and Society*, 24: 124–150.

Deakin, S. and Wilkinson, F. (1991) 'Labour law, social security and economic inequality' *Cambridge Journal of Economics*, 15: 125–148.

Deakin, S. and Wilkinson, F. (2000) ' "Capabilities", ordineo spontaneo del mercato, e diritti sociali' *Il diritto del mercato del lavoro*, 2: 317–344.

Deakin, S., Hobbs, R., Konzelmann, S. and Wilkinson, F. (2002) 'Partnership, ownership and control: the impact of corporate governance on employment relations' *Employee Relations*, 24: 335–352.

Deakin, S., Hobbs, R., Nash, D. and Slinger, G. (2003) 'Implicit contracts, takeovers and corporate governance: in the shadow of the City Code', in D. Campbell, H. Collins and J. Wightman (eds.) *Implicit Dimensions of Contract* (Oxford: Hart), 289–331.

Deaton, D. (1983) 'Unemployment', in G. Bain (ed.) *Industrial Relations in Britain* (Oxford: Blackwell), 237–262.

Dennett, D. (1995) *Darwin's Dangerous Idea: Evolution and the Meanings of Life* (Harmondsworth: Penguin).

Desmond, H. (2003) 'The generation game: pensions and retirement' *Industrial Law Journal*, 32: 218–222.

Dicey, A.V. (1905) *Lectures on the Relation between Law and Public Opinion in England in the Nineteenth Century* (London: Macmillan).

Dickens, L., Jones, M., Weekes, B. and Hart, M. (1985) *Dismissed: A Study of Unfair Dismissal and the Unfair Tribunal System* (Oxford: Blackwell).

Dickens, R. and Manning, A. (2003) 'Minimum wage, minimum impact', in R. Dickens et al. (eds.) *The Labour Market Under New Labour* (London: Palgrave), 201–213.

Digby, A. (1975) 'The labour market and the continuity of social policy after 1834: the case of the eastern counties' *Economic History Review* (NS), 28: 69–83.

Digby, A. (1976) 'The rural poor law' in D. Fraser (ed.) *The New Poor Law in the Nineteenth Century* (London: Macmillan), 149–170.

Digby, A. (1982) *The Poor Law in Nineteenth Century England and Wales* (London: Historical Association).

Dinwiddy, J. (1987) *From Luddism to the First Reform Bill: Reform in England, 1810–1832* (Oxford: Blackwell).

Dobson, C. (1980) *Masters and Journeymen: A Pre-History of Industrial Relations* (London, Croom Helm).

Dunlop, J.T. (1938) 'The movement of real and money wage rates' *Economic Journal*, 48: 413–434.

Easterbrook, F. and Fischel, D. (1991) *The Economic Structure of Corporate Law* (Cambridge, MA: Harvard University Press).

Eden, F. (1797) *The State of the Poor* (London: B. & J. White).

Elbaum, B. and Lazonick, W. (eds.) (1987) *The Decline of the British Economy* (Oxford: Clarendon Press).

Elbaum, B. and Wilkinson, F. (1979) 'Industrial relations and uneven development: a comparative study of the American and British steel industries' *Cambridge Journal of Economics*, 3: 275–303.

Elias, P. (1982) 'The structure of the employment contract' *Current Legal Problems*, 35: 95–116.

Elias, P. and Ewing, K. (1987) *Trade Union Democracy, Members' Rights and the Law* (London: Mansell).

Epstein, R. (1983) 'A common law for labor relations: a critique of the New Deal labor legislation' *Yale Law Journal*, 92: 1357–1408.

Erickson, C. (1959) *British Industrialists: Steel and Hosiery 1850–1950* (Cambridge: Cambridge University Press).

Ewald, F. (1987) 'Justice, equality, judgement: on "social justice" ', in G. Teubner (ed.) *Juridification of Social Spheres* (Berlin: de Gruyter, 91–110).

Ewing, K.D. (1998) 'The state and industrial relations: collective *laissez-faire* revisited' *Historical Studies in Industrial Relations*, 5: 1–31.

Feldman, D. (2004) 'Migrants, immigrants and welfare from the old poor law to the welfare state' *Transactions of the Royal Historical Society*, forthcoming.

Felkin, W. (1967) *History of the Machine-wrought Hosiery and Lace Manufactures* edited with an introduction by S.D. Chapman (Newton Abbot: David & Charles, 1967).

Fishman, N. (1999) ' "A vital element in British industrial relations": a Reassessment of Order 1305' *Historical Studies in Industrial Relations*, 12: 109–130.

Flanders, A. (1964) *The Fawley Productivity Agreements: A Case Study of Management and Collective Bargaining* (London: Faber).

Fögen, M.T. (2002) 'Legal history—history of the evolution of a social system. A proposal' *Rechtsgeschichte* September, English version available on line at: http://www.mpier. uni-frankfurt.de/Forschung/Mitarbeiter_Forschung/foegen-legal-history.htm.

Foster, K. (1983) 'The legal form of work in the nineteenth century: the myth of contract?', paper presented to the conference on *The History of Law, Labour and Crime*, University of Warwick.

Fox, A. (1974) *Beyond Contract: Work, Power and Trust Relations* (London: Allen & Unwin).

Fox, A. (1985) *History and Heritage: The Social Origins of the British Industrial Relations System* (London: Allen & Unwin).

Fredman, S. (1992) 'The new rights: labour law and ideology in the Thatcher years' *Oxford Journal of Legal Studies*, 12: 24–44.

Fredman, S. (1997) 'Reversing discrimination' *Law Quarterly Review*, 113: 575–600.

Fredman, S. (1997) *Women and the Law* (Oxford: Clarendon Press).

Freedland, M. (1976) *The Contract of Employment* (Oxford: Clarendon Press).

Freedland, M. (1983) 'Labour law and leaflet law: the Youth Training Scheme of 1983' *Industrial Law Journal*, 12: 220–235.

Freedland, M. (1992) 'The role of the Department of Employment—twenty years of industrial change', in W.E.J. McCarthy (ed.) *Legal Intervention in Industrial Relations: Gains and Losses* (Oxford: Blackwell), 274–295.

Freedland, M. (1995) 'The role of the contract of employment in modern labour law', in L. Betten (ed.) *The Employment Contract in Transforming Labour Relations* (Deventer: Kluwer), 17–27.

Freedland, M. (2003) *The Personal Employment Contract* (Oxford: Oxford University Press).

Freedland, M. and King, D. (2003) 'Contractual governance and illiberal contracts: some problems of contractualism as an instrument of behaviour management by agencies of government' *Cambridge Journal of Economics*, 27: 465–477.

Friedman, M. (1968) 'The role of monetary policy' *American Economic Review*, 58: 1–17.

Friedman, M. (1977) *Unemployment and Inflation* (London: Institute of Economic Affairs).

Gabora, L. (1997) 'The origin and evolution of culture and creativity' *Journal of Memetics*, 1: 1–27.

Gahan, P. (2003) 'Work, status and contract: another challenge for labour law' *Australian Journal of Labour Law*, 16: 249–258.

Gall, G. (2004) 'Trade union recognition in Britain, 1995–2002: turning a corner?' *Industrial Relations Journal*, 35: 249–270.

Gardiner, J. (2000) 'Rethinking self-sufficiency: employment, families and welfare' *Cambridge Journal of Economics*, 24: 671–689.

Gardiner, J. (2000) 'Alternative pathways to full employment' *Federation News*, 51: 25–26.

George, D. (1937) 'The Combination Laws reconsidered' *Economic Journal (Supplement) Economic History Series*, 2: 214–228.

Geremek, B. (1994) *Poverty: A History*, translated by A. Kolakowska (Oxford: Blackwell).

Gilbert, B.B. (1966) *The Evolution of National Insurance in Great Britain: The Origins of the Welfare State* (London: Michael Joseph).

Glen, R.C. (1898) *The General Orders of the Poor Law Commissioners, the Poor Law Board, and the Local Government Board relating to the Poor Law: with Explanatory Notes elucidating the Orders, Tables of Statutes, Cases and Index* (London: Knight).

Glen, W.C. (1847) *The General Consolidated Order Issued by the Poor Law Commissioners, 24th July, 1847: with a Commentary* (London: Knight).

Gordon, R. (1984) 'Critical legal histories' *Stanford Law Review*, 36: 57–125.

Gospel, H. (1998) 'Markets, institutions, and the development of national collective bargaining in Britain' *Economic History Review*, 51: 591–596.

Gospel, H. and Willman, P. (2003) 'High performance workplaces: the role of employee involvement in a modern economy. Evidence on the EU Directive establishing a general framework for informing and consulting employees' CEP Discussion Paper no. 562, February 2003 (London: LSE).

Gould, S.J. (2003) *The Structure of Evolutionary Theory* (Cambridge, MA: Belknap Press).

Granovetter, M. (1985) 'Economic action and social structure: the case of embeddedness' *American Journal of Sociology*, 91: 481–510.

Green, F. (2003) 'The demands of work', in R. Dickens, P. Gregg and J. Wadsworth (eds.) *The Labour Market Under New Labour. The State of Working Britain* (Basingstoke: Palgrave), 137–149.

Gregg, P. and Wadsworth, J. (2003) 'Workless households and the recovery', in R. Dickens, P. Gregg and J. Wadsworth (eds.) *The Labour Market Under New Labour: The State of Working Britain* (Basingstoke: Palgrave), 32–39.

Guest, D. (1987) 'Human resource management and industrial relations' *Journal of Management Studies*, 24: 503–521.

Hakim, C. (1987) 'Trends in the flexible workforce' *Employment Gazette*, 95: 549–560.

Hakim, C. (1990) 'Workforce restructuring, social insurance coverage and the black economy' *Journal of Social Policy*, 18: 471–503.

Hammond, J.L. and Hammond, B. (1913) *The Village Labourer, 1760–1832: A Study of the Government of England before the Reform Act*, 2nd ed. (London: Longmans, Green & Co.).

Hammond, J.L. and Hammond, B. (1919) *The Skilled Labourer. 1760–1832* (London: Longmans, Green & Co.), revised with an introduction by J. Rule, 1979 (London: Longman).

Hannah, L. (1974) 'Managerial innovation and the rise of the large-scale company in interwar Britain' *Economic History Review* (NS), 27: 252–270.

Hannah, L. (1983) *The Rise of the Corporate Economy*, 2nd ed. (London: Methuen).

Hansmann, H. (1996) *The Ownership of Enterprise* (Cambridge, MA: Belknap Press).

Hansmann, H. and Kraakman, R. (2004) 'What is corporate law?', in R. Kraakman, P. Davies, H. Hansmann, G. Hertig, H. Kanda, K. Hopt and E. Rock (eds.) *The Anatomy of Corporate Law: A Comparative and Functional Approach* (Oxford: Oxford University Press), 1–19.

Harkness, S. (2003) 'The household division of labour: changes in families' allocation of paid and unpaid work, 1992–2002', in R. Dickens, P. Gregg and J. Wadsworth (eds.) *The Labour Market Under New Labour: The State of Working Britain* (Basingstoke: Palgrave), 150–169.

Harris, J. (1972) *Unemployment and Politics: A Study in English Social Policy 1886–1914* (Oxford: Clarendon Press).

Harris, J. (1997) *William Beveridge: A Biography*, 2nd ed. (Oxford: Clarendon Press).

Harris, R. (2000) *Industrializing English Law: Entrepreneurship and Business Organization 1720–1844* (Cambridge: Cambridge University Press).

Harrison, R. (2000) *The Life and Times of Sidney and Beatrice Webb: The Formative Years 1858–1905* (London: Macmillan).

Hart, P. and Prais, S. (1956) 'The analysis of business concentration: a statistical approach' *Journal of the Royal Statistical Society Series A (General)*, 119: 150–191.

Harvey, C. and Press, J. (2000) 'Management and the Taff Vale strike of 1900' *Business History*, 42: 63–86.

Harvey, M. (2003) 'Productive systems, market and competition as "instituted economic process"', in B. Burchell, S. Deakin, J. Michie and J. Rubery (eds.) *Systems of Production: Markets, Organisations and Performance* (London: Routledge), 40–59.

Hay, D. (2000) 'Master and servant in England: using the law in the eighteenth and nineteenth centuries', in W. Steinmetz (ed.) *Private Law and Social Inequality in the Industrial Age: Comparing Legal Cultures in Britain, France, Germany and the United States* (Oxford: Oxford University Press), 227–264.

Hay, D. and Craven, P. (1994) 'The criminalisation of "free labour": master and servant in comparative perspective' *Slavery and Abolition*, 15: 71–101.

Hay, D. and Craven, P. (1995) 'Master and servant in England and the Empire: a comparative study' *Labour/Le Travail*, 31: 175–184.

Hayek, F.A. (1982) *Law, Legislation and Liberty. A New Statement of the Liberal Principles of Justice and Political Economy* (London: Routledge), consisting of: Vol. 1, *Rules and Order* (1973), Vol. 2, *The Mirage of Social Justice* (1976) and Vol. 3, *The Political Order of a Free People*.

Hayek, F.A. (1984) *1980s Unemployment and the Unions*, 2nd ed. (London: IEA).

Hennock, E.P. (1987) *British Social Reform and German Precedents: the Case of Social Insurance 1880–1914* (Oxford: Clarendon Press).

Hepple, B. (1981) 'A right to work?' *Industrial Law Journal*, 10: 65–83.

Hepple, B. (ed.) (1986) *The Making of Labour Law in Europe* (London: Mansell).

Hepple, B. (1995) 'The future of labour law' *Industrial Law Journal*, 24: 303–322.

Hepple, B. and Morris, G. (2002) 'The Employment Act 2002 and the crisis of individual employment rights' *Industrial Law Journal*, 31: 245–269.

Hepple, B.A. and O'Higgins, P. (1981) *Individual Employment Law*, 4th ed. (London: Sweet & Maxwell).

Hervey, T. and Kenner, J. (eds.) (2003) *Economic and Social Rights under the EU Charter of Fundamental Rights* (Oxford: Hart).

Hill, C. (1967) 'Pottage for freeborn Englishmen: attitudes to wage labour in the sixteenth and seventeenth centuries', in C.H. Feinstein (ed.) *Socialism, Capitalism and Economic Growth: Essays Presented to Maurice Dobb* (Cambridge: Cambridge University Press), 338–350.

Himmelfarb, G. (1983) *The Idea of Poverty. England in the Early Industrial Age* (New York: Knopf).

Hobsbawm, E. (1964) 'The machine breakers', in E. Hobsbawm, *Labouring Men* (London: Weidenfeld and Nicolson), 5–22.

Hobsbawm, E. (1969) *Industry and Empire* (Harmondsworth: Penguin).

Hobsbawm, E. and Rudé, G. (1973) *Captain Swing* (Harmondsworth: Penguin).

Hobson, J.A. (1922) *Economics of Unemployment* (London: Allen & Unwin).

Hodgson, G. (1998) *Economics and Utopia* (London: Routledge).

Hodgson, G. (2002) 'Darwinism in economics: from analogy to ontology' *Journal of Evolutionary Economics*, 12: 250–282.

Hodgson, G. (2002) 'The enforcement of contract and property rights: constitutive versus epiphenomenal conceptions of law', paper presented to the CRIC Polanyi conference, Manchester.

Hodgson, G. (2003) 'Darwinism and institutional economics' *Journal of Economic Issues*, 37: 85–97.

Holbrook-Jones, M. (1982) *Supremacy and Subordination of Labour: The Hierarchy of Work in the Early Labour Movement* (London: Heinemann Educational Books).

Holdsworth, W.R. (1938) *A History of English Law* (London: Methuen).

Hollway, W. (1991) *Work Psychology and Work Organisation* (London: Sage).

Holmes, O.W. Jr. (1968) *The Common Law*, ed. M. DeWolfe Howe (London: Macmillan).

Horrell, S. and Humphries, J. (1995) 'Women's labour force participation and the transition to the male breadwinner family, 1790–1865' *Economic History Review (NS)*, 43: 89–117.

Horwitz, M. (1977) *The Transformation of American Law 1780–1860* (Cambridge, MA: Harvard University Press).

Hoxie, R.F. (1915) *Scientific Management and Labour* (New York: Appleton).

Humphries, J. (1977) 'Class struggle and the persistence of the working class family' *Cambridge Journal of Economics*, 1: 241–258.

Humphries, J. (1987) ' "… The most free from objection …" The sexual division of labor and women's work in nineteenth century England' *Journal of Economic History*, 47: 929–949.

Humphries, J. (1990) 'Enclosures, common rights, and women: the proletarianization of families in the late eighteenth and early nineteenth centuries' *Journal of Economic History*, 50: 17–42.

Hutchins, B.L. and Harrison, A. (1926) *A History of Factory Legislation*, 3rd ed. (London: P.S. King).

Ibbetson, D.J. (1999) *An Historical Introduction to the Law of Obligations* (Oxford: Clarendon Press).

Ichino, A. and Ichino, P. (1998) 'A chi serve il diritto del lavoro? Riflessioni interdisciplinari sulla funzione economica e la giustificazione costituzionale dell'inderogabilitá delle norme giuslavoristiche', in A. Amendola (ed.) *Istituzione e mercato del lavoro* (Rome: Edizione Scientifiche Italiane), 67–102.

Ichniowski, C., Shaw, K. and Prennushi, G. (1997) 'The effects of human resource management practices on productivity: a study of steel finishing lines' *American Economic Review*, 87: 291–312.

Jacoby, S. (1985) *Employing Bureaucracy: Managers, Unions, and the Transformation of Work in American Industry 1900–1945* (New York: Columbia University Press).

Jacoby, S. (1985) 'The duration of indefinite employment contracts in the United States and England: an historical analysis' *Comparative Labor Law*, 10: 85–128.

Jaffe, J. (2003) 'The ambiguities of compulsory arbitration and the wartime experience of Order 1305' *Historical Studies in Industrial Relations*, 15: 1–25.

Jefferys, J. (1946) 'The denomination and character of shares' *Economic History Review*, 16: 45–55.

Jenner-Fust, H.R. (1907) *Poor Law Orders* (London: P.S. King), and *Supplement* (1912).

Jennings, I. (1936) *The Poor Law Code: Being the Poor Law Act 1930 and the Poor Law Orders Now in Force*, 2nd ed. (London: Knight).

Kahn-Freund, O. (1951) 'Servants and independent contractors' *Modern Law Review*, 14: 504–509.

Kahn-Freund, O. (1959) 'Labour law', in M. Ginsberg (ed.) *Law and Opinion in England in the 20th Century* (London: Stevens).

Kahn-Freund, O. (1967) 'A note on contract and status in labour law' *Modern Law Review*, 30: 635–644.

Kahn-Freund, O. (1978) 'Blackstone's neglected child: the contract of employment' *Law Quarterly Review*, 93: 508–528.

Karsten, P. (1997) *Heart and Head: Judge-Made Law in Nineteenth Century America* (Chapel Hill, NC: University of North Carolina Press).

Keegan, W. (1988) 'Lawson's miracle: is it all done with mirrors?' *The Guardian* (London), 7 November.

Kelsall, R.K. (1972) 'Wage regulations under the Statutes of Artificers', in W. Minchinton (ed.) *Wage Regulation in Pre-Industrial England* (Newton Abbot: David & Charles), 93–197.

Kerr, T. (1984) 'Contract doesn't live here any more?' *Modern Law Review*, 47: 30–47.

Keynes, J.M. (1936) *The General Theory of Employment, Interest and Money* (London: Macmillan), reprinted as *The Collected Writings of John Maynard Keynes* Vol. 7, 1973 (London: Macmillan).

Keynes, J.M. (1939) 'Relative movement of real wages and output' *Economic Journal*, 49: 34–51.

Kiesling, L. (1997) 'The long road to recovery' *Social Science History*, 21: 219–243.

Kirzner, I. (1997) *How Markets Work: Disequilibrium, Entrepreneurship and Discovery*, IEA Paper no. 133 (London: Institute of Economic Affairs).

Knell, J. (1999) *Partnership at Work* EMAR Research Series no. 7 (London: Department of Trade and Industry).

Knox, E. (2001) 'Blood on the tracks: railway employers and safety in late-Victorian and Edwardian Britain' *Historical Studies in Industrial Relations*, 12: 1–26.

Konzelmann, S., Forrant, R. and Wilkinson, F. (2004) 'Work systems, corporate strategy and global markets: creative shop floors or a "barge mentality"?' *Industrial Relations Journal*, 35: 216–232.

Kussmaul, A. (1981) *Servants in Husbandry in Early Modern England* (Cambridge: Cambridge University Press).

Landau, N. (1984) *The Justices of the Peace, 1679–1760* (Berkeley: University of California Press).

Landau, N. (1988) 'The laws of settlement and the surveillance of immigration in eighteenth-century Kent' *Continuity and Change*, 3: 391–420.

Landau, N. (1990) 'The regulation of immigration, economic structures and definitions of the poor in eighteenth-century England' *Historical Journal*, 33: 541–572.

Landau, N. (1995) 'Who was subjected to the laws of settlement? Procedure under the settlement laws in eighteenth-century England' *Agricultural History Review*, 43: 139–159.

Layard, R. and Nickell, S. (1985) 'The causes of British unemployment' *National Institute Economic Review*, 111: 62–85.

Lee, A. (2002) 'Law, economic theory, and corporate governance: the origins of UK legislation on company directors' conflicts of interests, 1862–1948' Ph.D. thesis, University of Cambridge.

Leeson, R. (1979) *Travelling Brothers: The Six Centuries' Road from Craft Fellowship to Trade Unionism* (London: Allen & Unwin).

Levine-Clark, M. (2000) 'Engendering relief: women, ablebodiedness and the new poor law in early Victorian England' *Journal of Women's History*, 11: 107–130.

Lewis, D. (1969) *Convention: A Philosophical Study* (Cambridge, MA: Harvard University Press).

Lewis, J. (2000) 'Reforming social insurance and social protection', presentation to SASE seminar on *The Transformation of Work and the Future of the Employment Relationship*, LSE, 8 July.

Lewis, R. (1986) 'The role of law in employment relations' in R. Lewis (ed.) *Labour Law in Britain* (Oxford: Blackwell).

Lindley, R.M. (1983) 'Active manpower policy', in G. Bain (ed.) *Industrial Relations in Britain* (Oxford: Blackwell), 339–360.

Lis, C. and Soly, H. (1979) *Poverty and Capitalism in Pre-Industrial Europe* (Hassocks: Harvester).

Littler, C. (1982) *The Development of the Labour Process in Capitalist Societies: A Comparative Study of the Transformation of Work Organisation in Britain, Japan and the United States* (London: Heinemann Educational Books).

Lowe, R. (1978) 'The erosion of state intervention in Britain 1917–24' *Economic History Review*, 31: 270–286.

Lowe, R. (1978) 'The failure of consensus in Britain: the National Industrial Conference, 1919–1921' *Historical Journal*, 21: 649–675.

Lowe, R. (1982) 'Hours of labour: negotiating industrial legislation in Britain, 1919–39' *Economic History Review*, 35: 254–271.

Lucas, R. and Sargent, T. (eds.) (1981) *Rational Expectations and Econometric Practice* (London: Macmillan).

Luhmann, N. (1995) *Social Systems*, translated by J. Bednarz Jr. with D. Baecker (Stanford, CA: Stanford University Press).

Lumley, W.G. (1845) *The New General Orders of the Poor Law Commissioners* (London: Shaw & Sons).

Lyon-Caen, A. and Affichard, J. (2004) 'From legal norms to statistical norms: employ- ment policies put to the test of coordination', in O. De Schutter and S. Deakin (eds.) *Social Rights and Market Forces: Is the Open Coordination of Employment and Social Policies the Future of Social Europe?* (Brussels: Bruylant).

Macneil, I. (1974) 'The many futures of contracts' (1974) *Southern California Law Review*, 47: 691–816.

Malthus, T.R. (1798) *An Essay on the Principle of Population, as it Affects the Future Improvement of Society. With Remarks on the Speculations of Mr. Godwin, M. Condorcet, and other Writers* (London: Johnson).

Mandeville, B. (1970) *The Fable of the Bees*, edited with an introduction by P. Harth (Harmondsworth: Penguin).

Mandler, P. (1987) 'The making of the new poor law *redivivus*' *Past and Present*, 117: 131–157.

Mandler, P. (1990) *Aristocratic Government in the Age of Reform: Whigs and Liberals 1830–1852* (Oxford: Clarendon Press).

Mansfield, M. (1994) 'Naissance d'une définition institutionelle du chômage en Grande- Bretagne (1860–1914)' in M. Mansfield, R. Salais and N. Whiteside (eds.) *Aux sources du chômage 1880–1914* (Paris: Belin), 295–323.

Marglin, S. and Schorr, J. (eds.) (1990) *The Golden Age of Capitalism: Reinterpreting the Postwar Experience* (Oxford: Clarendon Press).

Mark-Lawson, J. and Witz, A. (1988) 'From "family labour" to "family wage"? The case of women's labour in nineteenth century coal mining' *Social History*, 13: 151–174.

Marsden, D. (1996) 'Employment policy implications of new management systems' *Labour*, 9: 17–61.

Marsden, D. (1999) *A Theory of Employment Systems: Micro-Foundations of Societal Diversity* (Oxford: Oxford University Press).

Marsden, D. (1999) 'Breaking the link. Has the employment contract had its day?' *Centrepiece* (winter): 20–25.

Marsh, C. (1991) *Hours of Work of Women and Men in Great Britain* (London: DTI).

Marshall, A. (1949) *Principles of Economics: An Introductory Volume*, 8th ed. (London: Macmillan).

Marshall, J. (1985) *The Old Poor Law 1795–1834*, 2nd ed. (London: Macmillan).

Marshall, T.H. (1992) 'Citizenship and social class', reprinted in T.H. Marshall and T. Bottomore, *Citizenship and Social Class* (London: Pluto Press).

Marx, K. (1971) *A Contribution to the Critique of Political Economy*, ed. M. Dobb, transl. S. Ryazanskaya (London: Lawrence & Wishart).

McBriar, A. (1987) *An Edwardian Mixed Doubles: The Bosanquets versus the Webbs. A Study in British Social Policy 1890–1929* (Oxford: Clarendon Press).

McCarthy, W.E.J. (1992) 'The rise and fall of collective laissez-faire', in W.E.J. McCarthy (ed.) *Legal Intervention in Industrial Relations: Gains and Losses* (Oxford: Blackwell), 1–78.

McColgan, A. (2000) 'Missing the point: the Part-Time Workers (Prevention of Less Favourable Treatment) Regulations 2000 (SI 2000 No. 1551)' *Industrial Law Journal*, 29: 260–267.

McCormick, J. (1998) 'Prospects for pension reform', in J. McCormick and C. Oppenheim (eds.) *Welfare in Working Order* (London: Institute for Public Policy Research), 175–249.

McCormick, N. (1986) 'Spontaneous order and the rule of law: some problems' *Jahrbuch des Öffentlichen Rechts der Gegenwart*, 35: 1–13.

McKinnon, M. (1987) 'English poor law policy and the crusade against outdoor relief' *Journal of Economic History*, 47: 603–625.

Meade, J.E. (1982) *Stagflation Volume 1: Wage Fixing* (London: Allen & Unwin).

Merritt, A. (1982) ' "Control" v "economic reality": defining the contract of employment' *Australian Business Law Review*, 10: 105–124.

Merritt, A. (1982) 'The historical role of the law in the regulation of employment—abstentionist or interventionist?' (1982) *Australian Journal of Law and Society*, 1: 56–86.

Micklewright, J. (1989) 'The strange case of British earnings-related unemployment benefit' *Journal of Social Policy*, 18: 527–548.

Mill, J.S. (1909) *Principles of Political Economy, with some of their Applications to Social Philosophy*, edited by with an introduction by W.J. Ashley (London: Longmans, Green & Co.).

Miller, P. and Rose, N. (1998) 'Governing economic life', in G. Mabey, G. Salaman and J. Storey (eds.) *Strategic Human Resource Management: A Reader* (London: Sage), 46–57.

Milsom, S.F.C. (2003) *A Natural History of the Common Law* (New York: Columbia University Press).

Minford, P. (1986) *Unemployment: Cause and Cure* (Oxford: Blackwell, 1986).

Mitchell, R. (ed.) (1995) *Redefining Labour Law* (Melbourne: Centre for Employment and Labour Relations Law).

Mitchell, R. and Howe, J. (1999) 'The evolution of the contract of employment in Australia: a discussion' *Australian Journal of Labour Law*, 12: 113–130.

Moore, S. and Bewley, H. (2004) *The Content of New Voluntary Trade Union Recognition Agreements 1998–2002: Report of Preliminary Findings* EMAR Research Series no. 26 (London: Department of Trade and Industry).

Moore, S., Wood, S. and Ewing, K. (2003) 'The impact of the trade union recognition procedure under the Employment Relations Act 1999', in H. Gospel and S. Wood (eds.) *Representing Workers: Trade Union Membership and Recognition in Britain* (London: Routledge), 119–143.

Morris, J. (1986) *Women Workers and the Sweated Trades* (Aldershot: Gower).

Mückenberger, U. (2004) 'Alternative mechanisms of voice representation', presentation to joint Columbia University/Institute of Advanced Legal Studies seminar, London, July.

Mückenburger, U. and Deakin, S. (1989) 'From deregulation to a European floor of rights: labour law, flexibilisation and the European single market' *Zeitschrift für ausländisches und internationales Arbeits- und Sozialrecht*, 3: 153–207.

Napier, B.W. (1975) 'The contract of service: the concept and its application', Ph.D. Thesis, University of Cambridge.

Neuman, M. (1982) *The Speenhamland County: Poverty and the Poor Laws in Berkshire, 1782–1834* (New York: Garland).

Nickell, S. (1985) 'The government's policy for jobs, an analysis', *Oxford Review of Economic Policy*, 98–115.

Nickell, S. (1999) 'Unemployment in Britain', in P. Gregg and J. Wadsworth (eds.) *The State of Working Britain* (Manchester University Press), 7–28.

Njoya, W. (2002) 'Ownership and property rights in the company: a law and economics analysis of shareholder and employee interests', Ph.D. thesis, University of Cambridge.

Njoya, W. (2004) 'Employee ownership and efficiency: an evolutionary perspective' *Industrial Law Journal*, 30: 211–241.

Nolan, M. (1825) *A Treatise of the Laws for the Relief and Settlement of the Poor*, 4th ed. (London: Butterworth).

Ogus, A.I. (1982) 'Great Britain', in P. Köhler and H. Zacher (eds.) *The Evolution of Social Insurance 1881–1981. Studies of Germany, France, Great Britain, Austria, and Switzerland* (London: Pinter), 150–264.

Ogus, A.I. and Barendt, E.M. (1978) *The Law of Social Security*, 2nd ed. (London: Butterworths).

Orth, J. (1987) 'The English Combination Laws reconsidered', in F. Snyder and D. Hay (eds.) *Law, Labour and Crime: An Historical Perspective* (London: Tavistock).

Orth, J. (1991) *Combination and Conspiracy: A Legal History of Trade Unionism 1721–1906* (Oxford: Oxford University Press).

Oxenbridge, S., Brown, W., Deakin, S. and Pratten, C. (2003) 'Initial responses to the statutory recognition procedures of the Employment Relations Act 1999' *British Journal of Industrial Relations*, 41: 315–334.

Palmer, R. (1993) *English Law in the Age of the Black Death, 1348–1381: A Transformation of Governance and Law* (Chapel Hill, NC: University of North Carolina Press).

Panitch, L. (1976) *Social Democracy and Industrial Militancy: The Labour Party, the Trade Unions and Incomes Policy, 1945–1974* (Cambridge: Cambridge University Press).

Petersdorff, C. (1876) *A Practical Compendium of the Law of Master and Servant in General and Especially of Employers and Workmen under the Act of 1875* (London: Simpkin, Marshall & Co.).

Phelps-Brown, H. (1959) *The Growth of British Industrial Relations: A Study from the Perspective of 1906–14* (London: Macmillan).

Phillips, G. and Whiteside, N. (1986) *Casual Labour: The Unemployment Question in the Port Transport Industry 1880–1970* (Oxford: Oxford University Press).

Picchio del Mercado, A. (1992) *Social Reproduction, the Political Economy of the Labour Market* (Cambridge: Cambridge University Press).

Pinchbeck, I. (1981) *Women Workers and the Industrial Revolution 1750–1850*, edited with a new introduction by K. Hamilton (London: Virago).

Polanyi, K. (1957) 'The economy as instituted process', in K. Polanyi, C. Arensberg and H. Pearson (eds.) *Trade and Market in the Early Empires* (Glencoe, IL: Free Press), 243–270.

Polanyi, K. (1957) *The Great Transformation. The Political and Economic Origins of Our Time* (Boston: Beacon Press).

Pollard, S. (1965) *The Genesis of Modern Management: A Study of the Industrial Revolution in Great Britain* (Cambridge, MA: Harvard University Press).

Posner, R. (1999) *Economic Analysis of Law*, 5th ed. (New York: Aspen Law and Business).

Potter, D. and Stansfield, D. (1949) *National Insurance*, 2nd ed. (London: Butterworth).

Pound, R. (1959) *Jurisprudence* (St. Paul, MN: West Publishing Co.).

Power, M. (1999) 'Parasitic-industries analysis and arguments for a living wage for women in the early twentieth century United States' *Feminist Economics*, 5: 61–78.

Poynter, J.R. (1969) *Society and Pauperism: English Ideas on Poor Relief, 1795–1834* (London: Routledge and Kegan Paul).

Prothero, I. (1979) *Artisans and Politics in Early Nineteenth Century London: John Gast and His Times* (Folkestone: Dawson).

Putnam, B. (1908) *The Enforcement of the Statutes of Labourers in the First Decade after the Black Death 1349–1359* (New York: Columbia University Press).

Quintrell, B. (1980) 'The making of Charles I's Book of Orders' *English Historical Review*, 95: 553–572.

Ramm, T. (1987) 'Laissez-faire and state protection of workers', in B. Hepple (ed.) *The Making of Labour Law in Europe* (London: Mansell), 73–113.

Randall, A. (1991) *Before the Luddites: Custom, Community and Machinery in the English Woollen Industry, 1776–1809* (Cambridge, Cambridge University Press).

Reed, H. and Deakin, S. (1999) 'United Kingdom', in J. van Vugt and J. Peet (eds.) *Social Security and Solidarity in the European Union* (Heidelberg: Physica-Verlag), 182–222.

Reid, A. (1985) 'Dilution, trade unionism and the state', in S. Tolliday and J. Zeitlin (eds.) *Shop Floor Bargaining and the State* (Cambridge: Cambridge University Press).

Richardson, J.H. (1938) *Industrial Relations in Great Britain*, 2nd ed. (Geneva: ILO).

Robinson, H. (2003) 'Gender and labour market performance in the recovery', in R. Dickens, P. Gregg and J. Wadsworth (eds.) *The Labour Market Under New Labour. The State of Working Britain* (Basingstoke: Palgrave), 232–247.

Robinson, J. (1933) *The Economics of Imperfect Competition* (London: Macmillan).

Robinson, O. and Wallace, J. (1984) 'Growth and utilisation of part-time labour in Great Britain' *Employment Gazette*, 92: 391–397.

Roe, M. (1995) 'Chaos and evolution in law and economics' *Harvard Law Review*, 109: 641–668.

Rogowski, R. and Wilthagen, T. (1994) 'Reflexive labour law: an introduction', in R. Rogowski and T. Wilthagen (eds.) *Reflexive Labour Law* (Deventer: Kluwer).

Rose, S. (1988) 'Gender antagonism and class conflict: exclusionary strategies of male trade unionists in nineteenth century Britain' *Social History*, 13: 191–208.

Rostow, W.W. (1961) *The Stages of Economic Growth, A Non-Communist Manifesto* (Cambridge: Cambridge University Press).

Rubery, J., Deakin, S. and Horrell, S. (1992) 'Great Britain', in G. Bosch, P. Dawkins and F. Michon (eds.) *Times are Changing* (Geneva: IILS).

Rubin, G. (1987) *War, Law and Labour* (Oxford: Clarendon Press).

Rule, J. (1981) *The Experience of Labour in Eighteenth Century Industry* (London: Croom Helm).

Rule, J. (1988) *The Labouring Classes in Early Industrial England 1750–1850* (London: Longmans).

Saglio, J. (2000) 'Changing wages orders: France 1900–1950', in L. Clarke, P. de Gijsel and J. Jansenn (eds.) *The Dynamics of Wage Relations in Europe* (Dordrecht: Kluwer), 44–59.

Salais, R. (1999) 'Libertés du travail et capacités: une perspective pour une construction européenne?' *Droit Social* 467–471.

Samuel, G. (2003) *Epistemology and Method in Law* (Aldershot: Ashgate).

Saville, J. (1956) 'Sleeping partnership and limited liability, 1850–1856' *Economic History Review (NS)*, 8: 418–433.

Schotter, A. (1981) *The Economic Theory of Social Institutions* (Cambridge: Cambridge University Press).

Schwarz, L. (1999) 'English servants and their employers during the eighteenth and nineteenth centuries' *Economic History Review (NS)*, 52: 236–256.

Searle, G. (1987) *The Quest for National Efficiency* (Oxford: Blackwell).

Seccombe, W. (1986) 'Patriarchy stabilised: the construction of the male breadwinner wage norm in nineteenth century Britain' *Social History*, 11: 53–76.

Selznick, P. (1980) *Law, Society and Industrial Justice* (New Brunswick, NJ: Transaction Books).

Sen, A. (1985) *Commodities and Capabilities* (Deventer: North-Holland).

Sen, A. (1999) *Development as Freedom* (Oxford: Oxford University Press).

Sewell, G. and Wilkinson, B. (1998) 'Empowerment or emasculation? Shopfloor surveillances in a total quality organisation', in P. Blyton and P. Turnbull (eds.) *Reassessing Human Resource Management* (London: Sage), 97–115.

Shannon, H. (1933) 'The limited companies of 1866–1933' *Economic History Review*, 4: 290–316.

Simitis, S. (1987) 'Juridification of labour relations', in G. Teubner (ed.) *Juridification of Social Spheres* (Berlin: De Gruyter).

Simon, D. (1954) 'Master and servant', in J. Saville (ed.) *Democracy and the Labour Movement: Essays in Honour of Dona Torr* (London: Lawrence and Wishart), 160–200.

Simon, H. (1951) 'A formal theory of the employment relation' (1951) *Econometrica*, 19: 293–305.

Simpson, B. (1979) 'Judicial review of ACAS' *Industrial Law Journal*, 8: 420–426.

Simpson, B. (1999) 'A milestone in the legal regulation of pay: The National Minimum Wage Act 1998' *Industrial Law Journal*, 28: 1–32.

Simpson, B. (1999) Implementing the national minimum wage—the 1999 Regulations' *Industrial Law Journal*, 28: 171–182.

Slack, P. (1980) 'Books of Orders: the making of English social policy 1577–1631' *Transactions of the Royal Historical Society*, 5th Ser., 30: 1–22.

Slack, P. (1990) *The English Poor Law 1531–1782* (London: Macmillan).

Slinger, G. (1999) 'Spanning the gap: the theoretical principles that connect stakeholder policies to business performance' *Corporate Governance: an International Review*, 11: 136–151.

Smail, J. (1987) 'New languages for labour and capital: the transformation of discourse in the early years of the industrial revolution' *Social History*, 12: 54–61.

Smith, A. (1886) *An Inquiry into the Nature and Causes of the Wealth of Nations*, ed. with an introduction by J.S. Nicholson (London: T. Nelson and Sons).

Smith, C.M. (1860) *A Treatise on the Law of Master and Servant*, 2nd ed. (London: Sweet).

Snell, K.D.M. (1985) *Annals of the Labouring Poor* (Cambridge: Cambridge University Press).

Snell, K.D.M. and Millar, J. (1987) 'Lone parent families and the welfare state: past and present' *Continuity and Change*, 2: 387–422.

Solar, P. (1995) 'Poor relief and English economic development before the Industrial Revolution' *Economic History Review (NS)*, 42: 1–22.

Solow, R. (1990) *The Labour Market as a Social Institution* (Oxford: Blackwell).

Song, B.K. (1998) 'Landed interest, local government, and the labour market in England, 1750–1850' *Economic History Review (NS)*, 51: 465–488.

Stedman Jones, G. (1976) *Outcast London: A Study in the Relationship between Classes in Victorian Society* (Harmondsworth: Penguin).

Steedman, C. (2003) 'Servants and their relationship to the unconscious' *Journal of British Studies*, 42: 316–350.

Steedman, C. (2004) 'The servant's labour: the business of life, England, 1760–1820' *Social History*, 29: 1–29.

Steinfeld, R. (1991) *The Invention of Free Labor: The Employment Relation in English and American Law and Culture, 1350–1870* (Chapel Hill, NC: University of North Carolina Press).

Steinfeld, R. (2002) *Coercion, Contract and Free Labour in the Nineteenth Century* (Cambridge: Cambridge University Press).

Streeck, W. (1993) *Social Institutions and Economic Performance* (Cambridge: Polity).

Styles, P. (1963–4) 'The evolution of the law of settlement' *University of Birmingham Historical Journal*, 9: 32–63.

Sugden, R. (1986) *The Economics of Rights, Cooperation and Welfare* (Oxford: Blackwell).

Sugden, R. (1989) 'Spontaneous order' *Journal of Economic Perspectives*, 3: 85–97.

Sugden, R. (1998) 'Spontaneous order', in P. Newman (ed.) *The New Palgrave Dictionary of Economics and the Law* Vol. 3 (London: Macmillan), 485–495.

Supiot, A. (1994) *Critique du droit du travail* (Paris: Presses Universitaires de France).

Supiot, A. (1999) 'Introduction', in A. Supiot (ed.) *Au delà de l'emploi. Transformations du travail et devenir du droit du travail en Europe* (Paris: Flammarion), 7–24.

Supiot, A. (2003) 'The labyrinth of human rights: credo or common resource?' *New Left Review*, 21: 118–136.

Szyszczak, E. (1990) *Partial Unemployment: The Regulation of Short-Time Working in Britain* (London: Mansell).

Tarling, R. and Wilkinson, F. (1977) 'The Social Contract: post-war incomes policies and their inflationary impact' *Cambridge Journal of Economics*, 1: 395–414.

Tarling, R. and Wilkinson, F. (1982) 'The movement of real wages and the development of collective bargaining in the UK, 1855–1920' *Contributions to Political Economy*, 1: 1–35.

Tarshis, L. (1939) 'Changes in real and money wages' *Economic Journal*, 49: 150–157.

Tawney, R.H. (1914) *The Establishment of Minimum Rates in the Chainmaking Industry under the Trade Boards Act of 1909* (London: Bell).

Tawney, R.H. (1915) *The Establishment of Minimum Rates in the Tailoring Industry under the Trade Boards Act of 1909* (London: Bell).

Tawney, R.H. (1967) *The Agrarian Problem in the Sixteenth Century*, edited with an introduction by L. Stone (New York: Harper & Row).

Tawney, R.H. (1972) 'Assessment of wages in England by the Justices of the Peace', in W. Minchinton (ed.) *Wage Regulation in Pre-Industrial England* (Newton Abbot: David & Charles).

Taylor, F.W. (1911) *Principles of Scientific Management* (New York: Harper).

Taylor, J.S. (1976) 'The impact of pauper settlement' *Past and Present*, 73: 42–73.

Teubner, G. (1993) *Law as an Autopoietic System* (Oxford: Blackwell).

Thompson, E.P. (1967) 'Time, work-discipline, and industrial capitalism' *Past and Present*, 38: 36–97.

Thompson, E.P. (1968) *The Making of the English Working Class* (Harmondsworth: Penguin).

Thompson, E.P. (1971) 'The moral economy of the English crowd in the eighteenth century' *Past and Present*, 50: 76–136.

Thomson, D. (1984) 'The decline of social security: falling state support for the elderly since Victorian times' *Ageing and Society*, 4: 451–482.

Tillyard, F. (1928) *Industrial Law* (London: A. & C. Black).

Tomlins, C. (1993) *Law, Labor and Ideology in the Early American Republic* (Cambridge: Cambridge University Press).

Townsend, J. (1786) *A Dissertation on the Poor Laws: By a Well-Wisher to Mankind* (London: Dilly).

Toynbee, A. (1969) *Lectures on the Industrial Revolution in England*, ed. with an introduction by T.S. Ashton (Newton Abbot: A.M. Kelley).

Turner, H.A. (1957) 'Inflation and wage differentials in Great Britain', in J.T. Dunlop (ed.) *The Theory of Wage Determination* (London: Macmillan).

Turner, H.A. (1962) *Trade Union Growth, Structure and Policy: A Comparative Study of the Cotton Unions* (Toronto: University of Toronto Press).

Veneziani, B. (1986) 'The evolution of the contract of employment', in B. Hepple (ed.) *The Making of Labour Law in Europe* (London: Mansell), 31–72.

Walby, S. (1986) *Patriarchy at Work* (Cambridge: Polity).

Walton, R. and McKersie, R. (1965) *A Behavioural Theory of Labour Negotiations* (New York: McGraw-Hill).

Wareing, M. (1992) 'Working arrangements and patterns of working hours in Britain' *Employment Gazette*, 100: 88–100.

Warneryd, K. (1998) 'Conventions and transaction costs', in P. Newman (ed.) *The New Palgrave Dictionary of Economics and the Law* Vol. 1 (London: Macmillan, 1998), 461–465.

Webb, S. and Webb, B. (1894) *The History of Trade Unionism* (London: Longmans, Green and Co.), 2nd ed., 1911.

Webb, S. and Webb, B. (1897) *Industrial Democracy* (London: Longmans, Green and Co.), 2nd ed., 1920.

Webb, S. and Webb, B. (1909) *The Public Organisation of the Labour Market: Being Part Two of the Minority Report of the Poor Law Commission* (London: Longmans, Green & Co.).

Webb, S. and Webb, B. (1910) *English Poor Law Policy* (London: Longmans, Green & Co.).

Webb, S. and Webb, B. (1927) *English Poor Law History: Part I. The Old Poor Law* (London: Longmans, Green & Co.).

Webb, S. and Webb, B. (1927) *English Poor Law History Volume II: The Last Hundred Years* (London: Longmans, Green & Co.).

Weber, M. (1978) 'The origins of industrial capitalism in Europe', in W.G. Runciman (ed.) and E. Matthews (transl.), *Max Weber. Selections in Translation* (Cambridge: Cambridge University).

Wedderburn, K.W. (1967) *Cases and Materials on Labour Law* (Cambridge: Cambridge University Press).

Wedderburn, Lord (1984) 'Labour law now—a hold and a nudge' *Industrial Law Journal*, 13: 73–85.

Wedderburn, Lord (1985) 'The new policies in industrial relations law', in P. Fosh and C. Littler (eds.) *Industrial Relations and the Law in the 1980s: Issues and Future Trends* (Aldershot: Gower), 22–63.

Wedderburn, Lord (1986) *The Worker and the Law*, 3rd ed. (Harmondsworth: Penguin).

Wedderburn, Lord (1992) 'Inderogability, collective agreements and Community law' *Industrial Law Journal*, 21: 245–264.

Wedderburn, Lord (1993) 'Companies and employees: common law or social dimension?' *Law Quarterly Review*, 109: 220–262.

Wedderburn, Lord (1995) 'Change, struggle and ideology in British labour law', in Lord Wedderburn, (ed.) *Labour Law and Freedom* (London: Lawrence and Wishart).

Weekes, B., Mellish, M., Dickens, L. and Lloyd, J. (1975) *Industrial Relations and the Limits of the Law: The Industrial Effects of the Industrial Relations Act 1971* (Oxford: Blackwell).

Weinrib, E. (1997) 'The juridical classification of obligations' in P.B.H. Birks (ed.) *The Classification of Obligations* (Oxford: Clarendon Press, 1997), 37–55.

Wells, F.A. (1972) *The British Hosiery and Knitwear Industry: its History and Organisation*, revised edition (Newton Abbot: David & Charles).

Whiteside, N. (1991) *Bad Times: Unemployment in British Social and Political History* (London: Faber).

Whiteside, N. (1994) 'Définir le chômage: traditions syndicales et politique nationale en Grande-Bretagne avant la Première Guerre mondiale', in M. Mansfield, R. Salais and N. Whiteside (eds.) *Aux sources du chômage 1880–1914* (Paris: Belin), 381–411.

Whiteside, N. (2003) 'Historical perspectives and the politics of pension reform: constructing the public-private divide', in G. Clark and N. Whiteside (eds.) *Pension Security in the 21st Century* (Oxford: Oxford University Press).

Whiteside, N. and Gillespie, J. (1991) 'Deconstructing unemployment: developments in Britain in the inter-war years' *Economic History Review (NS)*, 44: 665–681.

Wikeley, N. (ed.) (1995) *Ogus, Barendt and Wikeley's Law of Social Security*, 4th ed. (London: Butterworths).

Wikeley, N. (ed.) (2002) *Wikeley, Ogus and Barendt's Law of Social Security*, 5th ed. (London: Butterworths).

Wilkinson, F. (1977) 'Collective bargaining in the steel industry in the 1930s', in A. Briggs and J. Saville (eds.) *Essays in Labour History 1918–1939* (London: Croom Helm), 102–132.

Wilkinson, F. (1983) 'Productive systems' *Cambridge Journal of Economics*, 7: 413–429.

Wilkinson, F. (1991) 'Industrial organization, collective bargaining and economic efficiency' *International Contributions to Labour Studies*, 1: 1–25.

Wilkinson, F. (2000) 'Inflation and employment: is there a Third Way?' *Cambridge Journal of Economics*, 24: 643–670.

Wilkinson, F. (2003) 'Productive systems and the structuring role of economic and social theories', in B. Burchell, S. Deakin, J. Michie and J. Rubery (eds.) *Systems of Production: Markets, Organisations and Performance* (London: Routledge), 10–39.

Williams, D. (1982) *Social Security Taxation* (London: Sweet & Maxwell).

Williams, K. (1981) *From Pauperism to Poverty* (London: Routledge and Kegan Paul).

Williamson, O. (1985) *The Economic Institutions of Capitalism* (New York: Free Press).

Williamson, O. (1996) *The Mechanisms of Governance* (Oxford: Oxford University Press).

Williamson, O., Wachter, M. and Harris, J. (1975) 'Understanding the employment relation: understanding the economics of idiosyncratic exchange' *Bell Journal of Economics and Management Science*, 6: 250–278.

Wood, S. (2000) 'From voluntarism to partnership: a third way overview of the public policy debate in British industrial relations', in H. Collins, P. Davies and R. Rideout (eds.) *Legal Regulation of the Employment Relation* (Deventer: Kluwer), 111–135.

Wood, S. and De Menezes, L. (1992) 'High commitment management in the UK: evidence from the Workplace Industrial Relations Survey and Employers' Manpower and Skill Practice Survey' *Human Relations*, 51: 485–515.

Woodroofe, K. (1977) 'The Royal Commission on the poor laws 1905–09' *International Review of Social History*, 22: 137–164.

Woods, D.C. (1982) 'The operation of the Master and Servant Acts in the Black Country, 1858–1875' *Midland History*, 7: 109–123.

Woodward, D. (1980) 'The background to the Statute of Artificers: the genesis of labour policy, 1558–63' *Economic History Review (NS)*, 33: 32–44.

Wordie, J.R. (1983) 'The chronology of English enclosure, 1500–1914' *Economic History Review (NS)*, 36: 483–505.

Wrigley, E.A. (1988) *Continuity, Chance and Change: The Character of the Industrial Revolution in England* (Cambridge: Cambridge University Press).

Wrigley, E.A. and Souden, D. (1986) 'Introduction', in E.A. Wrigley and D. Souden (eds.) *The Works of Thomas Robert Malthus* Vol. I (London: Pickering).

Young, H.P. (1998) *Individual Strategy and Social Structure: An Evolutionary Theory of Institutions* (Princeton, NJ: Princeton University Press).

Index

Index